KURT BRENT ERIC
BUSIEK ANDERSON
w r i t e r   a r t i s t

ALEX   ALEX   JG ROSHELL
SINCLAIR   ROSS   & COMICRAFT
colors   covers   lettering & design

BUSIEK, ANDERSON & ROSS
c u l t u r a l   h i s t o r i a n s

ASTRO CITY: THE DARK AGE

1: BROTHERS & OTHER STRANGERS

ANN HUNTINGTON BUSIEK
Managing Editor

RICHARD STARKINGS
Art Director

JIM LEE
Editorial Director

JOHN NEE
Senior VP—Business
Development

BEN ABERNATHY
Editor

KRISTY QUINN
Assistant Editor

ED ROEDER
Art Director

PAUL LEVITZ
President & Publisher

GEORG BREWER
VP—Design & DC Direct Creative

RICHARD BRUNING
Senior VP—Creative Director

PATRICK CALDON
Executive VP—Finance &
Operations

CHRIS CARAMALIS
VP—Finance

JOHN CUNNINGHAM
VP—Marketing

TERRI CUNNINGHAM
VP—Managing Editor

ALISON GILL
VP—Manufacturing

DAVID HYDE
VP—Publicity

HANK KANALZ
VP—General Manager,
WildStorm

PAULA LOWITT
Senior VP—Business & Legal
Affairs

MARYELLEN MCLAUGHLIN
VP—Advertising & Custom
Publishing

GREGORY NOVECK
Senior VP—Creative Affairs

SUE POHJA
VP—Book Trade Sales

STEVE ROTTERDAM
Senior VP—Sales & Marketing

CHERYL RUBIN
Senior VP—Brand Management

JEFF TROJAN
VP—Business Development,
DC Direct

BOB WAYNE
VP—Sales

Originally Published in ASTRO CITY/ARROWSMITH #1, ASTRO CITY: THE DARK
AGE BOOK ONE #1-4 and ASTRO CITY: THE DARK AGE BOOK TWO #1-4.

ASTRO CITY: THE DARK AGE 1: BROTHERS AND OTHER STRANGERS. Published by WildStorm
Productions. 888 Prospect St. #240, La Jolla, CA 92037. Cover, introduction, sketches and
compilation Copyright © 2008 Juke Box Productions. All Rights Reserved. Astro City, its
logos, symbols, prominent characters featured in this issue and the distinctive likenesses
thereof are trademarks of Juke Box Productions.

WildStorm and logo are trademarks of DC Comics. Any similarity to institutions or persons
living or dead is unintentional and purely coincidental. Printed on recyclable paper.
WildStorm does not read or accept unsolicited submissions of ideas, stories or artwork.
Printed in Canada.

DC Comics, a Warner Bros. Entertainment Company.

Hardcover ISBN 978-1-4012-1868-3 · Softcover ISBN 978-1-4012-2077-8

DC BOOKS BY THE SAME CREATORS:

ASTRO CITY: LIFE IN THE BIG CITY
ASTRO CITY: CONFESSION
ASTRO CITY: FAMILY ALBUM
ASTRO CITY: THE TARNISHED ANGEL
ASTRO CITY: LOCAL HEROES

BY KURT BUSIEK

AQUAMAN: ONCE AND FUTURE
(with Butch Guice)

ARROWSMITH: SO SMART IN THEIR FINE
UNIFORMS (with Carlos Pacheco)

JLA/AVENGERS (with George Pérez)

JLA: SYNDICATE RULES (with Ron Garney)

SUPERMAN: BACK IN ACTION
(with Fabian Nicieza & Pete Woods)

SUPERMAN: CAMELOT FALLS vol. 1-2
(with Carlos Pacheco)

SUPERMAN: REDEMPTION
(with Fabian Nicieza)

SUPERMAN: SECRET IDENTITY
(with Stuart Immonen)

SUPERMAN: 3-2-1-ACTION
(with Brad Walker)

SUPERMAN: UP, UP AND AWAY
(with Geoff Johns & Pete Woods)

THE WIZARD'S TALE (with David Wenzel)

BY BRENT ANDERSON

LEGACY: THE LAST WILL & TESTAMENT
OF HAL JORDAN (with Joe Kelly)

BY ALEX ROSS

BATMAN: WAR ON CRIME (with Paul Dini)

JLA: LIBERTY AND JUSTICE (with Paul Dini)

JUSTICE vol. 1-3
(with Jim Krueger & Doug Braithwaite)

KINGDOM COME (with Mark Waid)

MYTHOLOGY: THE DC COMICS
ART OF ALEX ROSS

SHAZAM: POWER OF HOPE (with Paul Dini)

SUPERMAN: PEACE ON EARTH (with Paul Dini)

UNCLE SAM (with Steve Darnall)

WONDER WOMAN: SPIRIT OF TRUTH
(with Paul Dini)

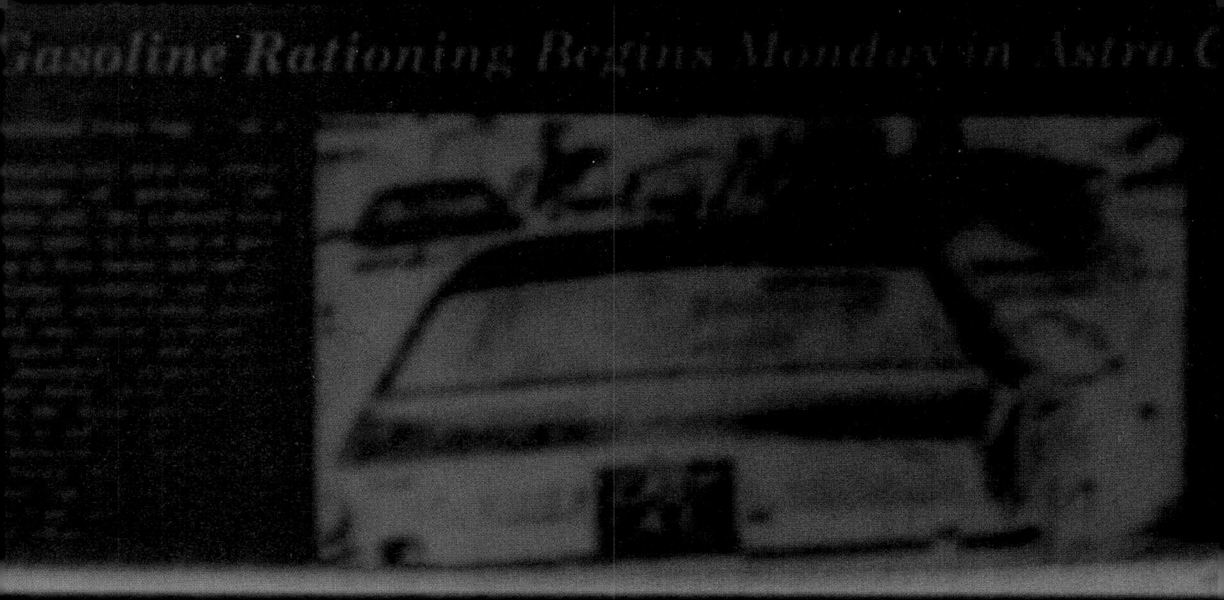
Gasoline Rationing Begins Monday in Astro

DEDICATIONS

For Dave, Ted, Steve, Randall and Guy,
my brothers-in-law....and one out-law...

— Kurt

For Alfredo Alcala, Dave Cockrum,
Steve Gerber, Jim Mooney and
Marshall Rogers. Masters of the
Universe, one and all.

— Brent

For Huggy Bear, without whom
this book would not exist.

— Alex

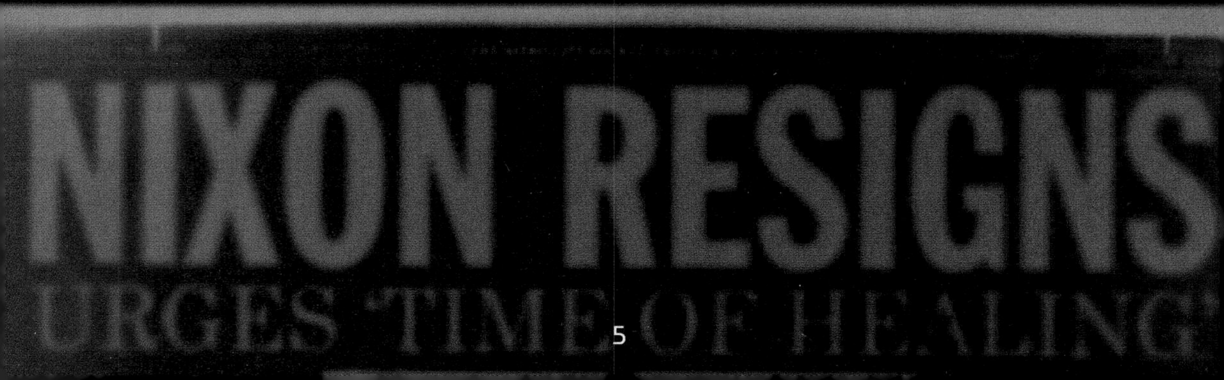
NIXON RESIGNS
URGES 'TIME OF HEALING'

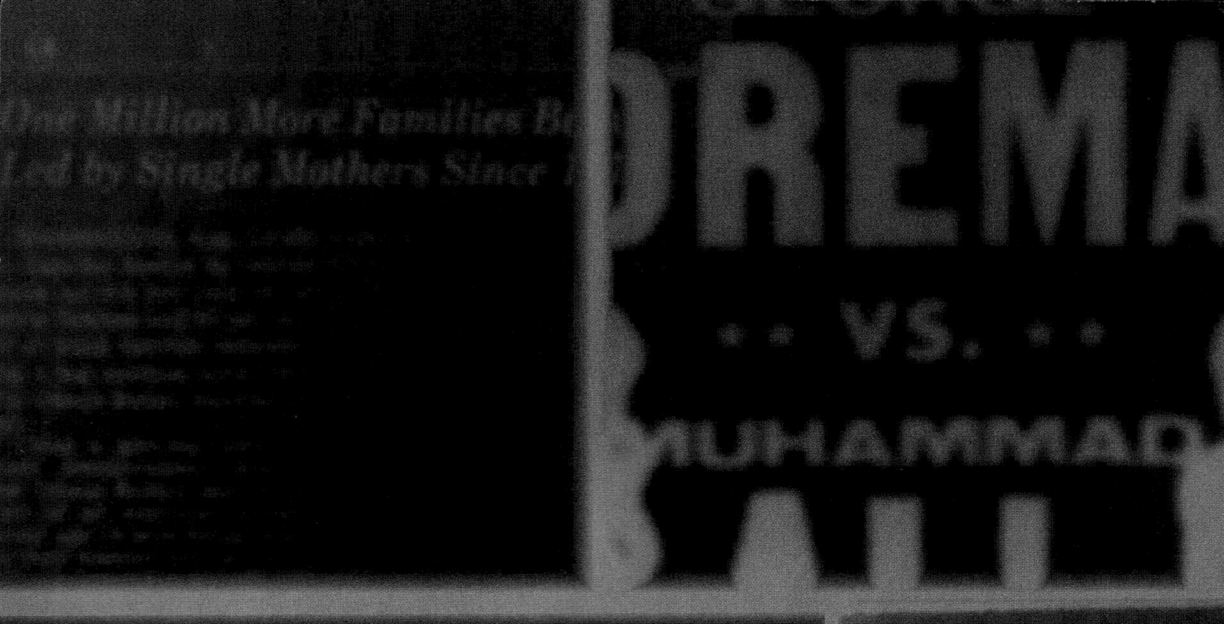
VS.
MUHAMMAD

CONTENTS

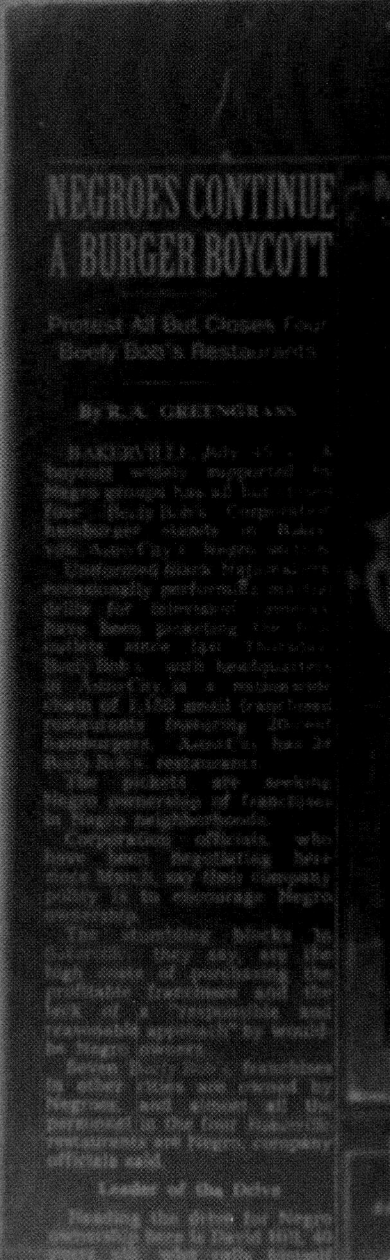
NEGROES CONTINUE
A BURGER BOYCOTT
Protest All But Closes Four
Beefy Bob's Restaurants
By R.A. GREENGRASS

i am one lucky bastard.

No, I'm not talking about my lovely wife and two equally lovely daughters (they're what make me one lucky S.O.B. — but that's the intro of a different book). I'm one lucky bastard because I'm a lifelong comic book fan who gets paid to write comic books. And for guys (in the gender-neutral sense) like me there are four types of comic books: books you don't read; books you do read; books you write; and books you wish you wrote.

Guess which category *Astro City* falls into?

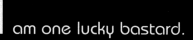

If you answered, "None of the Above," you're correct. For so many reasons, *Astro City* belongs in a category — nay, a *class* — by itself: Books you wish you'd *created*. Reading an issue of *Astro City* makes me sick with envy for Kurt Busiek's fertile imagination, encyclopedic knowledge of all things comic book, and inventiveness to combine the two into a sprawling epic that spans decades.

Now if you've read any of the previous *Astro City* stories, you might be tempted to write off the details and characters therein as random — little wisps of names and dates that were thrown in to add spice to the sauce, but not necessarily to promise some larger, specific story, not to suggest a grand plan.

Not to presage a sixteen-issue epic like *The Dark Age*.

You'd be justified in thinking that there wasn't something larger at work because, like a gifted prestidigitator, Mr. Busiek is employing sleight of hand to distract you from the larger saga he's laying the foundation for right beneath your feet and under your nose. The means of distraction he's using is a little thing we writer-types like to call "character."

In *Astro City*, the triumphs of good over evil, the collisions of worlds and the never-ending battles take a back seat to the people living, loving, working and sometimes dying in the shadows of such pivotal moments. Unlike other comics, where the clash of inter-dimensional civilizations would get a 12-issue maxi-series company-wide crossover, *Astro City* might — *might* — devote a panel to it. (Though you can be damn certain that Mr. Busiek has mapped out every plot twist and detail of the conflagration.)

Instead, the story would focus on the D-list villain looking to "make the big time" by taking advantage of the anarchy resulting from said inter-dimensional warfare. Or the hero who, faced with her own mortality in the aftermath of the inter-dimensional crisis, tries to make amends with her estranged sidekick. This is the brilliance of *Astro City*: in a book dealing with all forms of super-humanity, Mr. Busiek never loses sight of the fact that stories should be about *humanity*. In other words, heroes (and, yes, villains) are people, too.

Which is not to say that all of *Astro City*'s stories are concerned with the super-powered. Some of the best, in fact, have focused on very ordinary people, or "Average Joes" as the denizens of Astro City might be wont to call themselves. Case in point: *The Dark Age*, the first half of which you hold in your hand. It's fitting that for this, the most sweeping and ambitious of all of *Astro City*'s stories to date, Mr. Busiek would choose two very normal, all-too-human protagonists through which to weave his story: Charles and Royal Williams. I don't want to ruin your enjoyment of the story of the Williams brothers by telling you their tale here. Suffice it to say, it could stand on its own as a heartfelt drama of fraternal conflict and unrequited emotions — even if their lives didn't occasionally intersect with cosmic crises and crime syndicates.

But, like I said, that's par for the course when we're talking about *Astro City*.

What makes *The Dark Age* stand apart from earlier *Astro City* stories is that without ever losing the focus on character that makes this series so special, we also start to get a clearer picture of the grand epic I keep alluding to.

When you first read *Astro City* Volume 2, Number One, did you wonder what the inscription on the Silver Agent's tomb meant? For that matter, did you wonder how he died in the first place? Well, wonder no more. Were you curious how Rex joined the First Family? You soon won't be. How did the Deacon rise to the top of the criminal food chain? Find out here. (Hint: Royal Williams is to blame, at least partially.) Why did Alex Ross bother designing a costume for a hero (the Street Angel) who only showed up in two panels previously? Because Mr. Busiek's plan is so thorough he knew that S.A. (as his friends know him) would loom large in the *Dark Age* epic.

And there are probably a hundred more (at least) little seeds that were planted in previous issues of *Astro City* that sprout in *The Dark Age*, but I wasn't too smart to notice them. You see, I'm not nearly as smart a person, or as clever a writer, as Mr. Busiek. Nevertheless, he asked me to write this introduction.

Like I said, I'm one lucky bastard.

And if this book is your first exposure to *Astro City*, so are you.

Marc Guggenheim
March 11, 2008
Los Angeles, California

MARC GUGGENHEIM'S FIRST CLAIM TO FAME WAS COLORING THE SHORT STORY "ABSOLUTE ZERO" IN *MARVEL COMICS PRESENTS* #74. BUT HE WENT ON TO BIGGER AND BETTER THINGS—INCLUDING A LAW DEGREE AND WRITING CREDITS ON SUCH TV SERIES AS *THE PRACTICE*, *LAW & ORDER*, *JACK & BOBBY*, *CSI: MIAMI*, *BROTHERS & SISTERS* AND OTHERS—AND IS ALSO THE CO-CREATOR OF THE TV SERIES *ELI STONE*. COMICS NEVER QUITE LET GO, HOWEVER, AND SINCE WRITING AN *AQUAMAN* FILL-IN IN 2005, HE'S WORKED ON SUCH SERIES AS *THE FLASH*, *WOLVERINE*, *AMAZING SPIDER-MAN* AND HIS NEW *YOUNG X-MEN* SERIES. THESE DAYS, HE DIVIDES HIS TIME BETWEEN HOLLYWOOD, THE MARVEL UNIVERSE AND HIS CREATOR-OWNED SERIES *RESURRECTION*, AT ONI PRESS.

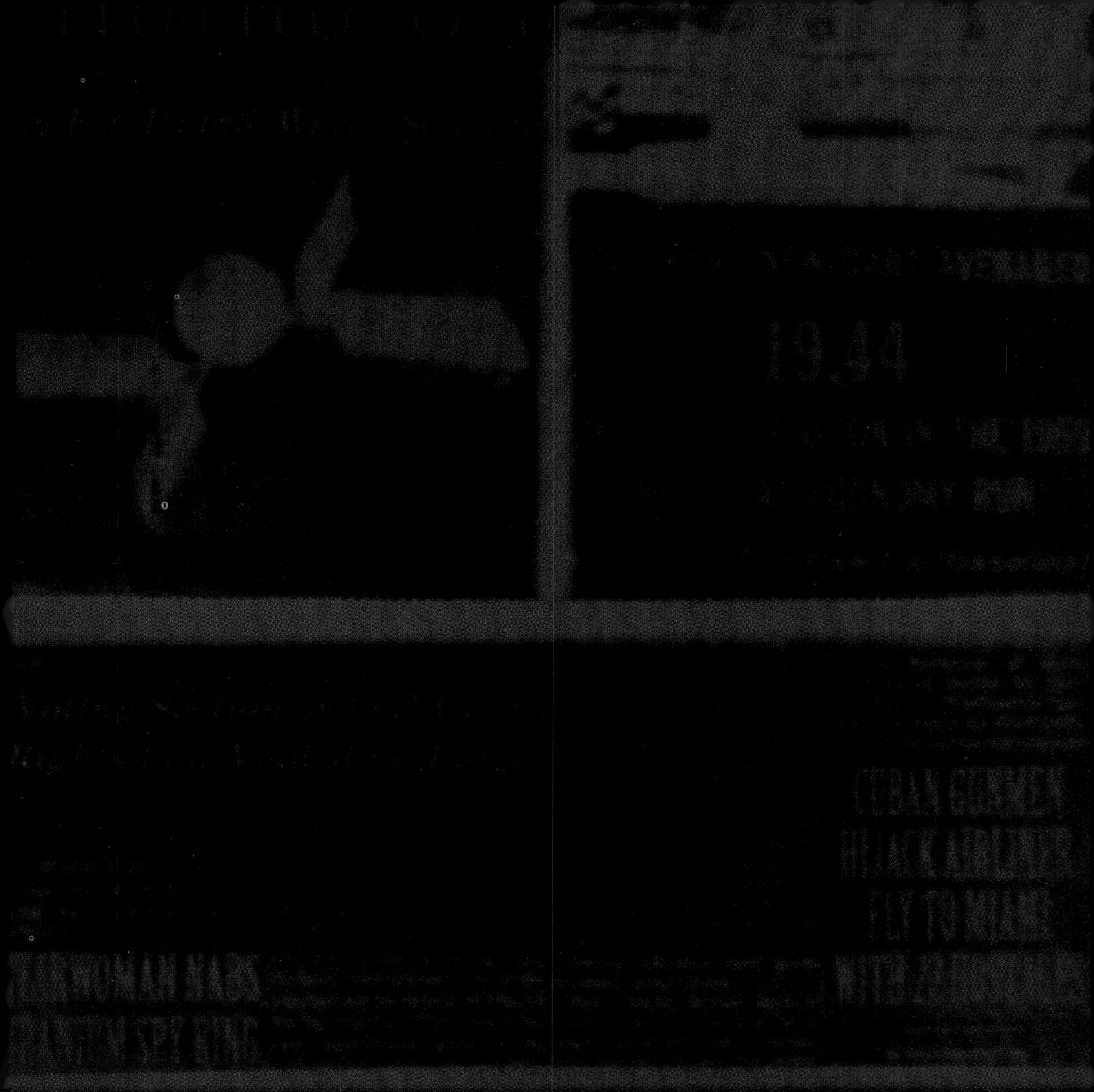

THE DARK AGE PRELUDE

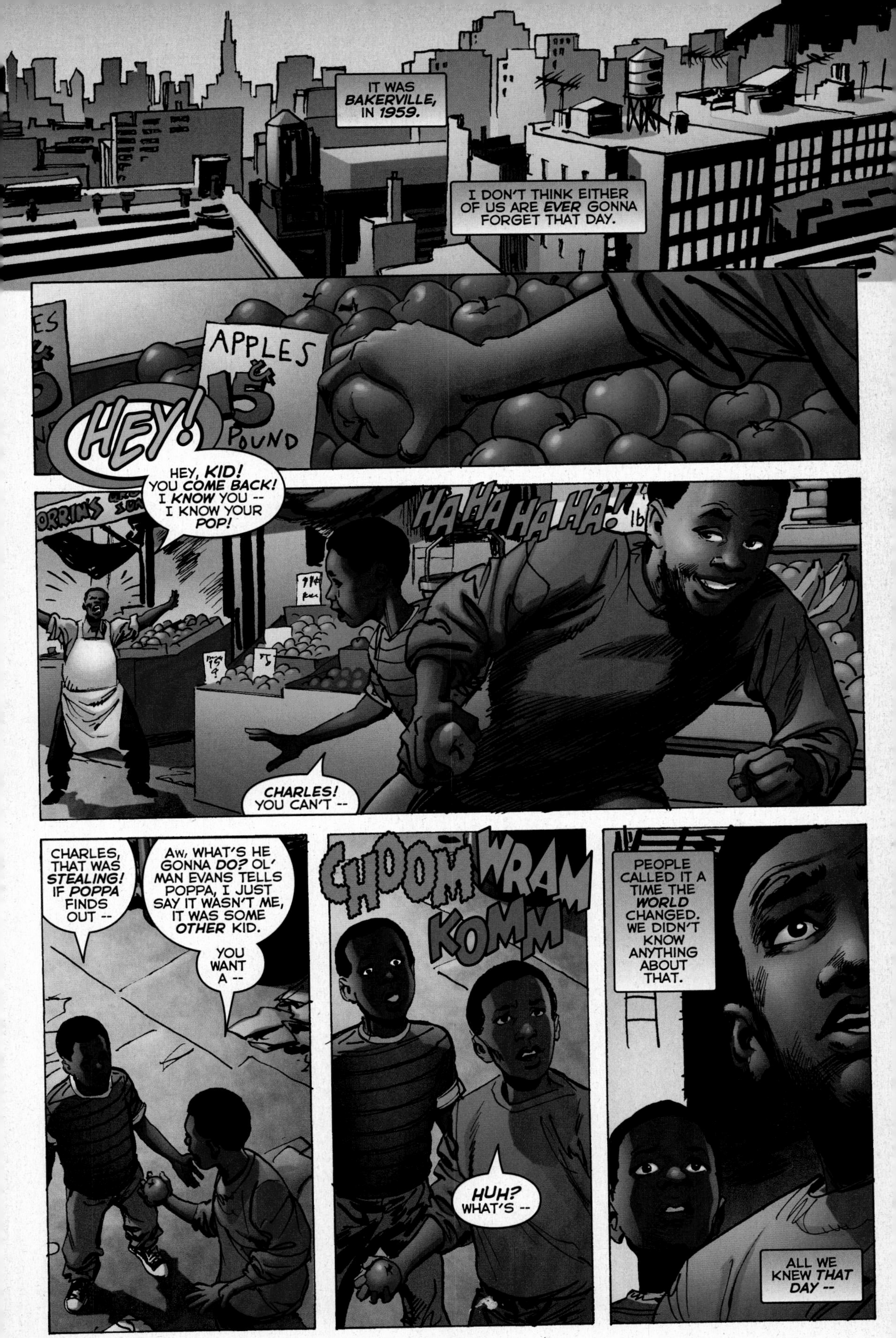
IT WAS BAKERVILLE, IN 1959.
I DON'T THINK EITHER OF US ARE EVER GONNA FORGET THAT DAY.
APPLES 15¢ POUND
HEY!
HEY, KID! YOU COME BACK! I KNOW YOU -- I KNOW YOUR POP!
HA HA HA HA HA!
CHARLES! YOU CAN'T --
CHARLES, THAT WAS STEALING! IF POPPA FINDS OUT --
AW, WHAT'S HE GONNA DO? OL' MAN EVANS TELLS POPPA, I JUST SAY IT WASN'T ME, IT WAS SOME OTHER KID.
YOU WANT A --
CHOOM WRAM KOMM
HUH? WHAT'S --
PEOPLE CALLED IT A TIME THE WORLD CHANGED. WE DIDN'T KNOW ANYTHING ABOUT THAT.
ALL WE KNEW THAT DAY --

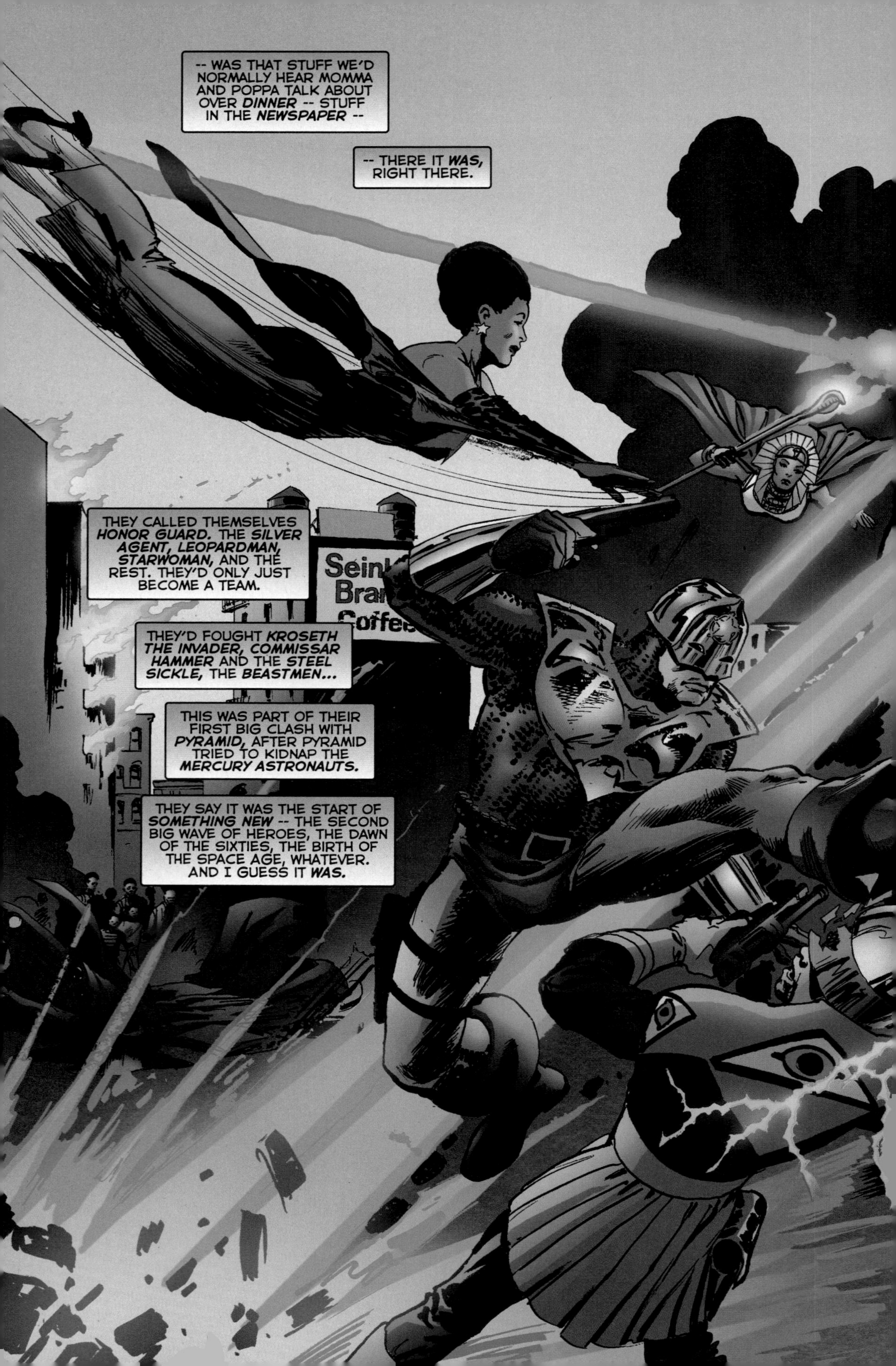

-- WAS THAT STUFF WE'D NORMALLY HEAR MOMMA AND POPPA TALK ABOUT OVER *DINNER* -- STUFF IN THE *NEWSPAPER* --
-- THERE IT *WAS*, RIGHT THERE.
THEY CALLED THEMSELVES *HONOR GUARD*. THE *SILVER AGENT*, *LEOPARDMAN*, *STARWOMAN*, AND THE REST. THEY'D ONLY JUST BECOME A TEAM.
THEY'D FOUGHT *KROSETH THE INVADER*, *COMMISSAR HAMMER* AND THE *STEEL SICKLE*, THE *BEASTMEN*...
THIS WAS PART OF THEIR FIRST BIG CLASH WITH *PYRAMID*, AFTER PYRAMID TRIED TO KIDNAP THE *MERCURY ASTRONAUTS*.
THEY SAY IT WAS THE START OF *SOMETHING NEW* -- THE SECOND BIG WAVE OF HEROES, THE DAWN OF THE SIXTIES, THE BIRTH OF THE SPACE AGE, WHATEVER. AND I GUESS IT *WAS*.

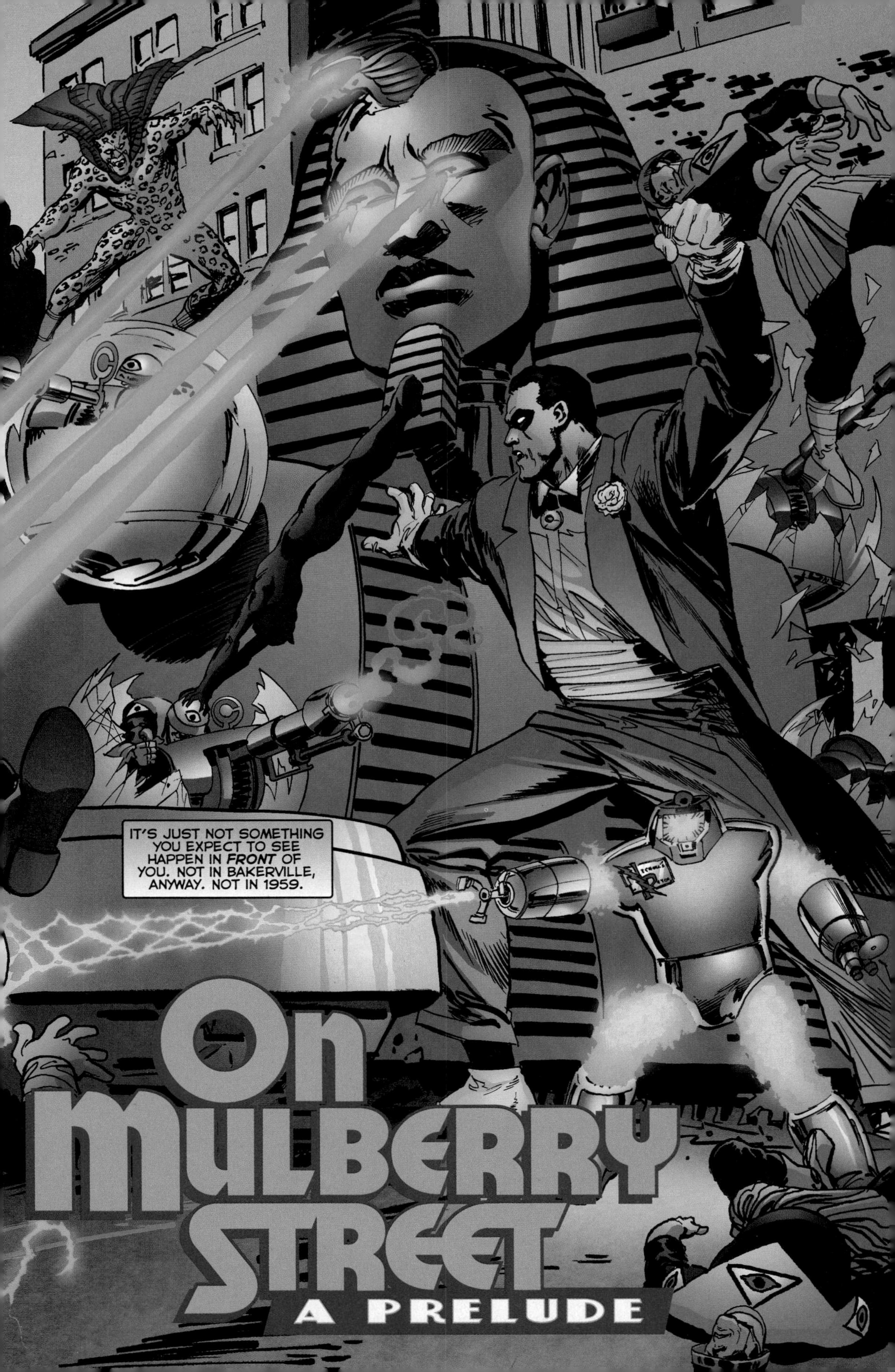
IT'S JUST NOT SOMETHING YOU EXPECT TO SEE HAPPEN IN FRONT OF YOU. NOT IN BAKERVILLE, ANYWAY. NOT IN 1959.
On Mulberry Street
A PRELUDE

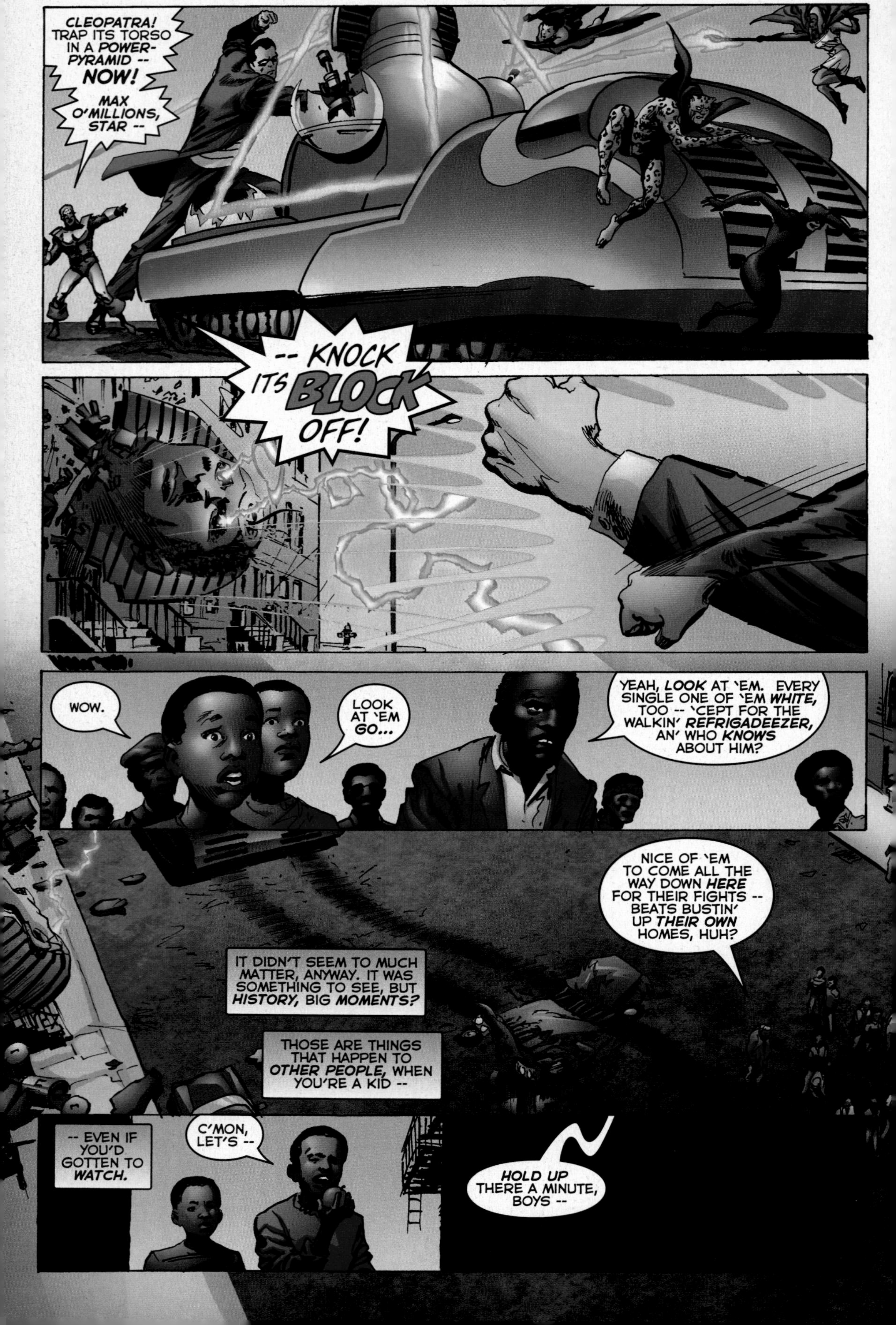
CLEOPATRA! TRAP ITS TORSO IN A POWER-PYRAMID -- NOW!
MAX O'MILLIONS, STAR --
-- KNOCK ITS BLOCK OFF!
WOW.
LOOK AT 'EM GO...
YEAH, LOOK AT 'EM. EVERY SINGLE ONE OF 'EM WHITE, TOO -- 'CEPT FOR THE WALKIN' REFRIGADEEZER, AN' WHO KNOWS ABOUT HIM?
NICE OF 'EM TO COME ALL THE WAY DOWN HERE FOR THEIR FIGHTS -- BEATS BUSTIN' UP THEIR OWN HOMES, HUH?
IT DIDN'T SEEM TO MUCH MATTER, ANYWAY. IT WAS SOMETHING TO SEE, BUT HISTORY, BIG MOMENTS?
THOSE ARE THINGS THAT HAPPEN TO OTHER PEOPLE, WHEN YOU'RE A KID --
-- EVEN IF YOU'D GOTTEN TO WATCH.
C'MON, LET'S --
HOLD UP THERE A MINUTE, BOYS --

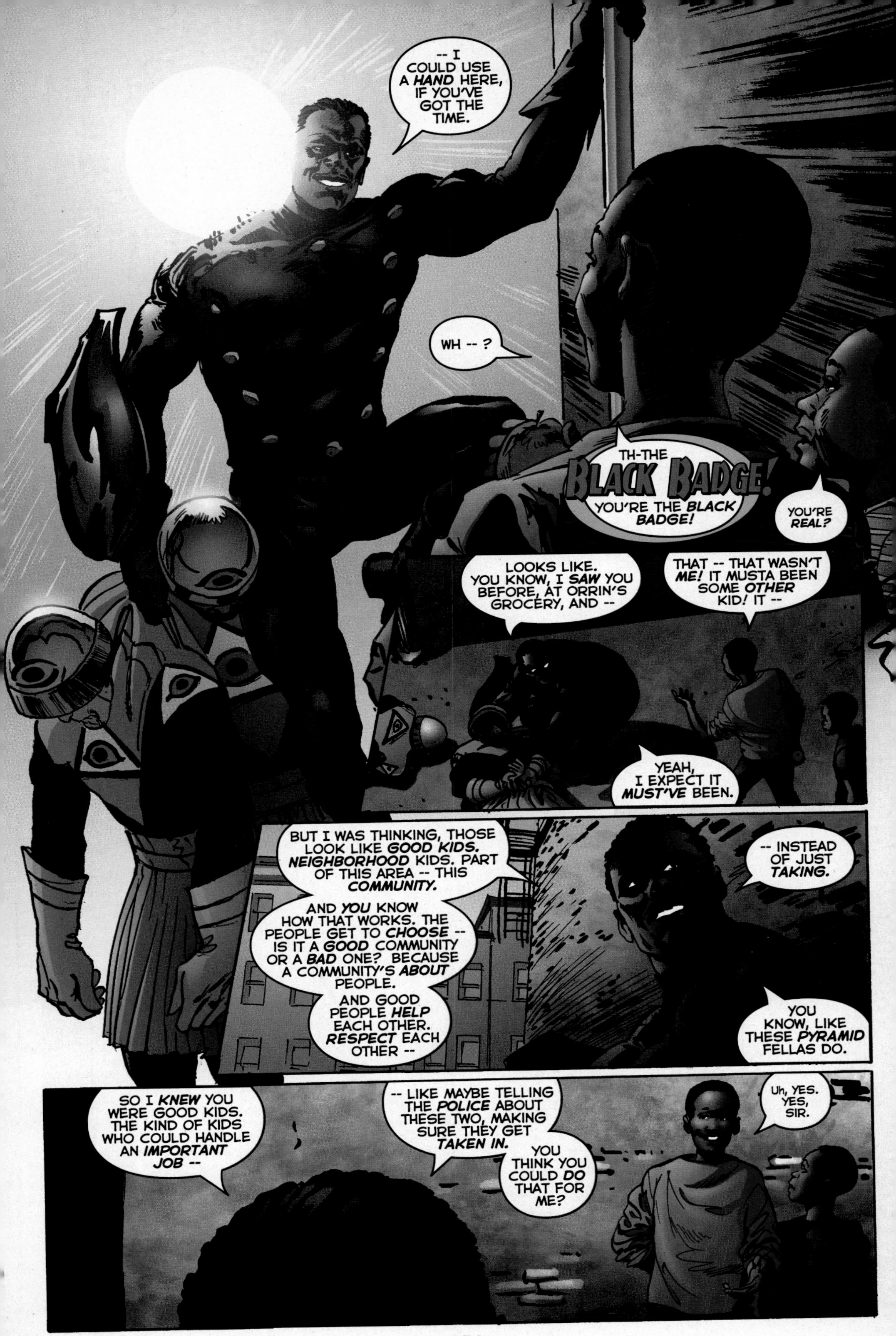

-- I COULD USE A HAND HERE, IF YOU'VE GOT THE TIME.
WH -- ?
TH-THE BLACK BADGE! YOU'RE THE BLACK BADGE!
YOU'RE REAL?
LOOKS LIKE. YOU KNOW, I SAW YOU BEFORE, AT ORRIN'S GROCERY, AND --
THAT -- THAT WASN'T ME! IT MUSTA BEEN SOME OTHER KID! IT --
YEAH, I EXPECT IT MUST'VE BEEN.
BUT I WAS THINKING, THOSE LOOK LIKE GOOD KIDS. NEIGHBORHOOD KIDS. PART OF THIS AREA -- THIS COMMUNITY.
AND YOU KNOW HOW THAT WORKS. THE PEOPLE GET TO CHOOSE -- IS IT A GOOD COMMUNITY OR A BAD ONE? BECAUSE A COMMUNITY'S ABOUT PEOPLE.
AND GOOD PEOPLE HELP EACH OTHER. RESPECT EACH OTHER --
-- INSTEAD OF JUST TAKING.
YOU KNOW, LIKE THESE PYRAMID FELLAS DO.
SO I KNEW YOU WERE GOOD KIDS. THE KIND OF KIDS WHO COULD HANDLE AN IMPORTANT JOB --
-- LIKE MAYBE TELLING THE POLICE ABOUT THESE TWO, MAKING SURE THEY GET TAKEN IN.
YOU THINK YOU COULD DO THAT FOR ME?
Uh, YES. YES, SIR.

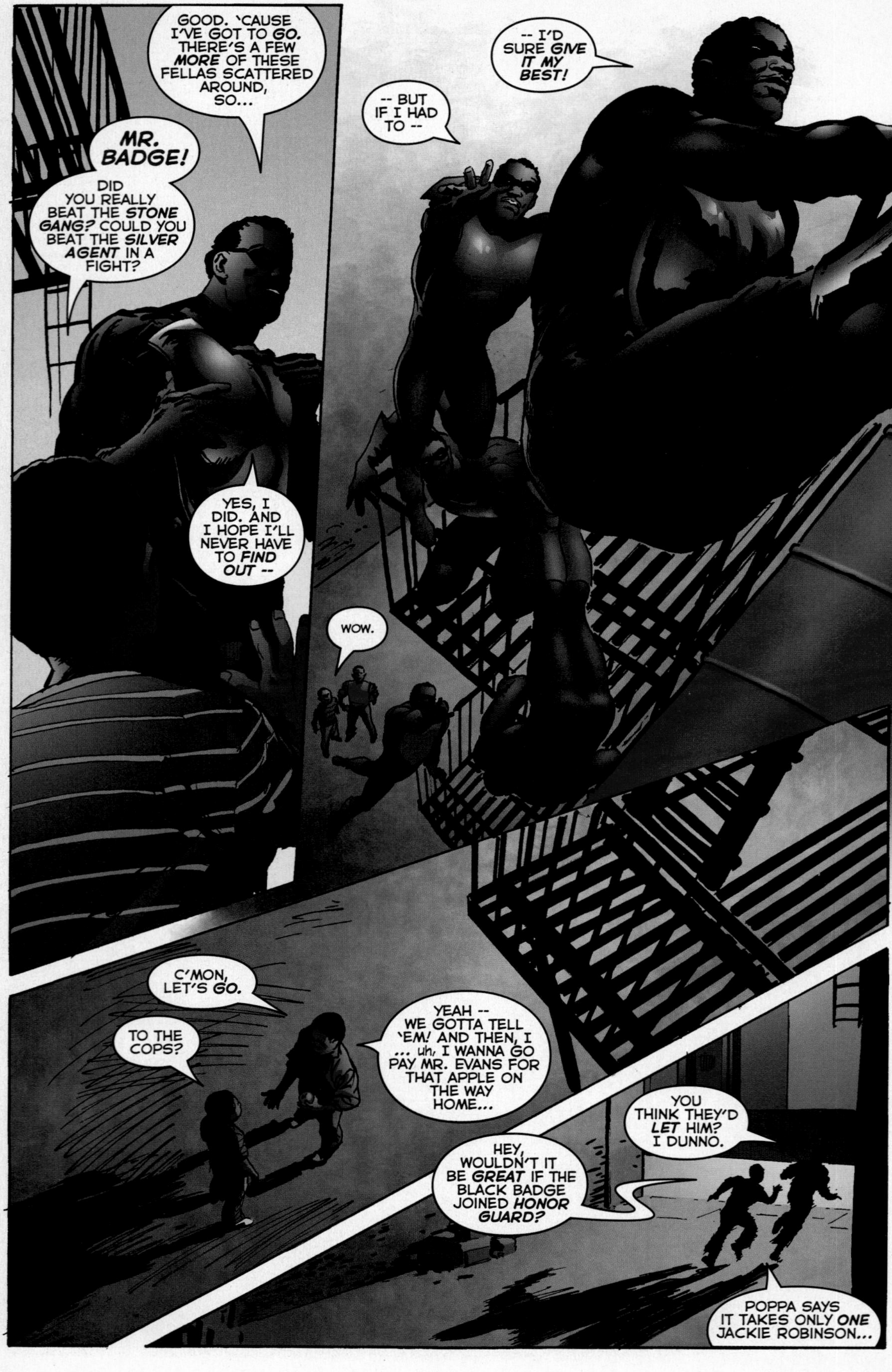
GOOD. 'CAUSE I'VE GOT TO GO. THERE'S A FEW MORE OF THESE FELLAS SCATTERED AROUND, SO...
MR. BADGE!
DID YOU REALLY BEAT THE STONE GANG? COULD YOU BEAT THE SILVER AGENT IN A FIGHT?
YES, I DID. AND I HOPE I'LL NEVER HAVE TO FIND OUT --
-- BUT IF I HAD TO --
-- I'D SURE GIVE IT MY BEST!
WOW.
C'MON, LET'S GO.
TO THE COPS?
YEAH -- WE GOTTA TELL 'EM! AND THEN, I ... uh, I WANNA GO PAY MR. EVANS FOR THAT APPLE ON THE WAY HOME...
HEY, WOULDN'T IT BE GREAT IF THE BLACK BADGE JOINED HONOR GUARD?
YOU THINK THEY'D LET HIM? I DUNNO.
POPPA SAYS IT TAKES ONLY ONE JACKIE ROBINSON...

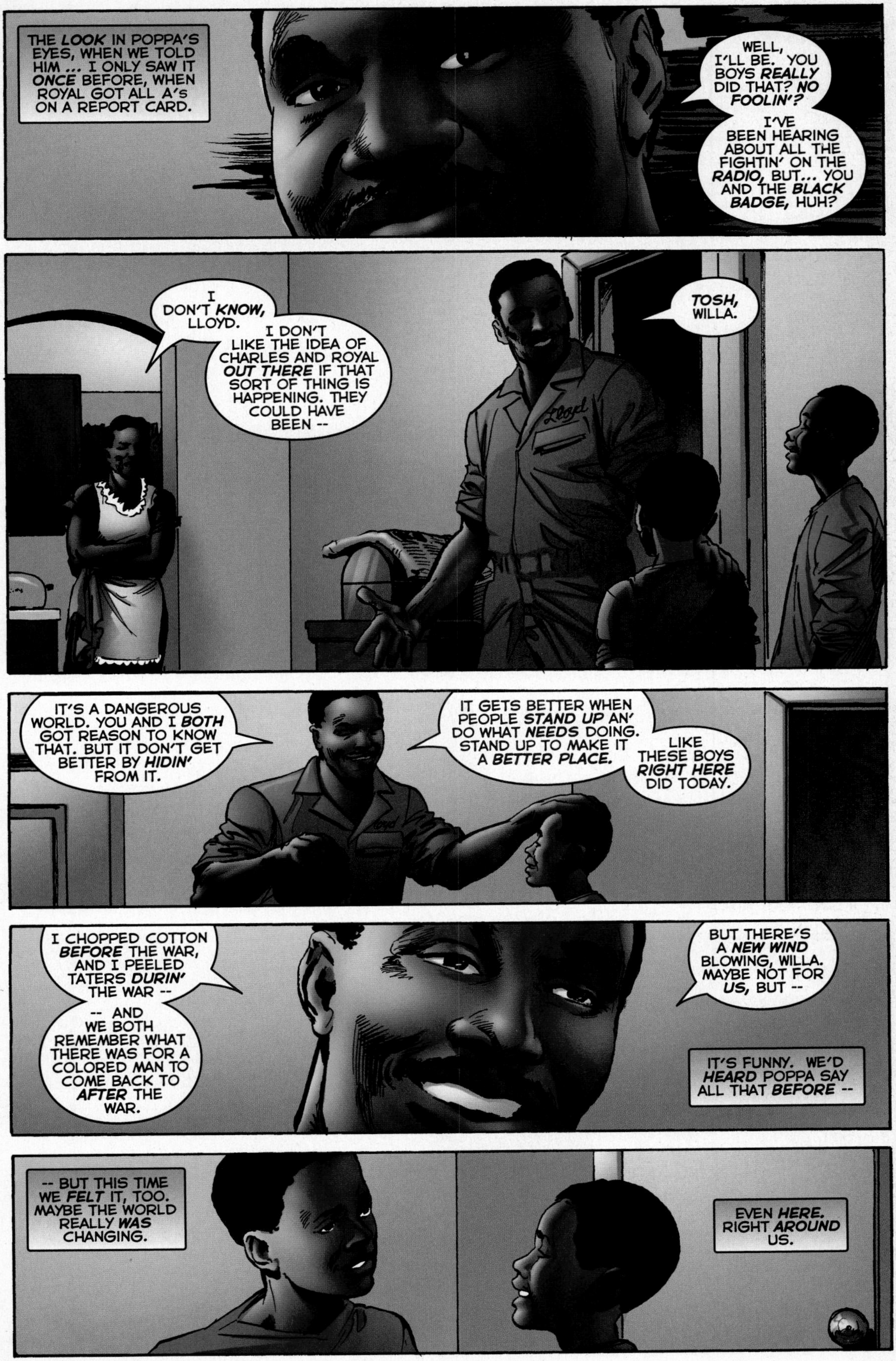

THE LOOK IN POPPA'S EYES, WHEN WE TOLD HIM ... I ONLY SAW IT ONCE BEFORE, WHEN ROYAL GOT ALL A's ON A REPORT CARD.
WELL, I'LL BE. YOU BOYS REALLY DID THAT? NO FOOLIN'?
I'VE BEEN HEARING ABOUT ALL THE FIGHTIN' ON THE RADIO, BUT... YOU AND THE BLACK BADGE, HUH?
I DON'T KNOW, LLOYD.
I DON'T LIKE THE IDEA OF CHARLES AND ROYAL OUT THERE IF THAT SORT OF THING IS HAPPENING. THEY COULD HAVE BEEN --
TOSH, WILLA.
IT'S A DANGEROUS WORLD. YOU AND I BOTH GOT REASON TO KNOW THAT. BUT IT DON'T GET BETTER BY HIDIN' FROM IT.
IT GETS BETTER WHEN PEOPLE STAND UP AN' DO WHAT NEEDS DOING. STAND UP TO MAKE IT A BETTER PLACE.
LIKE THESE BOYS RIGHT HERE DID TODAY.
I CHOPPED COTTON BEFORE THE WAR, AND I PEELED TATERS DURIN' THE WAR --
-- AND WE BOTH REMEMBER WHAT THERE WAS FOR A COLORED MAN TO COME BACK TO AFTER THE WAR.
BUT THERE'S A NEW WIND BLOWING, WILLA. MAYBE NOT FOR US, BUT --
IT'S FUNNY. WE'D HEARD POPPA SAY ALL THAT BEFORE --
-- BUT THIS TIME WE FELT IT, TOO. MAYBE THE WORLD REALLY WAS CHANGING.
EVEN HERE. RIGHT AROUND US.

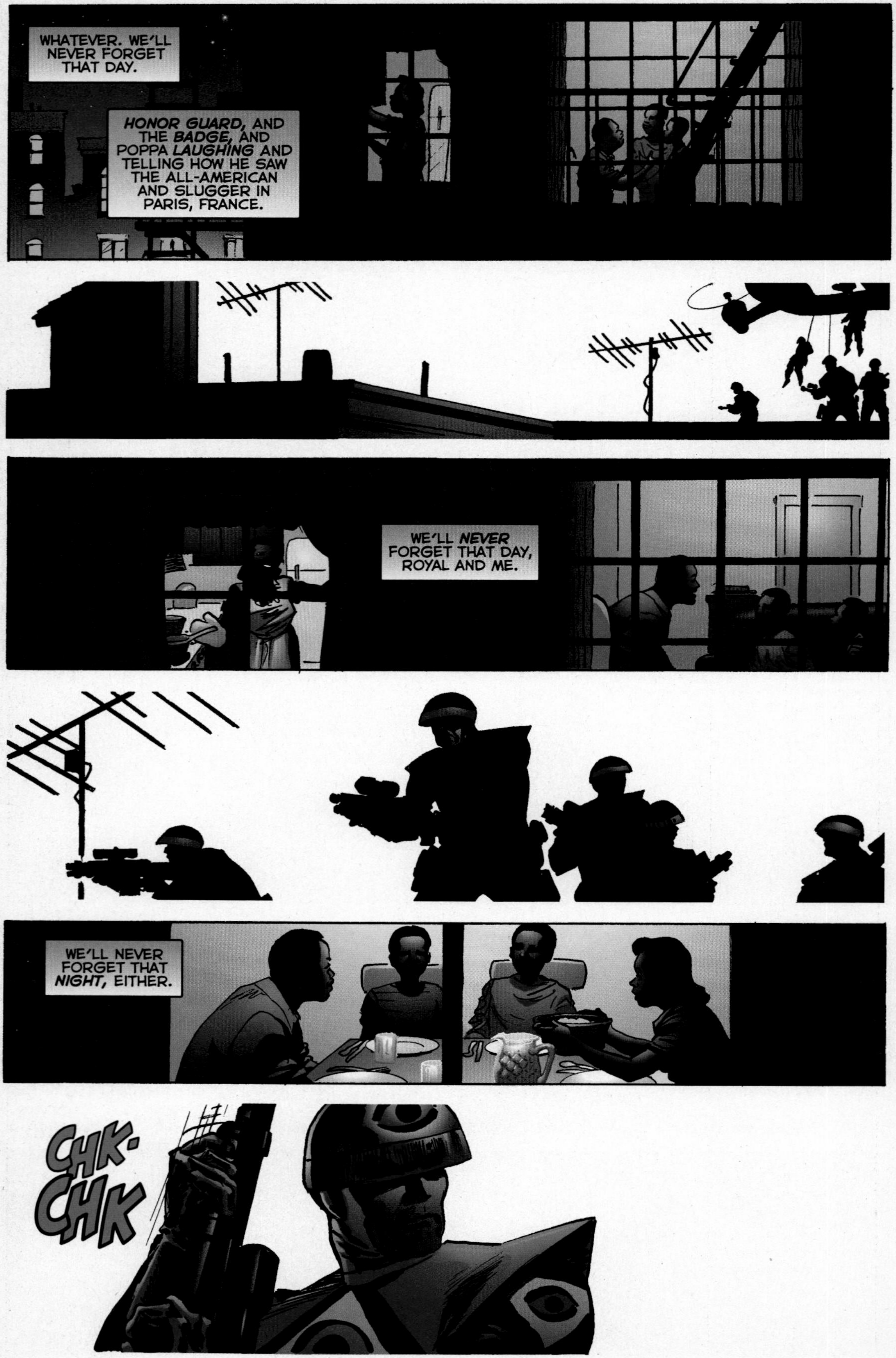
WHATEVER. WE'LL NEVER FORGET THAT DAY.
HONOR GUARD, AND THE BADGE, AND POPPA LAUGHING AND TELLING HOW HE SAW THE ALL-AMERICAN AND SLUGGER IN PARIS, FRANCE.
WE'LL NEVER FORGET THAT DAY, ROYAL AND ME.
WE'LL NEVER FORGET THAT NIGHT, EITHER.
CHK-CHK

BOOK ONE

THICKER THAN WATER

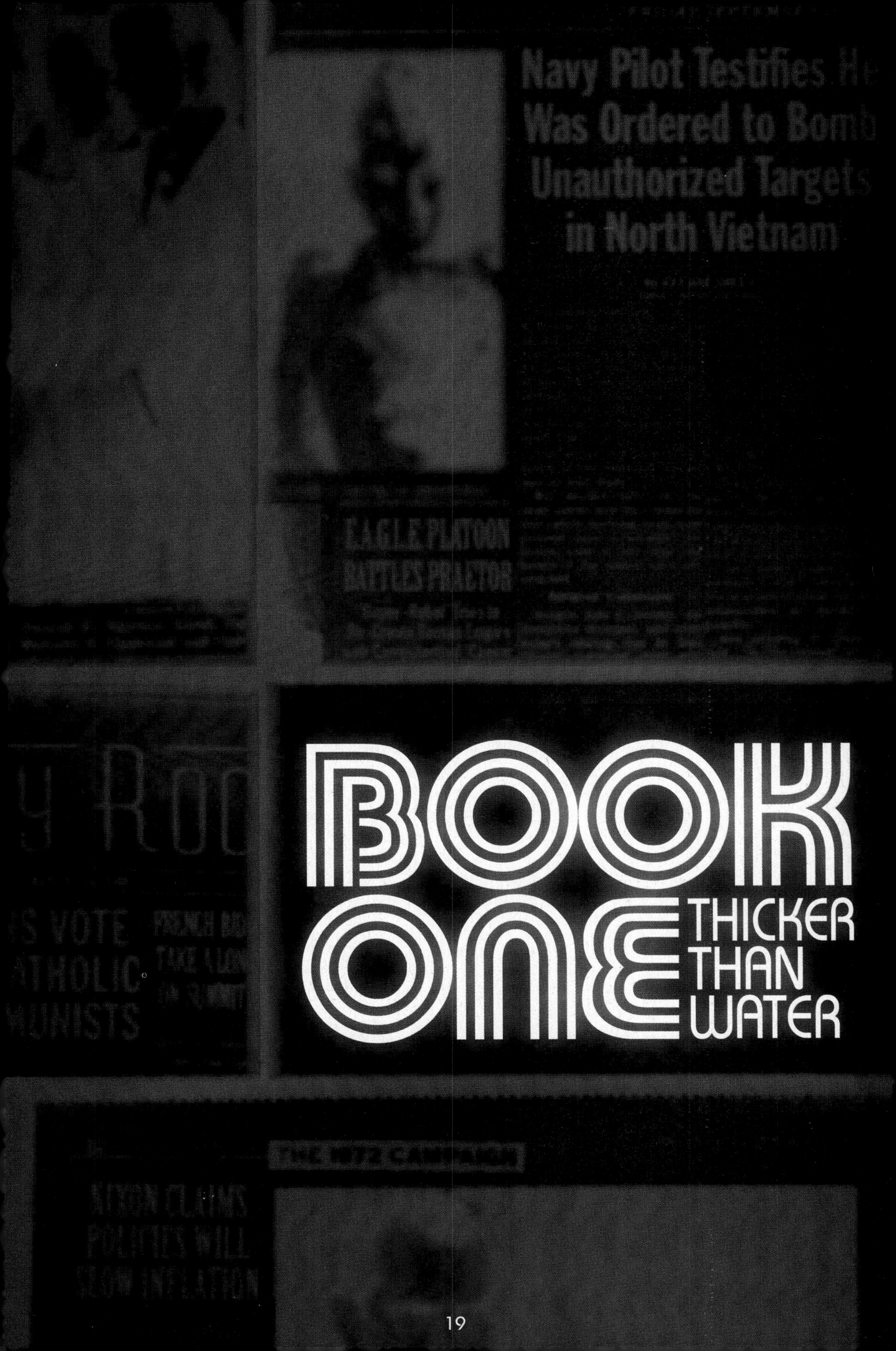
Navy Pilot Testifies He Was Ordered to Bomb Unauthorized Targets in North Vietnam
E.A.G.L.E. PLATOON BATTLES PRAECTOR
THE 1972 CAMPAIGN
NIXON CLAIMS POLICIES WILL SLOW INFLATION

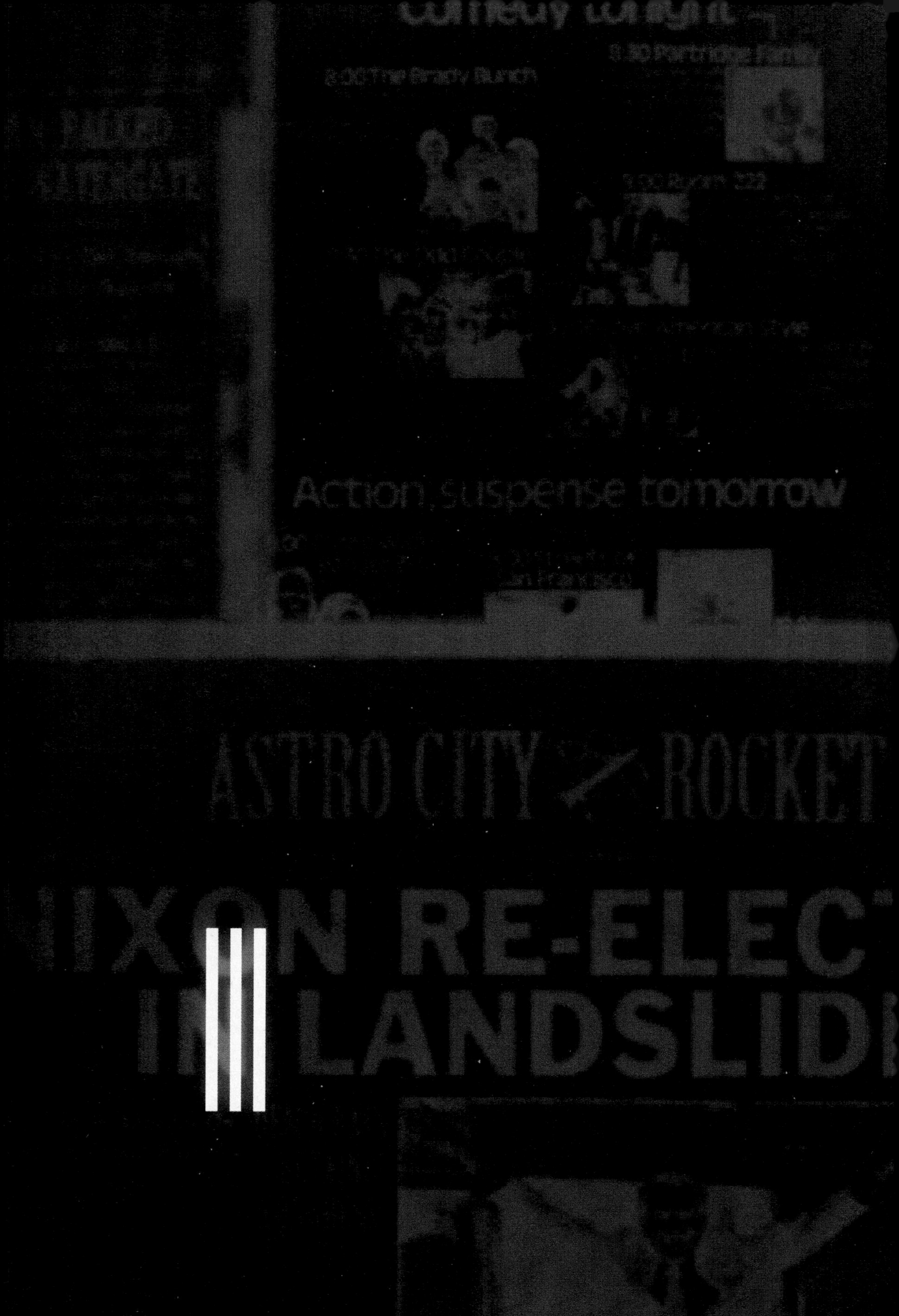

8:00 The Brady Bunch
Action, suspense tomorrow
ASTRO CITY
ROCKET
IXON RE-ELEC
LANDSLID

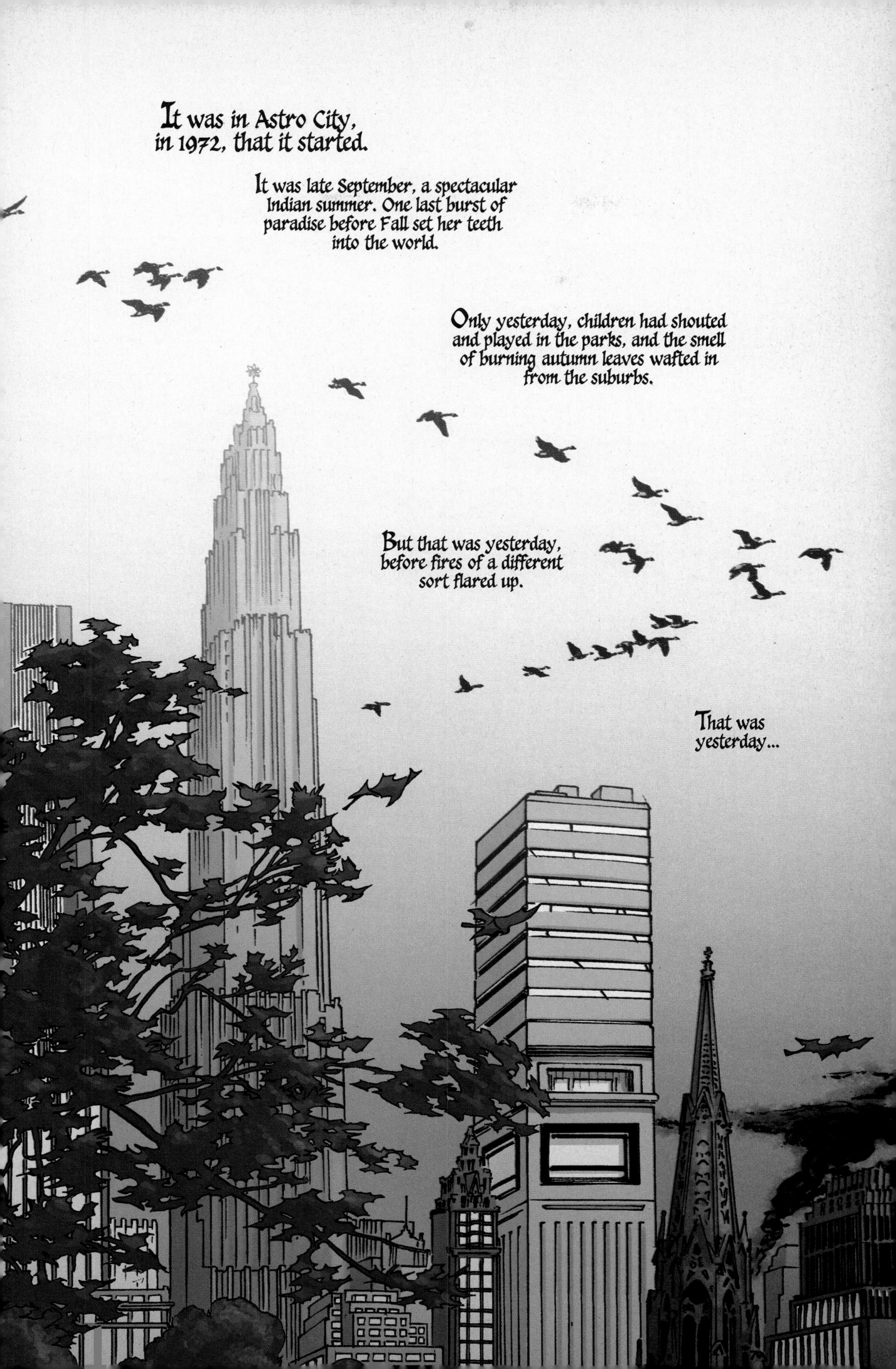
It was in Astro City, in 1972, that it started.
It was late September, a spectacular Indian summer. One last burst of paradise before Fall set her teeth into the world.
Only yesterday, children had shouted and played in the parks, and the smell of burning autumn leaves wafted in from the suburbs.
But that was yesterday, before fires of a different sort flared up.
That was yesterday...

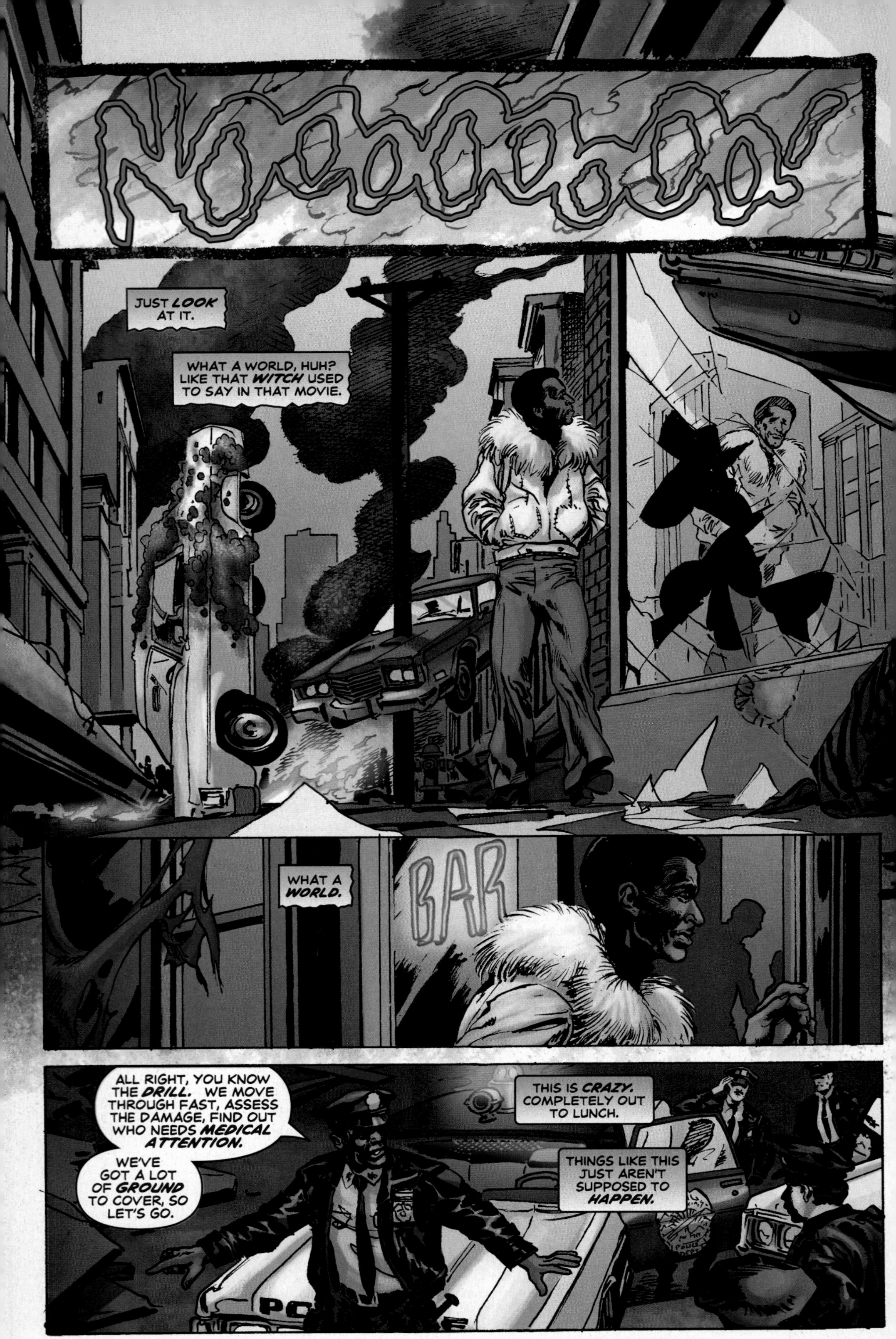
NOOOOOOOO!
JUST LOOK AT IT.
WHAT A WORLD, HUH? LIKE THAT WITCH USED TO SAY IN THAT MOVIE.
WHAT A WORLD.
BAR
ALL RIGHT, YOU KNOW THE DRILL. WE MOVE THROUGH FAST, ASSESS THE DAMAGE, FIND OUT WHO NEEDS MEDICAL ATTENTION.
WE'VE GOT A LOT OF GROUND TO COVER, SO LET'S GO.
THIS IS CRAZY. COMPLETELY OUT TO LUNCH.
THINGS LIKE THIS JUST AREN'T SUPPOSED TO HAPPEN.

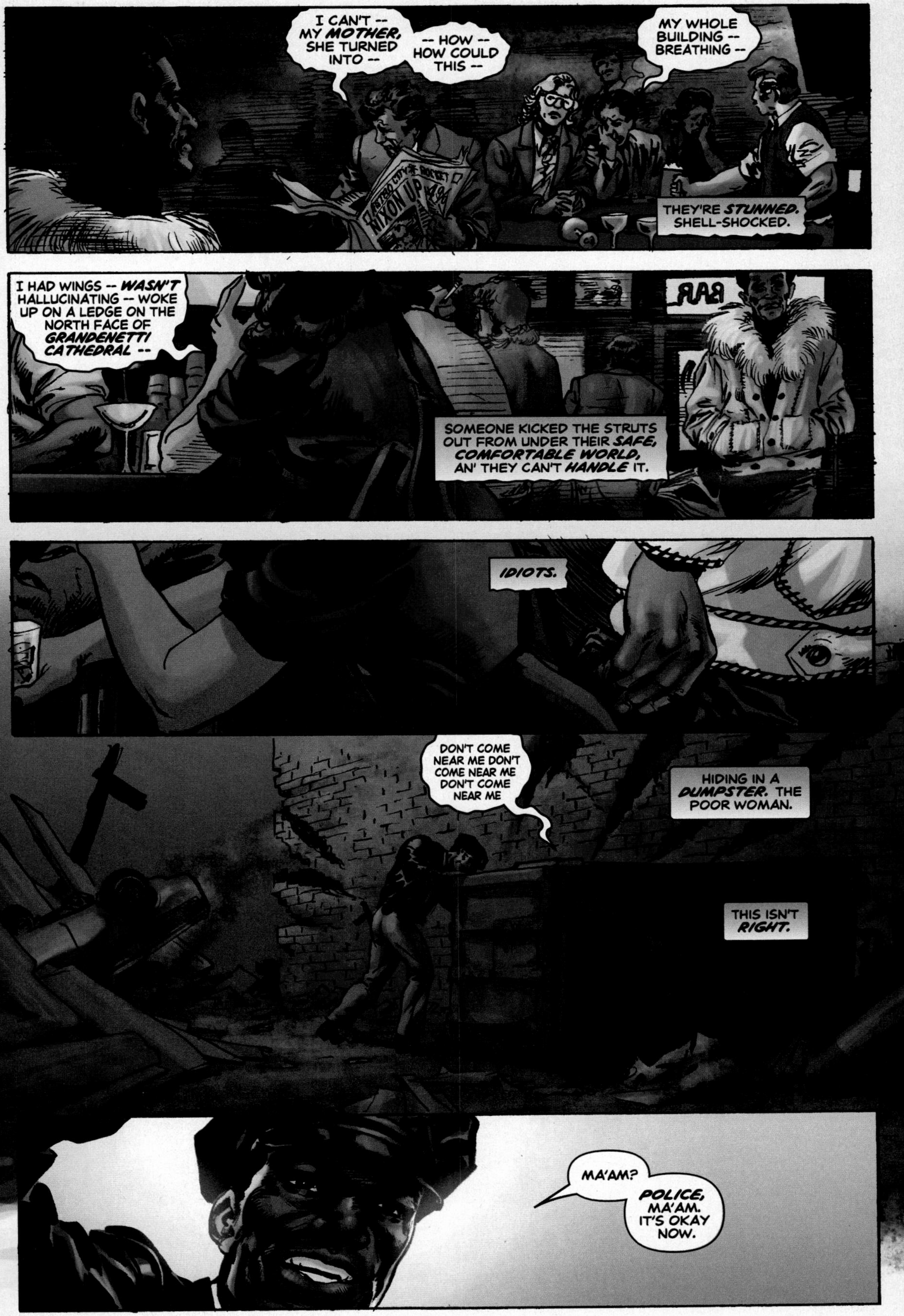
I CAN'T -- MY MOTHER, SHE TURNED INTO --
-- HOW -- HOW COULD THIS --
MY WHOLE BUILDING -- BREATHING --
NIXON UP
THEY'RE STUNNED. SHELL-SHOCKED.
I HAD WINGS -- WASN'T HALLUCINATING -- WOKE UP ON A LEDGE ON THE NORTH FACE OF GRANDENETTI CATHEDRAL --
BAR
SOMEONE KICKED THE STRUTS OUT FROM UNDER THEIR SAFE, COMFORTABLE WORLD, AN' THEY CAN'T HANDLE IT.
IDIOTS.
DON'T COME NEAR ME DON'T COME NEAR ME DON'T COME NEAR ME
HIDING IN A DUMPSTER. THE POOR WOMAN.
THIS ISN'T RIGHT.
MA'AM?
POLICE, MA'AM. IT'S OKAY NOW.

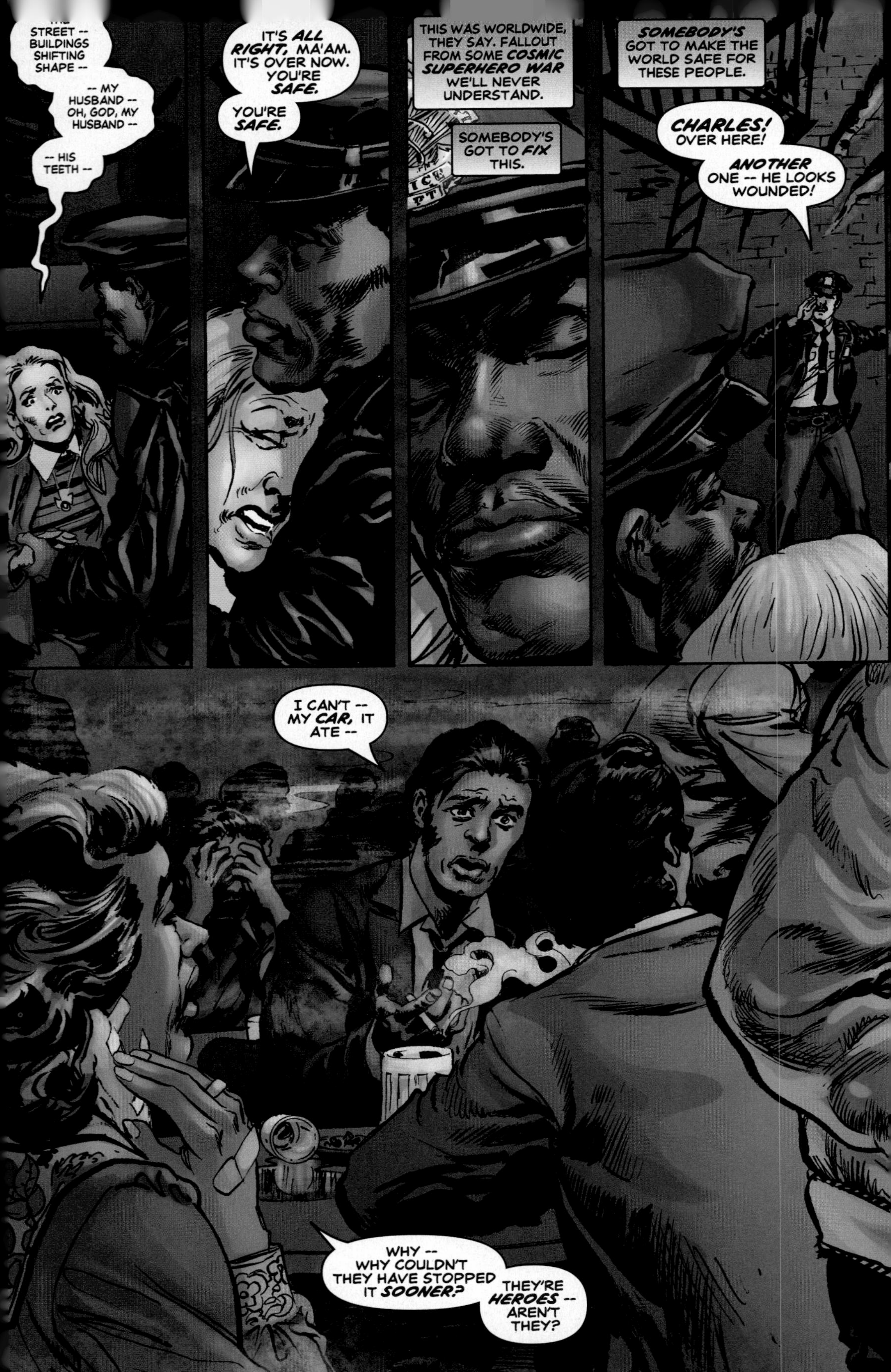
STREET -- BUILDINGS SHIFTING SHAPE --
-- MY HUSBAND -- OH, GOD, MY HUSBAND --
-- HIS TEETH --
IT'S ALL RIGHT, MA'AM. IT'S OVER NOW. YOU'RE SAFE.
YOU'RE SAFE.
THIS WAS WORLDWIDE, THEY SAY. FALLOUT FROM SOME COSMIC SUPERHERO WAR WE'LL NEVER UNDERSTAND.
SOMEBODY'S GOT TO FIX THIS.
SOMEBODY'S GOT TO MAKE THE WORLD SAFE FOR THESE PEOPLE.
CHARLES! OVER HERE!
ANOTHER ONE -- HE LOOKS WOUNDED!
I CAN'T -- MY CAR, IT ATE --
WHY -- WHY COULDN'T THEY HAVE STOPPED IT SOONER?
THEY'RE HEROES -- AREN'T THEY?

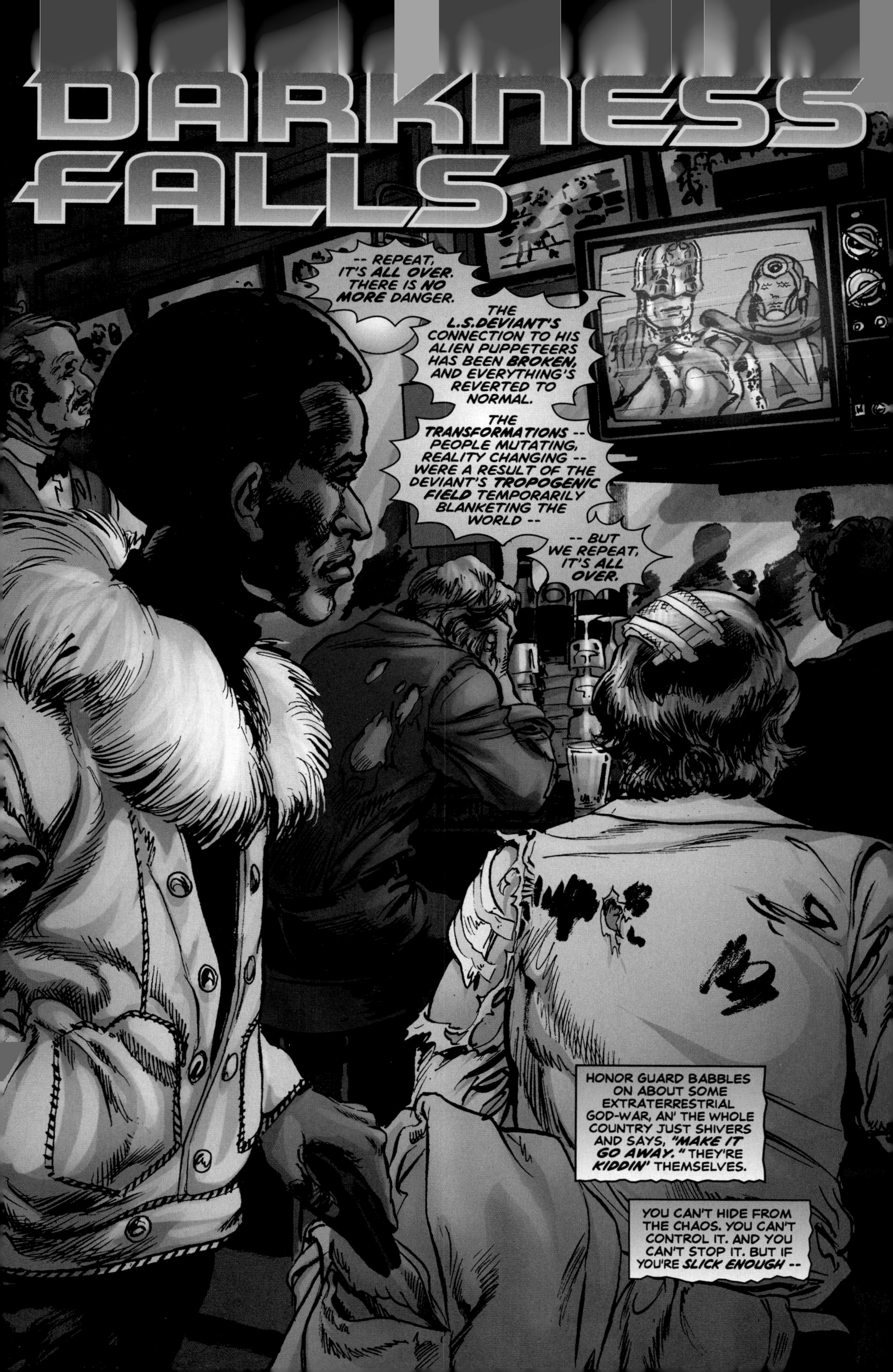
DARKNESS FALLS
-- REPEAT, IT'S ALL OVER. THERE IS NO MORE DANGER.
THE L.S.DEVIANT'S CONNECTION TO HIS ALIEN PUPPETEERS HAS BEEN BROKEN, AND EVERYTHING'S REVERTED TO NORMAL.
THE TRANSFORMATIONS -- PEOPLE MUTATING, REALITY CHANGING -- WERE A RESULT OF THE DEVIANT'S TROPOGENIC FIELD TEMPORARILY BLANKETING THE WORLD --
-- BUT WE REPEAT, IT'S ALL OVER.
HONOR GUARD BABBLES ON ABOUT SOME EXTRATERRESTRIAL GOD-WAR, AN' THE WHOLE COUNTRY JUST SHIVERS AND SAYS, "MAKE IT GO AWAY." THEY'RE KIDDIN' THEMSELVES.
YOU CAN'T HIDE FROM THE CHAOS. YOU CAN'T CONTROL IT. AND YOU CAN'T STOP IT. BUT IF YOU'RE SLICK ENOUGH --

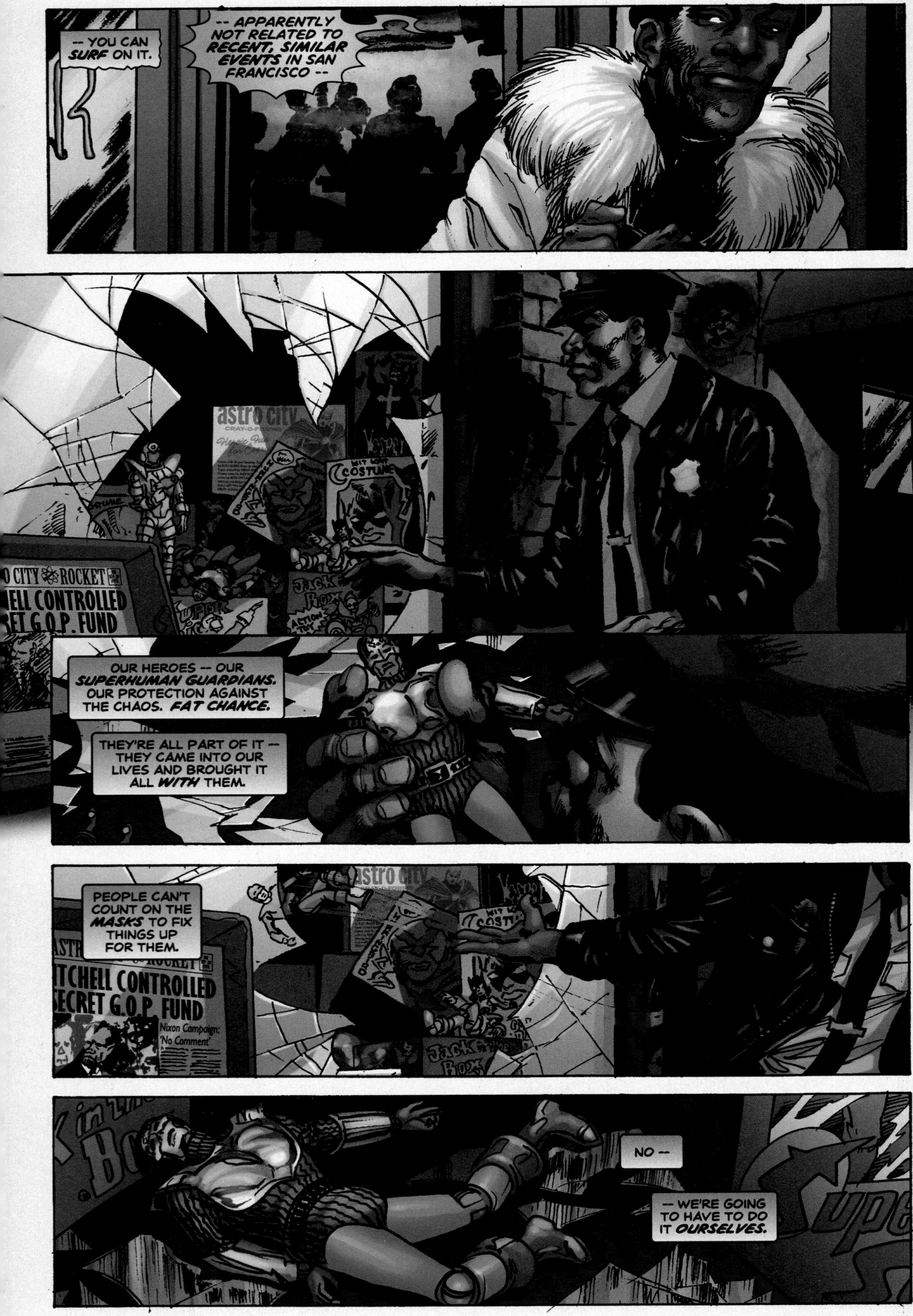
-- YOU CAN SURF ON IT.
-- APPARENTLY NOT RELATED TO RECENT, SIMILAR EVENTS IN SAN FRANCISCO --
astro city
COSTUME
ELL CONTROLLED
SET G.O.P. FUND
OUR HEROES -- OUR SUPERHUMAN GUARDIANS. OUR PROTECTION AGAINST THE CHAOS. FAT CHANCE.
THEY'RE ALL PART OF IT -- THEY CAME INTO OUR LIVES AND BROUGHT IT ALL WITH THEM.
PEOPLE CAN'T COUNT ON THE MASKS TO FIX THINGS UP FOR THEM.
ITCHELL CONTROLLED
SECRET G.O.P. FUND
Nixon Campaign: 'No Comment'
NO --
-- WE'RE GOING TO HAVE TO DO IT OURSELVES.

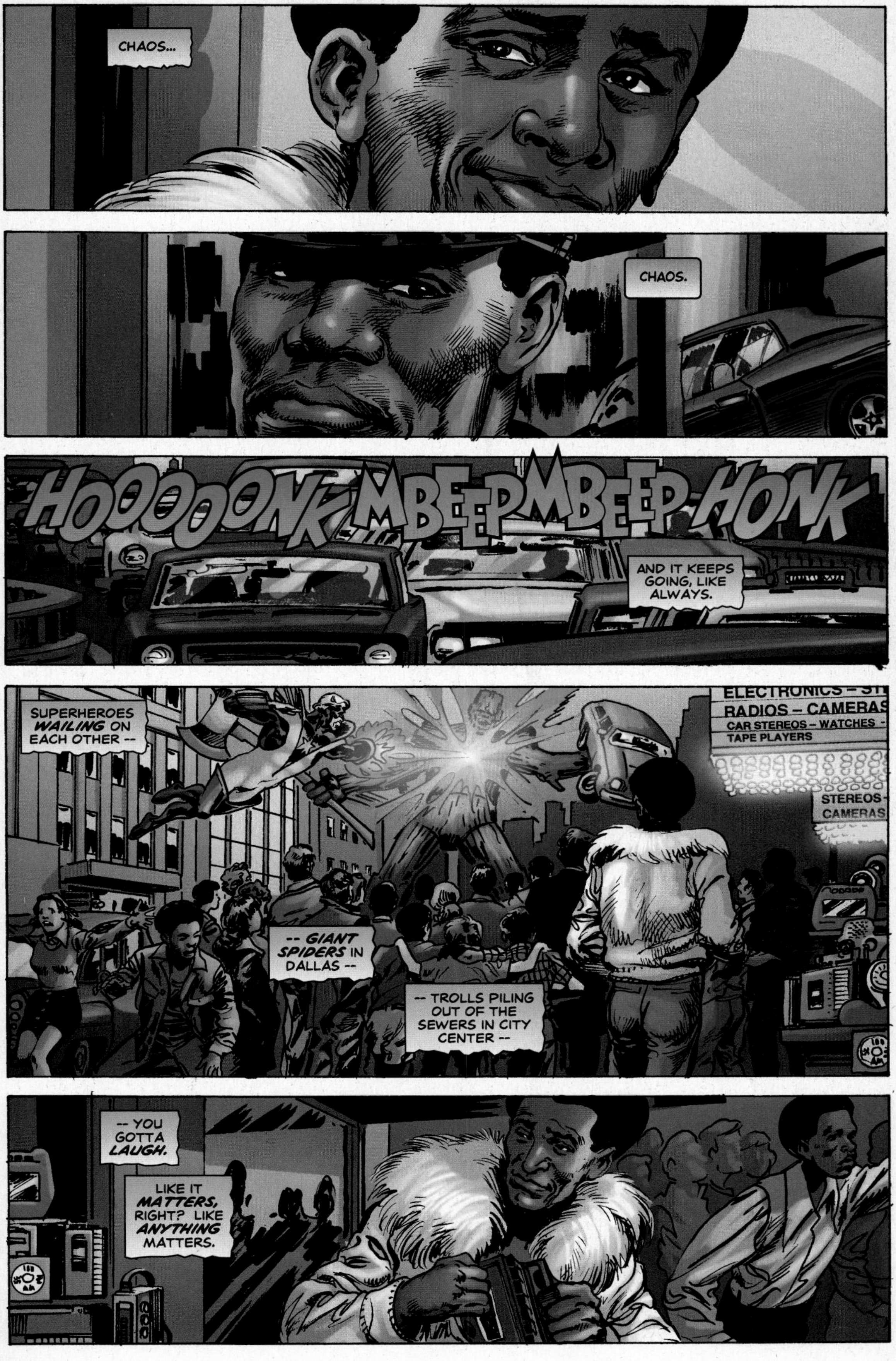
CHAOS...
CHAOS.
HOOOOOONK MBEEPMBEEP HONK
AND IT KEEPS GOING, LIKE ALWAYS.
SUPERHEROES WAILING ON EACH OTHER --
-- GIANT SPIDERS IN DALLAS --
-- TROLLS PILING OUT OF THE SEWERS IN CITY CENTER --
ELECTRONICS
RADIOS – CAMERAS
CAR STEREOS – WATCHES
TAPE PLAYERS
STEREOS
CAMERAS
-- YOU GOTTA LAUGH.
LIKE IT MATTERS, RIGHT? LIKE ANYTHING MATTERS.

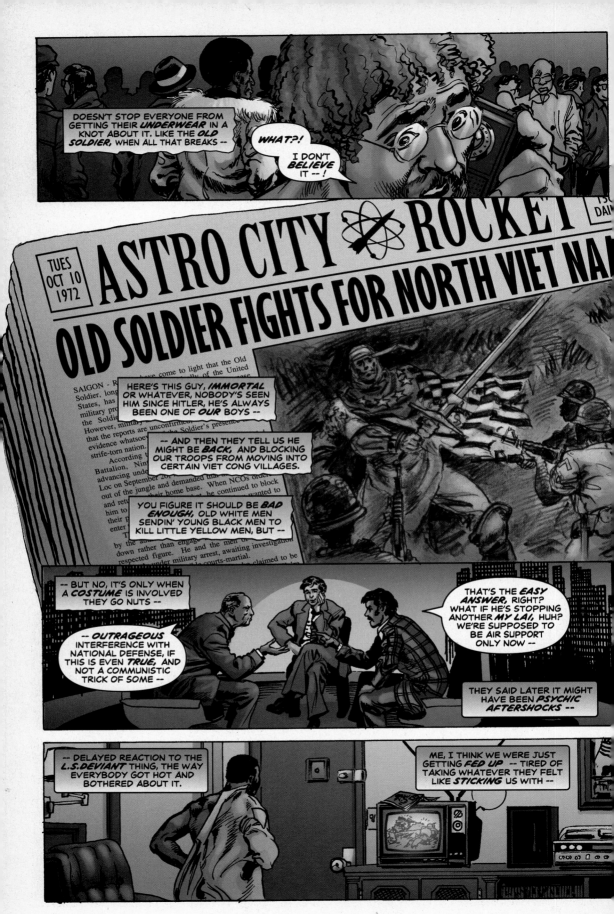

DOESN'T STOP EVERYONE FROM GETTING THEIR *UNDERWEAR* IN A KNOT ABOUT IT. LIKE THE *OLD SOLDIER,* WHEN ALL THAT BREAKS --

WHAT?!

I DON'T *BELIEVE* IT -- !

ASTRO CITY ROCKET

TUES OCT 10 1972

OLD SOLDIER FIGHTS FOR NORTH VIET NAM

HERE'S THIS GUY, *IMMORTAL* OR WHATEVER, NOBODY'S SEEN HIM SINCE HITLER, HE'S ALWAYS BEEN ONE OF *OUR* BOYS --

-- AND THEN THEY TELL US HE MIGHT BE *BACK,* AND BLOCKING OUR TROOPS FROM MOVING INTO CERTAIN VIET CONG VILLAGES.

YOU FIGURE IT SHOULD BE *BAD ENOUGH,* OLD WHITE MEN SENDIN' YOUNG BLACK MEN TO KILL LITTLE YELLOW MEN, BUT --

-- BUT NO, IT'S ONLY WHEN A *COSTUME* IS INVOLVED THEY GO NUTS --

-- *OUTRAGEOUS* INTERFERENCE WITH NATIONAL DEFENSE, IF THIS IS EVEN *TRUE,* AND NOT A COMMUNISTIC TRICK OF SOME --

THAT'S THE *EASY ANSWER,* RIGHT? WHAT IF HE'S STOPPING ANOTHER *MY LAI,* HUH? WE'RE SUPPOSED TO BE AIR SUPPORT ONLY NOW --

THEY SAID LATER IT MIGHT HAVE BEEN *PSYCHIC AFTERSHOCKS* --

-- DELAYED REACTION TO THE *L.S. DEVIANT* THING, THE WAY EVERYBODY GOT HOT AND BOTHERED ABOUT IT.

ME, I THINK WE WERE JUST GETTING *FED UP* -- TIRED OF TAKING WHATEVER THEY FELT LIKE *STICKING* US WITH --

28

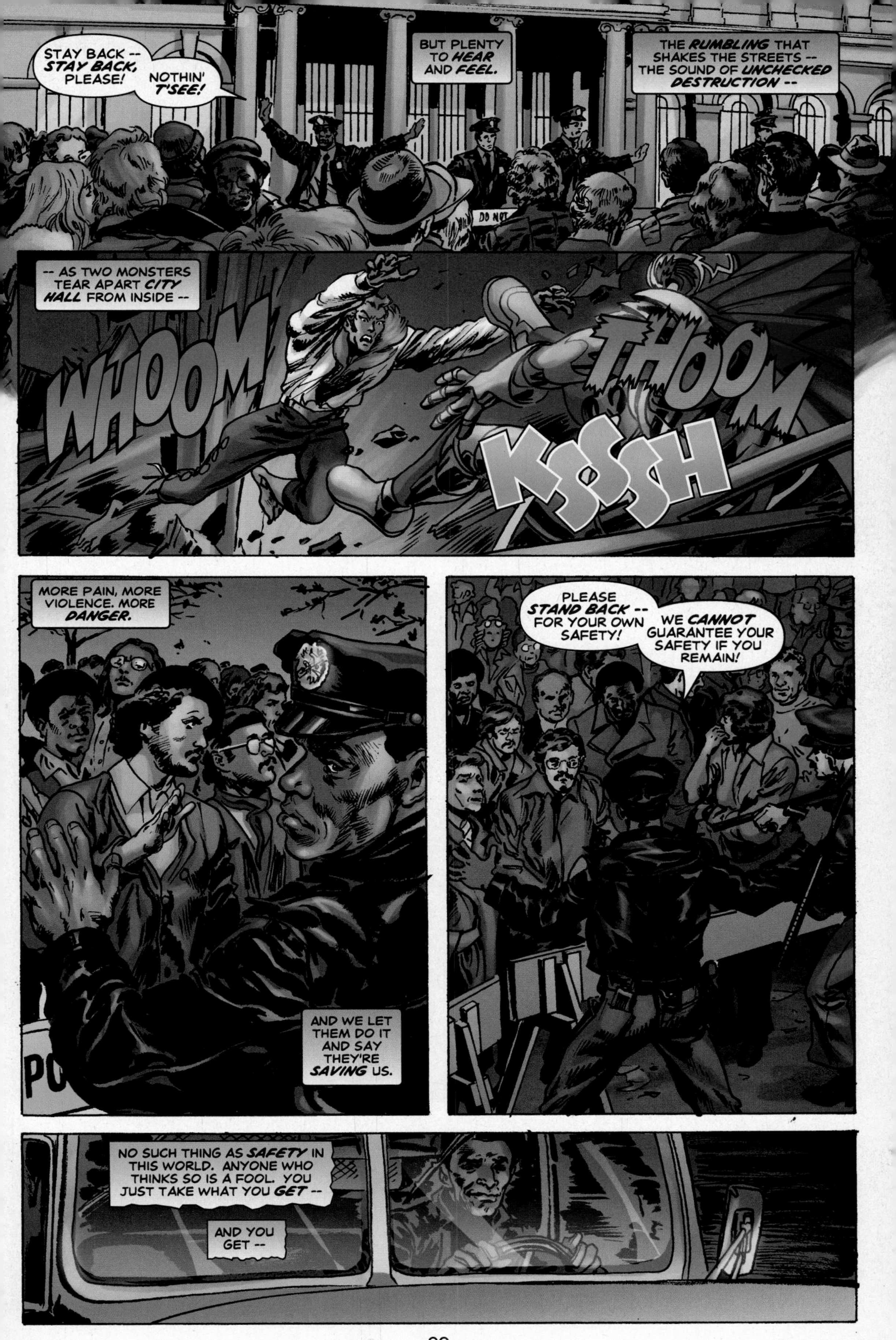
STAY BACK -- STAY BACK, PLEASE!
NOTHIN' T'SEE!
BUT PLENTY TO HEAR AND FEEL.
THE RUMBLING THAT SHAKES THE STREETS -- THE SOUND OF UNCHECKED DESTRUCTION --
DO NOT
-- AS TWO MONSTERS TEAR APART CITY HALL FROM INSIDE --
WHOOM
THOOM
KSSSH
MORE PAIN, MORE VIOLENCE. MORE DANGER.
AND WE LET THEM DO IT AND SAY THEY'RE SAVING US.
PO
PLEASE STAND BACK -- FOR YOUR OWN SAFETY!
WE CANNOT GUARANTEE YOUR SAFETY IF YOU REMAIN!
NO SUCH THING AS SAFETY IN THIS WORLD. ANYONE WHO THINKS SO IS A FOOL. YOU JUST TAKE WHAT YOU GET --
AND YOU GET --

-- WHAT YOU TAKE!

SKREEEEEEE

WHAT?!

HEY --!

T-KASSH

PERFECT! BULLET-PROOF GLASS, HAH!

THESE GUYS WERE FROM *OUT OF TOWN.* I DIDN'T KNOW 'EM -- BUT I KNEW GUYS WHO *KNEW* GUYS.

THEY NEEDED SOMEONE WHO KNEW *ASTRO* AND I NEEDED A SHOT, SO I *LIED* TO 'EM, SAID I WAS AN OLD HAND.

NIGHTY-NIGHT, RENT-A-COPS --

BUT EVERYBODY LIES. THE *WORLD'S* A LIE.

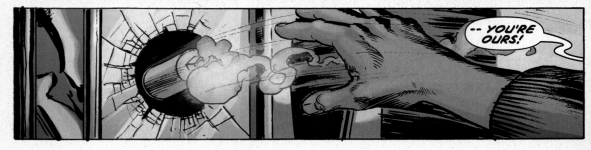

-- YOU'RE OURS!

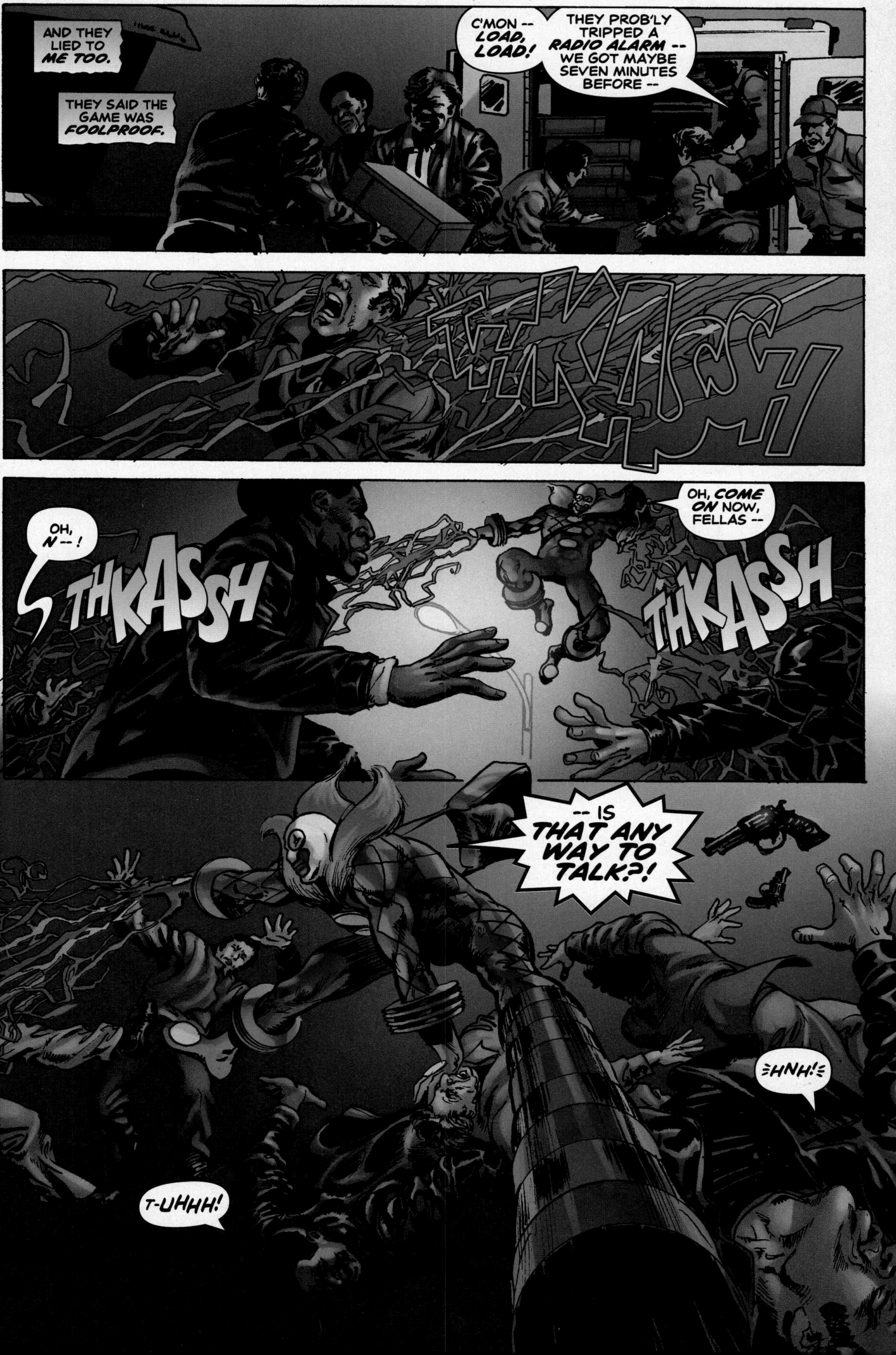
AND THEY LIED TO *ME TOO.*
THEY SAID THE GAME WAS *FOOLPROOF.*
C'MON -- *LOAD, LOAD!*
THEY PROB'LY TRIPPED A *RADIO ALARM* -- WE GOT MAYBE SEVEN MINUTES BEFORE --
THKASSH
OH, *N* -- !
THKASSH
OH, *COME ON* NOW, FELLAS --
THKASSH
-- IS *THAT ANY WAY TO TALK?!*
HNH!
T-UHHH!

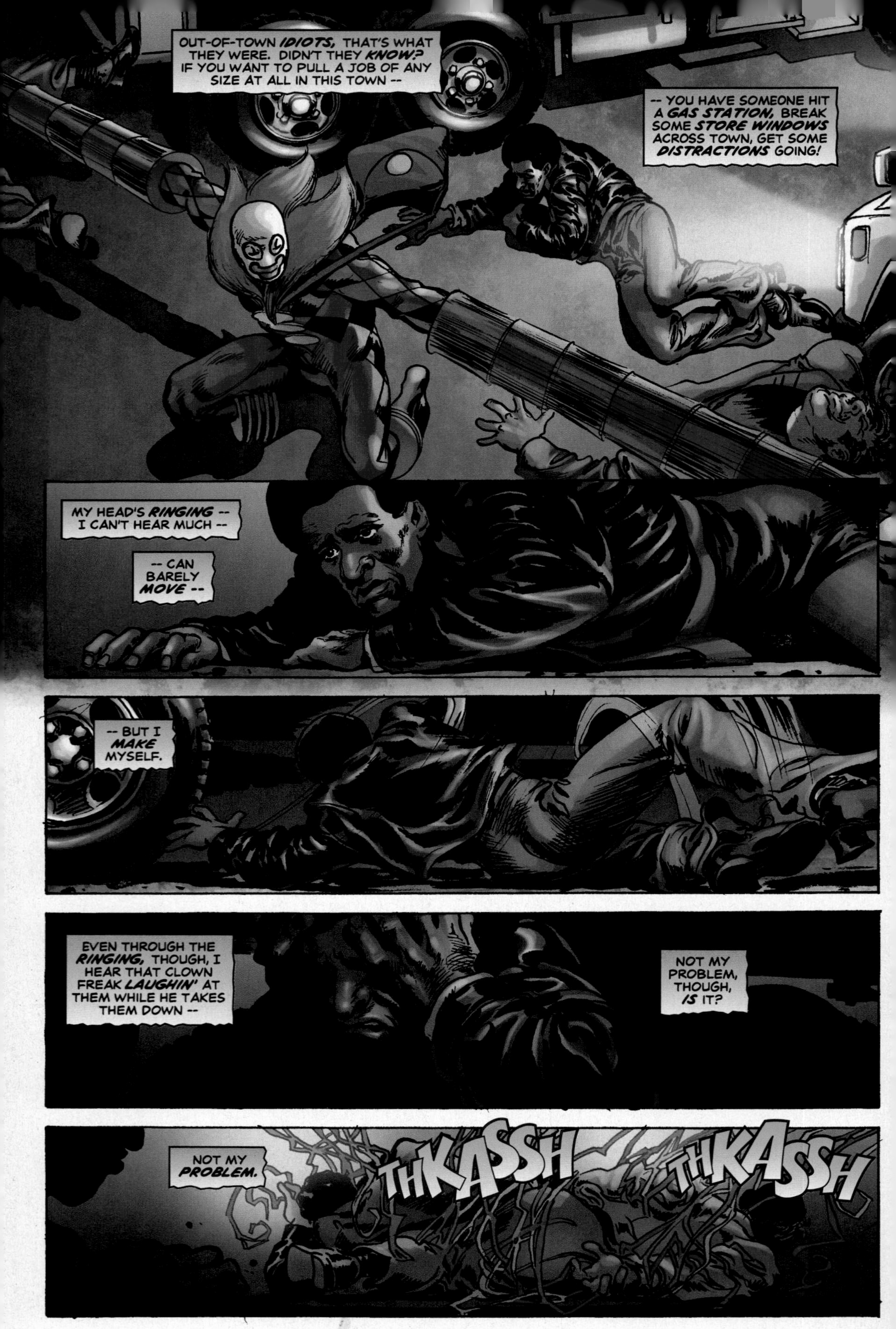
OUT-OF-TOWN *IDIOTS,* THAT'S WHAT THEY WERE. DIDN'T THEY *KNOW?* IF YOU WANT TO PULL A JOB OF ANY SIZE AT ALL IN THIS TOWN --
-- YOU HAVE SOMEONE HIT A *GAS STATION,* BREAK SOME *STORE WINDOWS* ACROSS TOWN, GET SOME *DISTRACTIONS* GOING!
MY HEAD'S *RINGING* -- I CAN'T HEAR MUCH --
-- CAN BARELY *MOVE* --
-- BUT I *MAKE* MYSELF.
EVEN THROUGH THE *RINGING,* THOUGH, I HEAR THAT CLOWN FREAK *LAUGHIN'* AT THEM WHILE HE TAKES THEM DOWN --
NOT MY PROBLEM, THOUGH, *IS* IT?
NOT MY *PROBLEM.*
THKASSH
THKASSH

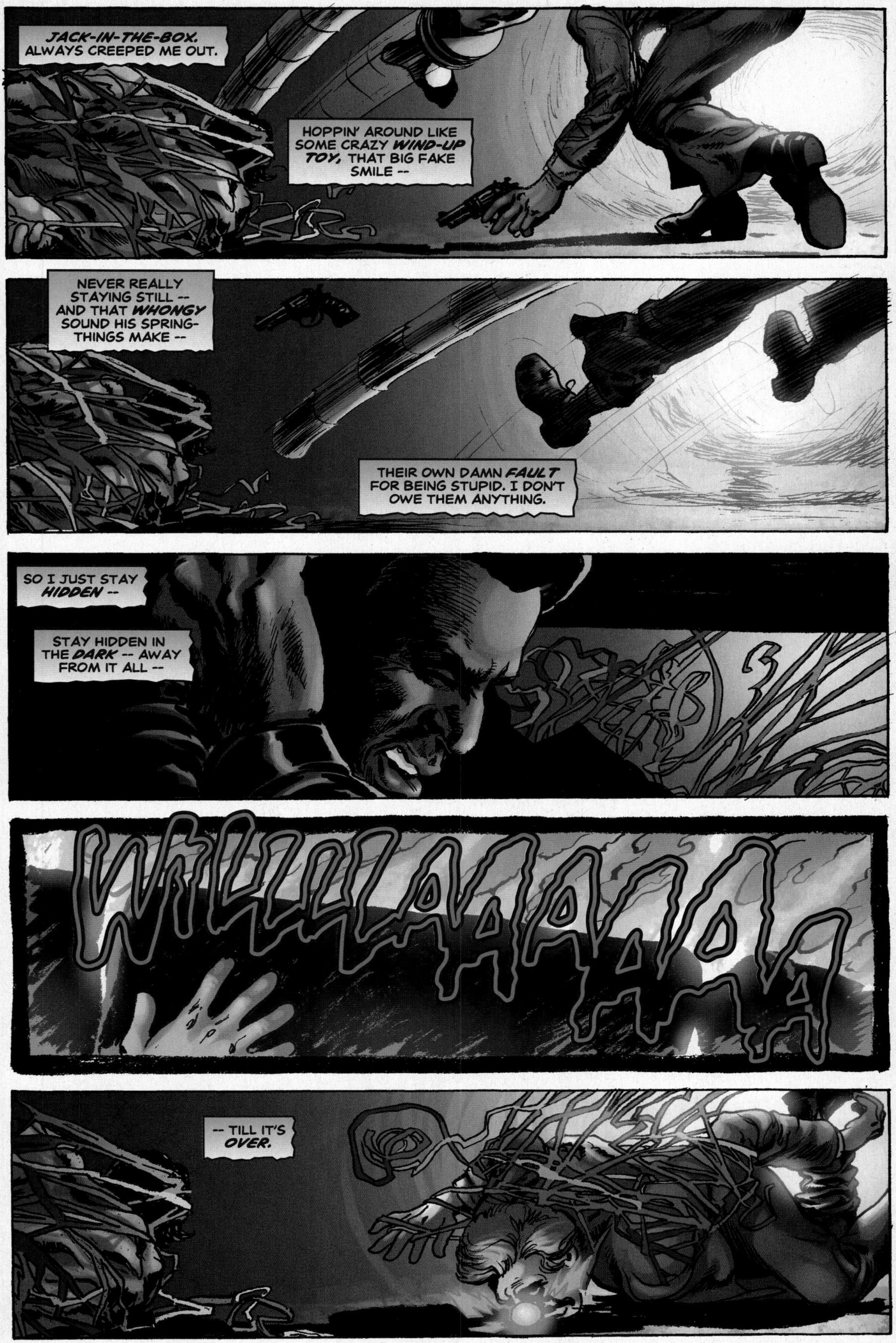
JACK-IN-THE-BOX. ALWAYS CREEPED ME OUT.
HOPPIN' AROUND LIKE SOME CRAZY WIND-UP TOY, THAT BIG FAKE SMILE --
NEVER REALLY STAYING STILL -- AND THAT WHONGY SOUND HIS SPRING-THINGS MAKE --
THEIR OWN DAMN FAULT FOR BEING STUPID. I DON'T OWE THEM ANYTHING.
SO I JUST STAY HIDDEN --
STAY HIDDEN IN THE DARK -- AWAY FROM IT ALL --
WHAAAAAAAA
-- TILL IT'S OVER.

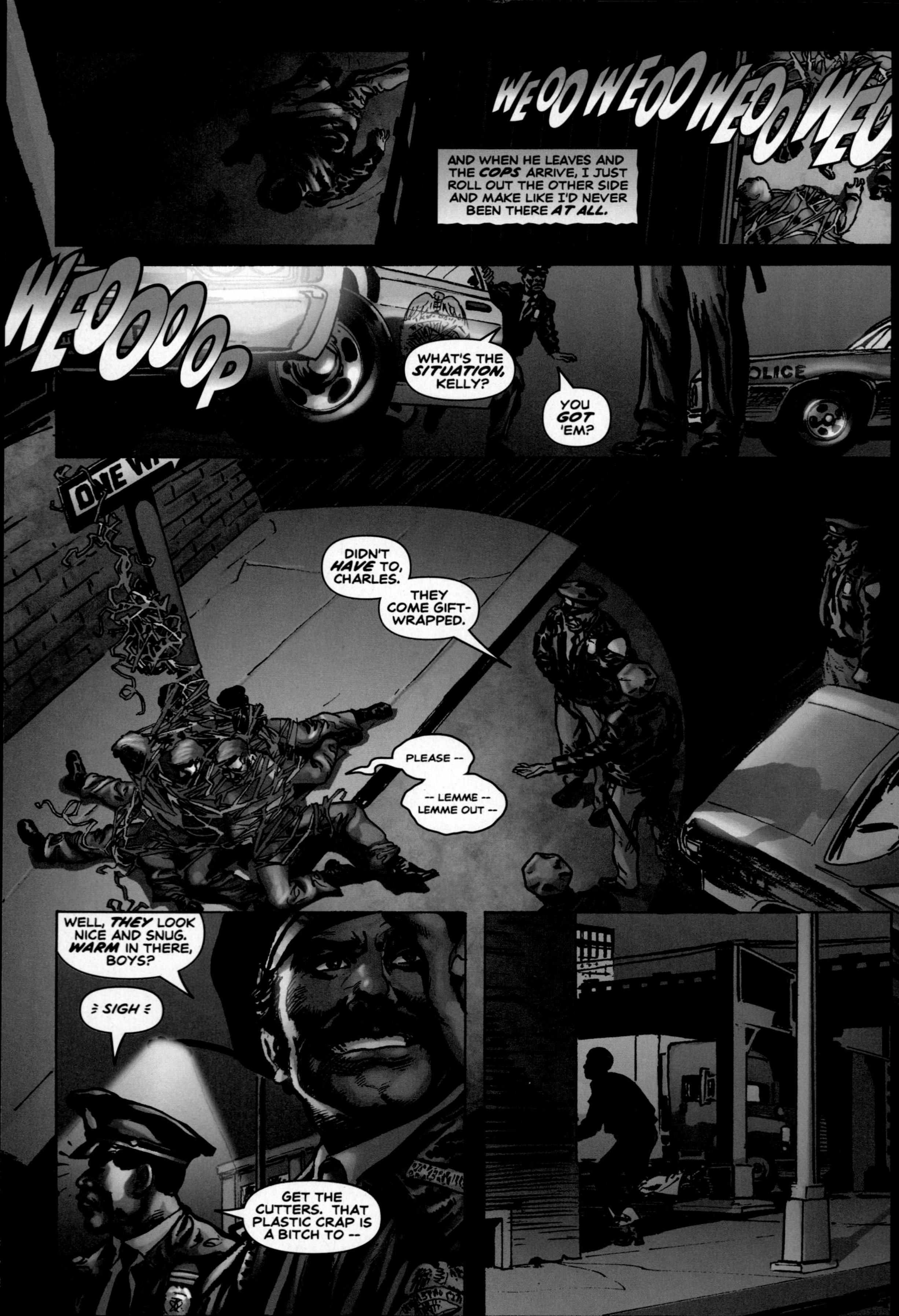
WEOO WEOO WEOO WEO
AND WHEN HE LEAVES AND THE COPS ARRIVE, I JUST ROLL OUT THE OTHER SIDE AND MAKE LIKE I'D NEVER BEEN THERE AT ALL.
WEOOOOOP
WHAT'S THE SITUATION, KELLY?
YOU GOT 'EM?
POLICE
ONE W
DIDN'T HAVE TO, CHARLES.
THEY COME GIFT-WRAPPED.
PLEASE --
-- LEMME -- LEMME OUT --
WELL, THEY LOOK NICE AND SNUG. WARM IN THERE, BOYS?
SIGH
GET THE CUTTERS. THAT PLASTIC CRAP IS A BITCH TO --

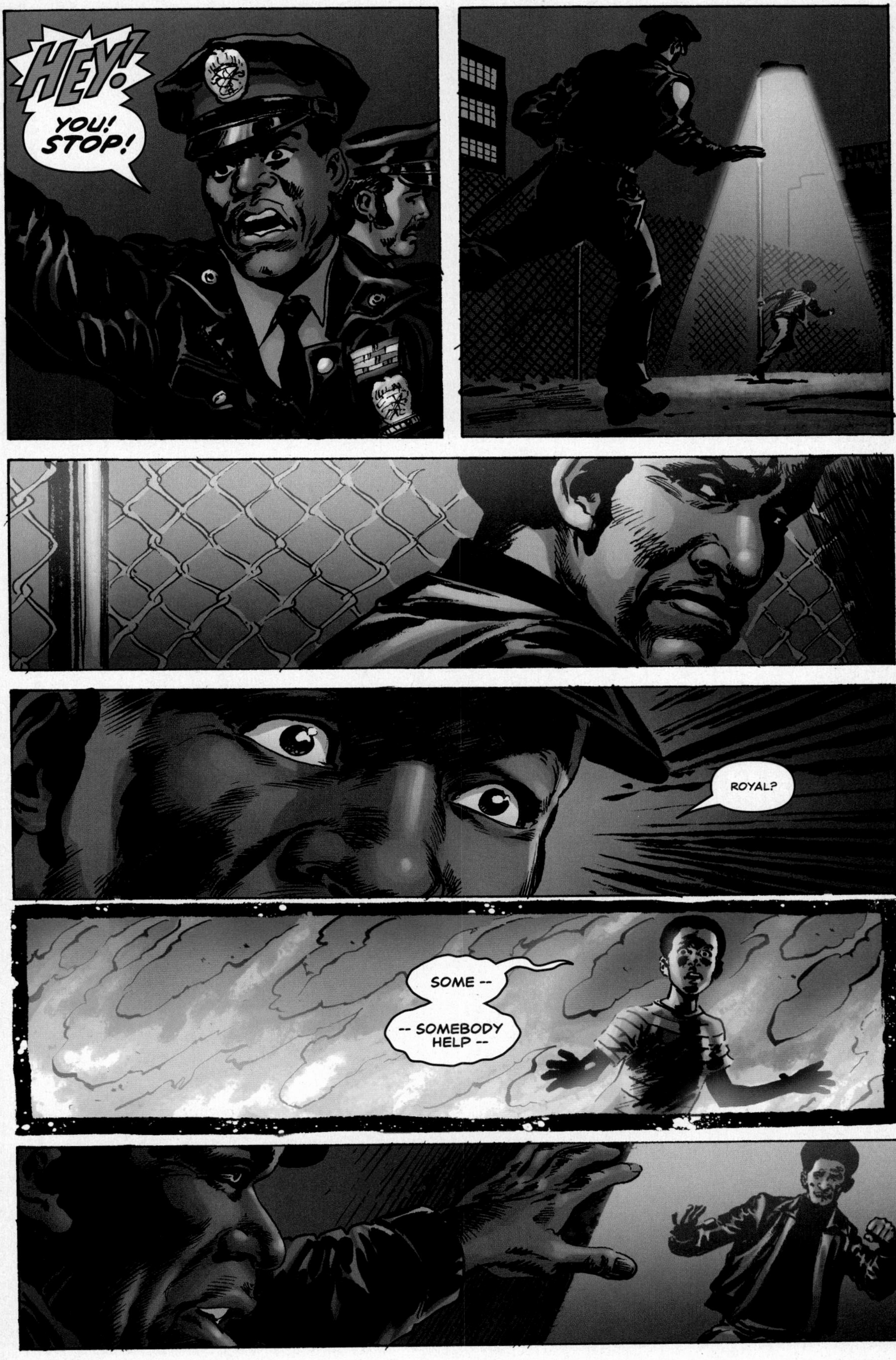
HEY!
YOU! STOP!
ROYAL?
SOME --
-- SOMEBODY HELP --

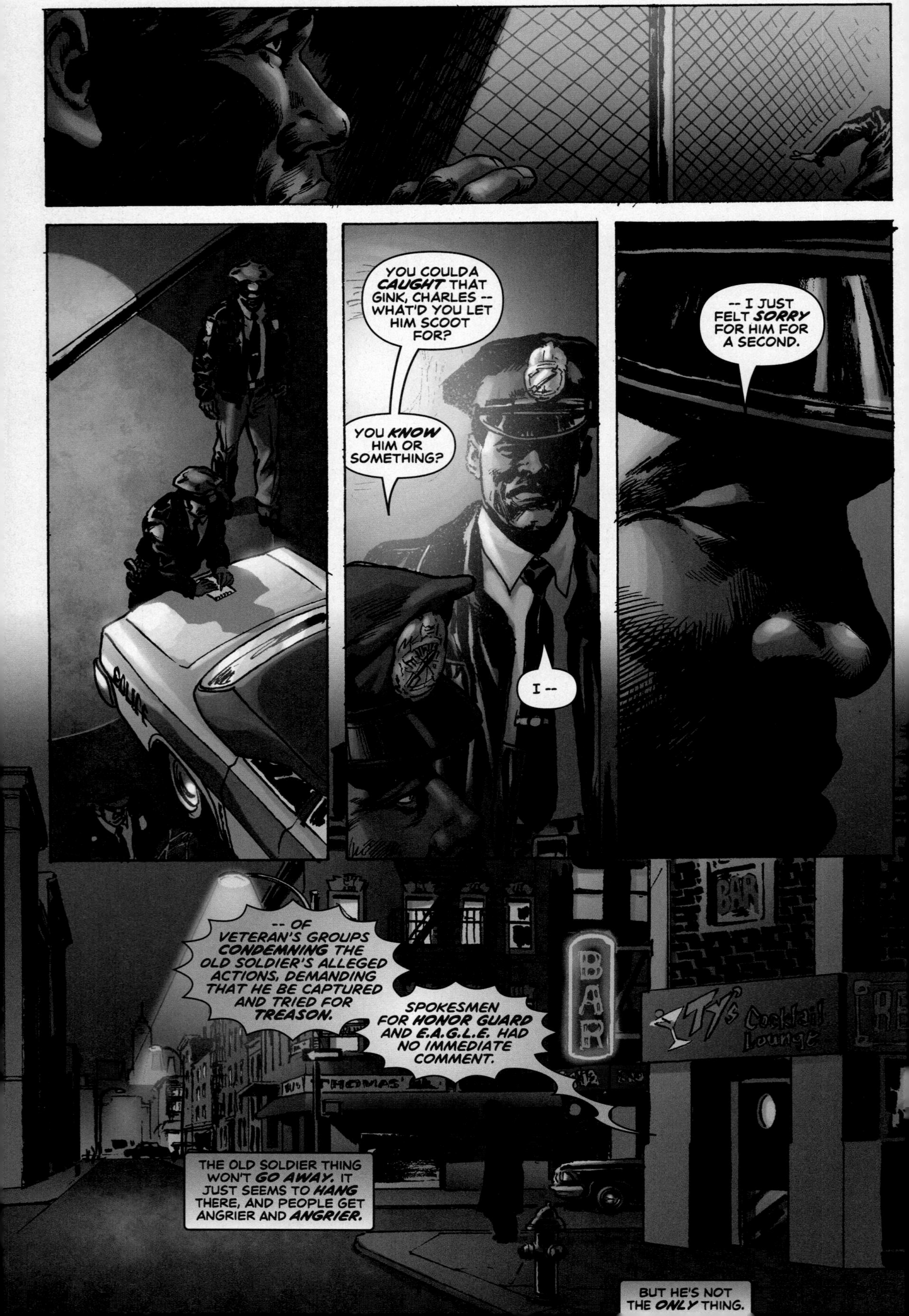
YOU COULDA CAUGHT THAT GINK, CHARLES -- WHAT'D YOU LET HIM SCOOT FOR?
YOU KNOW HIM OR SOMETHING?
I --
-- I JUST FELT SORRY FOR HIM FOR A SECOND.
-- OF VETERAN'S GROUPS CONDEMNING THE OLD SOLDIER'S ALLEGED ACTIONS, DEMANDING THAT HE BE CAPTURED AND TRIED FOR TREASON.
SPOKESMEN FOR HONOR GUARD AND E.A.G.L.E. HAD NO IMMEDIATE COMMENT.
BAR
BAR
Ty's Cocktail Lounge
THOMAS'
THE OLD SOLDIER THING WON'T GO AWAY. IT JUST SEEMS TO HANG THERE, AND PEOPLE GET ANGRIER AND ANGRIER.
BUT HE'S NOT THE ONLY THING.

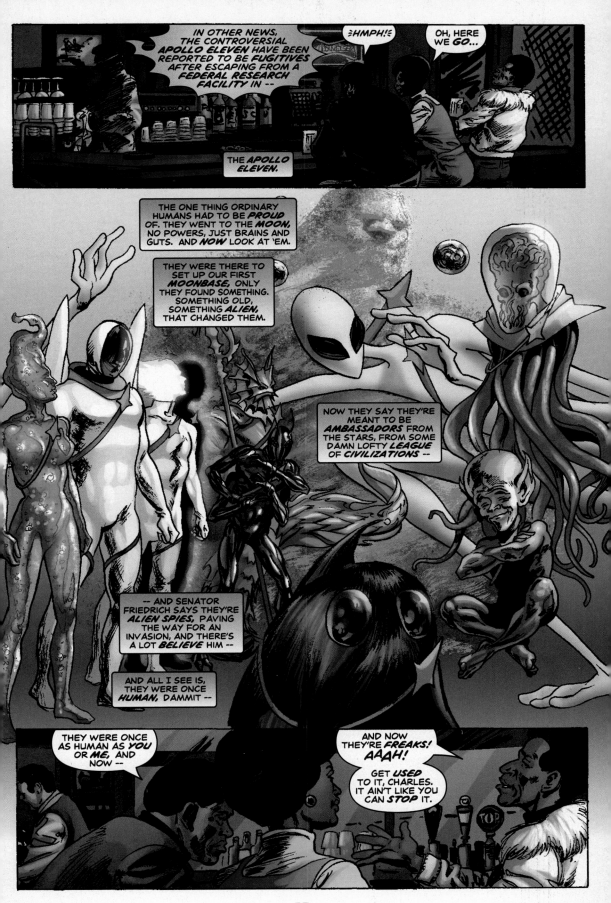

IN OTHER NEWS, THE CONTROVERSIAL *APOLLO ELEVEN* HAVE BEEN REPORTED TO BE *FUGITIVES* AFTER ESCAPING FROM A *FEDERAL RESEARCH FACILITY* IN --

⸘HMPH!⸘

OH, HERE WE *GO*...

THE *APOLLO ELEVEN.*

THE ONE THING ORDINARY HUMANS HAD TO BE *PROUD* OF. THEY WENT TO THE *MOON*, NO POWERS, JUST BRAINS AND GUTS. AND *NOW* LOOK AT 'EM.

THEY WERE THERE TO SET UP OUR FIRST *MOONBASE*, ONLY THEY FOUND SOMETHING. SOMETHING *OLD*, SOMETHING *ALIEN*, THAT CHANGED THEM.

NOW THEY SAY THEY'RE MEANT TO BE *AMBASSADORS* FROM THE STARS, FROM SOME DAMN LOFTY *LEAGUE* OF *CIVILIZATIONS* --

-- AND SENATOR FRIEDRICH SAYS THEY'RE *ALIEN SPIES*, PAVING THE WAY FOR AN INVASION, AND THERE'S A LOT *BELIEVE* HIM --

AND ALL I SEE IS, THEY WERE ONCE *HUMAN*, DAMMIT --

THEY WERE ONCE AS HUMAN AS *YOU* OR *ME*, AND NOW --

AND NOW THEY'RE *FREAKS!* AAAH!

GET *USED* TO IT, CHARLES. IT AIN'T LIKE YOU CAN *STOP* IT.

37

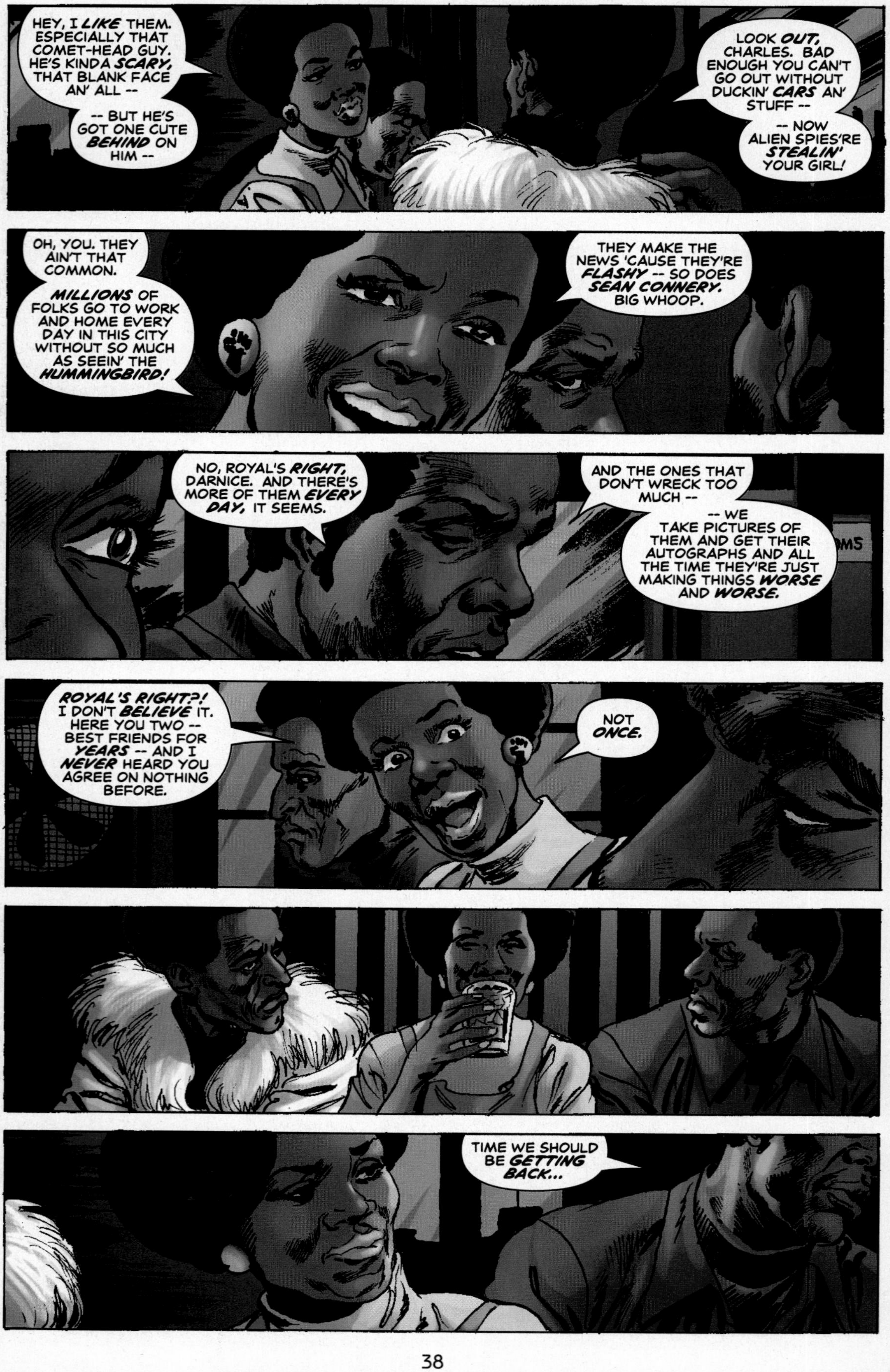
HEY, I LIKE THEM. ESPECIALLY THAT COMET-HEAD GUY. HE'S KINDA SCARY, THAT BLANK FACE AN' ALL --
-- BUT HE'S GOT ONE CUTE BEHIND ON HIM --
LOOK OUT, CHARLES. BAD ENOUGH YOU CAN'T GO OUT WITHOUT DUCKIN' CARS AN' STUFF --
-- NOW ALIEN SPIES'RE STEALIN' YOUR GIRL!
OH, YOU. THEY AIN'T THAT COMMON.
MILLIONS OF FOLKS GO TO WORK AND HOME EVERY DAY IN THIS CITY WITHOUT SO MUCH AS SEEIN' THE HUMMINGBIRD!
THEY MAKE THE NEWS 'CAUSE THEY'RE FLASHY -- SO DOES SEAN CONNERY. BIG WHOOP.
NO, ROYAL'S RIGHT, DARNICE. AND THERE'S MORE OF THEM EVERY DAY, IT SEEMS.
AND THE ONES THAT DON'T WRECK TOO MUCH --
-- WE TAKE PICTURES OF THEM AND GET THEIR AUTOGRAPHS AND ALL THE TIME THEY'RE JUST MAKING THINGS WORSE AND WORSE.
ROYAL'S RIGHT?! I DON'T BELIEVE IT. HERE YOU TWO -- BEST FRIENDS FOR YEARS -- AND I NEVER HEARD YOU AGREE ON NOTHING BEFORE.
NOT ONCE.
TIME WE SHOULD BE GETTING BACK...

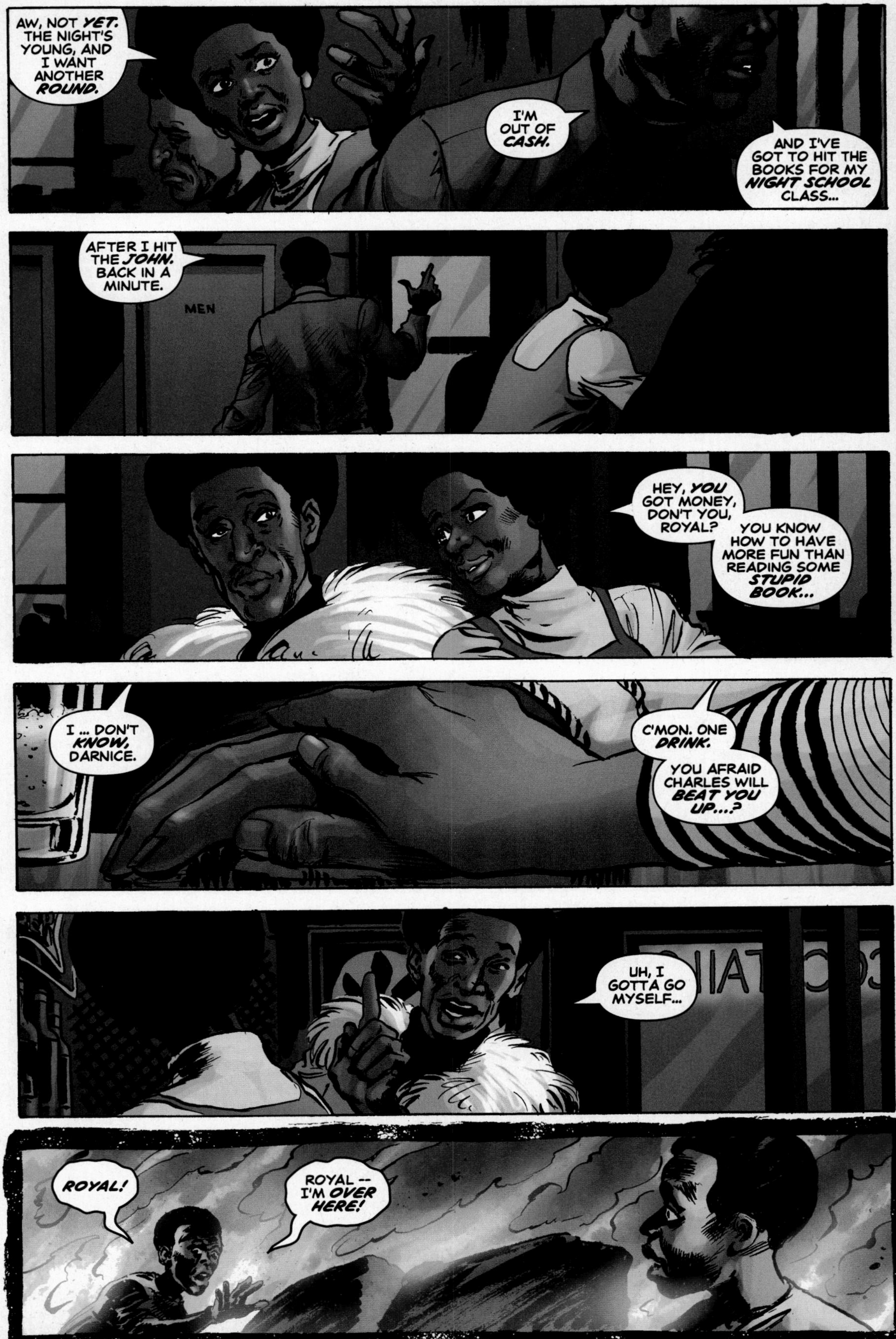
AW, NOT *YET.* THE NIGHT'S YOUNG, AND I WANT ANOTHER *ROUND.*
I'M OUT OF *CASH.*
AND I'VE GOT TO HIT THE BOOKS FOR MY *NIGHT SCHOOL* CLASS...
AFTER I HIT THE *JOHN.* BACK IN A MINUTE.
MEN
HEY, *YOU* GOT MONEY, DON'T YOU, ROYAL?
YOU KNOW HOW TO HAVE MORE FUN THAN READING SOME *STUPID BOOK...*
I ... DON'T *KNOW,* DARNICE.
C'MON. ONE *DRINK.*
YOU AFRAID CHARLES WILL *BEAT YOU UP...?*
UH, I GOTTA GO MYSELF...
ROYAL!
ROYAL -- I'M *OVER HERE!*

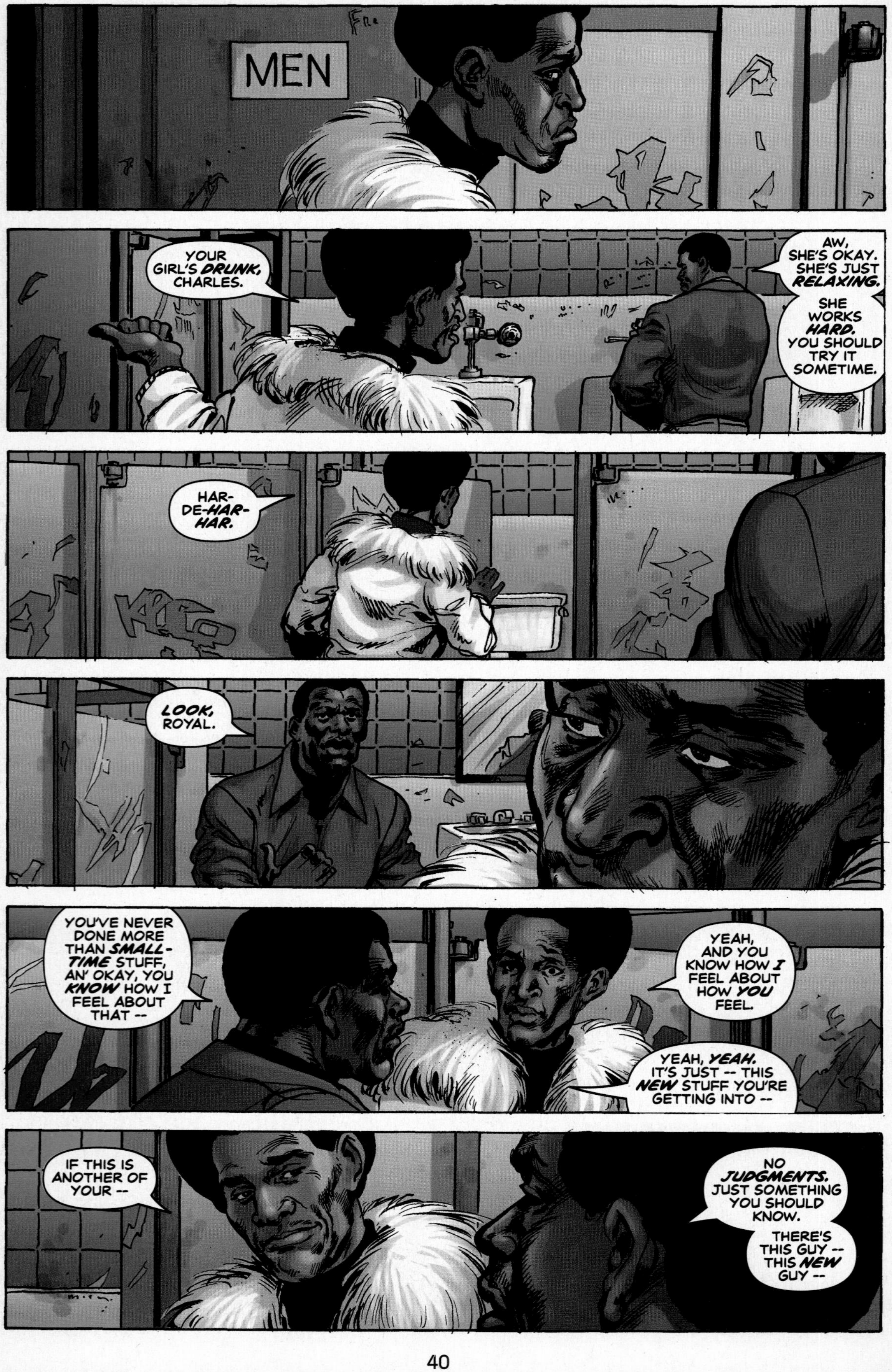
MEN
YOUR GIRL'S DRUNK, CHARLES.
AW, SHE'S OKAY. SHE'S JUST RELAXING.
SHE WORKS HARD. YOU SHOULD TRY IT SOMETIME.
HAR-DE-HAR-HAR.
LOOK, ROYAL.
YOU'VE NEVER DONE MORE THAN SMALL-TIME STUFF, AN' OKAY, YOU KNOW HOW I FEEL ABOUT THAT --
YEAH, AND YOU KNOW HOW I FEEL ABOUT HOW YOU FEEL.
YEAH, YEAH. IT'S JUST -- THIS NEW STUFF YOU'RE GETTING INTO --
IF THIS IS ANOTHER OF YOUR --
NO JUDGMENTS. JUST SOMETHING YOU SHOULD KNOW.
THERE'S THIS GUY -- THIS NEW GUY --

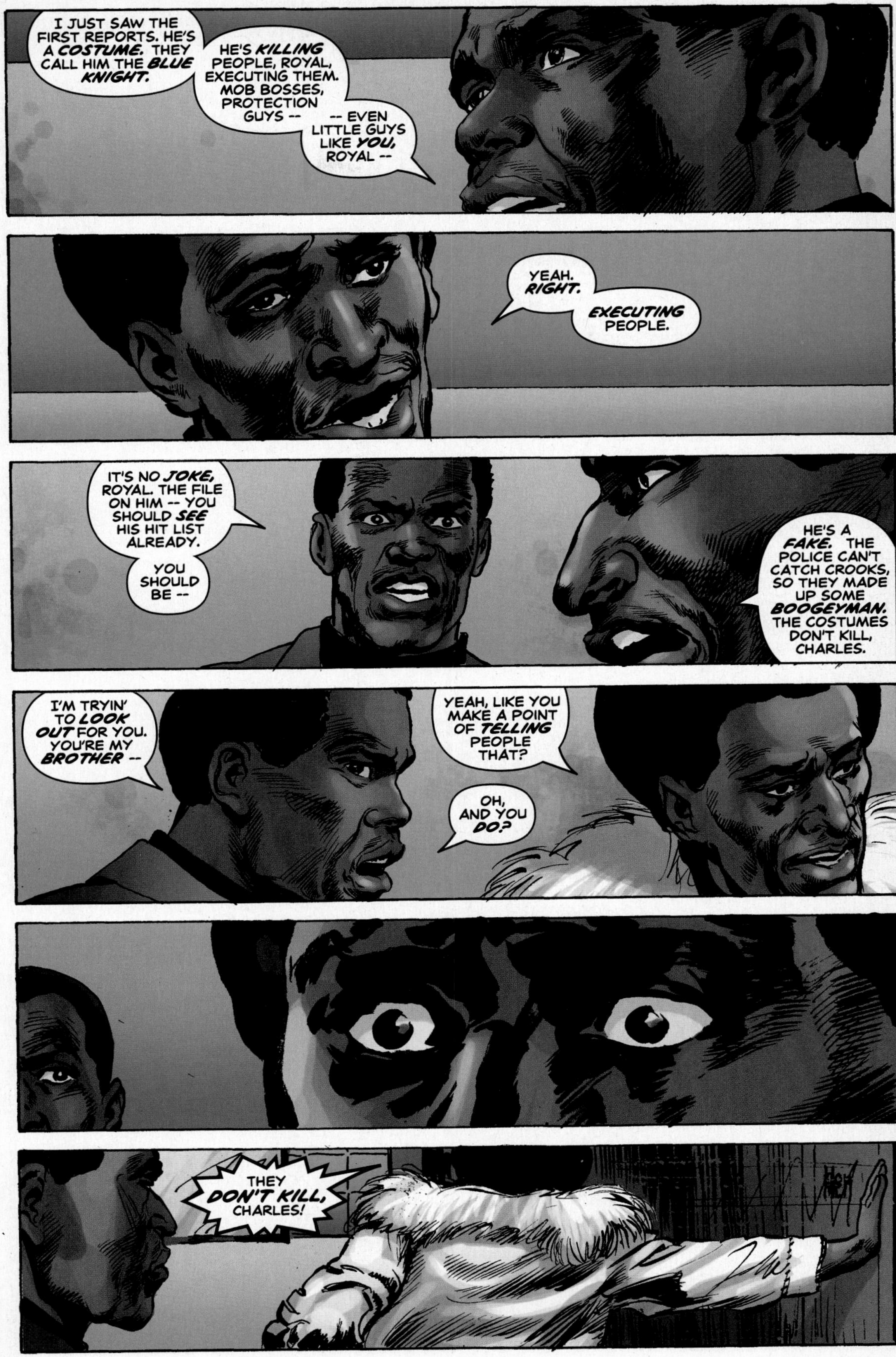
I JUST SAW THE FIRST REPORTS. HE'S A COSTUME. THEY CALL HIM THE BLUE KNIGHT.
HE'S KILLING PEOPLE, ROYAL, EXECUTING THEM. MOB BOSSES, PROTECTION GUYS --
-- EVEN LITTLE GUYS LIKE YOU, ROYAL --
YEAH. RIGHT.
EXECUTING PEOPLE.
IT'S NO JOKE, ROYAL. THE FILE ON HIM -- YOU SHOULD SEE HIS HIT LIST ALREADY.
YOU SHOULD BE --
HE'S A FAKE. THE POLICE CAN'T CATCH CROOKS, SO THEY MADE UP SOME BOOGEYMAN. THE COSTUMES DON'T KILL, CHARLES.
I'M TRYIN' TO LOOK OUT FOR YOU. YOU'RE MY BROTHER --
YEAH, LIKE YOU MAKE A POINT OF TELLING PEOPLE THAT?
OH, AND YOU DO?
THEY DON'T KILL, CHARLES!

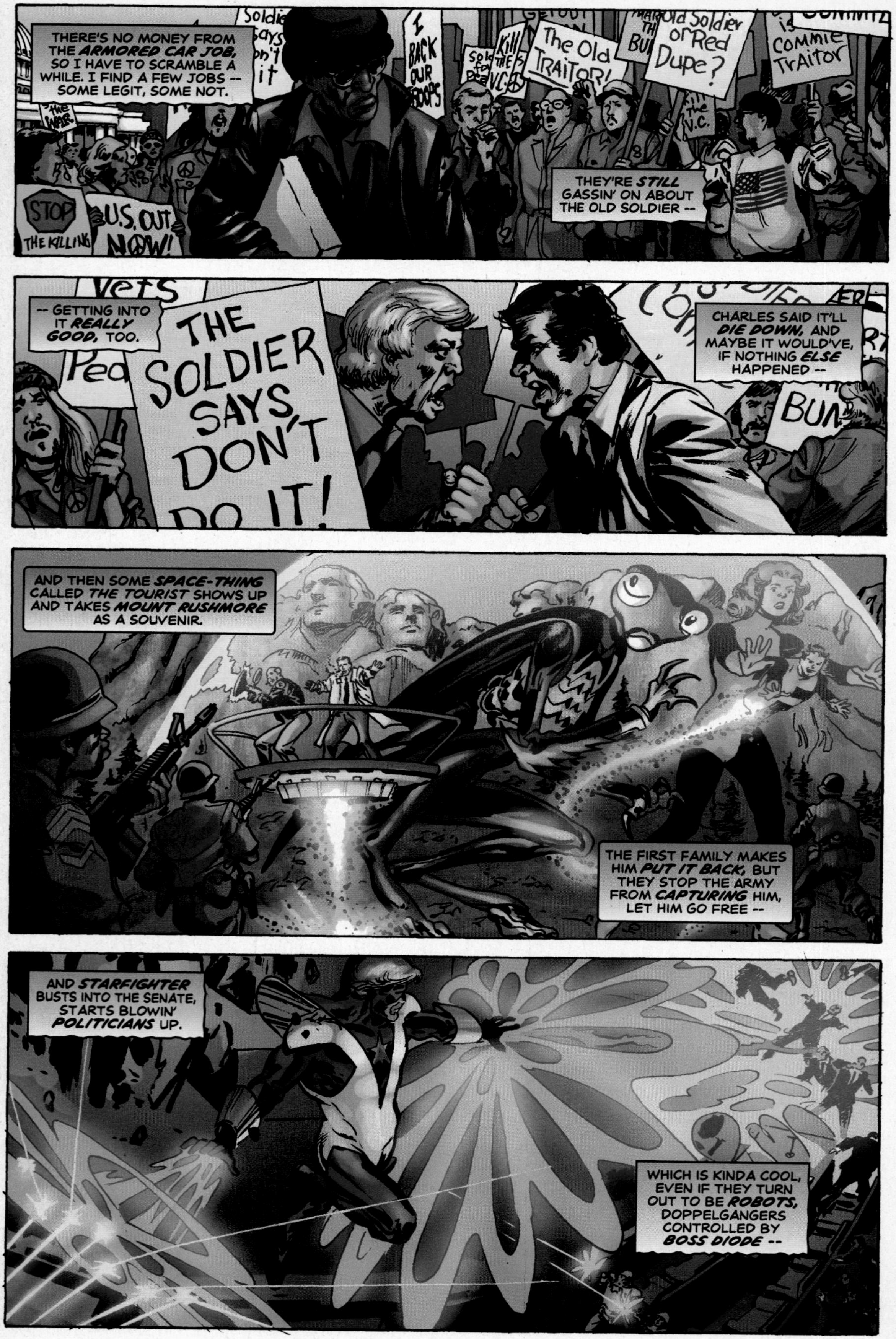
THERE'S NO MONEY FROM THE ARMORED CAR JOB, SO I HAVE TO SCRAMBLE A WHILE. I FIND A FEW JOBS -- SOME LEGIT, SOME NOT.
I BACK OUR TROOPS
The Old TRAITOR!
Old Soldier or Red Dupe?
Commie Traitor
STOP THE KILLING
U.S. OUT NOW!
THEY'RE STILL GASSIN' ON ABOUT THE OLD SOLDIER --
-- GETTING INTO IT REALLY GOOD, TOO.
THE SOLDIER SAYS DON'T DO IT!
CHARLES SAID IT'LL DIE DOWN, AND MAYBE IT WOULD'VE, IF NOTHING ELSE HAPPENED --
AND THEN SOME SPACE-THING CALLED THE TOURIST SHOWS UP AND TAKES MOUNT RUSHMORE AS A SOUVENIR.
THE FIRST FAMILY MAKES HIM PUT IT BACK, BUT THEY STOP THE ARMY FROM CAPTURING HIM, LET HIM GO FREE --
AND STARFIGHTER BUSTS INTO THE SENATE, STARTS BLOWIN' POLITICIANS UP.
WHICH IS KINDA COOL, EVEN IF THEY TURN OUT TO BE ROBOTS, DOPPELGANGERS CONTROLLED BY BOSS DIODE --

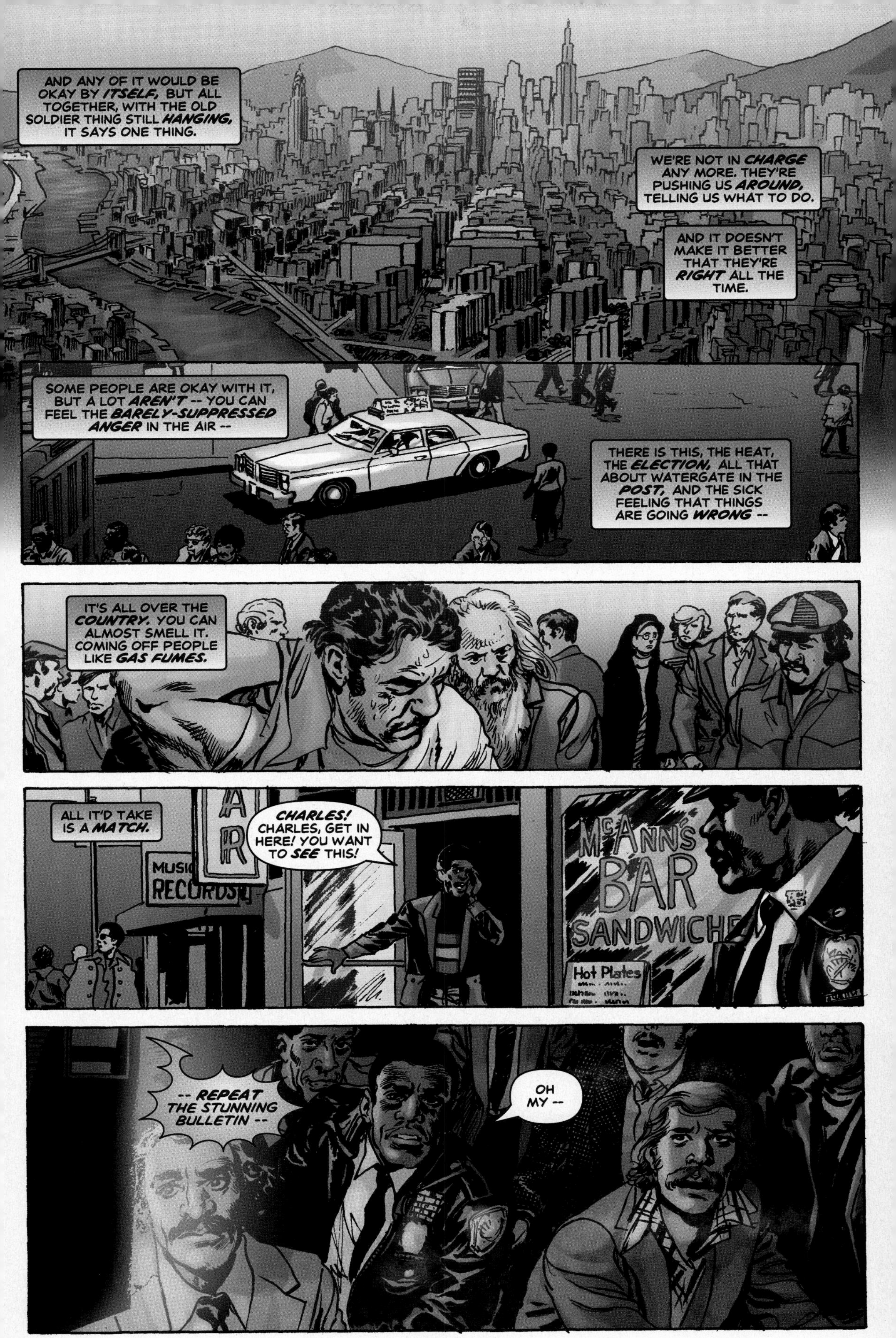
AND ANY OF IT WOULD BE OKAY BY ITSELF, BUT ALL TOGETHER, WITH THE OLD SOLDIER THING STILL HANGING, IT SAYS ONE THING.
WE'RE NOT IN CHARGE ANY MORE. THEY'RE PUSHING US AROUND, TELLING US WHAT TO DO.
AND IT DOESN'T MAKE IT BETTER THAT THEY'RE RIGHT ALL THE TIME.
SOME PEOPLE ARE OKAY WITH IT, BUT A LOT AREN'T -- YOU CAN FEEL THE BARELY-SUPPRESSED ANGER IN THE AIR --
THERE IS THIS, THE HEAT, THE ELECTION, ALL THAT ABOUT WATERGATE IN THE POST, AND THE SICK FEELING THAT THINGS ARE GOING WRONG --
IT'S ALL OVER THE COUNTRY. YOU CAN ALMOST SMELL IT. COMING OFF PEOPLE LIKE GAS FUMES.
ALL IT'D TAKE IS A MATCH.
CHARLES! CHARLES, GET IN HERE! YOU WANT TO SEE THIS!
MUSIC
RECORDS
McANN'S BAR SANDWICHE
Hot Plates
-- REPEAT THE STUNNING BULLETIN --
OH MY --

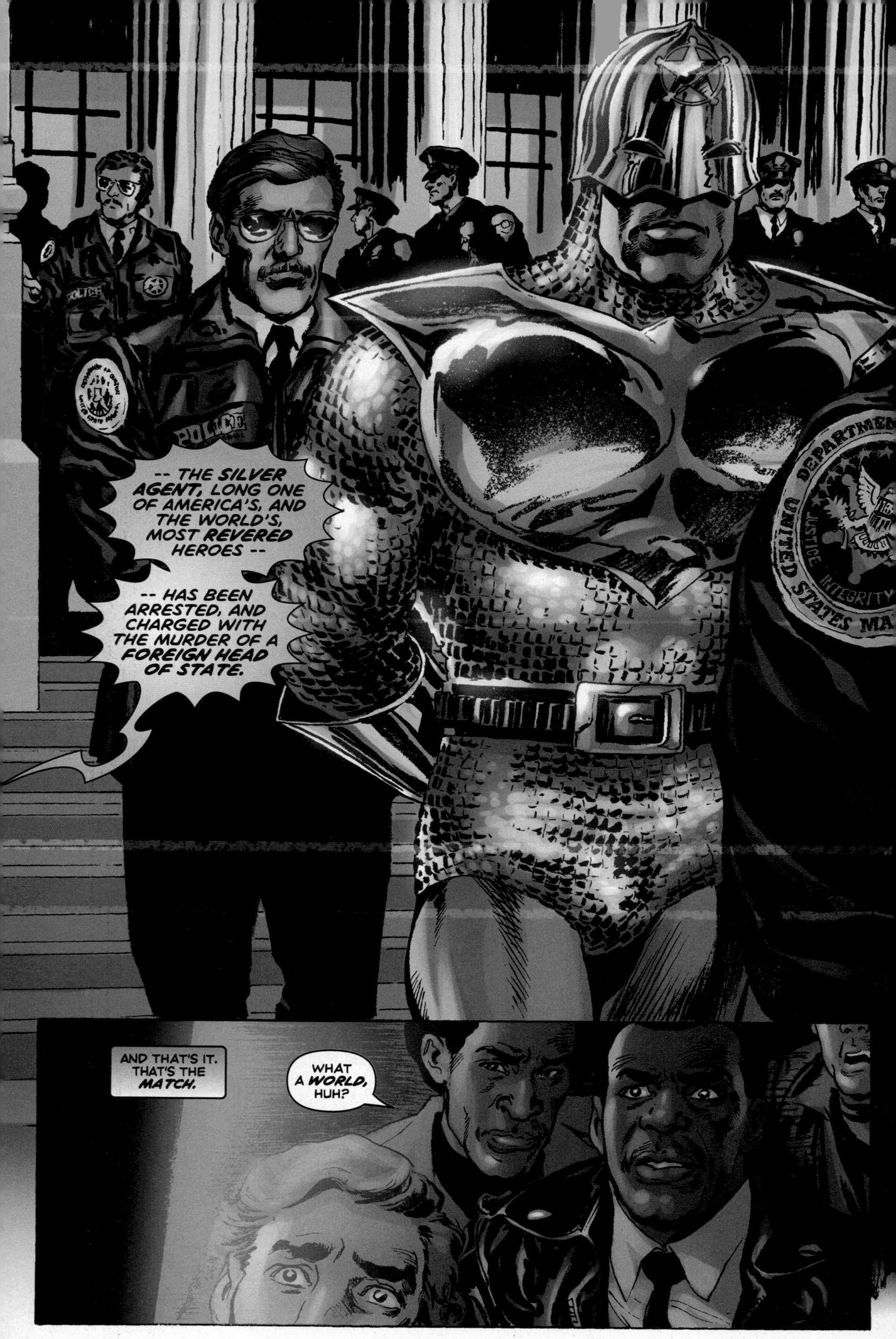
-- THE SILVER AGENT, LONG ONE OF AMERICA'S, AND THE WORLD'S, MOST REVERED HEROES --
-- HAS BEEN ARRESTED, AND CHARGED WITH THE MURDER OF A FOREIGN HEAD OF STATE.
AND THAT'S IT. THAT'S THE MATCH.
WHAT A WORLD, HUH?

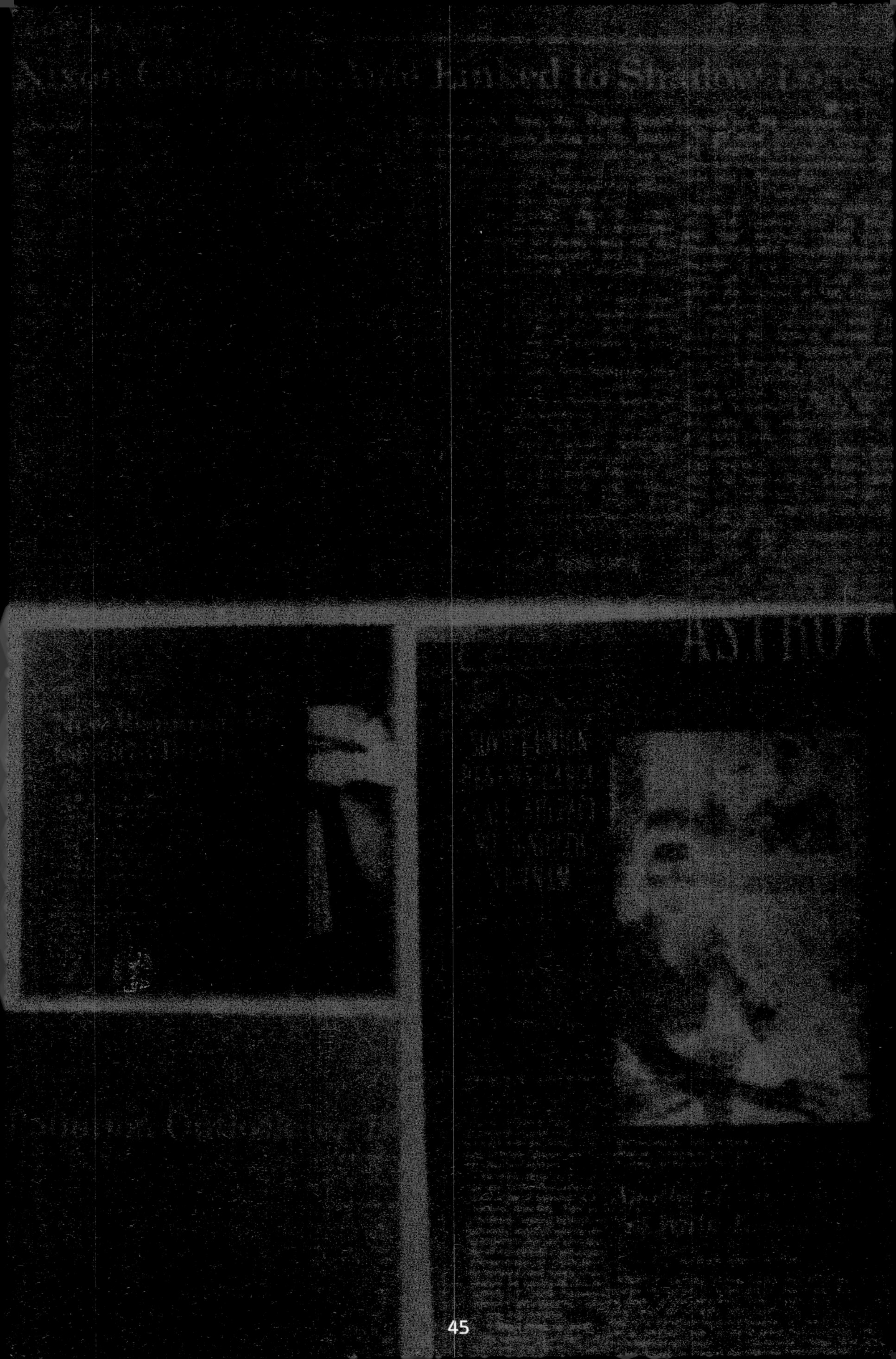

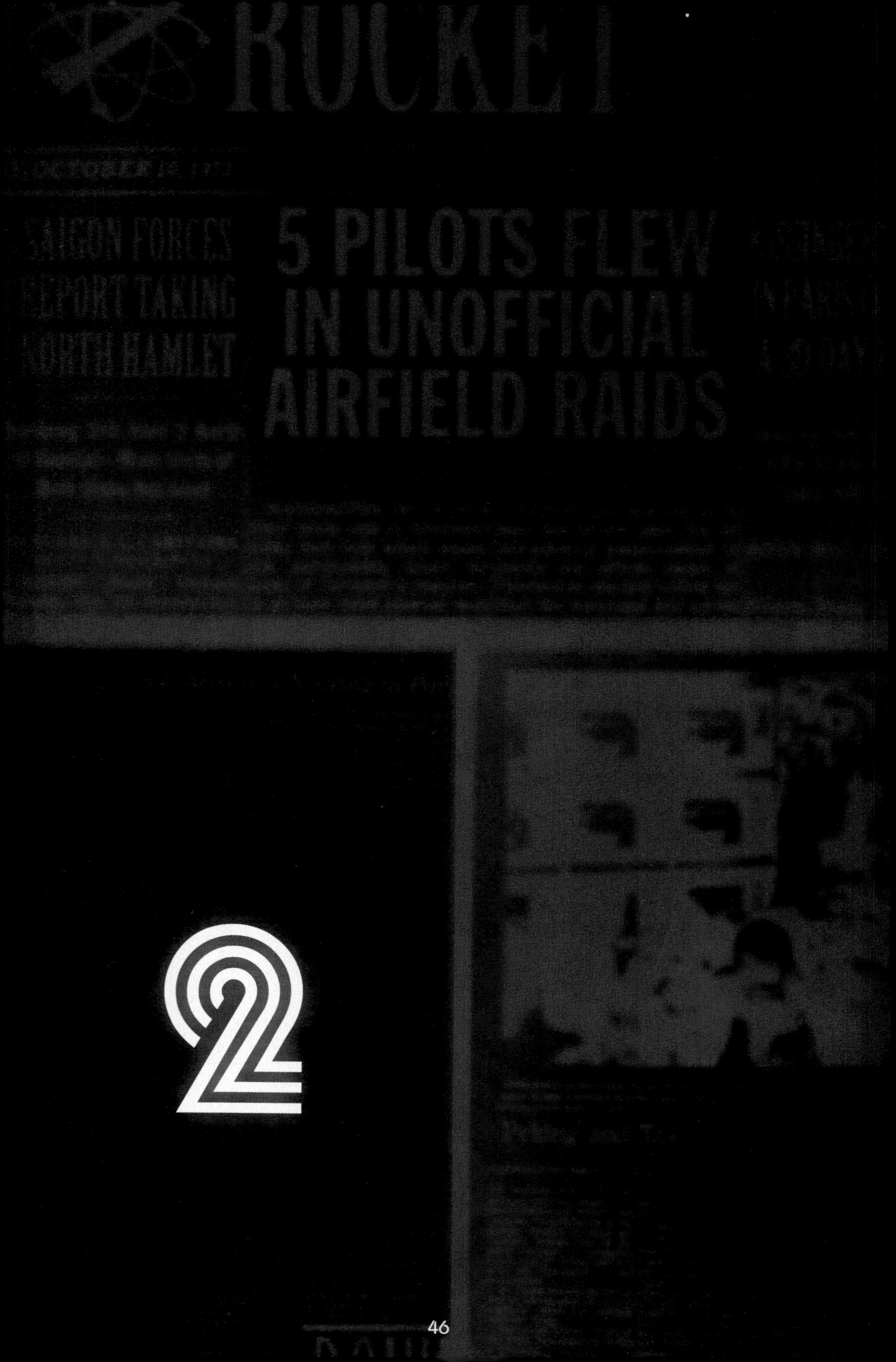
SAIGON FORCES REPORT TAKING NORTH HAMLET
5 PILOTS FLEW IN UNOFFICIAL AIRFIELD RAIDS

2

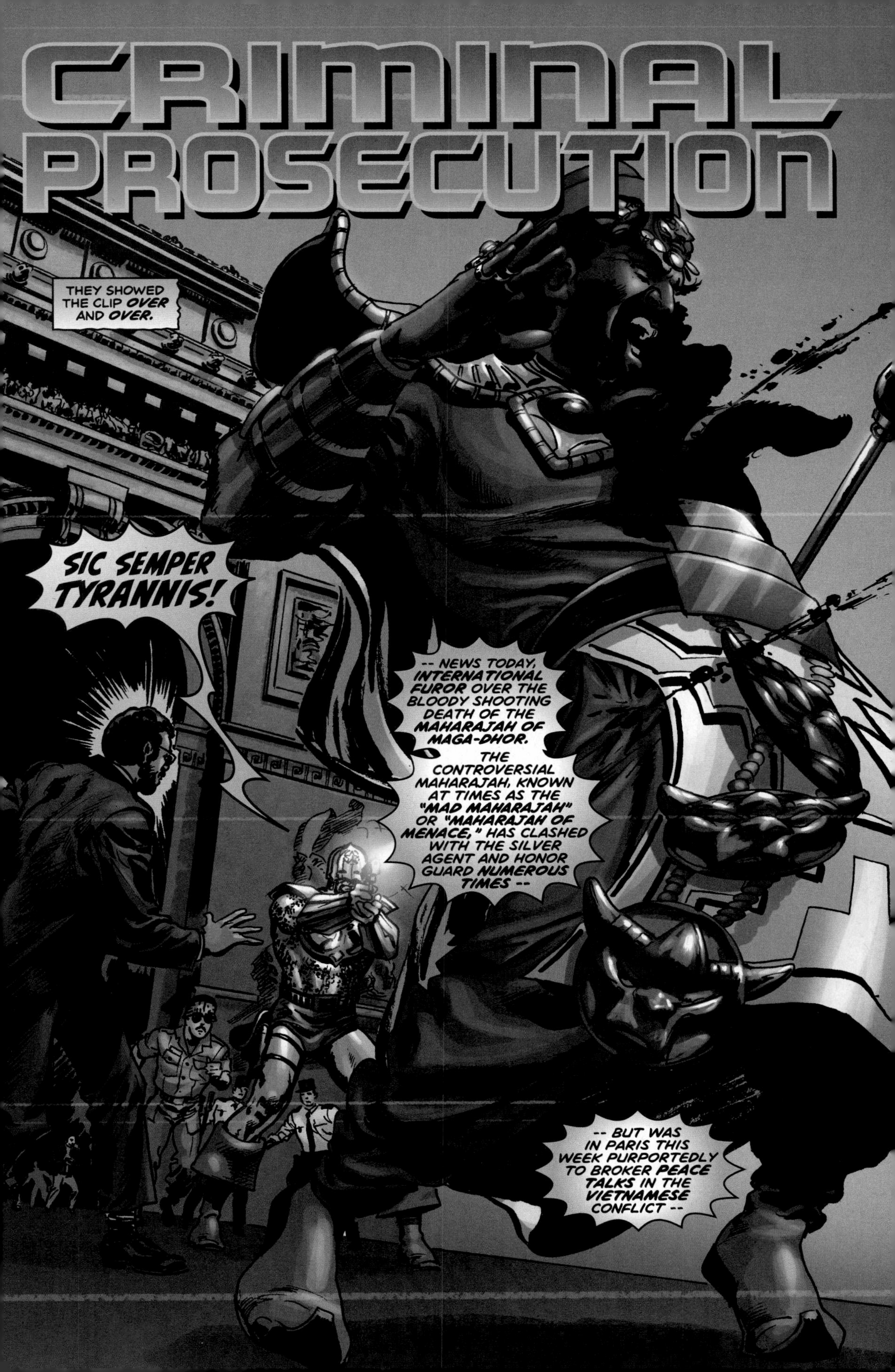
CRIMINAL PROSECUTION
THEY SHOWED THE CLIP OVER AND OVER.
SIC SEMPER TYRANNIS!
-- NEWS TODAY, INTERNATIONAL FUROR OVER THE BLOODY SHOOTING DEATH OF THE MAHARAJAH OF MAGA-DHOR.
THE CONTROVERSIAL MAHARAJAH, KNOWN AT TIMES AS THE "MAD MAHARAJAH" OR "MAHARAJAH OF MENACE," HAS CLASHED WITH THE SILVER AGENT AND HONOR GUARD NUMEROUS TIMES --
-- BUT WAS IN PARIS THIS WEEK PURPORTEDLY TO BROKER PEACE TALKS IN THE VIETNAMESE CONFLICT --

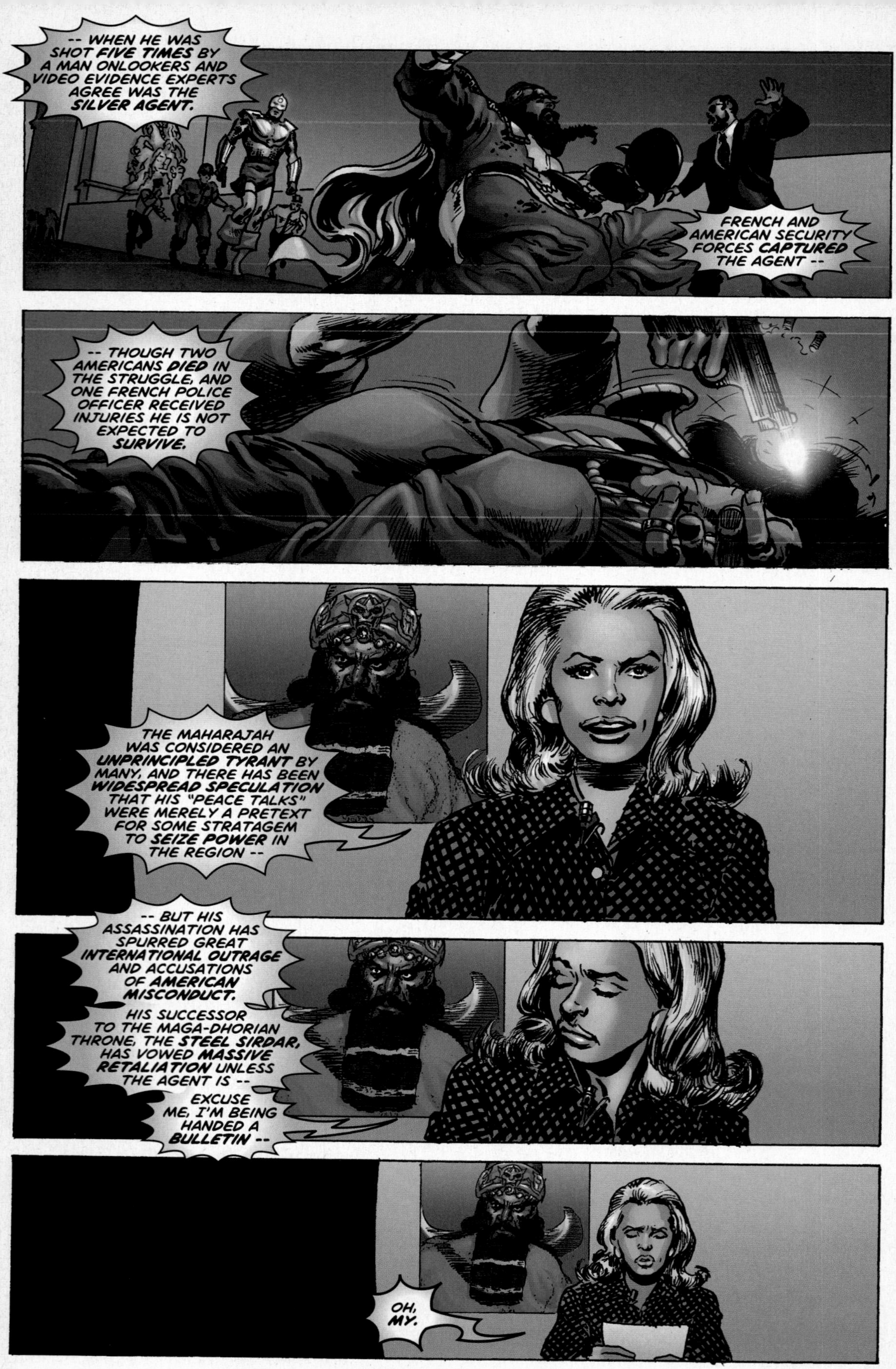
-- WHEN HE WAS SHOT FIVE TIMES BY A MAN ONLOOKERS AND VIDEO EVIDENCE EXPERTS AGREE WAS THE SILVER AGENT.
FRENCH AND AMERICAN SECURITY FORCES CAPTURED THE AGENT --
-- THOUGH TWO AMERICANS DIED IN THE STRUGGLE, AND ONE FRENCH POLICE OFFICER RECEIVED INJURIES HE IS NOT EXPECTED TO SURVIVE.
THE MAHARAJAH WAS CONSIDERED AN UNPRINCIPLED TYRANT BY MANY, AND THERE HAS BEEN WIDESPREAD SPECULATION THAT HIS "PEACE TALKS" WERE MERELY A PRETEXT FOR SOME STRATAGEM TO SEIZE POWER IN THE REGION --
-- BUT HIS ASSASSINATION HAS SPURRED GREAT INTERNATIONAL OUTRAGE AND ACCUSATIONS OF AMERICAN MISCONDUCT.
HIS SUCCESSOR TO THE MAGA-DHORIAN THRONE, THE STEEL SIRDAR, HAS VOWED MASSIVE RETALIATION UNLESS THE AGENT IS --
EXCUSE ME, I'M BEING HANDED A BULLETIN --
OH, MY.

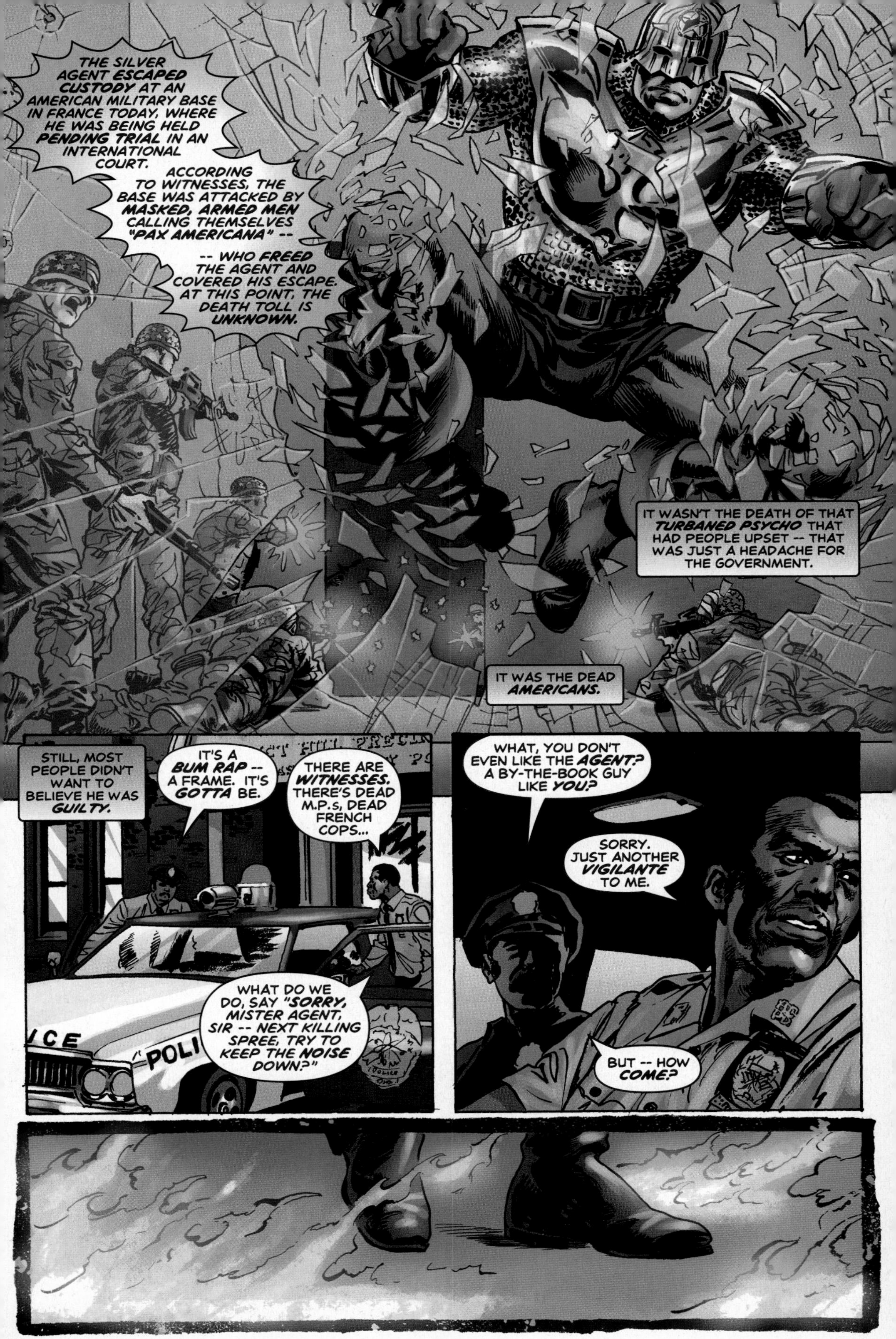
THE SILVER AGENT ESCAPED CUSTODY AT AN AMERICAN MILITARY BASE IN FRANCE TODAY, WHERE HE WAS BEING HELD PENDING TRIAL IN AN INTERNATIONAL COURT.
ACCORDING TO WITNESSES, THE BASE WAS ATTACKED BY MASKED, ARMED MEN CALLING THEMSELVES "PAX AMERICANA" --
-- WHO FREED THE AGENT AND COVERED HIS ESCAPE. AT THIS POINT, THE DEATH TOLL IS UNKNOWN.
IT WASN'T THE DEATH OF THAT TURBANED PSYCHO THAT HAD PEOPLE UPSET -- THAT WAS JUST A HEADACHE FOR THE GOVERNMENT.
IT WAS THE DEAD AMERICANS.
STILL, MOST PEOPLE DIDN'T WANT TO BELIEVE HE WAS GUILTY.
IT'S A BUM RAP -- A FRAME. IT'S GOTTA BE.
THERE ARE WITNESSES. THERE'S DEAD M.P.s, DEAD FRENCH COPS...
WHAT DO WE DO, SAY "SORRY, MISTER AGENT, SIR -- NEXT KILLING SPREE, TRY TO KEEP THE NOISE DOWN?"
ICE
POLI
WHAT, YOU DON'T EVEN LIKE THE AGENT? A BY-THE-BOOK GUY LIKE YOU?
SORRY. JUST ANOTHER VIGILANTE TO ME.
BUT -- HOW COME?

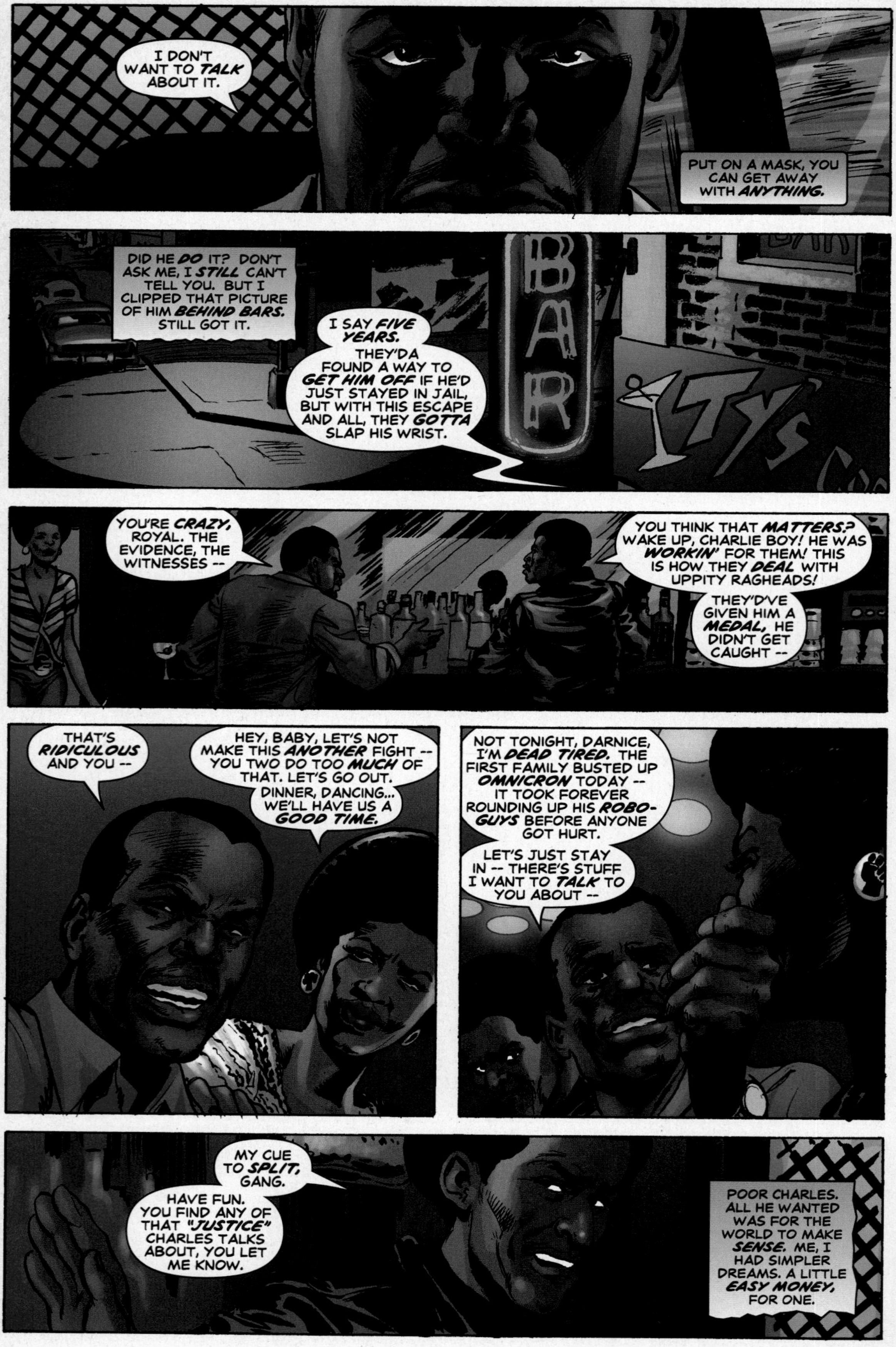
I DON'T WANT TO TALK ABOUT IT.
PUT ON A MASK, YOU CAN GET AWAY WITH ANYTHING.
DID HE DO IT? DON'T ASK ME, I STILL CAN'T TELL YOU. BUT I CLIPPED THAT PICTURE OF HIM BEHIND BARS. STILL GOT IT.
I SAY FIVE YEARS.
THEY'DA FOUND A WAY TO GET HIM OFF IF HE'D JUST STAYED IN JAIL, BUT WITH THIS ESCAPE AND ALL, THEY GOTTA SLAP HIS WRIST.
BAR
YOU'RE CRAZY, ROYAL. THE EVIDENCE, THE WITNESSES --
YOU THINK THAT MATTERS? WAKE UP, CHARLIE BOY! HE WAS WORKIN' FOR THEM! THIS IS HOW THEY DEAL WITH UPPITY RAGHEADS!
THEY'D'VE GIVEN HIM A MEDAL, HE DIDN'T GET CAUGHT --
THAT'S RIDICULOUS AND YOU --
HEY, BABY, LET'S NOT MAKE THIS ANOTHER FIGHT -- YOU TWO DO TOO MUCH OF THAT. LET'S GO OUT. DINNER, DANCING... WE'LL HAVE US A GOOD TIME.
NOT TONIGHT, DARNICE, I'M DEAD TIRED. THE FIRST FAMILY BUSTED UP OMNICRON TODAY -- IT TOOK FOREVER ROUNDING UP HIS ROBO-GUYS BEFORE ANYONE GOT HURT.
LET'S JUST STAY IN -- THERE'S STUFF I WANT TO TALK TO YOU ABOUT --
MY CUE TO SPLIT, GANG.
HAVE FUN. YOU FIND ANY OF THAT "JUSTICE" CHARLES TALKS ABOUT, YOU LET ME KNOW.
POOR CHARLES. ALL HE WANTED WAS FOR THE WORLD TO MAKE SENSE. ME, I HAD SIMPLER DREAMS. A LITTLE EASY MONEY, FOR ONE.

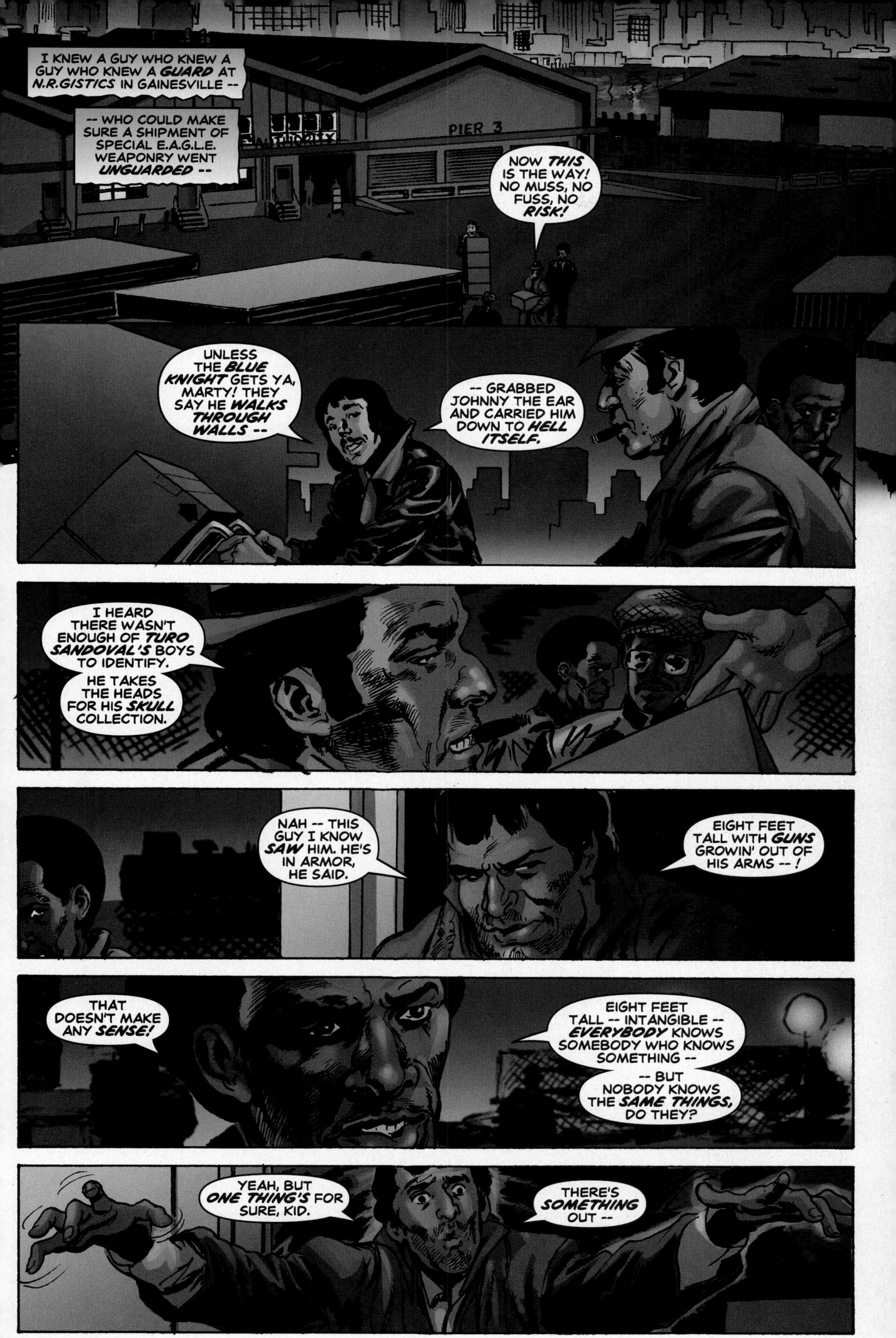
I KNEW A GUY WHO KNEW A GUY WHO KNEW A GUARD AT N.R.GISTICS IN GAINESVILLE --
-- WHO COULD MAKE SURE A SHIPMENT OF SPECIAL E.A.G.L.E. WEAPONRY WENT UNGUARDED --
PIER 3
NOW THIS IS THE WAY! NO MUSS, NO FUSS, NO RISK!
UNLESS THE BLUE KNIGHT GETS YA, MARTY! THEY SAY HE WALKS THROUGH WALLS --
-- GRABBED JOHNNY THE EAR AND CARRIED HIM DOWN TO HELL ITSELF.
I HEARD THERE WASN'T ENOUGH OF TURO SANDOVAL'S BOYS TO IDENTIFY.
HE TAKES THE HEADS FOR HIS SKULL COLLECTION.
NAH -- THIS GUY I KNOW SAW HIM. HE'S IN ARMOR, HE SAID.
EIGHT FEET TALL WITH GUNS GROWIN' OUT OF HIS ARMS -- !
THAT DOESN'T MAKE ANY SENSE!
EIGHT FEET TALL -- INTANGIBLE -- EVERYBODY KNOWS SOMEBODY WHO KNOWS SOMETHING --
-- BUT NOBODY KNOWS THE SAME THINGS, DO THEY?
YEAH, BUT ONE THING'S FOR SURE, KID.
THERE'S SOMETHING OUT --

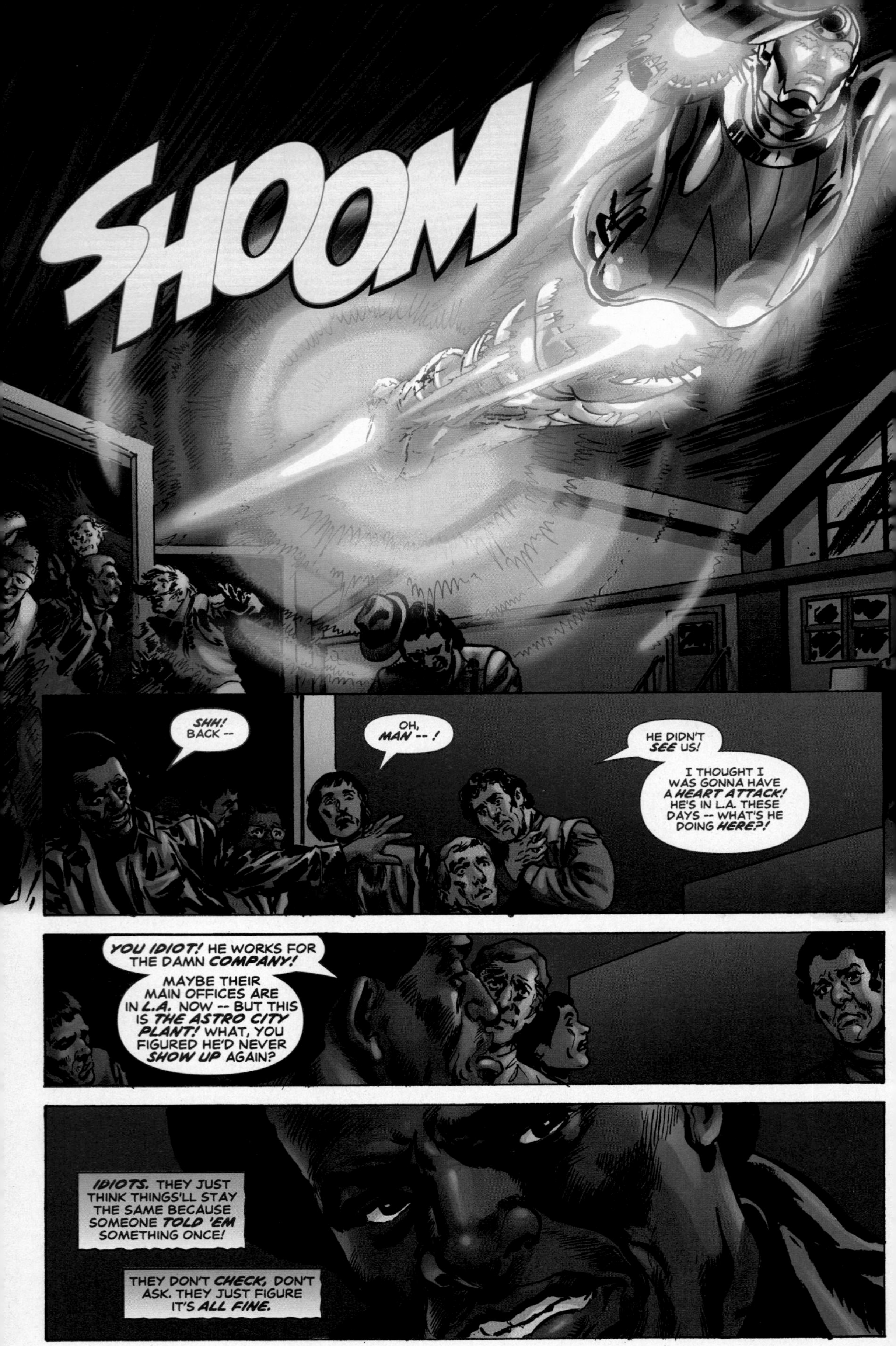
SHOOM
SHH! BACK --
OH, MAN -- !
HE DIDN'T SEE US!
I THOUGHT I WAS GONNA HAVE A HEART ATTACK! HE'S IN L.A. THESE DAYS -- WHAT'S HE DOING HERE?!
YOU IDIOT! HE WORKS FOR THE DAMN COMPANY!
MAYBE THEIR MAIN OFFICES ARE IN L.A. NOW -- BUT THIS IS THE ASTRO CITY PLANT! WHAT, YOU FIGURED HE'D NEVER SHOW UP AGAIN?
IDIOTS. THEY JUST THINK THINGS'LL STAY THE SAME BECAUSE SOMEONE TOLD 'EM SOMETHING ONCE!
THEY DON'T CHECK, DON'T ASK. THEY JUST FIGURE IT'S ALL FINE.

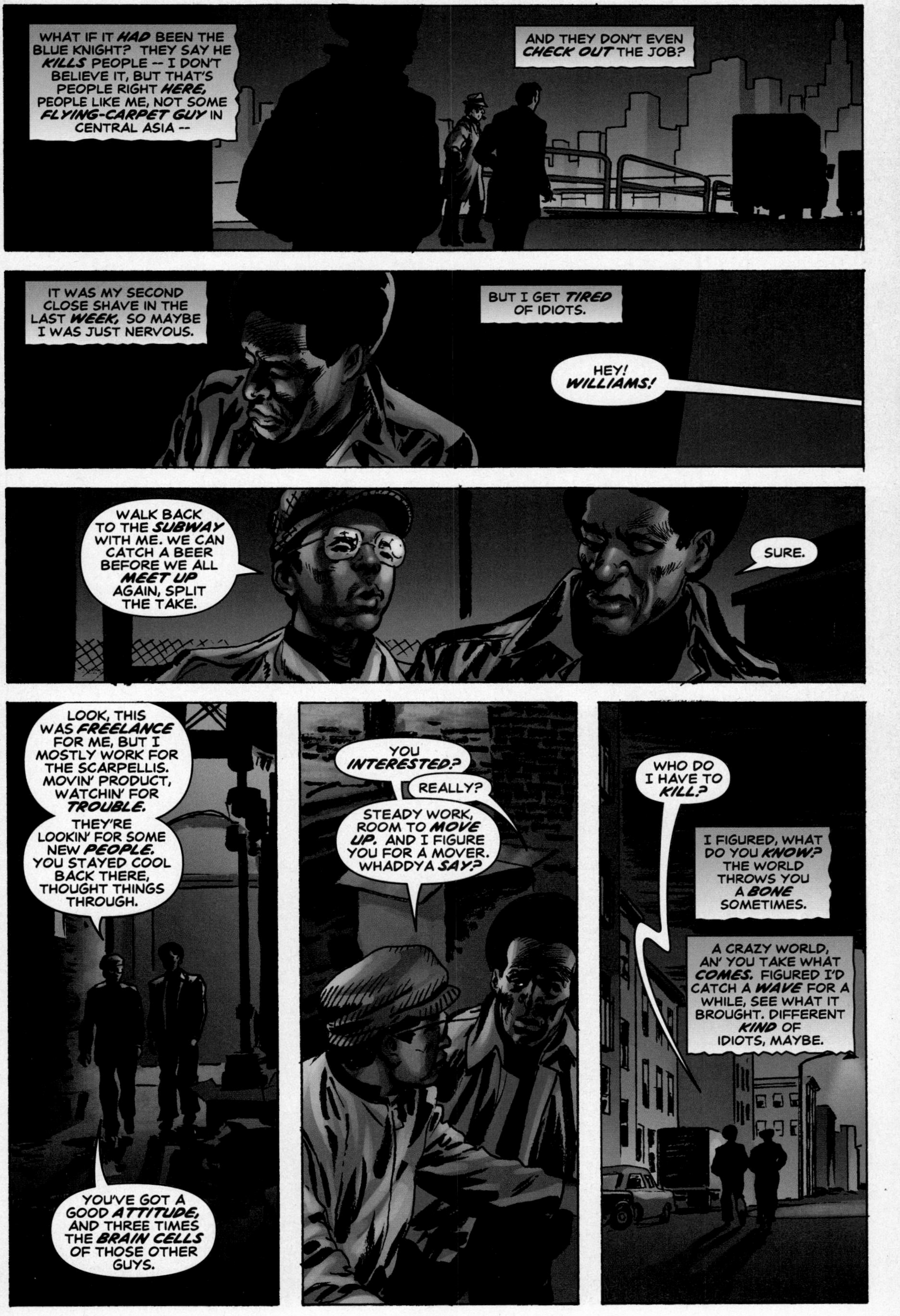
WHAT IF IT HAD BEEN THE BLUE KNIGHT? THEY SAY HE KILLS PEOPLE -- I DON'T BELIEVE IT, BUT THAT'S PEOPLE RIGHT HERE, PEOPLE LIKE ME, NOT SOME FLYING-CARPET GUY IN CENTRAL ASIA --
AND THEY DON'T EVEN CHECK OUT THE JOB?
IT WAS MY SECOND CLOSE SHAVE IN THE LAST WEEK, SO MAYBE I WAS JUST NERVOUS.
BUT I GET TIRED OF IDIOTS.
HEY! WILLIAMS!
WALK BACK TO THE SUBWAY WITH ME. WE CAN CATCH A BEER BEFORE WE ALL MEET UP AGAIN, SPLIT THE TAKE.
SURE.
LOOK, THIS WAS FREELANCE FOR ME, BUT I MOSTLY WORK FOR THE SCARPELLIS. MOVIN' PRODUCT, WATCHIN' FOR TROUBLE.
THEY'RE LOOKIN' FOR SOME NEW PEOPLE. YOU STAYED COOL BACK THERE, THOUGHT THINGS THROUGH.
YOU'VE GOT A GOOD ATTITUDE, AND THREE TIMES THE BRAIN CELLS OF THOSE OTHER GUYS.
YOU INTERESTED?
REALLY?
STEADY WORK, ROOM TO MOVE UP. AND I FIGURE YOU FOR A MOVER. WHADDYA SAY?
WHO DO I HAVE TO KILL?
I FIGURED, WHAT DO YOU KNOW? THE WORLD THROWS YOU A BONE SOMETIMES.
A CRAZY WORLD, AN' YOU TAKE WHAT COMES. FIGURED I'D CATCH A WAVE FOR A WHILE, SEE WHAT IT BROUGHT. DIFFERENT KIND OF IDIOTS, MAYBE.

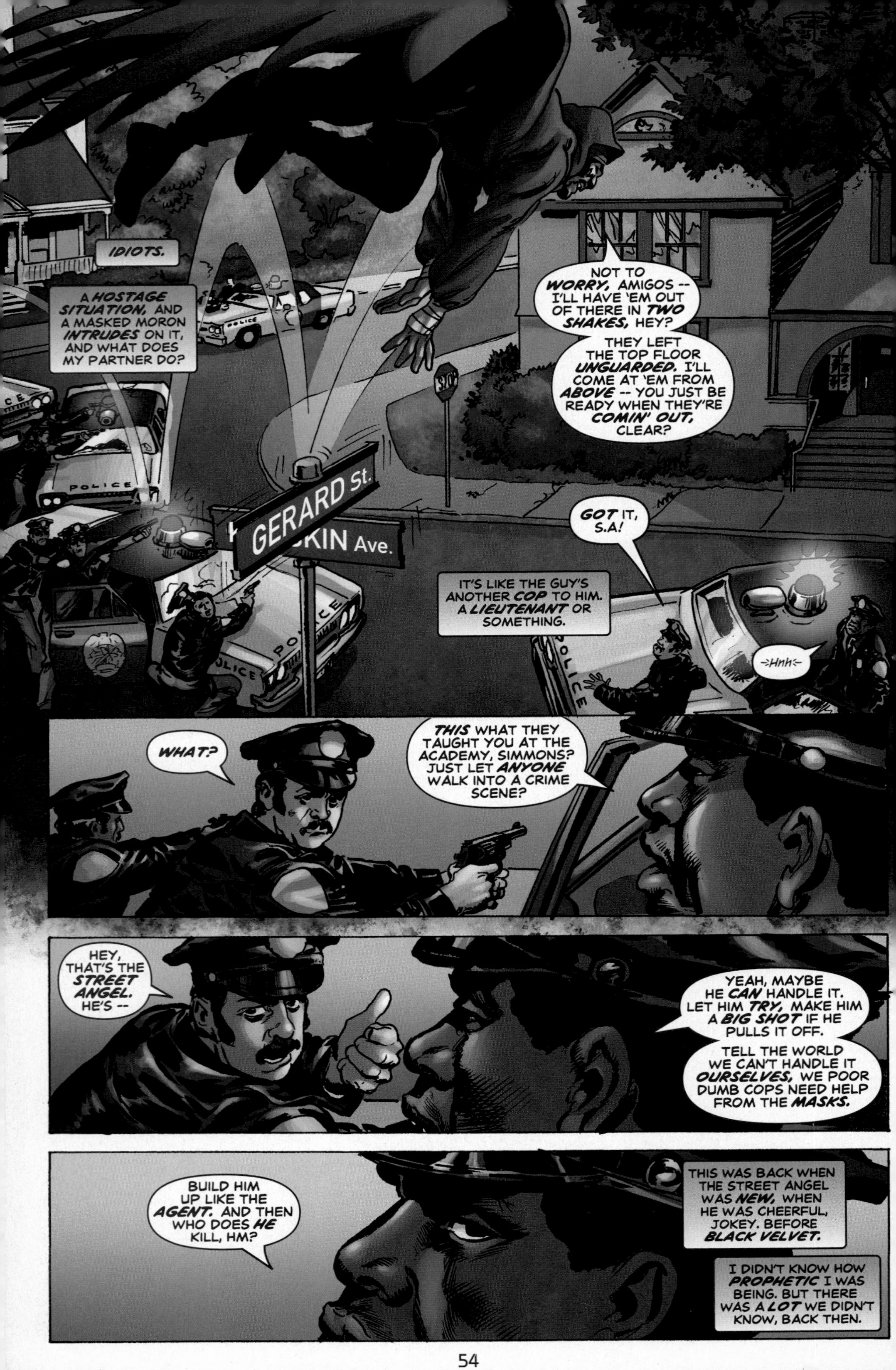
IDIOTS.
A HOSTAGE SITUATION, AND A MASKED MORON INTRUDES ON IT, AND WHAT DOES MY PARTNER DO?
NOT TO WORRY, AMIGOS -- I'LL HAVE 'EM OUT OF THERE IN TWO SHAKES, HEY?
THEY LEFT THE TOP FLOOR UNGUARDED. I'LL COME AT 'EM FROM ABOVE -- YOU JUST BE READY WHEN THEY'RE COMIN' OUT, CLEAR?
GERARD St.
KIN Ave.
GOT IT, S.A!
IT'S LIKE THE GUY'S ANOTHER COP TO HIM. A LIEUTENANT OR SOMETHING.
Hnh
WHAT?
THIS WHAT THEY TAUGHT YOU AT THE ACADEMY, SIMMONS? JUST LET ANYONE WALK INTO A CRIME SCENE?
HEY, THAT'S THE STREET ANGEL. HE'S --
YEAH, MAYBE HE CAN HANDLE IT. LET HIM TRY, MAKE HIM A BIG SHOT IF HE PULLS IT OFF.
TELL THE WORLD WE CAN'T HANDLE IT OURSELVES, WE POOR DUMB COPS NEED HELP FROM THE MASKS.
BUILD HIM UP LIKE THE AGENT. AND THEN WHO DOES HE KILL, HM?
THIS WAS BACK WHEN THE STREET ANGEL WAS NEW, WHEN HE WAS CHEERFUL, JOKEY. BEFORE BLACK VELVET.
I DIDN'T KNOW HOW PROPHETIC I WAS BEING. BUT THERE WAS A LOT WE DIDN'T KNOW, BACK THEN.

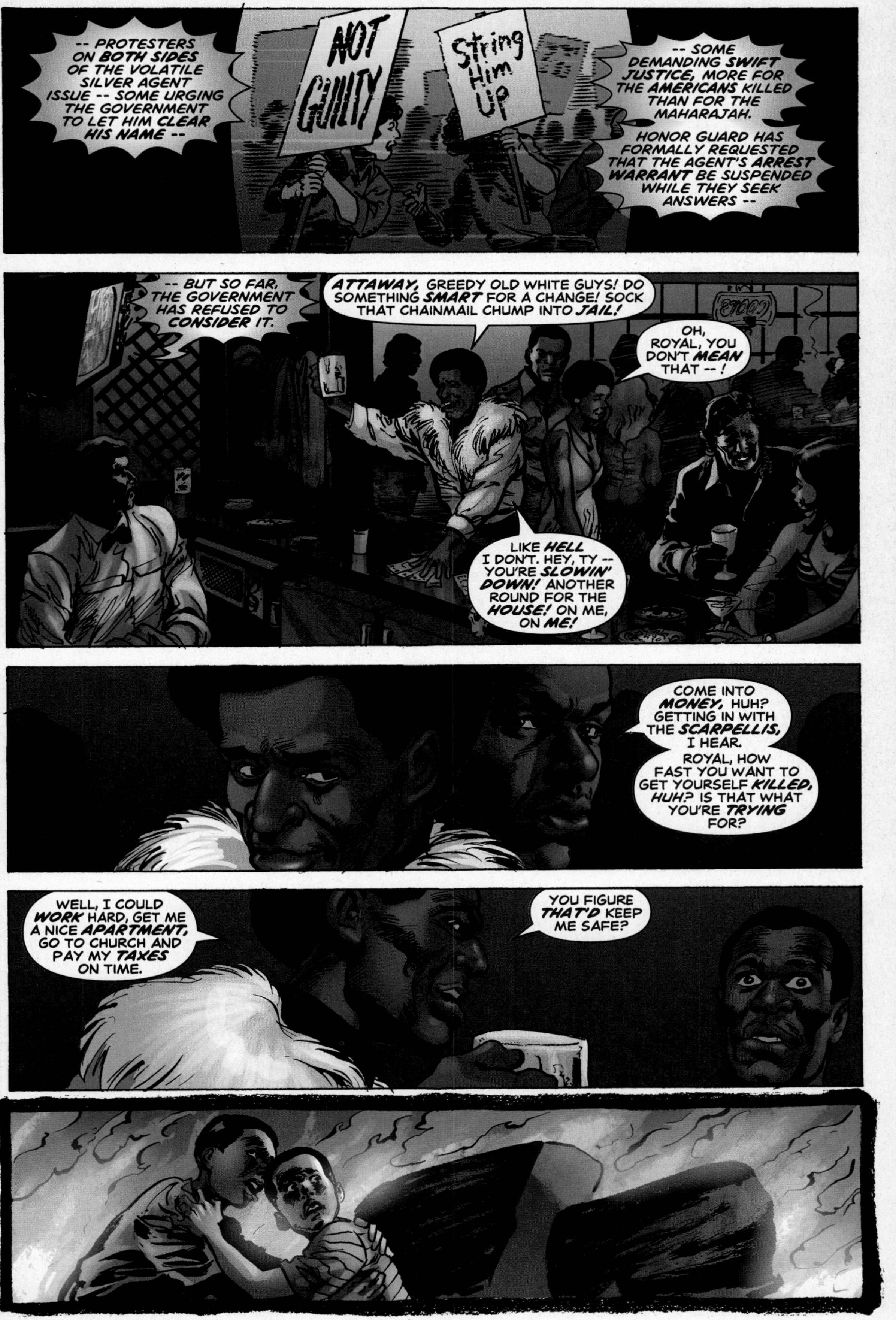
-- PROTESTERS ON BOTH SIDES OF THE VOLATILE SILVER AGENT ISSUE -- SOME URGING THE GOVERNMENT TO LET HIM CLEAR HIS NAME --
NOT GUILTY
String Him Up
-- SOME DEMANDING SWIFT JUSTICE, MORE FOR THE AMERICANS KILLED THAN FOR THE MAHARAJAH.
HONOR GUARD HAS FORMALLY REQUESTED THAT THE AGENT'S ARREST WARRANT BE SUSPENDED WHILE THEY SEEK ANSWERS --
-- BUT SO FAR, THE GOVERNMENT HAS REFUSED TO CONSIDER IT.
ATTAWAY, GREEDY OLD WHITE GUYS! DO SOMETHING SMART FOR A CHANGE! SOCK THAT CHAINMAIL CHUMP INTO JAIL!
OH, ROYAL, YOU DON'T MEAN THAT -- !
LIKE HELL I DON'T. HEY, TY -- YOU'RE SLOWIN' DOWN! ANOTHER ROUND FOR THE HOUSE! ON ME, ON ME!
COME INTO MONEY, HUH? GETTING IN WITH THE SCARPELLIS, I HEAR.
ROYAL, HOW FAST YOU WANT TO GET YOURSELF KILLED, HUH? IS THAT WHAT YOU'RE TRYING FOR?
WELL, I COULD WORK HARD, GET ME A NICE APARTMENT, GO TO CHURCH AND PAY MY TAXES ON TIME.
YOU FIGURE THAT'D KEEP ME SAFE?

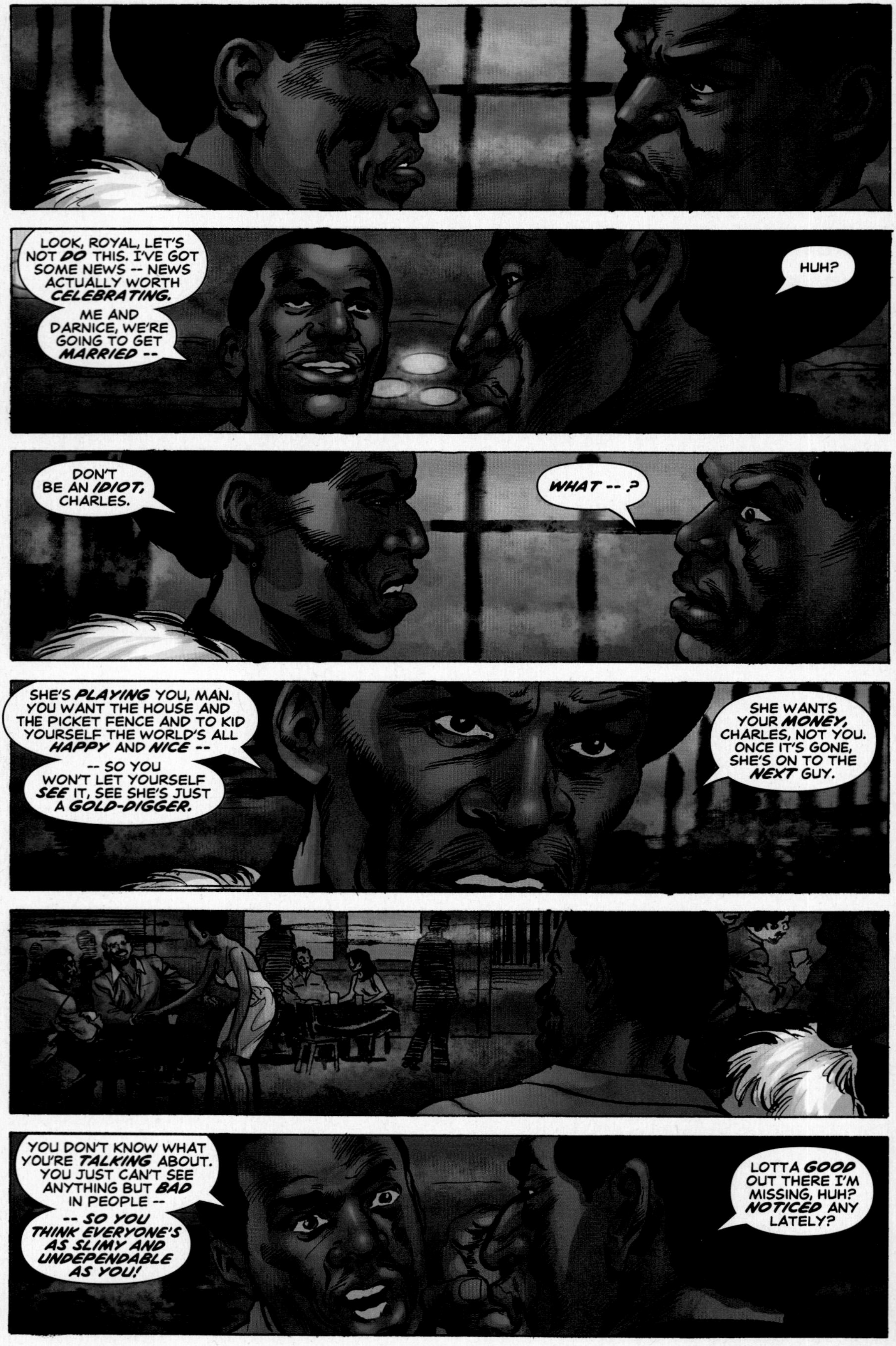

LOOK, ROYAL, LET'S NOT DO THIS. I'VE GOT SOME NEWS -- NEWS ACTUALLY WORTH CELEBRATING.
ME AND DARNICE, WE'RE GOING TO GET MARRIED --
HUH?
DON'T BE AN IDIOT, CHARLES.
WHAT -- ?
SHE'S PLAYING YOU, MAN. YOU WANT THE HOUSE AND THE PICKET FENCE AND TO KID YOURSELF THE WORLD'S ALL HAPPY AND NICE --
-- SO YOU WON'T LET YOURSELF SEE IT, SEE SHE'S JUST A GOLD-DIGGER.
SHE WANTS YOUR MONEY, CHARLES, NOT YOU. ONCE IT'S GONE, SHE'S ON TO THE NEXT GUY.
YOU DON'T KNOW WHAT YOU'RE TALKING ABOUT. YOU JUST CAN'T SEE ANYTHING BUT BAD IN PEOPLE --
-- SO YOU THINK EVERYONE'S AS SLIMY AND UNDEPENDABLE AS YOU!
LOTTA GOOD OUT THERE I'M MISSING, HUH? NOTICED ANY LATELY?

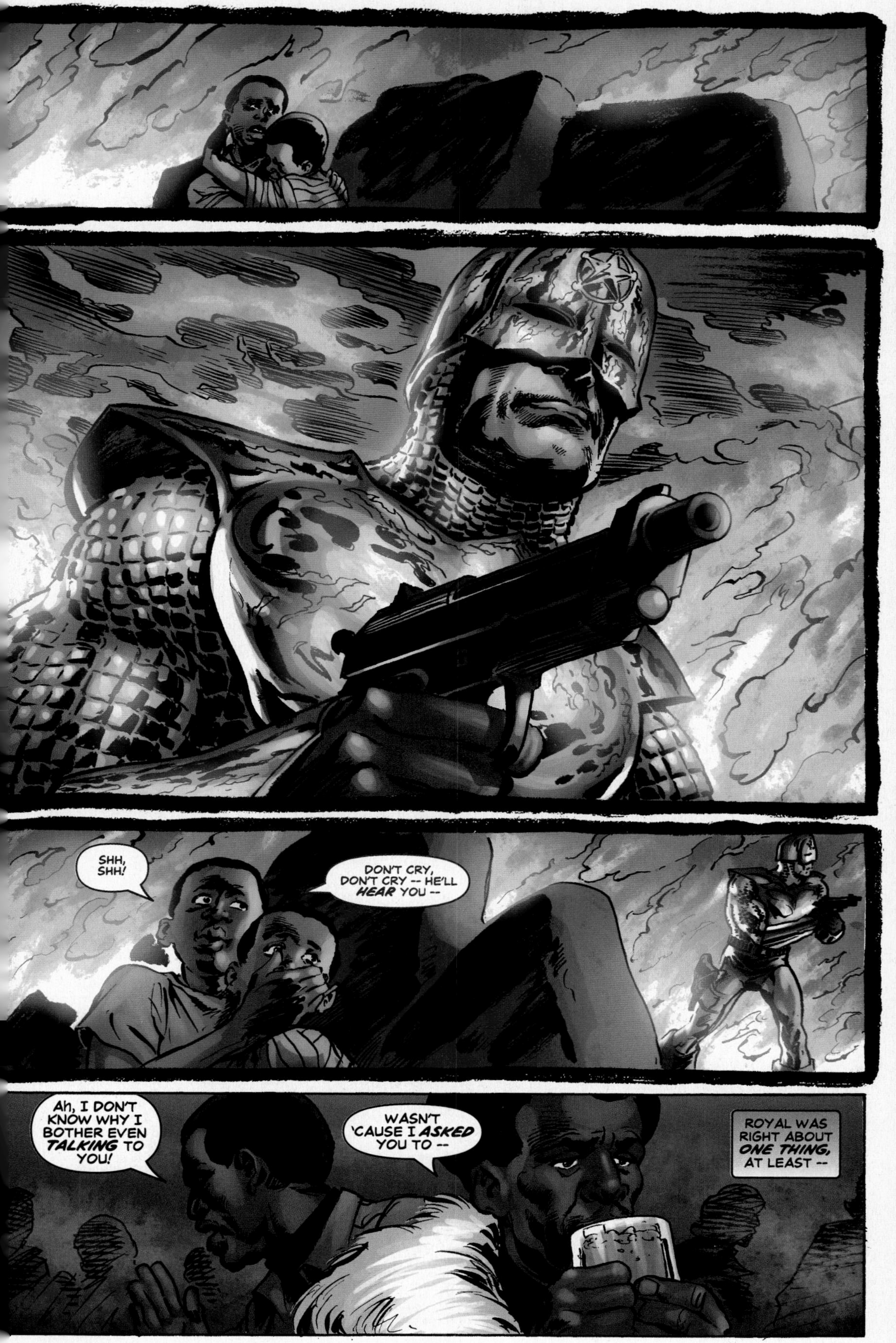
SHH, SHH!
DON'T CRY, DON'T CRY -- HE'LL HEAR YOU --
Ah, I DON'T KNOW WHY I BOTHER EVEN TALKING TO YOU!
WASN'T 'CAUSE I ASKED YOU TO --
ROYAL WAS RIGHT ABOUT ONE THING, AT LEAST --

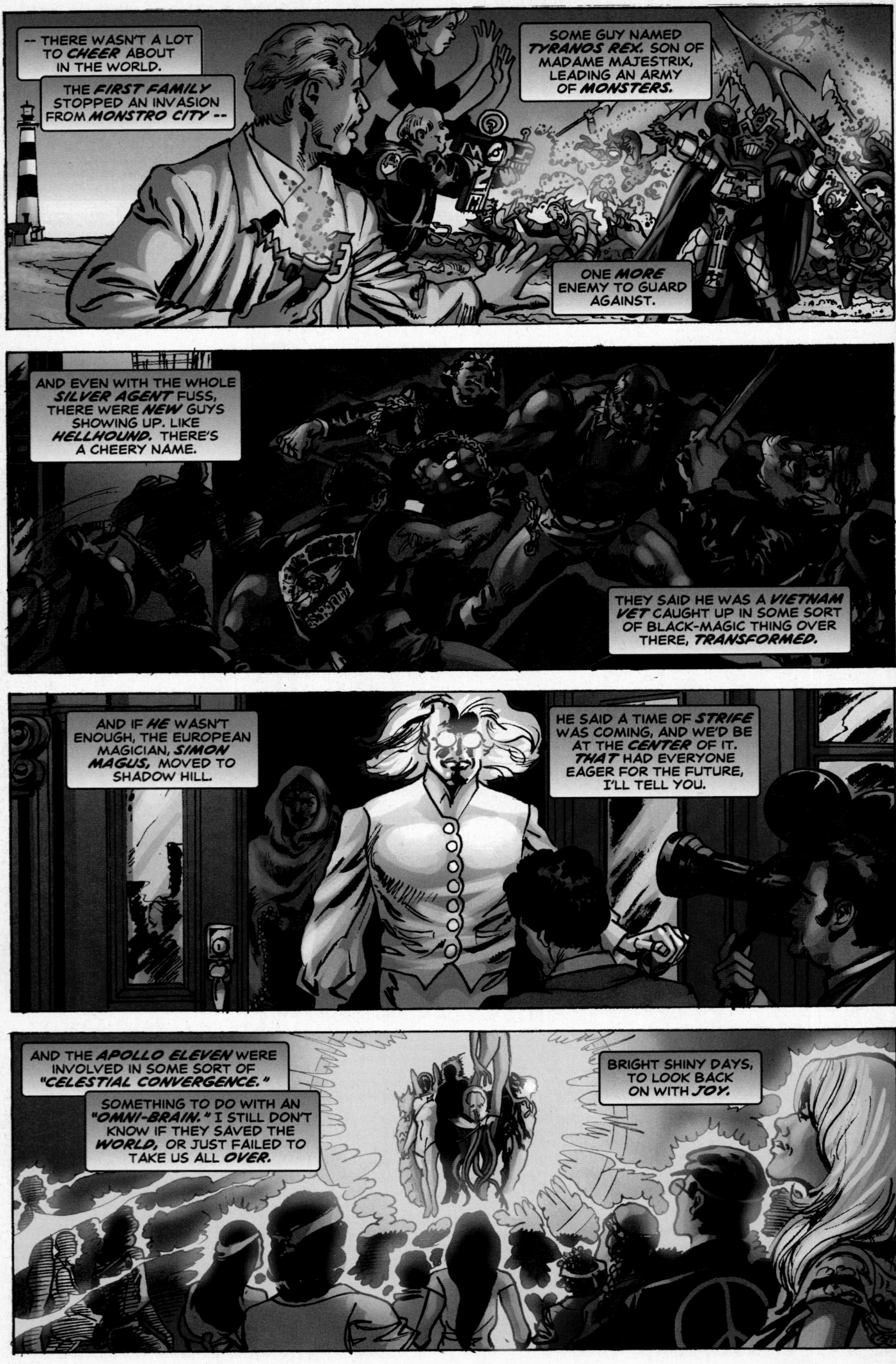
-- THERE WASN'T A LOT TO CHEER ABOUT IN THE WORLD.
THE FIRST FAMILY STOPPED AN INVASION FROM MONSTRO CITY --
SOME GUY NAMED TYRANOS REX. SON OF MADAME MAJESTRIX, LEADING AN ARMY OF MONSTERS.
ONE MORE ENEMY TO GUARD AGAINST.
AND EVEN WITH THE WHOLE SILVER AGENT FUSS, THERE WERE NEW GUYS SHOWING UP. LIKE HELLHOUND. THERE'S A CHEERY NAME.
THEY SAID HE WAS A VIETNAM VET CAUGHT UP IN SOME SORT OF BLACK-MAGIC THING OVER THERE, TRANSFORMED.
AND IF HE WASN'T ENOUGH, THE EUROPEAN MAGICIAN, SIMON MAGUS, MOVED TO SHADOW HILL.
HE SAID A TIME OF STRIFE WAS COMING, AND WE'D BE AT THE CENTER OF IT. THAT HAD EVERYONE EAGER FOR THE FUTURE, I'LL TELL YOU.
AND THE APOLLO ELEVEN WERE INVOLVED IN SOME SORT OF "CELESTIAL CONVERGENCE."
SOMETHING TO DO WITH AN "OMNI-BRAIN." I STILL DON'T KNOW IF THEY SAVED THE WORLD, OR JUST FAILED TO TAKE US ALL OVER.
BRIGHT SHINY DAYS, TO LOOK BACK ON WITH JOY.

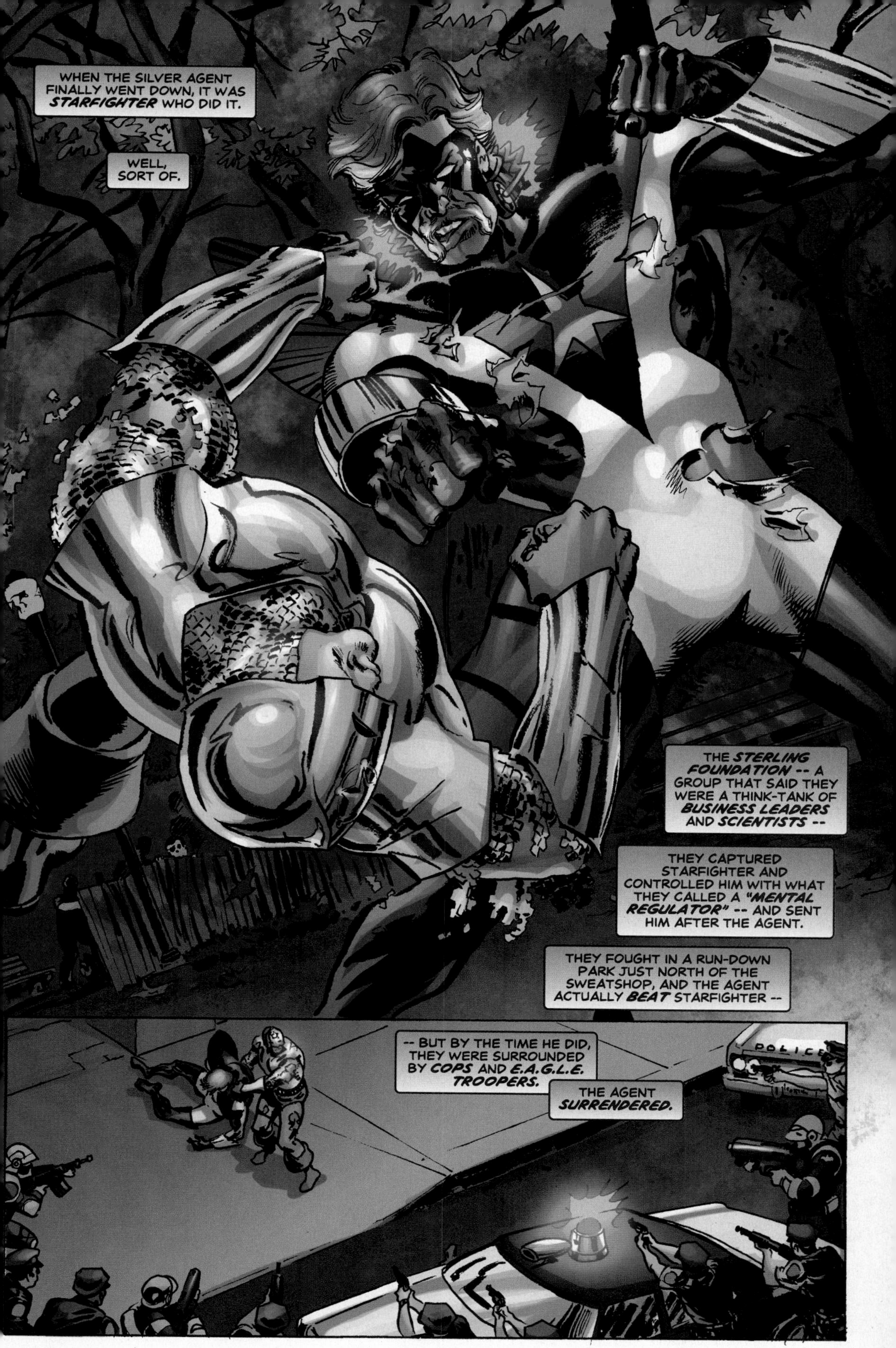
WHEN THE SILVER AGENT FINALLY WENT DOWN, IT WAS STARFIGHTER WHO DID IT.
WELL, SORT OF.
THE STERLING FOUNDATION -- A GROUP THAT SAID THEY WERE A THINK-TANK OF BUSINESS LEADERS AND SCIENTISTS --
THEY CAPTURED STARFIGHTER AND CONTROLLED HIM WITH WHAT THEY CALLED A "MENTAL REGULATOR" -- AND SENT HIM AFTER THE AGENT.
THEY FOUGHT IN A RUN-DOWN PARK JUST NORTH OF THE SWEATSHOP, AND THE AGENT ACTUALLY BEAT STARFIGHTER --
-- BUT BY THE TIME HE DID, THEY WERE SURROUNDED BY COPS AND E.A.G.L.E. TROOPERS.
THE AGENT SURRENDERED.
POLICE

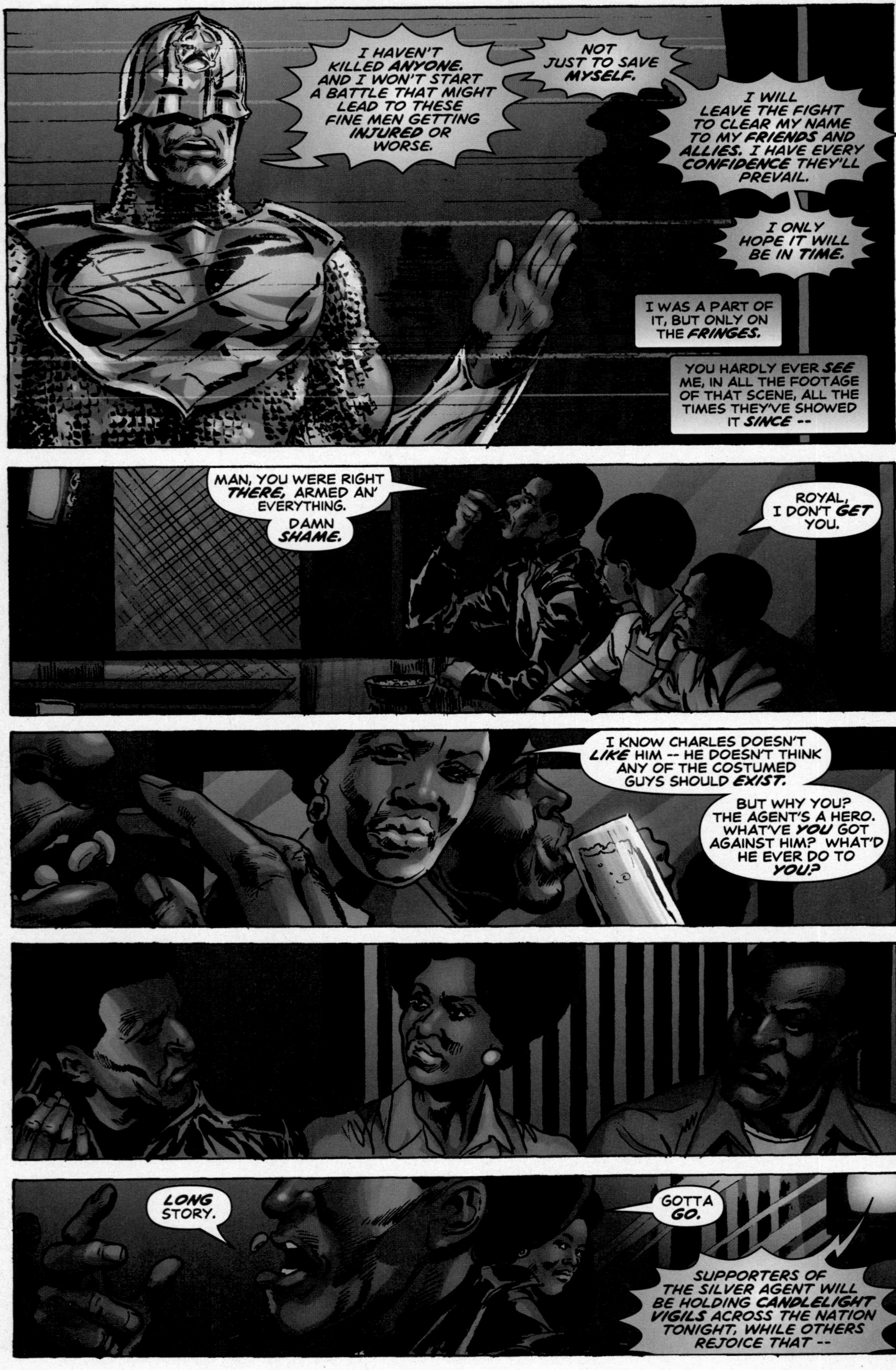
I HAVEN'T KILLED ANYONE. AND I WON'T START A BATTLE THAT MIGHT LEAD TO THESE FINE MEN GETTING INJURED OR WORSE.
NOT JUST TO SAVE MYSELF.
I WILL LEAVE THE FIGHT TO CLEAR MY NAME TO MY FRIENDS AND ALLIES. I HAVE EVERY CONFIDENCE THEY'LL PREVAIL.
I ONLY HOPE IT WILL BE IN TIME.
I WAS A PART OF IT, BUT ONLY ON THE FRINGES.
YOU HARDLY EVER SEE ME, IN ALL THE FOOTAGE OF THAT SCENE, ALL THE TIMES THEY'VE SHOWED IT SINCE --
MAN, YOU WERE RIGHT THERE, ARMED AN' EVERYTHING.
DAMN SHAME.
ROYAL, I DON'T GET YOU.
I KNOW CHARLES DOESN'T LIKE HIM -- HE DOESN'T THINK ANY OF THE COSTUMED GUYS SHOULD EXIST.
BUT WHY YOU? THE AGENT'S A HERO. WHAT'VE YOU GOT AGAINST HIM? WHAT'D HE EVER DO TO YOU?
LONG STORY.
GOTTA GO.
SUPPORTERS OF THE SILVER AGENT WILL BE HOLDING CANDLELIGHT VIGILS ACROSS THE NATION TONIGHT, WHILE OTHERS REJOICE THAT --

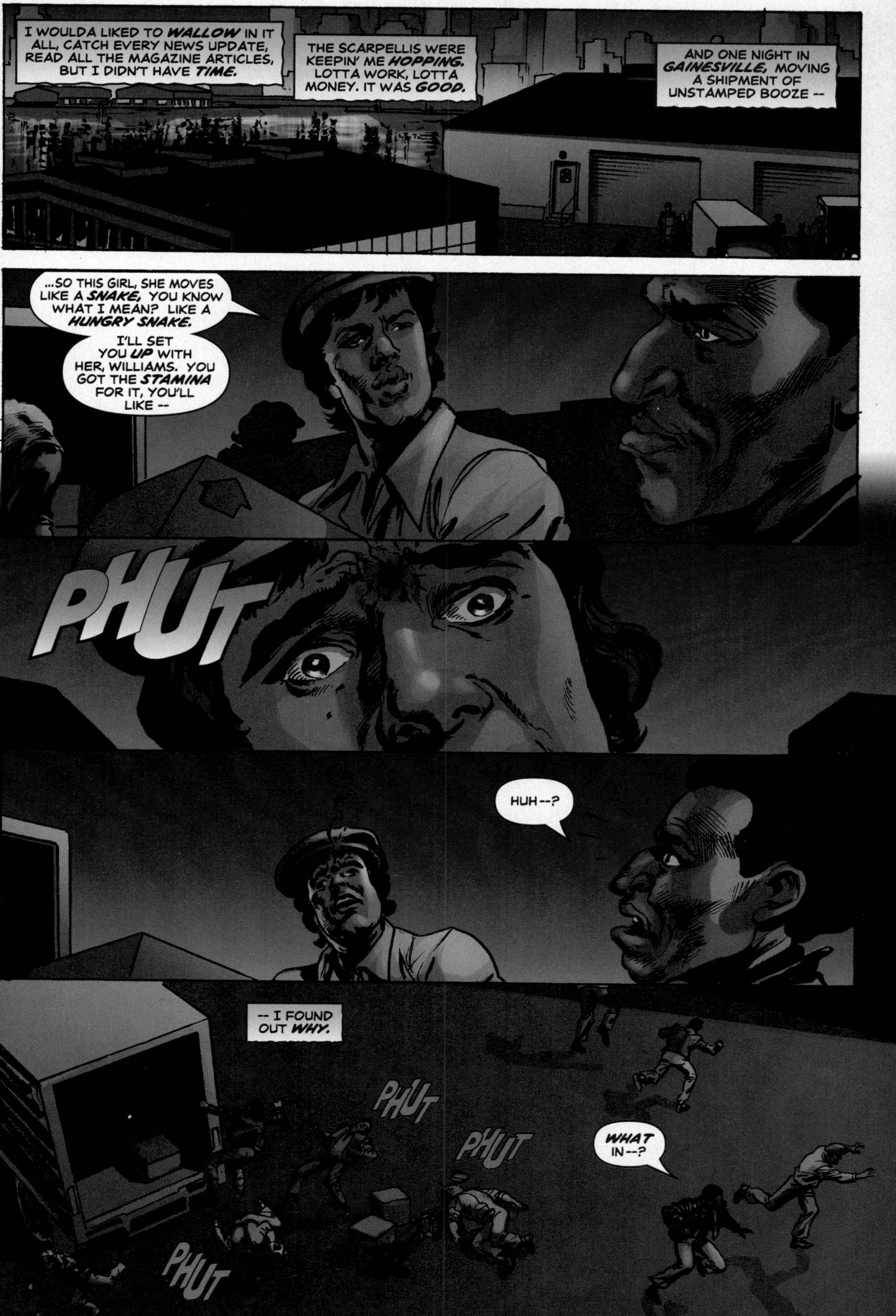
I WOULDA LIKED TO WALLOW IN IT ALL, CATCH EVERY NEWS UPDATE, READ ALL THE MAGAZINE ARTICLES, BUT I DIDN'T HAVE TIME.
THE SCARPELLIS WERE KEEPIN' ME HOPPING. LOTTA WORK, LOTTA MONEY. IT WAS GOOD.
AND ONE NIGHT IN GAINESVILLE, MOVING A SHIPMENT OF UNSTAMPED BOOZE --
...SO THIS GIRL, SHE MOVES LIKE A SNAKE, YOU KNOW WHAT I MEAN? LIKE A HUNGRY SNAKE.
I'LL SET YOU UP WITH HER, WILLIAMS. YOU GOT THE STAMINA FOR IT, YOU'LL LIKE --
PHUT
HUH --?
-- I FOUND OUT WHY.
PHUT
PHUT
WHAT IN --?
PHUT

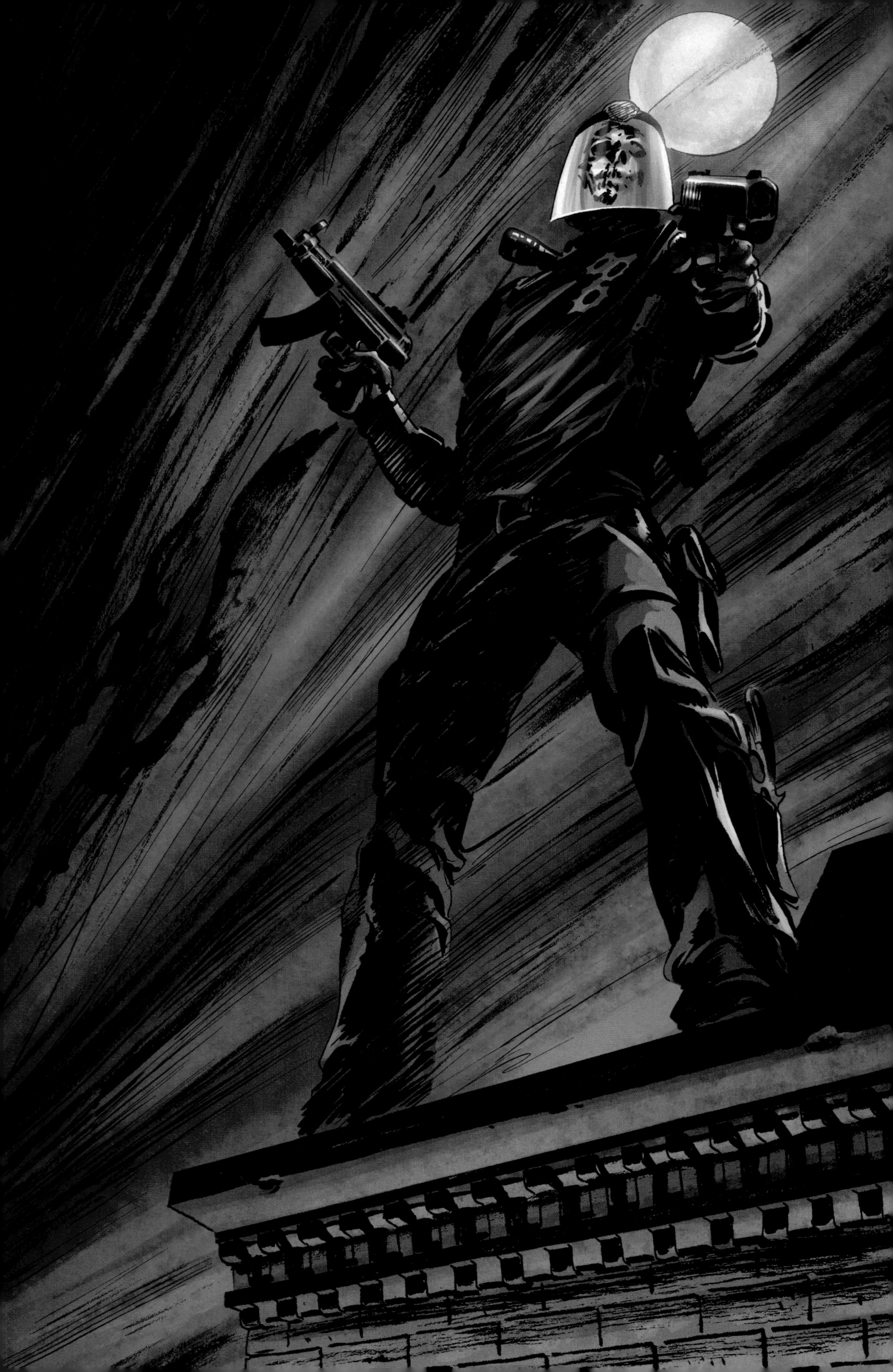

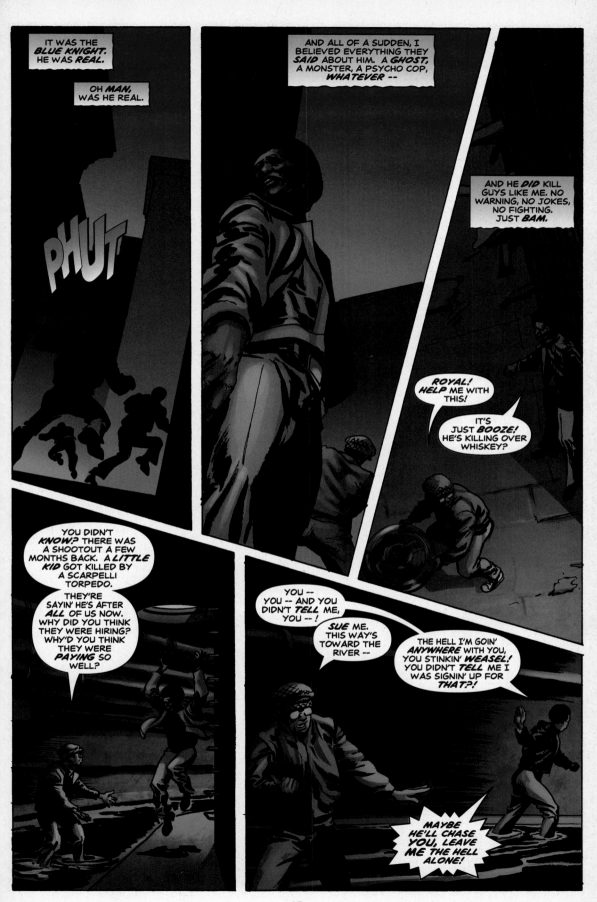

IT WAS THE *BLUE KNIGHT*. HE WAS *REAL*.

OH *MAN*, WAS HE REAL.

AND ALL OF A SUDDEN, I BELIEVED EVERYTHING THEY *SAID* ABOUT HIM. A *GHOST*, A MONSTER, A PSYCHO COP, *WHATEVER* --

AND HE *DID* KILL GUYS LIKE ME. NO WARNING, NO JOKES, NO FIGHTING. JUST *BAM*.

PHUT

ROYAL! *HELP* ME WITH THIS!

IT'S JUST *BOOZE!* HE'S KILLING OVER WHISKEY?

YOU DIDN'T *KNOW?* THERE WAS A SHOOTOUT A FEW MONTHS BACK. A *LITTLE KID* GOT KILLED BY A SCARPELLI TORPEDO.

THEY'RE SAYIN' HE'S AFTER *ALL* OF US NOW. WHY DID YOU THINK THEY WERE HIRING? WHY'D YOU THINK THEY WERE *PAYING* SO WELL?

YOU -- YOU -- AND YOU DIDN'T *TELL* ME, YOU -- !

SUE ME. THIS WAY'S TOWARD THE RIVER --

THE HELL I'M GOIN' *ANYWHERE* WITH YOU, YOU STINKIN' *WEASEL!* YOU DIDN'T *TELL* ME I WAS SIGNIN' UP FOR *THAT?!*

MAYBE HE'LL CHASE *YOU*, LEAVE *ME* THE HELL ALONE!

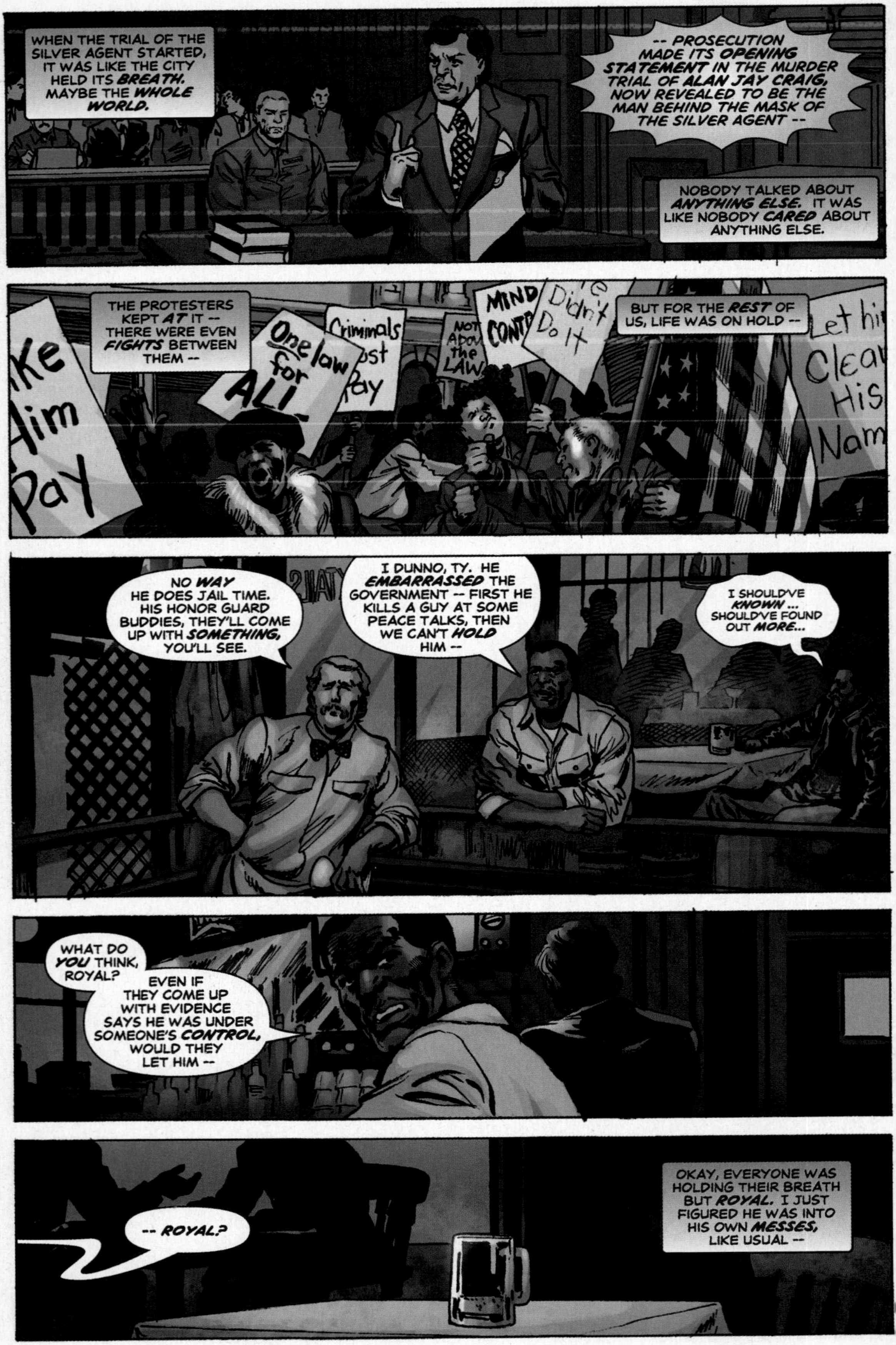

WHEN THE TRIAL OF THE SILVER AGENT STARTED, IT WAS LIKE THE CITY HELD ITS BREATH. MAYBE THE WHOLE WORLD.
-- PROSECUTION MADE ITS OPENING STATEMENT IN THE MURDER TRIAL OF ALAN JAY CRAIG, NOW REVEALED TO BE THE MAN BEHIND THE MASK OF THE SILVER AGENT --
NOBODY TALKED ABOUT ANYTHING ELSE. IT WAS LIKE NOBODY CARED ABOUT ANYTHING ELSE.
THE PROTESTERS KEPT AT IT -- THERE WERE EVEN FIGHTS BETWEEN THEM --
One law for ALL
Criminals
MIND
Didn't Do It
BUT FOR THE REST OF US, LIFE WAS ON HOLD --
NO WAY HE DOES JAIL TIME. HIS HONOR GUARD BUDDIES, THEY'LL COME UP WITH SOMETHING, YOU'LL SEE.
I DUNNO, TY. HE EMBARRASSED THE GOVERNMENT -- FIRST HE KILLS A GUY AT SOME PEACE TALKS, THEN WE CAN'T HOLD HIM --
I SHOULD'VE KNOWN... SHOULD'VE FOUND OUT MORE...
WHAT DO YOU THINK, ROYAL?
EVEN IF THEY COME UP WITH EVIDENCE SAYS HE WAS UNDER SOMEONE'S CONTROL, WOULD THEY LET HIM --
-- ROYAL?
OKAY, EVERYONE WAS HOLDING THEIR BREATH BUT ROYAL. I JUST FIGURED HE WAS INTO HIS OWN MESSES, LIKE USUAL --

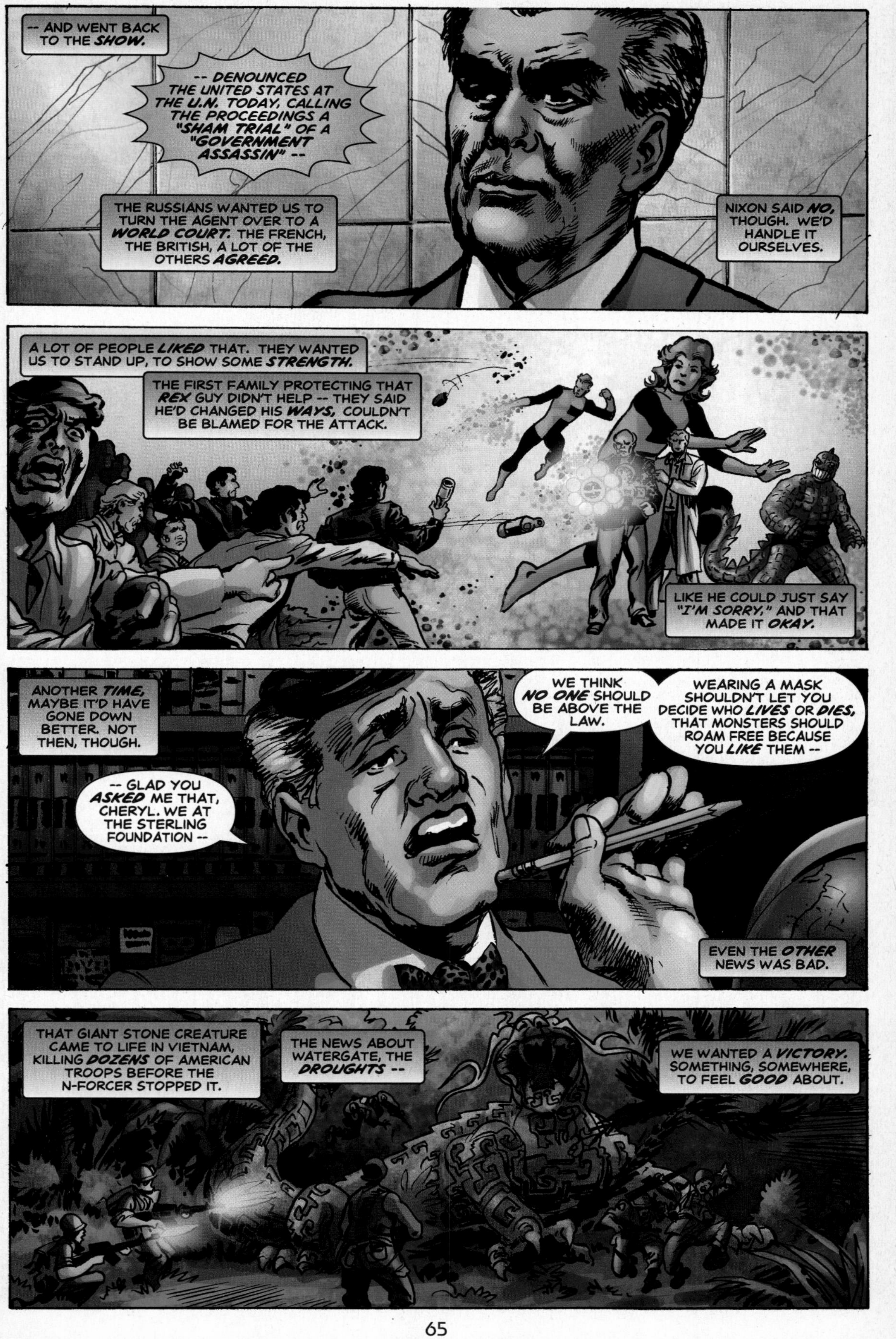
-- AND WENT BACK TO THE SHOW.
-- DENOUNCED THE UNITED STATES AT THE U.N. TODAY, CALLING THE PROCEEDINGS A "SHAM TRIAL" OF A "GOVERNMENT ASSASSIN" --
THE RUSSIANS WANTED US TO TURN THE AGENT OVER TO A WORLD COURT. THE FRENCH, THE BRITISH, A LOT OF THE OTHERS AGREED.
NIXON SAID NO, THOUGH. WE'D HANDLE IT OURSELVES.
A LOT OF PEOPLE LIKED THAT. THEY WANTED US TO STAND UP, TO SHOW SOME STRENGTH.
THE FIRST FAMILY PROTECTING THAT REX GUY DIDN'T HELP -- THEY SAID HE'D CHANGED HIS WAYS, COULDN'T BE BLAMED FOR THE ATTACK.
LIKE HE COULD JUST SAY "I'M SORRY," AND THAT MADE IT OKAY.
ANOTHER TIME, MAYBE IT'D HAVE GONE DOWN BETTER. NOT THEN, THOUGH.
-- GLAD YOU ASKED ME THAT, CHERYL. WE AT THE STERLING FOUNDATION --
WE THINK NO ONE SHOULD BE ABOVE THE LAW.
WEARING A MASK SHOULDN'T LET YOU DECIDE WHO LIVES OR DIES, THAT MONSTERS SHOULD ROAM FREE BECAUSE YOU LIKE THEM --
EVEN THE OTHER NEWS WAS BAD.
THAT GIANT STONE CREATURE CAME TO LIFE IN VIETNAM, KILLING DOZENS OF AMERICAN TROOPS BEFORE THE N-FORCER STOPPED IT.
THE NEWS ABOUT WATERGATE, THE DROUGHTS --
WE WANTED A VICTORY. SOMETHING, SOMEWHERE, TO FEEL GOOD ABOUT.

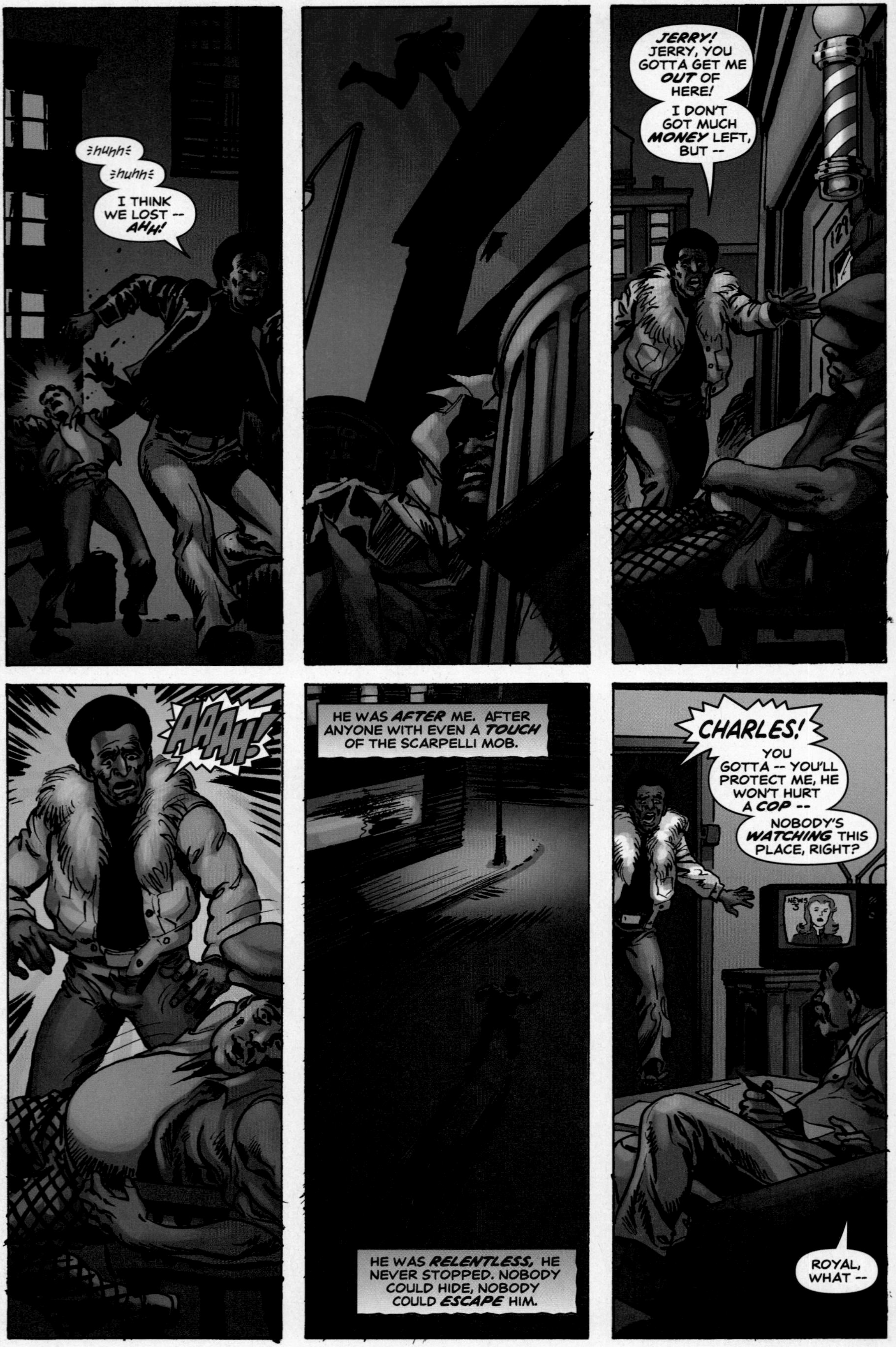

huhh
huhh
I THINK WE LOST -- AHH!
JERRY! JERRY, YOU GOTTA GET ME OUT OF HERE!
I DON'T GOT MUCH MONEY LEFT, BUT --
129
AAAH!
HE WAS AFTER ME. AFTER ANYONE WITH EVEN A TOUCH OF THE SCARPELLI MOB.
HE WAS RELENTLESS, HE NEVER STOPPED. NOBODY COULD HIDE, NOBODY COULD ESCAPE HIM.
CHARLES!
YOU GOTTA -- YOU'LL PROTECT ME, HE WON'T HURT A COP --
NOBODY'S WATCHING THIS PLACE, RIGHT?
NEWS 3
ROYAL, WHAT --

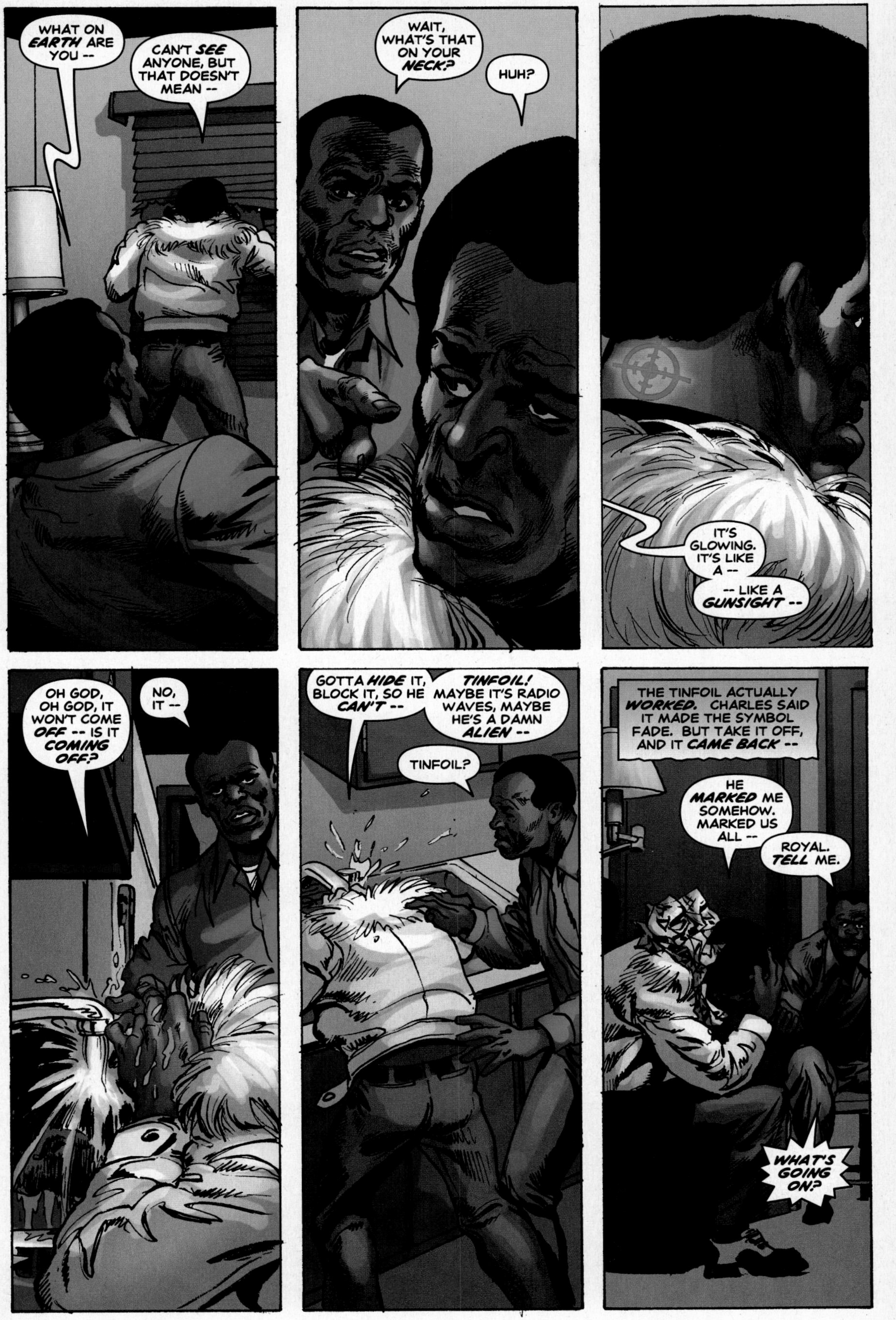
WHAT ON EARTH ARE YOU --
CAN'T SEE ANYONE, BUT THAT DOESN'T MEAN --
WAIT, WHAT'S THAT ON YOUR NECK?
HUH?
IT'S GLOWING. IT'S LIKE A --
-- LIKE A GUNSIGHT --
OH GOD, OH GOD, IT WON'T COME OFF -- IS IT COMING OFF?
NO, IT --
GOTTA HIDE IT, BLOCK IT, SO HE CAN'T --
TINFOIL! MAYBE IT'S RADIO WAVES, MAYBE HE'S A DAMN ALIEN --
TINFOIL?
THE TINFOIL ACTUALLY WORKED. CHARLES SAID IT MADE THE SYMBOL FADE. BUT TAKE IT OFF, AND IT CAME BACK --
HE MARKED ME SOMEHOW. MARKED US ALL --
ROYAL. TELL ME.
WHAT'S GOING ON?

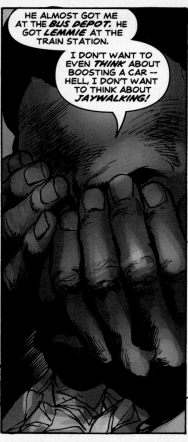

I TOLD HIM. *ALL* OF IT.

OH, ROYAL...

I DIDN'T *KNOW,* ALL RIGHT? *I DIDN'T KNOW!*

WHAT DO I *DO,* HUH? YOU'RE THE *SMART* ONE, YOU WENT TO COP SCHOOL. WHAT DO I *DO?*

WELL, HE'S NEVER BEEN SIGHTED OUTSIDE THE *CITY* --

HE ALMOST GOT ME AT THE *BUS DEPOT.* HE GOT *LEMMIE* AT THE TRAIN STATION.

I DON'T WANT TO EVEN *THINK* ABOUT BOOSTING A CAR -- HELL, I DON'T WANT TO THINK ABOUT *JAYWALKING!*

CHARLES.

I DON'T *KILL* PEOPLE. DON'T EVEN *BEAT* PEOPLE *UP.* I NICK *PURSES.* MOVE BOXES THAT FELL OFF OF TRUCKS. HELP *STEAL* THINGS. I DON'T DO ANYTHING WORTH DYING FOR!

NOT *DYING!*

WELL, I HATE TO SAY IT, BUT MAYBE YOU SHOULD HAVE *THOUGHT* OF THAT BEFORE --

DON'T *SAY* THAT! *DON'T YOU SAY THAT!!*

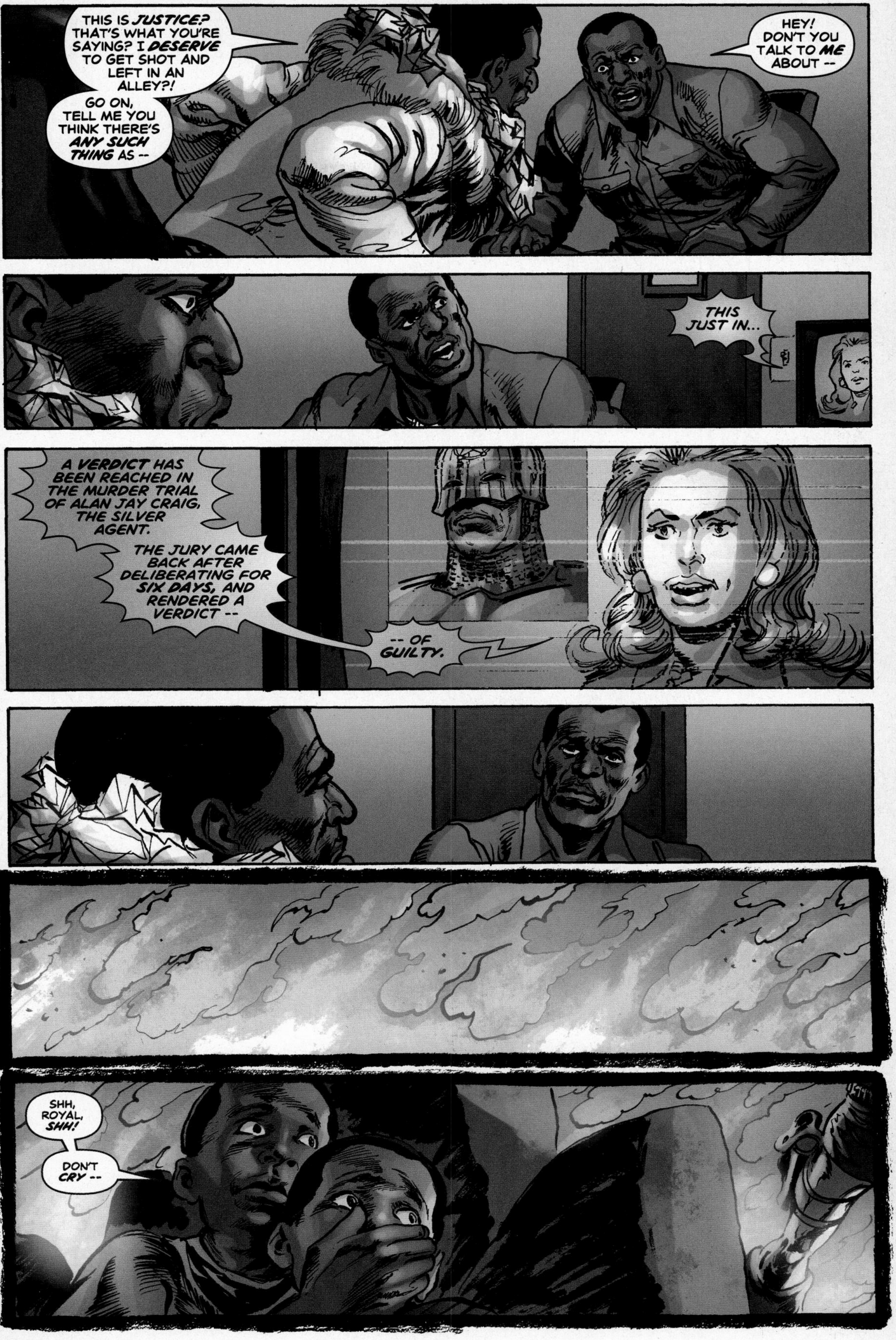
THIS IS JUSTICE? THAT'S WHAT YOU'RE SAYING? I DESERVE TO GET SHOT AND LEFT IN AN ALLEY?!
GO ON, TELL ME YOU THINK THERE'S ANY SUCH THING AS --
HEY! DON'T YOU TALK TO ME ABOUT --
THIS JUST IN...
A VERDICT HAS BEEN REACHED IN THE MURDER TRIAL OF ALAN JAY CRAIG, THE SILVER AGENT.
THE JURY CAME BACK AFTER DELIBERATING FOR SIX DAYS, AND RENDERED A VERDICT --
-- OF GUILTY.
SHH, ROYAL, SHH!
DON'T CRY --

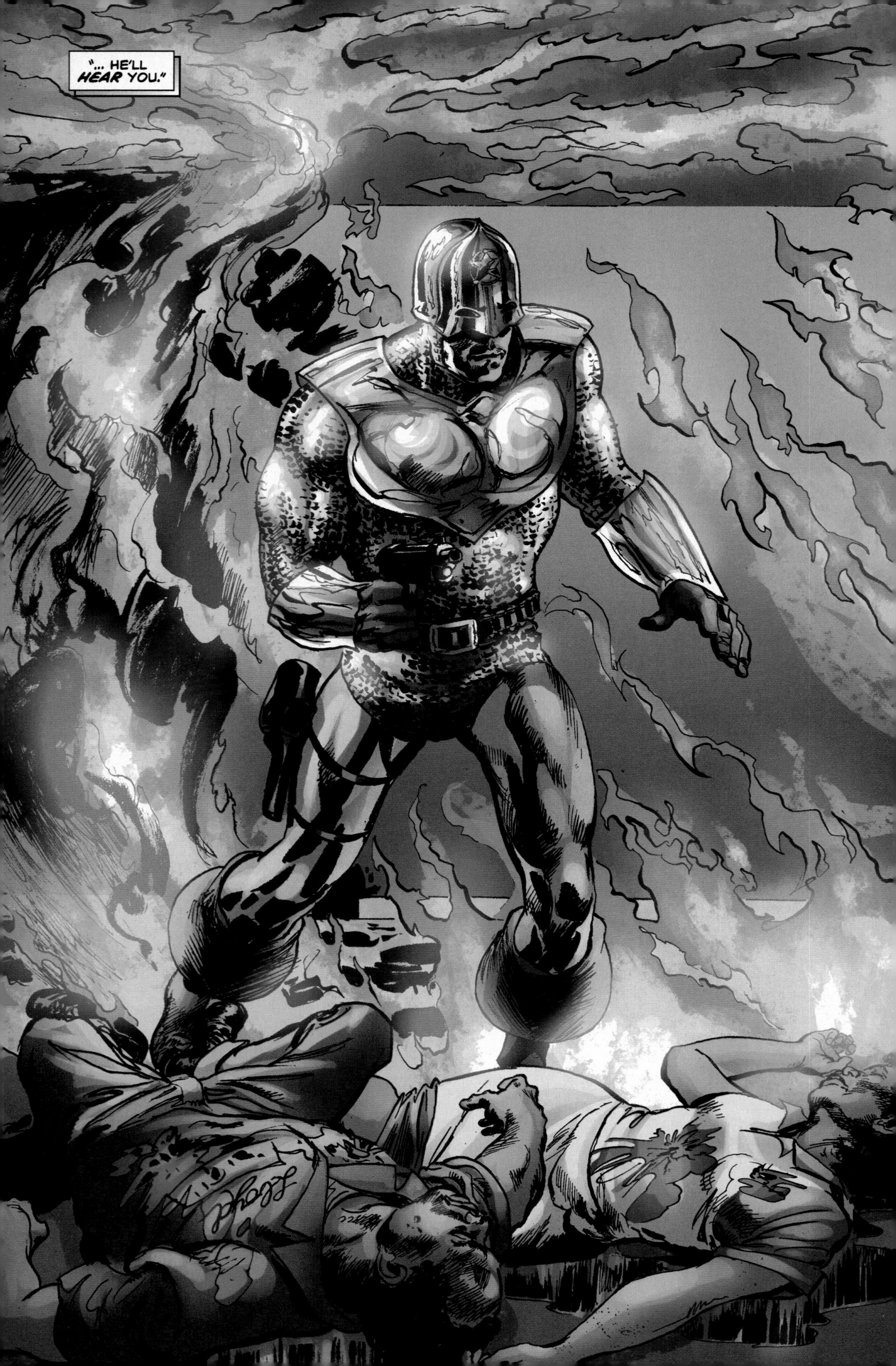
"... HE'LL HEAR YOU."

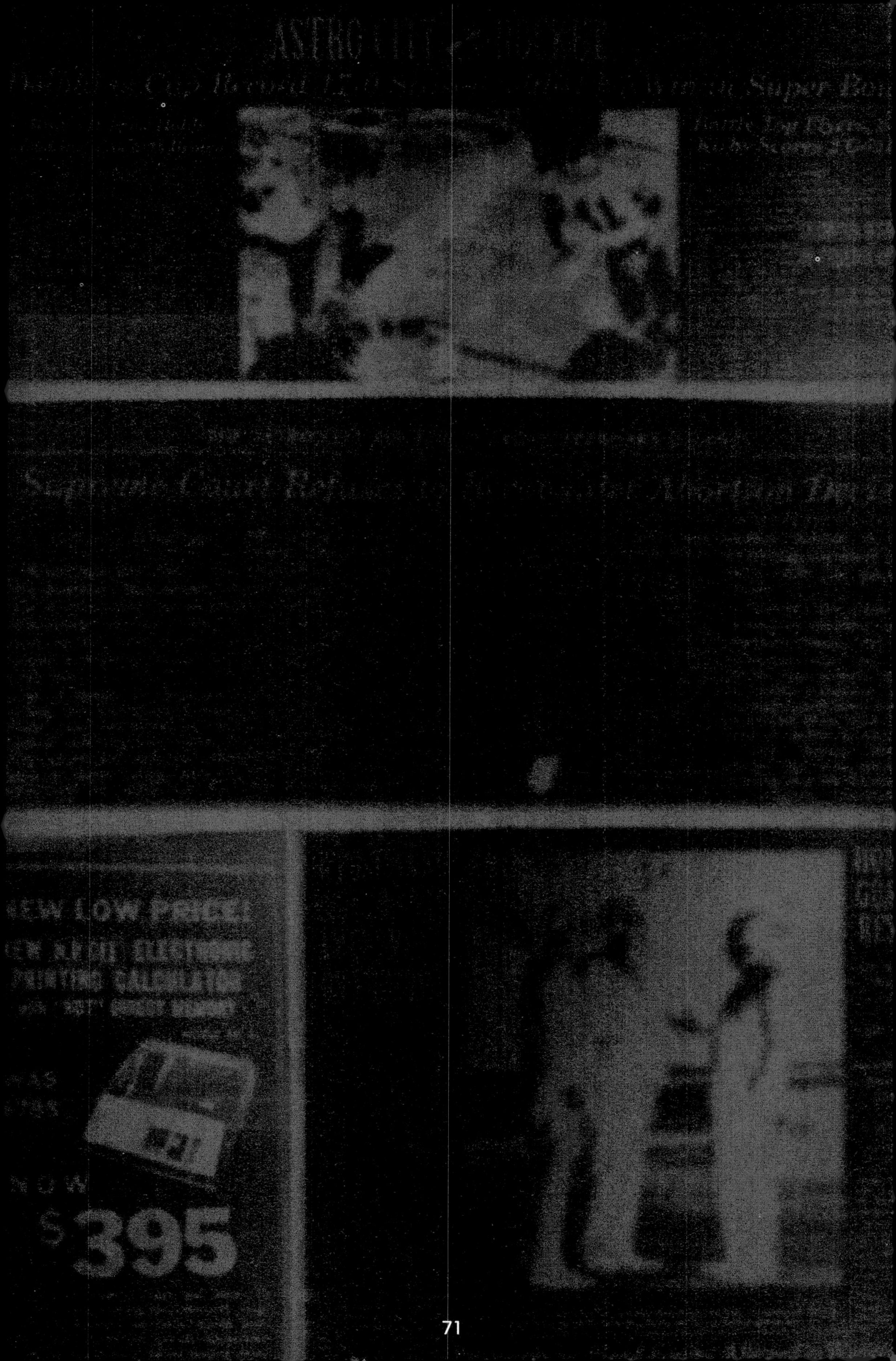
NOW
$395

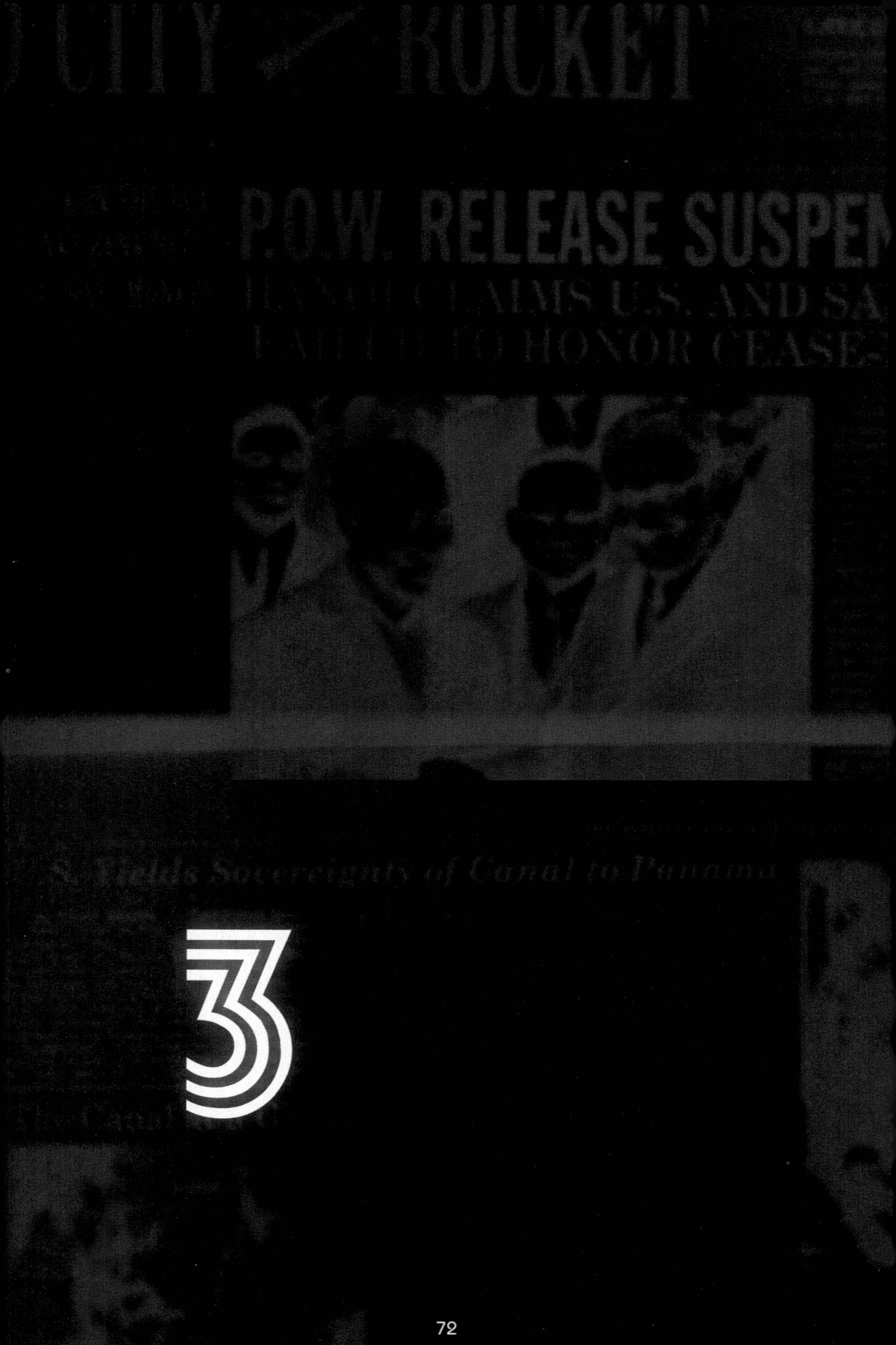
ROCKET
P.O.W. RELEASE
HANOI CLAIMS U.S. AND
FAILED TO HONOR
Yields Sovereignty of Canal to Panama

3

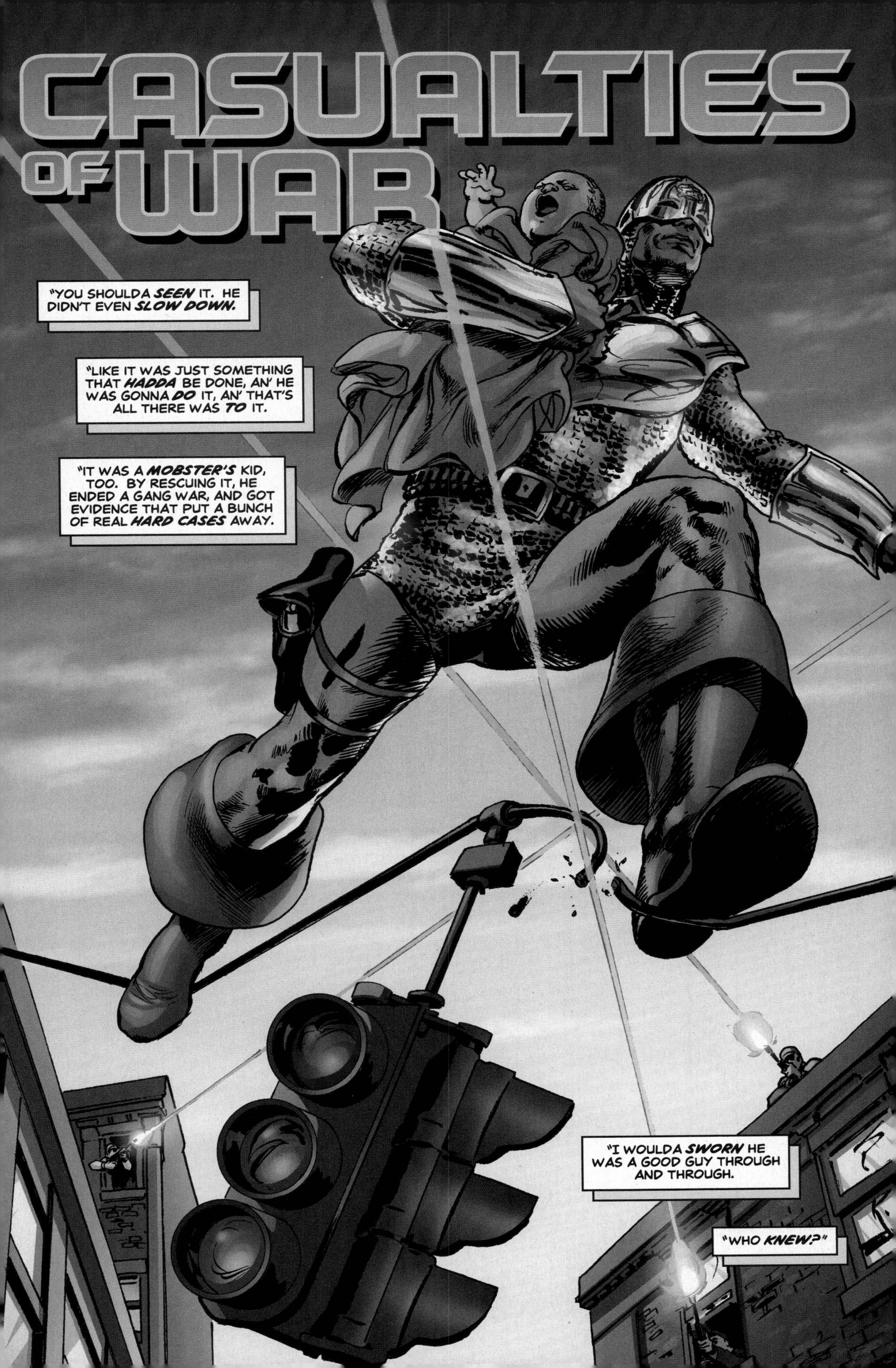
CASUALTIES OF WAR
"YOU SHOULDA SEEN IT. HE DIDN'T EVEN SLOW DOWN.
"LIKE IT WAS JUST SOMETHING THAT HADDA BE DONE, AN' HE WAS GONNA DO IT, AN' THAT'S ALL THERE WAS TO IT.
"IT WAS A MOBSTER'S KID, TOO. BY RESCUING IT, HE ENDED A GANG WAR, AND GOT EVIDENCE THAT PUT A BUNCH OF REAL HARD CASES AWAY.
"I WOULDA SWORN HE WAS A GOOD GUY THROUGH AND THROUGH.
"WHO KNEW?"

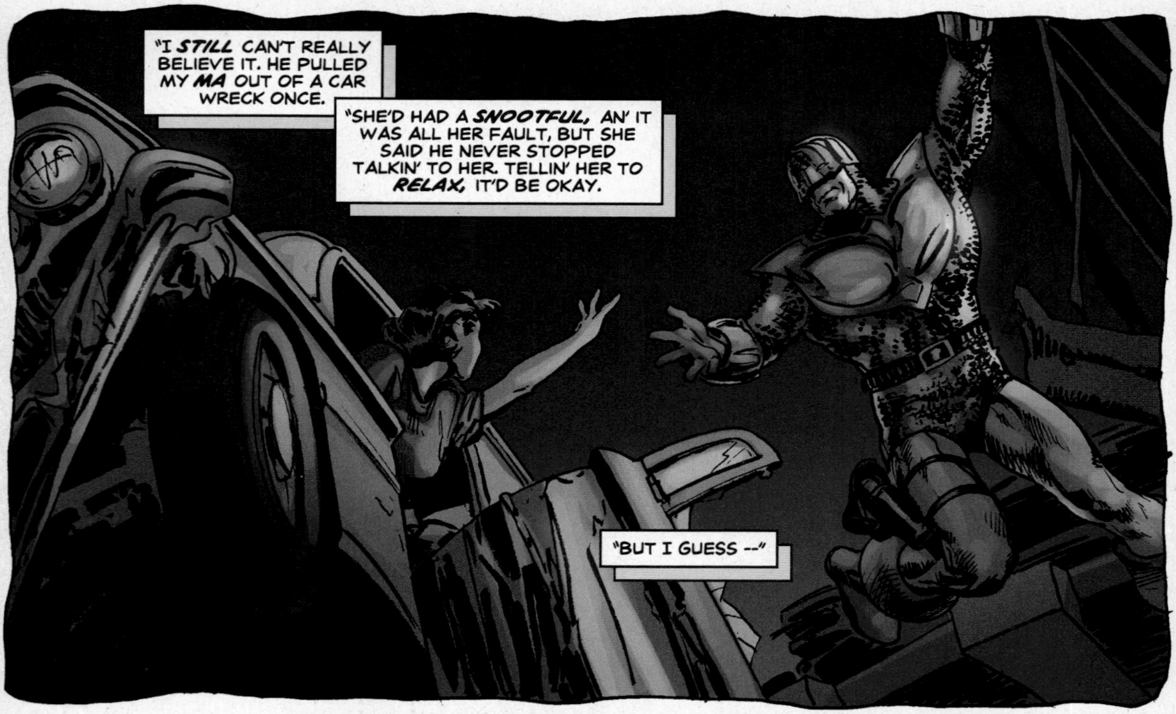
"I STILL CAN'T REALLY BELIEVE IT. HE PULLED MY MA OUT OF A CAR WRECK ONCE.
"SHE'D HAD A SNOOTFUL, AN' IT WAS ALL HER FAULT, BUT SHE SAID HE NEVER STOPPED TALKIN' TO HER. TELLIN' HER TO RELAX, IT'D BE OKAY.
"BUT I GUESS --"

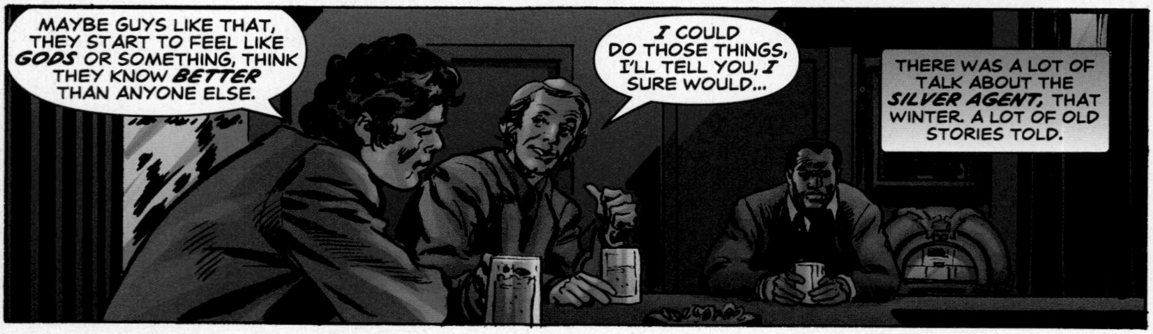
MAYBE GUYS LIKE THAT, THEY START TO FEEL LIKE GODS OR SOMETHING, THINK THEY KNOW BETTER THAN ANYONE ELSE.
I COULD DO THOSE THINGS, I'LL TELL YOU, I SURE WOULD...
THERE WAS A LOT OF TALK ABOUT THE SILVER AGENT, THAT WINTER. A LOT OF OLD STORIES TOLD.

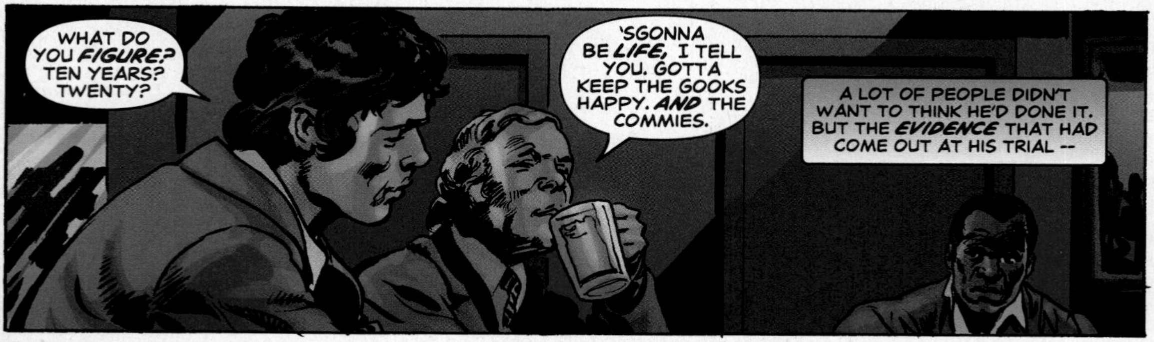
WHAT DO YOU FIGURE? TEN YEARS? TWENTY?
'SGONNA BE LIFE, I TELL YOU. GOTTA KEEP THE GOOKS HAPPY. AND THE COMMIES.
A LOT OF PEOPLE DIDN'T WANT TO THINK HE'D DONE IT. BUT THE EVIDENCE THAT HAD COME OUT AT HIS TRIAL --

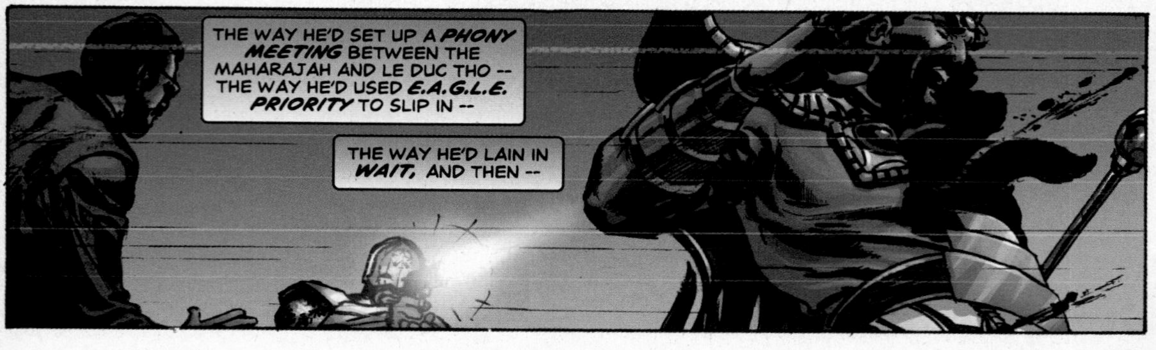
THE WAY HE'D SET UP A PHONY MEETING BETWEEN THE MAHARAJAH AND LE DUC THO -- THE WAY HE'D USED E.A.G.L.E. PRIORITY TO SLIP IN --
THE WAY HE'D LAIN IN WAIT, AND THEN --

TUES FEB 27 1973

ASTRO CITY ⚛ ROCKET

15¢ DAILY

GUILTY

[WASHINGTON, DC] After deliberating ___ days, the jury returned a guilty ___ on all counts in the murder trial ___ Ray Craig, better known as the ___. Craig had been on trial for ___ rated murder of the Maharajah ___ or in Paris, only weeks ago. ___ ave asked for a sentence of ___ ecution, and a sen ___

HE WAS GUILTY. MOST PEOPLE *ACCEPTED* THAT.

IT WAS JUST DOWN TO *SENTENCING.*

HE'D MESSED UP THE PARIS *PEACE TALKS* SOMETHING FIERCE. HERE IT WAS LATE FEBRUARY AND THEY WEREN'T *DONE.*

WORD WAS, *THO* WOULDN'T SIGN UNLESS THE AGENT GOT THE DEATH PENALTY, AND *THIEU* WOULDN'T SIGN UNLESS THO DID.

AND WE JUST WANTED *OUT.* OUT OF VIETNAM AND DON'T LOOK *BACK.*

THE PROTESTERS WE SAW ON THE *NEWS* EVERY NIGHT --

THE *ANTIWAR* GUYS WERE THERE. THE GUYS WHO WANTED THE MASKS *SLAPPED DOWN* WERE THERE.

NO ONE ABOVE THE LAW

Bring Our Boys Home

GUILTY

END THE WAR

THE GUYS WHO *BELIEVED* IN THE AGENT WHEN HE SAID HE WAS INNOCENT -- THEY'D *GIVEN UP.*

IT WAS FINE WITH *ME.* GO AHEAD AND *KILL* HIM, IF THAT'S WHAT IT TOOK.

BUT THEN, THEY'D NEVER HAVE LET ME *SERVE* ON THAT JURY.

AND I HAD *OTHER* THINGS TO THINK ABOUT, ANYWAY.

DELI

ROYAL?

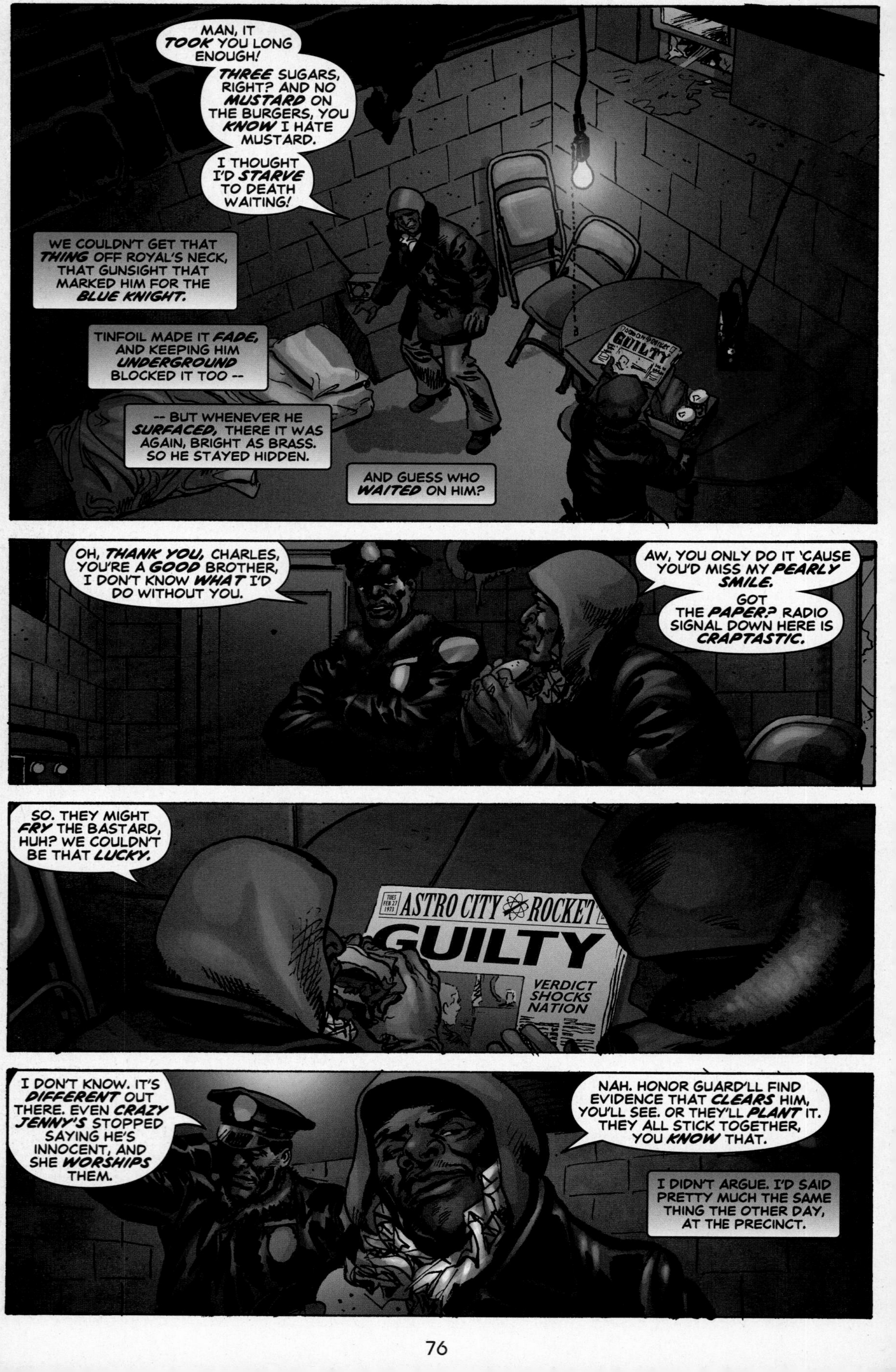
MAN, IT *TOOK* YOU LONG ENOUGH!
THREE SUGARS, RIGHT? AND NO *MUSTARD* ON THE BURGERS, YOU *KNOW* I HATE MUSTARD.
I THOUGHT I'D *STARVE* TO DEATH WAITING!
WE COULDN'T GET THAT *THING* OFF ROYAL'S NECK, THAT GUNSIGHT THAT MARKED HIM FOR THE *BLUE KNIGHT.*
TINFOIL MADE IT *FADE,* AND KEEPING HIM *UNDERGROUND* BLOCKED IT TOO --
-- BUT WHENEVER HE *SURFACED,* THERE IT WAS AGAIN, BRIGHT AS BRASS. SO HE STAYED HIDDEN.
AND GUESS WHO *WAITED* ON HIM?
OH, *THANK YOU,* CHARLES, YOU'RE A *GOOD* BROTHER, I DON'T KNOW *WHAT* I'D DO WITHOUT YOU.
AW, YOU ONLY DO IT 'CAUSE YOU'D MISS MY *PEARLY SMILE.*
GOT THE *PAPER?* RADIO SIGNAL DOWN HERE IS *CRAPTASTIC.*
SO. THEY MIGHT *FRY* THE BASTARD, HUH? WE COULDN'T BE THAT *LUCKY.*
ASTRO CITY ROCKET
GUILTY
VERDICT SHOCKS NATION
I DON'T KNOW. IT'S *DIFFERENT* OUT THERE. EVEN *CRAZY JENNY'S* STOPPED SAYING HE'S INNOCENT, AND SHE *WORSHIPS* THEM.
NAH. HONOR GUARD'LL FIND EVIDENCE THAT *CLEARS* HIM, YOU'LL SEE. OR THEY'LL *PLANT* IT. THEY ALL STICK TOGETHER, YOU *KNOW* THAT.
I DIDN'T ARGUE. I'D SAID PRETTY MUCH THE SAME THING THE OTHER DAY, AT THE PRECINCT.

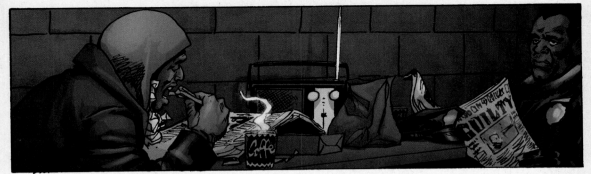

WELL, I SHOULD --

YOU NEVER *TOLD* HER.

WHAT?

DARNICE ASKED ME HOW COME I DON'T LIKE THE *SILVER AGENT.* YOU HAVEN'T TOLD HER ABOUT IT.

ROYAL, DON'T *START* WITH --

NOT *STARTIN'* NOTHING, I'M JUST SAYING...

YOU THINK I DON'T *KNOW* WHAT YOU'RE SAYING?

CHARLES --

YOU THINK I'M SOME DAMN FOOL?

YOU THINK DARNICE IS *NO GOOD,* AND I'M A *FOOL* FOR MARRYING HER WHEN SHE DOESN'T MEET YOUR *OH-SO-LOFTY* STANDARDS, WHEN *YOU'LL* JUMP ANYTHING IN *NYLONS!*

YOU -- YOU --

YOU JUST DON'T WANT ME *GETTING OUT!* BUILDING SOMETHING, BUILDING A *LIFE!* YOU DON'T WANT TO LOSE YOUR *PROTECTION!*

YOU'RE SCARED I WON'T BE THERE TO BRING YOU *BURGERS,* CLEAN UP YOUR MESSES -- HIDE YOU FROM *PSYCHO KILLERS!*

YEAH?

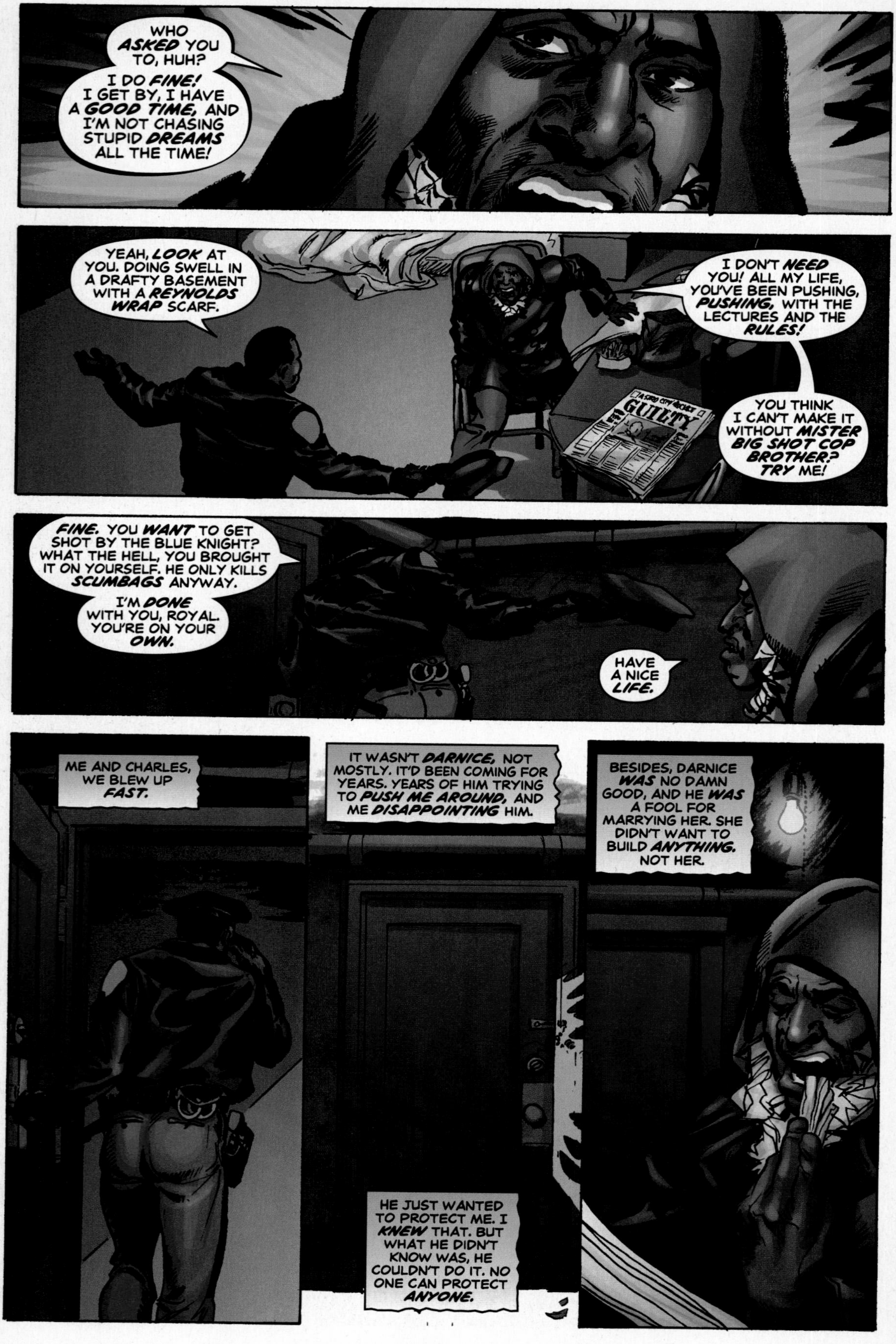

WHO ASKED YOU TO, HUH?
I DO FINE! I GET BY, I HAVE A GOOD TIME, AND I'M NOT CHASING STUPID DREAMS ALL THE TIME!
YEAH, LOOK AT YOU. DOING SWELL IN A DRAFTY BASEMENT WITH A REYNOLDS WRAP SCARF.
I DON'T NEED YOU! ALL MY LIFE, YOU'VE BEEN PUSHING, PUSHING, WITH THE LECTURES AND THE RULES!
YOU THINK I CAN'T MAKE IT WITHOUT MISTER BIG SHOT COP BROTHER? TRY ME!
GUILTY
FINE. YOU WANT TO GET SHOT BY THE BLUE KNIGHT? WHAT THE HELL, YOU BROUGHT IT ON YOURSELF. HE ONLY KILLS SCUMBAGS ANYWAY.
I'M DONE WITH YOU, ROYAL. YOU'RE ON YOUR OWN.
HAVE A NICE LIFE.
ME AND CHARLES, WE BLEW UP FAST.
IT WASN'T DARNICE, NOT MOSTLY. IT'D BEEN COMING FOR YEARS. YEARS OF HIM TRYING TO PUSH ME AROUND, AND ME DISAPPOINTING HIM.
BESIDES, DARNICE WAS NO DAMN GOOD, AND HE WAS A FOOL FOR MARRYING HER. SHE DIDN'T WANT TO BUILD ANYTHING. NOT HER.
HE JUST WANTED TO PROTECT ME. I KNEW THAT. BUT WHAT HE DIDN'T KNOW WAS, HE COULDN'T DO IT. NO ONE CAN PROTECT ANYONE.

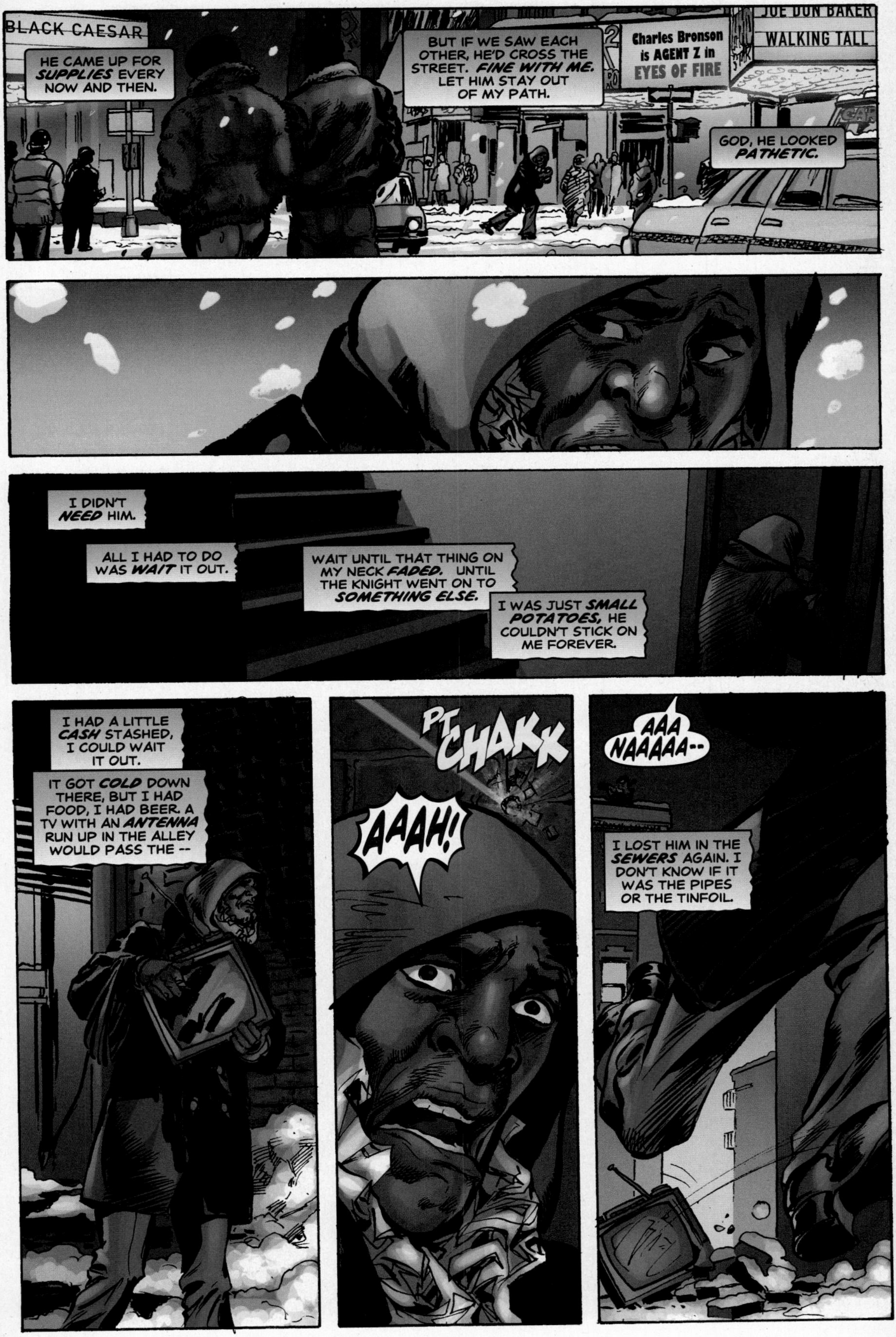
BLACK CAESAR
HE CAME UP FOR SUPPLIES EVERY NOW AND THEN.
BUT IF WE SAW EACH OTHER, HE'D CROSS THE STREET. FINE WITH ME. LET HIM STAY OUT OF MY PATH.
Charles Bronson is AGENT Z in EYES OF FIRE
JOE DON BAKER
WALKING TALL
GOD, HE LOOKED PATHETIC.
I DIDN'T NEED HIM.
ALL I HAD TO DO WAS WAIT IT OUT.
WAIT UNTIL THAT THING ON MY NECK FADED. UNTIL THE KNIGHT WENT ON TO SOMETHING ELSE.
I WAS JUST SMALL POTATOES, HE COULDN'T STICK ON ME FOREVER.
I HAD A LITTLE CASH STASHED, I COULD WAIT IT OUT.
IT GOT COLD DOWN THERE, BUT I HAD FOOD, I HAD BEER. A TV WITH AN ANTENNA RUN UP IN THE ALLEY WOULD PASS THE --
PT CHAKK
AAAH!
AAA NAAAAA--
I LOST HIM IN THE SEWERS AGAIN. I DON'T KNOW IF IT WAS THE PIPES OR THE TINFOIL.

I WENT BACK FOR THE TV AT DAWN. IT STILL *WORKED*, MOSTLY.

AND IT WAS A *SHOW*, ALL RIGHT.

NIXON MADE AN *ADDRESS*, TOLD THE COUNTRY THE AGENT MESS WAS *"A CRUCIAL MOMENT, A MOMENT FOR DELIBERATION, FOR JUSTICE."*

HE HAD AIDES PLEADING *GUILTY*, BEING CONVICTED LEFT AND RIGHT OVER WATERGATE. WHO'D BELIEVE A *WORD* HE SAID?

BUT THEY *WANTED* TO.

THEY WANTED *SOMETHING*. JACK-IN-THE-BOX CAUGHT *RICHIE FORGIONE*. DRUG TRAFFICKING. LOOKED LIKE THE FORGIONES WERE *DONE*.

BUT THE WITNESSES *VANISHED*, AND RICHIE WALKED.

HE ALWAYS KNEW HOW TO HAVE A *GOOD TIME*, BUT YOU DIDN'T WANT TO SIT TOO *CLOSE* -- BOY HAD A TEMPER.

THE *U.N.* AND *E.A.G.L.E.* HAD TOLD HONOR GUARD TO STAY OUT OF KHANISTAN --

-- BUT WORD WAS THEY WERE THERE *ANYWAY*, STILL TRYING TO CLEAR THE AGENT. IT LOOKED LIKE IT MIGHT BLOW THE PEACE TALKS *AGAIN*.

ONE *MORE* THING FOR THE PUBLIC TO FEEL GOOD ABOUT.

AND THE *FIRST FAMILY*, UP ON THE HILL --

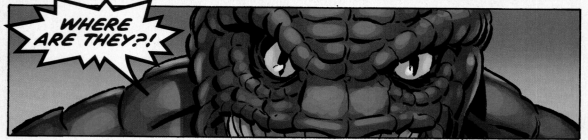

WHERE ARE THEY?!

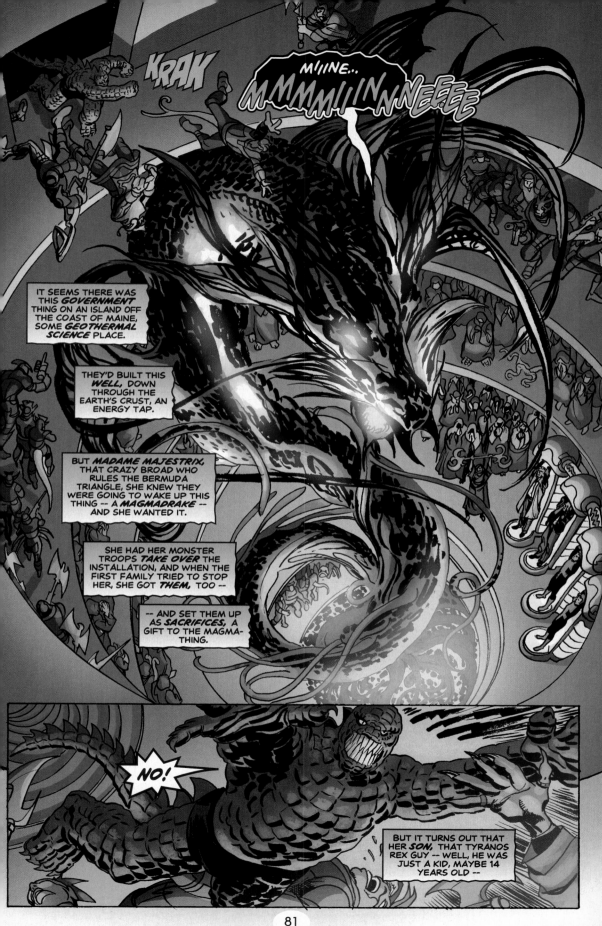

KRAK

MIINE...
MMMMIINNEEEE

IT SEEMS THERE WAS THIS **GOVERNMENT** THING ON AN ISLAND OFF THE COAST OF MAINE, SOME **GEOTHERMAL SCIENCE** PLACE.

THEY'D BUILT THIS **WELL,** DOWN THROUGH THE EARTH'S CRUST, AN ENERGY TAP.

BUT **MADAME MAJESTRIX,** THAT CRAZY BROAD WHO RULES THE BERMUDA TRIANGLE, SHE KNEW THEY WERE GOING TO WAKE UP THIS THING -- A **MAGMADRAKE** -- AND SHE WANTED IT.

SHE HAD HER MONSTER TROOPS **TAKE OVER** THE INSTALLATION, AND WHEN THE FIRST FAMILY TRIED TO STOP HER, SHE GOT **THEM,** TOO --

-- AND SET THEM UP AS **SACRIFICES,** A GIFT TO THE MAGMA-THING.

NO!

BUT IT TURNS OUT THAT HER **SON,** THAT TYRANOS REX GUY -- WELL, HE WAS JUST A KID, MAYBE 14 YEARS OLD --

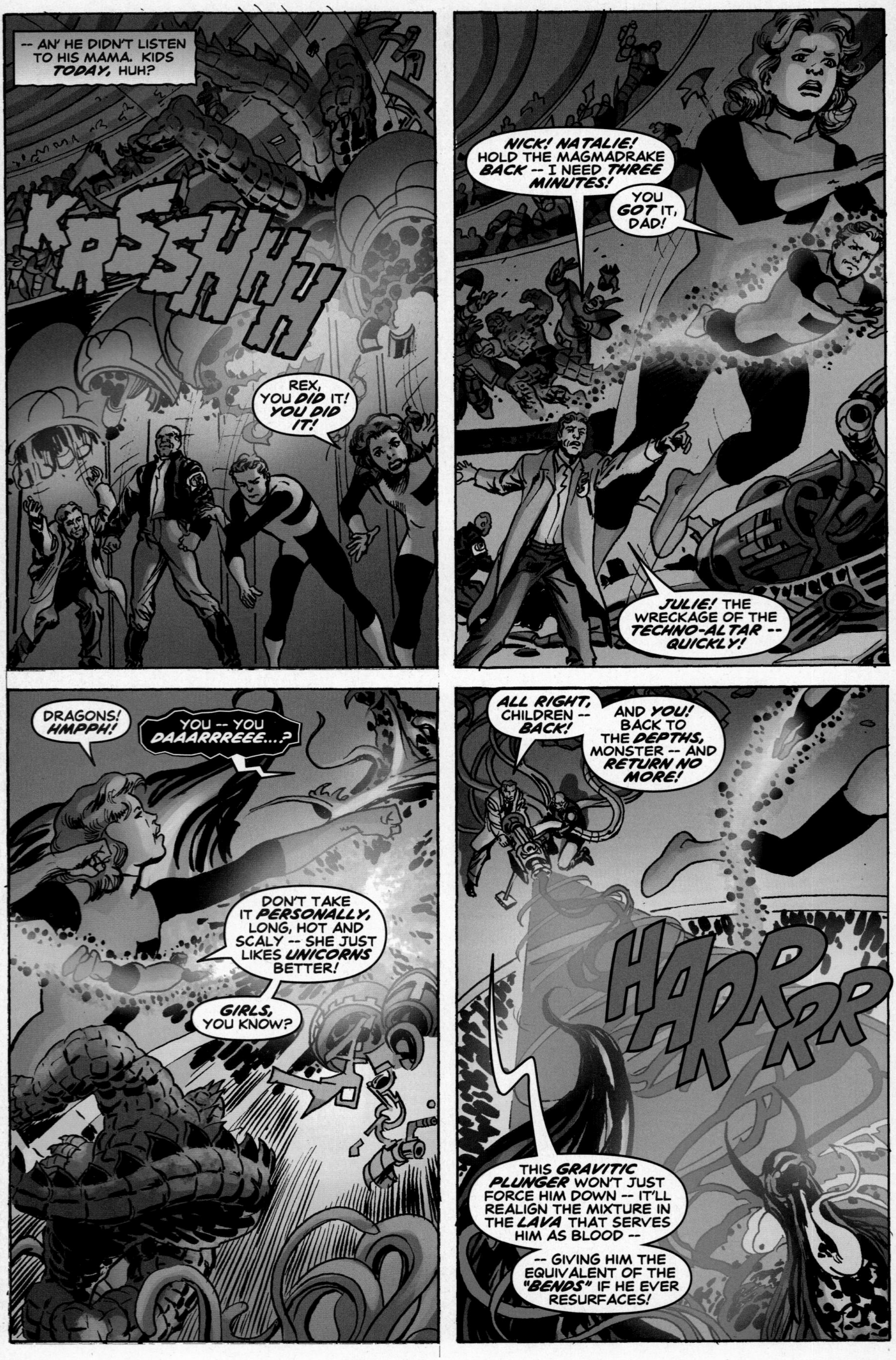
-- AN' HE DIDN'T LISTEN TO HIS MAMA. KIDS TODAY, HUH?
KRSHHH
REX, YOU DID IT! YOU DID IT!
NICK! NATALIE! HOLD THE MAGMADRAKE BACK -- I NEED THREE MINUTES!
YOU GOT IT, DAD!
JULIE! THE WRECKAGE OF THE TECHNO-ALTAR -- QUICKLY!
DRAGONS! HMPPH!
YOU -- YOU DAAARRREEE...?
DON'T TAKE IT PERSONALLY, LONG, HOT AND SCALY -- SHE JUST LIKES UNICORNS BETTER!
GIRLS, YOU KNOW?
ALL RIGHT, CHILDREN -- BACK!
AND YOU! BACK TO THE DEPTHS, MONSTER -- AND RETURN NO MORE!
HARRRRR
THIS GRAVITIC PLUNGER WON'T JUST FORCE HIM DOWN -- IT'LL REALIGN THE MIXTURE IN THE LAVA THAT SERVES HIM AS BLOOD --
-- GIVING HIM THE EQUIVALENT OF THE "BENDS" IF HE EVER RESURFACES!

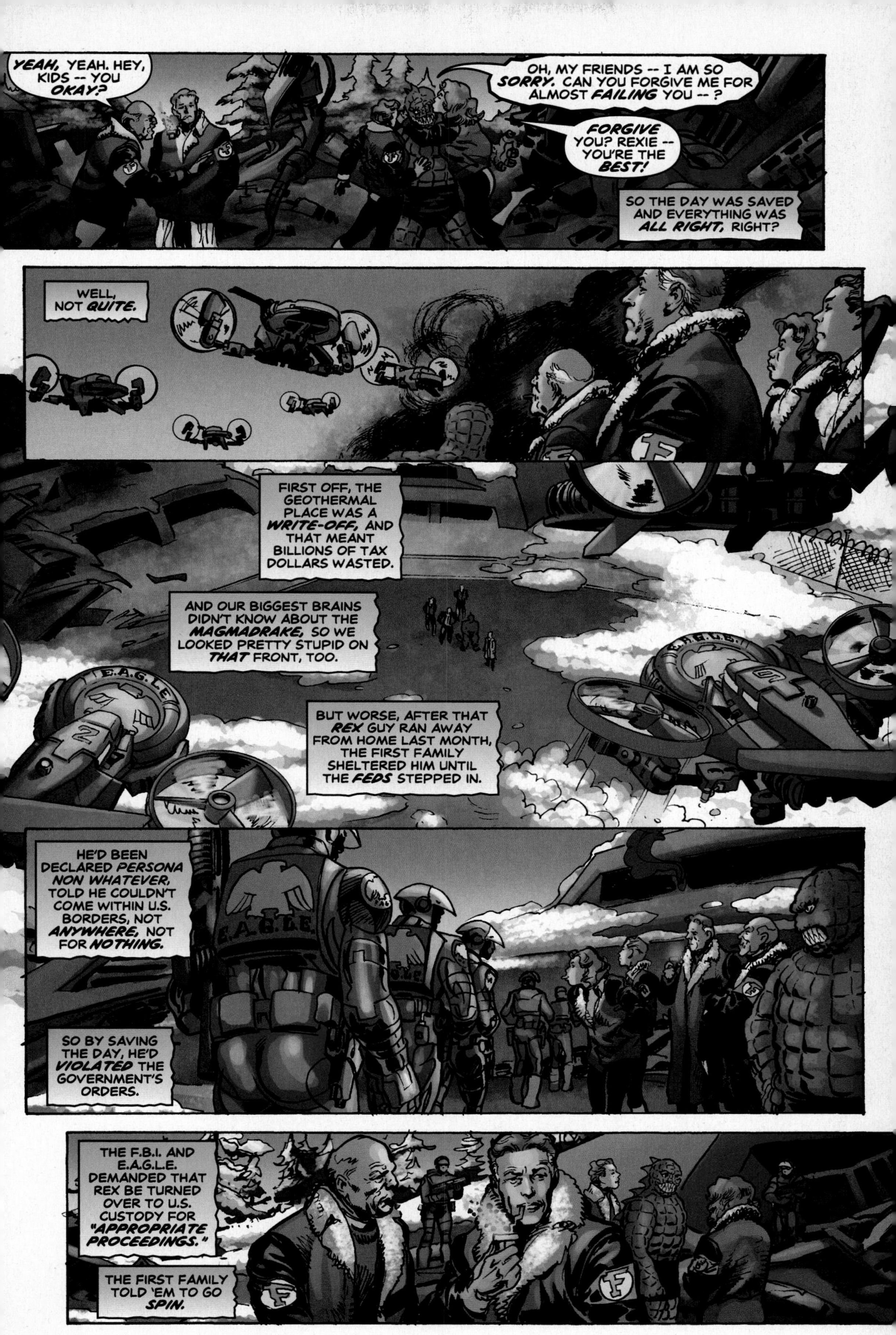
YEAH, YEAH. HEY, KIDS -- YOU OKAY?
OH, MY FRIENDS -- I AM SO SORRY. CAN YOU FORGIVE ME FOR ALMOST FAILING YOU -- ?
FORGIVE YOU? REXIE -- YOU'RE THE BEST!
SO THE DAY WAS SAVED AND EVERYTHING WAS ALL RIGHT, RIGHT?
WELL, NOT QUITE.
FIRST OFF, THE GEOTHERMAL PLACE WAS A WRITE-OFF, AND THAT MEANT BILLIONS OF TAX DOLLARS WASTED.
AND OUR BIGGEST BRAINS DIDN'T KNOW ABOUT THE MAGMADRAKE, SO WE LOOKED PRETTY STUPID ON THAT FRONT, TOO.
BUT WORSE, AFTER THAT REX GUY RAN AWAY FROM HOME LAST MONTH, THE FIRST FAMILY SHELTERED HIM UNTIL THE FEDS STEPPED IN.
HE'D BEEN DECLARED PERSONA NON WHATEVER, TOLD HE COULDN'T COME WITHIN U.S. BORDERS, NOT ANYWHERE, NOT FOR NOTHING.
SO BY SAVING THE DAY, HE'D VIOLATED THE GOVERNMENT'S ORDERS.
THE F.B.I. AND E.A.G.L.E. DEMANDED THAT REX BE TURNED OVER TO U.S. CUSTODY FOR "APPROPRIATE PROCEEDINGS."
THE FIRST FAMILY TOLD 'EM TO GO SPIN.

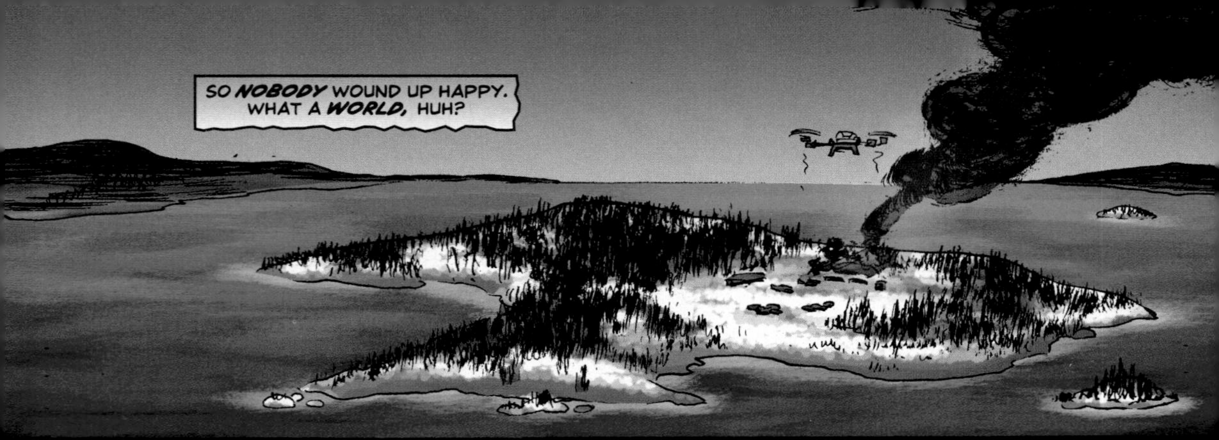
SO ***NOBODY*** WOUND UP HAPPY. WHAT A ***WORLD,*** HUH?

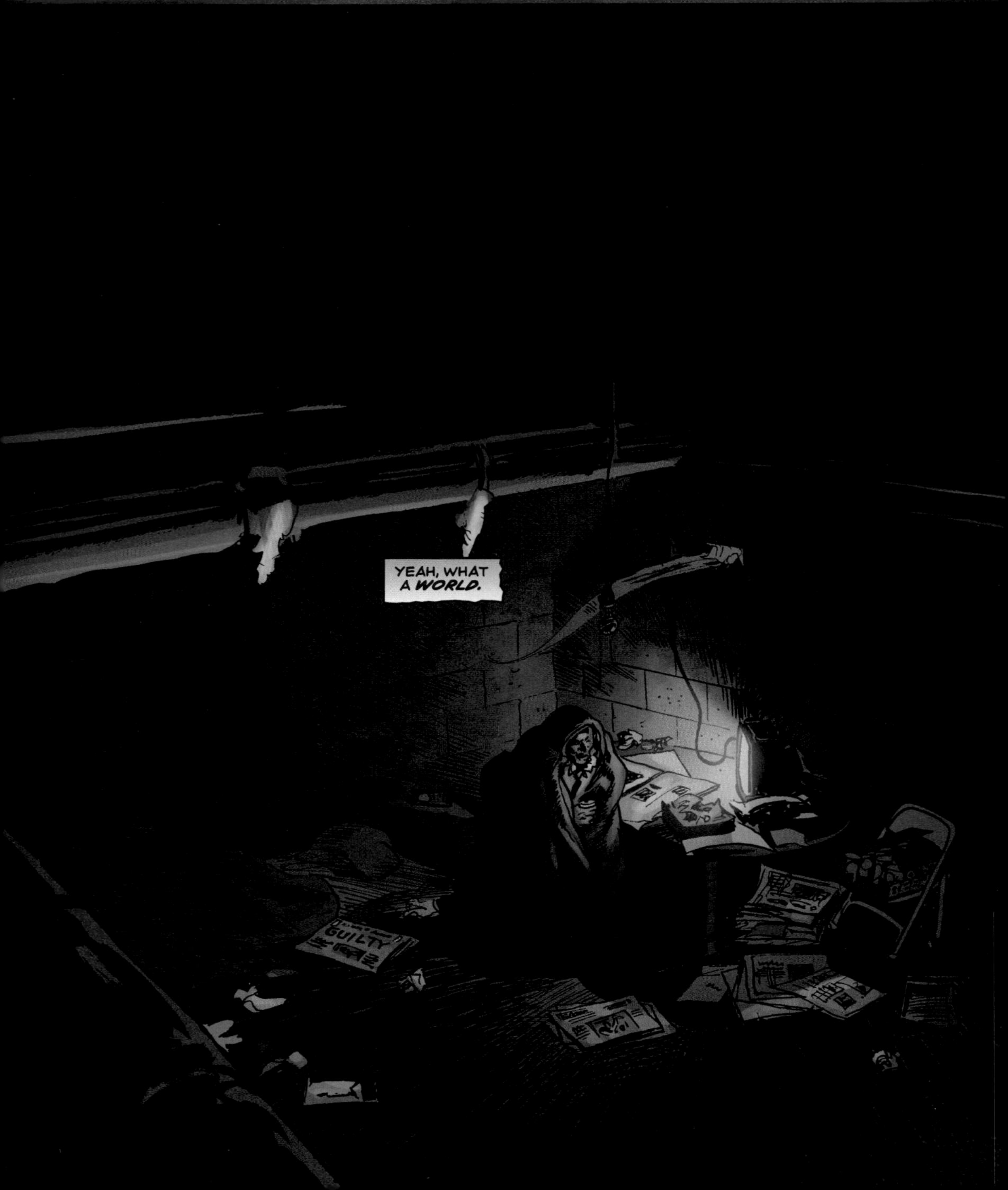
YEAH, WHAT A ***WORLD.***
GUILTY

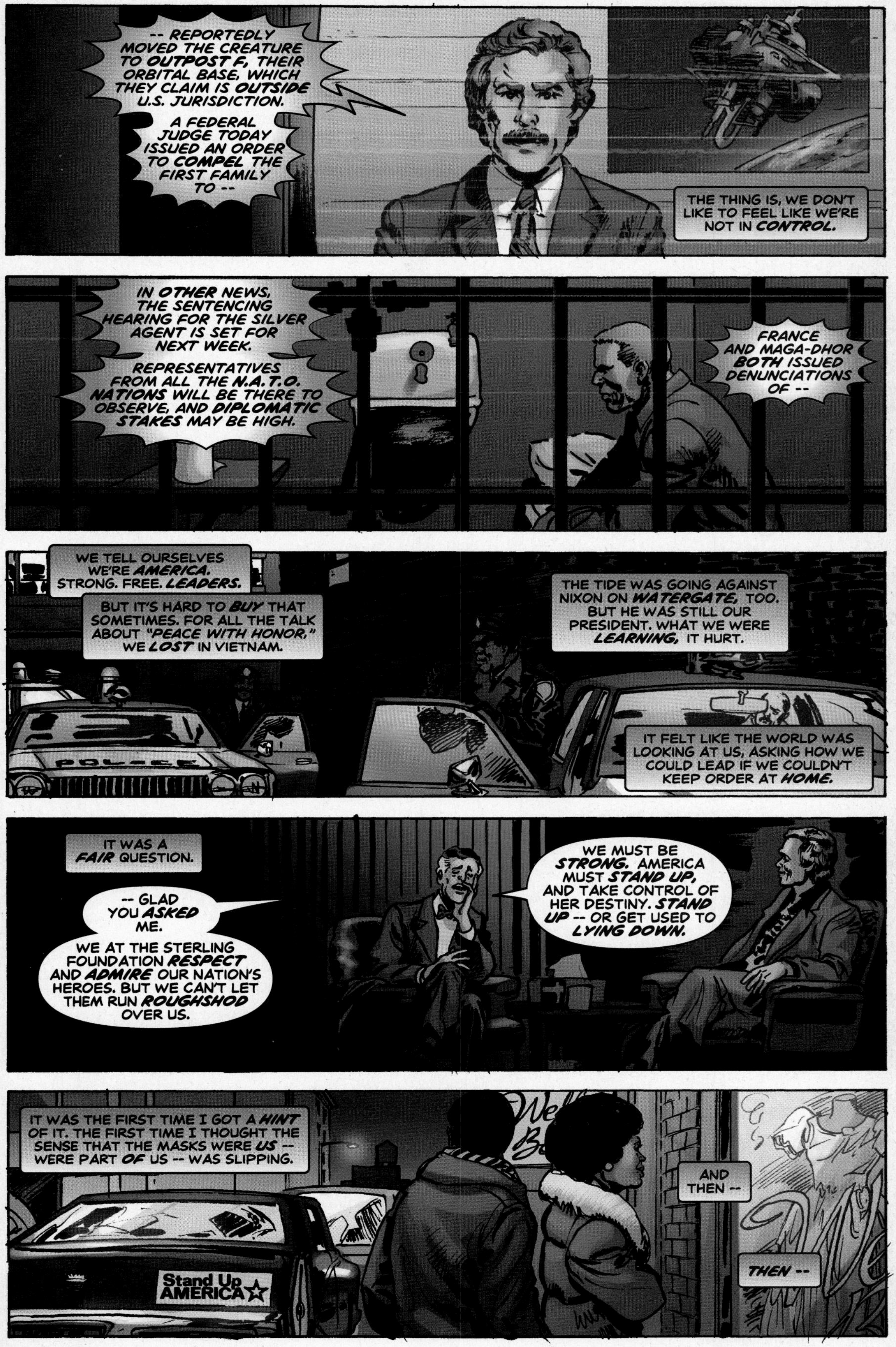
-- REPORTEDLY MOVED THE CREATURE TO OUTPOST F, THEIR ORBITAL BASE, WHICH THEY CLAIM IS OUTSIDE U.S. JURISDICTION.
A FEDERAL JUDGE TODAY ISSUED AN ORDER TO COMPEL THE FIRST FAMILY TO --
THE THING IS, WE DON'T LIKE TO FEEL LIKE WE'RE NOT IN CONTROL.
IN OTHER NEWS, THE SENTENCING HEARING FOR THE SILVER AGENT IS SET FOR NEXT WEEK.
REPRESENTATIVES FROM ALL THE N.A.T.O. NATIONS WILL BE THERE TO OBSERVE, AND DIPLOMATIC STAKES MAY BE HIGH.
FRANCE AND MAGA-DHOR BOTH ISSUED DENUNCIATIONS OF --
WE TELL OURSELVES WE'RE AMERICA. STRONG. FREE. LEADERS.
BUT IT'S HARD TO BUY THAT SOMETIMES. FOR ALL THE TALK ABOUT "PEACE WITH HONOR," WE LOST IN VIETNAM.
THE TIDE WAS GOING AGAINST NIXON ON WATERGATE, TOO. BUT HE WAS STILL OUR PRESIDENT. WHAT WE WERE LEARNING, IT HURT.
IT FELT LIKE THE WORLD WAS LOOKING AT US, ASKING HOW WE COULD LEAD IF WE COULDN'T KEEP ORDER AT HOME.
IT WAS A FAIR QUESTION.
-- GLAD YOU ASKED ME.
WE AT THE STERLING FOUNDATION RESPECT AND ADMIRE OUR NATION'S HEROES. BUT WE CAN'T LET THEM RUN ROUGHSHOD OVER US.
WE MUST BE STRONG. AMERICA MUST STAND UP, AND TAKE CONTROL OF HER DESTINY. STAND UP -- OR GET USED TO LYING DOWN.
IT WAS THE FIRST TIME I GOT A HINT OF IT. THE FIRST TIME I THOUGHT THE SENSE THAT THE MASKS WERE US -- WERE PART OF US -- WAS SLIPPING.
Stand Up AMERICA
AND THEN --
THEN --

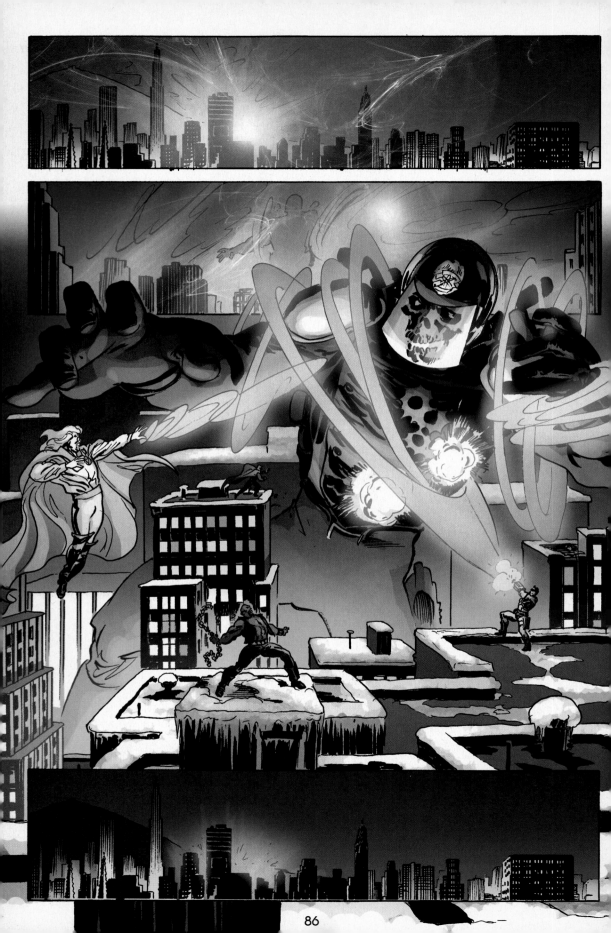

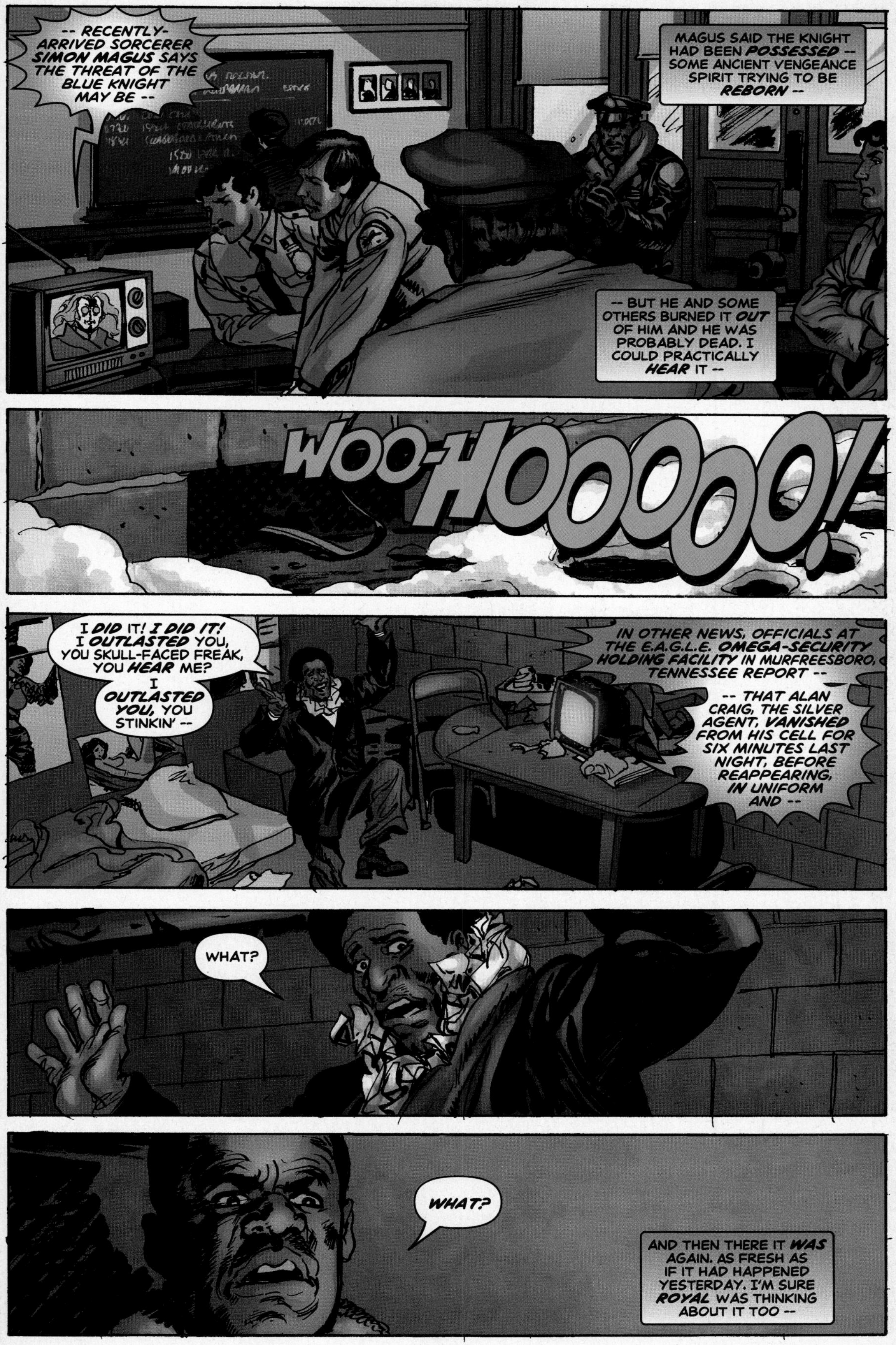
-- RECENTLY-ARRIVED SORCERER SIMON MAGUS SAYS THE THREAT OF THE BLUE KNIGHT MAY BE --
MAGUS SAID THE KNIGHT HAD BEEN POSSESSED -- SOME ANCIENT VENGEANCE SPIRIT TRYING TO BE REBORN --
-- BUT HE AND SOME OTHERS BURNED IT OUT OF HIM AND HE WAS PROBABLY DEAD. I COULD PRACTICALLY HEAR IT --
WOO-HOOOOOO!
I DID IT! I DID IT! I OUTLASTED YOU, YOU SKULL-FACED FREAK, YOU HEAR ME?
I OUTLASTED YOU, YOU STINKIN' --
IN OTHER NEWS, OFFICIALS AT THE E.A.G.L.E. OMEGA-SECURITY HOLDING FACILITY IN MURFREESBORO, TENNESSEE REPORT --
-- THAT ALAN CRAIG, THE SILVER AGENT, VANISHED FROM HIS CELL FOR SIX MINUTES LAST NIGHT, BEFORE REAPPEARING, IN UNIFORM AND --
WHAT?
WHAT?
AND THEN THERE IT WAS AGAIN. AS FRESH AS IF IT HAD HAPPENED YESTERDAY. I'M SURE ROYAL WAS THINKING ABOUT IT TOO --

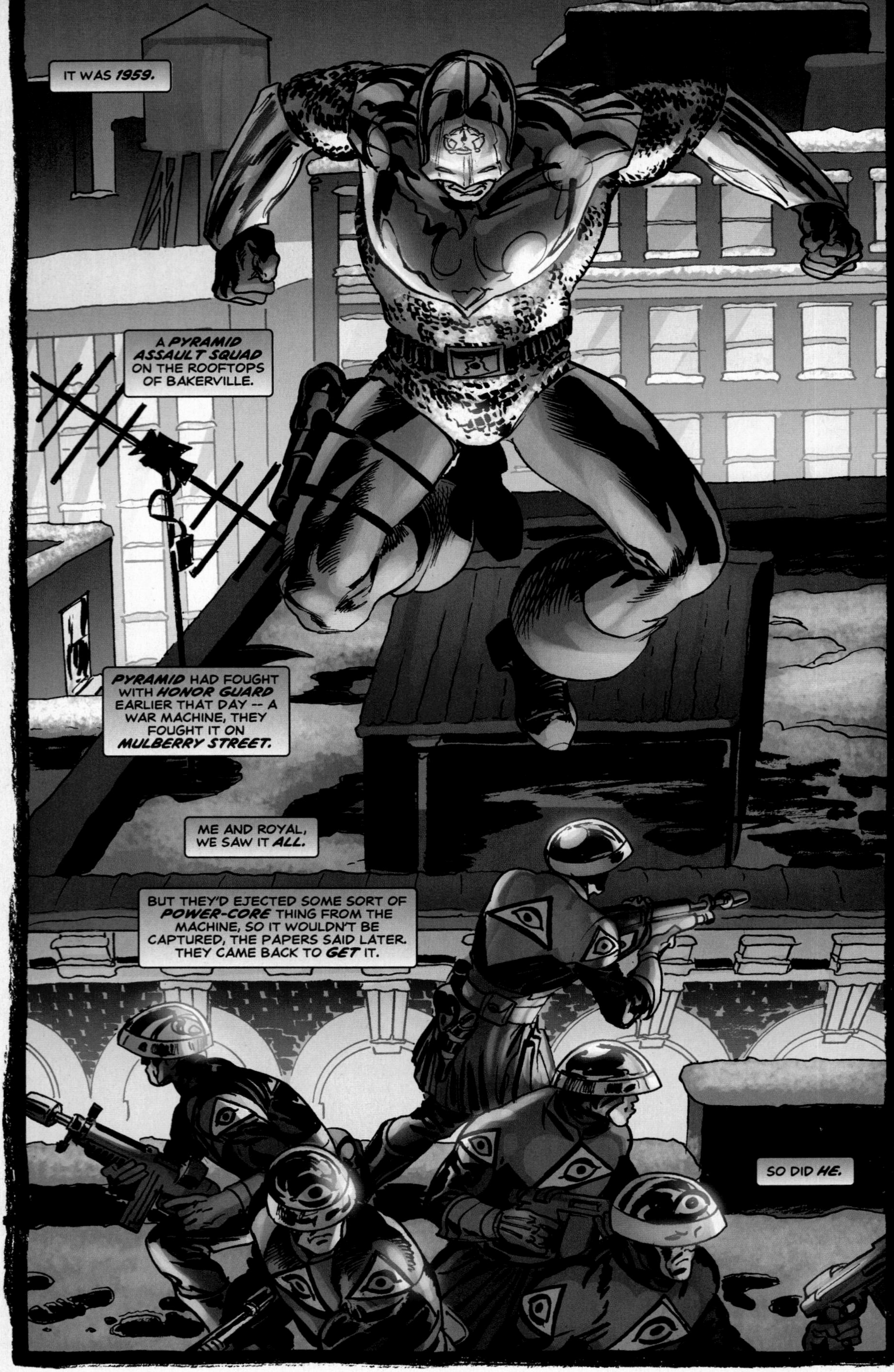
IT WAS 1959.
A PYRAMID ASSAULT SQUAD ON THE ROOFTOPS OF BAKERVILLE.
PYRAMID HAD FOUGHT WITH HONOR GUARD EARLIER THAT DAY -- A WAR MACHINE, THEY FOUGHT IT ON MULBERRY STREET.
ME AND ROYAL, WE SAW IT ALL.
BUT THEY'D EJECTED SOME SORT OF POWER-CORE THING FROM THE MACHINE, SO IT WOULDN'T BE CAPTURED, THE PAPERS SAID LATER. THEY CAME BACK TO GET IT.
SO DID HE.

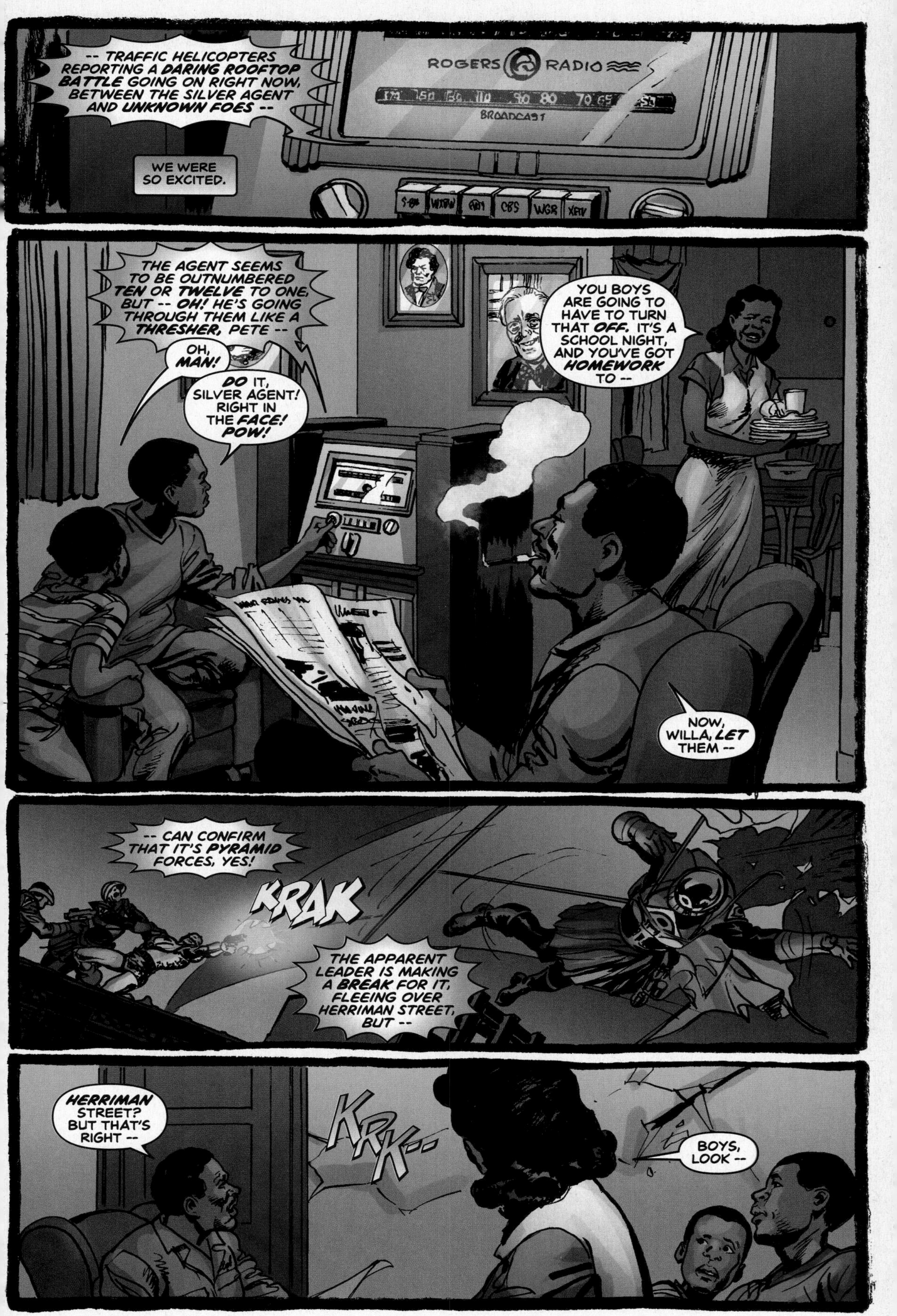
-- TRAFFIC HELICOPTERS REPORTING A DARING ROOFTOP BATTLE GOING ON RIGHT NOW, BETWEEN THE SILVER AGENT AND UNKNOWN FOES --
ROGERS RADIO
BROADCAST
WE WERE SO EXCITED.
THE AGENT SEEMS TO BE OUTNUMBERED TEN OR TWELVE TO ONE, BUT -- OH! HE'S GOING THROUGH THEM LIKE A THRESHER, PETE --
OH, MAN!
DO IT, SILVER AGENT! RIGHT IN THE FACE! POW!
YOU BOYS ARE GOING TO HAVE TO TURN THAT OFF. IT'S A SCHOOL NIGHT, AND YOU'VE GOT HOMEWORK TO --
NOW, WILLA, LET THEM --
-- CAN CONFIRM THAT IT'S PYRAMID FORCES, YES!
KRAK
THE APPARENT LEADER IS MAKING A BREAK FOR IT, FLEEING OVER HERRIMAN STREET, BUT --
HERRIMAN STREET? BUT THAT'S RIGHT --
KRK--
BOYS, LOOK --

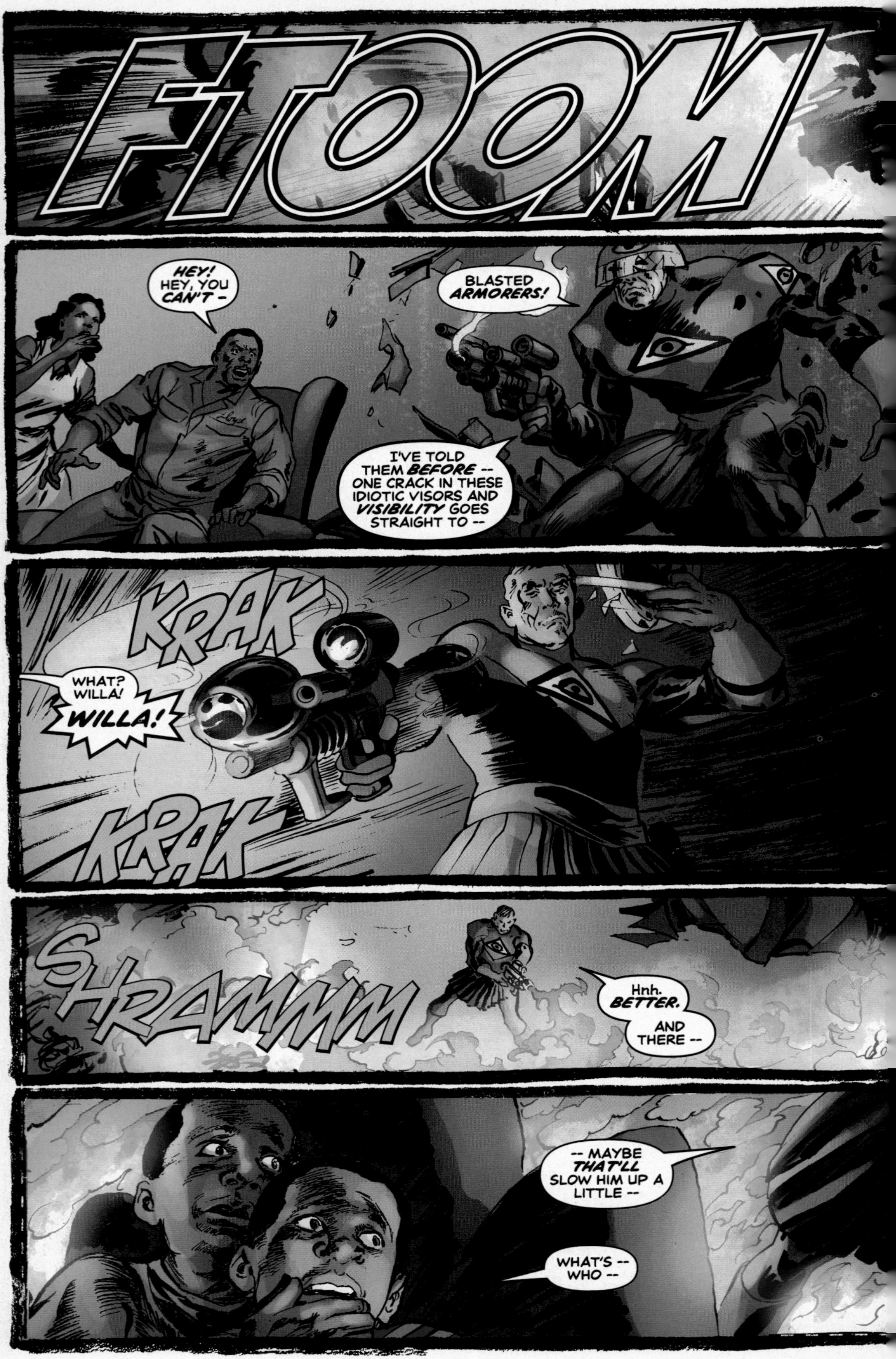
F-TOOM
HEY! HEY, YOU CAN'T --
BLASTED ARMORERS!
I'VE TOLD THEM BEFORE -- ONE CRACK IN THESE IDIOTIC VISORS AND VISIBILITY GOES STRAIGHT TO --
KRAK
WHAT? WILLA!
WILLA!
KRAK
SHRAMMMM
Hnh. BETTER.
AND THERE --
-- MAYBE THAT'LL SLOW HIM UP A LITTLE --
WHAT'S -- WHO --

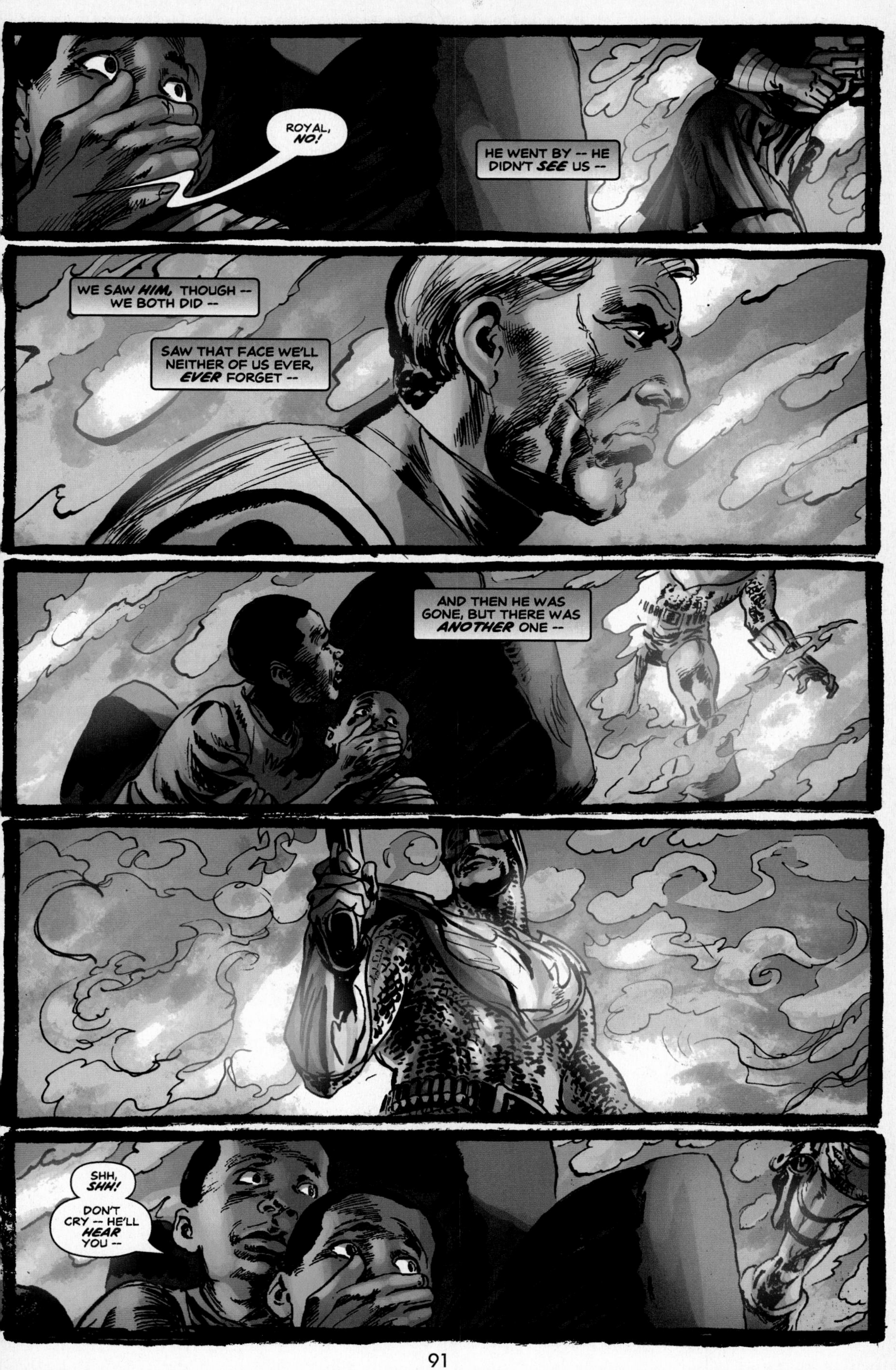
ROYAL, NO!
HE WENT BY -- HE DIDN'T SEE US --
WE SAW HIM, THOUGH -- WE BOTH DID --
SAW THAT FACE WE'LL NEITHER OF US EVER, EVER FORGET --
AND THEN HE WAS GONE, BUT THERE WAS ANOTHER ONE --
SHH, SHH!
DON'T CRY -- HE'LL HEAR YOU --

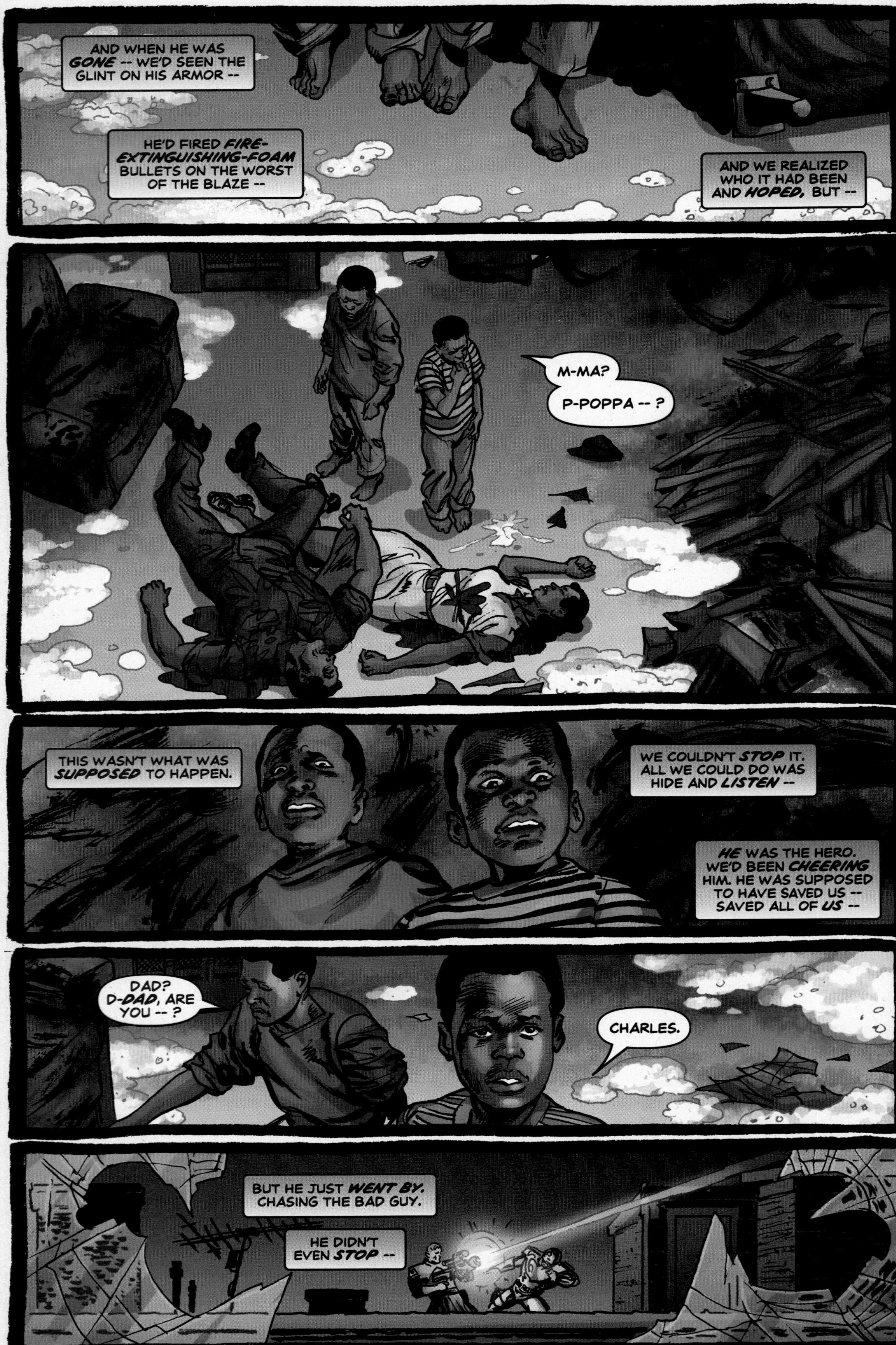
AND WHEN HE WAS GONE -- WE'D SEEN THE GLINT ON HIS ARMOR --
HE'D FIRED FIRE-EXTINGUISHING-FOAM BULLETS ON THE WORST OF THE BLAZE --
AND WE REALIZED WHO IT HAD BEEN AND HOPED, BUT --
M-MA?
P-POPPA -- ?
THIS WASN'T WHAT WAS SUPPOSED TO HAPPEN.
WE COULDN'T STOP IT. ALL WE COULD DO WAS HIDE AND LISTEN --
HE WAS THE HERO. WE'D BEEN CHEERING HIM. HE WAS SUPPOSED TO HAVE SAVED US -- SAVED ALL OF US --
DAD? D-DAD, ARE YOU -- ?
CHARLES.
BUT HE JUST WENT BY. CHASING THE BAD GUY.
HE DIDN'T EVEN STOP --

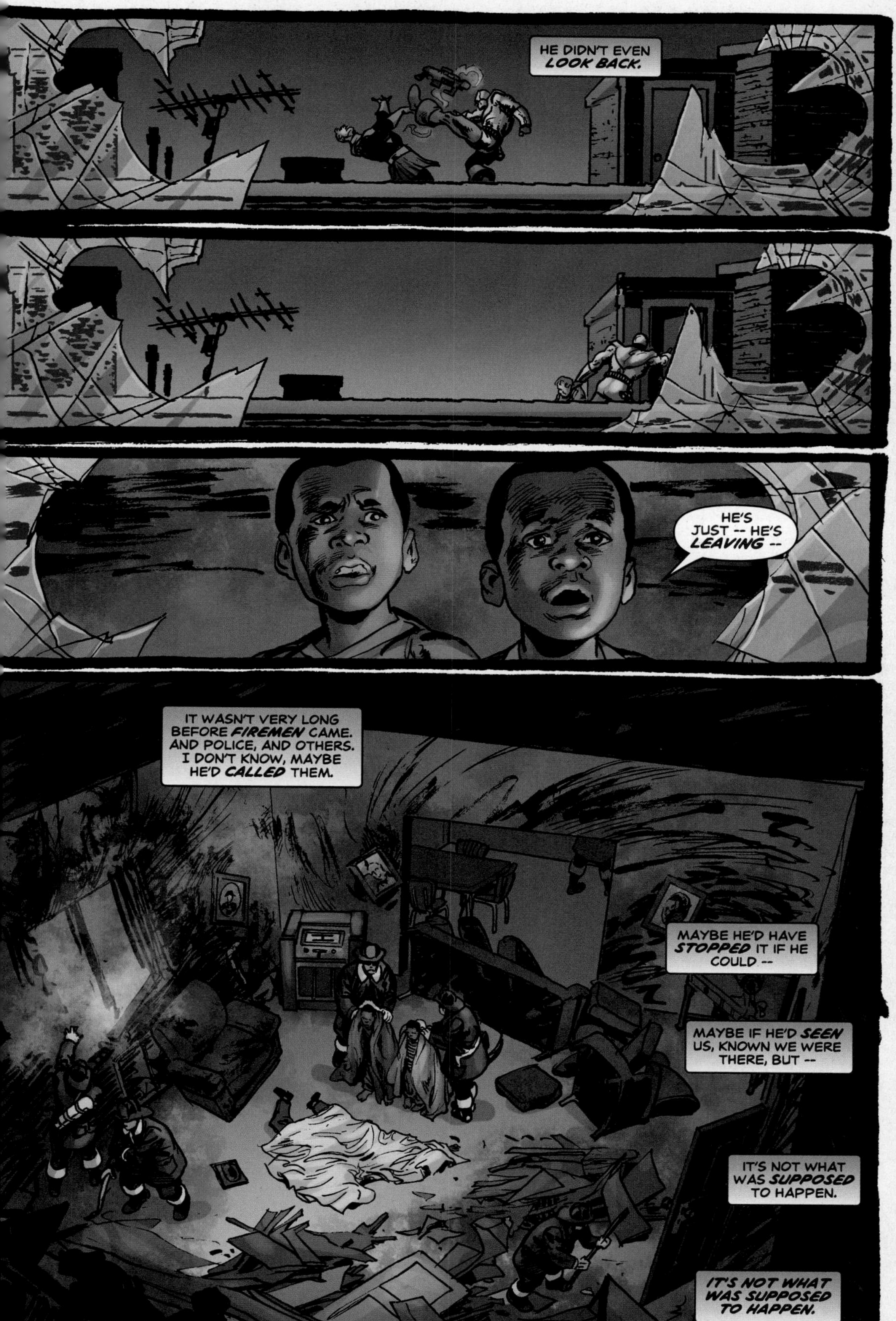
HE DIDN'T EVEN LOOK BACK.
HE'S JUST -- HE'S LEAVING --
IT WASN'T VERY LONG BEFORE FIREMEN CAME. AND POLICE, AND OTHERS. I DON'T KNOW, MAYBE HE'D CALLED THEM.
MAYBE HE'D HAVE STOPPED IT IF HE COULD --
MAYBE IF HE'D SEEN US, KNOWN WE WERE THERE, BUT --
IT'S NOT WHAT WAS SUPPOSED TO HAPPEN.
IT'S NOT WHAT WAS SUPPOSED TO HAPPEN.

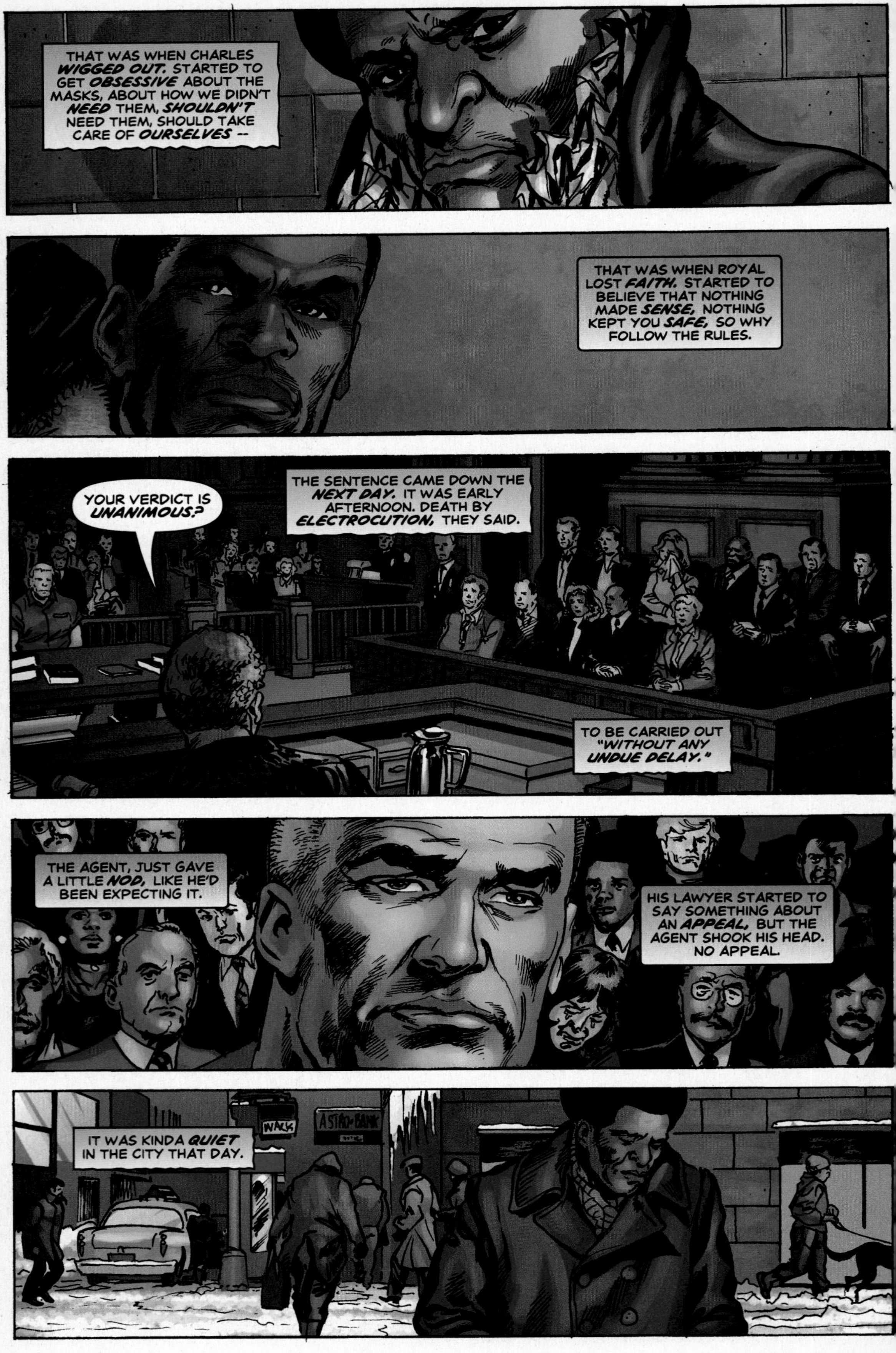
THAT WAS WHEN CHARLES WIGGED OUT. STARTED TO GET OBSESSIVE ABOUT THE MASKS, ABOUT HOW WE DIDN'T NEED THEM, SHOULDN'T NEED THEM, SHOULD TAKE CARE OF OURSELVES --
THAT WAS WHEN ROYAL LOST FAITH. STARTED TO BELIEVE THAT NOTHING MADE SENSE, NOTHING KEPT YOU SAFE, SO WHY FOLLOW THE RULES.
YOUR VERDICT IS UNANIMOUS?
THE SENTENCE CAME DOWN THE NEXT DAY. IT WAS EARLY AFTERNOON. DEATH BY ELECTROCUTION, THEY SAID.
TO BE CARRIED OUT "WITHOUT ANY UNDUE DELAY."
THE AGENT, JUST GAVE A LITTLE NOD, LIKE HE'D BEEN EXPECTING IT.
HIS LAWYER STARTED TO SAY SOMETHING ABOUT AN APPEAL, BUT THE AGENT SHOOK HIS HEAD. NO APPEAL.
IT WAS KINDA QUIET IN THE CITY THAT DAY.

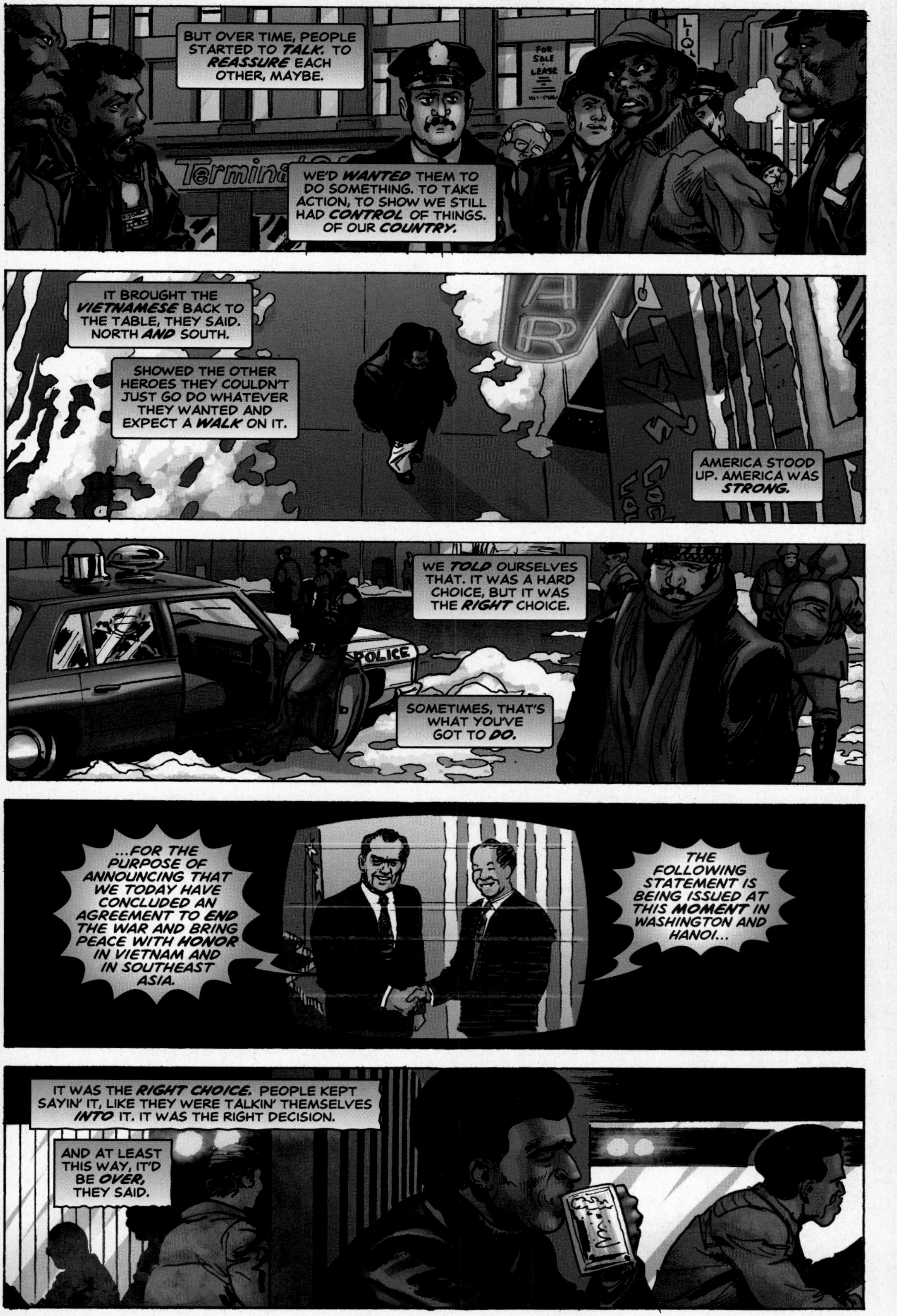
BUT OVER TIME, PEOPLE STARTED TO TALK. TO REASSURE EACH OTHER, MAYBE.
FOR SALE LEASE
WE'D WANTED THEM TO DO SOMETHING. TO TAKE ACTION, TO SHOW WE STILL HAD CONTROL OF THINGS. OF OUR COUNTRY.
IT BROUGHT THE VIETNAMESE BACK TO THE TABLE, THEY SAID. NORTH AND SOUTH.
SHOWED THE OTHER HEROES THEY COULDN'T JUST GO DO WHATEVER THEY WANTED AND EXPECT A WALK ON IT.
AMERICA STOOD UP. AMERICA WAS STRONG.
WE TOLD OURSELVES THAT. IT WAS A HARD CHOICE, BUT IT WAS THE RIGHT CHOICE.
POLICE
SOMETIMES, THAT'S WHAT YOU'VE GOT TO DO.
...FOR THE PURPOSE OF ANNOUNCING THAT WE TODAY HAVE CONCLUDED AN AGREEMENT TO END THE WAR AND BRING PEACE WITH HONOR IN VIETNAM AND IN SOUTHEAST ASIA.
THE FOLLOWING STATEMENT IS BEING ISSUED AT THIS MOMENT IN WASHINGTON AND HANOI...
IT WAS THE RIGHT CHOICE. PEOPLE KEPT SAYIN' IT, LIKE THEY WERE TALKIN' THEMSELVES INTO IT. IT WAS THE RIGHT DECISION.
AND AT LEAST THIS WAY, IT'D BE OVER, THEY SAID.

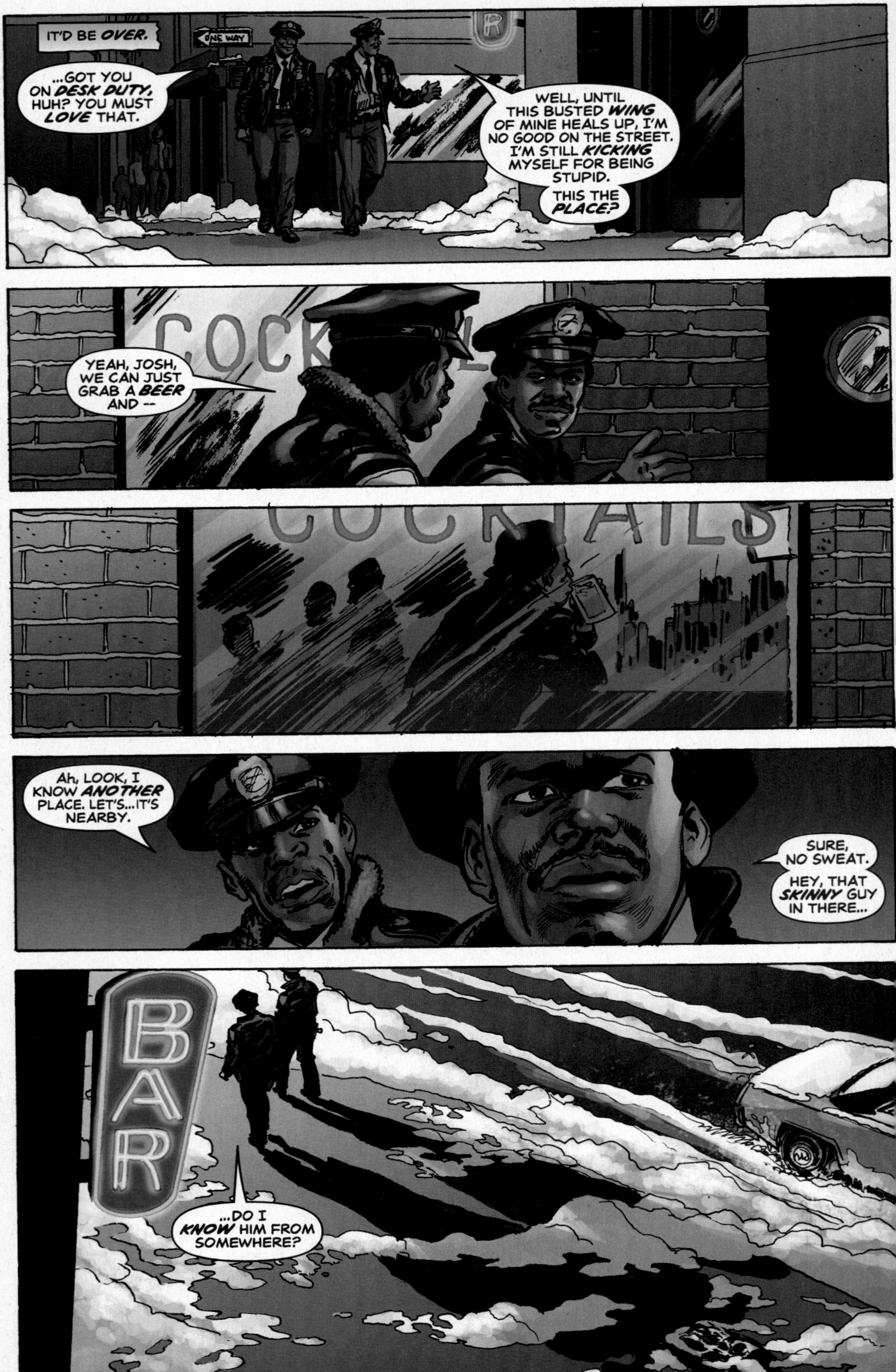
IT'D BE OVER.
ONE WAY
...GOT YOU ON DESK DUTY, HUH? YOU MUST LOVE THAT.
WELL, UNTIL THIS BUSTED WING OF MINE HEALS UP, I'M NO GOOD ON THE STREET. I'M STILL KICKING MYSELF FOR BEING STUPID.
THIS THE PLACE?
YEAH, JOSH, WE CAN JUST GRAB A BEER AND --
COCKTAILS
Ah, LOOK, I KNOW ANOTHER PLACE. LET'S...IT'S NEARBY.
SURE, NO SWEAT.
HEY, THAT SKINNY GUY IN THERE...
BAR
...DO I KNOW HIM FROM SOMEWHERE?

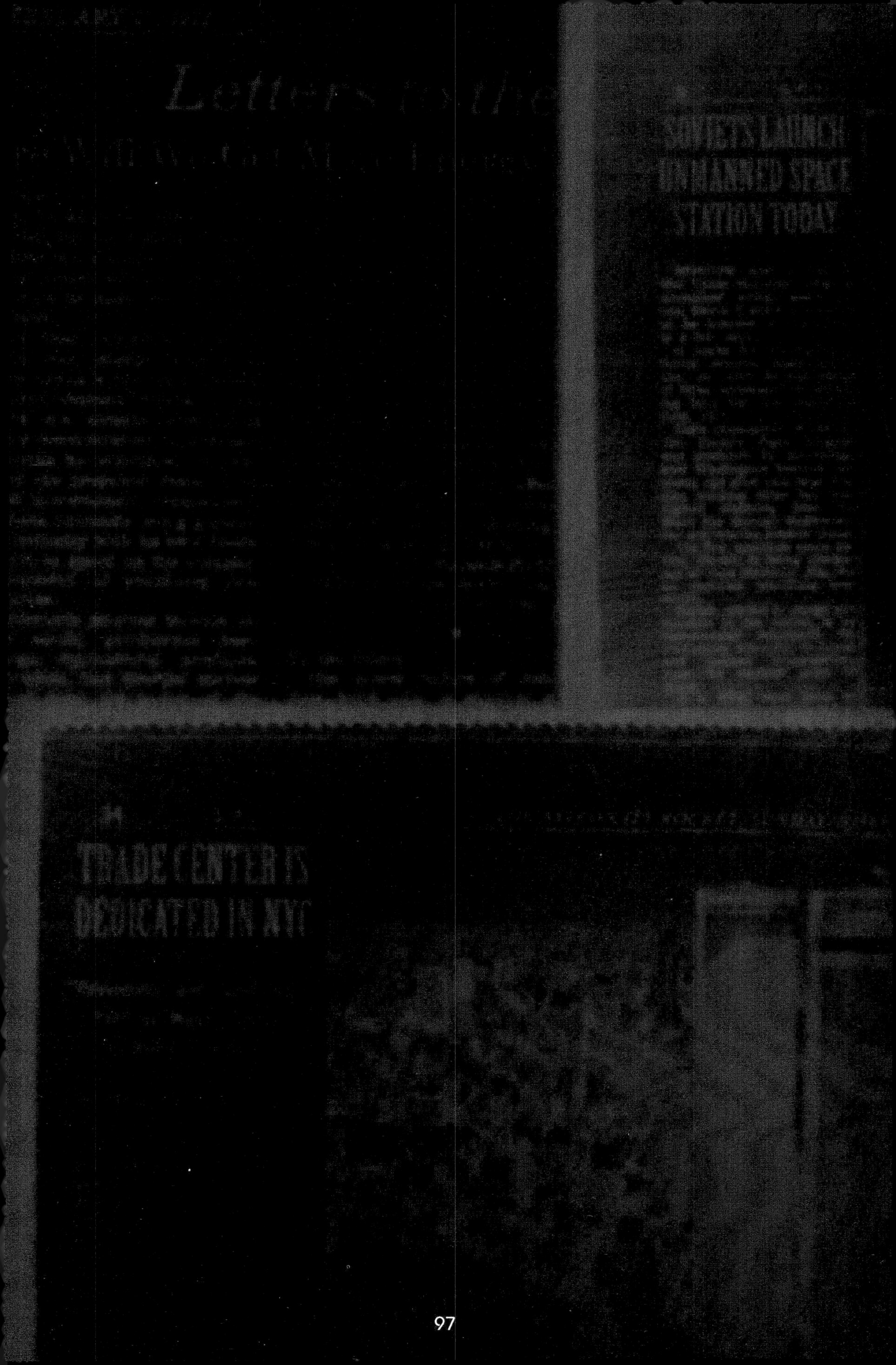
Letters to the
SOVIETS LAUNCH UNMANNED SPACE STATION TODAY
TRADE CENTER IS DEDICATED IN NYC

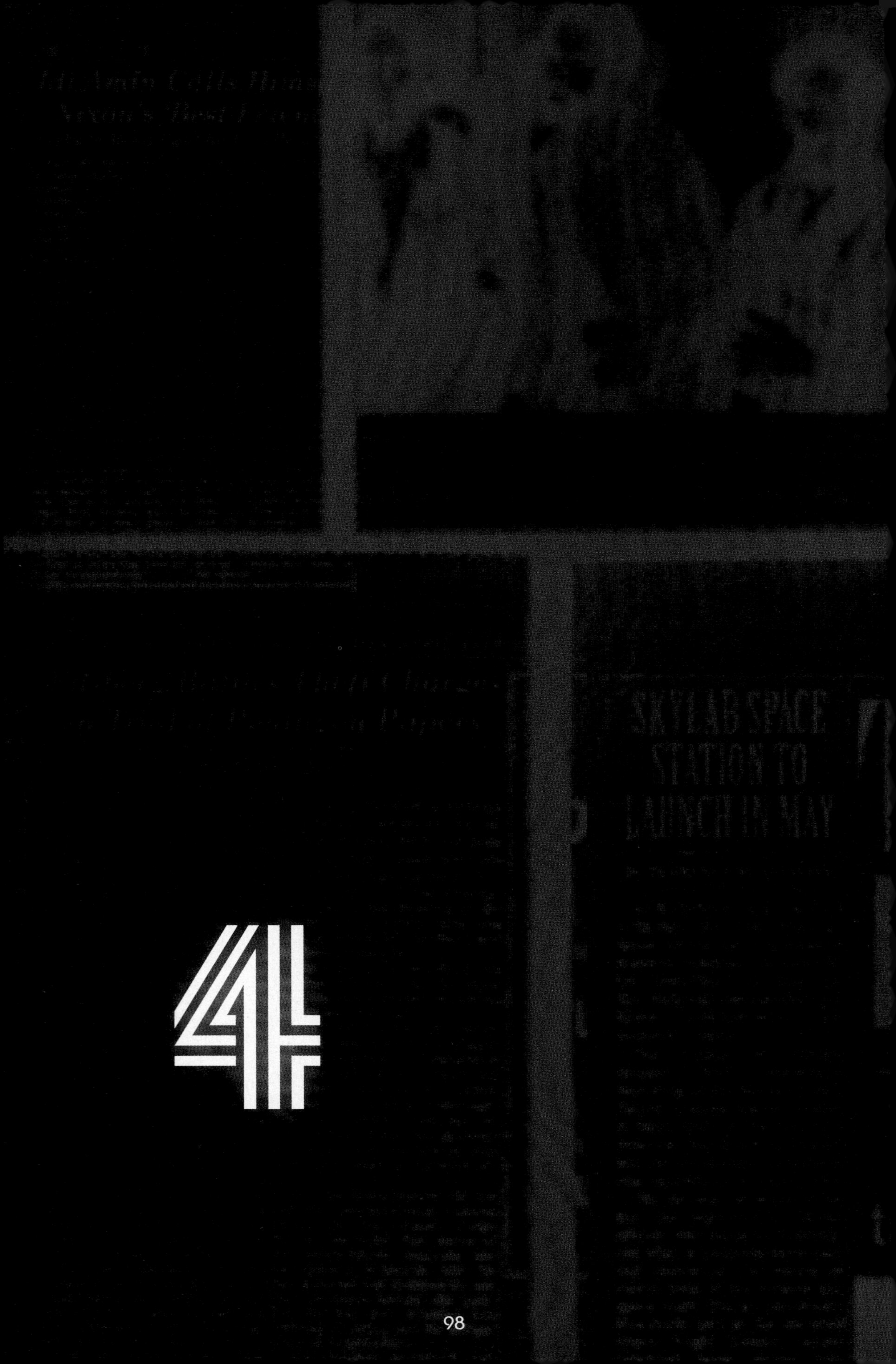
SKYLAB SPACE
STATION TO
LAUNCH IN MAY

4

HUMANS! HOMO SAPIENS -- YOU WHO CALL YOURSELF "THINKING MEN" -- HEAR ME! YOU OF NORTH AMERICA HAVE TRANSGRESSED AGAINST MADAME MAJESTRIX--
-- AND YOUR LIVES ARE THEREFORE FORFEIT!
OF ALL THE THINGS WE COULD HAVE EXPECTED TO HAPPEN THAT DAY, THE LAST ONE WAS HER.
EXECUTION DAY

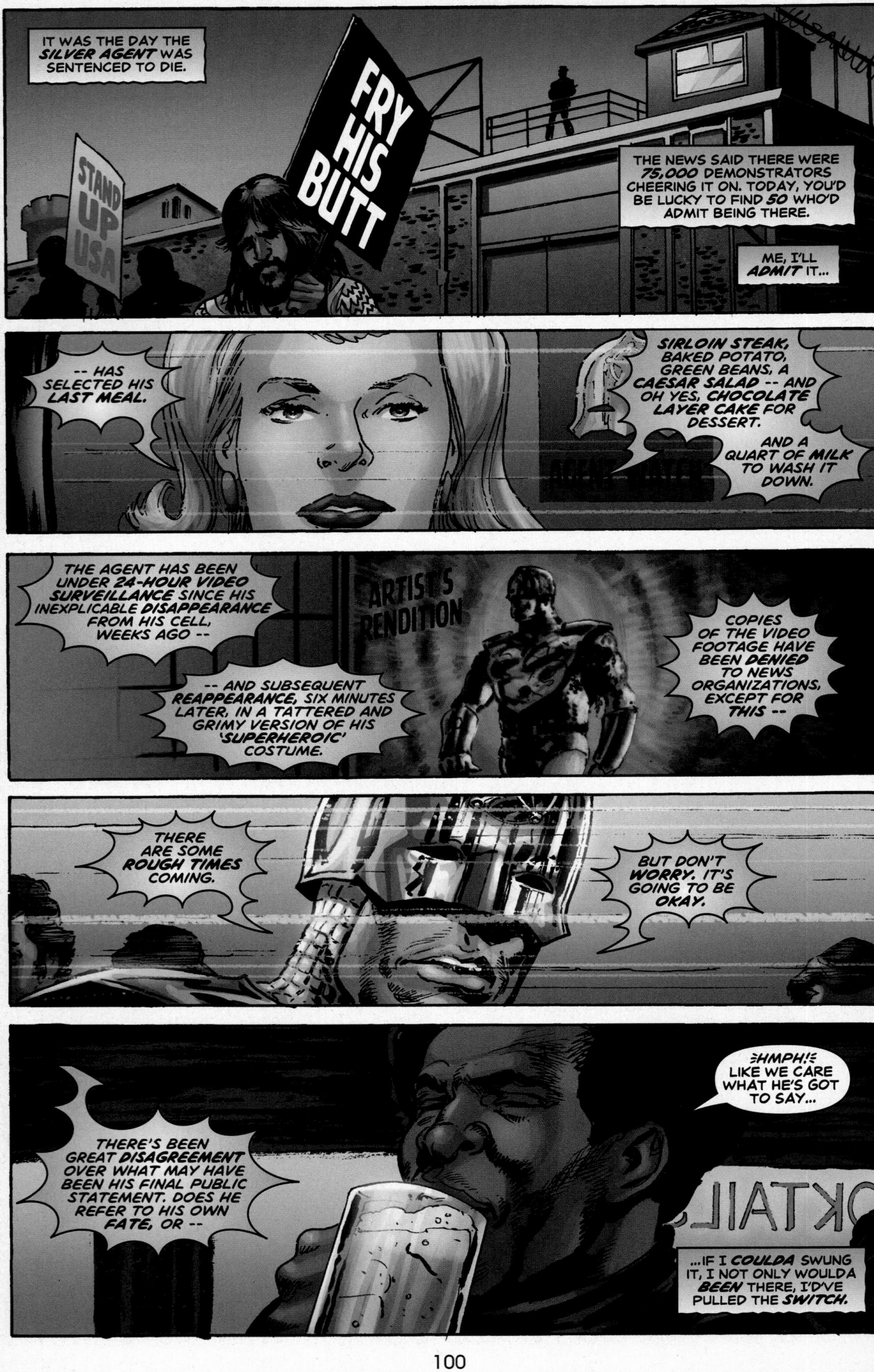
IT WAS THE DAY THE SILVER AGENT WAS SENTENCED TO DIE.
FRY HIS BUTT
STAND UP USA
THE NEWS SAID THERE WERE 75,000 DEMONSTRATORS CHEERING IT ON. TODAY, YOU'D BE LUCKY TO FIND 50 WHO'D ADMIT BEING THERE.
ME, I'LL ADMIT IT...
-- HAS SELECTED HIS LAST MEAL.
SIRLOIN STEAK, BAKED POTATO, GREEN BEANS, A CAESAR SALAD -- AND OH YES, CHOCOLATE LAYER CAKE FOR DESSERT.
AND A QUART OF MILK TO WASH IT DOWN.
THE AGENT HAS BEEN UNDER 24-HOUR VIDEO SURVEILLANCE SINCE HIS INEXPLICABLE DISAPPEARANCE FROM HIS CELL, WEEKS AGO --
ARTIST'S RENDITION
-- AND SUBSEQUENT REAPPEARANCE, SIX MINUTES LATER, IN A TATTERED AND GRIMY VERSION OF HIS 'SUPERHEROIC' COSTUME.
COPIES OF THE VIDEO FOOTAGE HAVE BEEN DENIED TO NEWS ORGANIZATIONS, EXCEPT FOR THIS --
THERE ARE SOME ROUGH TIMES COMING.
BUT DON'T WORRY. IT'S GOING TO BE OKAY.
HMPH! LIKE WE CARE WHAT HE'S GOT TO SAY...
THERE'S BEEN GREAT DISAGREEMENT OVER WHAT MAY HAVE BEEN HIS FINAL PUBLIC STATEMENT. DOES HE REFER TO HIS OWN FATE, OR --
...IF I COULDA SWUNG IT, I NOT ONLY WOULDA BEEN THERE, I'D'VE PULLED THE SWITCH.

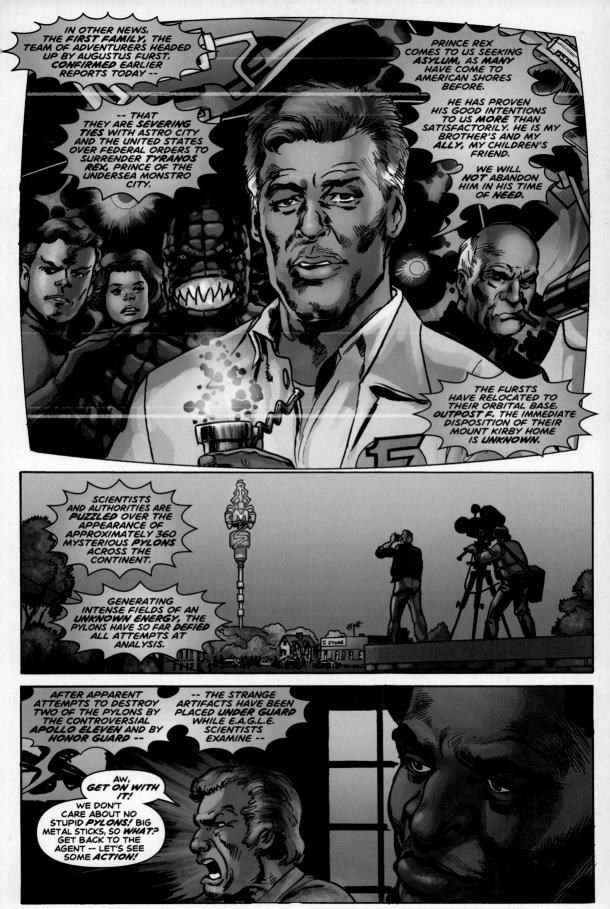

IN OTHER NEWS, THE *FIRST FAMILY,* THE TEAM OF ADVENTURERS HEADED UP BY AUGUSTUS FURST, *CONFIRMED* EARLIER REPORTS TODAY --

-- THAT THEY ARE *SEVERING* TIES WITH ASTRO CITY AND THE UNITED STATES OVER FEDERAL ORDERS TO SURRENDER TYRANOS REX, PRINCE OF THE UNDERSEA MONSTRO CITY.

PRINCE REX COMES TO US SEEKING *ASYLUM,* AS *MANY* HAVE COME TO AMERICAN SHORES BEFORE.

HE HAS PROVEN HIS GOOD INTENTIONS TO US *MORE* THAN SATISFACTORILY. HE IS MY *BROTHER'S* AND MY *ALLY,* MY *CHILDREN'S* FRIEND.

WE WILL *NOT* ABANDON HIM IN HIS TIME OF *NEED.*

THE FURSTS HAVE RELOCATED TO THEIR ORBITAL BASE, *OUTPOST F.* THE IMMEDIATE DISPOSITION OF THEIR MOUNT KIRBY HOME IS *UNKNOWN.*

SCIENTISTS AND AUTHORITIES ARE *PUZZLED* OVER THE APPEARANCE OF APPROXIMATELY 360 MYSTERIOUS *PYLONS* ACROSS THE CONTINENT.

GENERATING INTENSE FIELDS OF AN *UNKNOWN* ENERGY, THE PYLONS HAVE SO FAR *DEFIED* ALL ATTEMPTS AT ANALYSIS.

AFTER APPARENT ATTEMPTS TO DESTROY TWO OF THE PYLONS BY THE CONTROVERSIAL *APOLLO ELEVEN* AND BY *HONOR GUARD* --

-- THE STRANGE ARTIFACTS HAVE BEEN PLACED *UNDER GUARD* WHILE E.A.G.L.E. SCIENTISTS EXAMINE --

AW, *GET ON WITH IT!* WE DON'T CARE ABOUT NO STUPID *PYLONS!* BIG METAL STICKS, SO *WHAT?* GET BACK TO THE AGENT -- LET'S SEE SOME *ACTION!*

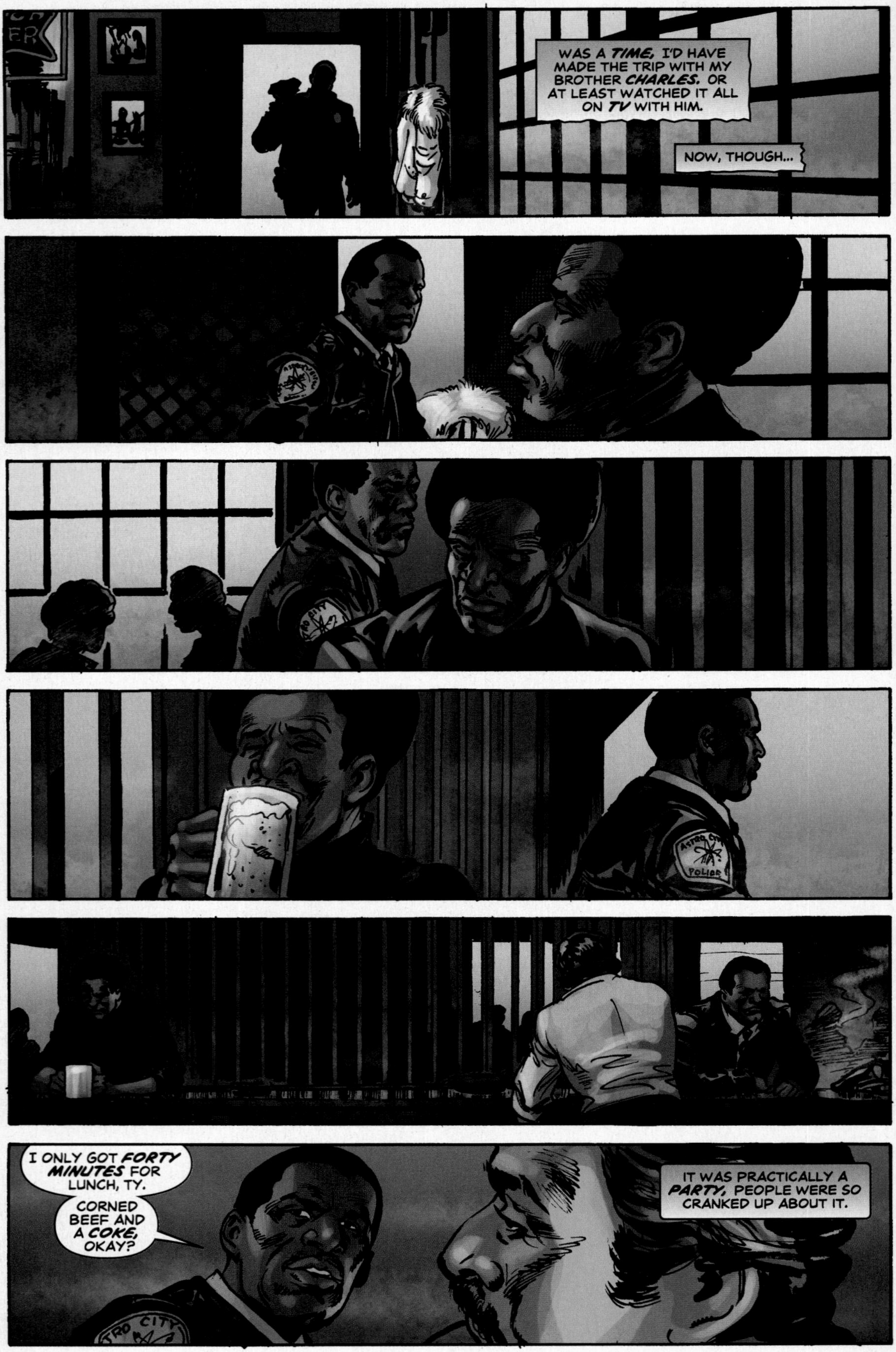

WAS A TIME, I'D HAVE MADE THE TRIP WITH MY BROTHER CHARLES. OR AT LEAST WATCHED IT ALL ON TV WITH HIM.
NOW, THOUGH...
IT WAS PRACTICALLY A PARTY, PEOPLE WERE SO CRANKED UP ABOUT IT.
I ONLY GOT FORTY MINUTES FOR LUNCH, TY.
CORNED BEEF AND A COKE, OKAY?

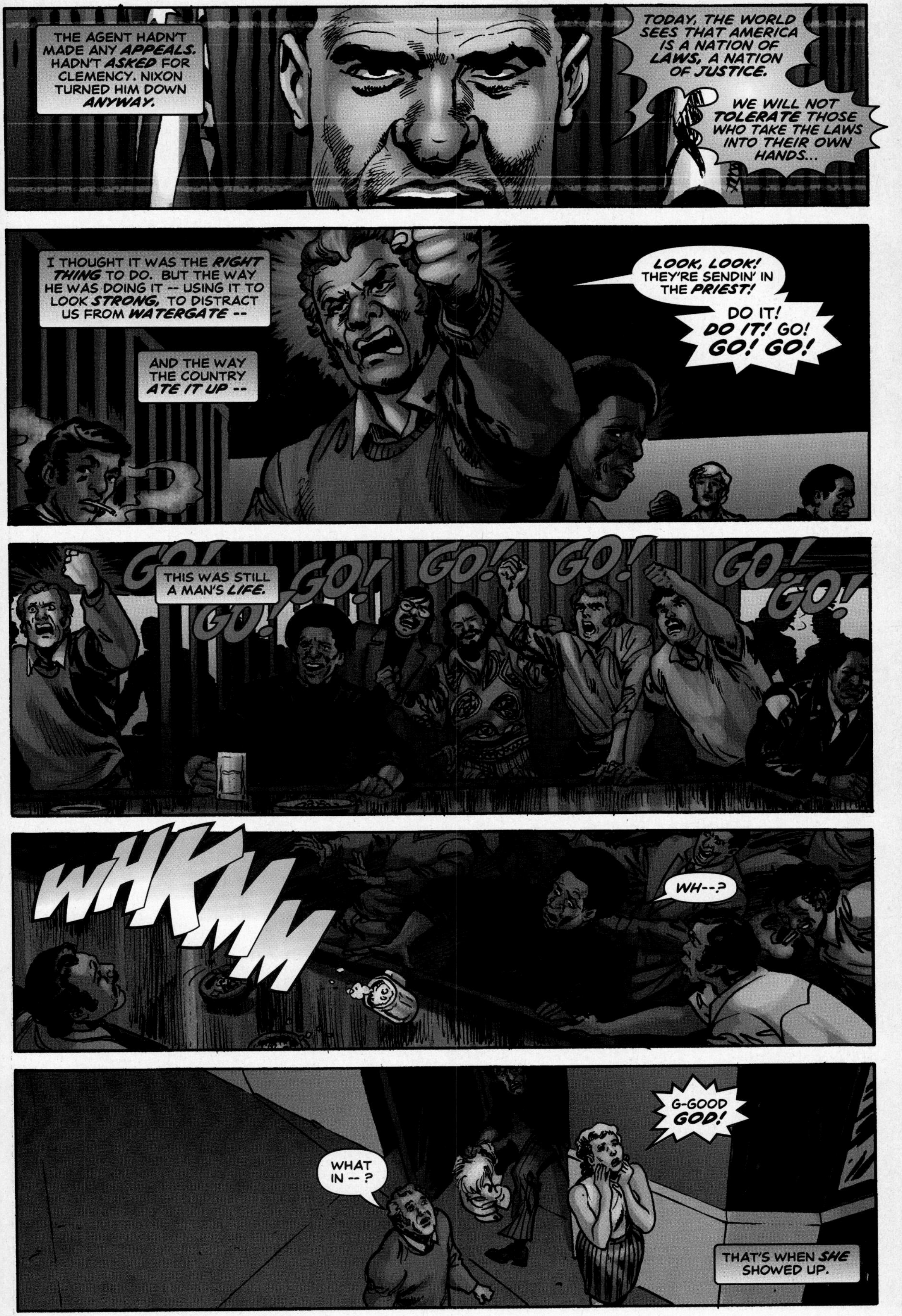
THE AGENT HADN'T MADE ANY APPEALS. HADN'T ASKED FOR CLEMENCY. NIXON TURNED HIM DOWN ANYWAY.
TODAY, THE WORLD SEES THAT AMERICA IS A NATION OF LAWS, A NATION OF JUSTICE.
WE WILL NOT TOLERATE THOSE WHO TAKE THE LAWS INTO THEIR OWN HANDS...
I THOUGHT IT WAS THE RIGHT THING TO DO. BUT THE WAY HE WAS DOING IT -- USING IT TO LOOK STRONG, TO DISTRACT US FROM WATERGATE --
LOOK, LOOK! THEY'RE SENDIN' IN THE PRIEST!
DO IT! DO IT! GO! GO! GO!
AND THE WAY THE COUNTRY ATE IT UP --
GO!
THIS WAS STILL A MAN'S LIFE.
GO!
GO!
GO!
GO!
GO!
GO!
GO!
WHKMM
WH--?
G-GOOD GOD!
WHAT IN -- ?
THAT'S WHEN SHE SHOWED UP.

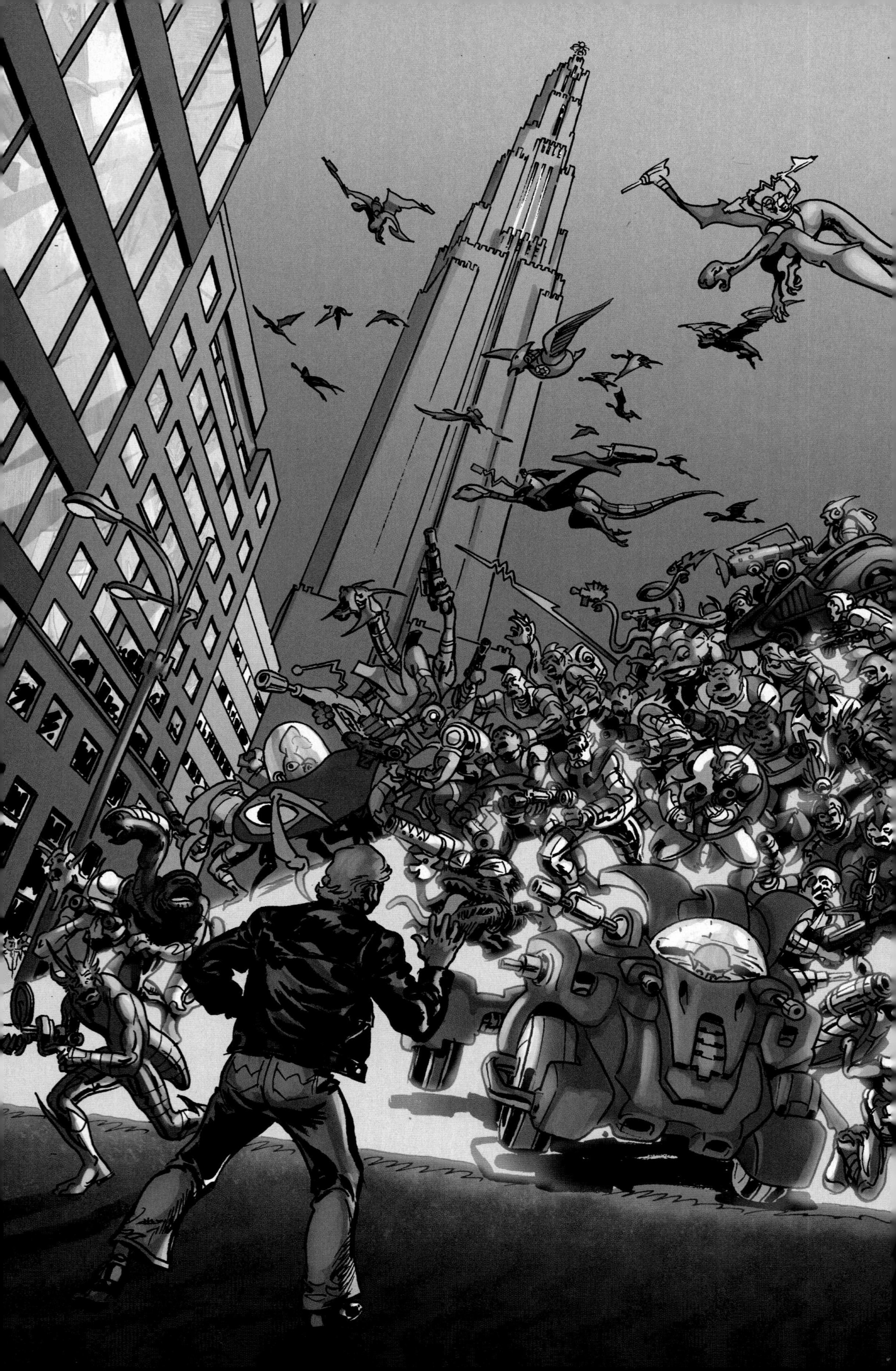

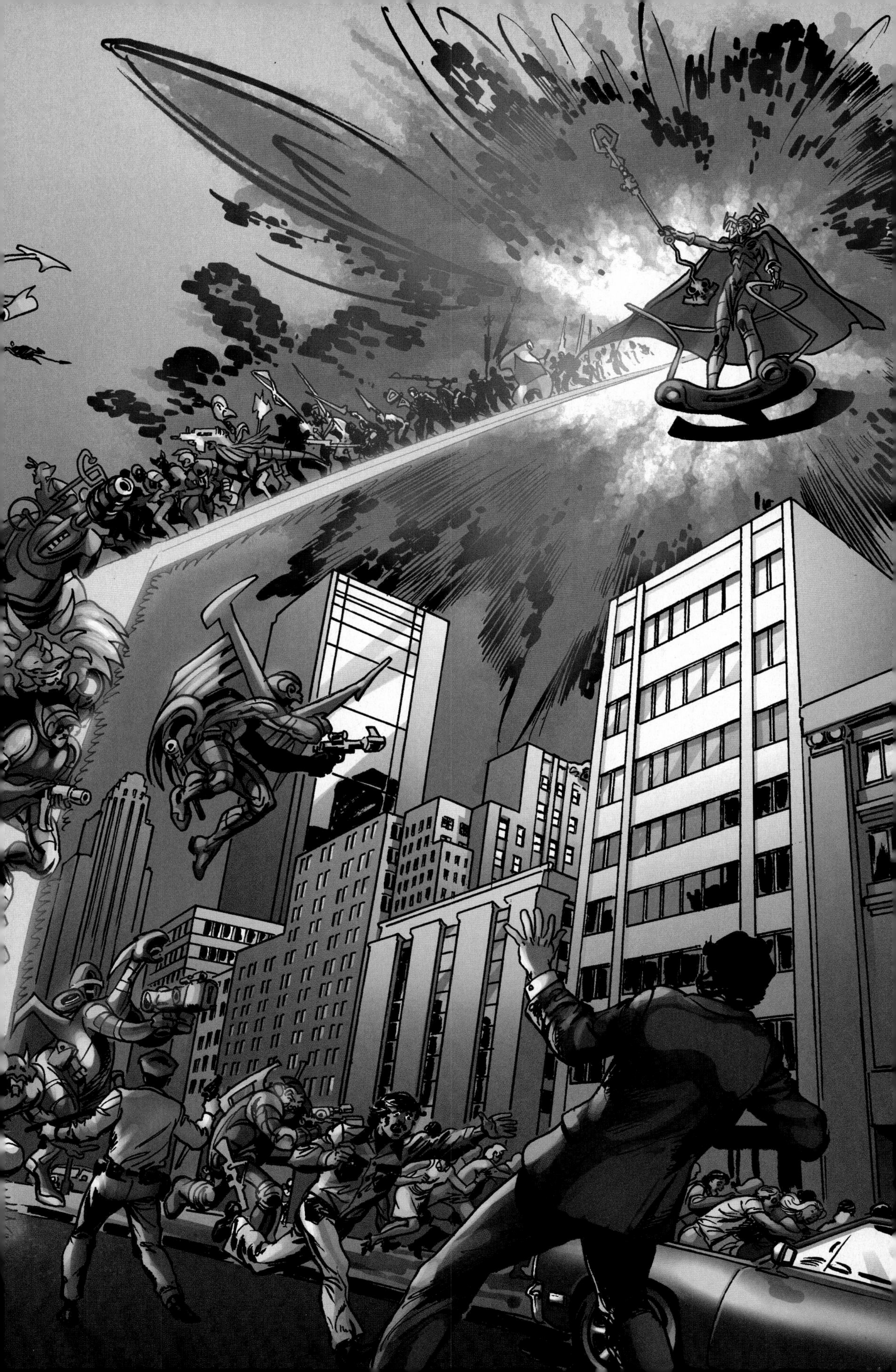

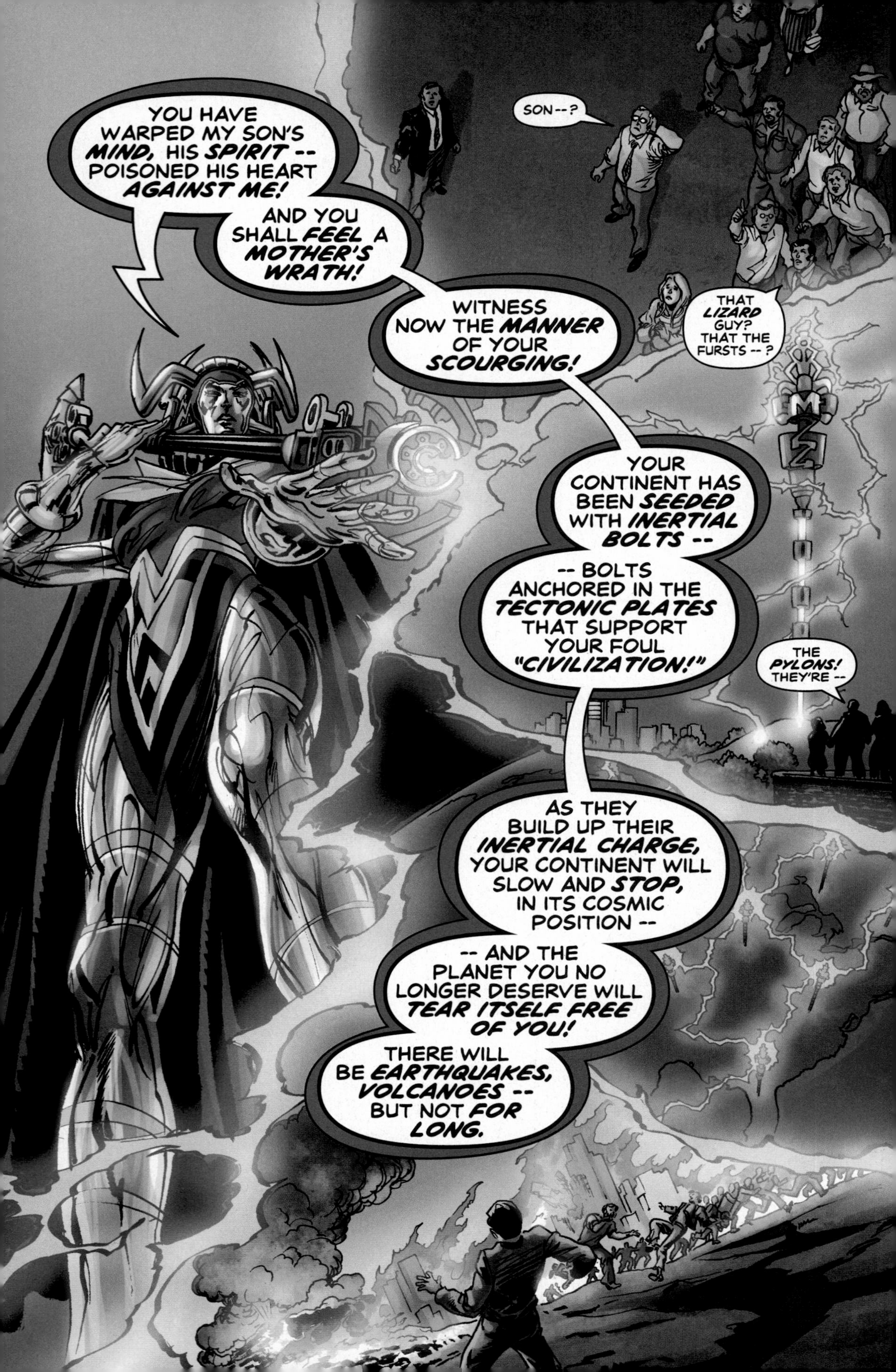
YOU HAVE WARPED MY SON'S MIND, HIS SPIRIT -- POISONED HIS HEART AGAINST ME!
AND YOU SHALL FEEL A MOTHER'S WRATH!
SON--?
WITNESS NOW THE MANNER OF YOUR SCOURGING!
THAT LIZARD GUY? THAT THE FURSTS -- ?
YOUR CONTINENT HAS BEEN SEEDED WITH INERTIAL BOLTS --
-- BOLTS ANCHORED IN THE TECTONIC PLATES THAT SUPPORT YOUR FOUL "CIVILIZATION!"
THE PYLONS! THEY'RE --
AS THEY BUILD UP THEIR INERTIAL CHARGE, YOUR CONTINENT WILL SLOW AND STOP, IN ITS COSMIC POSITION --
-- AND THE PLANET YOU NO LONGER DESERVE WILL TEAR ITSELF FREE OF YOU!
THERE WILL BE EARTHQUAKES, VOLCANOES -- BUT NOT FOR LONG.

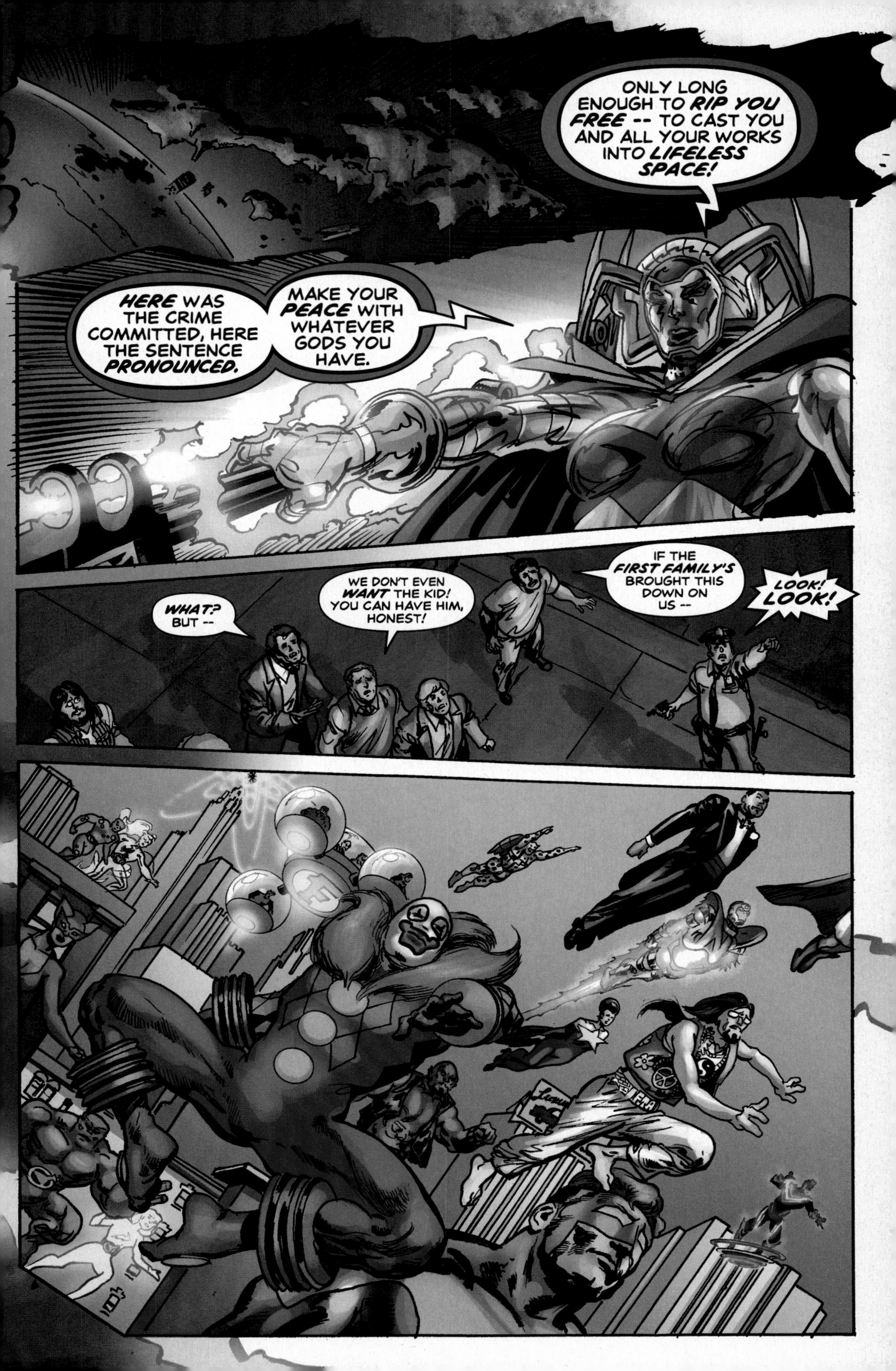
ONLY LONG ENOUGH TO *RIP YOU FREE* -- TO CAST YOU AND ALL YOUR WORKS INTO *LIFELESS SPACE!*
HERE WAS THE CRIME COMMITTED, HERE THE SENTENCE *PRONOUNCED.*
MAKE YOUR *PEACE* WITH WHATEVER GODS YOU HAVE.
WHAT? BUT --
WE DON'T EVEN *WANT* THE KID! YOU CAN HAVE HIM, HONEST!
IF THE *FIRST FAMILY'S* BROUGHT THIS DOWN ON US --
LOOK! LOOK!

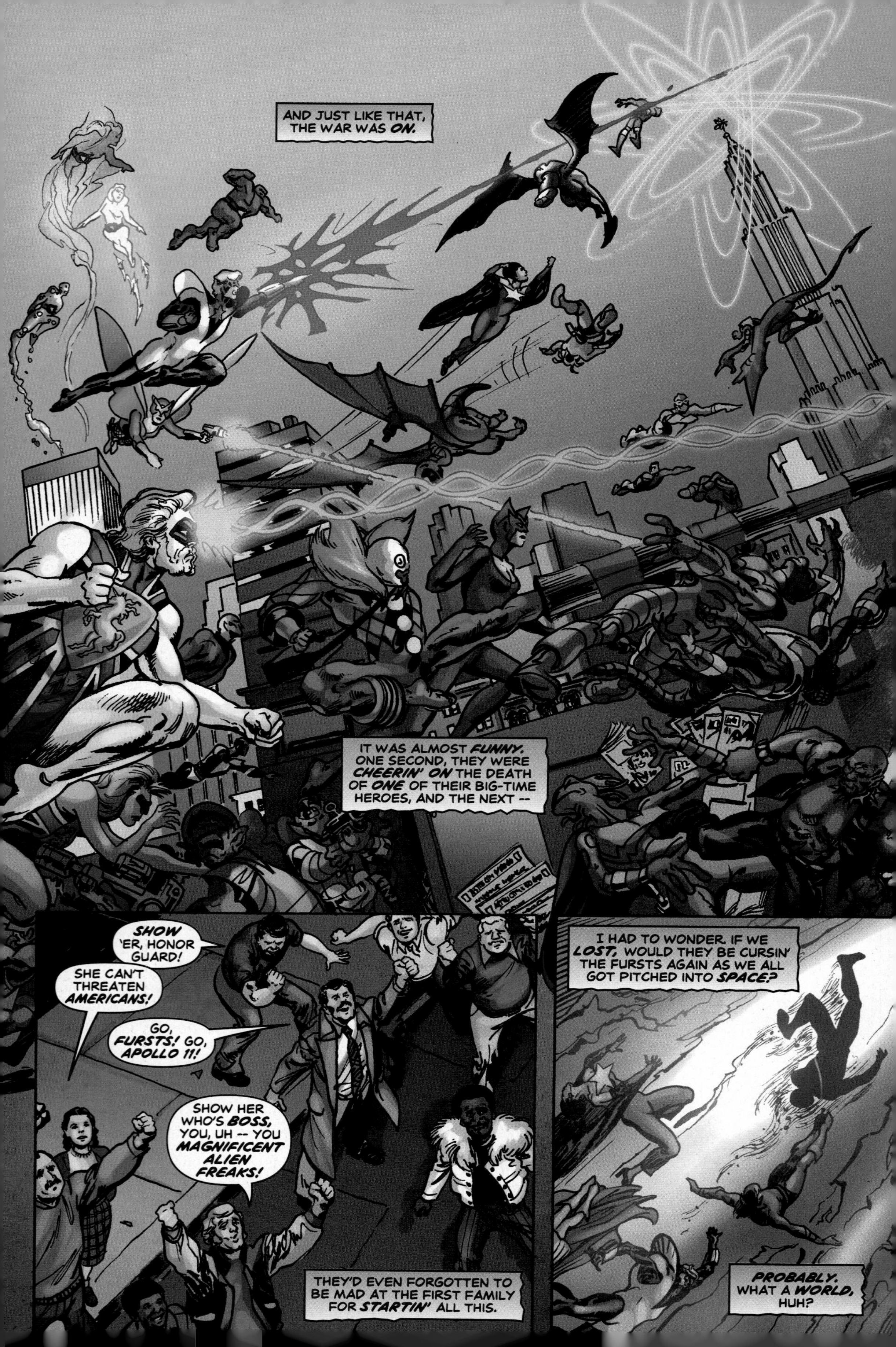
AND JUST LIKE THAT, THE WAR WAS ON.
IT WAS ALMOST FUNNY. ONE SECOND, THEY WERE CHEERIN' ON THE DEATH OF ONE OF THEIR BIG-TIME HEROES, AND THE NEXT --
SHOW 'ER, HONOR GUARD!
SHE CAN'T THREATEN AMERICANS!
GO, FURSTS! GO, APOLLO 11!
SHOW HER WHO'S BOSS, YOU, UH -- YOU MAGNIFICENT ALIEN FREAKS!
THEY'D EVEN FORGOTTEN TO BE MAD AT THE FIRST FAMILY FOR STARTIN' ALL THIS.
I HAD TO WONDER. IF WE LOST, WOULD THEY BE CURSIN' THE FURSTS AGAIN AS WE ALL GOT PITCHED INTO SPACE?
PROBABLY. WHAT A WORLD, HUH?

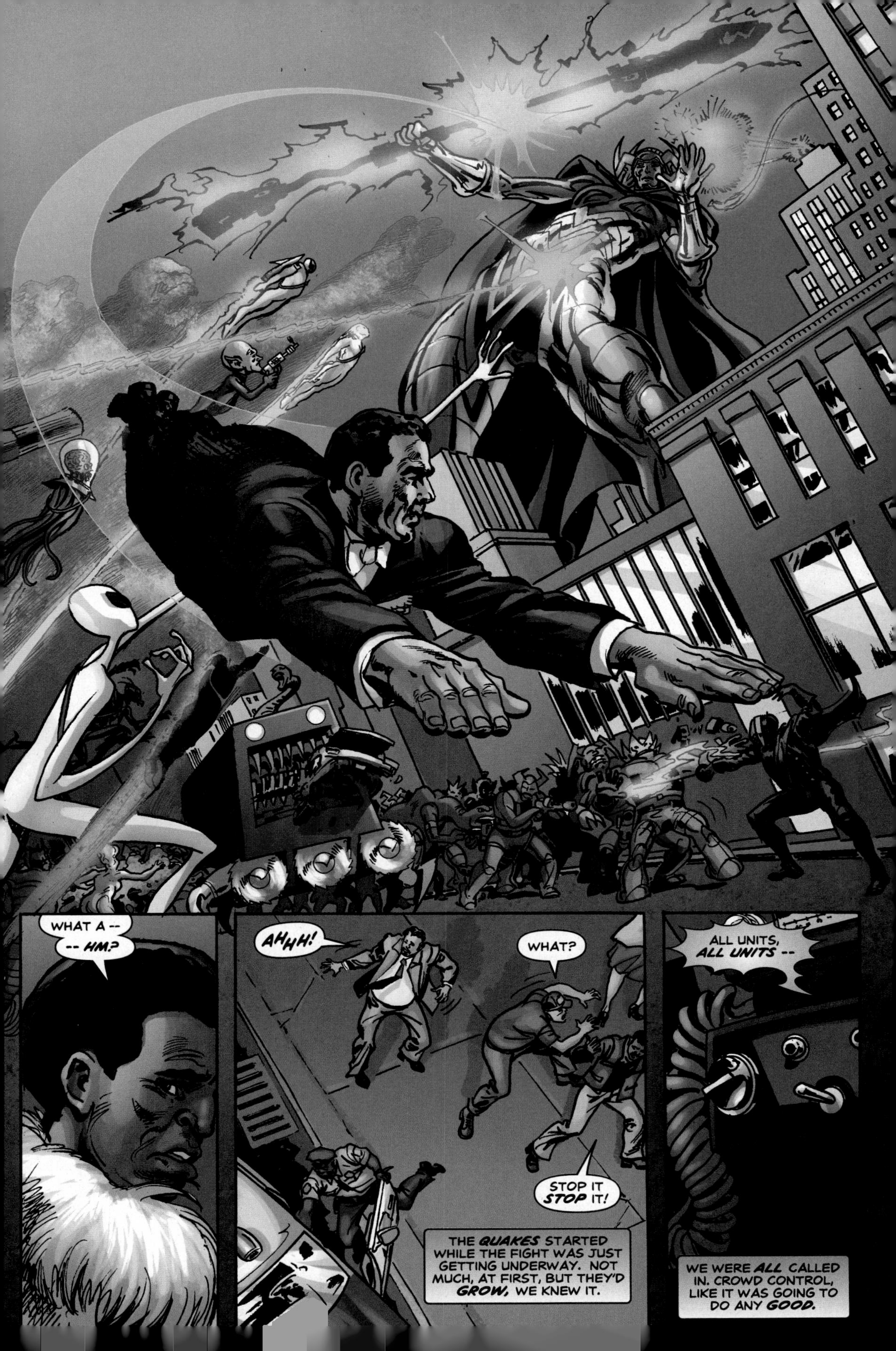
WHAT A --
-- HM?
AHHH!
WHAT?
STOP IT STOP IT!
THE QUAKES STARTED WHILE THE FIGHT WAS JUST GETTING UNDERWAY. NOT MUCH, AT FIRST, BUT THEY'D GROW, WE KNEW IT.
ALL UNITS, ALL UNITS --
WE WERE ALL CALLED IN. CROWD CONTROL, LIKE IT WAS GOING TO DO ANY GOOD.

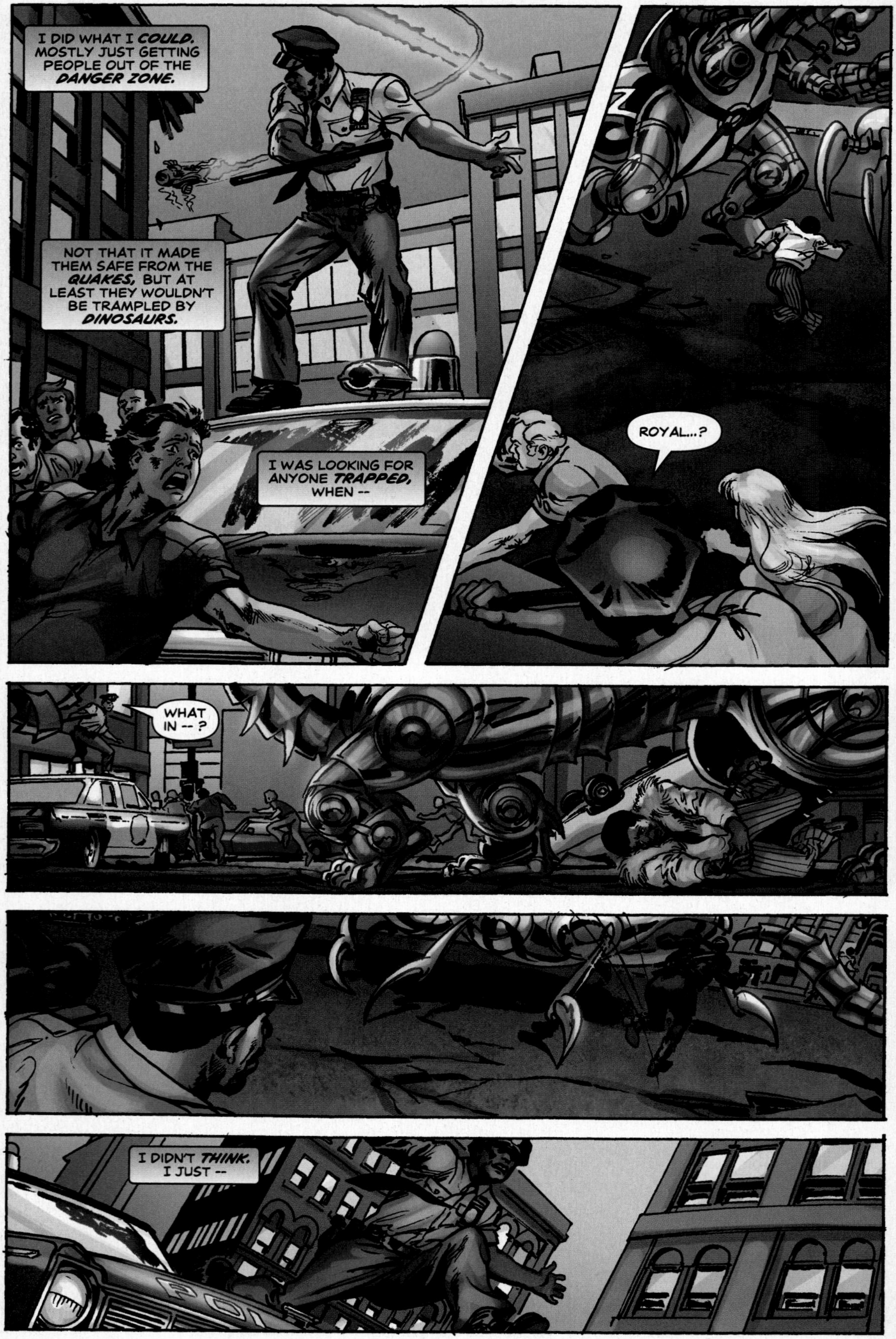
I DID WHAT I COULD. MOSTLY JUST GETTING PEOPLE OUT OF THE DANGER ZONE.
NOT THAT IT MADE THEM SAFE FROM THE QUAKES, BUT AT LEAST THEY WOULDN'T BE TRAMPLED BY DINOSAURS.
I WAS LOOKING FOR ANYONE TRAPPED, WHEN --
ROYAL...?
WHAT IN -- ?
I DIDN'T THINK. I JUST --

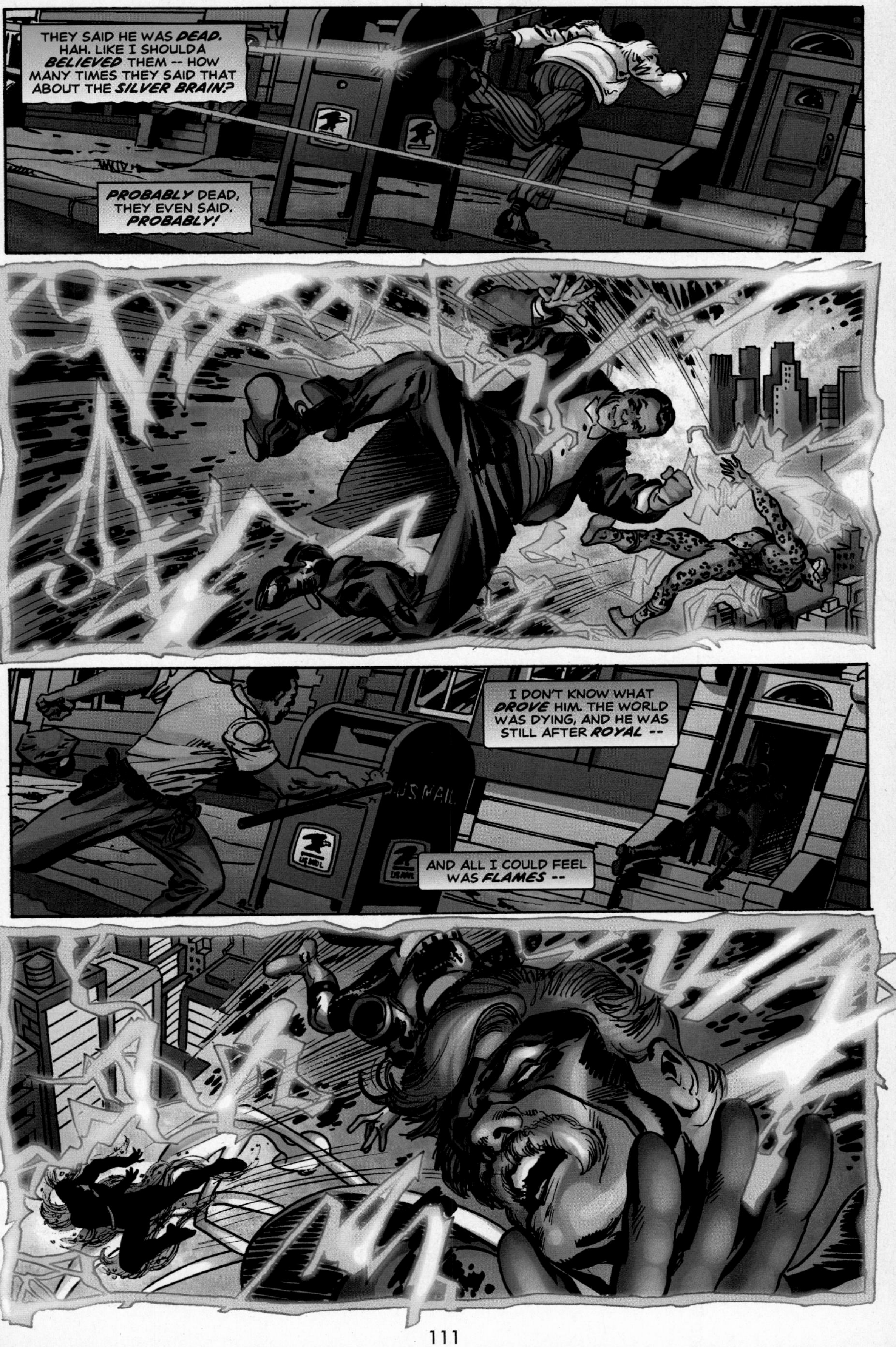
THEY SAID HE WAS DEAD. HAH. LIKE I SHOULDA BELIEVED THEM -- HOW MANY TIMES THEY SAID THAT ABOUT THE SILVER BRAIN?
PROBABLY DEAD, THEY EVEN SAID. PROBABLY!
I DON'T KNOW WHAT DROVE HIM. THE WORLD WAS DYING, AND HE WAS STILL AFTER ROYAL --
AND ALL I COULD FEEL WAS FLAMES --

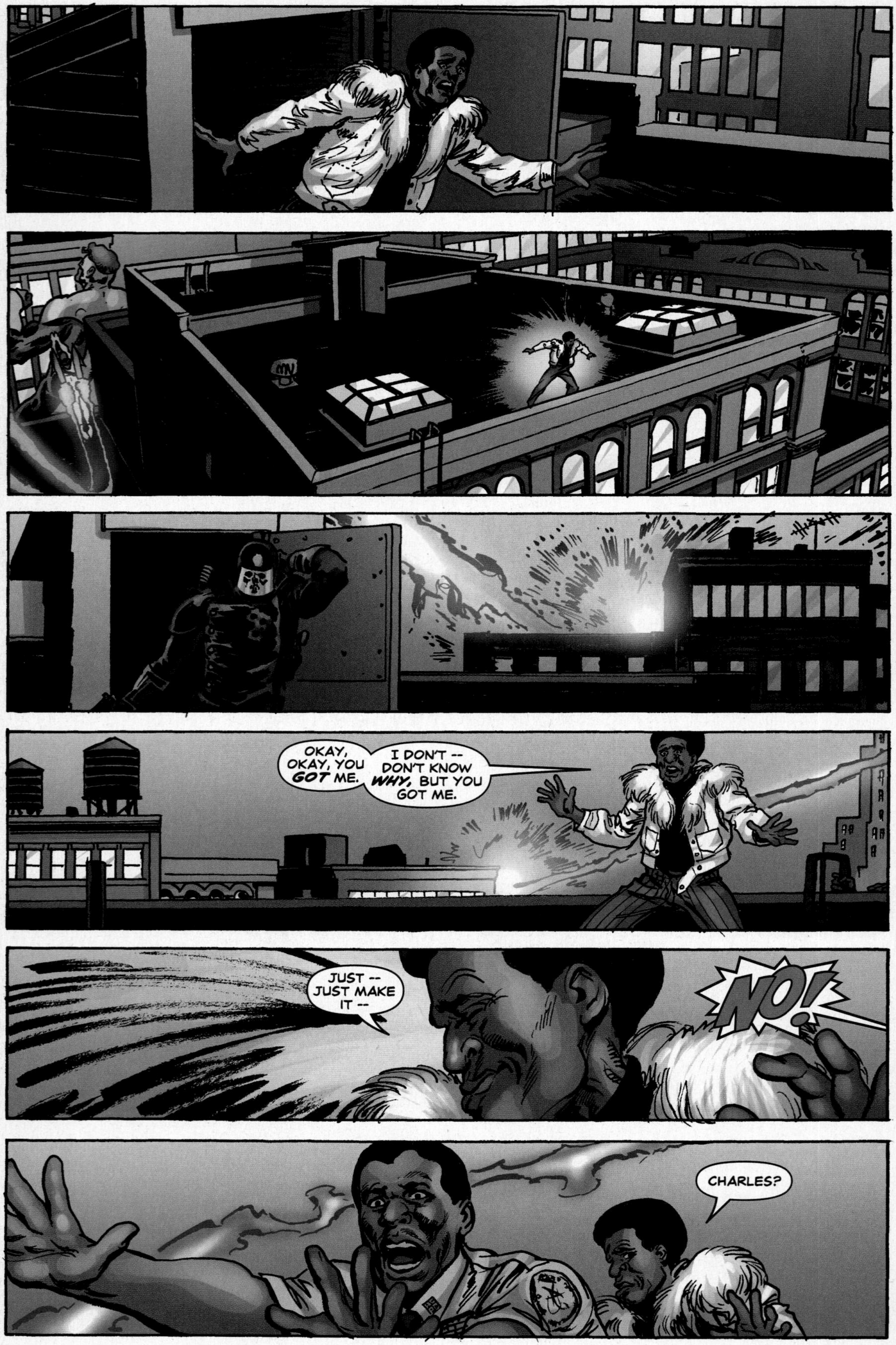
OKAY, OKAY, YOU GOT ME.
I DON'T -- DON'T KNOW WHY, BUT YOU GOT ME.
JUST -- JUST MAKE IT --
NO!
CHARLES?

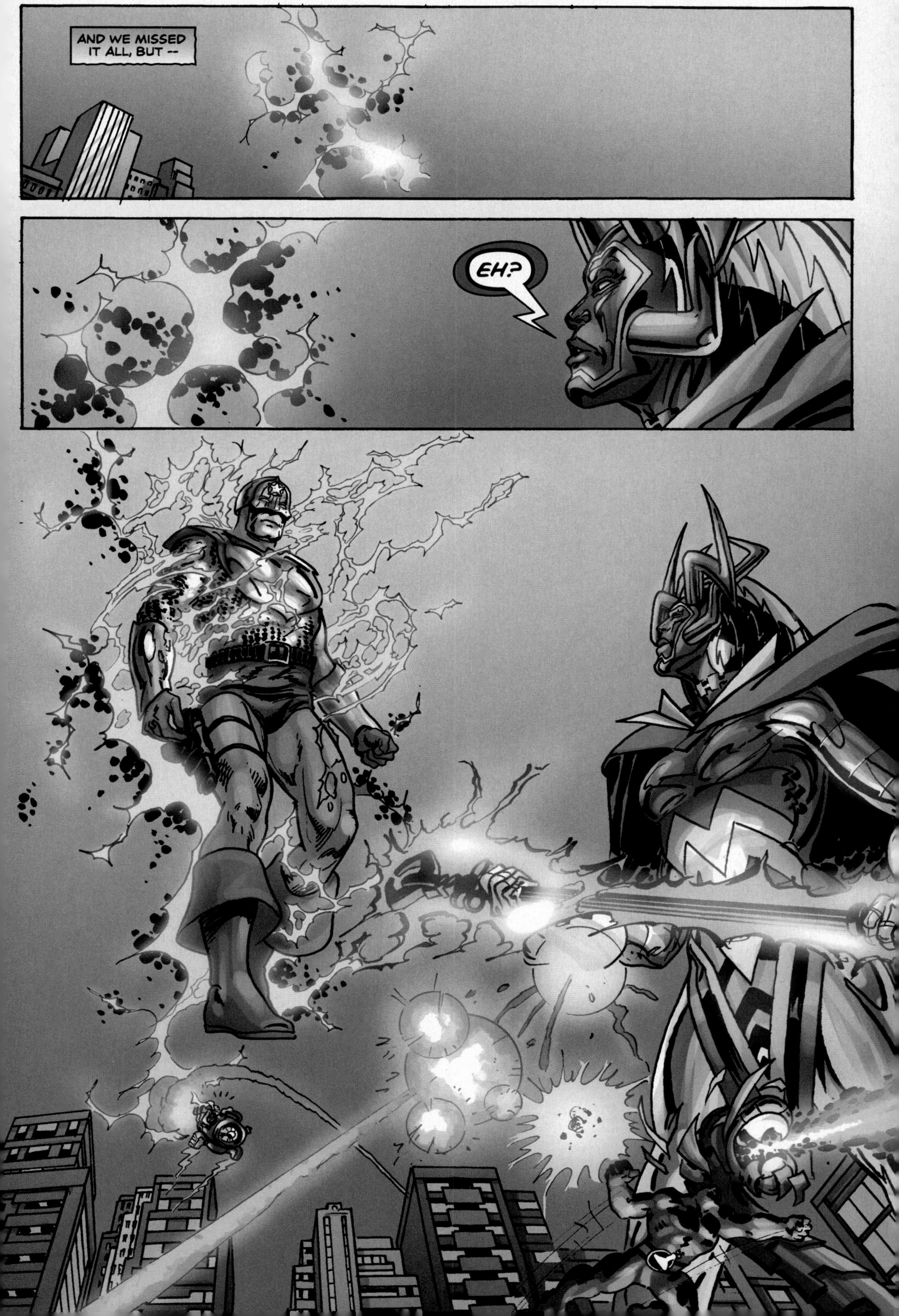
AND WE MISSED IT ALL, BUT --
EH?

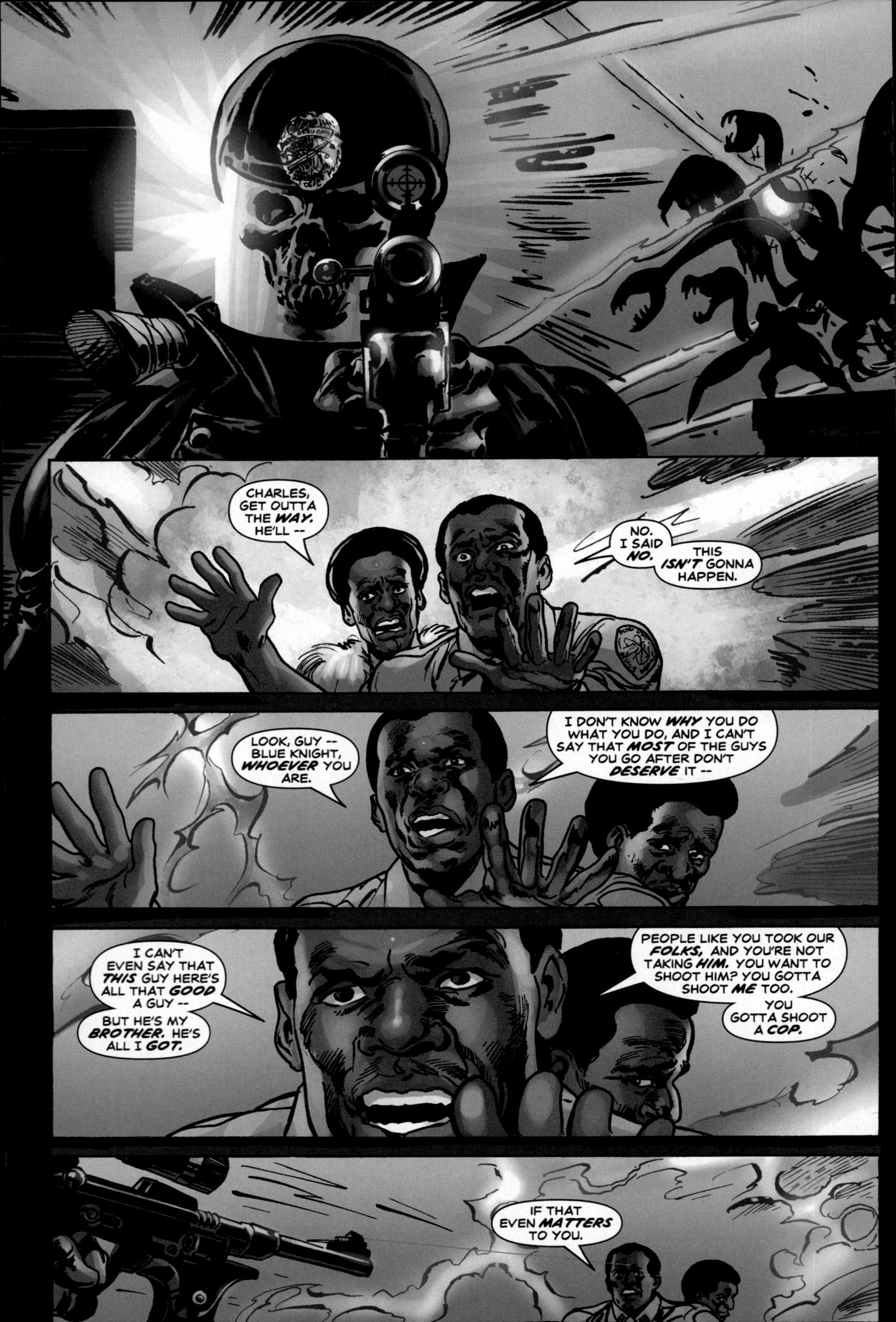
CHARLES, GET OUTTA THE WAY. HE'LL --
NO. I SAID NO.
THIS ISN'T GONNA HAPPEN.
LOOK, GUY -- BLUE KNIGHT, WHOEVER YOU ARE.
I DON'T KNOW WHY YOU DO WHAT YOU DO, AND I CAN'T SAY THAT MOST OF THE GUYS YOU GO AFTER DON'T DESERVE IT --
I CAN'T EVEN SAY THAT THIS GUY HERE'S ALL THAT GOOD A GUY --
BUT HE'S MY BROTHER. HE'S ALL I GOT.
PEOPLE LIKE YOU TOOK OUR FOLKS, AND YOU'RE NOT TAKING HIM. YOU WANT TO SHOOT HIM? YOU GOTTA SHOOT ME TOO.
YOU GOTTA SHOOT A COP.
IF THAT EVEN MATTERS TO YOU.

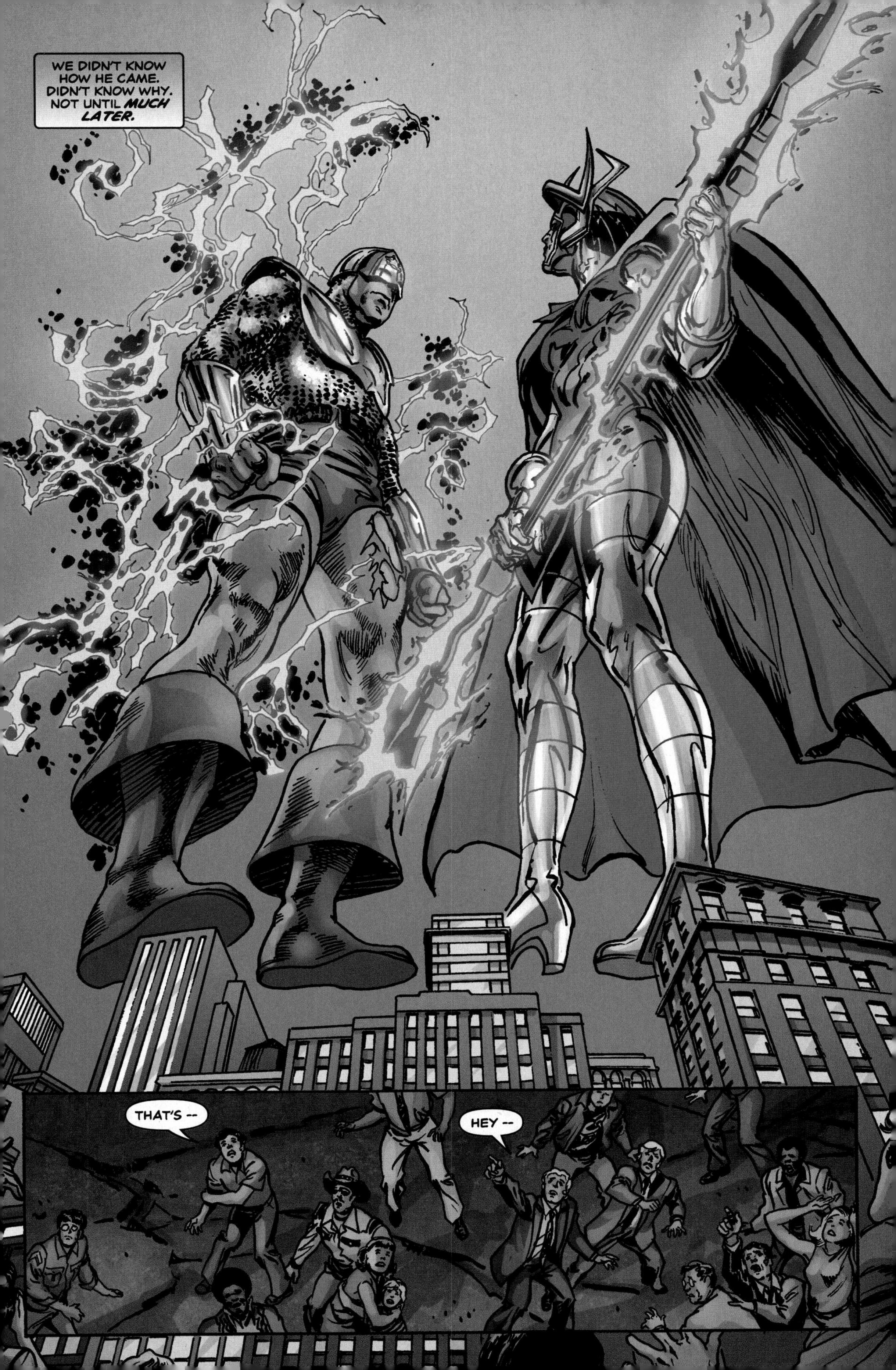
WE DIDN'T KNOW HOW HE CAME. DIDN'T KNOW WHY. NOT UNTIL *MUCH LATER.*
THAT'S --
HEY --

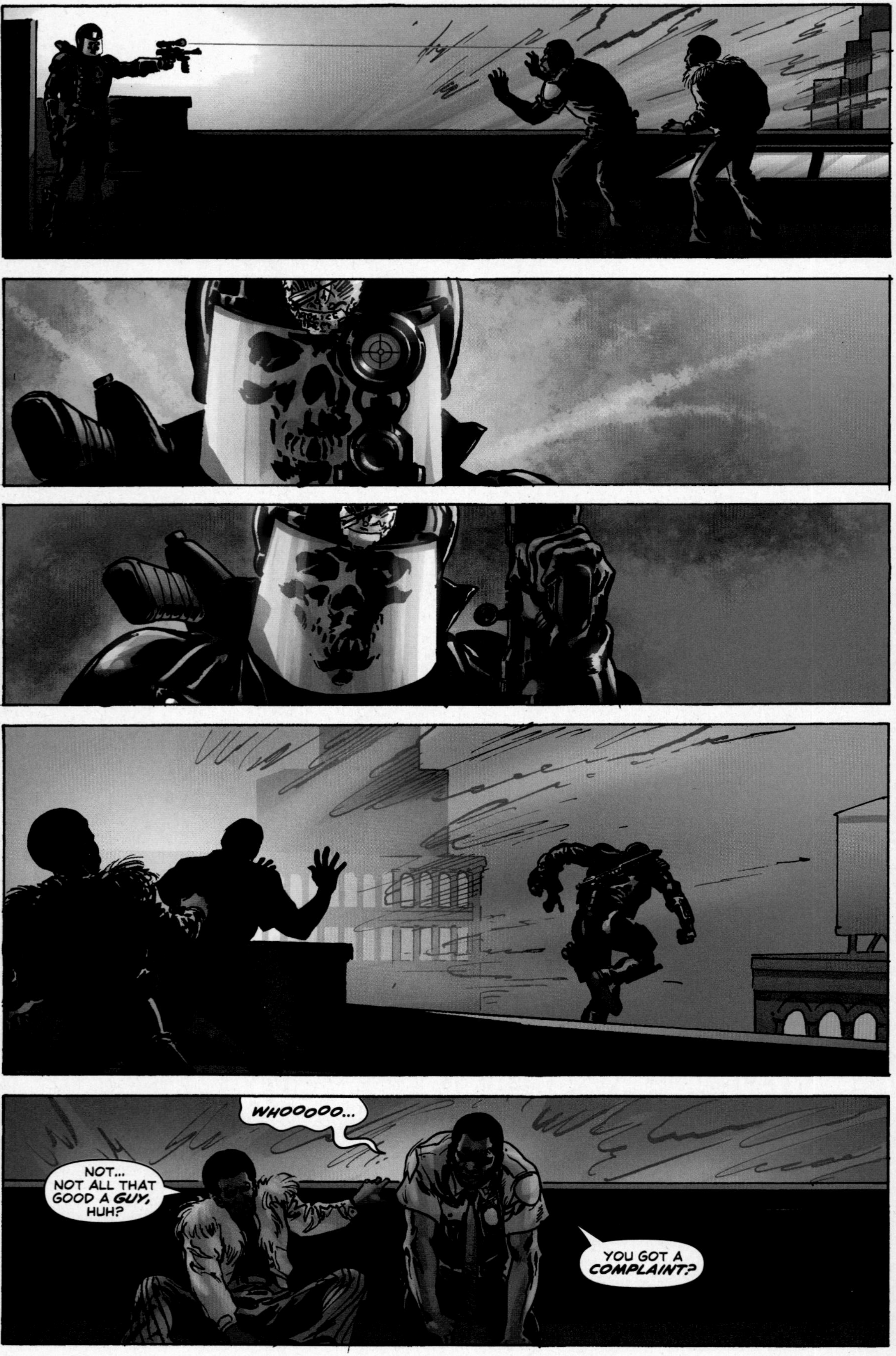
WHOOOOO...
NOT... NOT ALL THAT GOOD A GUY, HUH?
YOU GOT A COMPLAINT?

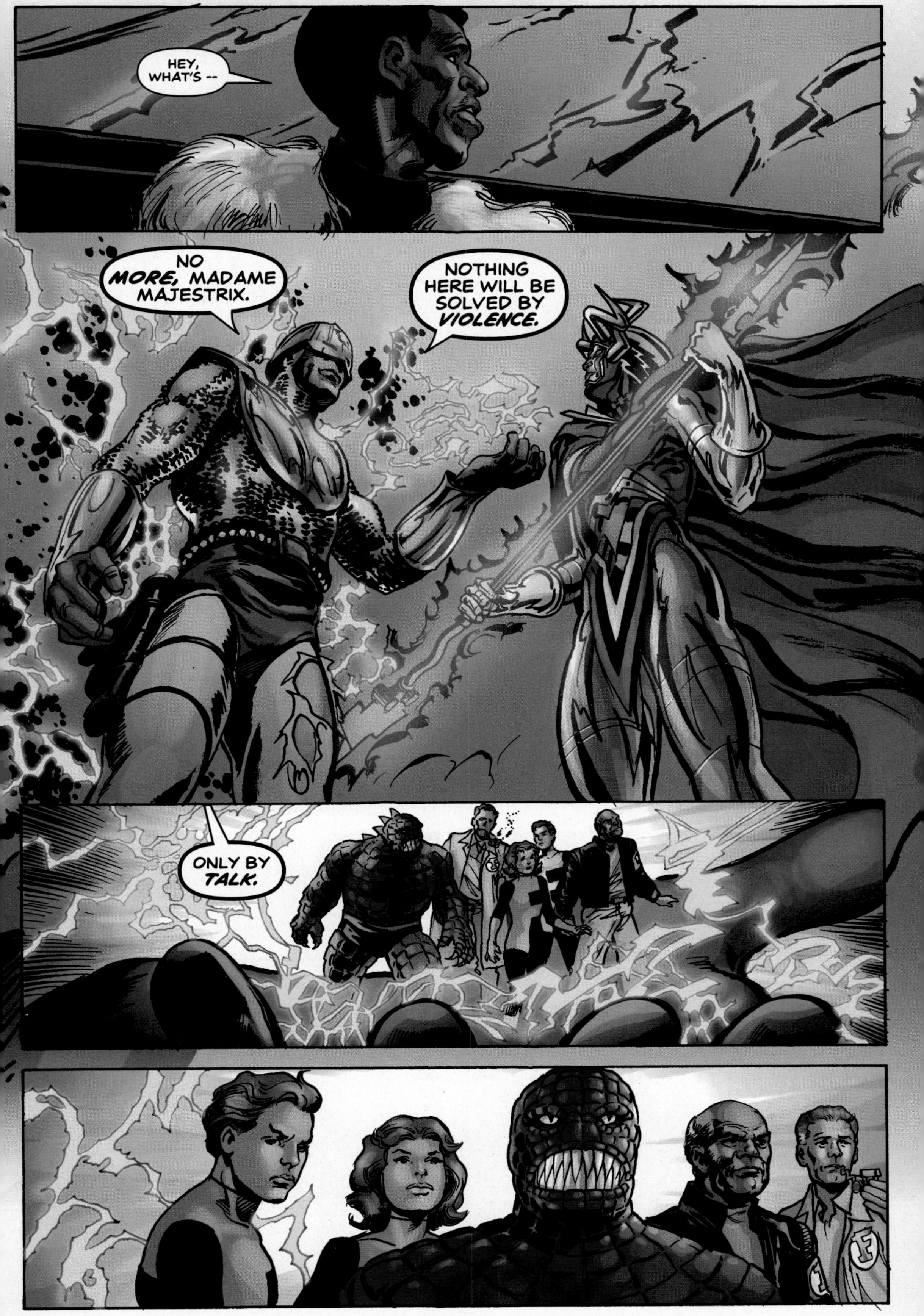
HEY, WHAT'S --
NO *MORE,* MADAME MAJESTRIX.
NOTHING HERE WILL BE SOLVED BY *VIOLENCE.*
ONLY BY *TALK.*

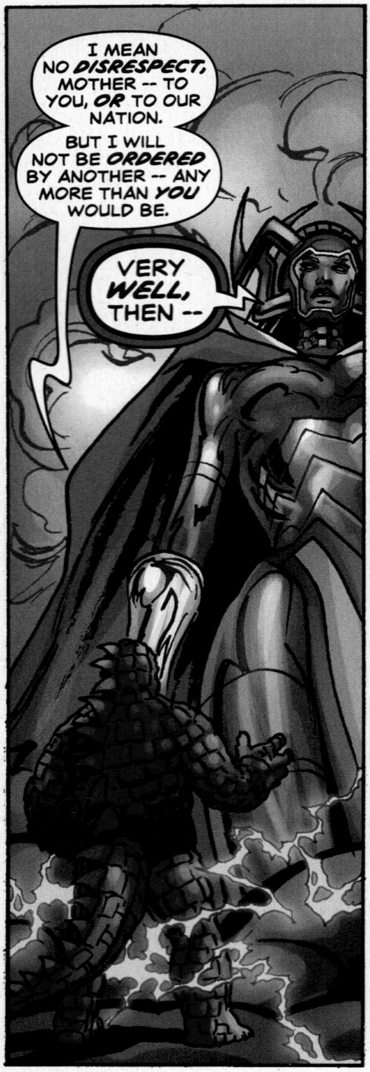
I MEAN NO DISRESPECT, MOTHER -- TO YOU, OR TO OUR NATION.
BUT I WILL NOT BE ORDERED BY ANOTHER -- ANY MORE THAN YOU WOULD BE.
VERY WELL, THEN --

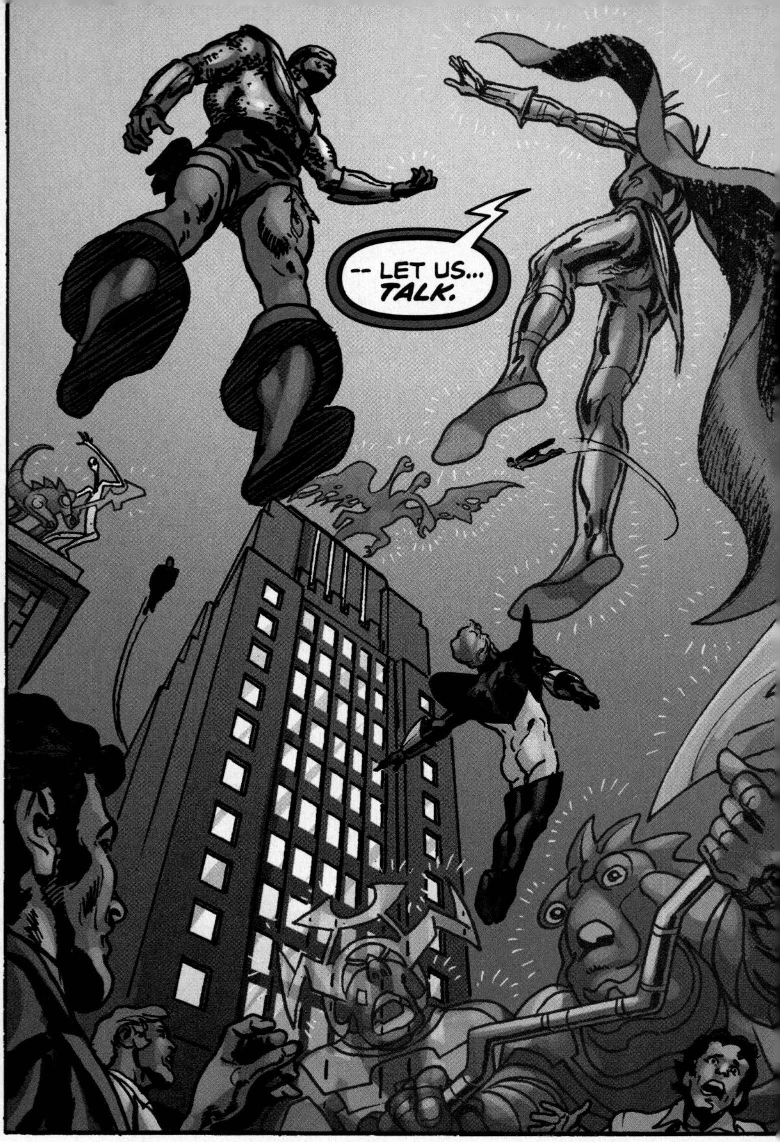
-- LET US... TALK.

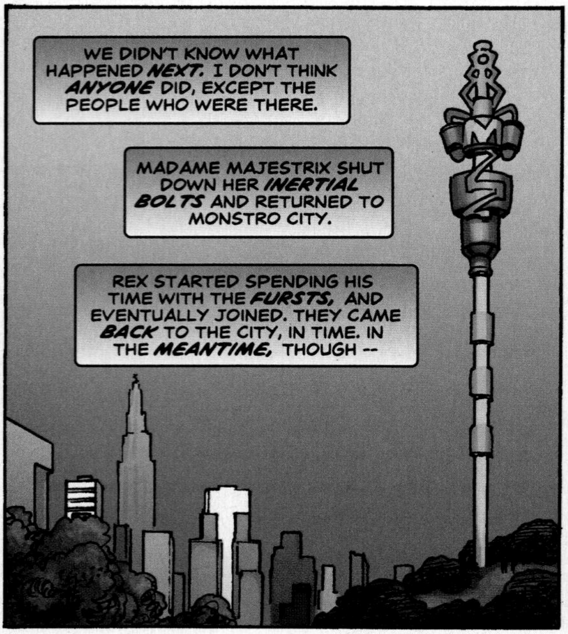
WE DIDN'T KNOW WHAT HAPPENED NEXT. I DON'T THINK ANYONE DID, EXCEPT THE PEOPLE WHO WERE THERE.
MADAME MAJESTRIX SHUT DOWN HER INERTIAL BOLTS AND RETURNED TO MONSTRO CITY.
REX STARTED SPENDING HIS TIME WITH THE FURSTS, AND EVENTUALLY JOINED. THEY CAME BACK TO THE CITY, IN TIME. IN THE MEANTIME, THOUGH --

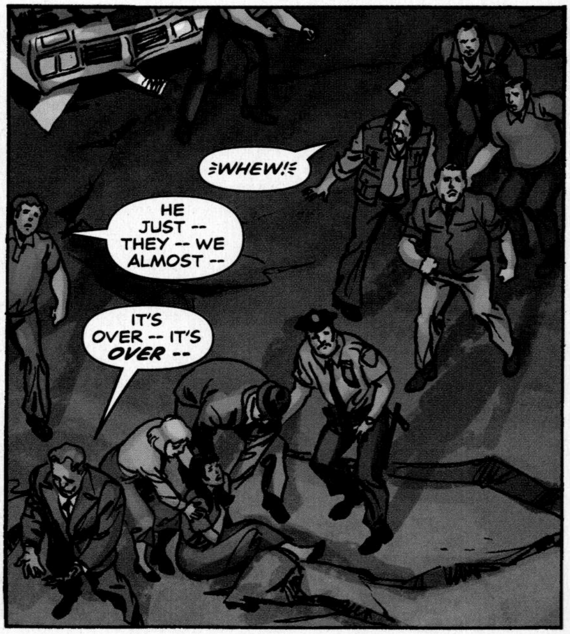
WHEW!
HE JUST -- THEY -- WE ALMOST --
IT'S OVER -- IT'S OVER --

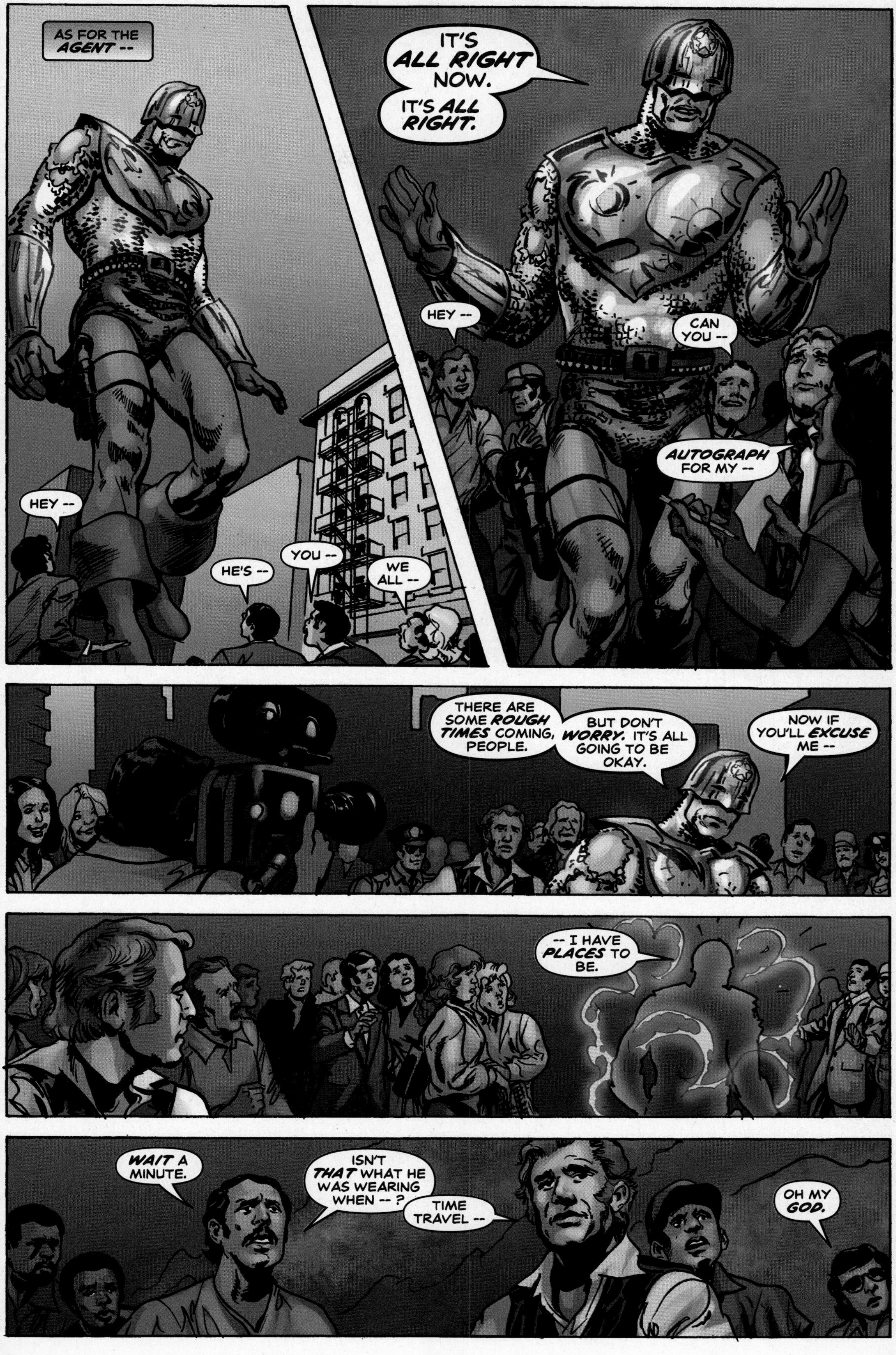

AS FOR THE AGENT --
HEY --
HE'S --
YOU --
WE ALL --
IT'S ALL RIGHT NOW.
IT'S ALL RIGHT.
HEY --
CAN YOU --
AUTOGRAPH FOR MY --
THERE ARE SOME ROUGH TIMES COMING, PEOPLE.
BUT DON'T WORRY. IT'S ALL GOING TO BE OKAY.
NOW IF YOU'LL EXCUSE ME --
-- I HAVE PLACES TO BE.
WAIT A MINUTE.
ISN'T THAT WHAT HE WAS WEARING WHEN -- ?
TIME TRAVEL --
OH MY GOD.

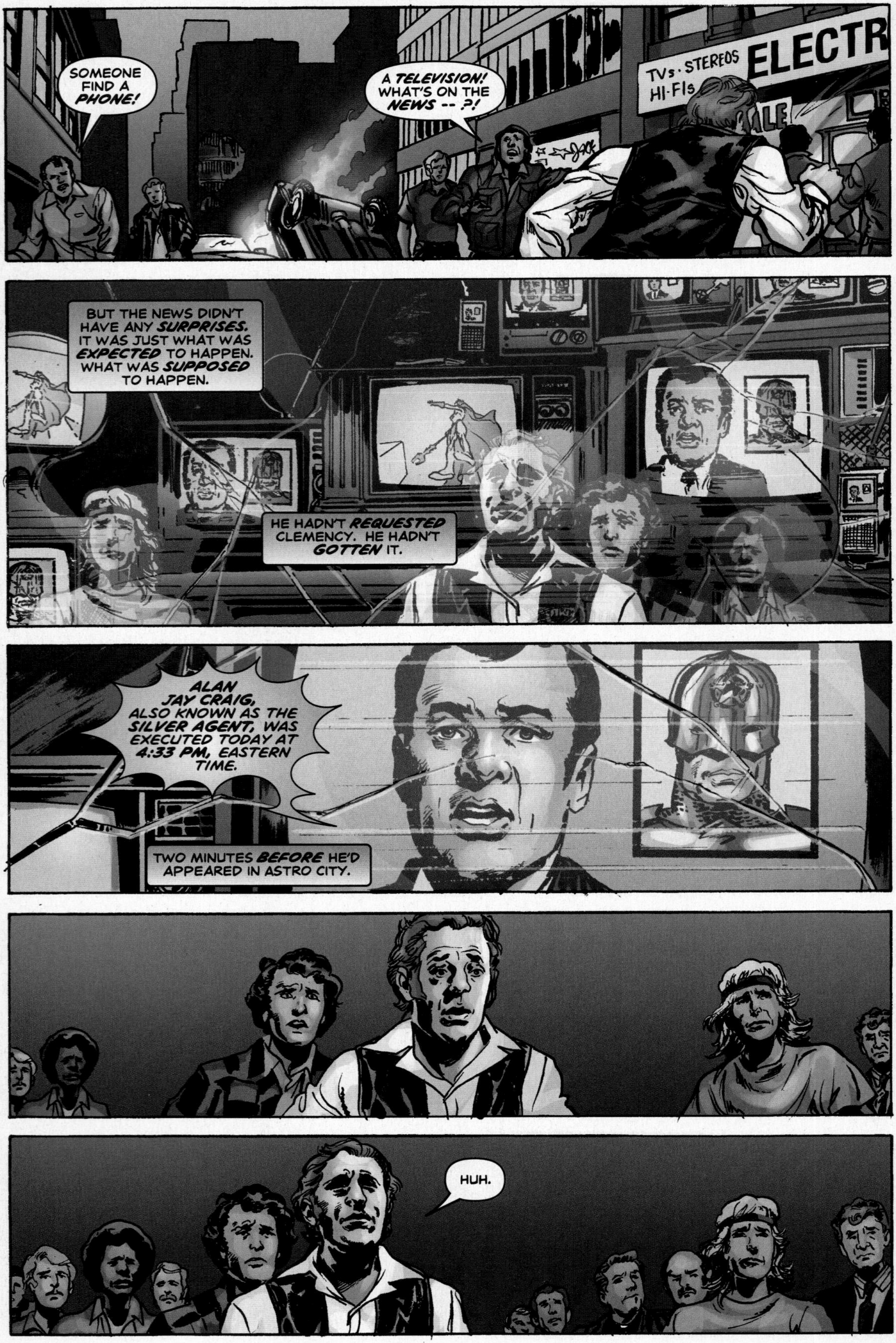
SOMEONE FIND A PHONE!
A TELEVISION! WHAT'S ON THE NEWS -- ?!
TVs · STEREOS HI-FIs
ELECTR
BUT THE NEWS DIDN'T HAVE ANY SURPRISES. IT WAS JUST WHAT WAS EXPECTED TO HAPPEN. WHAT WAS SUPPOSED TO HAPPEN.
HE HADN'T REQUESTED CLEMENCY. HE HADN'T GOTTEN IT.
ALAN JAY CRAIG, ALSO KNOWN AS THE SILVER AGENT, WAS EXECUTED TODAY AT 4:33 PM, EASTERN TIME.
TWO MINUTES BEFORE HE'D APPEARED IN ASTRO CITY.
HUH.

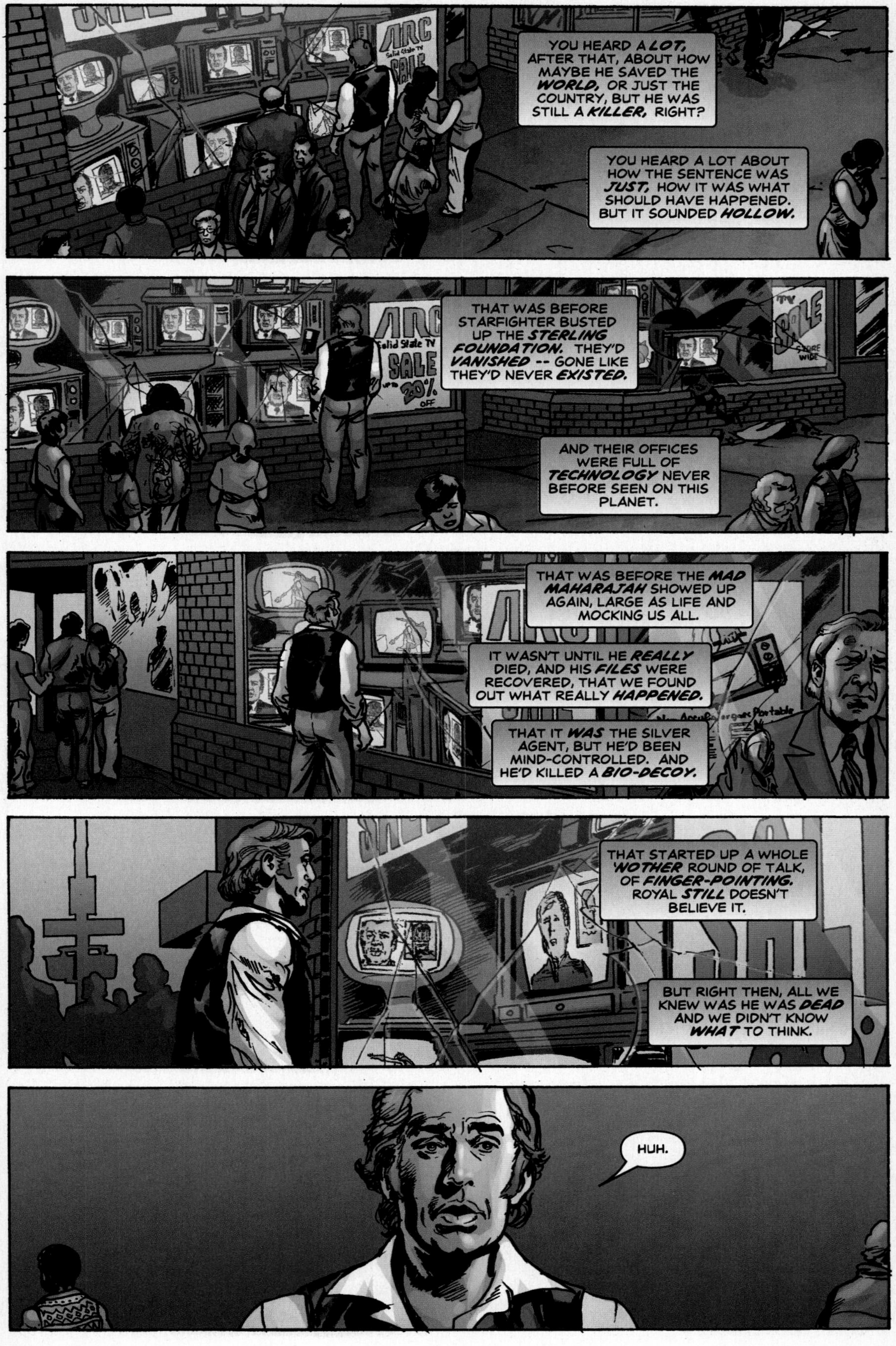
SALE
ARC Solid State TV SALE
YOU HEARD A LOT, AFTER THAT, ABOUT HOW MAYBE HE SAVED THE WORLD, OR JUST THE COUNTRY, BUT HE WAS STILL A KILLER, RIGHT?
YOU HEARD A LOT ABOUT HOW THE SENTENCE WAS JUST, HOW IT WAS WHAT SHOULD HAVE HAPPENED. BUT IT SOUNDED HOLLOW.
ARC Solid State TV SALE UP TO 20% OFF
THAT WAS BEFORE STARFIGHTER BUSTED UP THE STERLING FOUNDATION. THEY'D VANISHED -- GONE LIKE THEY'D NEVER EXISTED.
TV SALE STORE WIDE
AND THEIR OFFICES WERE FULL OF TECHNOLOGY NEVER BEFORE SEEN ON THIS PLANET.
THAT WAS BEFORE THE MAD MAHARAJAH SHOWED UP AGAIN, LARGE AS LIFE AND MOCKING US ALL.
IT WASN'T UNTIL HE REALLY DIED, AND HIS FILES WERE RECOVERED, THAT WE FOUND OUT WHAT REALLY HAPPENED.
THAT IT WAS THE SILVER AGENT, BUT HE'D BEEN MIND-CONTROLLED. AND HE'D KILLED A BIO-DECOY.
THAT STARTED UP A WHOLE 'WOTHER ROUND OF TALK, OF FINGER-POINTING. ROYAL STILL DOESN'T BELIEVE IT.
BUT RIGHT THEN, ALL WE KNEW WAS HE WAS DEAD AND WE DIDN'T KNOW WHAT TO THINK.
HUH.

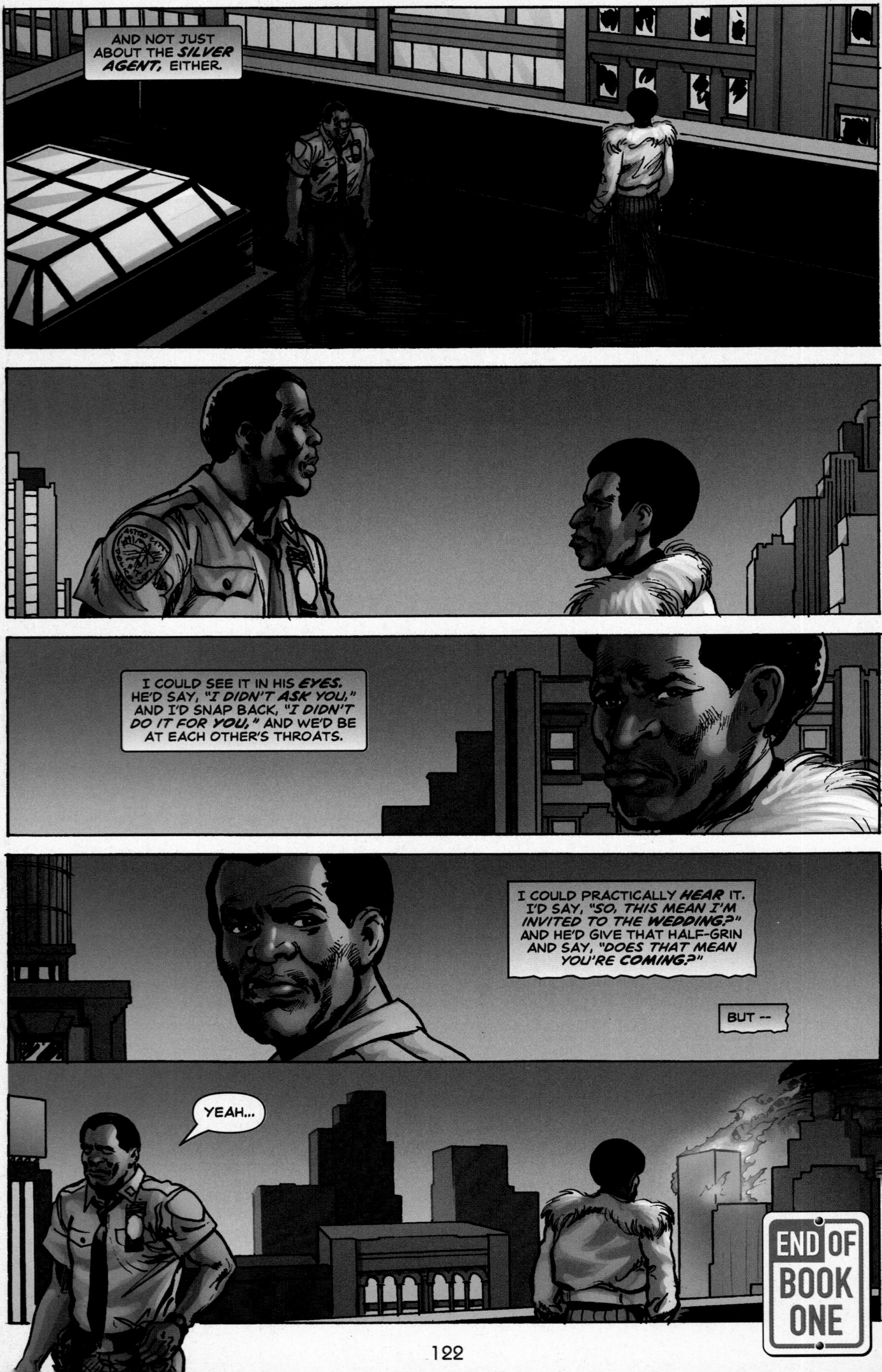
AND NOT JUST ABOUT THE SILVER AGENT, EITHER.
I COULD SEE IT IN HIS EYES. HE'D SAY, "I DIDN'T ASK YOU," AND I'D SNAP BACK, "I DIDN'T DO IT FOR YOU," AND WE'D BE AT EACH OTHER'S THROATS.
I COULD PRACTICALLY HEAR IT. I'D SAY, "SO, THIS MEAN I'M INVITED TO THE WEDDING?" AND HE'D GIVE THAT HALF-GRIN AND SAY, "DOES THAT MEAN YOU'RE COMING?"
BUT --
YEAH...
END OF BOOK ONE

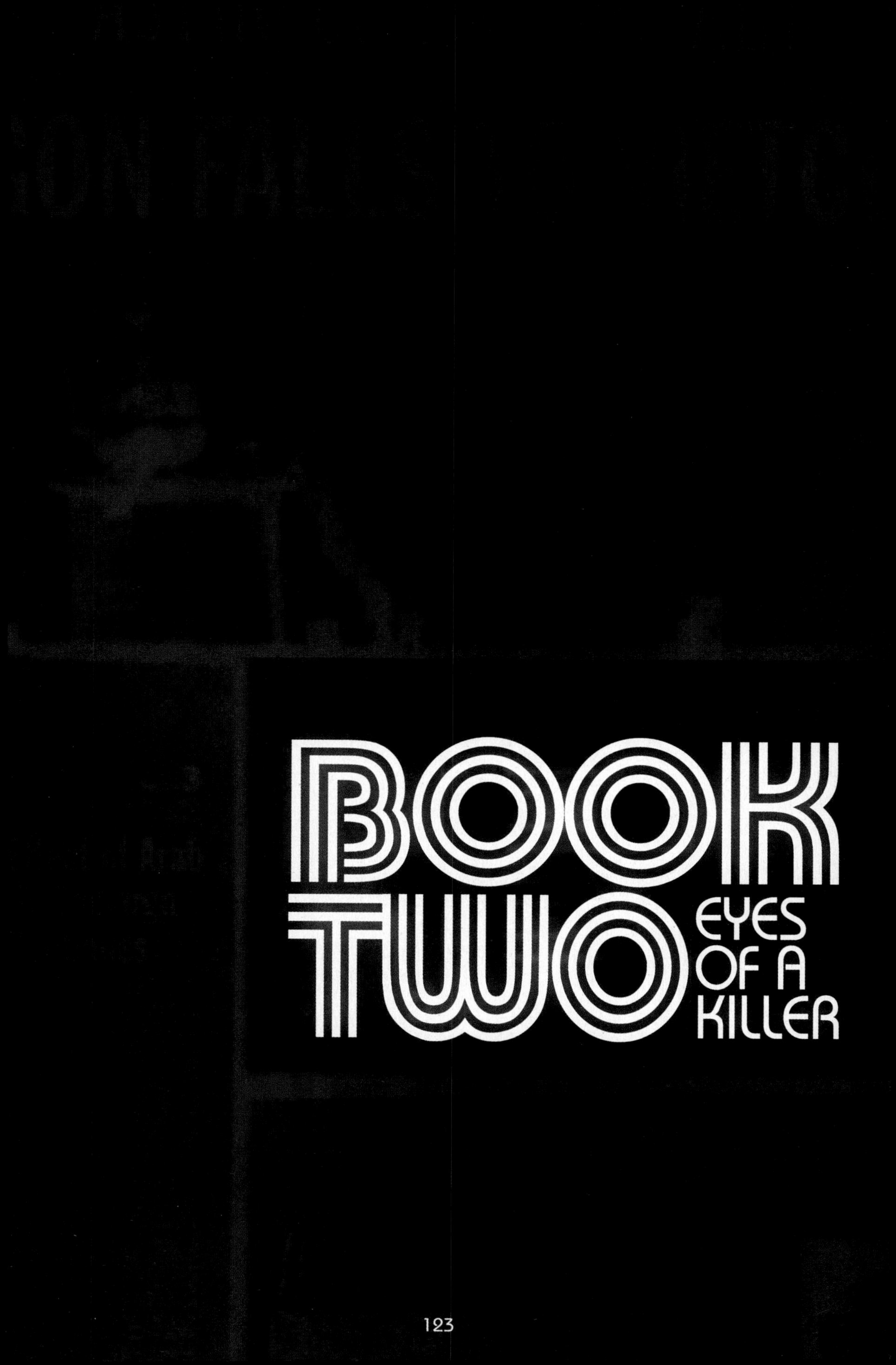

BOOK TWO

EYES OF A KILLER

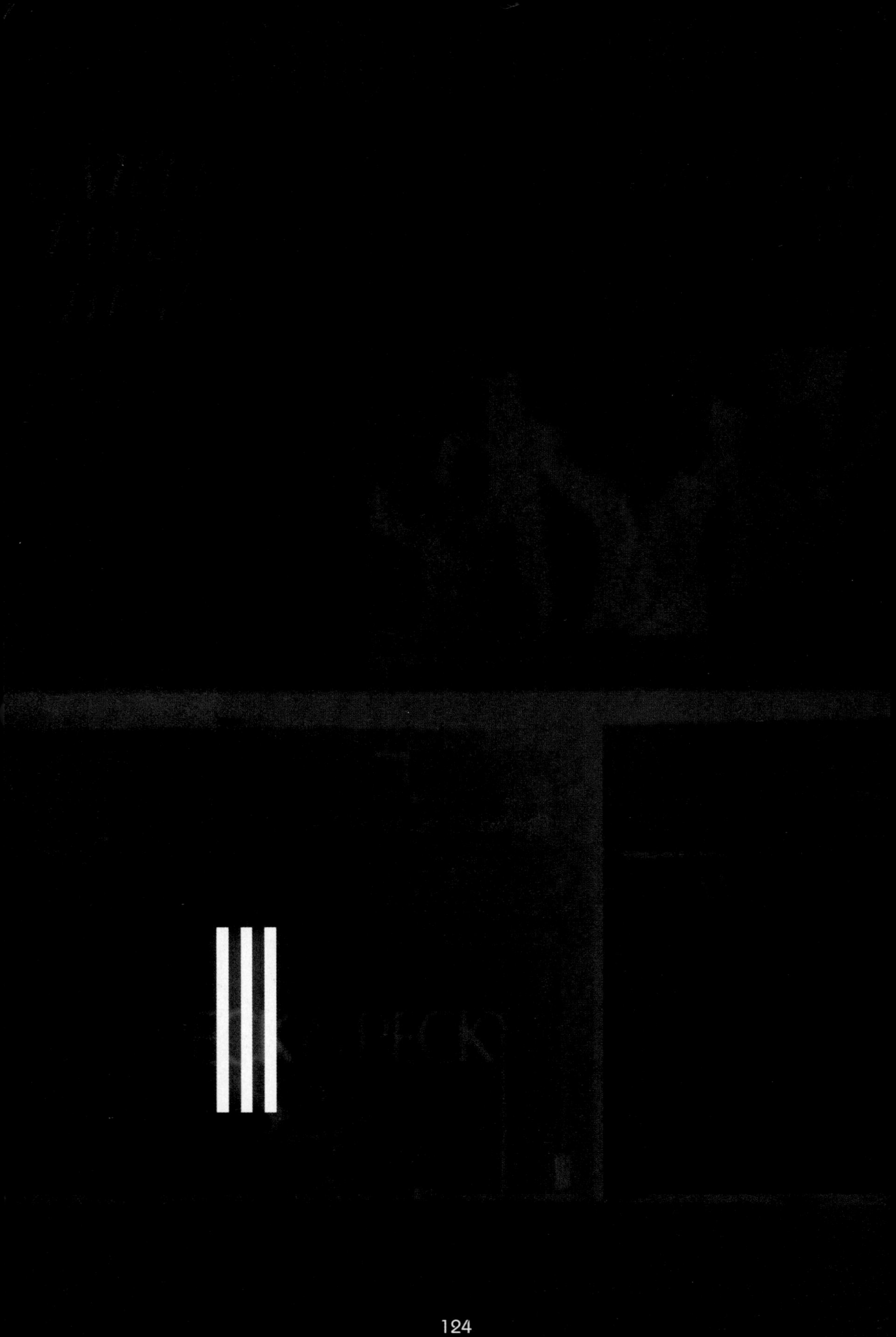
III

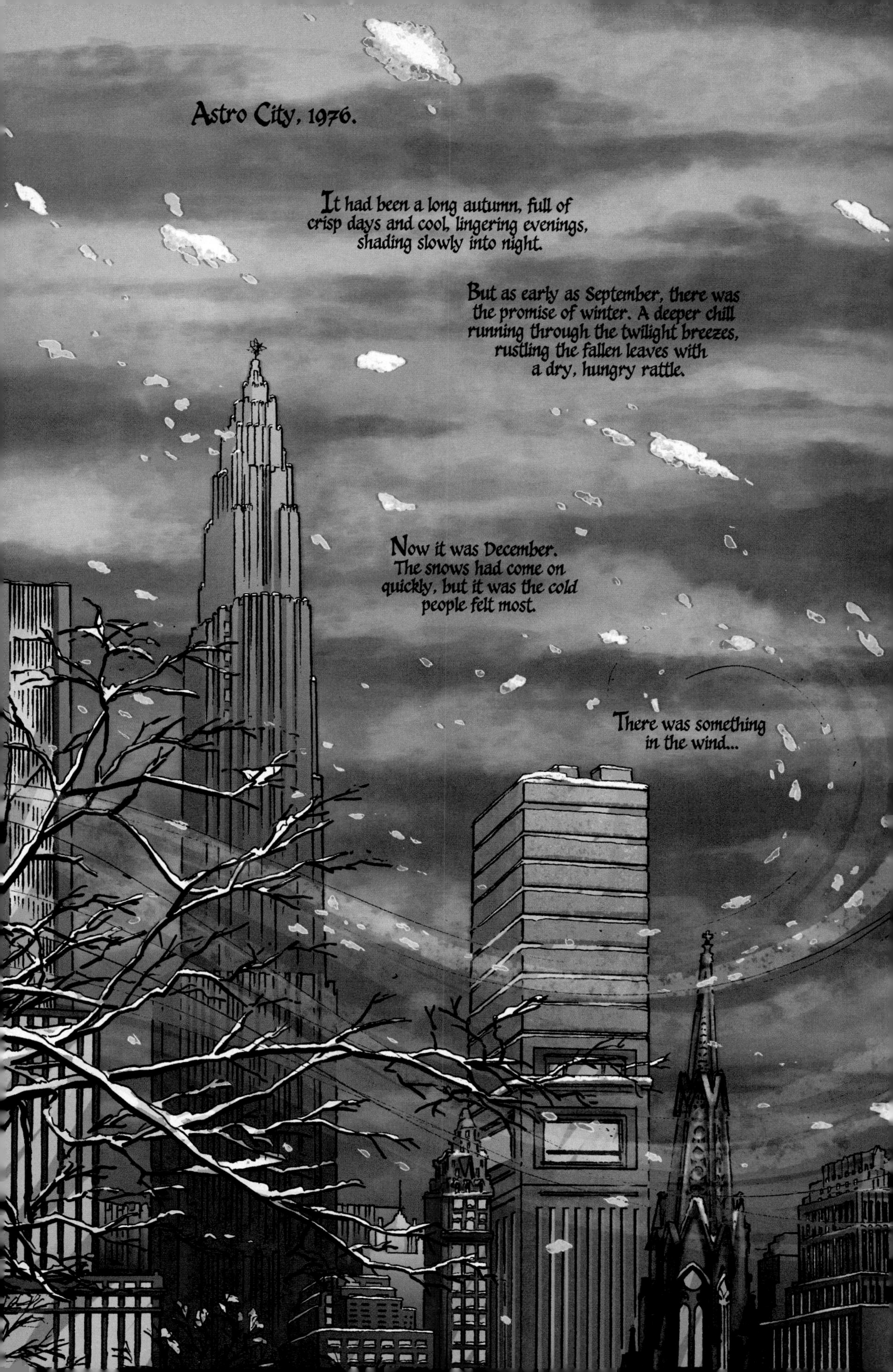
Astro City, 1976.
It had been a long autumn, full of crisp days and cool, lingering evenings, shading slowly into night.
But as early as September, there was the promise of winter. A deeper chill running through the twilight breezes, rustling the fallen leaves with a dry, hungry rattle.
Now it was December. The snows had come on quickly, but it was the cold people felt most.
There was something in the wind...

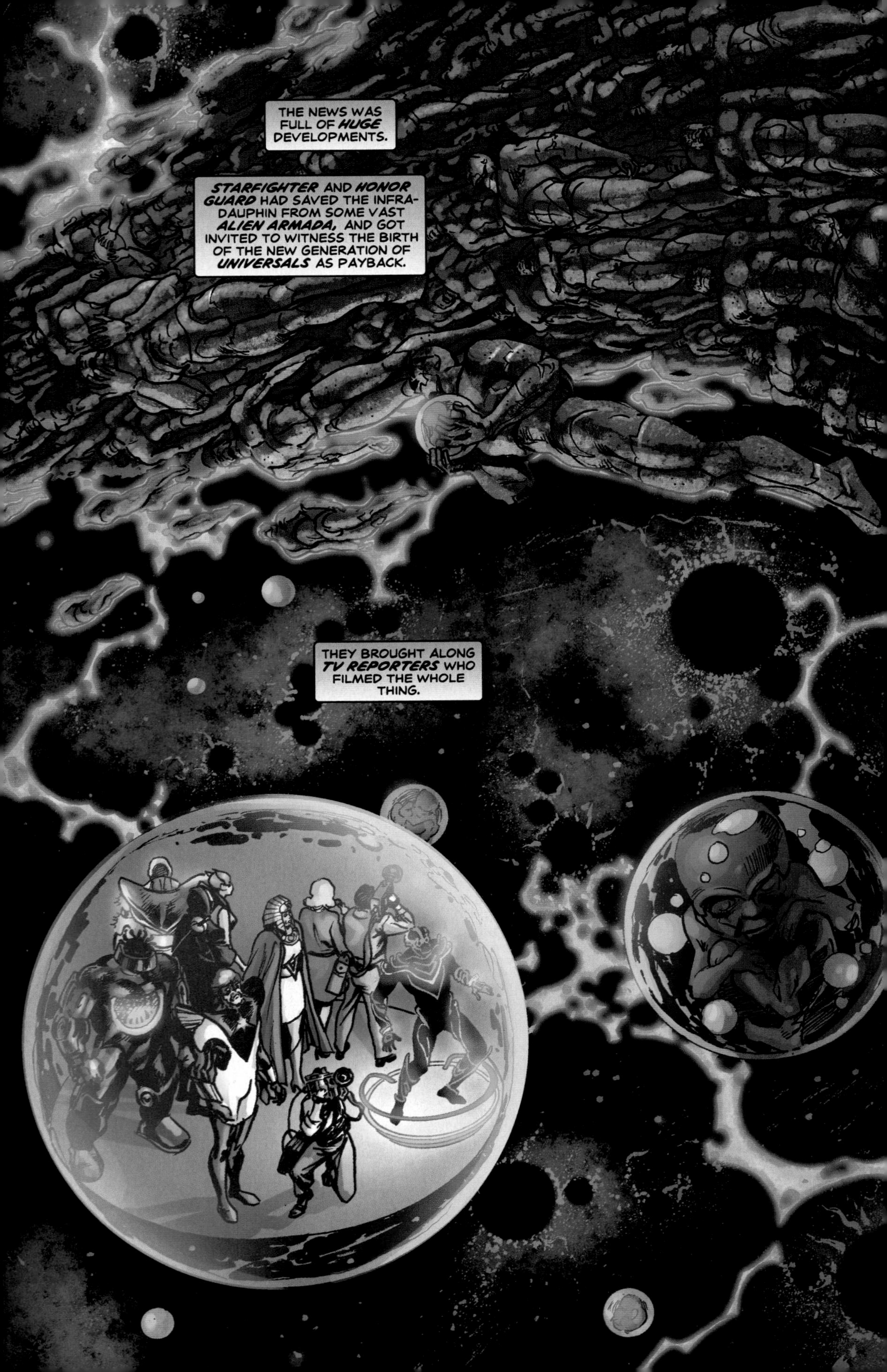
THE NEWS WAS FULL OF HUGE DEVELOPMENTS.
STARFIGHTER AND HONOR GUARD HAD SAVED THE INFRA-DAUPHIN FROM SOME VAST ALIEN ARMADA, AND GOT INVITED TO WITNESS THE BIRTH OF THE NEW GENERATION OF UNIVERSALS AS PAYBACK.
THEY BROUGHT ALONG TV REPORTERS WHO FILMED THE WHOLE THING.

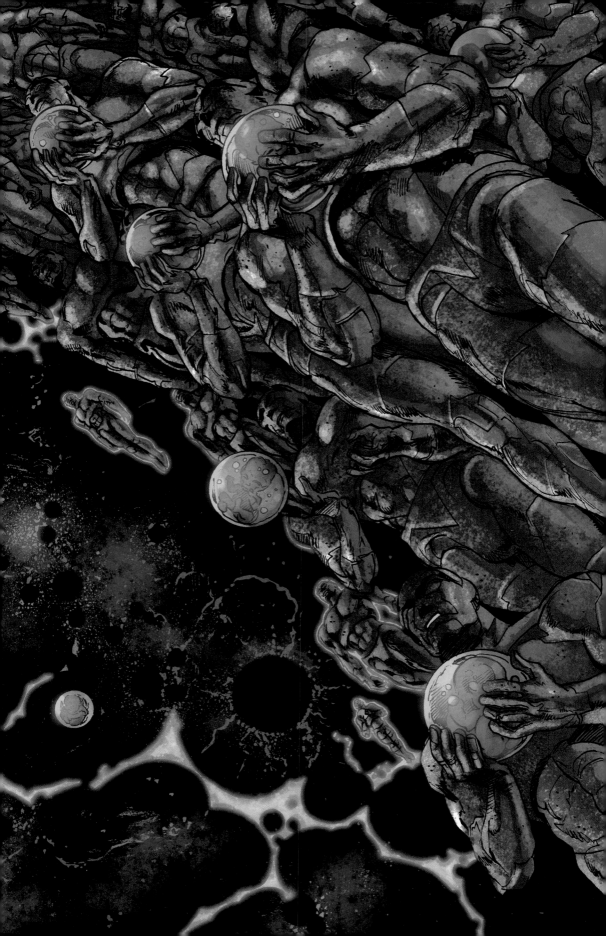

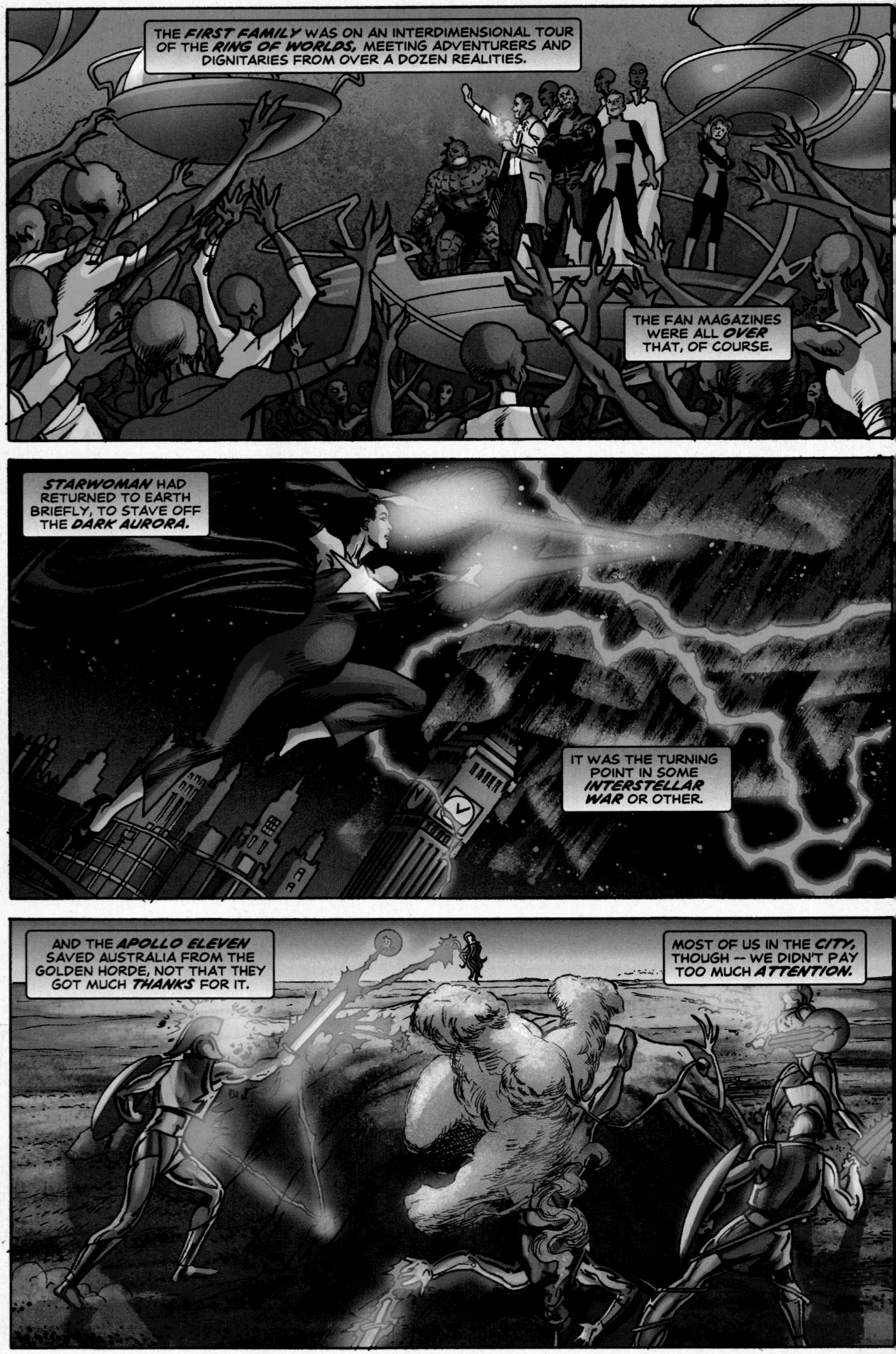
THE FIRST FAMILY WAS ON AN INTERDIMENSIONAL TOUR OF THE RING OF WORLDS, MEETING ADVENTURERS AND DIGNITARIES FROM OVER A DOZEN REALITIES.
THE FAN MAGAZINES WERE ALL OVER THAT, OF COURSE.
STARWOMAN HAD RETURNED TO EARTH BRIEFLY, TO STAVE OFF THE DARK AURORA.
IT WAS THE TURNING POINT IN SOME INTERSTELLAR WAR OR OTHER.
AND THE APOLLO ELEVEN SAVED AUSTRALIA FROM THE GOLDEN HORDE, NOT THAT THEY GOT MUCH THANKS FOR IT.
MOST OF US IN THE CITY, THOUGH -- WE DIDN'T PAY TOO MUCH ATTENTION.

WE HAD *OTHER THINGS* TO DEAL WITH.
玉龍酒樓
CHINESE AMERICAN FOOD
CHINESE AMERICAN FOOD
A COLD WIND BLOWING

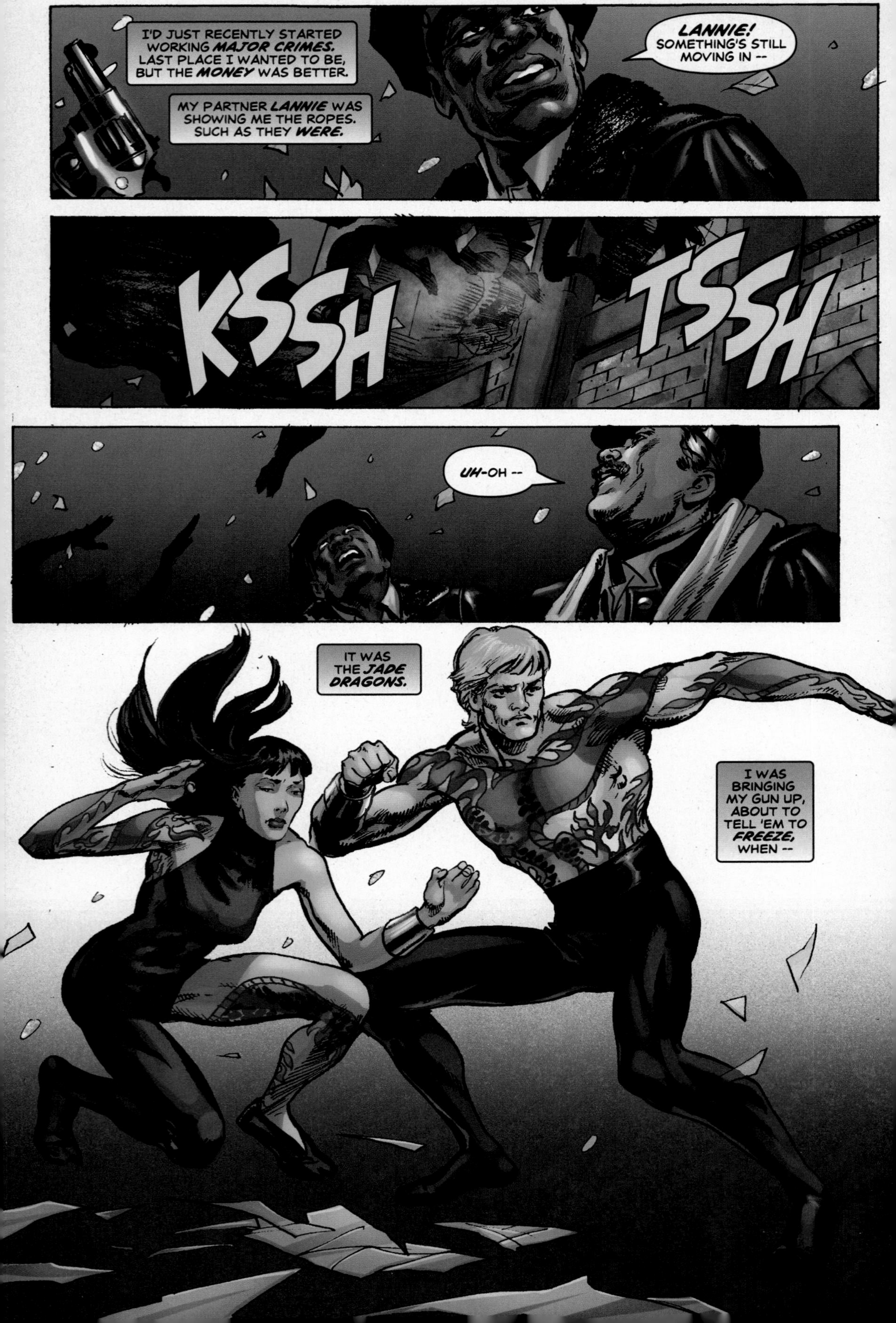
I'D JUST RECENTLY STARTED WORKING MAJOR CRIMES. LAST PLACE I WANTED TO BE, BUT THE MONEY WAS BETTER.
MY PARTNER LANNIE WAS SHOWING ME THE ROPES. SUCH AS THEY WERE.
LANNIE! SOMETHING'S STILL MOVING IN --
KSSH
TSSH
UH-OH --
IT WAS THE JADE DRAGONS.
I WAS BRINGING MY GUN UP, ABOUT TO TELL 'EM TO FREEZE, WHEN --

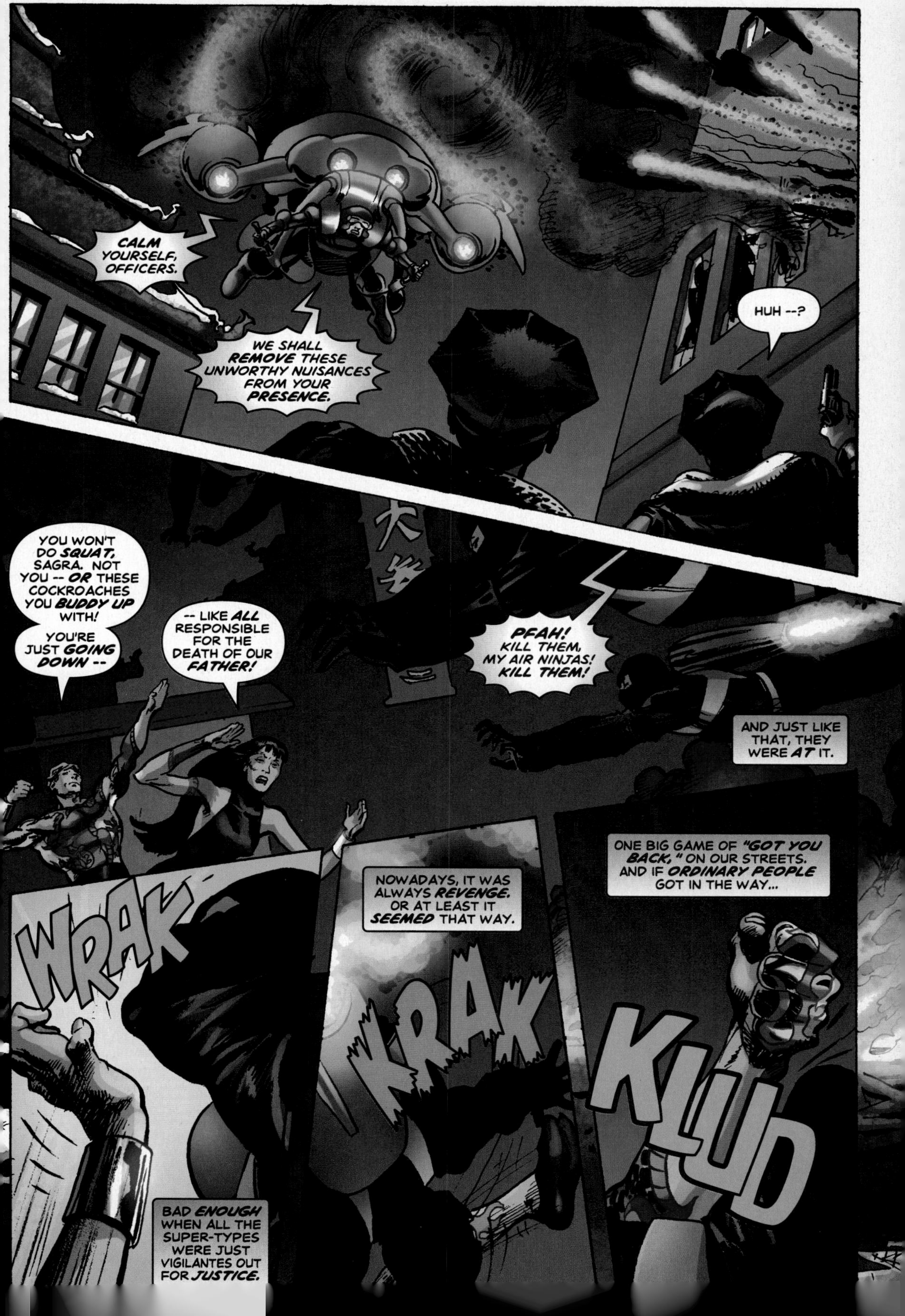
CALM YOURSELF, OFFICERS.
WE SHALL REMOVE THESE UNWORTHY NUISANCES FROM YOUR PRESENCE.
HUH --?
YOU WON'T DO SQUAT, SAGRA. NOT YOU -- OR THESE COCKROACHES YOU BUDDY UP WITH!
YOU'RE JUST GOING DOWN --
-- LIKE ALL RESPONSIBLE FOR THE DEATH OF OUR FATHER!
PFAH! KILL THEM, MY AIR NINJAS! KILL THEM!
AND JUST LIKE THAT, THEY WERE AT IT.
WRAK
BAD ENOUGH WHEN ALL THE SUPER-TYPES WERE JUST VIGILANTES OUT FOR JUSTICE.
NOWADAYS, IT WAS ALWAYS REVENGE. OR AT LEAST IT SEEMED THAT WAY.
KRAK
ONE BIG GAME OF "GOT YOU BACK," ON OUR STREETS. AND IF ORDINARY PEOPLE GOT IN THE WAY...
KLUD

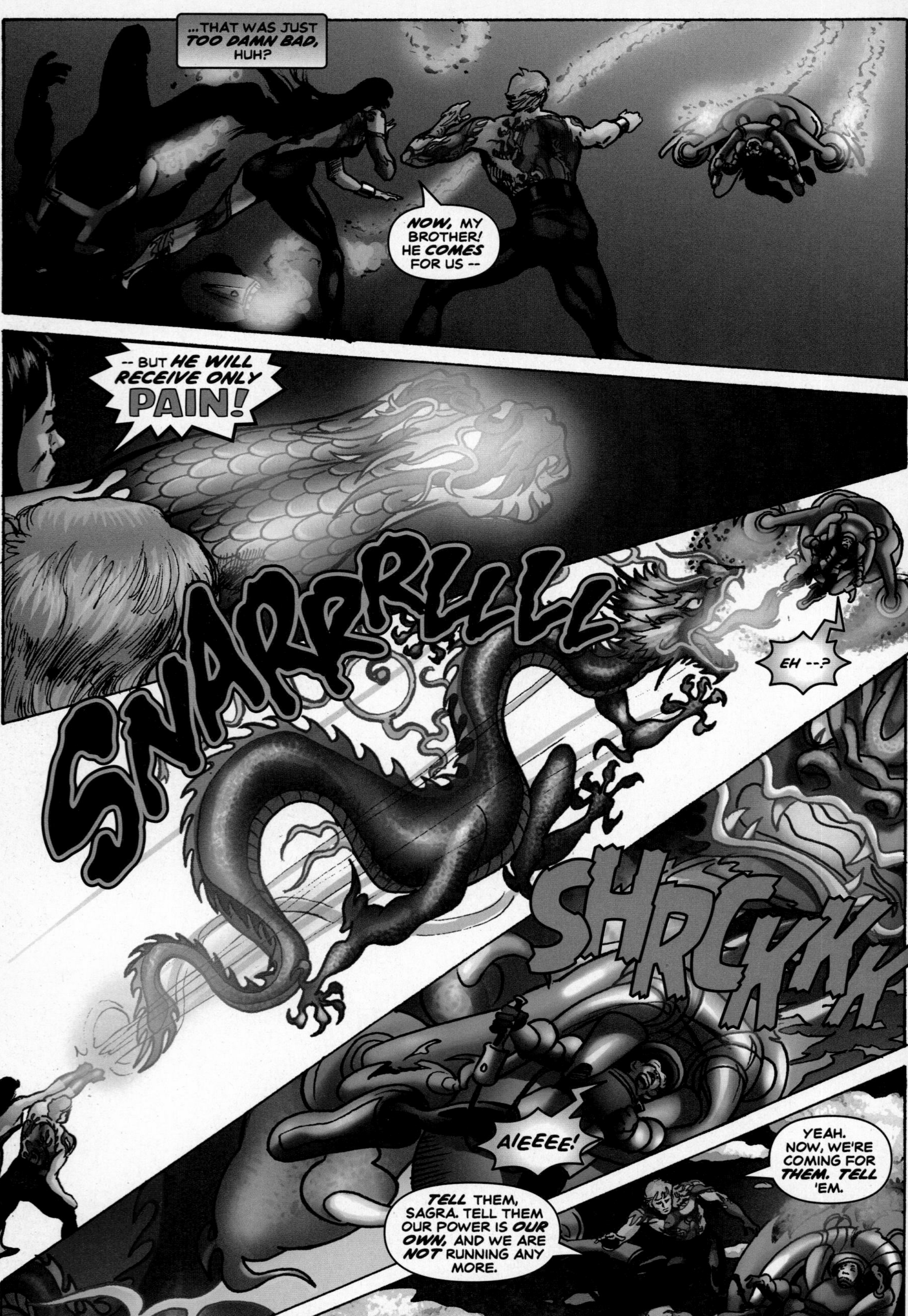
...THAT WAS JUST TOO DAMN BAD, HUH?
NOW, MY BROTHER! HE COMES FOR US --
-- BUT HE WILL RECEIVE ONLY PAIN!
SNARRRLLLL
EH --?
SHRCKKK
AIEEEE!
TELL THEM, SAGRA. TELL THEM OUR POWER IS OUR OWN, AND WE ARE NOT RUNNING ANY MORE.
YEAH. NOW, WE'RE COMING FOR THEM. TELL 'EM.

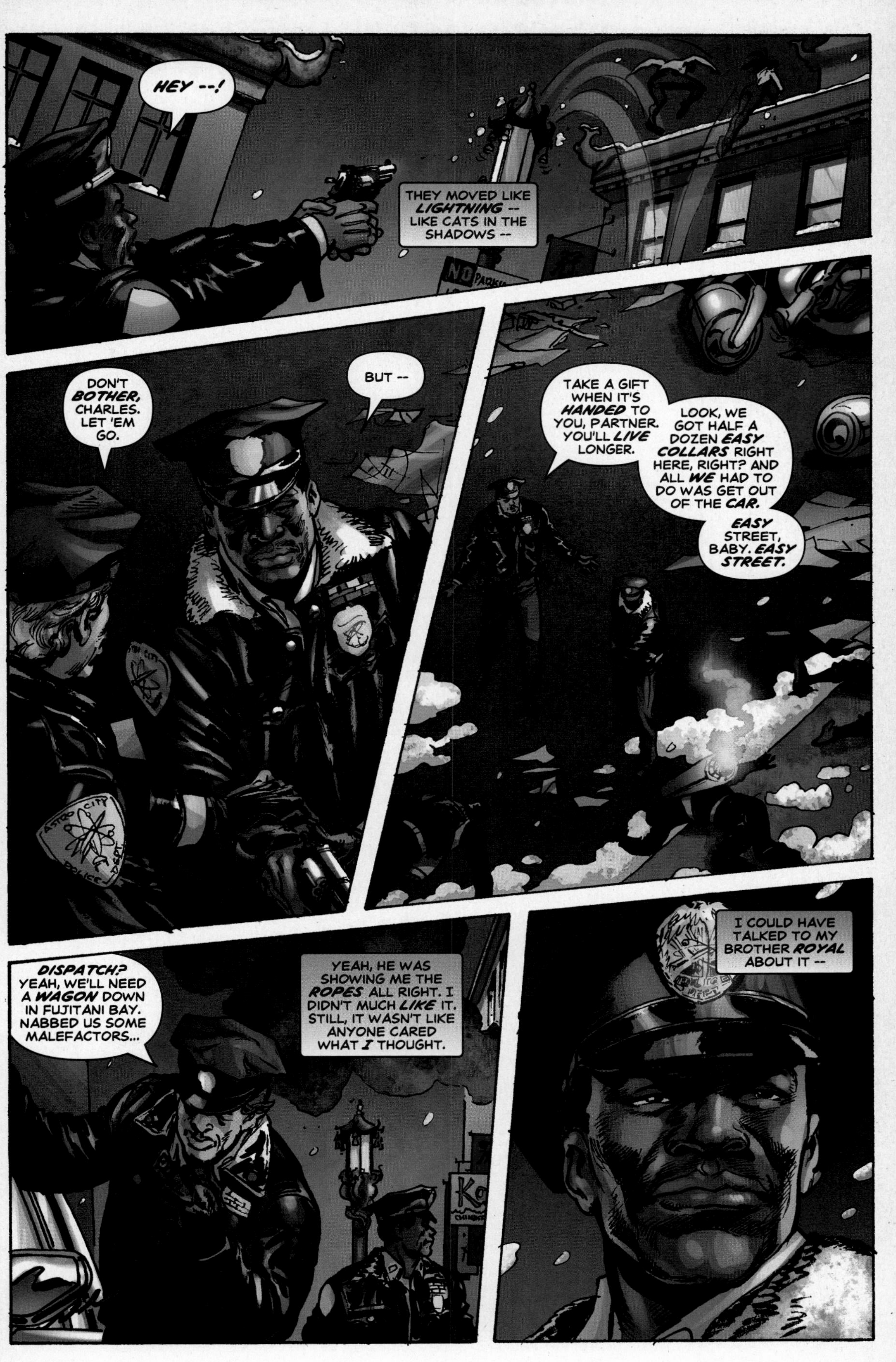
HEY --!
THEY MOVED LIKE LIGHTNING -- LIKE CATS IN THE SHADOWS --
NO PARKI
DON'T BOTHER, CHARLES. LET 'EM GO.
BUT --
TAKE A GIFT WHEN IT'S HANDED TO YOU, PARTNER. YOU'LL LIVE LONGER.
LOOK, WE GOT HALF A DOZEN EASY COLLARS RIGHT HERE, RIGHT? AND ALL WE HAD TO DO WAS GET OUT OF THE CAR.
EASY STREET, BABY. EASY STREET.
DISPATCH? YEAH, WE'LL NEED A WAGON DOWN IN FUJITANI BAY. NABBED US SOME MALEFACTORS...
YEAH, HE WAS SHOWING ME THE ROPES ALL RIGHT. I DIDN'T MUCH LIKE IT. STILL, IT WASN'T LIKE ANYONE CARED WHAT I THOUGHT.
I COULD HAVE TALKED TO MY BROTHER ROYAL ABOUT IT --

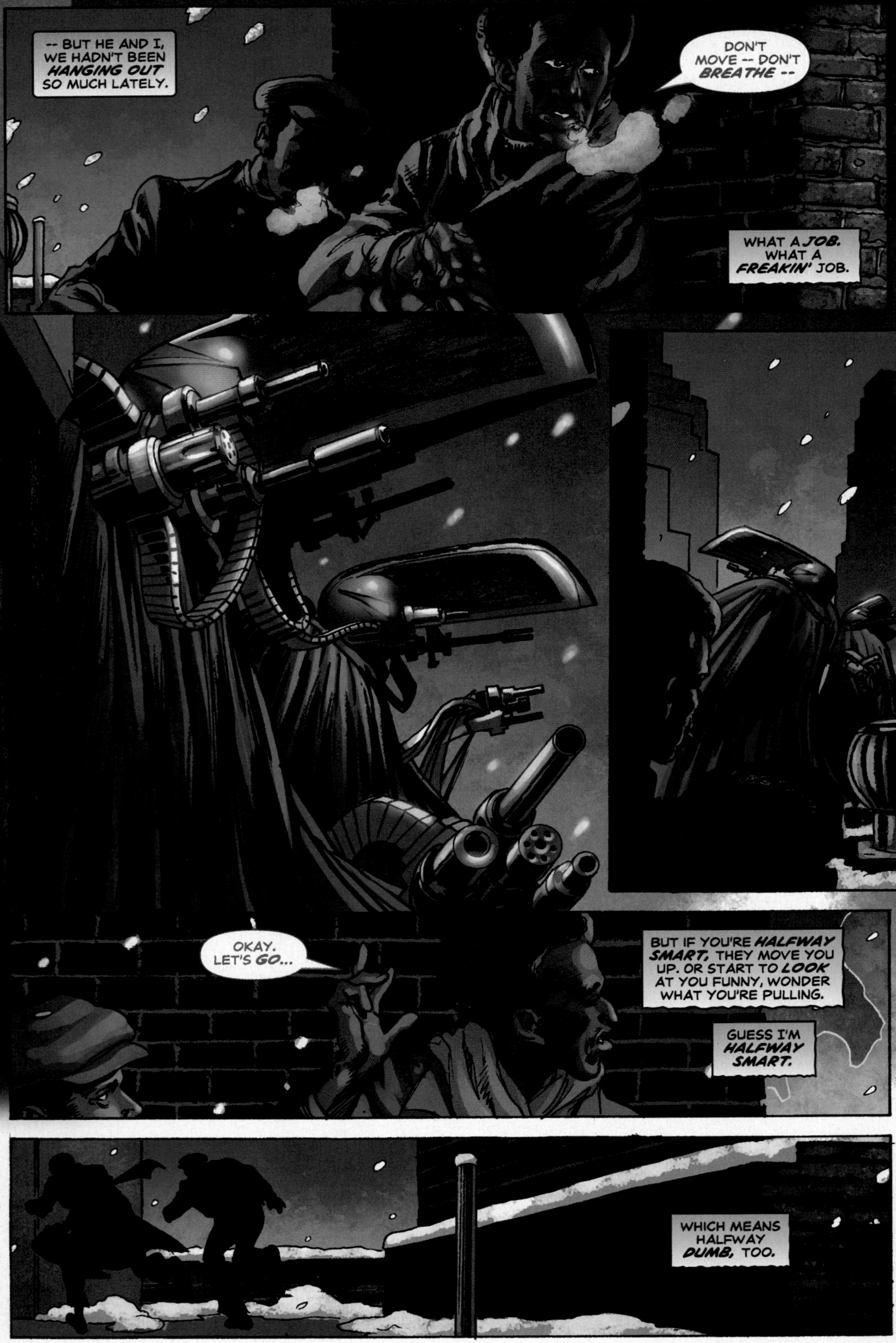
-- BUT HE AND I, WE HADN'T BEEN HANGING OUT SO MUCH LATELY.
DON'T MOVE -- DON'T BREATHE --
WHAT A JOB. WHAT A FREAKIN' JOB.
OKAY. LET'S GO...
BUT IF YOU'RE HALFWAY SMART, THEY MOVE YOU UP. OR START TO LOOK AT YOU FUNNY, WONDER WHAT YOU'RE PULLING.
GUESS I'M HALFWAY SMART.
WHICH MEANS HALFWAY DUMB, TOO.

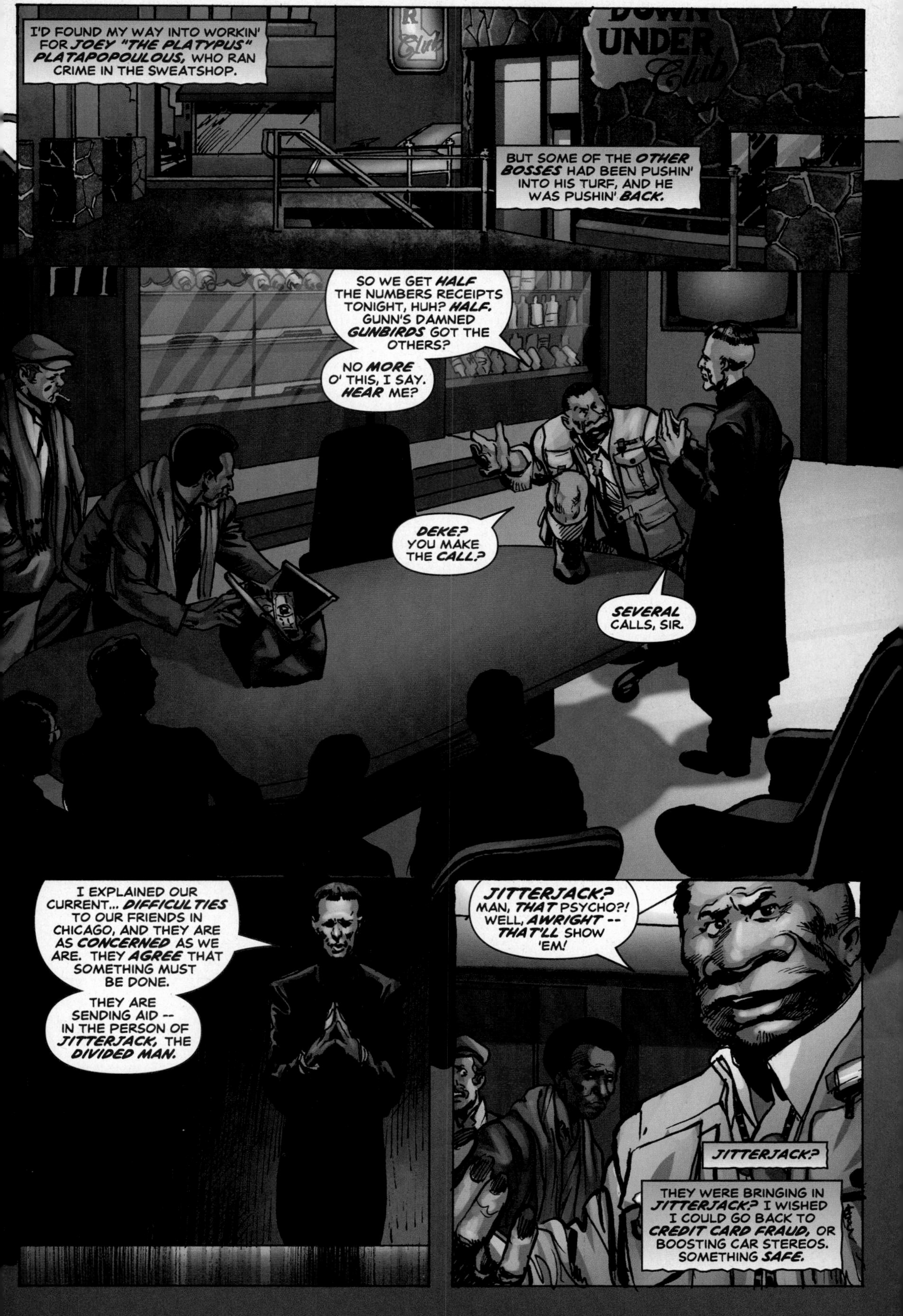
I'D FOUND MY WAY INTO WORKIN' FOR JOEY "THE PLATYPUS" PLATAPOPOULOUS, WHO RAN CRIME IN THE SWEATSHOP.
R Club
DOWN UNDER Club
BUT SOME OF THE OTHER BOSSES HAD BEEN PUSHIN' INTO HIS TURF, AND HE WAS PUSHIN' BACK.
SO WE GET HALF THE NUMBERS RECEIPTS TONIGHT, HUH? HALF. GUNN'S DAMNED GUNBIRDS GOT THE OTHERS?
NO MORE O' THIS, I SAY. HEAR ME?
DEKE? YOU MAKE THE CALL?
SEVERAL CALLS, SIR.
I EXPLAINED OUR CURRENT... DIFFICULTIES TO OUR FRIENDS IN CHICAGO, AND THEY ARE AS CONCERNED AS WE ARE. THEY AGREE THAT SOMETHING MUST BE DONE.
THEY ARE SENDING AID -- IN THE PERSON OF JITTERJACK, THE DIVIDED MAN.
JITTERJACK? MAN, THAT PSYCHO?! WELL, AWRIGHT -- THAT'LL SHOW 'EM!
JITTERJACK?
THEY WERE BRINGING IN JITTERJACK? I WISHED I COULD GO BACK TO CREDIT CARD FRAUD, OR BOOSTING CAR STEREOS. SOMETHING SAFE.

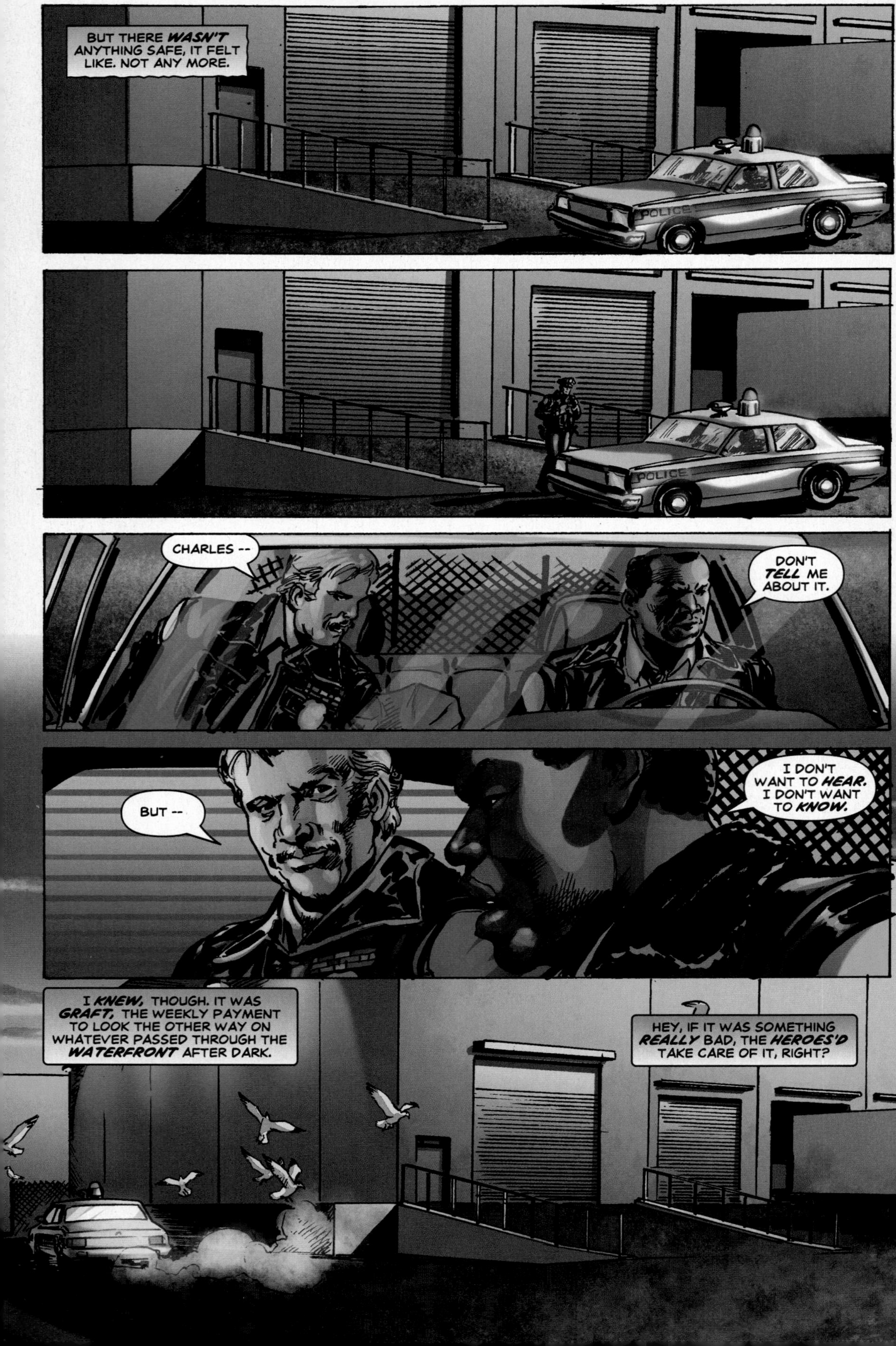

BUT THERE WASN'T ANYTHING SAFE, IT FELT LIKE. NOT ANY MORE.
POLICE
POLICE
CHARLES --
DON'T TELL ME ABOUT IT.
BUT --
I DON'T WANT TO HEAR. I DON'T WANT TO KNOW.
I KNEW, THOUGH. IT WAS GRAFT, THE WEEKLY PAYMENT TO LOOK THE OTHER WAY ON WHATEVER PASSED THROUGH THE WATERFRONT AFTER DARK.
HEY, IF IT WAS SOMETHING REALLY BAD, THE HEROES'D TAKE CARE OF IT, RIGHT?

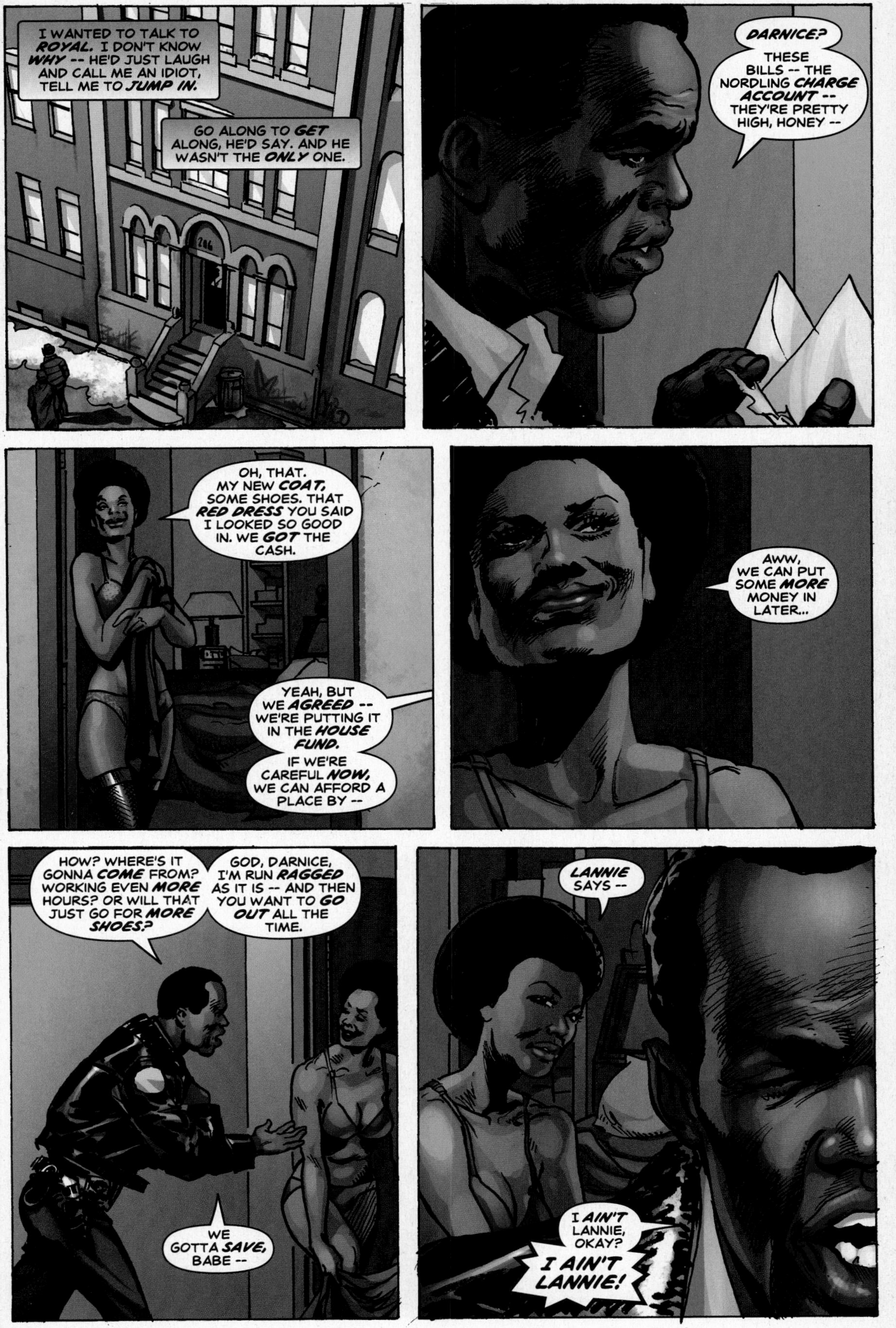
I WANTED TO TALK TO ROYAL. I DON'T KNOW WHY -- HE'D JUST LAUGH AND CALL ME AN IDIOT, TELL ME TO JUMP IN.
GO ALONG TO GET ALONG, HE'D SAY. AND HE WASN'T THE ONLY ONE.
DARNICE?
THESE BILLS -- THE NORDLING CHARGE ACCOUNT -- THEY'RE PRETTY HIGH, HONEY --
OH, THAT. MY NEW COAT, SOME SHOES. THAT RED DRESS YOU SAID I LOOKED SO GOOD IN. WE GOT THE CASH.
YEAH, BUT WE AGREED -- WE'RE PUTTING IT IN THE HOUSE FUND.
IF WE'RE CAREFUL NOW, WE CAN AFFORD A PLACE BY --
AWW, WE CAN PUT SOME MORE MONEY IN LATER...
WE GOTTA SAVE, BABE --
HOW? WHERE'S IT GONNA COME FROM? WORKING EVEN MORE HOURS? OR WILL THAT JUST GO FOR MORE SHOES?
GOD, DARNICE, I'M RUN RAGGED AS IT IS -- AND THEN YOU WANT TO GO OUT ALL THE TIME.
LANNIE SAYS --
I AIN'T LANNIE, OKAY?
I AIN'T LANNIE!

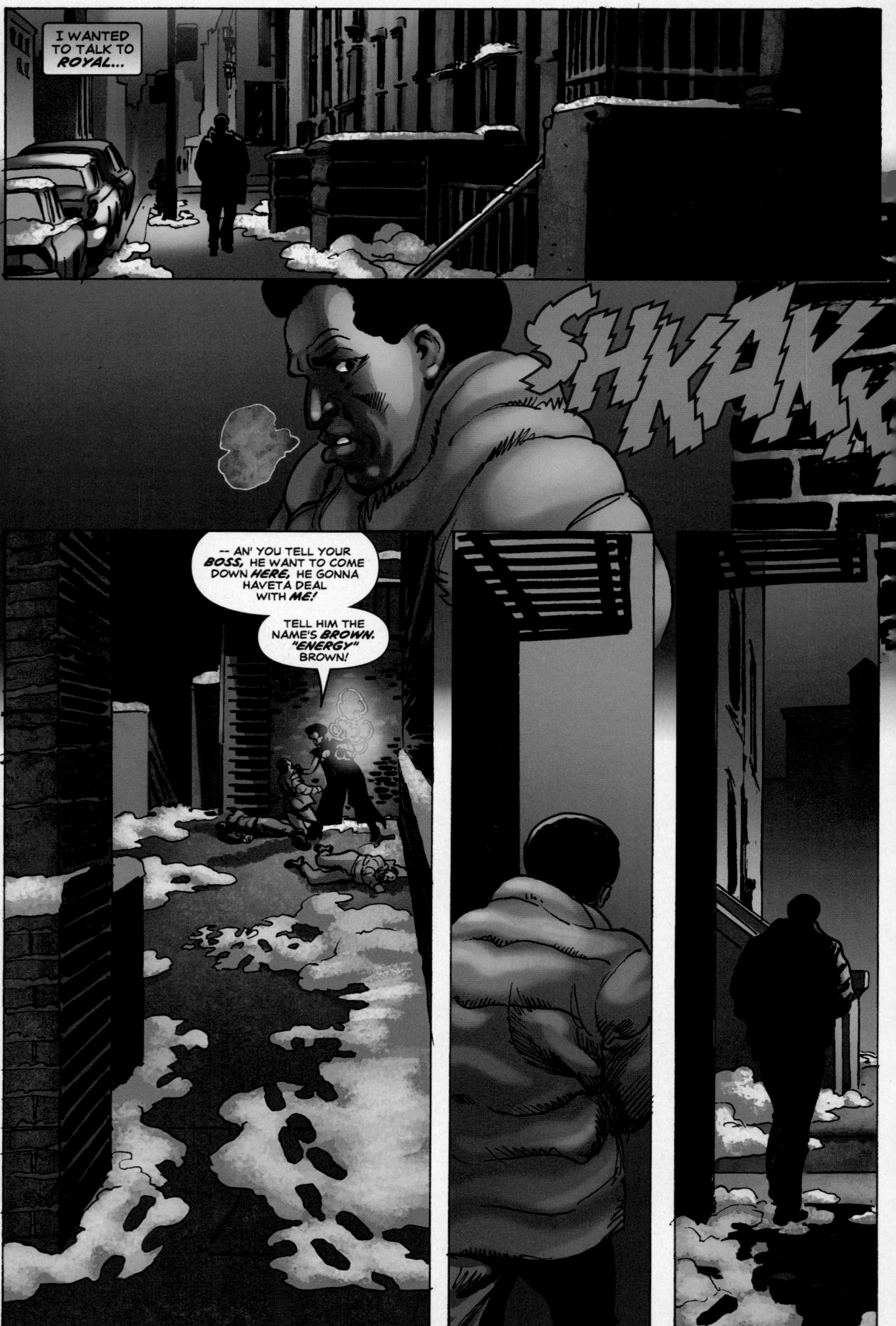
I WANTED TO TALK TO ROYAL...
SHKAK
-- AN' YOU TELL YOUR BOSS, HE WANT TO COME DOWN HERE, HE GONNA HAVETA DEAL WITH ME!
TELL HIM THE NAME'S BROWN. "ENERGY" BROWN!

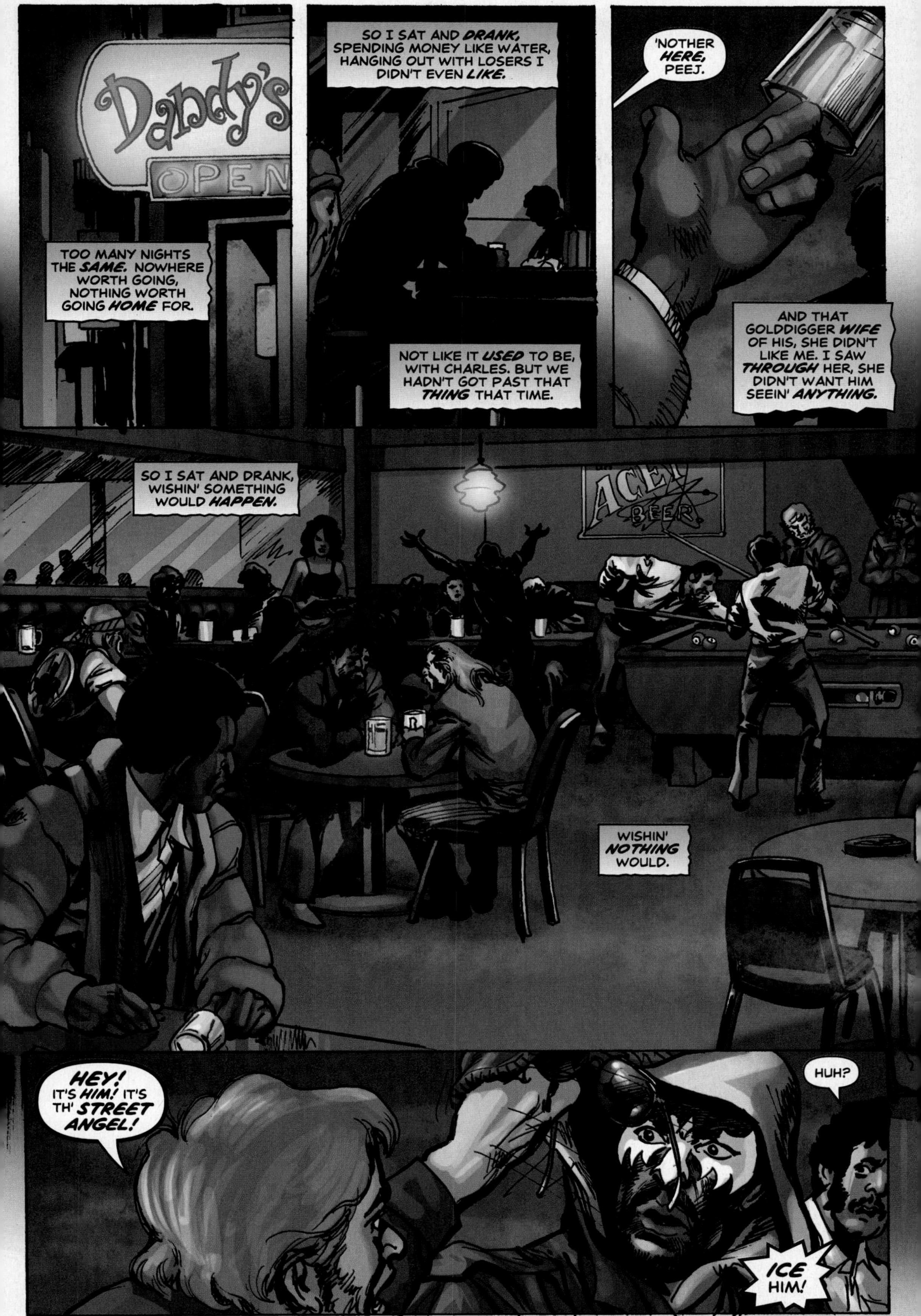
Dandy's
OPEN
TOO MANY NIGHTS THE SAME. NOWHERE WORTH GOING, NOTHING WORTH GOING HOME FOR.
SO I SAT AND DRANK, SPENDING MONEY LIKE WATER, HANGING OUT WITH LOSERS I DIDN'T EVEN LIKE.
NOT LIKE IT USED TO BE, WITH CHARLES. BUT WE HADN'T GOT PAST THAT THING THAT TIME.
'NOTHER HERE, PEEJ.
AND THAT GOLDDIGGER WIFE OF HIS, SHE DIDN'T LIKE ME. I SAW THROUGH HER, SHE DIDN'T WANT HIM SEEIN' ANYTHING.
SO I SAT AND DRANK, WISHIN' SOMETHING WOULD HAPPEN.
BEER
WISHIN' NOTHING WOULD.
HEY! IT'S HIM! IT'S TH' STREET ANGEL!
HUH?
ICE HIM!

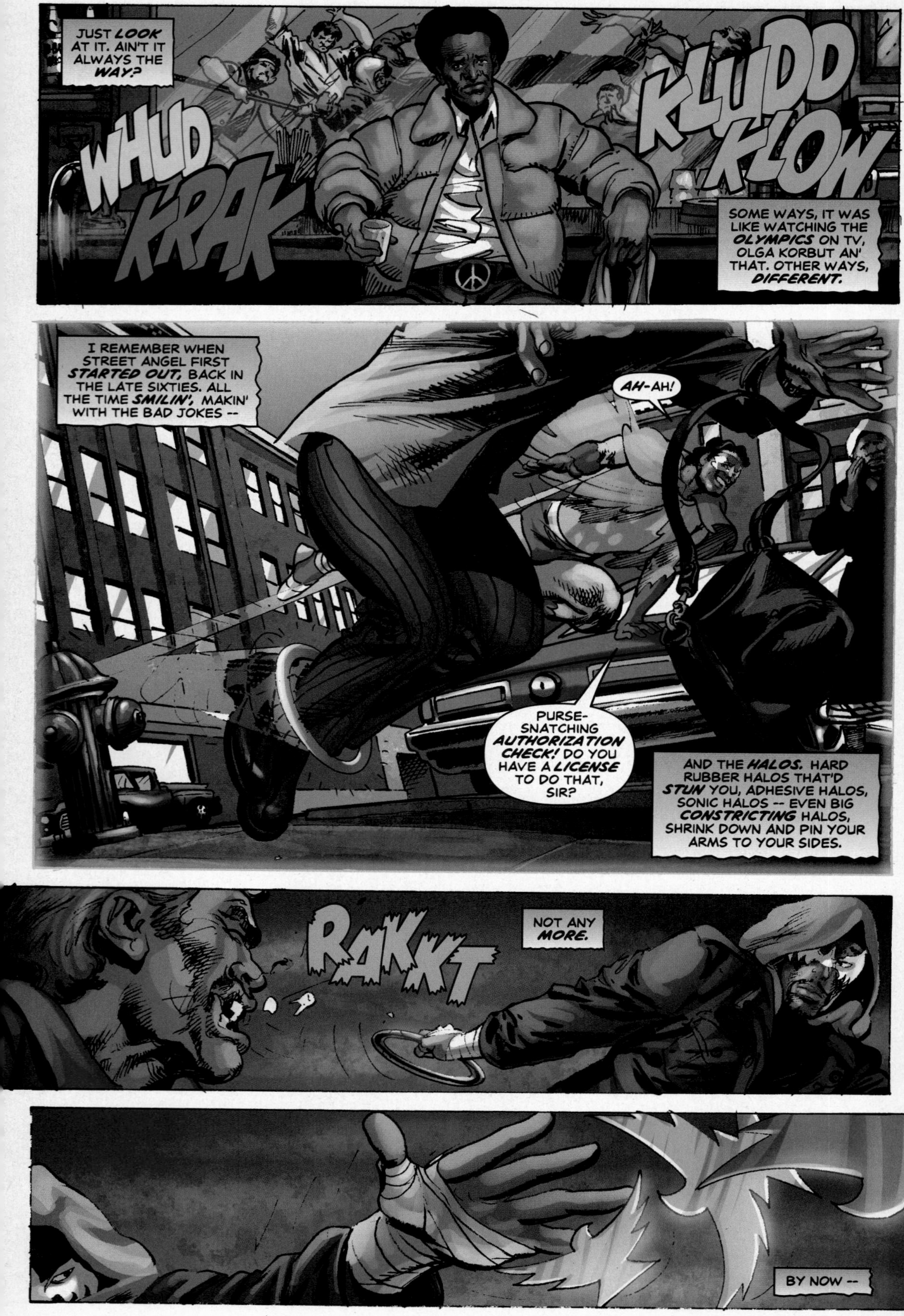
JUST LOOK AT IT. AIN'T IT ALWAYS THE WAY?
WHUD
KRAK
KLUDD
KLOW
SOME WAYS, IT WAS LIKE WATCHING THE OLYMPICS ON TV, OLGA KORBUT AN' THAT. OTHER WAYS, DIFFERENT.
I REMEMBER WHEN STREET ANGEL FIRST STARTED OUT, BACK IN THE LATE SIXTIES. ALL THE TIME SMILIN', MAKIN' WITH THE BAD JOKES --
AH-AH!
PURSE-SNATCHING AUTHORIZATION CHECK! DO YOU HAVE A LICENSE TO DO THAT, SIR?
AND THE HALOS. HARD RUBBER HALOS THAT'D STUN YOU, ADHESIVE HALOS, SONIC HALOS -- EVEN BIG CONSTRICTING HALOS, SHRINK DOWN AND PIN YOUR ARMS TO YOUR SIDES.
RAKKKT
NOT ANY MORE.
BY NOW --

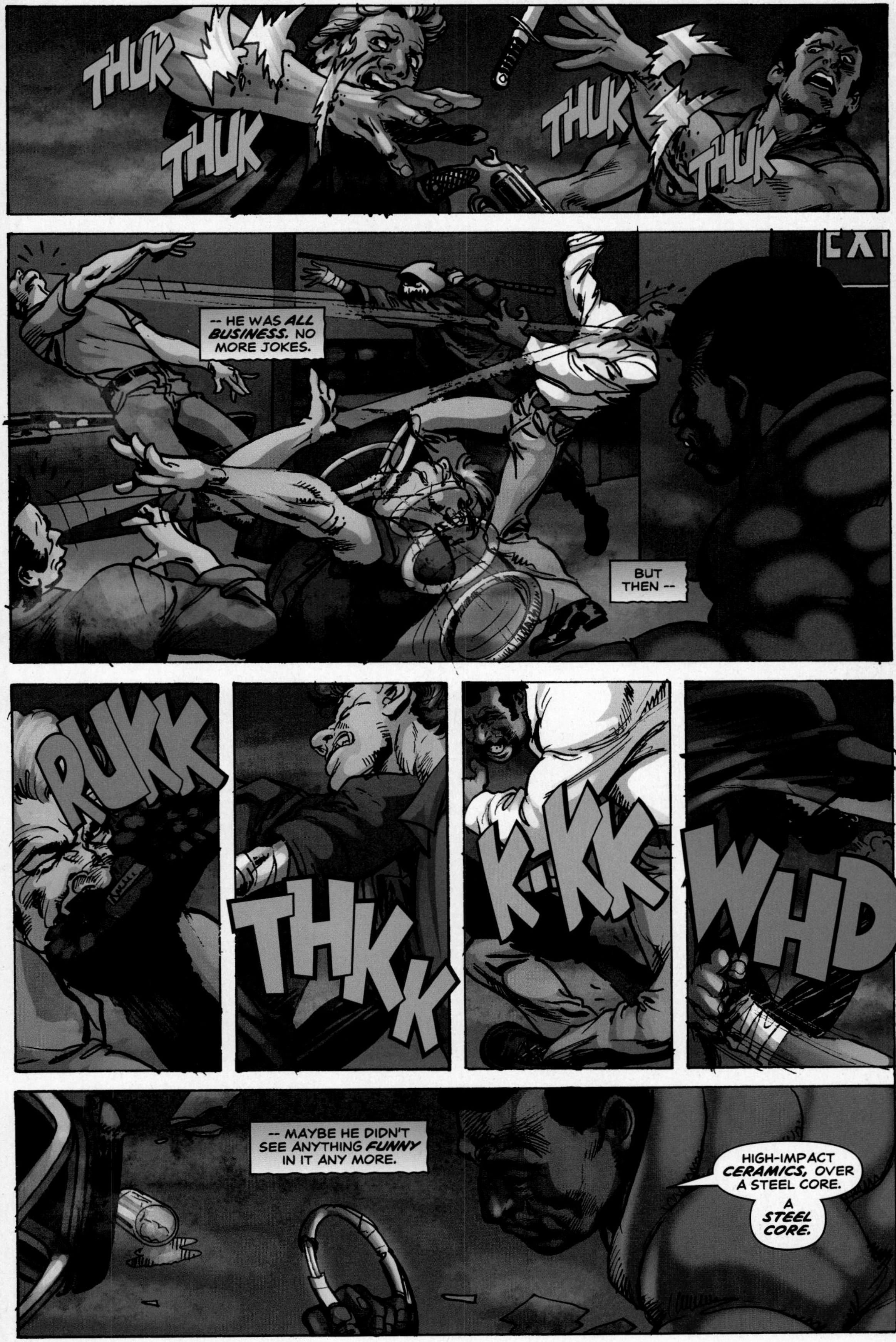
THUK
THUK
THUK
THUK
-- HE WAS ALL BUSINESS. NO MORE JOKES.
BUT THEN --
RUKK
THKK
K-KK
WHD
-- MAYBE HE DIDN'T SEE ANYTHING FUNNY IN IT ANY MORE.
HIGH-IMPACT CERAMICS, OVER A STEEL CORE.
A STEEL CORE.

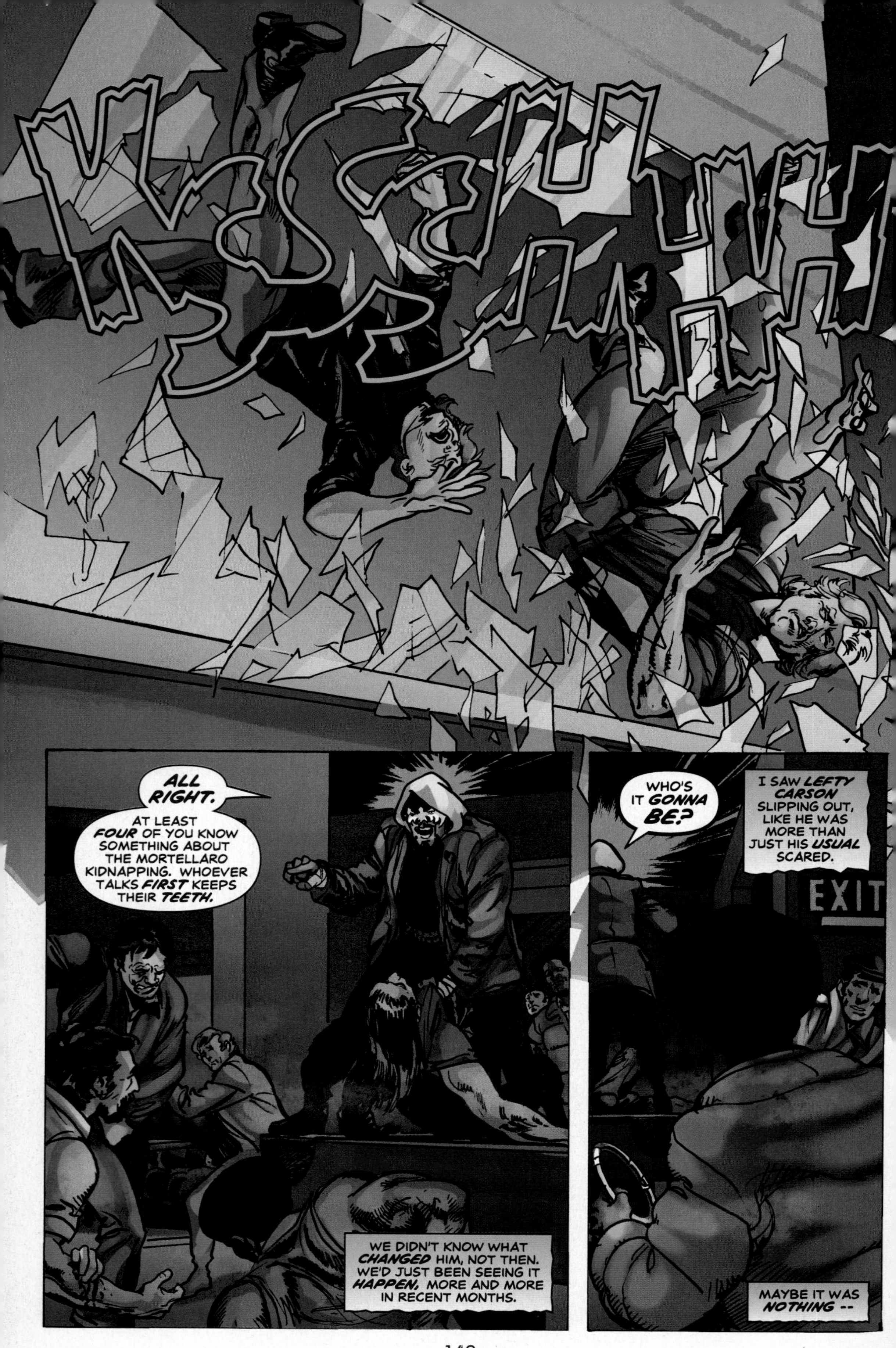
ALL RIGHT.
AT LEAST FOUR OF YOU KNOW SOMETHING ABOUT THE MORTELLARO KIDNAPPING. WHOEVER TALKS FIRST KEEPS THEIR TEETH.
WE DIDN'T KNOW WHAT CHANGED HIM, NOT THEN. WE'D JUST BEEN SEEING IT HAPPEN, MORE AND MORE IN RECENT MONTHS.
WHO'S IT GONNA BE?
I SAW LEFTY CARSON SLIPPING OUT, LIKE HE WAS MORE THAN JUST HIS USUAL SCARED.
EXIT
MAYBE IT WAS NOTHING --

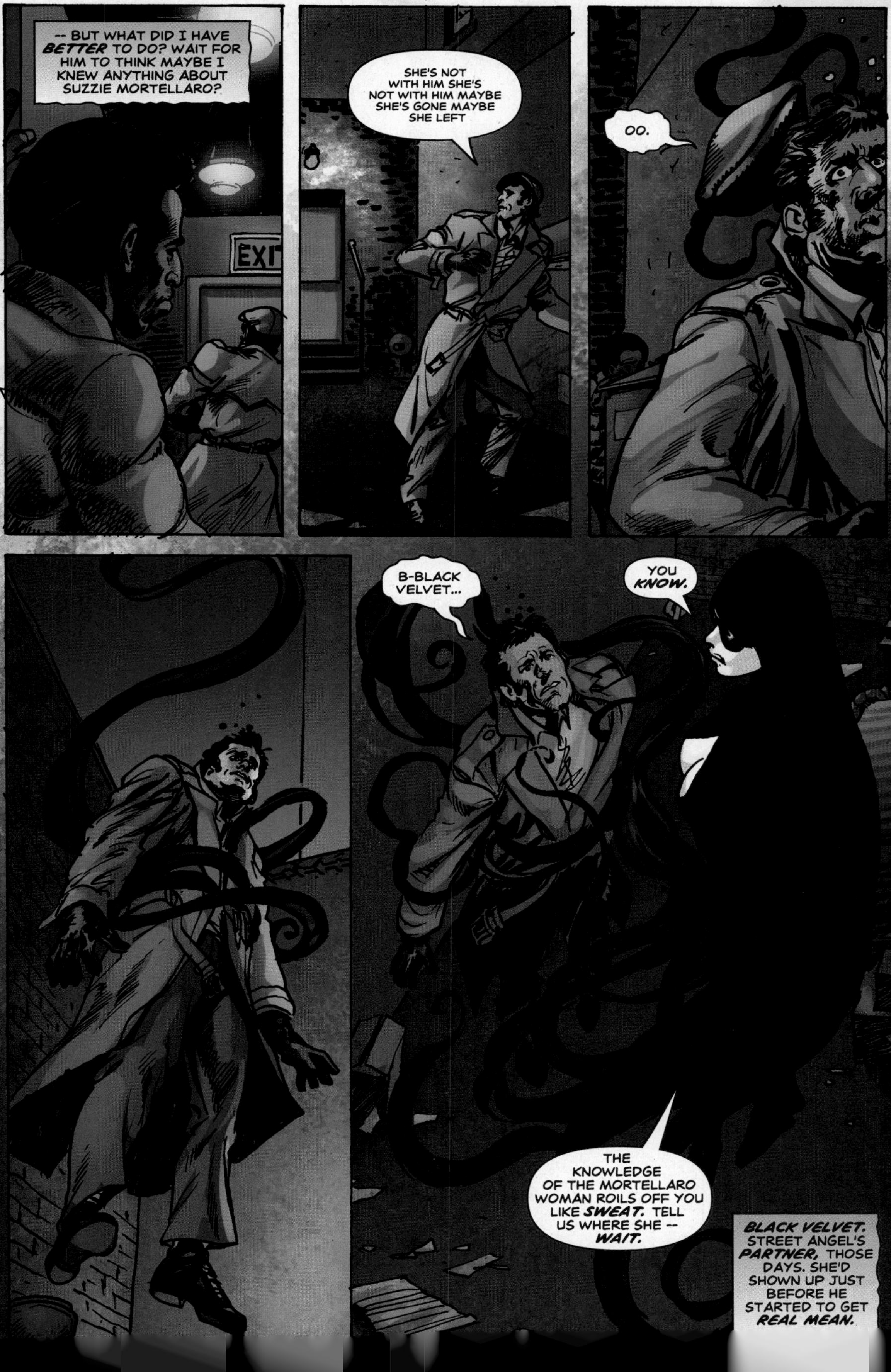
-- BUT WHAT DID I HAVE BETTER TO DO? WAIT FOR HIM TO THINK MAYBE I KNEW ANYTHING ABOUT SUZZIE MORTELLARO?
EXIT
SHE'S NOT WITH HIM SHE'S NOT WITH HIM MAYBE SHE'S GONE MAYBE SHE LEFT
OO.
B-BLACK VELVET...
YOU KNOW.
THE KNOWLEDGE OF THE MORTELLARO WOMAN ROILS OFF YOU LIKE SWEAT. TELL US WHERE SHE -- WAIT.
BLACK VELVET. STREET ANGEL'S PARTNER, THOSE DAYS. SHE'D SHOWN UP JUST BEFORE HE STARTED TO GET REAL MEAN.

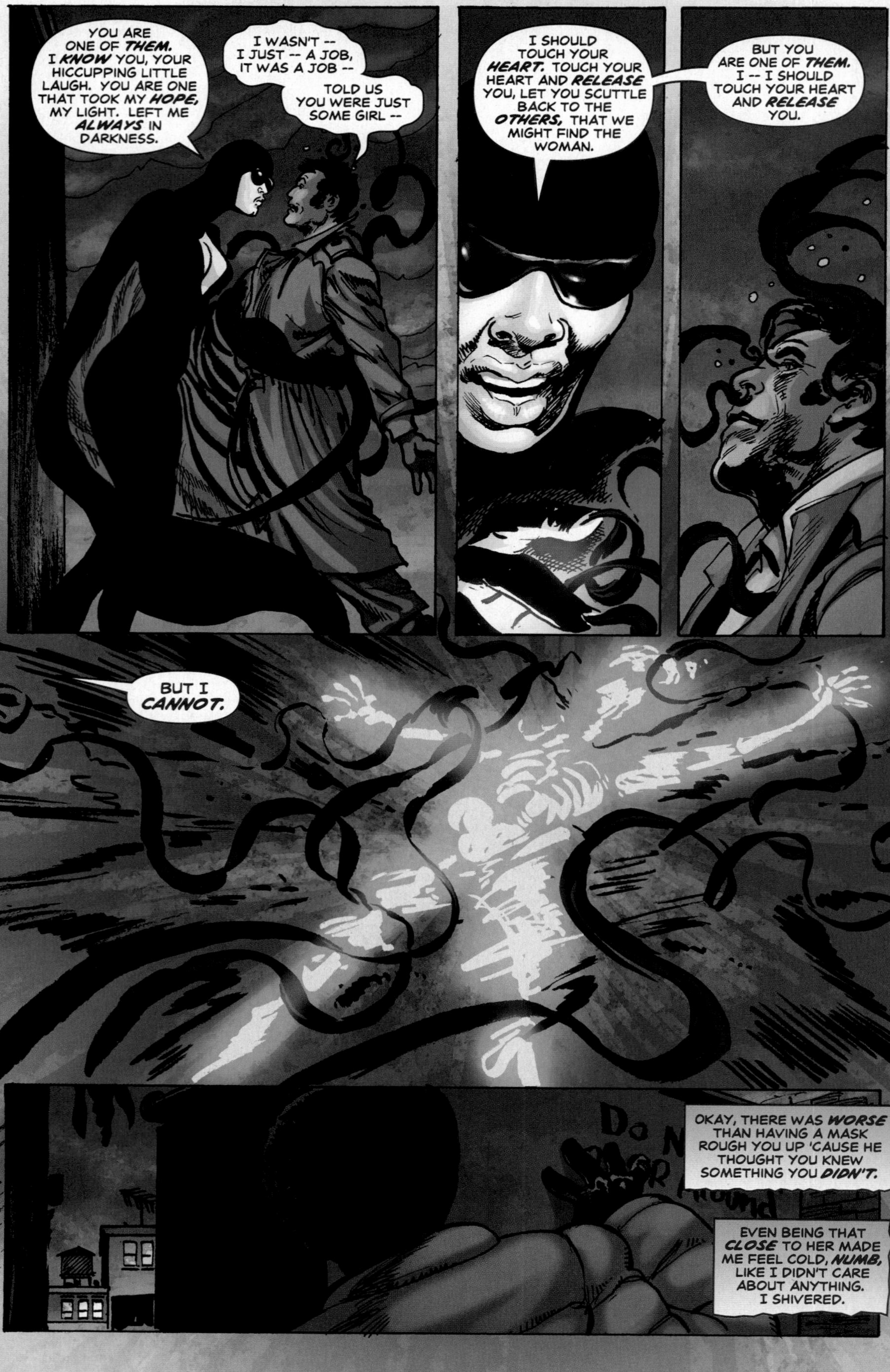
YOU ARE ONE OF THEM. I KNOW YOU, YOUR HICCUPPING LITTLE LAUGH. YOU ARE ONE THAT TOOK MY HOPE, MY LIGHT. LEFT ME ALWAYS IN DARKNESS.
I WASN'T -- I JUST -- A JOB, IT WAS A JOB --
TOLD US YOU WERE JUST SOME GIRL --
I SHOULD TOUCH YOUR HEART. TOUCH YOUR HEART AND RELEASE YOU, LET YOU SCUTTLE BACK TO THE OTHERS, THAT WE MIGHT FIND THE WOMAN.
BUT YOU ARE ONE OF THEM. I -- I SHOULD TOUCH YOUR HEART AND RELEASE YOU.
BUT I CANNOT.
OKAY, THERE WAS WORSE THAN HAVING A MASK ROUGH YOU UP 'CAUSE HE THOUGHT YOU KNEW SOMETHING YOU DIDN'T.
EVEN BEING THAT CLOSE TO HER MADE ME FEEL COLD, NUMB, LIKE I DIDN'T CARE ABOUT ANYTHING. I SHIVERED.

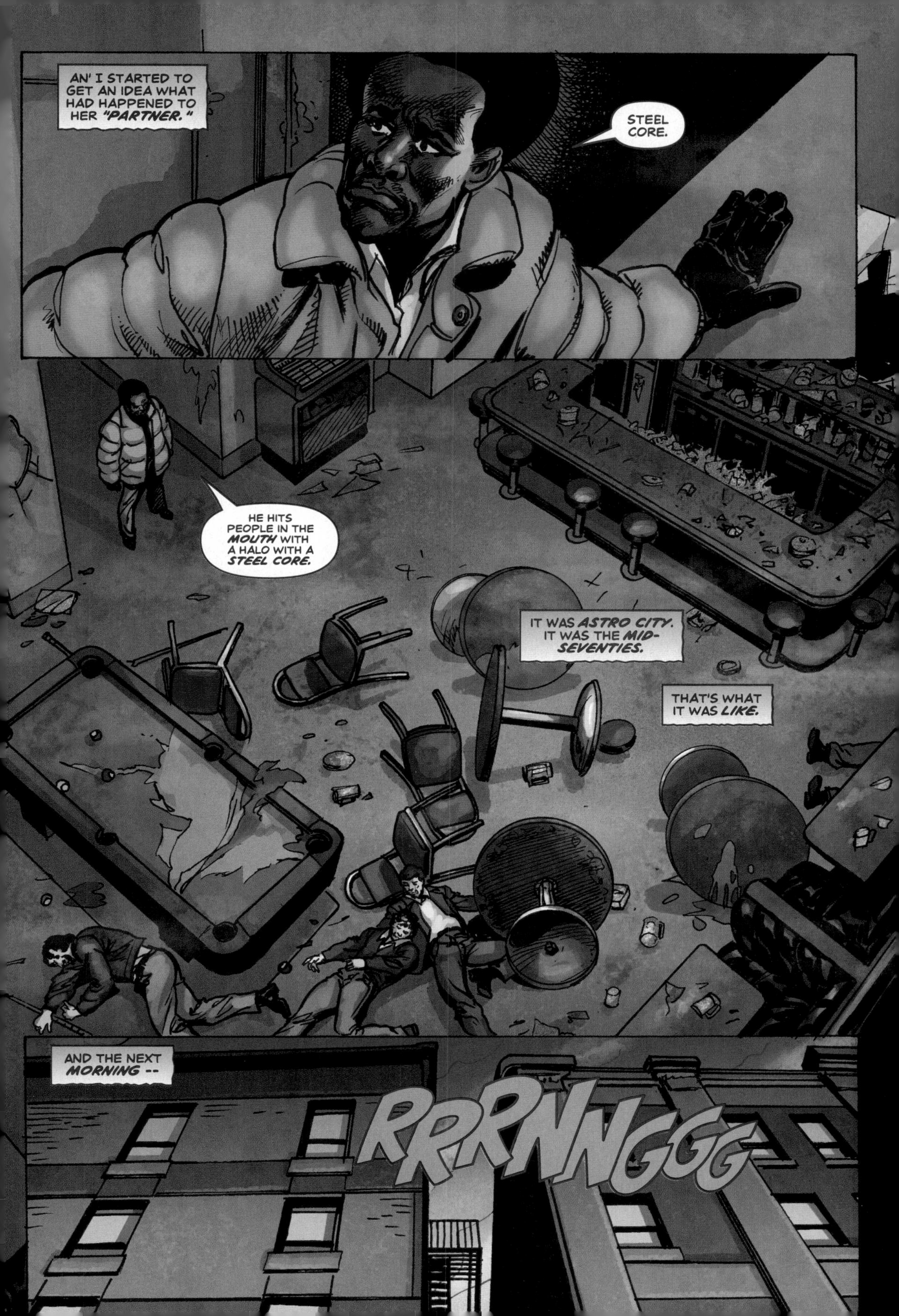
AN' I STARTED TO GET AN IDEA WHAT HAD HAPPENED TO HER "PARTNER."
STEEL CORE.
HE HITS PEOPLE IN THE MOUTH WITH A HALO WITH A STEEL CORE.
IT WAS ASTRO CITY. IT WAS THE MID-SEVENTIES.
THAT'S WHAT IT WAS LIKE.
AND THE NEXT MORNING --
RRRNNGGG

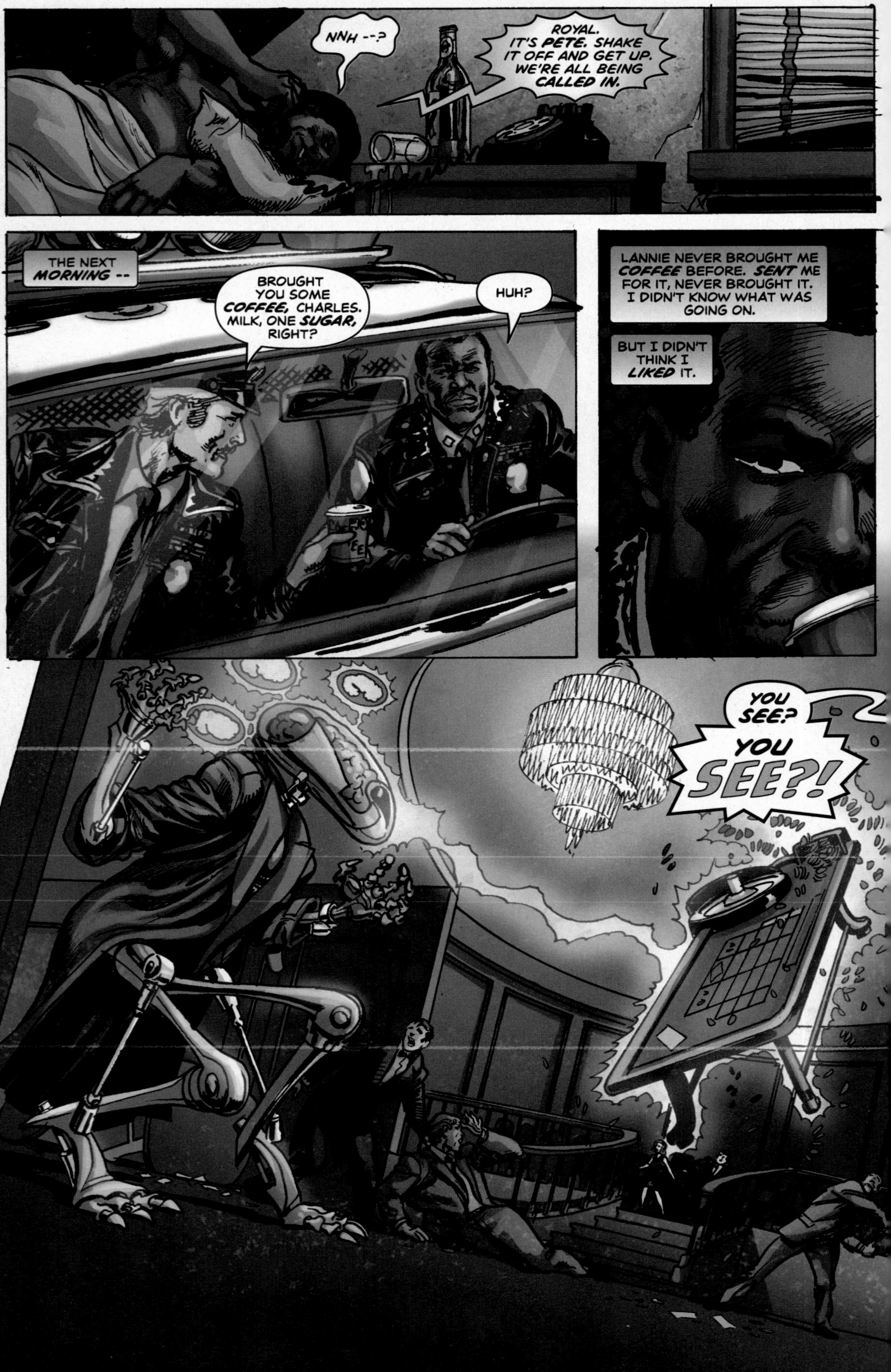
NNH --?
ROYAL. IT'S PETE. SHAKE IT OFF AND GET UP. WE'RE ALL BEING CALLED IN.
THE NEXT MORNING --
BROUGHT YOU SOME COFFEE, CHARLES. MILK, ONE SUGAR, RIGHT?
HUH?
LANNIE NEVER BROUGHT ME COFFEE BEFORE. SENT ME FOR IT, NEVER BROUGHT IT. I DIDN'T KNOW WHAT WAS GOING ON.
BUT I DIDN'T THINK I LIKED IT.
YOU SEE?
YOU SEE?!

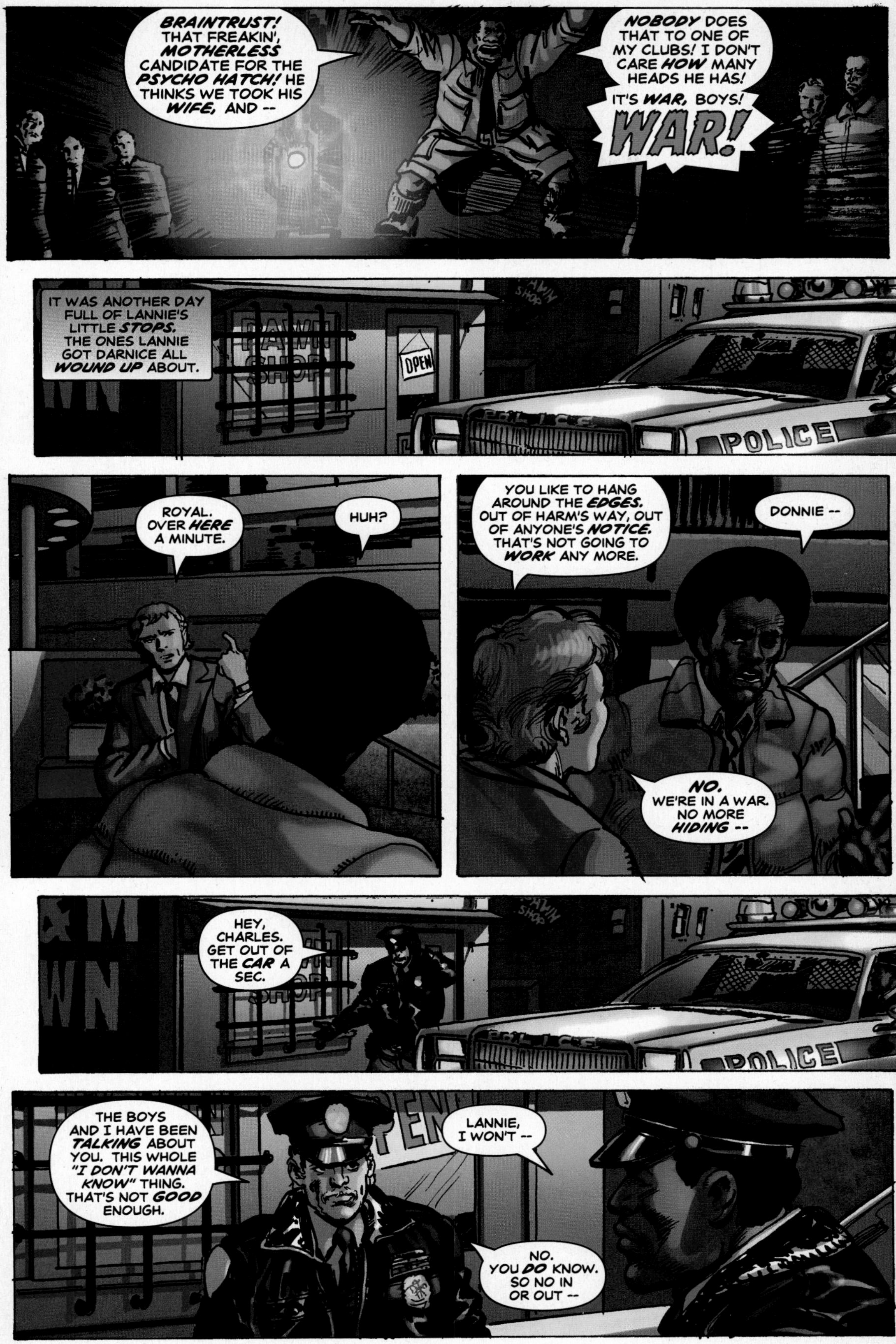
BRAINTRUST! THAT FREAKIN', MOTHERLESS CANDIDATE FOR THE PSYCHO HATCH! HE THINKS WE TOOK HIS WIFE, AND --
NOBODY DOES THAT TO ONE OF MY CLUBS! I DON'T CARE HOW MANY HEADS HE HAS!
IT'S WAR, BOYS! WAR!
IT WAS ANOTHER DAY FULL OF LANNIE'S LITTLE STOPS. THE ONES LANNIE GOT DARNICE ALL WOUND UP ABOUT.
PAWN SHOP
OPEN
POLICE
ROYAL. OVER HERE A MINUTE.
HUH?
YOU LIKE TO HANG AROUND THE EDGES. OUT OF HARM'S WAY, OUT OF ANYONE'S NOTICE. THAT'S NOT GOING TO WORK ANY MORE.
DONNIE --
NO. WE'RE IN A WAR. NO MORE HIDING --
HEY, CHARLES. GET OUT OF THE CAR A SEC.
POLICE
THE BOYS AND I HAVE BEEN TALKING ABOUT YOU. THIS WHOLE "I DON'T WANNA KNOW" THING. THAT'S NOT GOOD ENOUGH.
LANNIE, I WON'T --
NO. YOU DO KNOW. SO NO IN OR OUT --

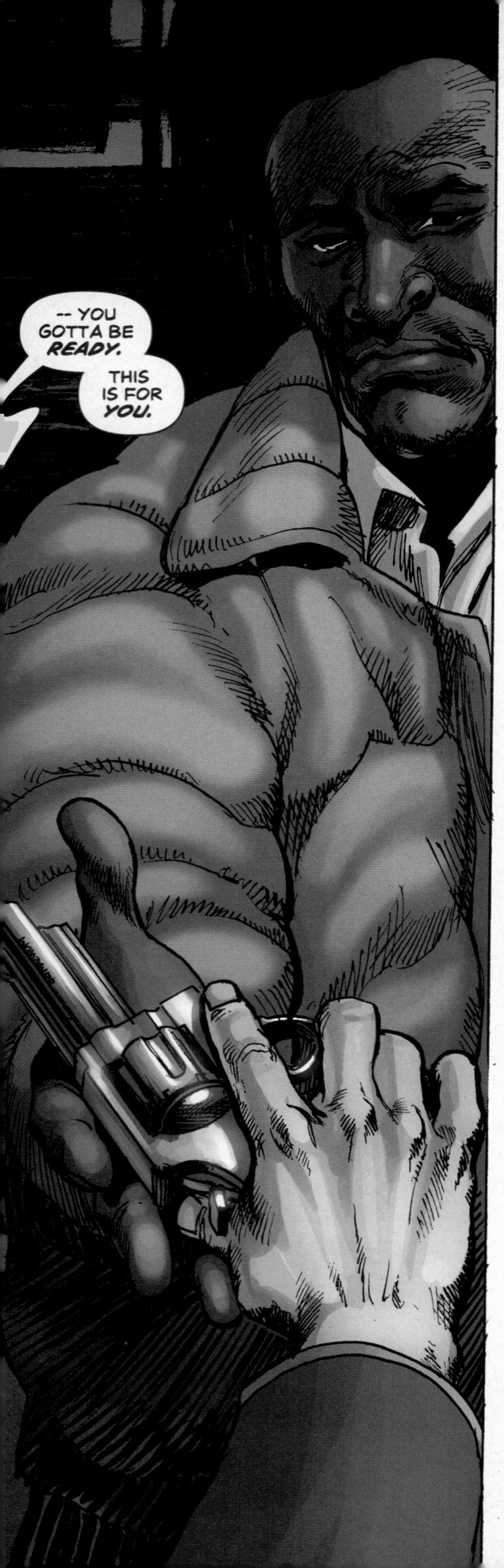
-- YOU GOTTA BE *READY.*
THIS IS FOR *YOU.*

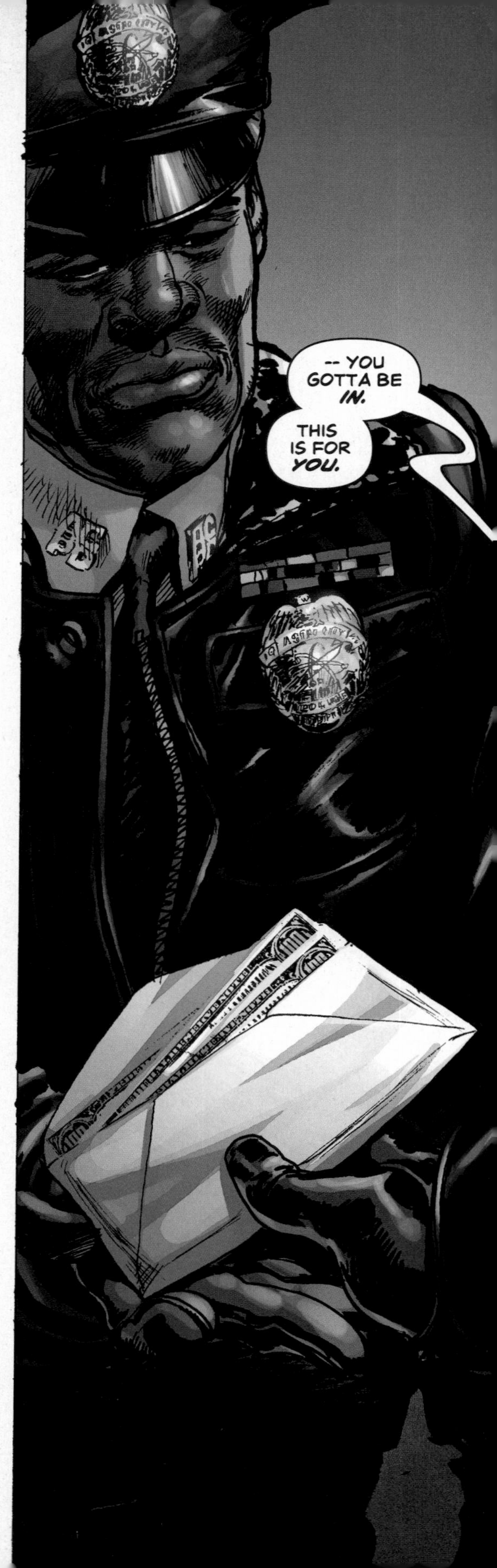
-- YOU GOTTA BE *IN.*
THIS IS FOR *YOU.*

JANUARY 19, 1977.

IF YOU WERE LIVING IN ASTRO CITY -- OR ABOUT *ANYWHERE* IN THE U.S. -- ODDS ARE YOU *REMEMBER* THAT DAY.

WRAK

BAK

KAKK

BUT NOT BECAUSE ME AND *SOME OTHER GUYS* FROM THE PLATYPUS MOB AMBUSHED A COUPLE OF *GUNBIRDS*.

AN' THAT'S *IT.*

LOTTA HELP *YOU* WERE, ROYAL.

BLAM

AH --

I DON'T -- DIDN'T THINK YOU *NEEDED* --

NO, IF YOU REMEMBER *THAT* DAY...

WHAT THE *HELL* IS -- ?

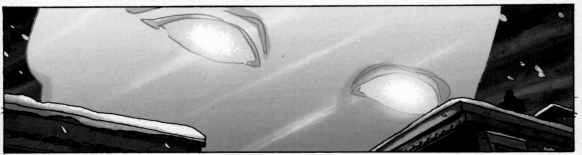

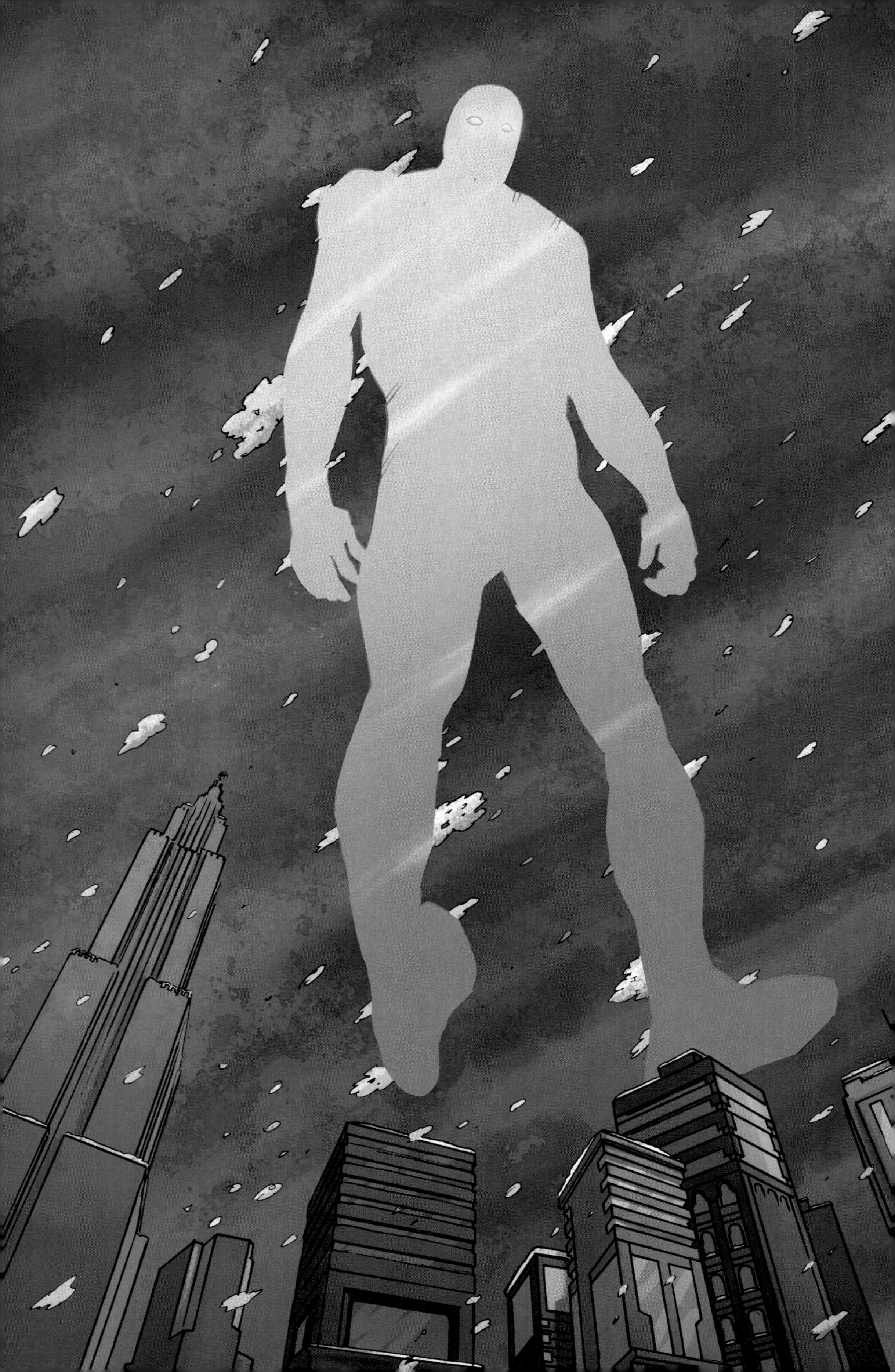

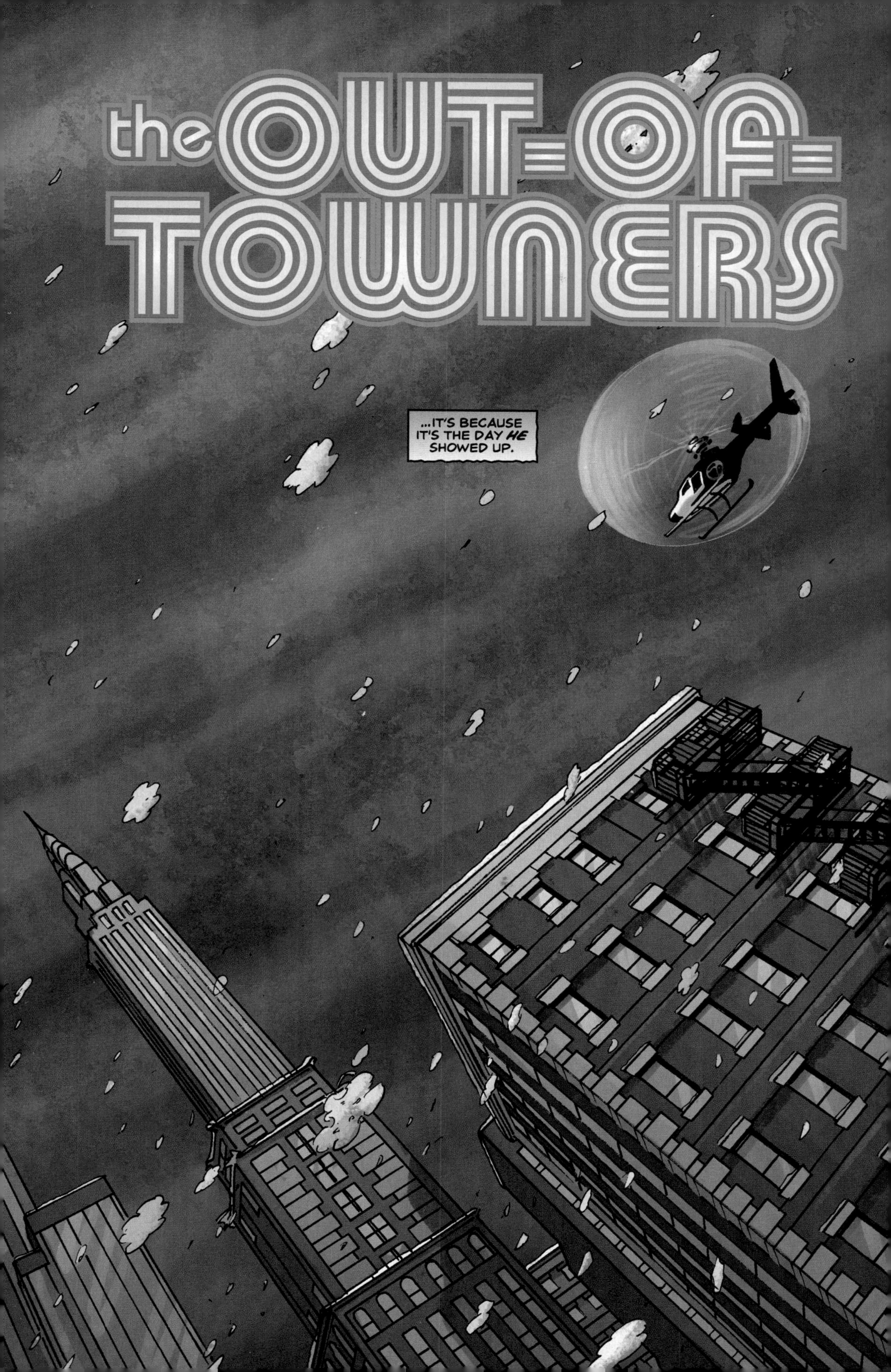
the OUT-OF-TOWNERS
...IT'S BECAUSE IT'S THE DAY HE SHOWED UP.

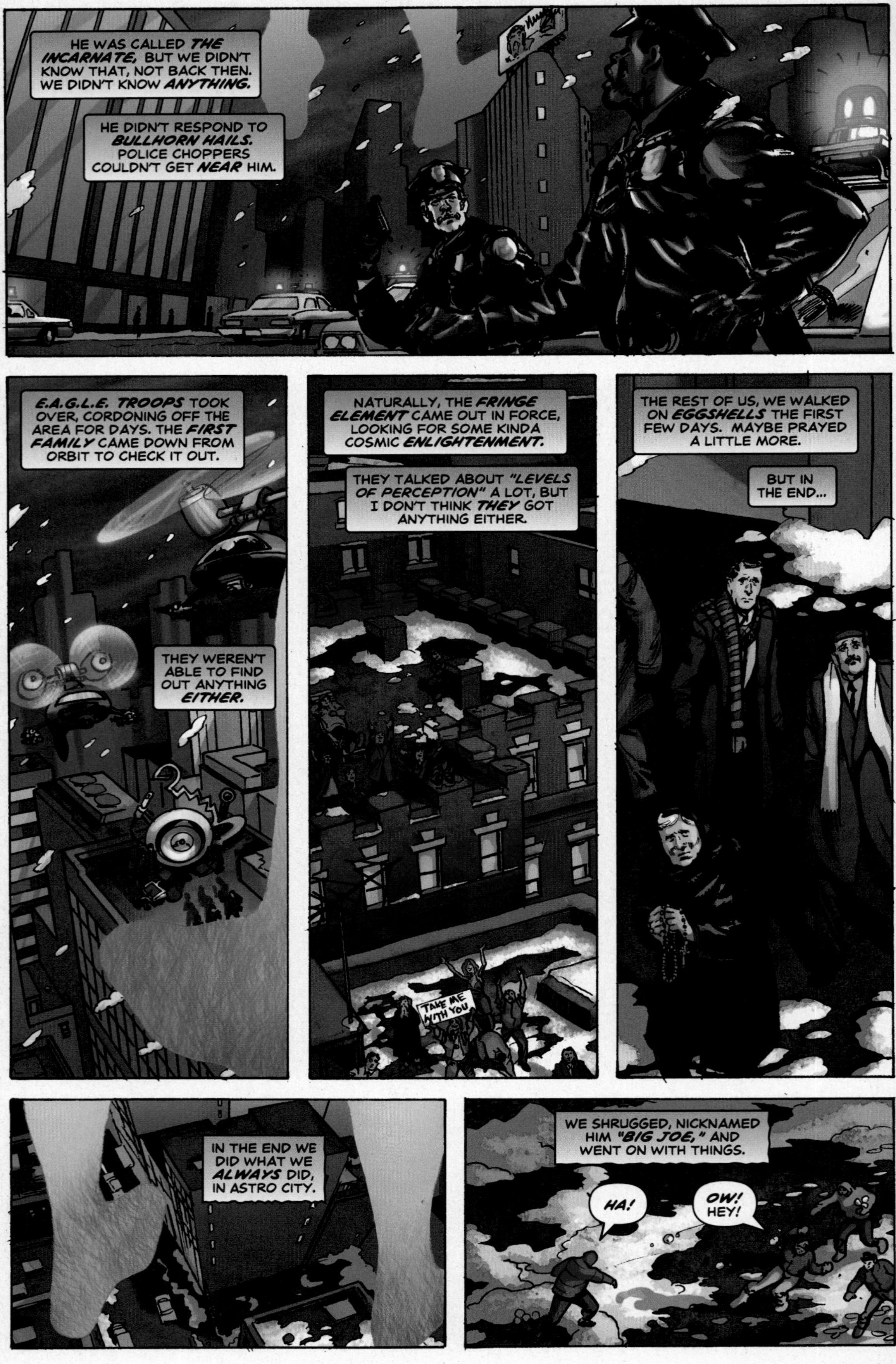
HE WAS CALLED THE INCARNATE, BUT WE DIDN'T KNOW THAT, NOT BACK THEN. WE DIDN'T KNOW ANYTHING.
HE DIDN'T RESPOND TO BULLHORN HAILS. POLICE CHOPPERS COULDN'T GET NEAR HIM.
E.A.G.L.E. TROOPS TOOK OVER, CORDONING OFF THE AREA FOR DAYS. THE FIRST FAMILY CAME DOWN FROM ORBIT TO CHECK IT OUT.
THEY WEREN'T ABLE TO FIND OUT ANYTHING EITHER.
NATURALLY, THE FRINGE ELEMENT CAME OUT IN FORCE, LOOKING FOR SOME KINDA COSMIC ENLIGHTENMENT.
THEY TALKED ABOUT "LEVELS OF PERCEPTION" A LOT, BUT I DON'T THINK THEY GOT ANYTHING EITHER.
TAKE ME WITH YOU
THE REST OF US, WE WALKED ON EGGSHELLS THE FIRST FEW DAYS. MAYBE PRAYED A LITTLE MORE.
BUT IN THE END...
IN THE END WE DID WHAT WE ALWAYS DID, IN ASTRO CITY.
WE SHRUGGED, NICKNAMED HIM "BIG JOE," AND WENT ON WITH THINGS.
HA!
OW! HEY!

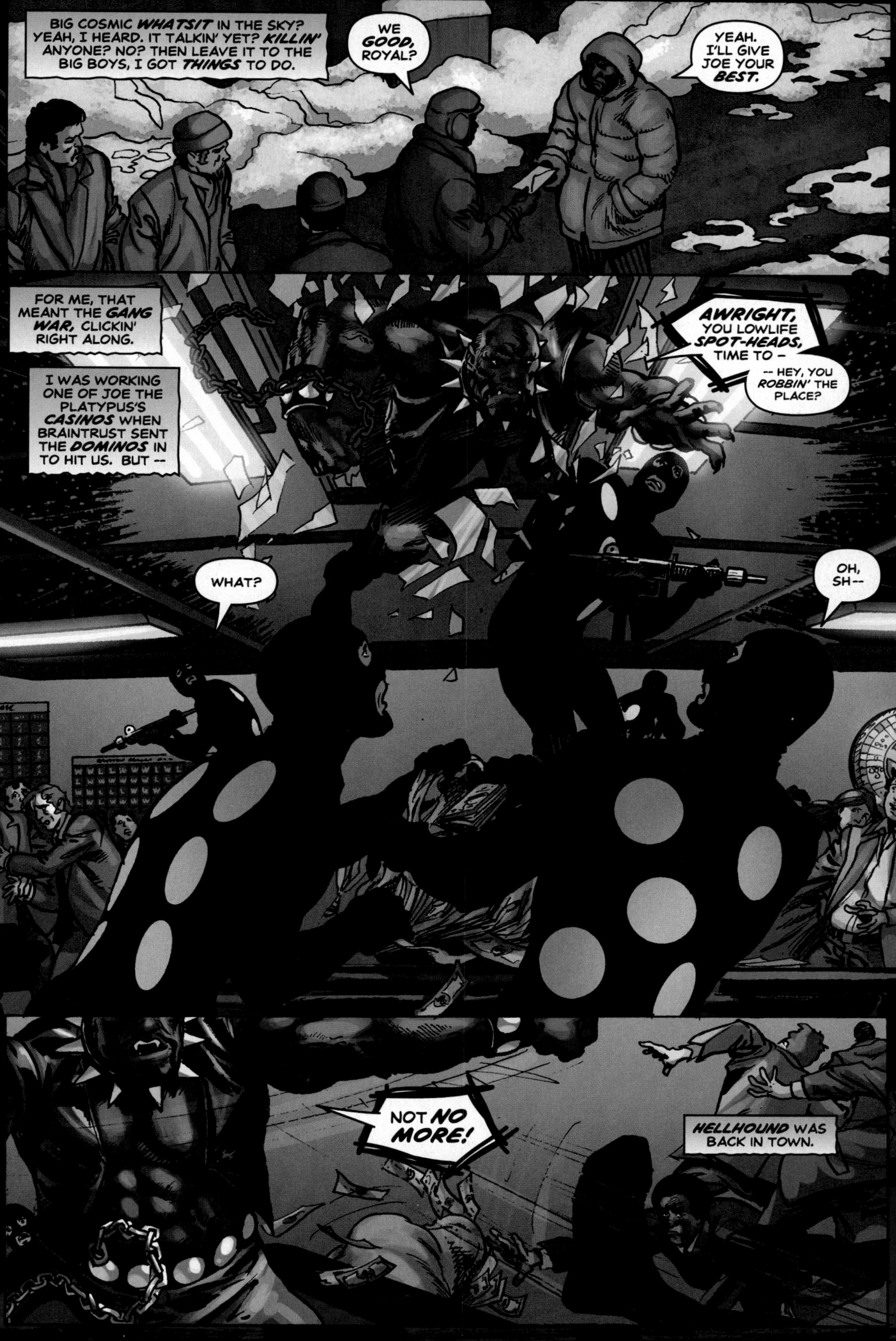
BIG COSMIC WHATSIT IN THE SKY? YEAH, I HEARD. IT TALKIN' YET? KILLIN' ANYONE? NO? THEN LEAVE IT TO THE BIG BOYS, I GOT THINGS TO DO.
WE GOOD, ROYAL?
YEAH. I'LL GIVE JOE YOUR BEST.
FOR ME, THAT MEANT THE GANG WAR, CLICKIN' RIGHT ALONG.
I WAS WORKING ONE OF JOE THE PLATYPUS'S CASINOS WHEN BRAINTRUST SENT THE DOMINOS IN TO HIT US. BUT --
AWRIGHT, YOU LOWLIFE SPOT-HEADS, TIME TO –
-- HEY, YOU ROBBIN' THE PLACE?
WHAT?
OH, SH--
NOT NO MORE!
HELLHOUND WAS BACK IN TOWN.

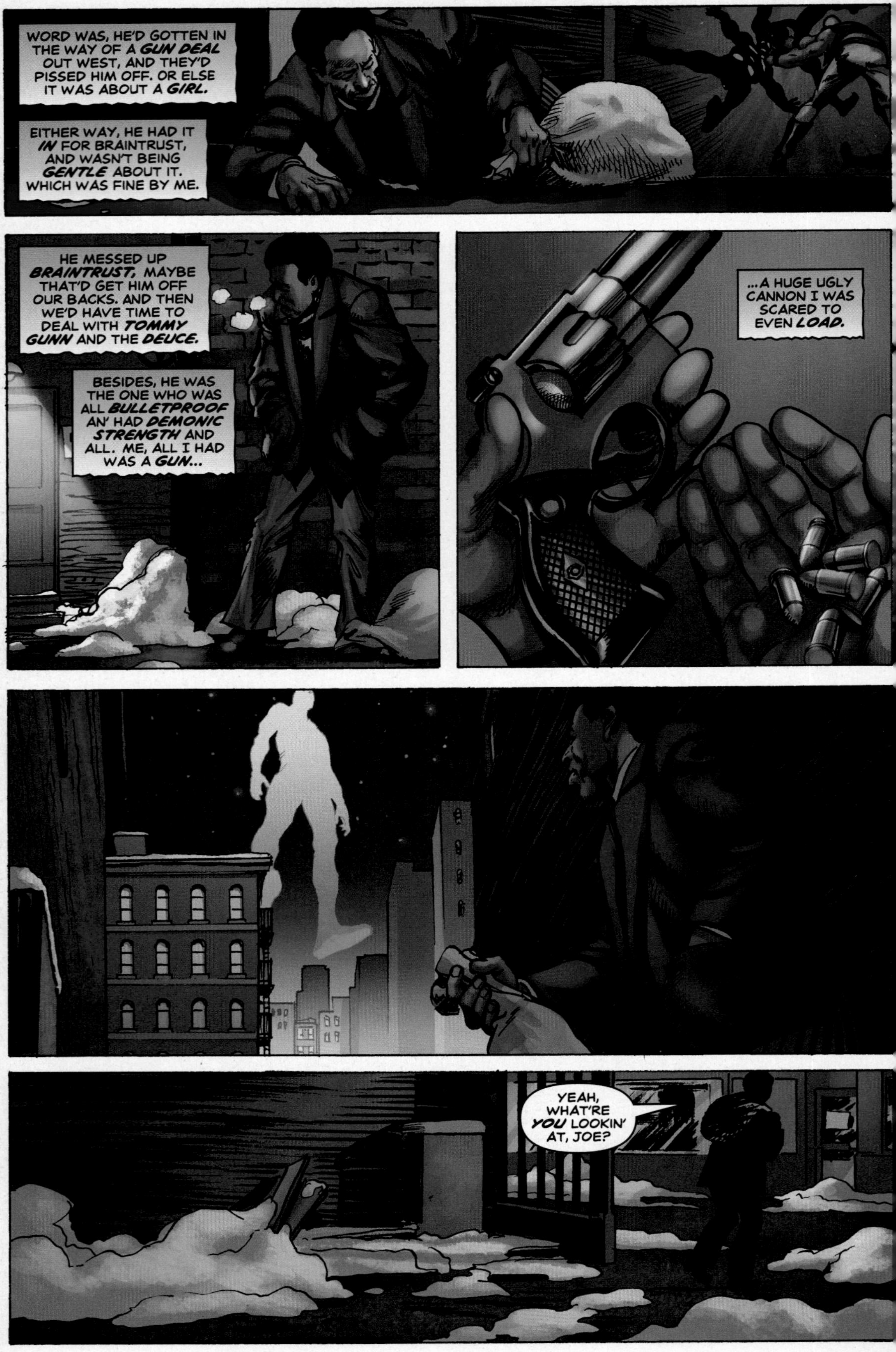
WORD WAS, HE'D GOTTEN IN THE WAY OF A GUN DEAL OUT WEST, AND THEY'D PISSED HIM OFF. OR ELSE IT WAS ABOUT A GIRL.
EITHER WAY, HE HAD IT IN FOR BRAINTRUST, AND WASN'T BEING GENTLE ABOUT IT. WHICH WAS FINE BY ME.
HE MESSED UP BRAINTRUST, MAYBE THAT'D GET HIM OFF OUR BACKS. AND THEN WE'D HAVE TIME TO DEAL WITH TOMMY GUNN AND THE DEUCE.
BESIDES, HE WAS THE ONE WHO WAS ALL BULLETPROOF AN' HAD DEMONIC STRENGTH AND ALL. ME, ALL I HAD WAS A GUN...
...A HUGE UGLY CANNON I WAS SCARED TO EVEN LOAD.
YEAH, WHAT'RE YOU LOOKIN' AT, JOE?

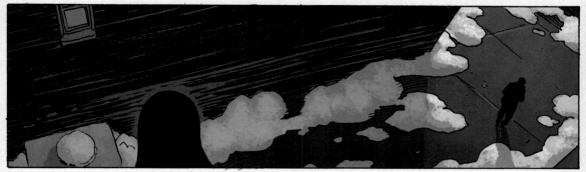

NO. NOT *YOU*.

I SMELL A FILM OF *CORRUPTION* AROUND YOU, AND THE TAINT OF DARKNESS. BUT YOU ARE NOT ONE OF THEM.

NOT ONE I SEEK *REVENGE* ON -- NOR ONE I HUNT FOR *OTHER* REASONS.

STILL, I FEEL ONE OF THEM *NEARBY.* ONE OF THOSE WHO *VIOLATED* ME, WHO STOLE MY LIGHT, MY *SELF.*

SOMEWHERE. SOMEWHERE *NEAR...*

WHEN I WAS AT THE *PRECINCT HOUSE*, I SPENT A LOT OF MY TIME IN THE RECORDS ROOM.

AND NOT JUST BECAUSE I DIDN'T WANT TO *DEAL* WITH ANYONE.

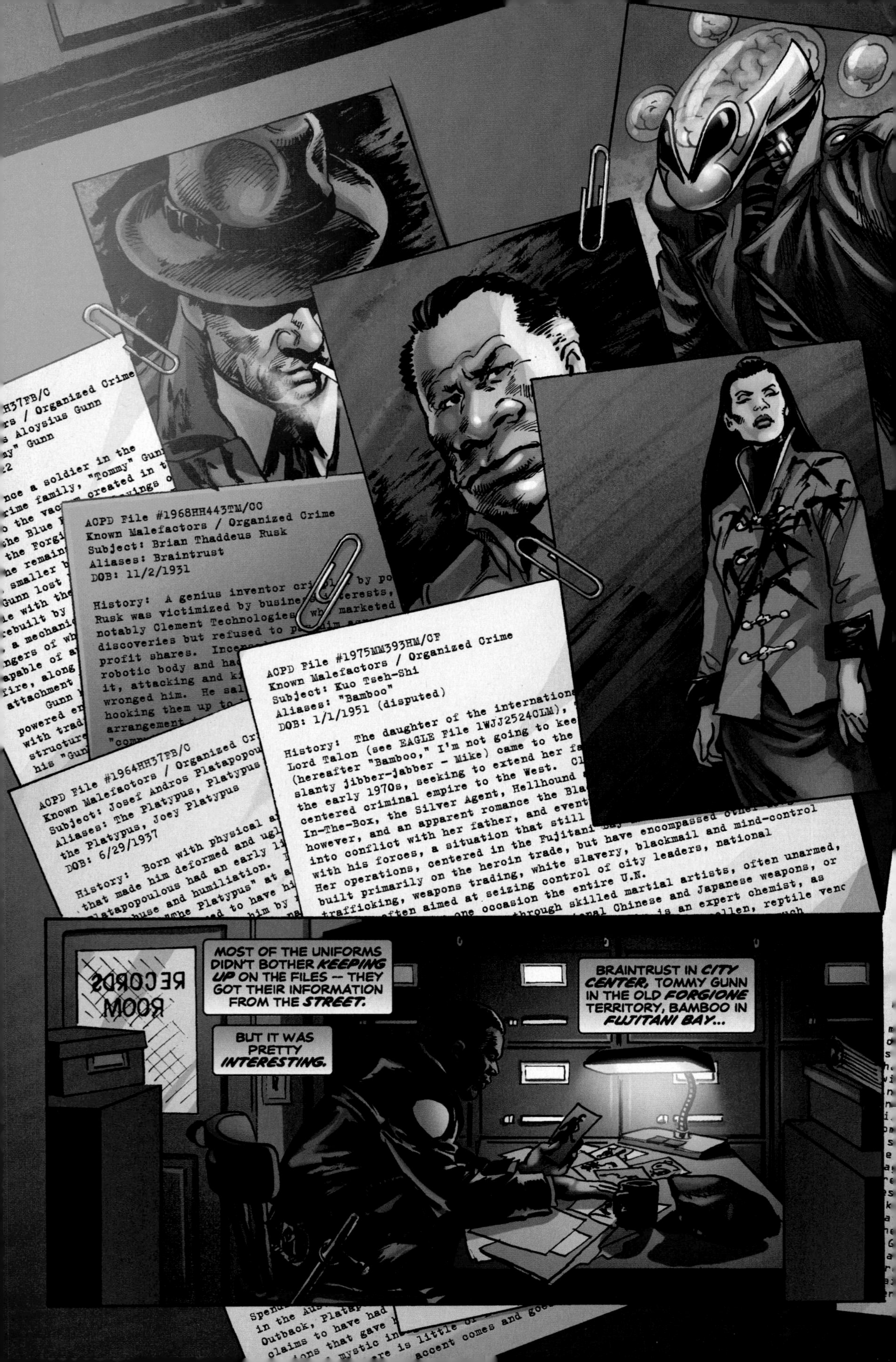
ACPD File #1968HH443TM/CC
Known Malefactors / Organized Crime
Subject: Brian Thaddeus Rusk
Aliases: Braintrust
DOB: 11/2/1931
ACPD File #1975MM393HM/CF
Known Malefactors / Organized Crime
Subject: Kuo Tseh-Shi
Aliases: "Bamboo"
DOB: 1/1/1951 (disputed)
ACPD File #1964HH37FB/C
Known Malefactors / Organized Cr
Subject: Josef Andros Platapopou
Aliases: The Platypus, Platypus
the Platypus, Joey Platypus
DOB: 6/29/1937
RECORDS ROOM
MOST OF THE UNIFORMS DIDN'T BOTHER KEEPING UP ON THE FILES -- THEY GOT THEIR INFORMATION FROM THE STREET.
BUT IT WAS PRETTY INTERESTING.
BRAINTRUST IN CITY CENTER, TOMMY GUNN IN THE OLD FORGIONE TERRITORY, BAMBOO IN FUJITANI BAY...

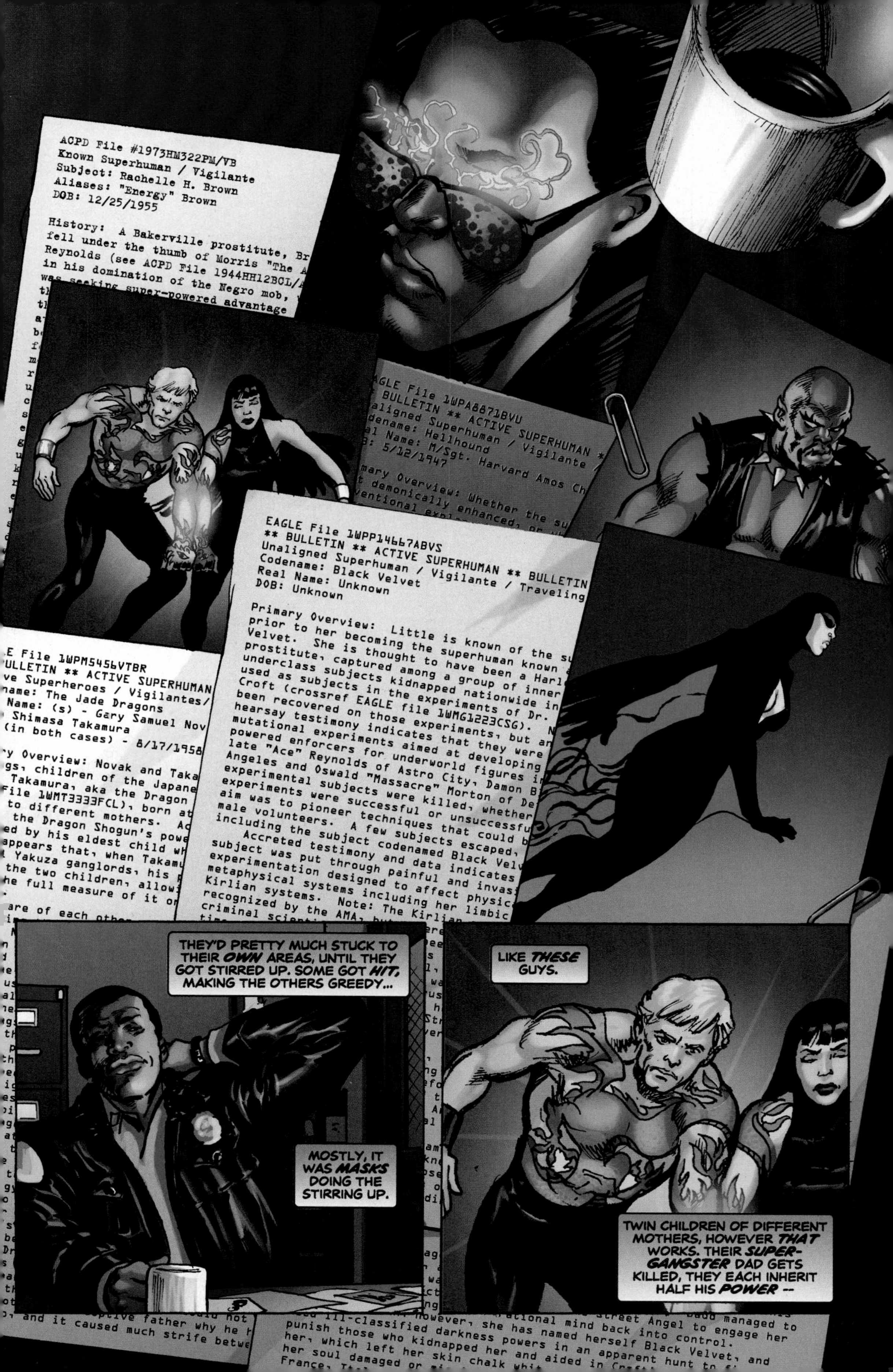

ACPD File #1973HM322PM/VB
Known Superhuman / Vigilante
Subject: Rachelle H. Brown
Aliases: "Energy" Brown
DOB: 12/25/1955
EAGLE File 1WPP14667ABVS
** BULLETIN ** ACTIVE SUPERHUMAN ** BULLETIN
Unaligned Superhuman / Vigilante / Traveling
Codename: Black Velvet
Real Name: Unknown
DOB: Unknown
THEY'D PRETTY MUCH STUCK TO THEIR OWN AREAS, UNTIL THEY GOT STIRRED UP. SOME GOT HIT, MAKING THE OTHERS GREEDY...
MOSTLY, IT WAS MASKS DOING THE STIRRING UP.
LIKE THESE GUYS.
TWIN CHILDREN OF DIFFERENT MOTHERS, HOWEVER THAT WORKS. THEIR SUPER-GANGSTER DAD GETS KILLED, THEY EACH INHERIT HALF HIS POWER --

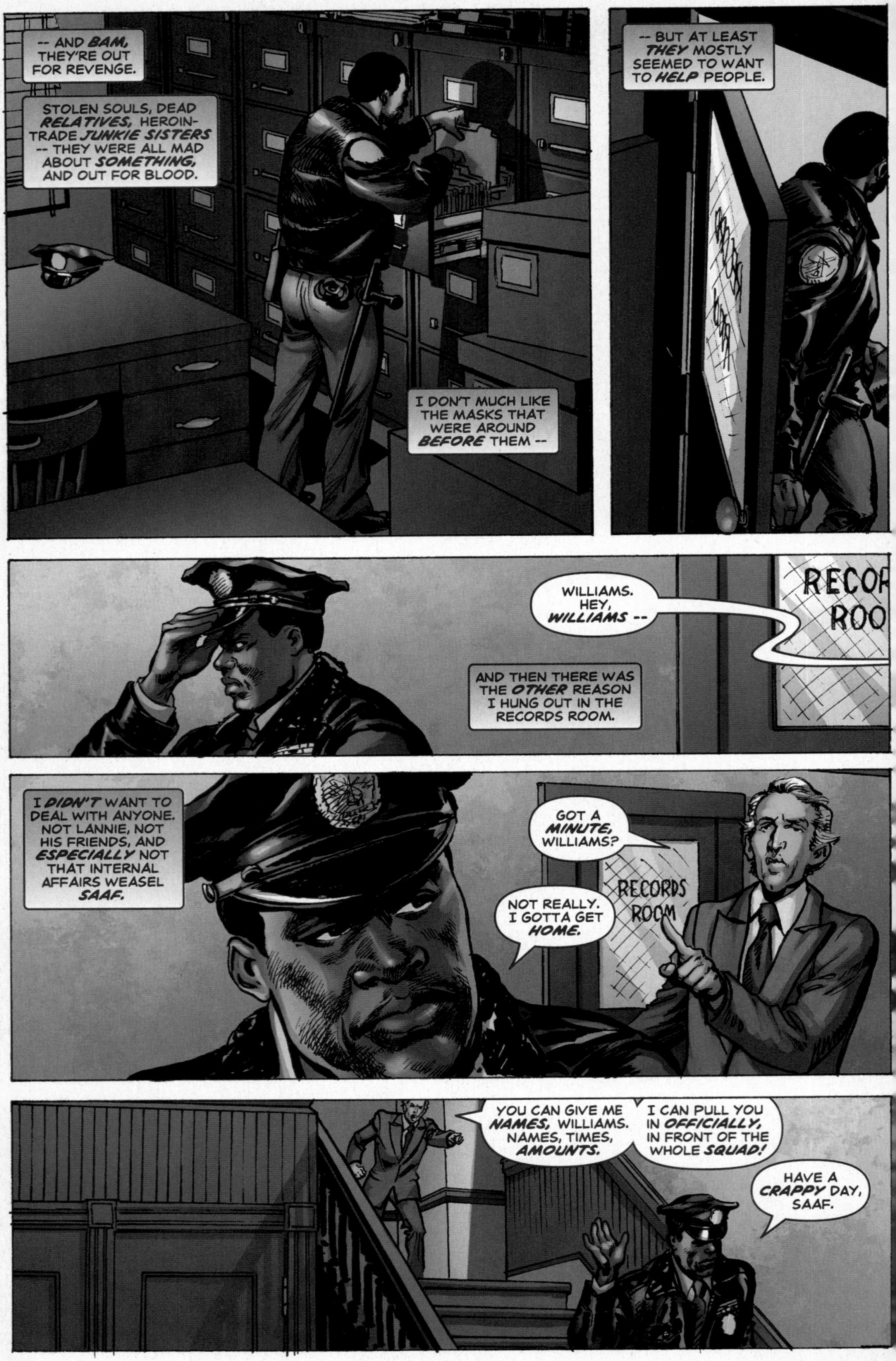
-- AND BAM, THEY'RE OUT FOR REVENGE.
STOLEN SOULS, DEAD RELATIVES, HEROIN-TRADE JUNKIE SISTERS -- THEY WERE ALL MAD ABOUT SOMETHING, AND OUT FOR BLOOD.
I DON'T MUCH LIKE THE MASKS THAT WERE AROUND BEFORE THEM --
-- BUT AT LEAST THEY MOSTLY SEEMED TO WANT TO HELP PEOPLE.
RECORDS ROOM
WILLIAMS. HEY, WILLIAMS --
AND THEN THERE WAS THE OTHER REASON I HUNG OUT IN THE RECORDS ROOM.
I DIDN'T WANT TO DEAL WITH ANYONE. NOT LANNIE, NOT HIS FRIENDS, AND ESPECIALLY NOT THAT INTERNAL AFFAIRS WEASEL SAAF.
GOT A MINUTE, WILLIAMS?
RECORDS ROOM
NOT REALLY. I GOTTA GET HOME.
YOU CAN GIVE ME NAMES, WILLIAMS. NAMES, TIMES, AMOUNTS.
I CAN PULL YOU IN OFFICIALLY, IN FRONT OF THE WHOLE SQUAD!
HAVE A CRAPPY DAY, SAAF.

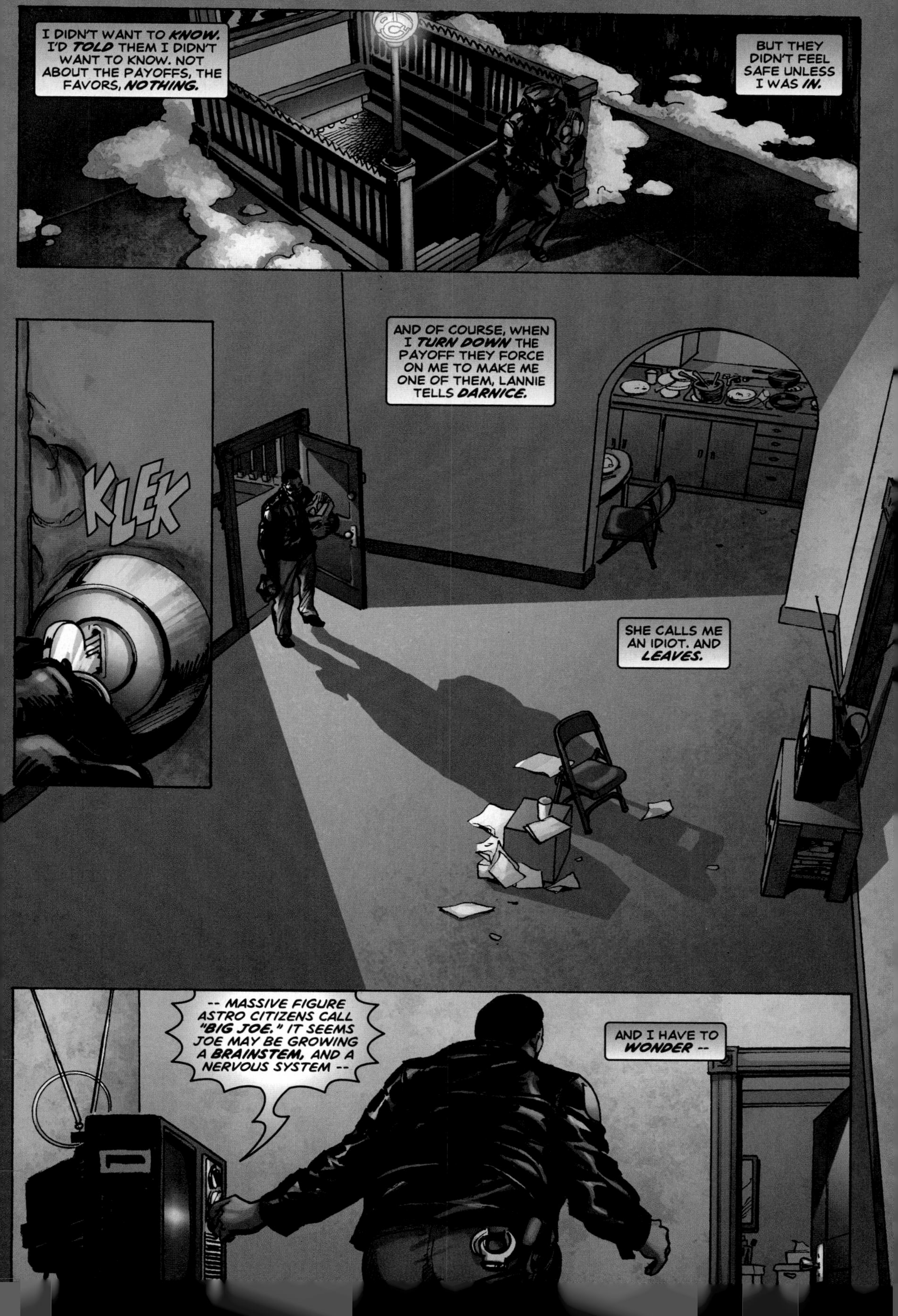
I DIDN'T WANT TO KNOW. I'D TOLD THEM I DIDN'T WANT TO KNOW. NOT ABOUT THE PAYOFFS, THE FAVORS, NOTHING.
BUT THEY DIDN'T FEEL SAFE UNLESS I WAS IN.
KLEK
AND OF COURSE, WHEN I TURN DOWN THE PAYOFF THEY FORCE ON ME TO MAKE ME ONE OF THEM, LANNIE TELLS DARNICE.
SHE CALLS ME AN IDIOT. AND LEAVES.
-- MASSIVE FIGURE ASTRO CITIZENS CALL "BIG JOE." IT SEEMS JOE MAY BE GROWING A BRAINSTEM, AND A NERVOUS SYSTEM --
AND I HAVE TO WONDER --

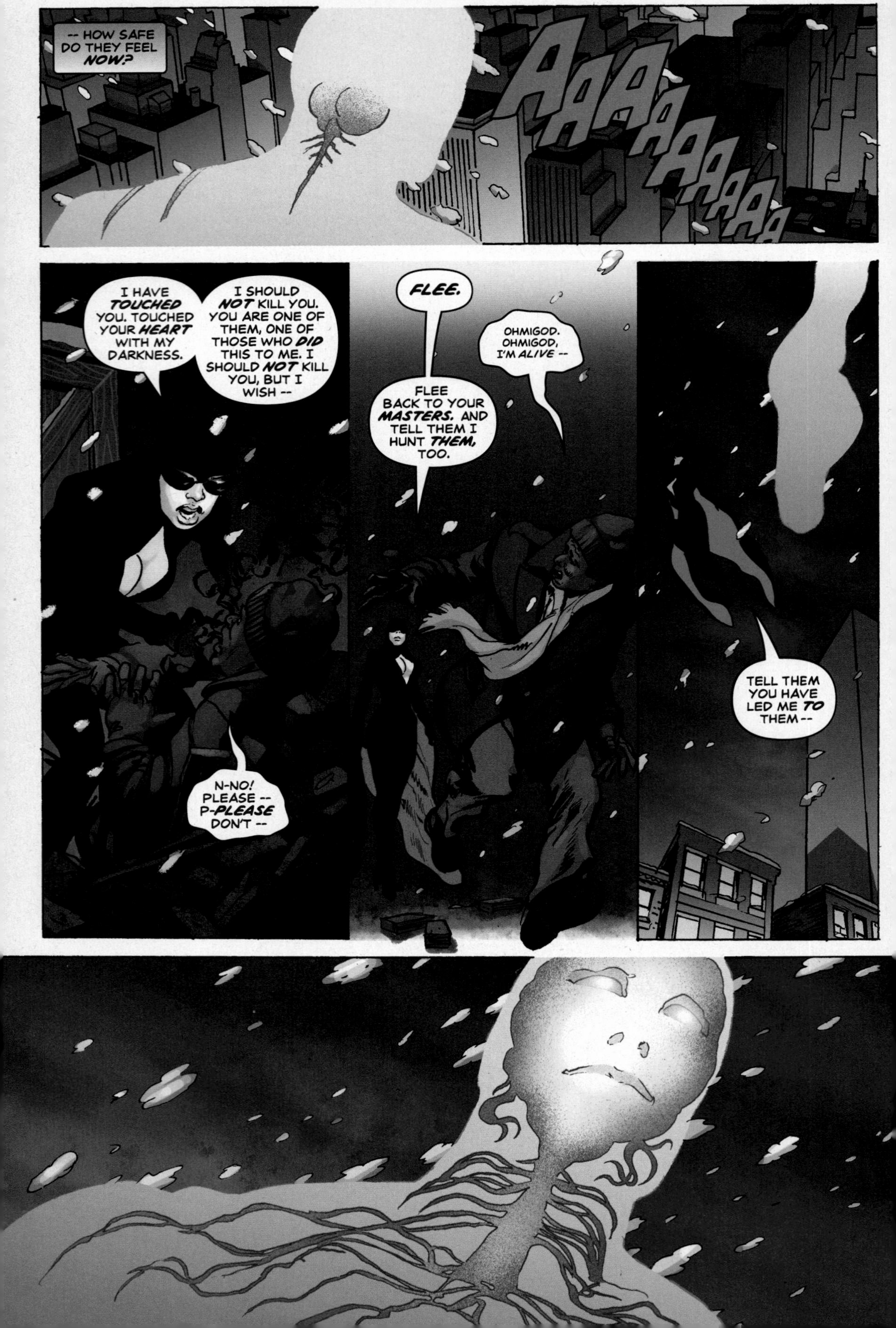
-- HOW SAFE DO THEY FEEL *NOW?*
AAAAAAAAAAAAA
I HAVE *TOUCHED* YOU. TOUCHED YOUR *HEART* WITH MY DARKNESS.
I SHOULD *NOT* KILL YOU. YOU ARE ONE OF THEM, ONE OF THOSE WHO *DID* THIS TO ME. I SHOULD *NOT* KILL YOU, BUT I WISH --
N-NO! PLEASE -- P-*PLEASE* DON'T --
FLEE.
FLEE BACK TO YOUR *MASTERS.* AND TELL THEM I HUNT *THEM,* TOO.
OHMIGOD. OHMIGOD, I'M *ALIVE* --
TELL THEM YOU HAVE LED ME *TO* THEM --

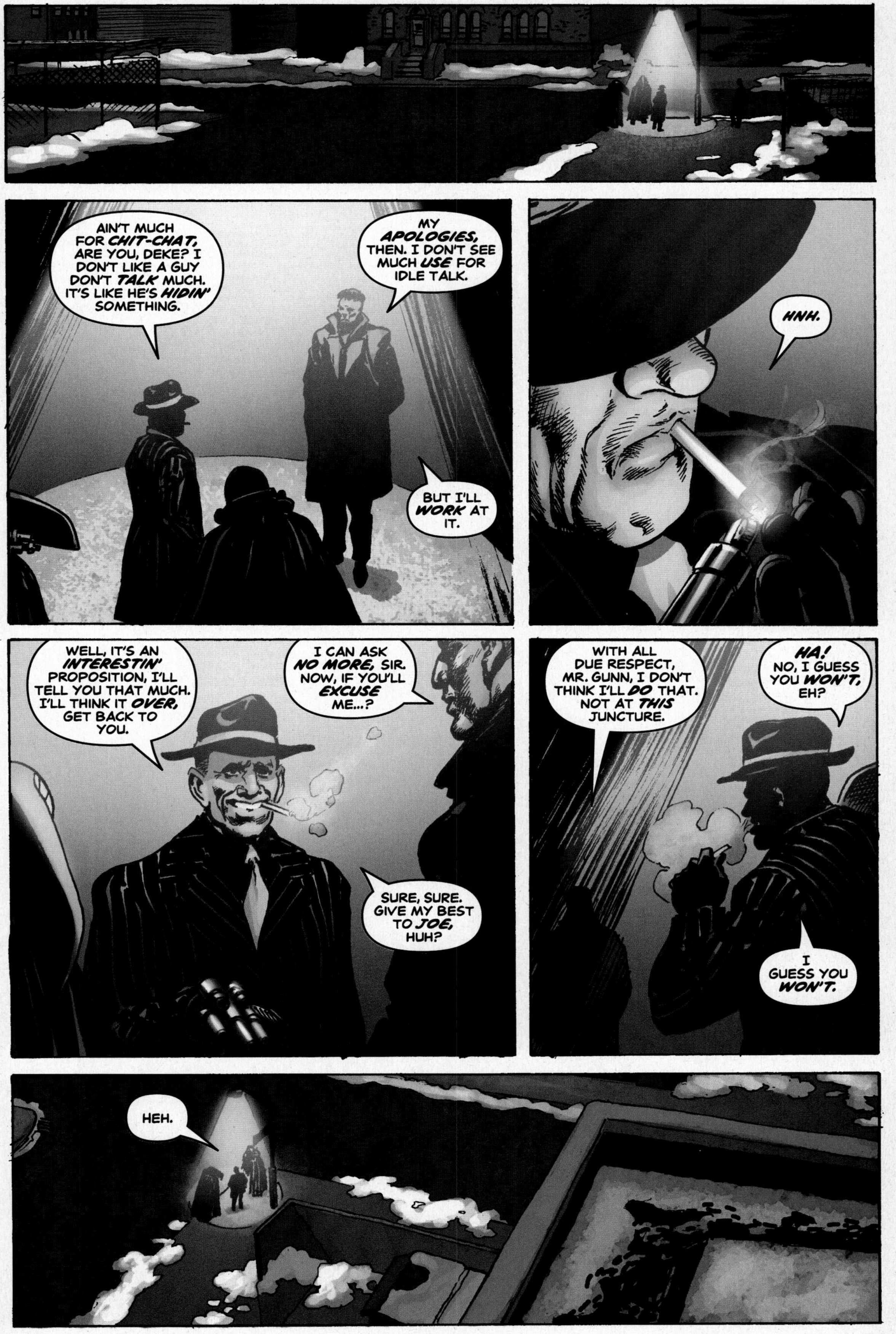
AIN'T MUCH FOR CHIT-CHAT, ARE YOU, DEKE? I DON'T LIKE A GUY DON'T TALK MUCH. IT'S LIKE HE'S HIDIN' SOMETHING.
MY APOLOGIES, THEN. I DON'T SEE MUCH USE FOR IDLE TALK.
BUT I'LL WORK AT IT.
HNH.
WELL, IT'S AN INTERESTIN' PROPOSITION, I'LL TELL YOU THAT MUCH. I'LL THINK IT OVER, GET BACK TO YOU.
I CAN ASK NO MORE, SIR. NOW, IF YOU'LL EXCUSE ME...?
SURE, SURE. GIVE MY BEST TO JOE, HUH?
WITH ALL DUE RESPECT, MR. GUNN, I DON'T THINK I'LL DO THAT. NOT AT THIS JUNCTURE.
HA! NO, I GUESS YOU WON'T, EH?
I GUESS YOU WON'T.
HEH.

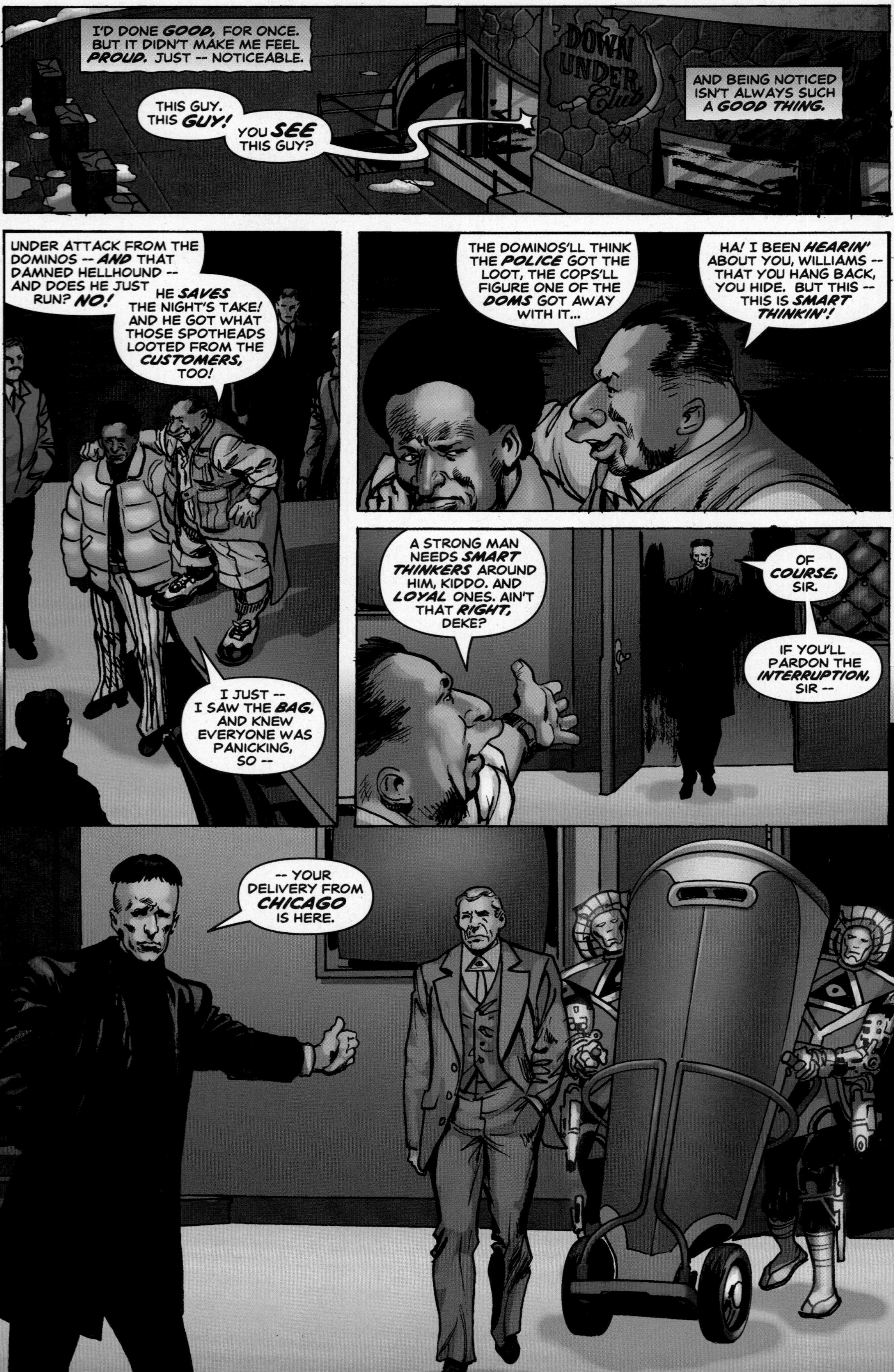
I'D DONE GOOD, FOR ONCE. BUT IT DIDN'T MAKE ME FEEL PROUD. JUST -- NOTICEABLE.
THIS GUY. THIS GUY!
YOU SEE THIS GUY?
AND BEING NOTICED ISN'T ALWAYS SUCH A GOOD THING.
DOWN UNDER Club
UNDER ATTACK FROM THE DOMINOS -- AND THAT DAMNED HELLHOUND -- AND DOES HE JUST RUN? NO!
HE SAVES THE NIGHT'S TAKE! AND HE GOT WHAT THOSE SPOTHEADS LOOTED FROM THE CUSTOMERS, TOO!
I JUST -- I SAW THE BAG, AND KNEW EVERYONE WAS PANICKING, SO --
THE DOMINOS'LL THINK THE POLICE GOT THE LOOT, THE COPS'LL FIGURE ONE OF THE DOMS GOT AWAY WITH IT...
HA! I BEEN HEARIN' ABOUT YOU, WILLIAMS -- THAT YOU HANG BACK, YOU HIDE. BUT THIS -- THIS IS SMART THINKIN'!
A STRONG MAN NEEDS SMART THINKERS AROUND HIM, KIDDO. AND LOYAL ONES. AIN'T THAT RIGHT, DEKE?
OF COURSE, SIR.
IF YOU'LL PARDON THE INTERRUPTION, SIR --
-- YOUR DELIVERY FROM CHICAGO IS HERE.

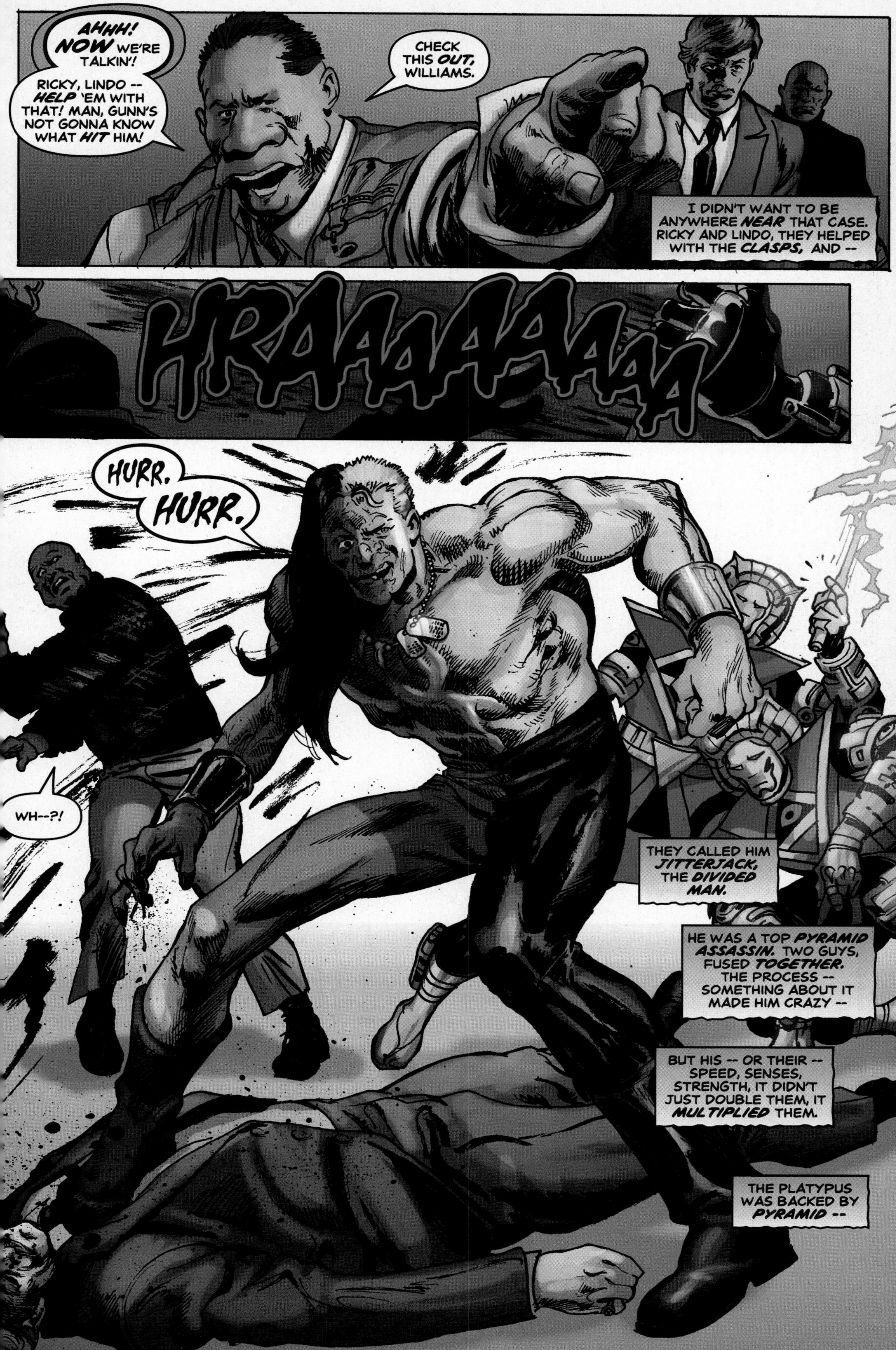
AHHH! NOW WE'RE TALKIN'!
RICKY, LINDO -- HELP 'EM WITH THAT! MAN, GUNN'S NOT GONNA KNOW WHAT HIT HIM!
CHECK THIS OUT, WILLIAMS.
I DIDN'T WANT TO BE ANYWHERE NEAR THAT CASE. RICKY AND LINDO, THEY HELPED WITH THE CLASPS, AND --
HRAAAAAAAAAA
HURR. HURR.
WH--?!
THEY CALLED HIM JITTERJACK, THE DIVIDED MAN.
HE WAS A TOP PYRAMID ASSASSIN. TWO GUYS, FUSED TOGETHER. THE PROCESS -- SOMETHING ABOUT IT MADE HIM CRAZY --
BUT HIS -- OR THEIR -- SPEED, SENSES, STRENGTH, IT DIDN'T JUST DOUBLE THEM, IT MULTIPLIED THEM.
THE PLATYPUS WAS BACKED BY PYRAMID --

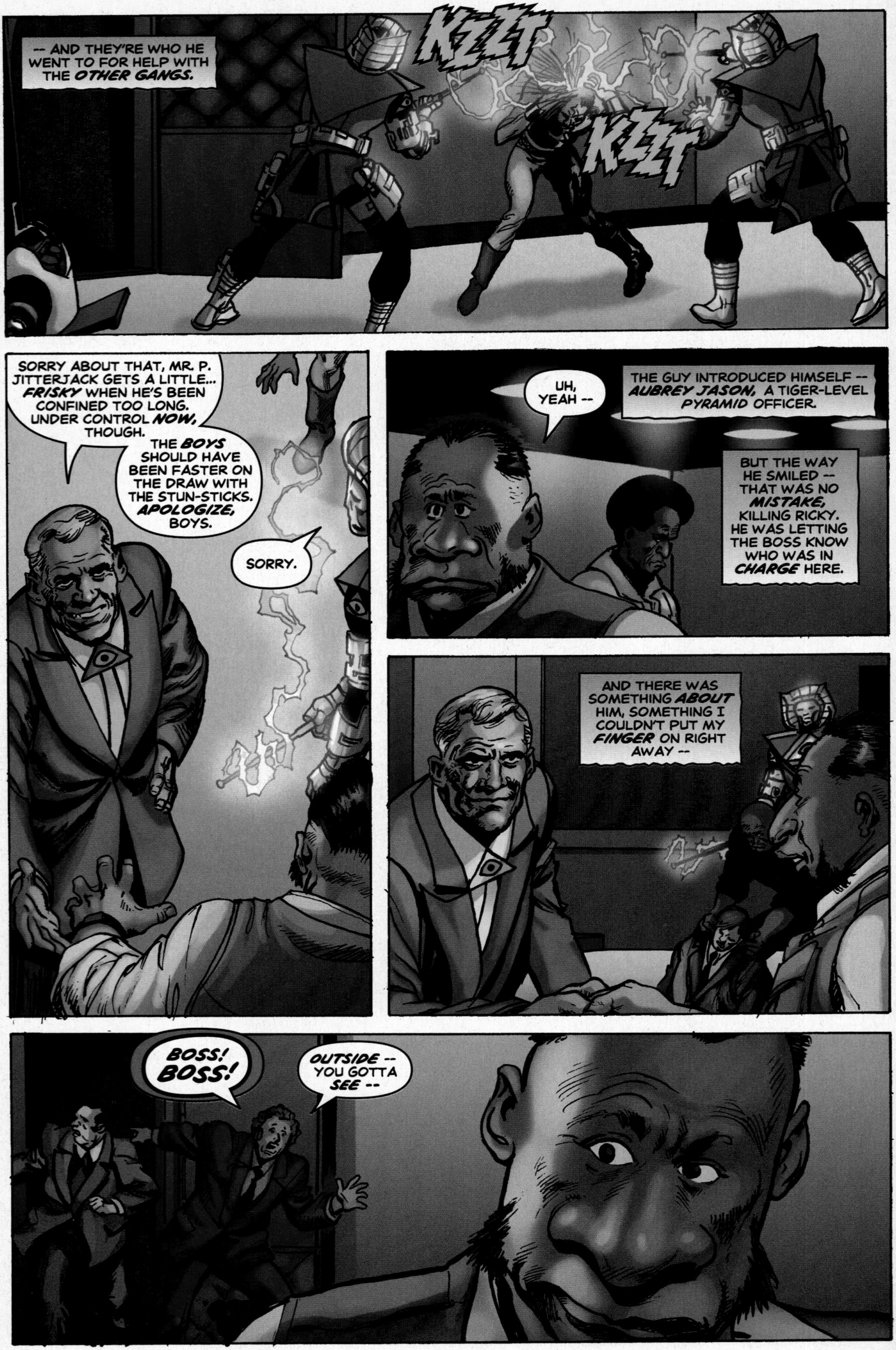

-- AND THEY'RE WHO HE WENT TO FOR HELP WITH THE OTHER GANGS.
KZZZT
KZZZT
SORRY ABOUT THAT, MR. P. JITTERJACK GETS A LITTLE... FRISKY WHEN HE'S BEEN CONFINED TOO LONG. UNDER CONTROL NOW, THOUGH.
THE BOYS SHOULD HAVE BEEN FASTER ON THE DRAW WITH THE STUN-STICKS. APOLOGIZE, BOYS.
SORRY.
UH, YEAH --
THE GUY INTRODUCED HIMSELF -- AUBREY JASON, A TIGER-LEVEL PYRAMID OFFICER.
BUT THE WAY HE SMILED -- THAT WAS NO MISTAKE, KILLING RICKY. HE WAS LETTING THE BOSS KNOW WHO WAS IN CHARGE HERE.
AND THERE WAS SOMETHING ABOUT HIM, SOMETHING I COULDN'T PUT MY FINGER ON RIGHT AWAY --
BOSS! BOSS!
OUTSIDE -- YOU GOTTA SEE --

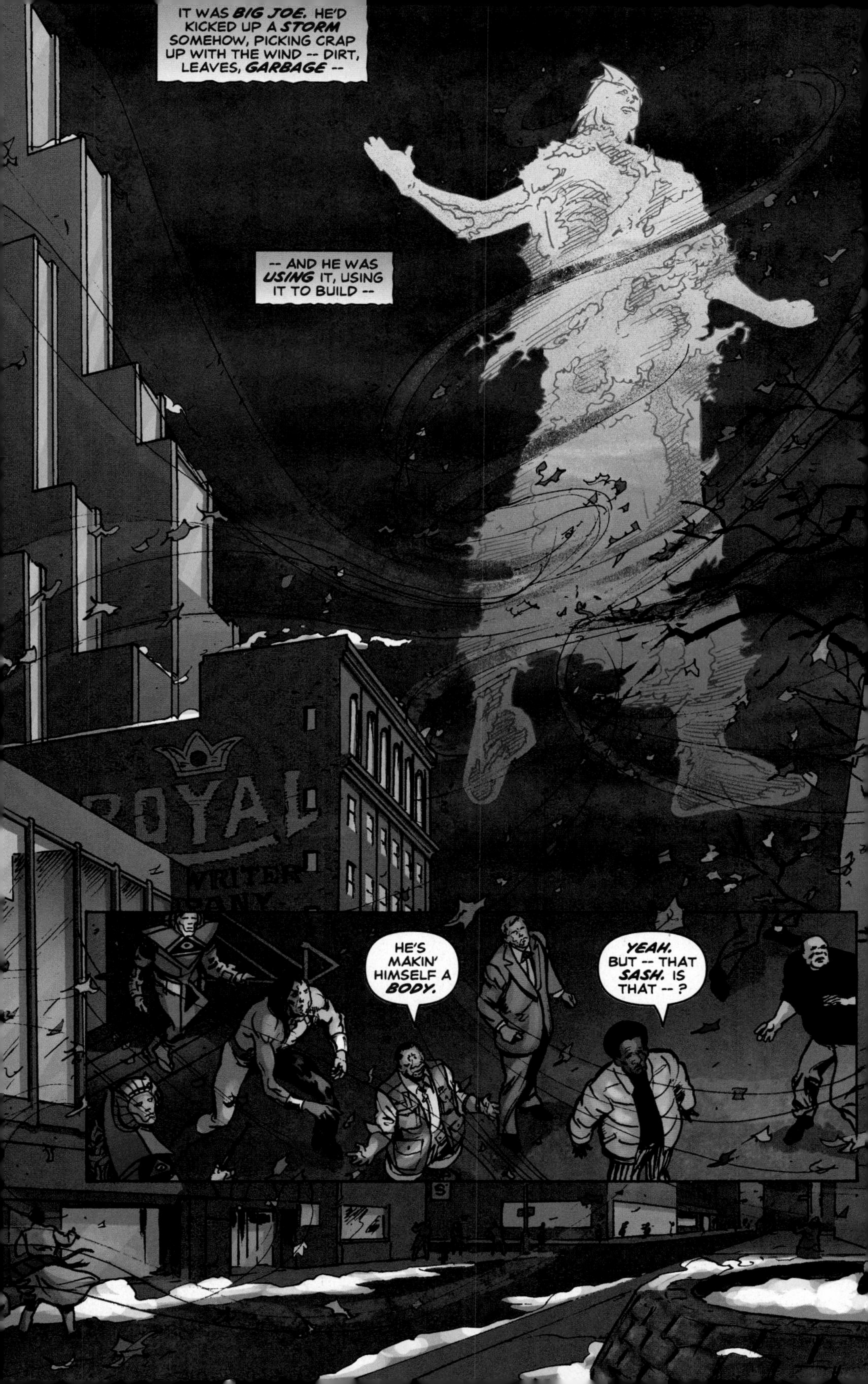

IT WAS BIG JOE. HE'D KICKED UP A STORM SOMEHOW, PICKING CRAP UP WITH THE WIND -- DIRT, LEAVES, GARBAGE --
-- AND HE WAS USING IT, USING IT TO BUILD --
ROYAL
HE'S MAKIN' HIMSELF A BODY.
YEAH. BUT -- THAT SASH. IS THAT -- ?

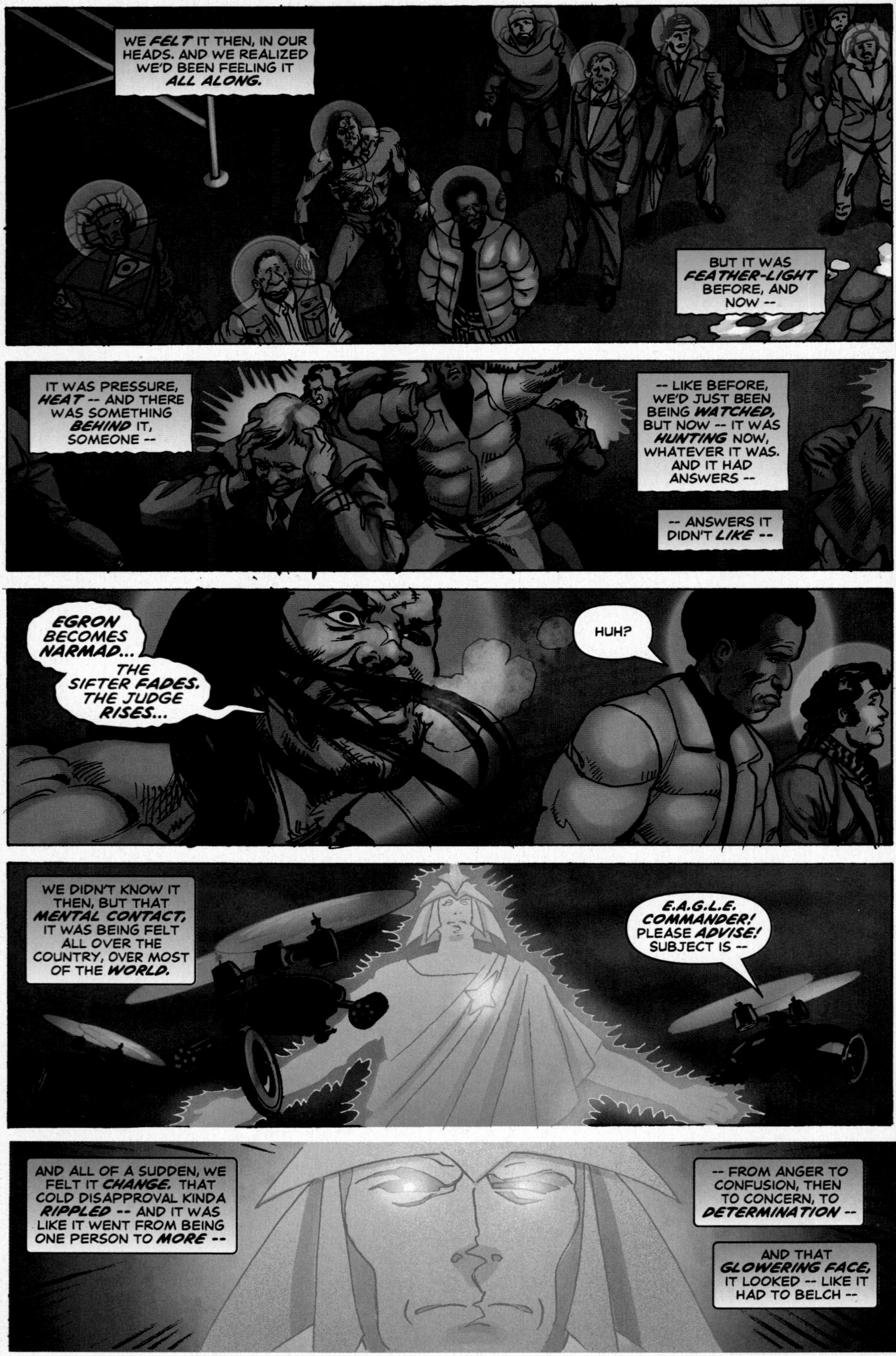
WE FELT IT THEN, IN OUR HEADS. AND WE REALIZED WE'D BEEN FEELING IT ALL ALONG.
BUT IT WAS FEATHER-LIGHT BEFORE, AND NOW --
IT WAS PRESSURE, HEAT -- AND THERE WAS SOMETHING BEHIND IT, SOMEONE --
-- LIKE BEFORE, WE'D JUST BEEN BEING WATCHED, BUT NOW -- IT WAS HUNTING NOW, WHATEVER IT WAS. AND IT HAD ANSWERS --
-- ANSWERS IT DIDN'T LIKE --
EGRON BECOMES NARMAD... THE SIFTER FADES. THE JUDGE RISES...
HUH?
WE DIDN'T KNOW IT THEN, BUT THAT MENTAL CONTACT, IT WAS BEING FELT ALL OVER THE COUNTRY, OVER MOST OF THE WORLD.
E.A.G.L.E. COMMANDER! PLEASE ADVISE! SUBJECT IS --
AND ALL OF A SUDDEN, WE FELT IT CHANGE. THAT COLD DISAPPROVAL KINDA RIPPLED -- AND IT WAS LIKE IT WENT FROM BEING ONE PERSON TO MORE --
-- FROM ANGER TO CONFUSION, THEN TO CONCERN, TO DETERMINATION --
AND THAT GLOWERING FACE, IT LOOKED -- LIKE IT HAD TO BELCH --

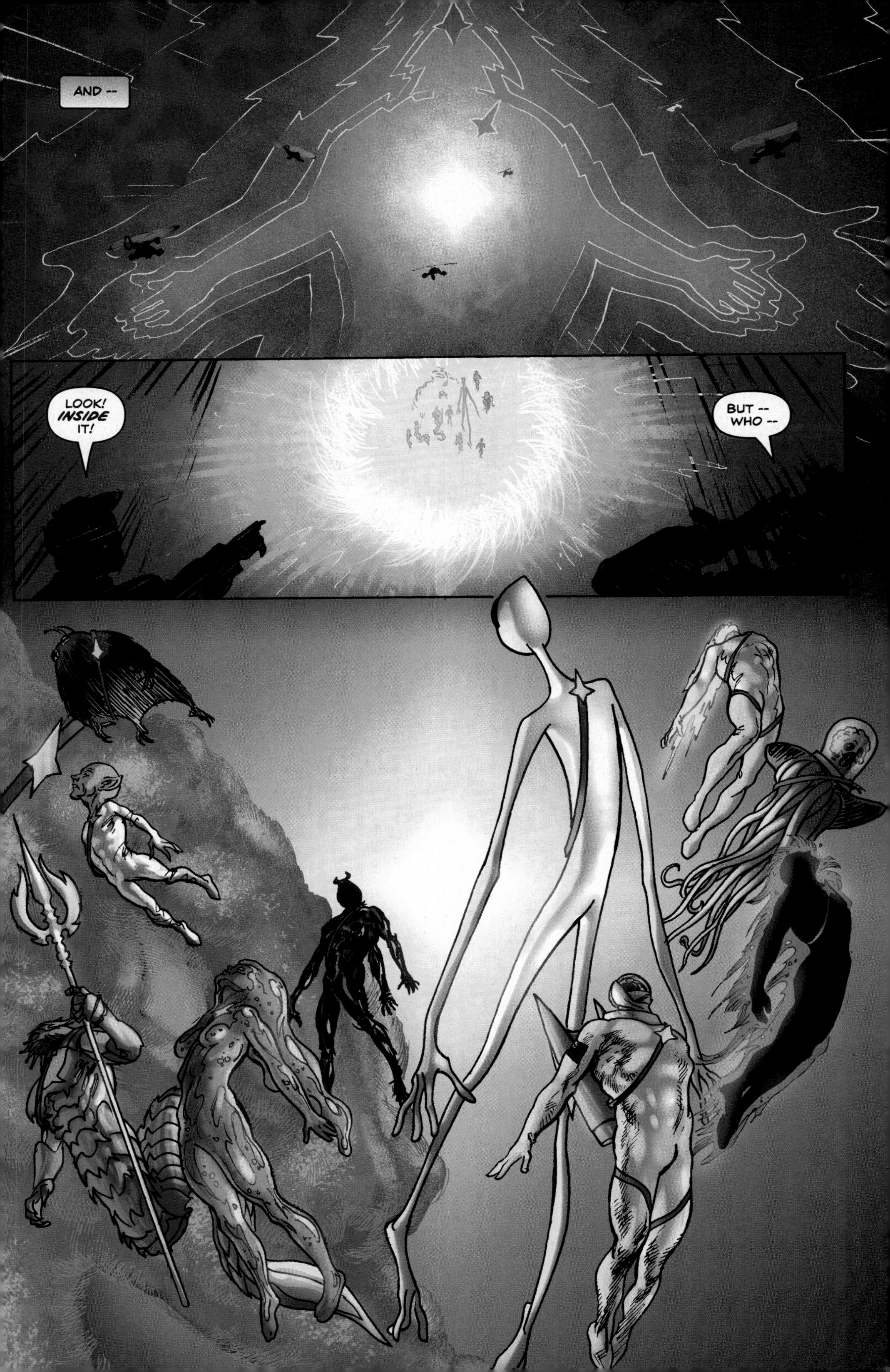
AND --
LOOK! *INSIDE* IT!
BUT -- WHO --

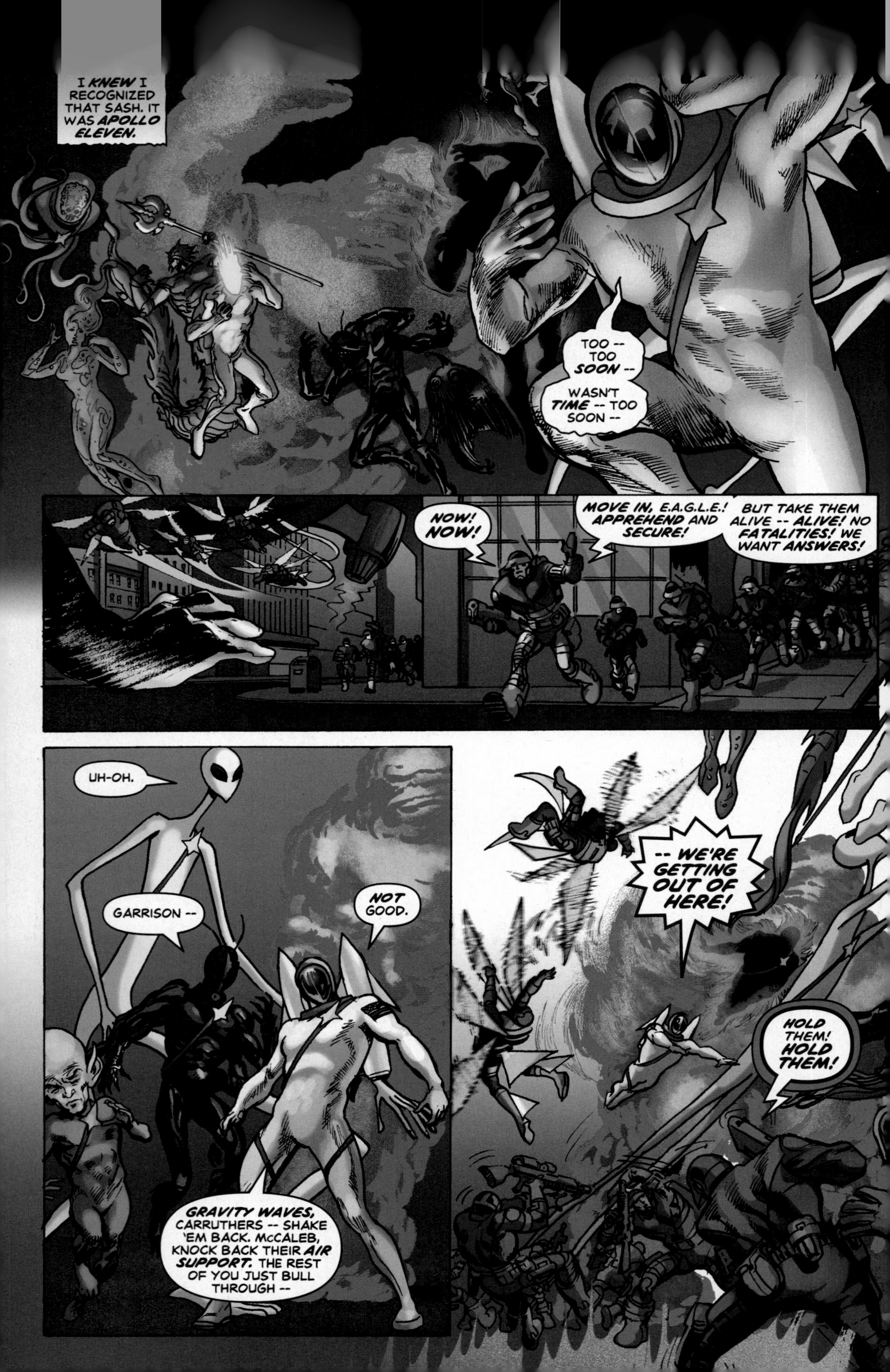
I KNEW I RECOGNIZED THAT SASH. IT WAS APOLLO ELEVEN.
TOO -- TOO SOON --
WASN'T TIME -- TOO SOON --
NOW! NOW!
MOVE IN, E.A.G.L.E.! APPREHEND AND SECURE!
BUT TAKE THEM ALIVE -- ALIVE! NO FATALITIES! WE WANT ANSWERS!
UH-OH.
GARRISON --
NOT GOOD.
GRAVITY WAVES, CARRUTHERS -- SHAKE 'EM BACK. McCALEB, KNOCK BACK THEIR AIR SUPPORT. THE REST OF YOU JUST BULL THROUGH --
-- WE'RE GETTING OUT OF HERE!
HOLD THEM! HOLD THEM!

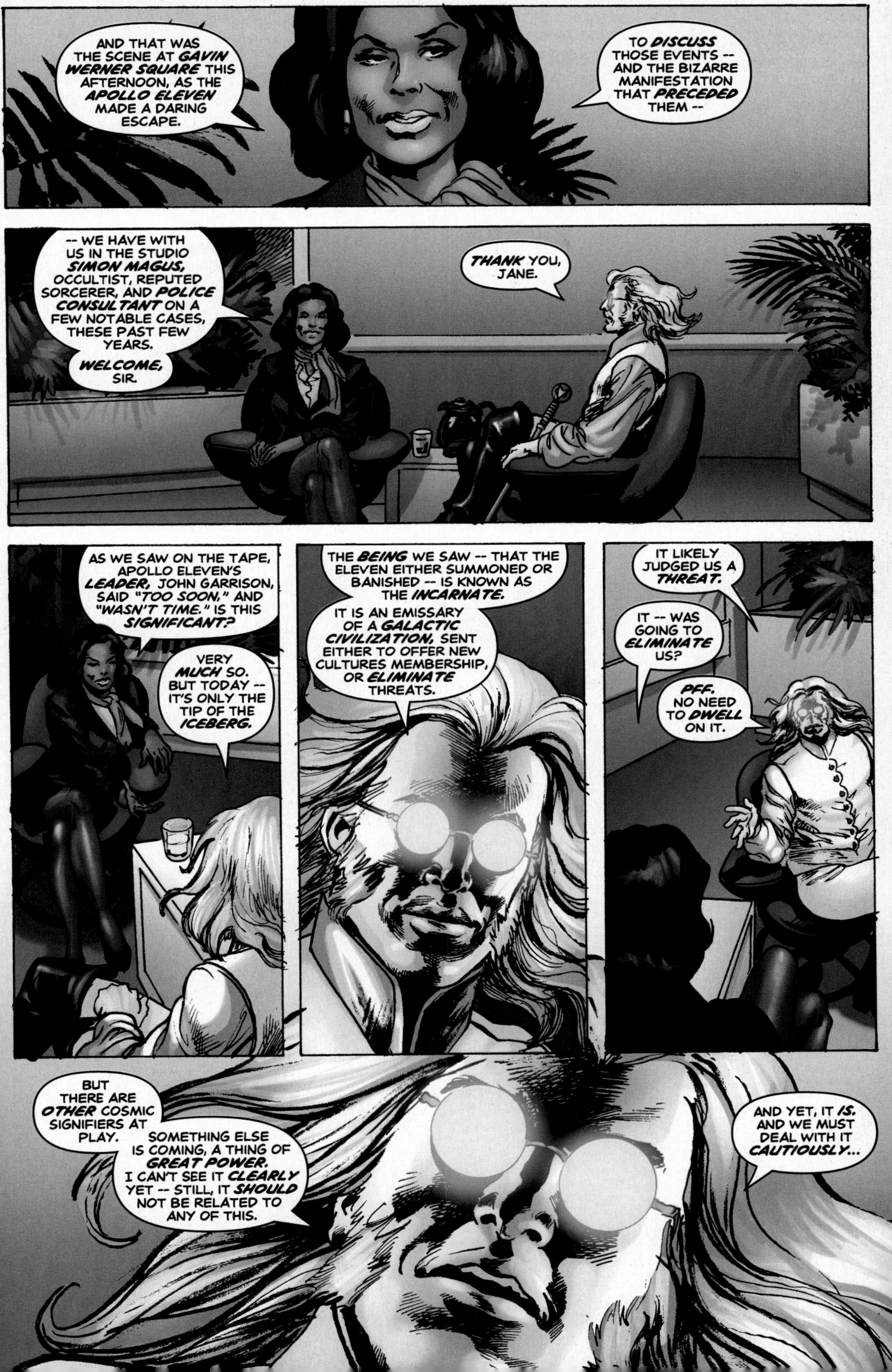
AND THAT WAS THE SCENE AT GAVIN WERNER SQUARE THIS AFTERNOON, AS THE APOLLO ELEVEN MADE A DARING ESCAPE.
TO DISCUSS THOSE EVENTS -- AND THE BIZARRE MANIFESTATION THAT PRECEDED THEM --
-- WE HAVE WITH US IN THE STUDIO SIMON MAGUS, OCCULTIST, REPUTED SORCERER, AND POLICE CONSULTANT ON A FEW NOTABLE CASES, THESE PAST FEW YEARS.
WELCOME, SIR.
THANK YOU, JANE.
AS WE SAW ON THE TAPE, APOLLO ELEVEN'S LEADER, JOHN GARRISON, SAID "TOO SOON," AND "WASN'T TIME." IS THIS SIGNIFICANT?
VERY MUCH SO. BUT TODAY -- IT'S ONLY THE TIP OF THE ICEBERG.
THE BEING WE SAW -- THAT THE ELEVEN EITHER SUMMONED OR BANISHED -- IS KNOWN AS THE INCARNATE.
IT IS AN EMISSARY OF A GALACTIC CIVILIZATION, SENT EITHER TO OFFER NEW CULTURES MEMBERSHIP, OR ELIMINATE THREATS.
IT LIKELY JUDGED US A THREAT.
IT -- WAS GOING TO ELIMINATE US?
PFF. NO NEED TO DWELL ON IT.
BUT THERE ARE OTHER COSMIC SIGNIFIERS AT PLAY.
SOMETHING ELSE IS COMING, A THING OF GREAT POWER. I CAN'T SEE IT CLEARLY YET -- STILL, IT SHOULD NOT BE RELATED TO ANY OF THIS.
AND YET, IT IS. AND WE MUST DEAL WITH IT CAUTIOUSLY...

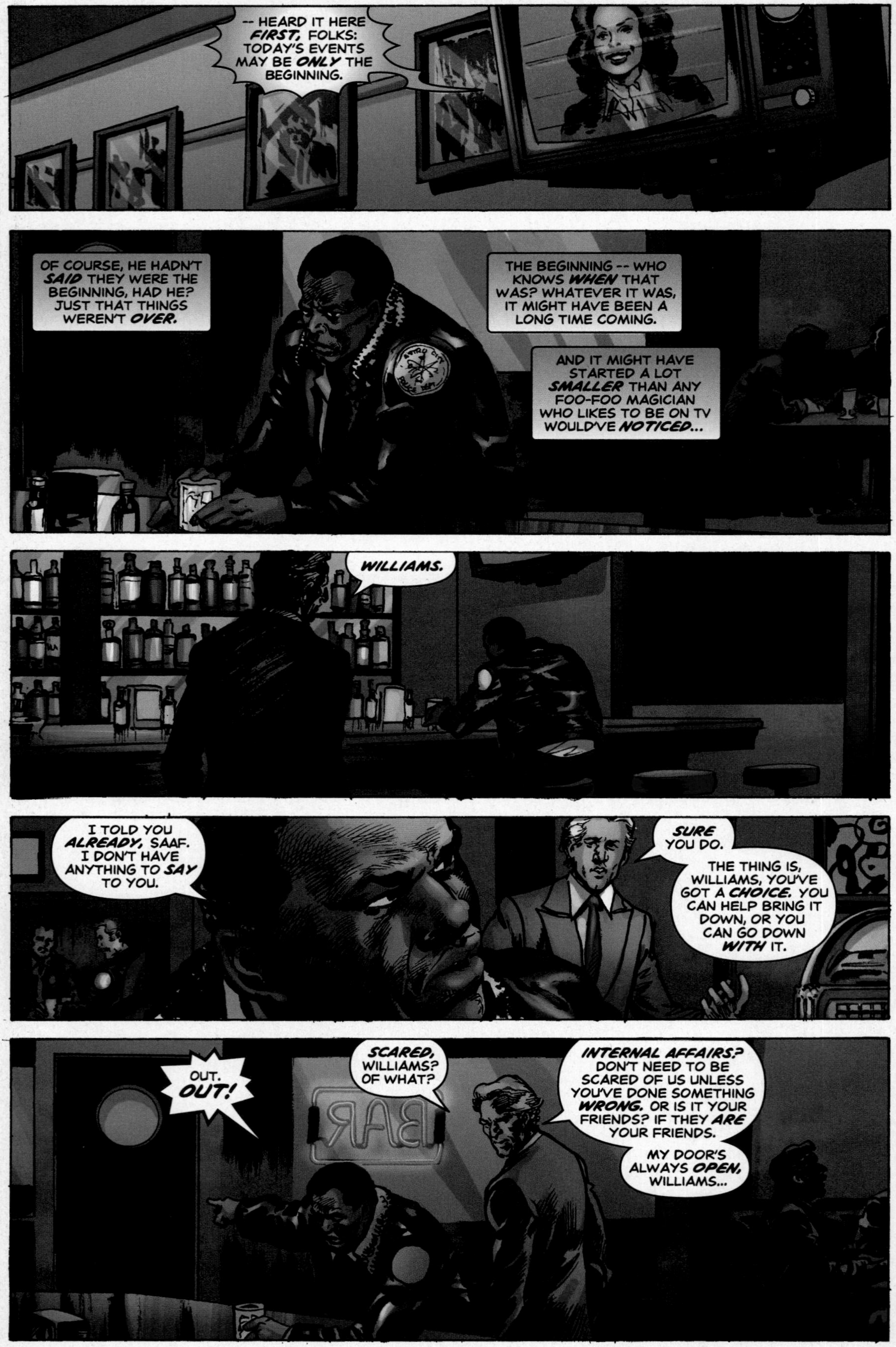
-- HEARD IT HERE FIRST, FOLKS: TODAY'S EVENTS MAY BE ONLY THE BEGINNING.
OF COURSE, HE HADN'T SAID THEY WERE THE BEGINNING, HAD HE? JUST THAT THINGS WEREN'T OVER.
THE BEGINNING -- WHO KNOWS WHEN THAT WAS? WHATEVER IT WAS, IT MIGHT HAVE BEEN A LONG TIME COMING.
AND IT MIGHT HAVE STARTED A LOT SMALLER THAN ANY FOO-FOO MAGICIAN WHO LIKES TO BE ON TV WOULD'VE NOTICED...
WILLIAMS.
I TOLD YOU ALREADY, SAAF. I DON'T HAVE ANYTHING TO SAY TO YOU.
SURE YOU DO.
THE THING IS, WILLIAMS, YOU'VE GOT A CHOICE. YOU CAN HELP BRING IT DOWN, OR YOU CAN GO DOWN WITH IT.
OUT. OUT!
SCARED, WILLIAMS? OF WHAT?
INTERNAL AFFAIRS? DON'T NEED TO BE SCARED OF US UNLESS YOU'VE DONE SOMETHING WRONG. OR IS IT YOUR FRIENDS? IF THEY ARE YOUR FRIENDS.
MY DOOR'S ALWAYS OPEN, WILLIAMS...
BAR

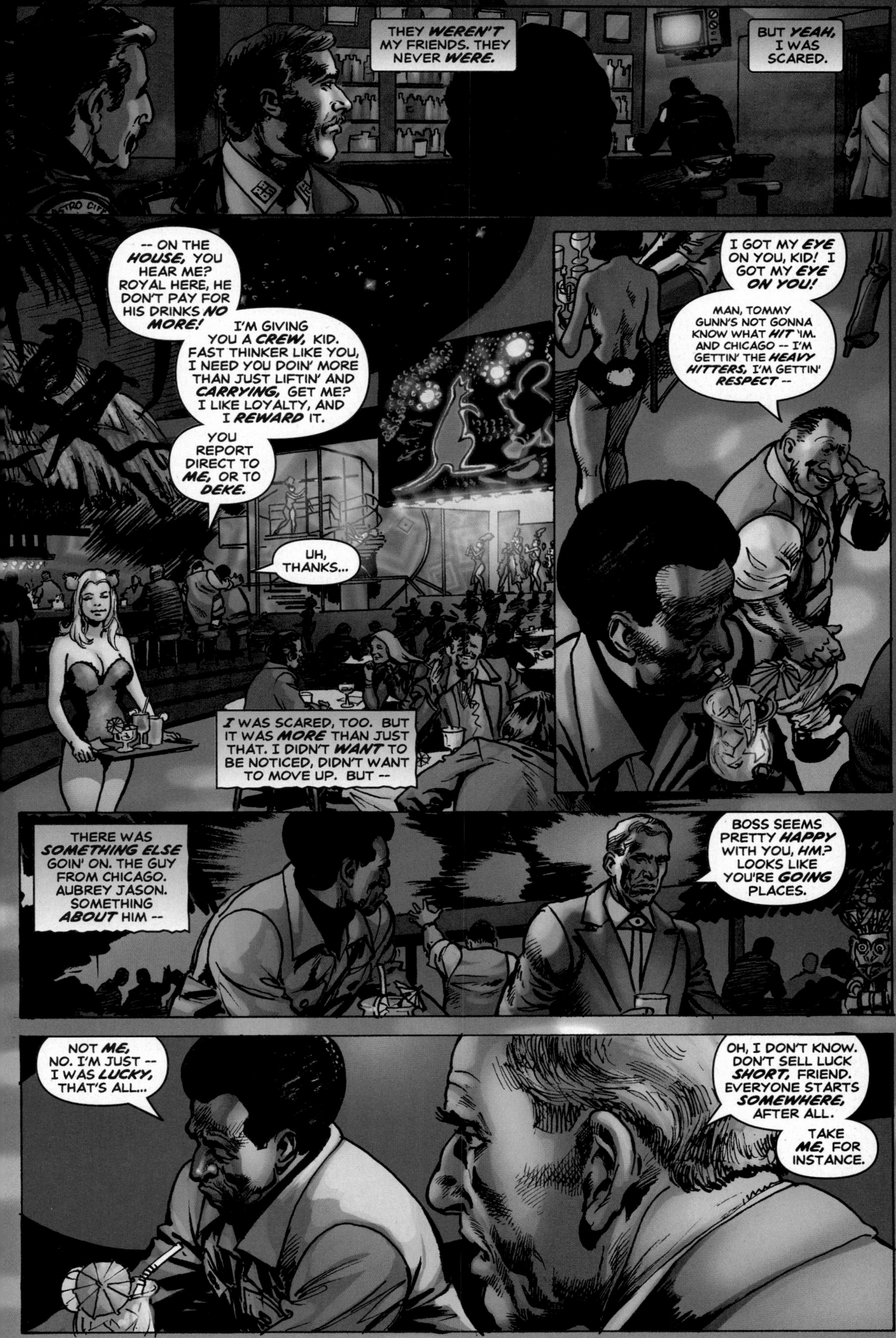
THEY WEREN'T MY FRIENDS. THEY NEVER WERE.
BUT YEAH, I WAS SCARED.
-- ON THE HOUSE, YOU HEAR ME? ROYAL HERE, HE DON'T PAY FOR HIS DRINKS NO MORE!
I'M GIVING YOU A CREW, KID. FAST THINKER LIKE YOU, I NEED YOU DOIN' MORE THAN JUST LIFTIN' AND CARRYING, GET ME? I LIKE LOYALTY, AND I REWARD IT.
YOU REPORT DIRECT TO ME, OR TO DEKE.
UH, THANKS...
I WAS SCARED, TOO. BUT IT WAS MORE THAN JUST THAT. I DIDN'T WANT TO BE NOTICED, DIDN'T WANT TO MOVE UP. BUT --
I GOT MY EYE ON YOU, KID! I GOT MY EYE ON YOU!
MAN, TOMMY GUNN'S NOT GONNA KNOW WHAT HIT 'IM. AND CHICAGO -- I'M GETTIN' THE HEAVY HITTERS, I'M GETTIN' RESPECT --
THERE WAS SOMETHING ELSE GOIN' ON. THE GUY FROM CHICAGO. AUBREY JASON. SOMETHING ABOUT HIM --
BOSS SEEMS PRETTY HAPPY WITH YOU, HM? LOOKS LIKE YOU'RE GOING PLACES.
NOT ME, NO. I'M JUST -- I WAS LUCKY, THAT'S ALL...
OH, I DON'T KNOW. DON'T SELL LUCK SHORT, FRIEND. EVERYONE STARTS SOMEWHERE, AFTER ALL.
TAKE ME, FOR INSTANCE.

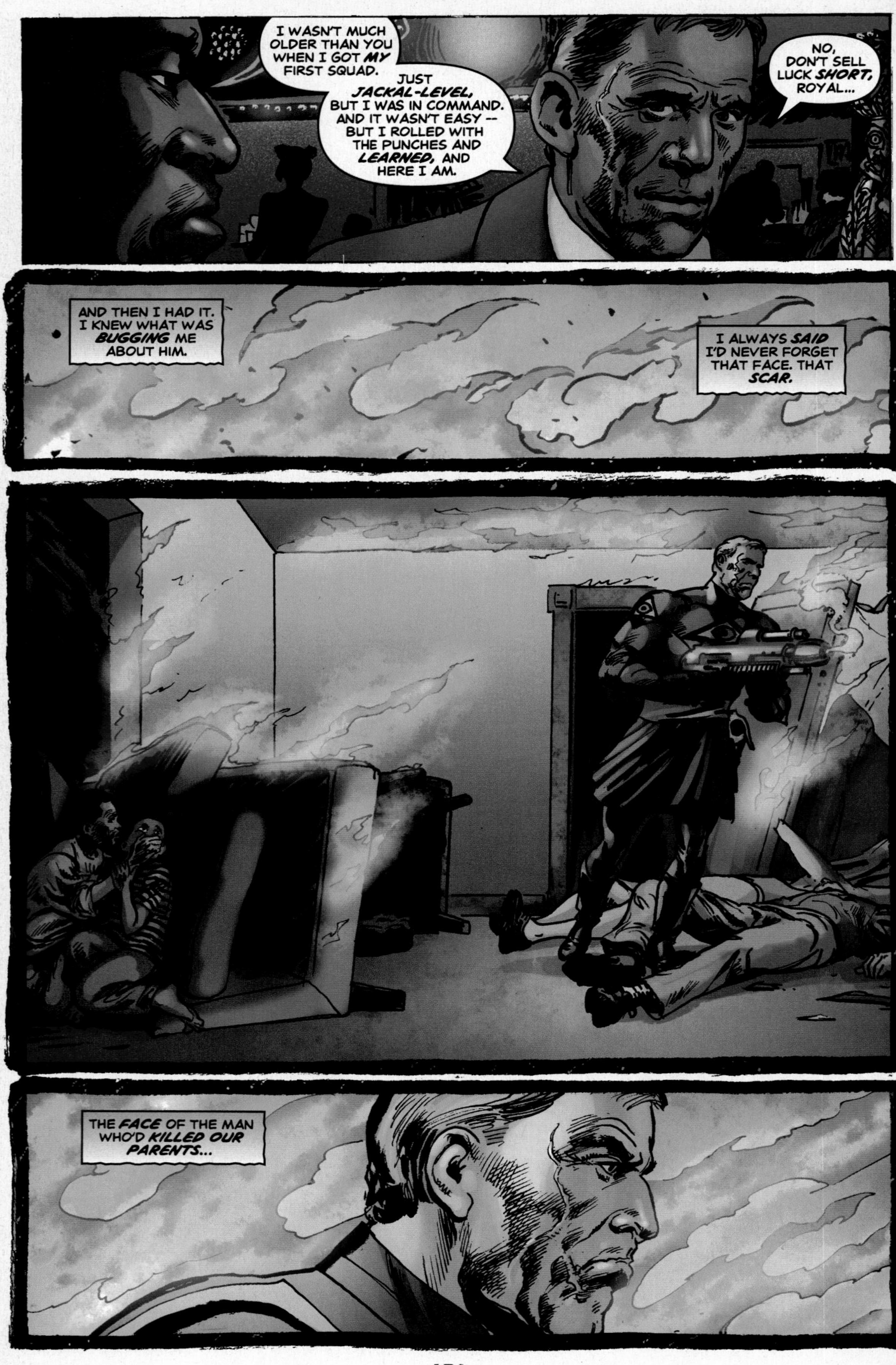

I WASN'T MUCH OLDER THAN YOU WHEN I GOT MY FIRST SQUAD.
JUST JACKAL-LEVEL, BUT I WAS IN COMMAND. AND IT WASN'T EASY -- BUT I ROLLED WITH THE PUNCHES AND LEARNED, AND HERE I AM.
NO, DON'T SELL LUCK SHORT, ROYAL...
AND THEN I HAD IT. I KNEW WHAT WAS BUGGING ME ABOUT HIM.
I ALWAYS SAID I'D NEVER FORGET THAT FACE. THAT SCAR.
THE FACE OF THE MAN WHO'D KILLED OUR PARENTS...

ARABS SET TO
AGREE ON WEST
BANK STATE FOR

Television

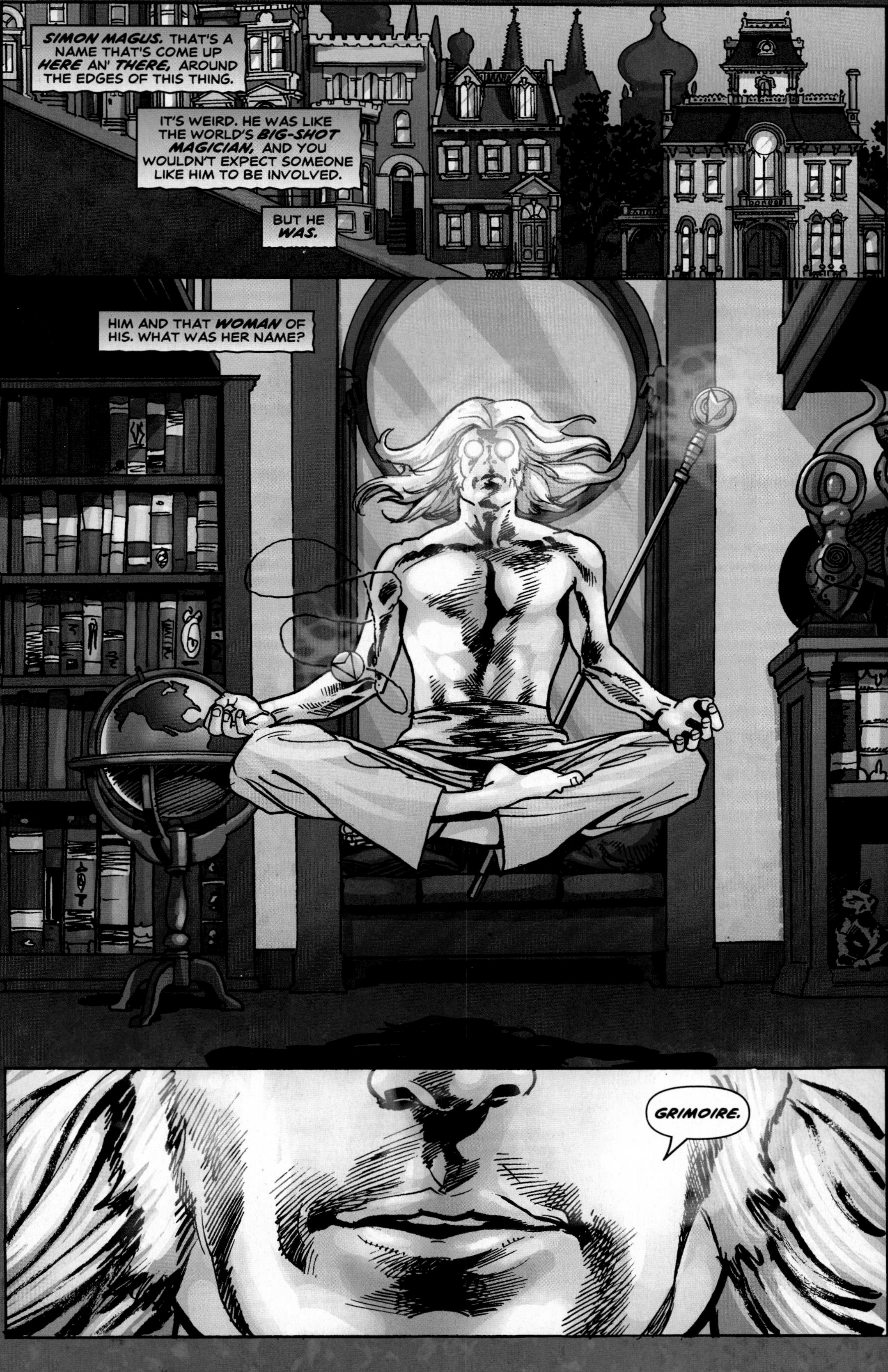
SIMON MAGUS. THAT'S A NAME THAT'S COME UP HERE AN' THERE, AROUND THE EDGES OF THIS THING.
IT'S WEIRD. HE WAS LIKE THE WORLD'S BIG-SHOT MAGICIAN, AND YOU WOULDN'T EXPECT SOMEONE LIKE HIM TO BE INVOLVED.
BUT HE WAS.
HIM AND THAT WOMAN OF HIS. WHAT WAS HER NAME?
GRIMOIRE.

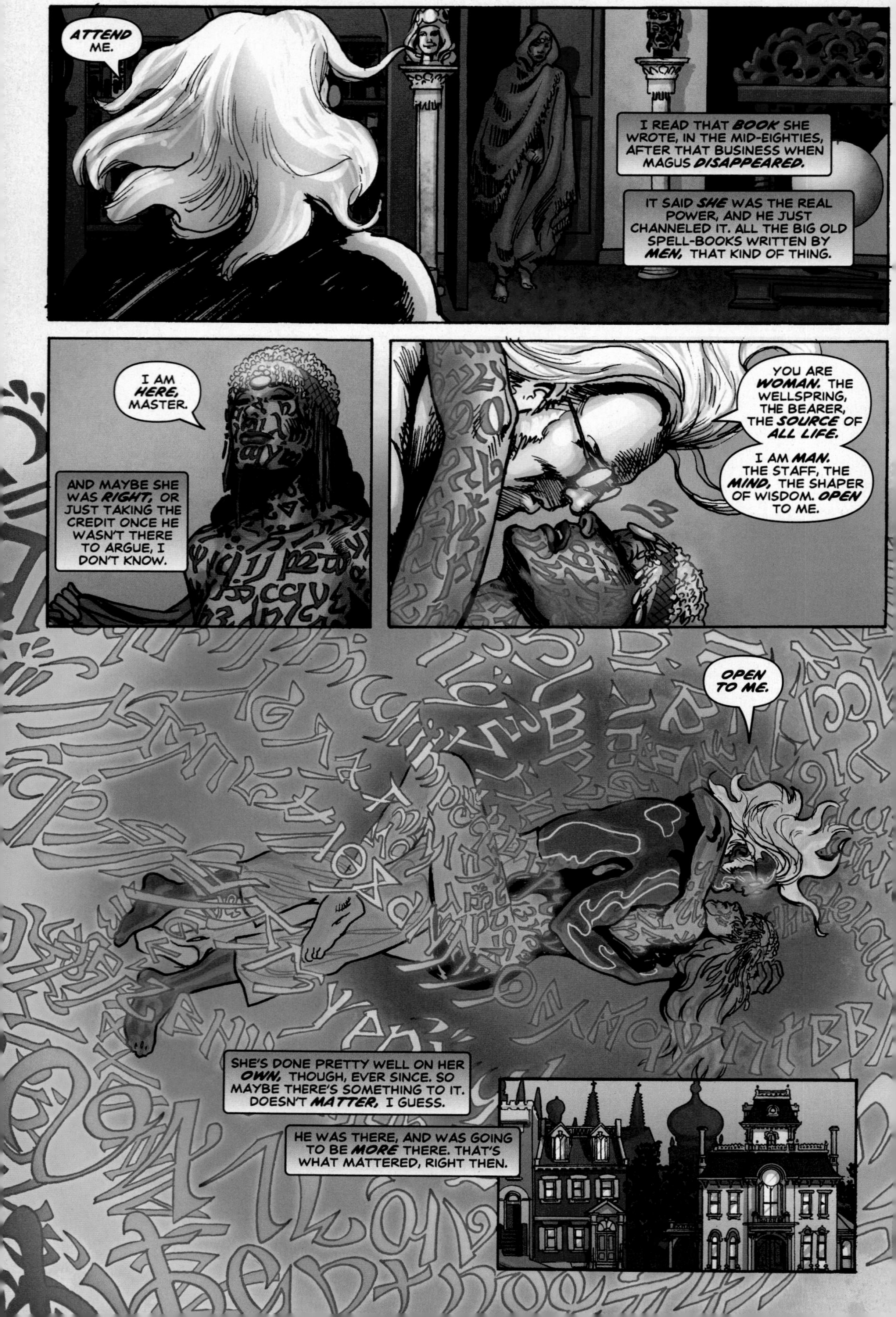
ATTEND ME.
I READ THAT BOOK SHE WROTE, IN THE MID-EIGHTIES, AFTER THAT BUSINESS WHEN MAGUS DISAPPEARED.
IT SAID SHE WAS THE REAL POWER, AND HE JUST CHANNELED IT. ALL THE BIG OLD SPELL-BOOKS WRITTEN BY MEN, THAT KIND OF THING.
I AM HERE, MASTER.
AND MAYBE SHE WAS RIGHT, OR JUST TAKING THE CREDIT ONCE HE WASN'T THERE TO ARGUE, I DON'T KNOW.
YOU ARE WOMAN. THE WELLSPRING, THE BEARER, THE SOURCE OF ALL LIFE.
I AM MAN. THE STAFF, THE MIND, THE SHAPER OF WISDOM. OPEN TO ME.
OPEN TO ME.
SHE'S DONE PRETTY WELL ON HER OWN, THOUGH, EVER SINCE. SO MAYBE THERE'S SOMETHING TO IT. DOESN'T MATTER, I GUESS.
HE WAS THERE, AND WAS GOING TO BE MORE THERE. THAT'S WHAT MATTERED, RIGHT THEN.

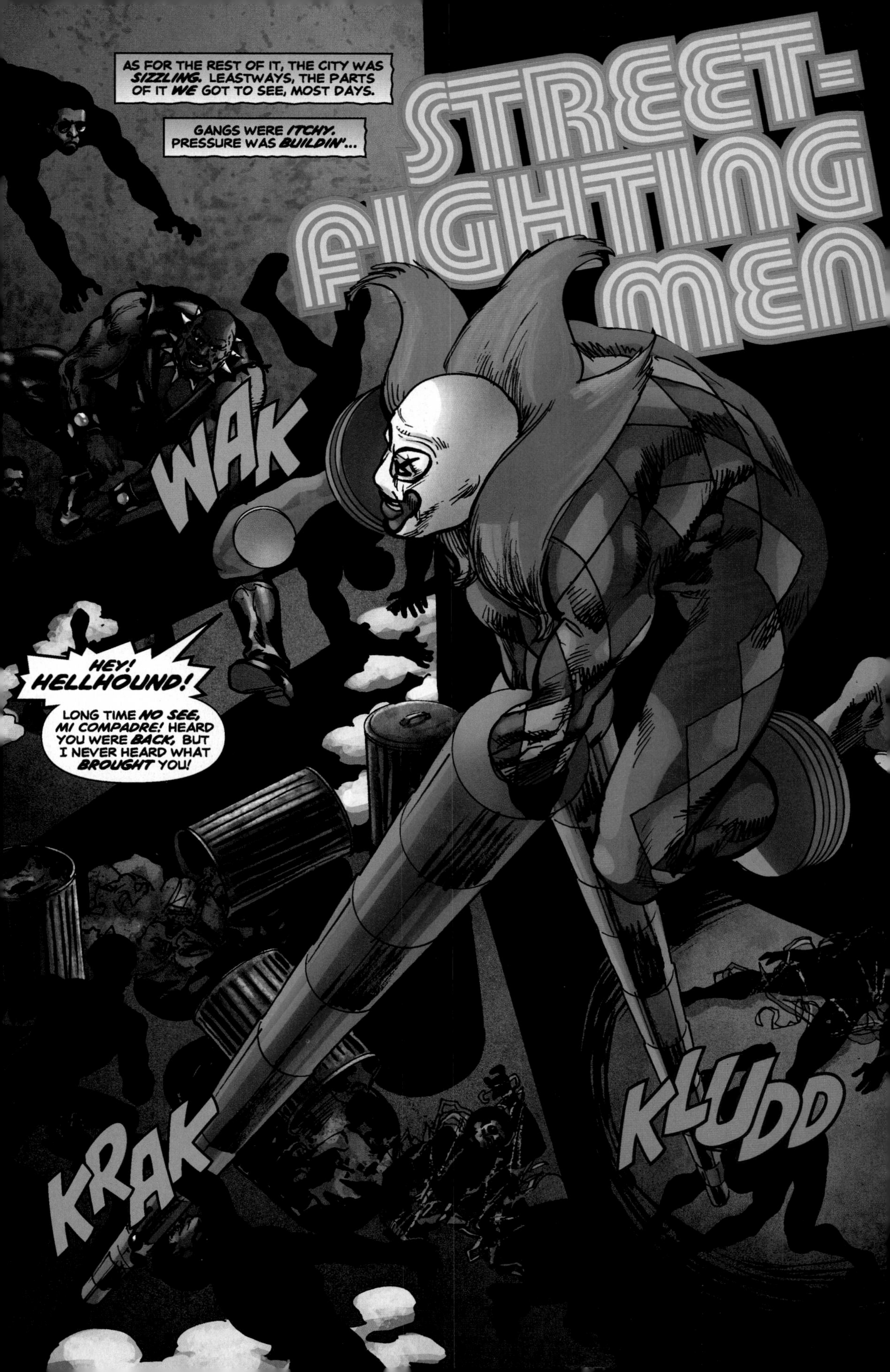
AS FOR THE REST OF IT, THE CITY WAS SIZZLING. LEASTWAYS, THE PARTS OF IT WE GOT TO SEE, MOST DAYS.
GANGS WERE ITCHY. PRESSURE WAS BUILDIN'...
STREET-FIGHTING MEN
WAK
HEY! HELLHOUND!
LONG TIME NO SEE, MI COMPADRE! HEARD YOU WERE BACK, BUT I NEVER HEARD WHAT BROUGHT YOU!
KRAK
KLUDD

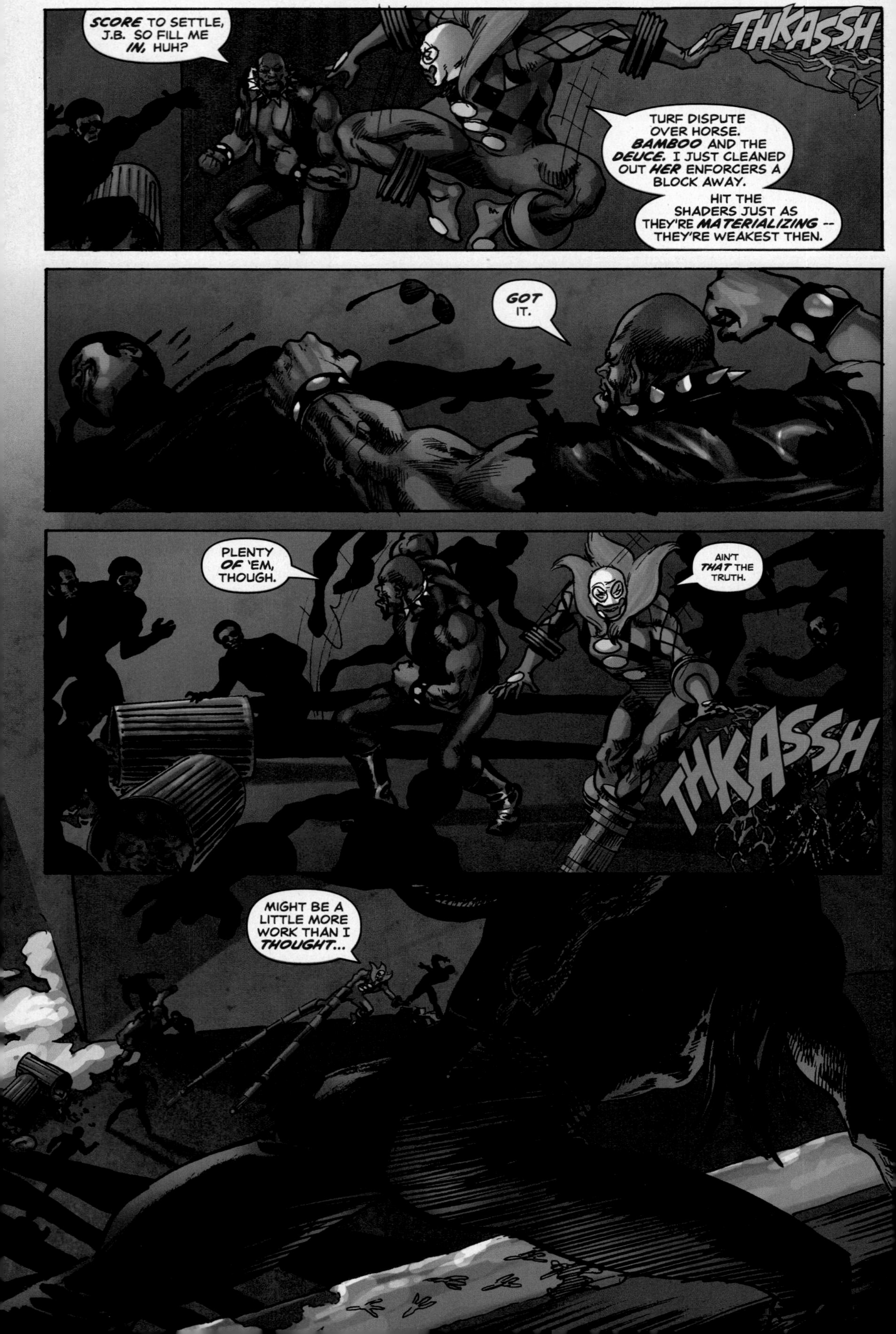
SCORE TO SETTLE, J.B. SO FILL ME IN, HUH?
THKASSH
TURF DISPUTE OVER HORSE. BAMBOO AND THE DEUCE. I JUST CLEANED OUT HER ENFORCERS A BLOCK AWAY.
HIT THE SHADERS JUST AS THEY'RE MATERIALIZING -- THEY'RE WEAKEST THEN.
GOT IT.
PLENTY OF 'EM, THOUGH.
AIN'T THAT THE TRUTH.
THKASSH
MIGHT BE A LITTLE MORE WORK THAN I THOUGHT...

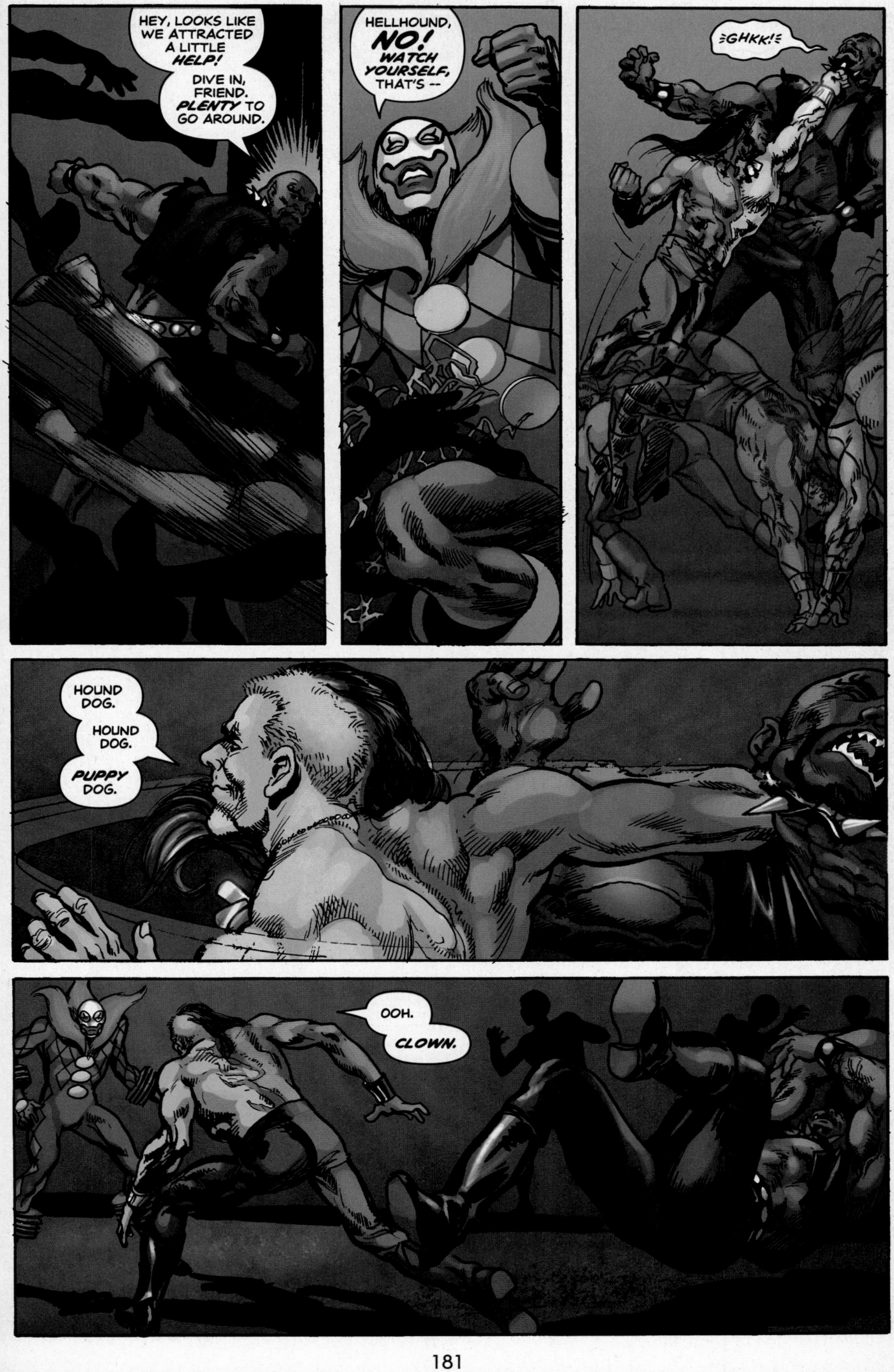
HEY, LOOKS LIKE WE ATTRACTED A LITTLE HELP!
DIVE IN, FRIEND. PLENTY TO GO AROUND.
HELLHOUND, NO! WATCH YOURSELF, THAT'S --
GHKK!
HOUND DOG.
HOUND DOG.
PUPPY DOG.
OOH.
CLOWN.

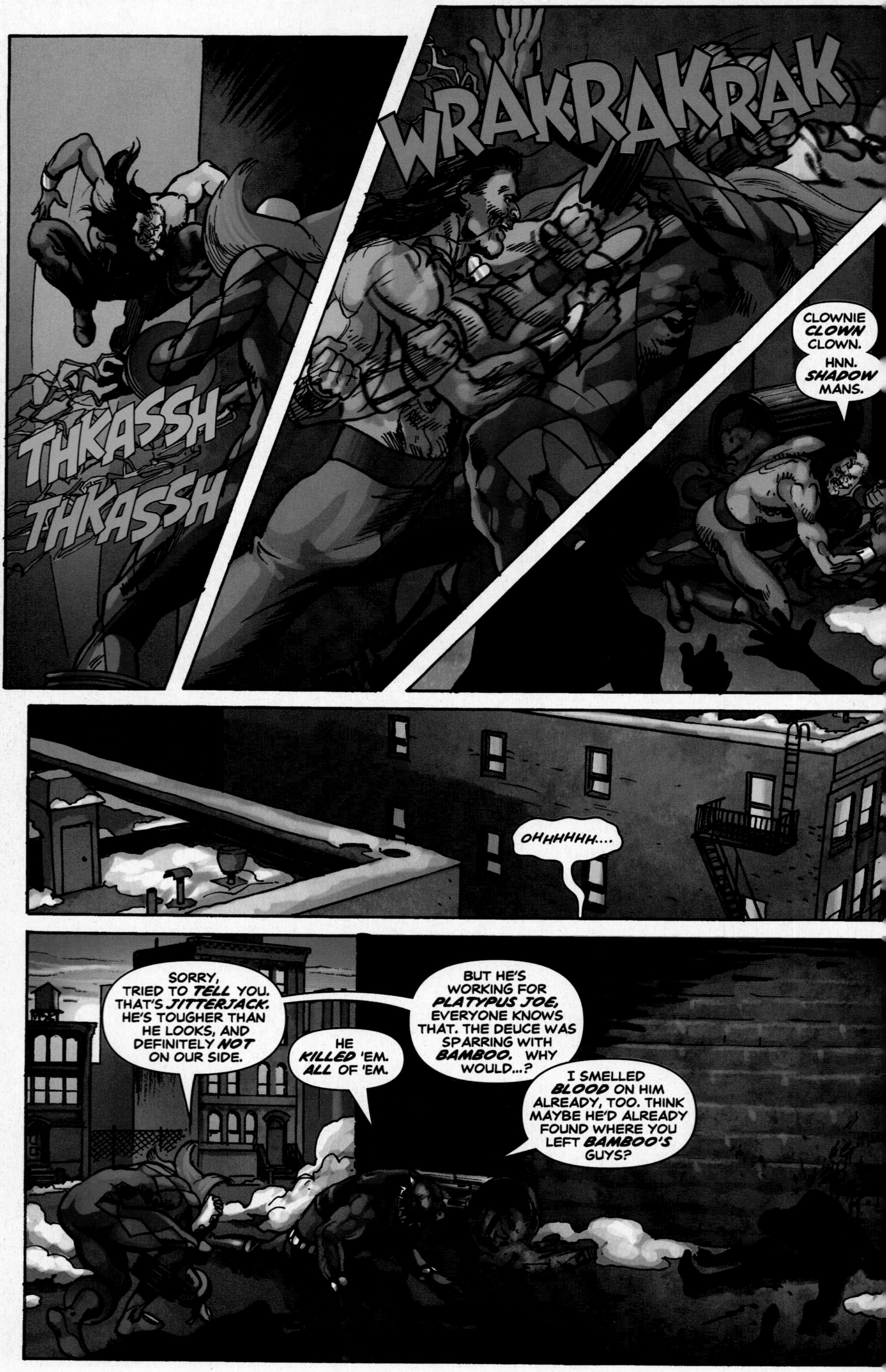
WRAKRAKRAK
THKASSH
THKASSH
CLOWNIE CLOWN CLOWN.
HNN. SHADOW MANS.
OHHHHHH....
SORRY, TRIED TO TELL YOU. THAT'S JITTERJACK. HE'S TOUGHER THAN HE LOOKS, AND DEFINITELY NOT ON OUR SIDE.
BUT HE'S WORKING FOR PLATYPUS JOE, EVERYONE KNOWS THAT. THE DEUCE WAS SPARRING WITH BAMBOO. WHY WOULD...?
HE KILLED 'EM. ALL OF 'EM.
I SMELLED BLOOD ON HIM ALREADY, TOO. THINK MAYBE HE'D ALREADY FOUND WHERE YOU LEFT BAMBOO'S GUYS?

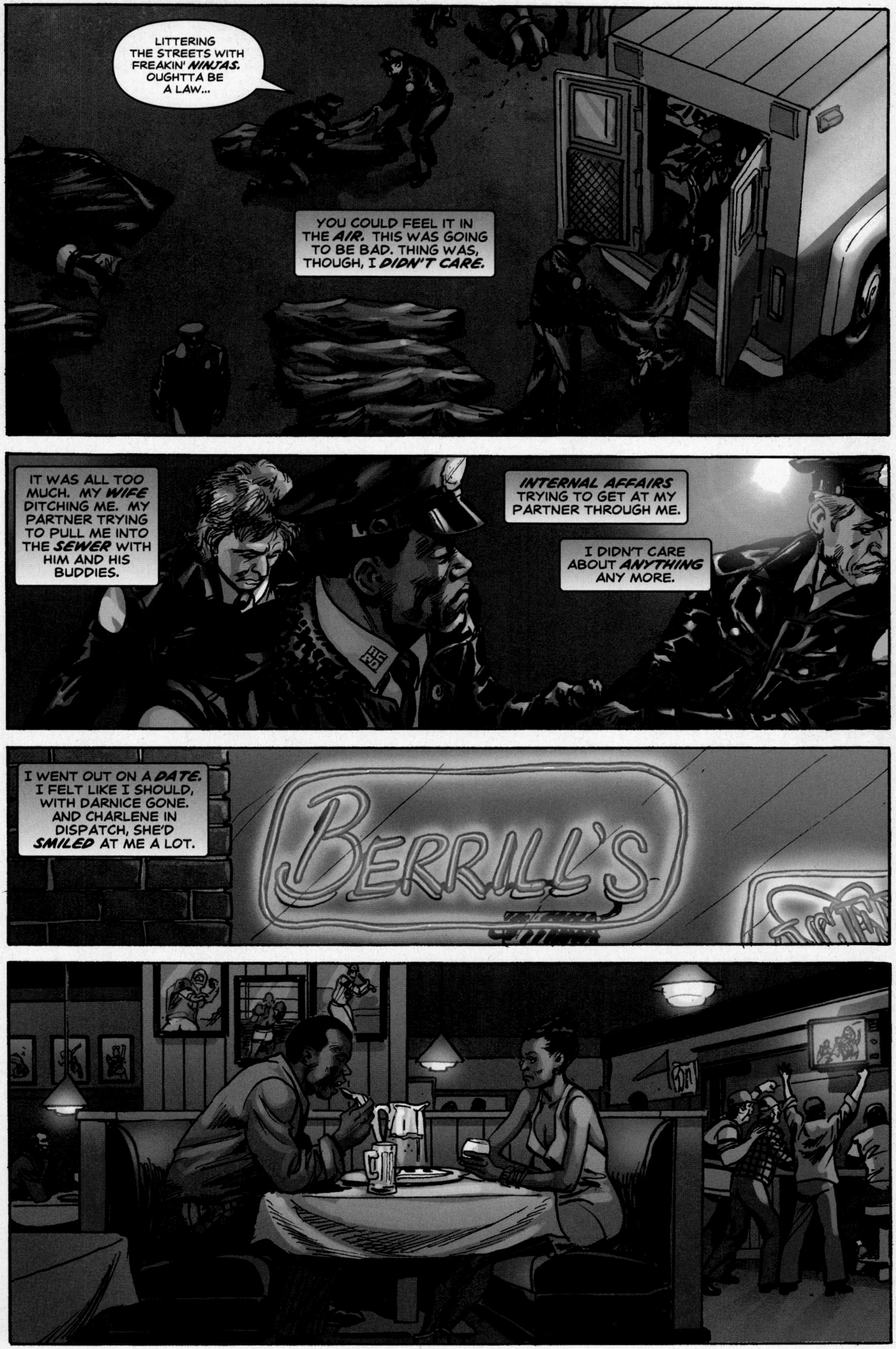
LITTERING THE STREETS WITH FREAKIN' NINJAS. OUGHTTA BE A LAW...
YOU COULD FEEL IT IN THE AIR. THIS WAS GOING TO BE BAD. THING WAS, THOUGH, I DIDN'T CARE.
IT WAS ALL TOO MUCH. MY WIFE DITCHING ME. MY PARTNER TRYING TO PULL ME INTO THE SEWER WITH HIM AND HIS BUDDIES.
INTERNAL AFFAIRS TRYING TO GET AT MY PARTNER THROUGH ME.
I DIDN'T CARE ABOUT ANYTHING ANY MORE.
I WENT OUT ON A DATE. I FELT LIKE I SHOULD, WITH DARNICE GONE. AND CHARLENE IN DISPATCH, SHE'D SMILED AT ME A LOT.
BERRILL'S

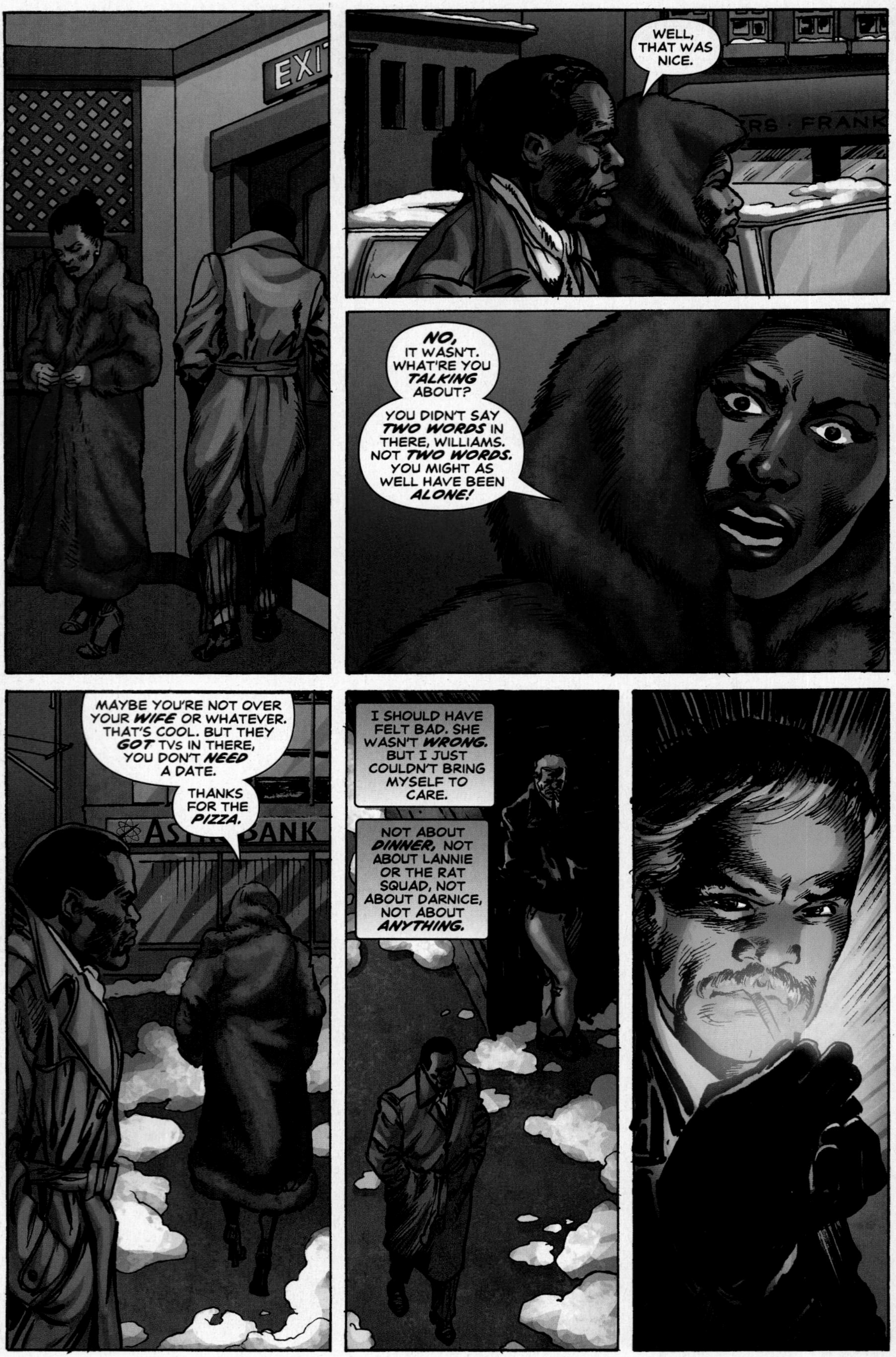
EXIT
WELL, THAT WAS NICE.
NO, IT WASN'T. WHAT'RE YOU TALKING ABOUT?
YOU DIDN'T SAY TWO WORDS IN THERE, WILLIAMS. NOT TWO WORDS. YOU MIGHT AS WELL HAVE BEEN ALONE!
MAYBE YOU'RE NOT OVER YOUR WIFE OR WHATEVER. THAT'S COOL. BUT THEY GOT TVs IN THERE, YOU DON'T NEED A DATE.
THANKS FOR THE PIZZA.
I SHOULD HAVE FELT BAD. SHE WASN'T WRONG. BUT I JUST COULDN'T BRING MYSELF TO CARE.
NOT ABOUT DINNER, NOT ABOUT LANNIE OR THE RAT SQUAD, NOT ABOUT DARNICE, NOT ABOUT ANYTHING.

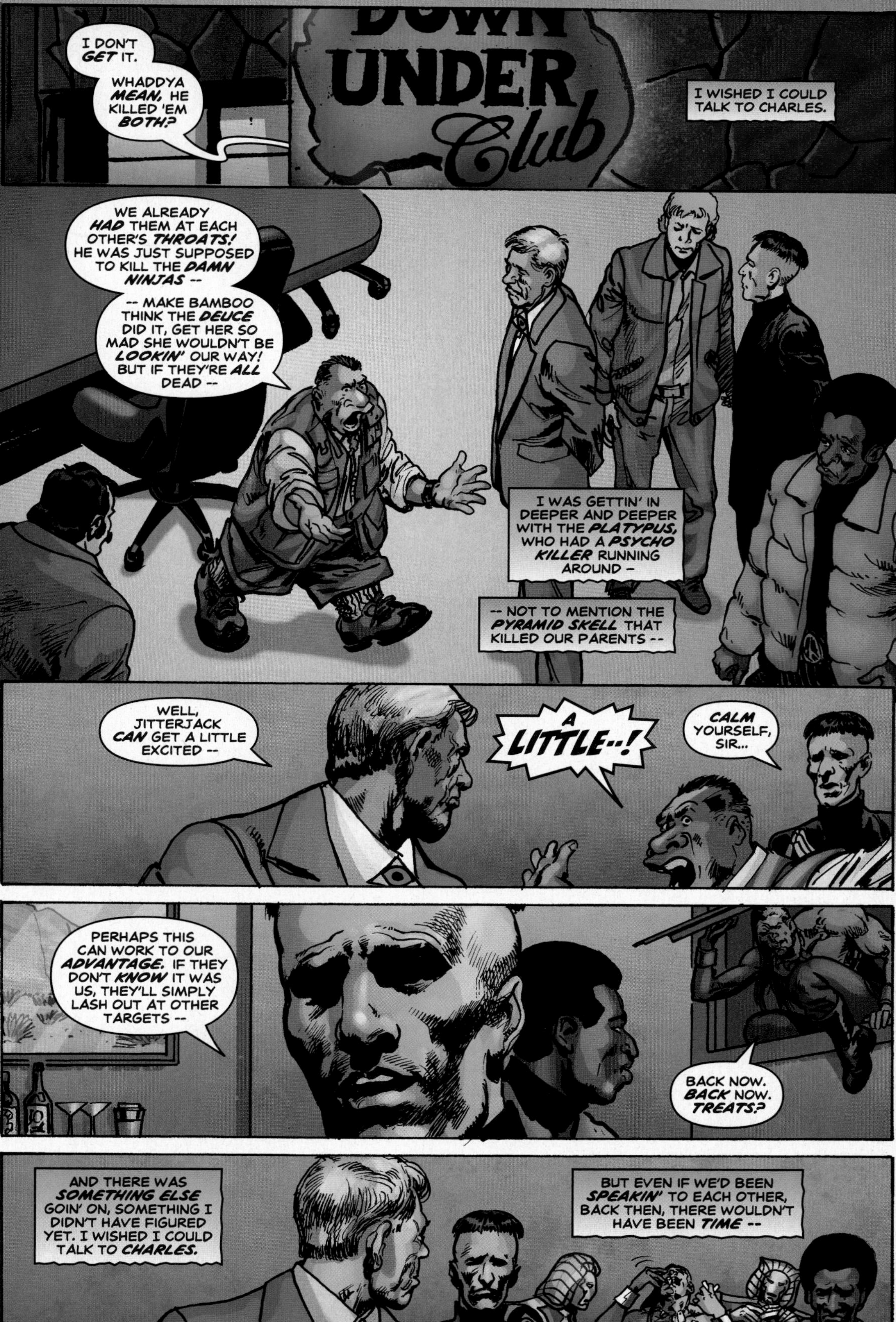

I DON'T GET IT.
WHADDYA MEAN, HE KILLED 'EM BOTH?
DOWN UNDER Club
I WISHED I COULD TALK TO CHARLES.
WE ALREADY HAD THEM AT EACH OTHER'S THROATS! HE WAS JUST SUPPOSED TO KILL THE DAMN NINJAS --
-- MAKE BAMBOO THINK THE DEUCE DID IT, GET HER SO MAD SHE WOULDN'T BE LOOKIN' OUR WAY! BUT IF THEY'RE ALL DEAD --
I WAS GETTIN' IN DEEPER AND DEEPER WITH THE PLATYPUS, WHO HAD A PSYCHO KILLER RUNNING AROUND –
-- NOT TO MENTION THE PYRAMID SKELL THAT KILLED OUR PARENTS --
WELL, JITTERJACK CAN GET A LITTLE EXCITED --
A LITTLE--!
CALM YOURSELF, SIR...
PERHAPS THIS CAN WORK TO OUR ADVANTAGE. IF THEY DON'T KNOW IT WAS US, THEY'LL SIMPLY LASH OUT AT OTHER TARGETS --
BACK NOW. BACK NOW. TREATS?
AND THERE WAS SOMETHING ELSE GOIN' ON, SOMETHING I DIDN'T HAVE FIGURED YET. I WISHED I COULD TALK TO CHARLES.
BUT EVEN IF WE'D BEEN SPEAKIN' TO EACH OTHER, BACK THEN, THERE WOULDN'T HAVE BEEN TIME --

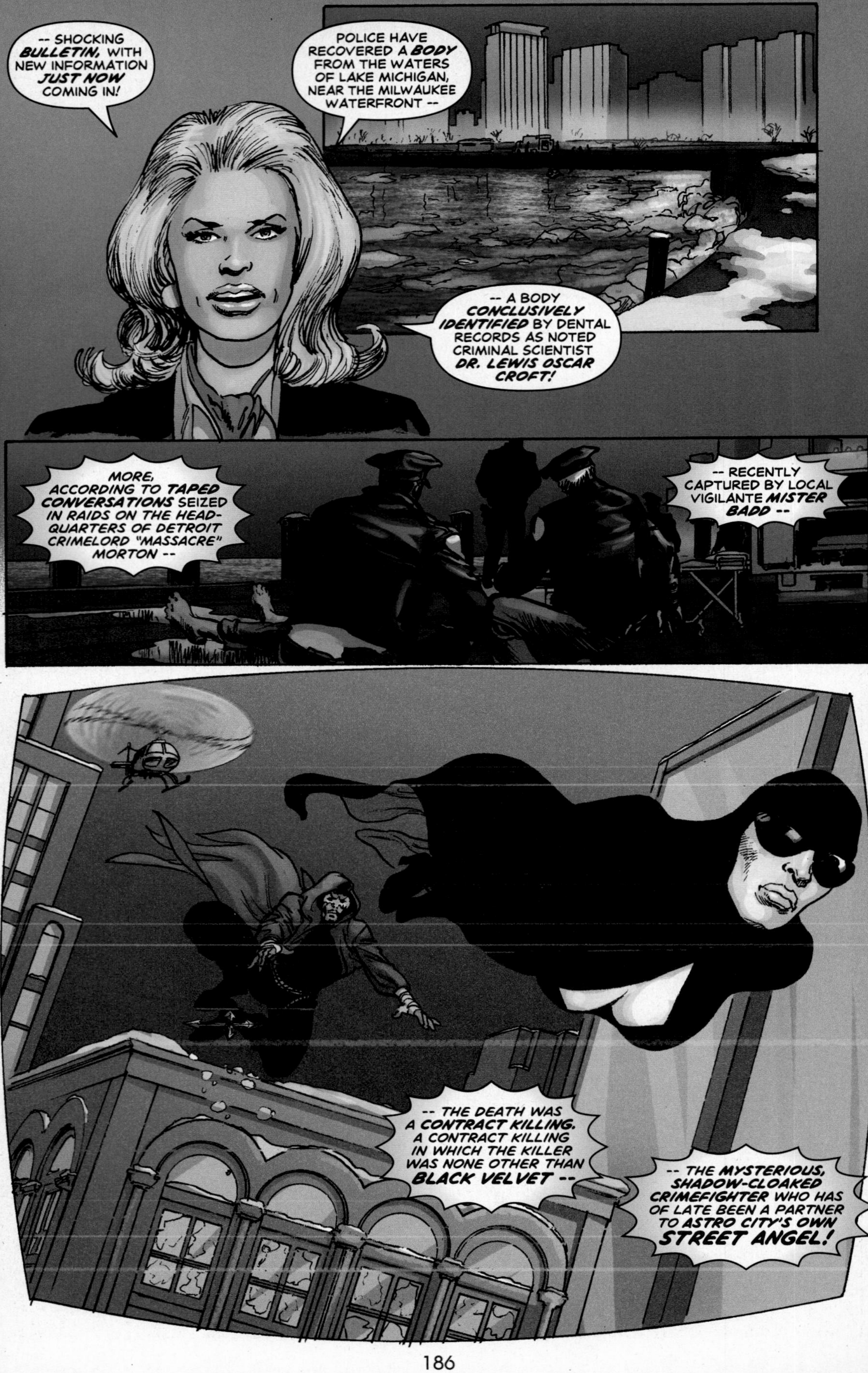
-- SHOCKING BULLETIN, WITH NEW INFORMATION JUST NOW COMING IN!
POLICE HAVE RECOVERED A BODY FROM THE WATERS OF LAKE MICHIGAN, NEAR THE MILWAUKEE WATERFRONT --
-- A BODY CONCLUSIVELY IDENTIFIED BY DENTAL RECORDS AS NOTED CRIMINAL SCIENTIST DR. LEWIS OSCAR CROFT!
MORE, ACCORDING TO TAPED CONVERSATIONS SEIZED IN RAIDS ON THE HEAD-QUARTERS OF DETROIT CRIMELORD "MASSACRE" MORTON --
-- RECENTLY CAPTURED BY LOCAL VIGILANTE MISTER BADD --
-- THE DEATH WAS A CONTRACT KILLING. A CONTRACT KILLING IN WHICH THE KILLER WAS NONE OTHER THAN BLACK VELVET --
-- THE MYSTERIOUS, SHADOW-CLOAKED CRIMEFIGHTER WHO HAS OF LATE BEEN A PARTNER TO ASTRO CITY'S OWN STREET ANGEL!

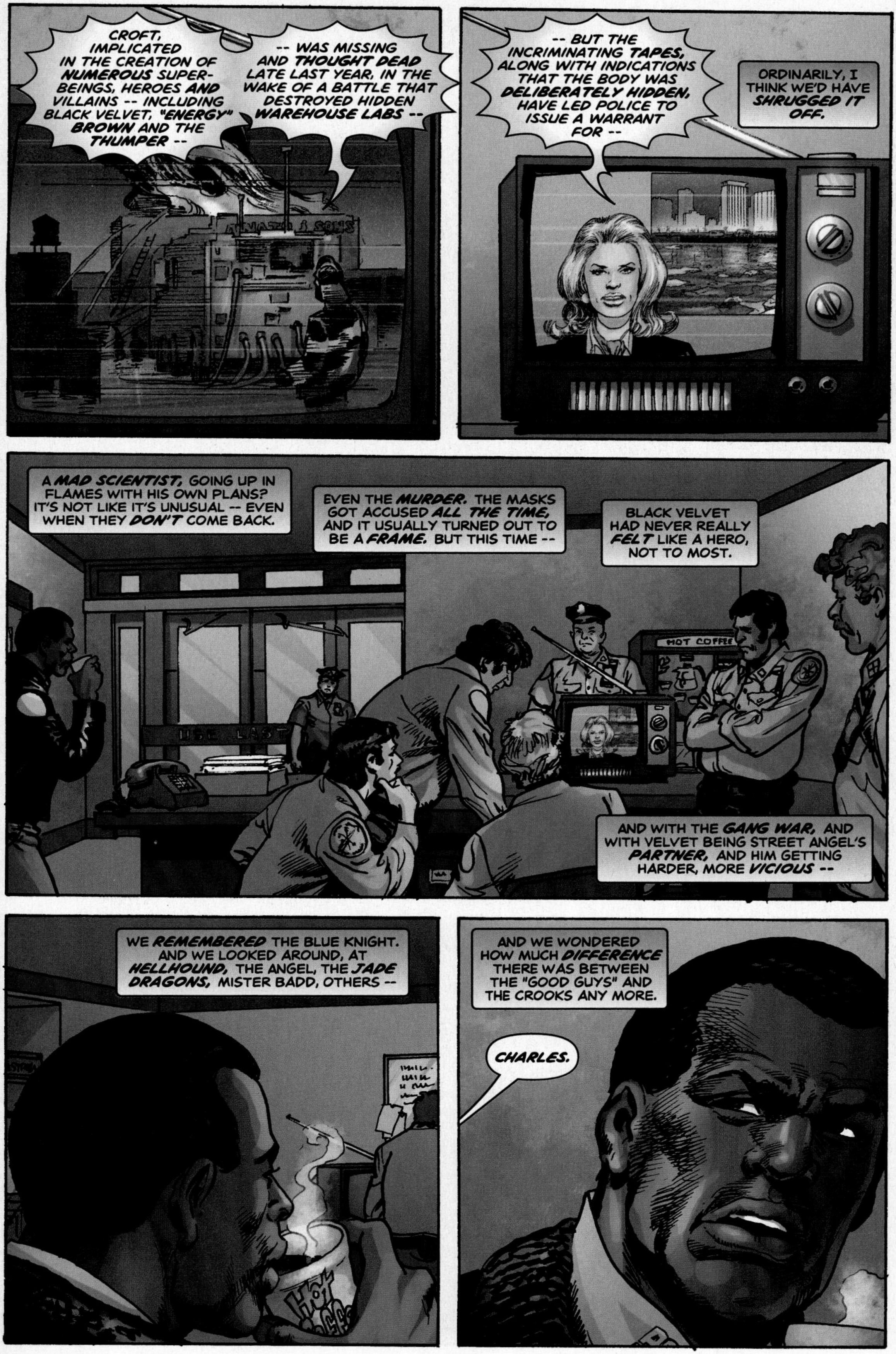
CROFT, IMPLICATED IN THE CREATION OF NUMEROUS SUPER-BEINGS, HEROES AND VILLAINS -- INCLUDING BLACK VELVET, "ENERGY" BROWN AND THE THUMPER --
-- WAS MISSING AND THOUGHT DEAD LATE LAST YEAR, IN THE WAKE OF A BATTLE THAT DESTROYED HIDDEN WAREHOUSE LABS --
-- BUT THE INCRIMINATING TAPES, ALONG WITH INDICATIONS THAT THE BODY WAS DELIBERATELY HIDDEN, HAVE LED POLICE TO ISSUE A WARRANT FOR --
ORDINARILY, I THINK WE'D HAVE SHRUGGED IT OFF.
A MAD SCIENTIST, GOING UP IN FLAMES WITH HIS OWN PLANS? IT'S NOT LIKE IT'S UNUSUAL -- EVEN WHEN THEY DON'T COME BACK.
EVEN THE MURDER. THE MASKS GOT ACCUSED ALL THE TIME, AND IT USUALLY TURNED OUT TO BE A FRAME. BUT THIS TIME --
BLACK VELVET HAD NEVER REALLY FELT LIKE A HERO, NOT TO MOST.
AND WITH THE GANG WAR, AND WITH VELVET BEING STREET ANGEL'S PARTNER, AND HIM GETTING HARDER, MORE VICIOUS --
WE REMEMBERED THE BLUE KNIGHT. AND WE LOOKED AROUND, AT HELLHOUND, THE ANGEL, THE JADE DRAGONS, MISTER BADD, OTHERS --
AND WE WONDERED HOW MUCH DIFFERENCE THERE WAS BETWEEN THE "GOOD GUYS" AND THE CROOKS ANY MORE.
CHARLES.

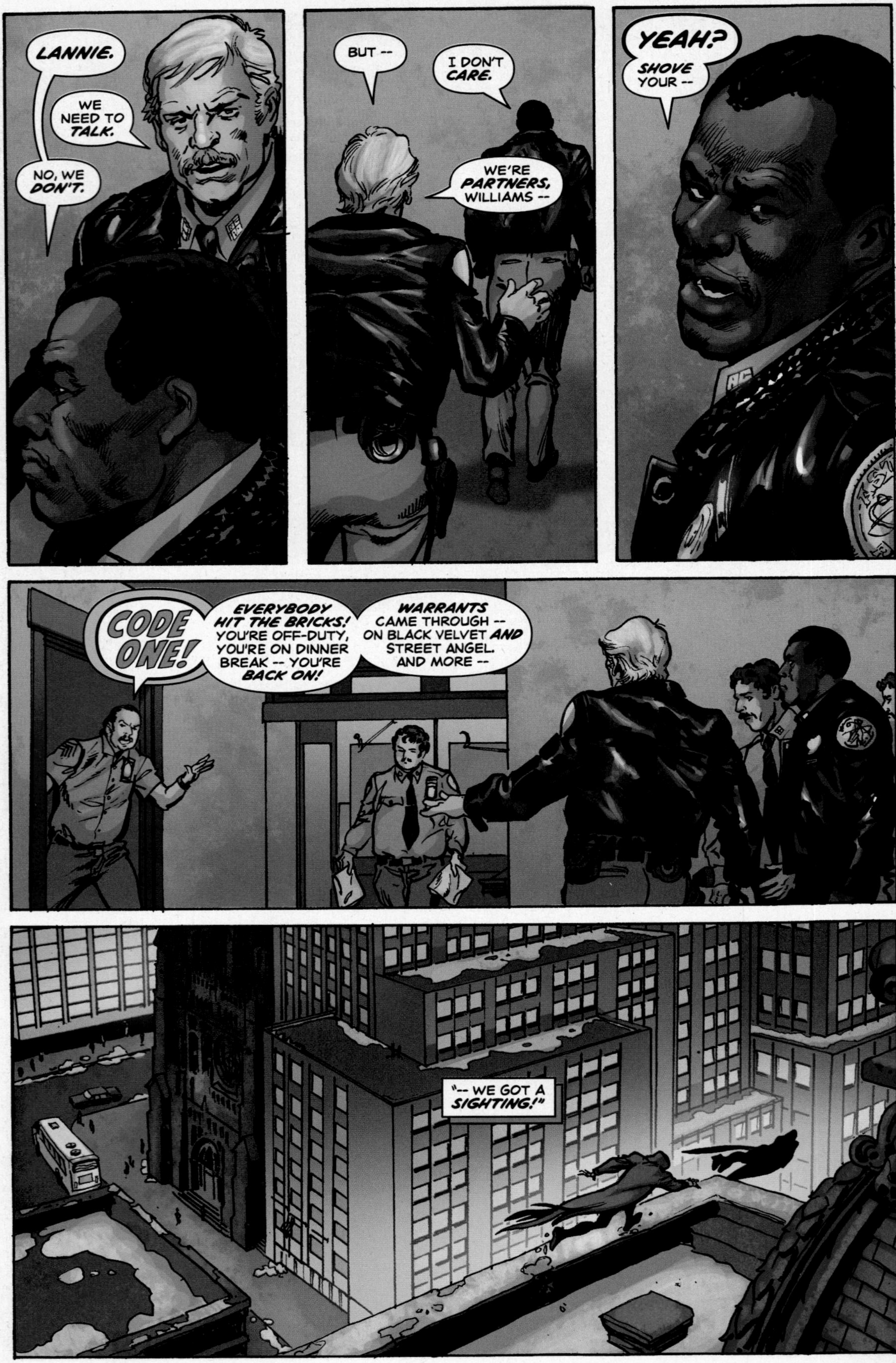
LANNIE.
WE NEED TO TALK.
NO, WE DON'T.
BUT --
I DON'T CARE.
WE'RE PARTNERS, WILLIAMS --
YEAH? SHOVE YOUR --
CODE ONE!
EVERYBODY HIT THE BRICKS! YOU'RE OFF-DUTY, YOU'RE ON DINNER BREAK -- YOU'RE BACK ON!
WARRANTS CAME THROUGH -- ON BLACK VELVET AND STREET ANGEL. AND MORE --
"-- WE GOT A SIGHTING!"

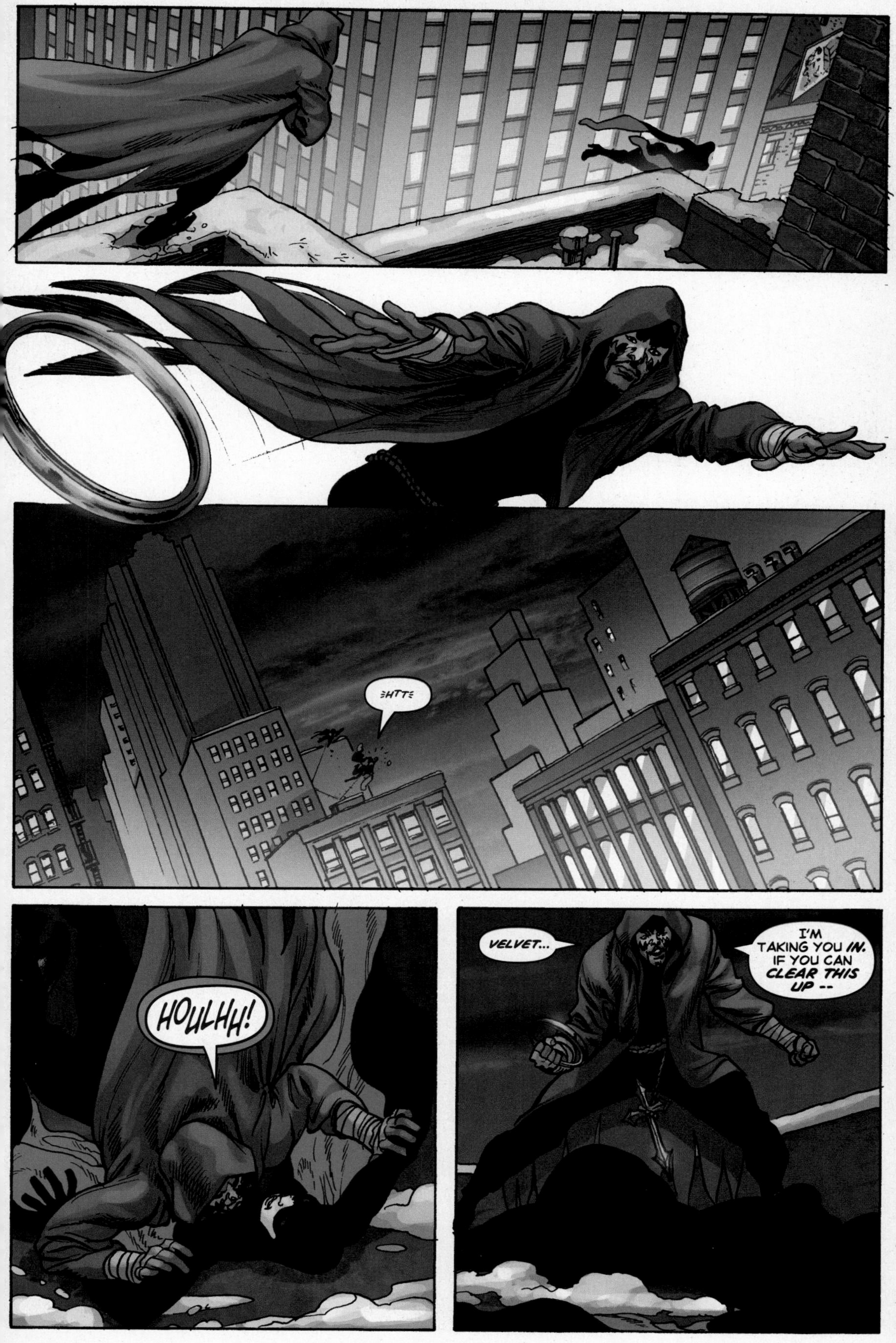

HTT
HOULHH!
VELVET...
I'M TAKING YOU IN. IF YOU CAN CLEAR THIS UP --

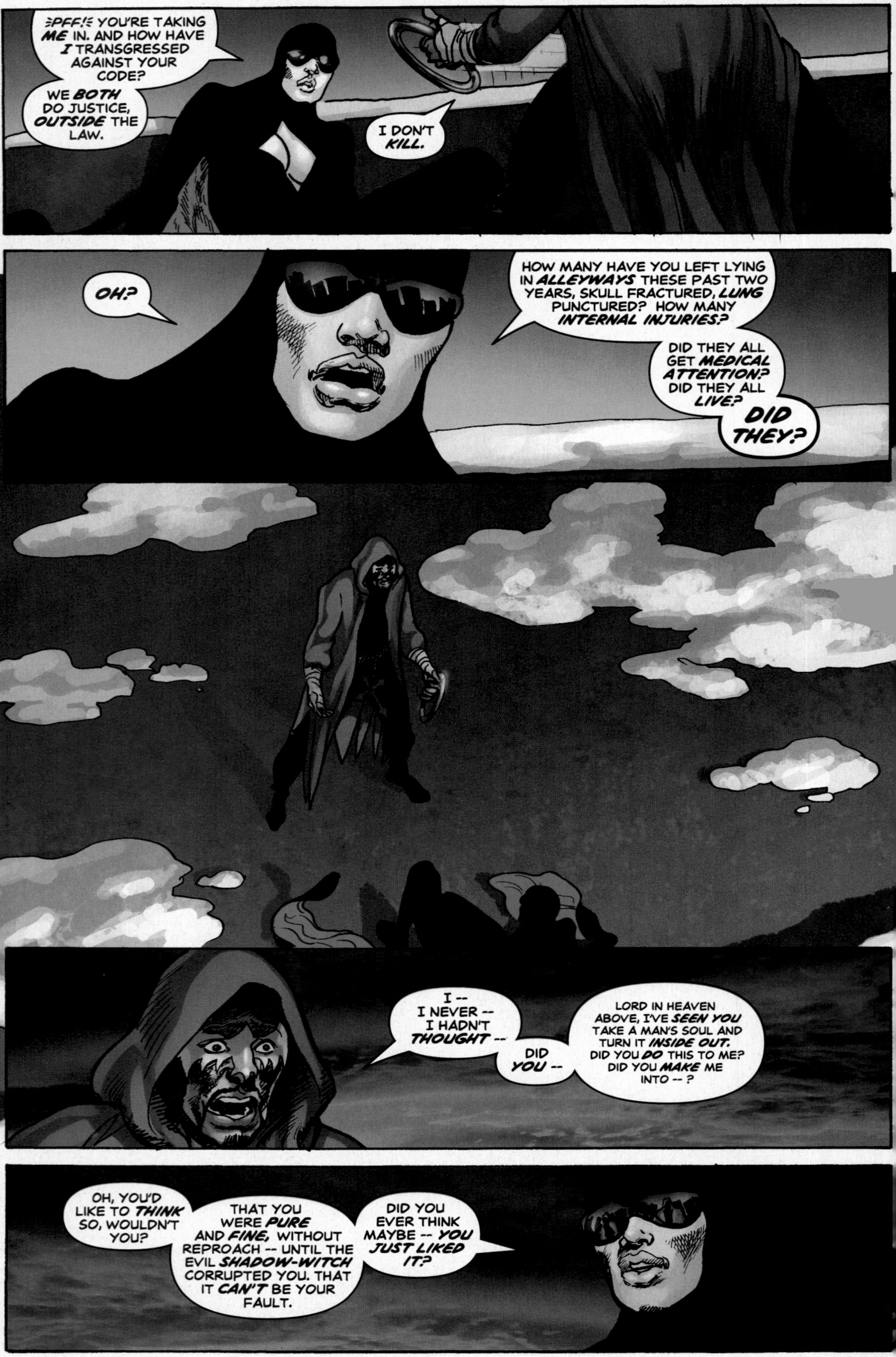
PFF! YOU'RE TAKING ME IN. AND HOW HAVE I TRANSGRESSED AGAINST YOUR CODE?
WE BOTH DO JUSTICE, OUTSIDE THE LAW.
I DON'T KILL.
OH?
HOW MANY HAVE YOU LEFT LYING IN ALLEYWAYS THESE PAST TWO YEARS, SKULL FRACTURED, LUNG PUNCTURED? HOW MANY INTERNAL INJURIES?
DID THEY ALL GET MEDICAL ATTENTION? DID THEY ALL LIVE?
DID THEY?
I -- I NEVER -- I HADN'T THOUGHT --
DID YOU --
LORD IN HEAVEN ABOVE, I'VE SEEN YOU TAKE A MAN'S SOUL AND TURN IT INSIDE OUT. DID YOU DO THIS TO ME? DID YOU MAKE ME INTO -- ?
OH, YOU'D LIKE TO THINK SO, WOULDN'T YOU?
THAT YOU WERE PURE AND FINE, WITHOUT REPROACH -- UNTIL THE EVIL SHADOW-WITCH CORRUPTED YOU. THAT IT CAN'T BE YOUR FAULT.
DID YOU EVER THINK MAYBE -- YOU JUST LIKED IT?

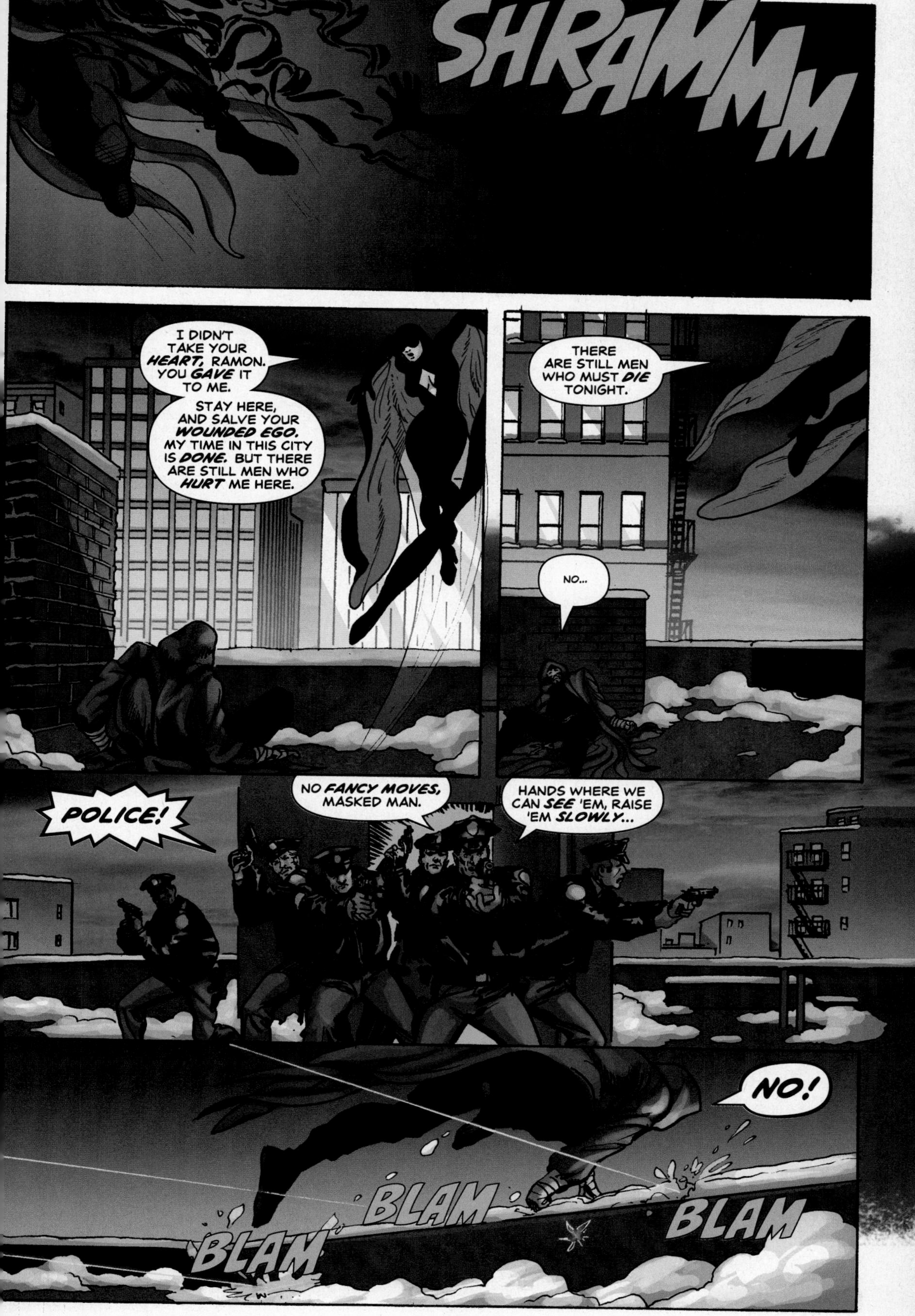
SHRAMMM
I DIDN'T TAKE YOUR HEART, RAMON. YOU GAVE IT TO ME.
STAY HERE, AND SALVE YOUR WOUNDED EGO. MY TIME IN THIS CITY IS DONE. BUT THERE ARE STILL MEN WHO HURT ME HERE.
THERE ARE STILL MEN WHO MUST DIE TONIGHT.
NO...
POLICE!
NO FANCY MOVES, MASKED MAN.
HANDS WHERE WE CAN SEE 'EM, RAISE 'EM SLOWLY...
NO!
BLAM
BLAM
BLAM

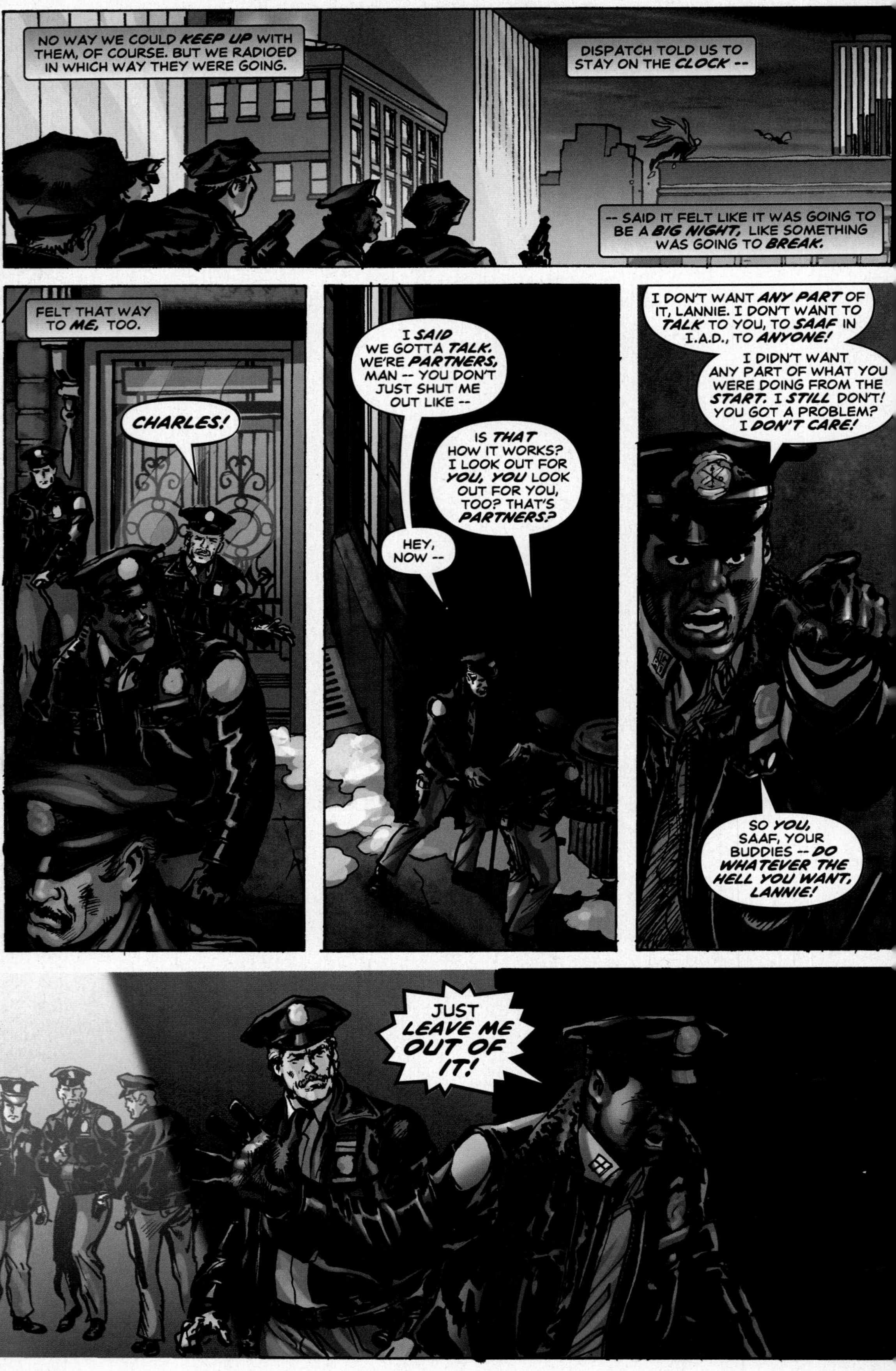
NO WAY WE COULD KEEP UP WITH THEM, OF COURSE. BUT WE RADIOED IN WHICH WAY THEY WERE GOING.
DISPATCH TOLD US TO STAY ON THE CLOCK --
-- SAID IT FELT LIKE IT WAS GOING TO BE A BIG NIGHT, LIKE SOMETHING WAS GOING TO BREAK.
FELT THAT WAY TO ME, TOO.
CHARLES!
I SAID WE GOTTA TALK. WE'RE PARTNERS, MAN -- YOU DON'T JUST SHUT ME OUT LIKE --
IS THAT HOW IT WORKS? I LOOK OUT FOR YOU, YOU LOOK OUT FOR YOU, TOO? THAT'S PARTNERS?
HEY, NOW --
I DON'T WANT ANY PART OF IT, LANNIE. I DON'T WANT TO TALK TO YOU, TO SAAF IN I.A.D., TO ANYONE!
I DIDN'T WANT ANY PART OF WHAT YOU WERE DOING FROM THE START. I STILL DON'T! YOU GOT A PROBLEM? I DON'T CARE!
SO YOU, SAAF, YOUR BUDDIES -- DO WHATEVER THE HELL YOU WANT, LANNIE!
JUST LEAVE ME OUT OF IT!

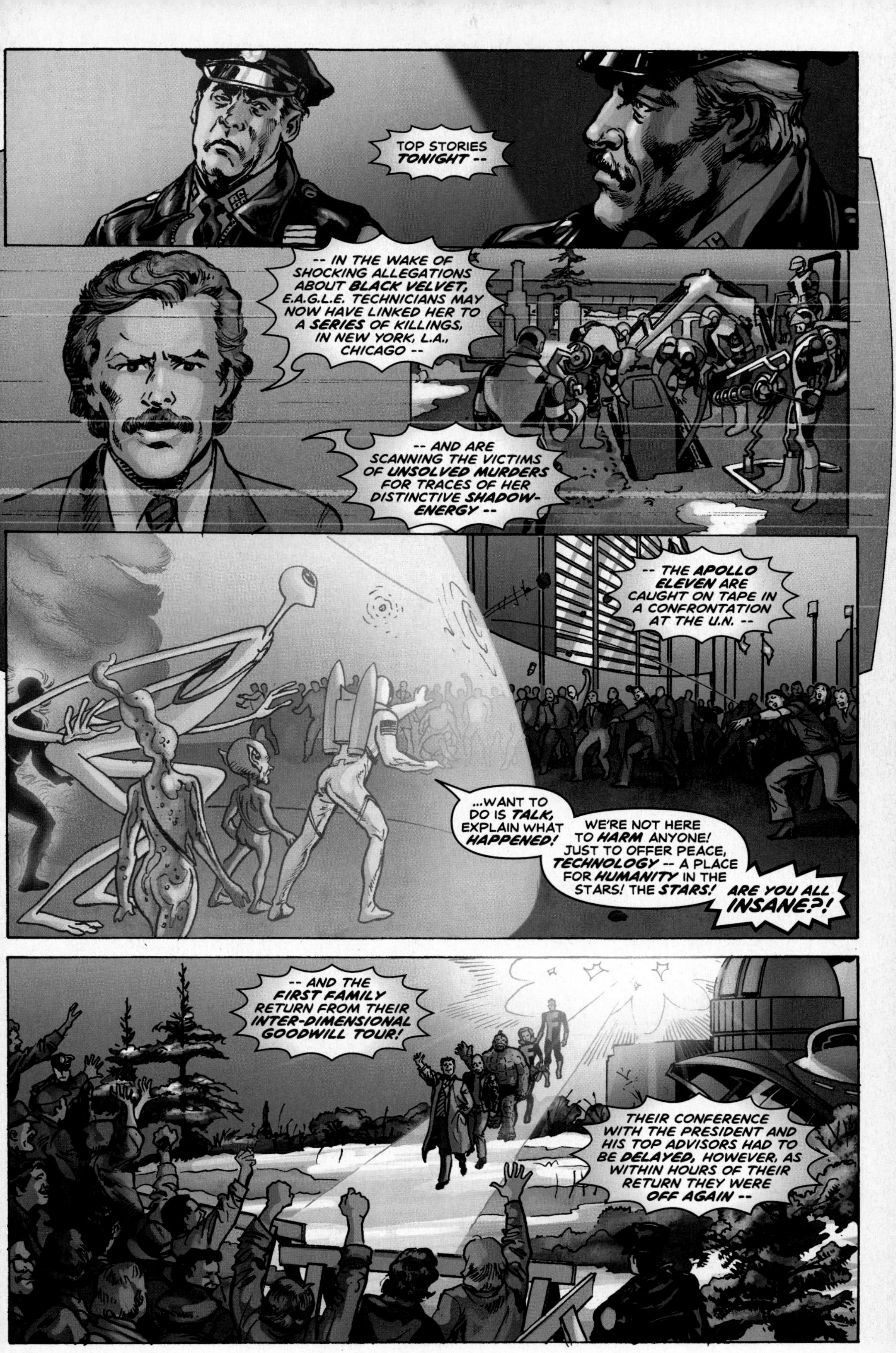
TOP STORIES TONIGHT --
-- IN THE WAKE OF SHOCKING ALLEGATIONS ABOUT BLACK VELVET, E.A.G.L.E. TECHNICIANS MAY NOW HAVE LINKED HER TO A SERIES OF KILLINGS, IN NEW YORK, L.A., CHICAGO --
-- AND ARE SCANNING THE VICTIMS OF UNSOLVED MURDERS FOR TRACES OF HER DISTINCTIVE SHADOW-ENERGY --
-- THE APOLLO ELEVEN ARE CAUGHT ON TAPE IN A CONFRONTATION AT THE U.N. --
...WANT TO DO IS TALK, EXPLAIN WHAT HAPPENED!
WE'RE NOT HERE TO HARM ANYONE! JUST TO OFFER PEACE, TECHNOLOGY -- A PLACE FOR HUMANITY IN THE STARS! THE STARS!
ARE YOU ALL INSANE?!
-- AND THE FIRST FAMILY RETURN FROM THEIR INTER-DIMENSIONAL GOODWILL TOUR!
THEIR CONFERENCE WITH THE PRESIDENT AND HIS TOP ADVISORS HAD TO BE DELAYED, HOWEVER, AS WITHIN HOURS OF THEIR RETURN THEY WERE OFF AGAIN --

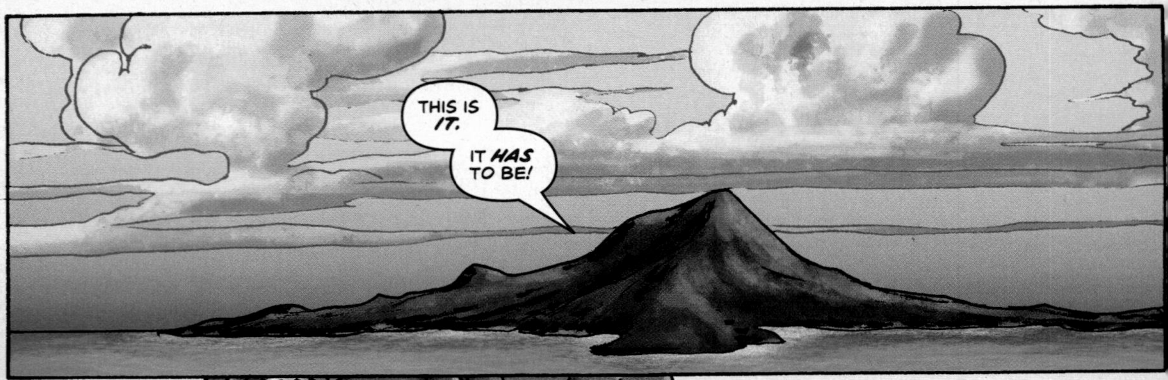
THIS IS *IT.*
IT *HAS* TO BE!

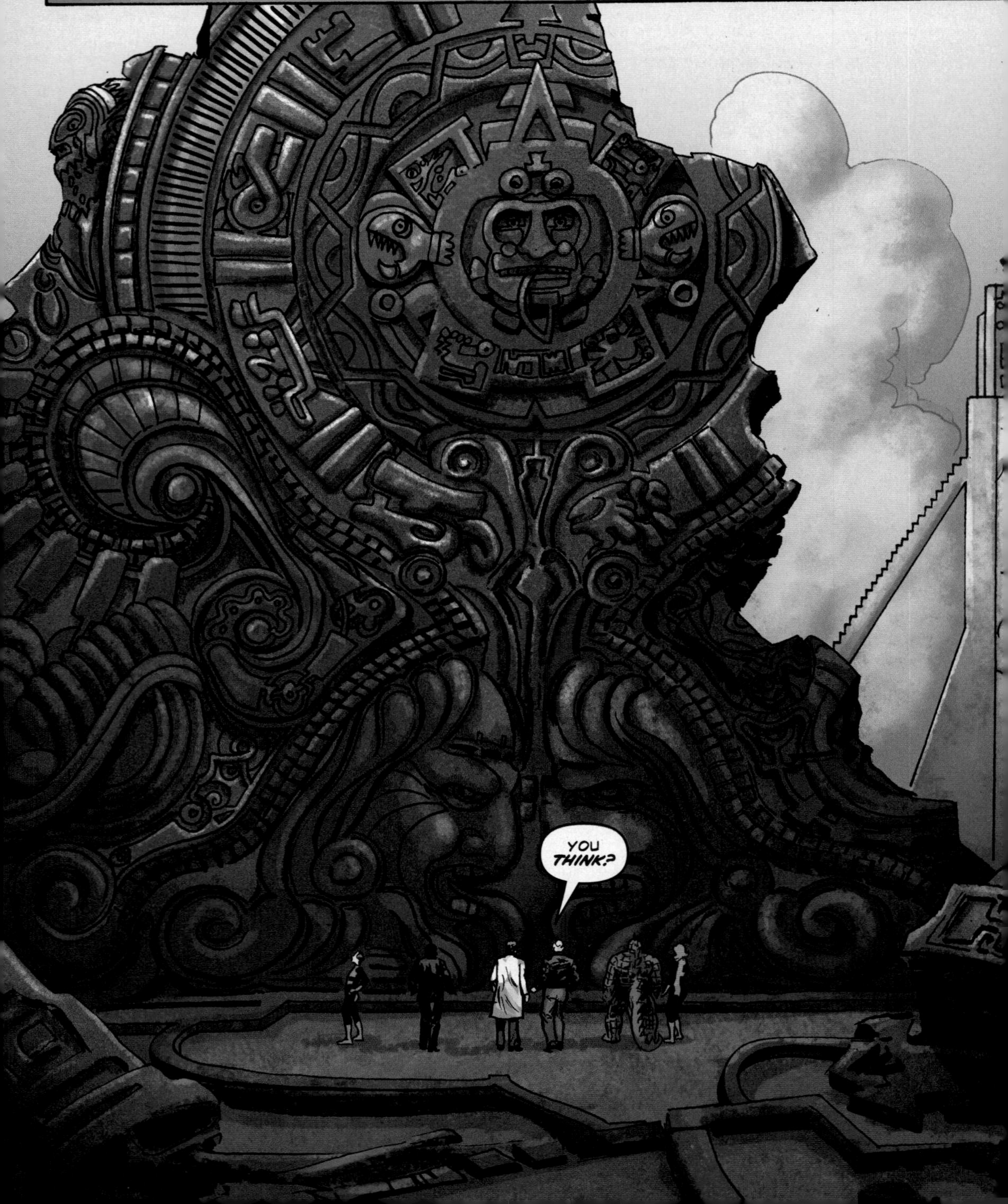
YOU *THINK?*

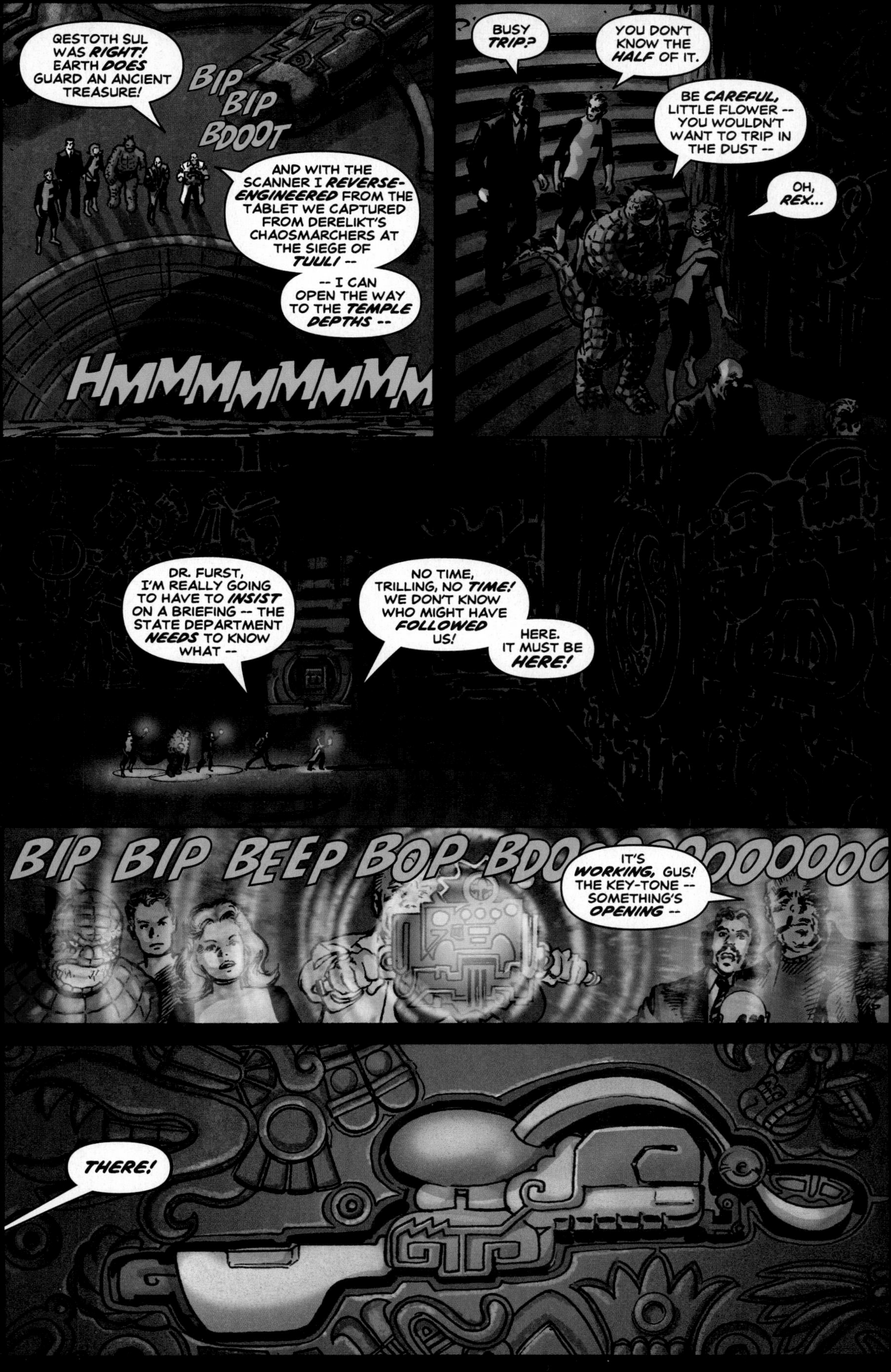
QESTOTH SUL WAS RIGHT! EARTH DOES GUARD AN ANCIENT TREASURE!
BIP BIP BDOOT
AND WITH THE SCANNER I REVERSE-ENGINEERED FROM THE TABLET WE CAPTURED FROM DERELIKT'S CHAOSMARCHERS AT THE SIEGE OF TUULI --
-- I CAN OPEN THE WAY TO THE TEMPLE DEPTHS --
HMMMMMMMMM
BUSY TRIP?
YOU DON'T KNOW THE HALF OF IT.
BE CAREFUL, LITTLE FLOWER -- YOU WOULDN'T WANT TO TRIP IN THE DUST --
OH, REX...
DR. FURST, I'M REALLY GOING TO HAVE TO INSIST ON A BRIEFING -- THE STATE DEPARTMENT NEEDS TO KNOW WHAT --
NO TIME, TRILLING, NO TIME! WE DON'T KNOW WHO MIGHT HAVE FOLLOWED US!
HERE. IT MUST BE HERE!
BIP BIP BEEP BOP BDOOOOOOOOOO
IT'S WORKING, GUS! THE KEY-TONE -- SOMETHING'S OPENING --
THERE!

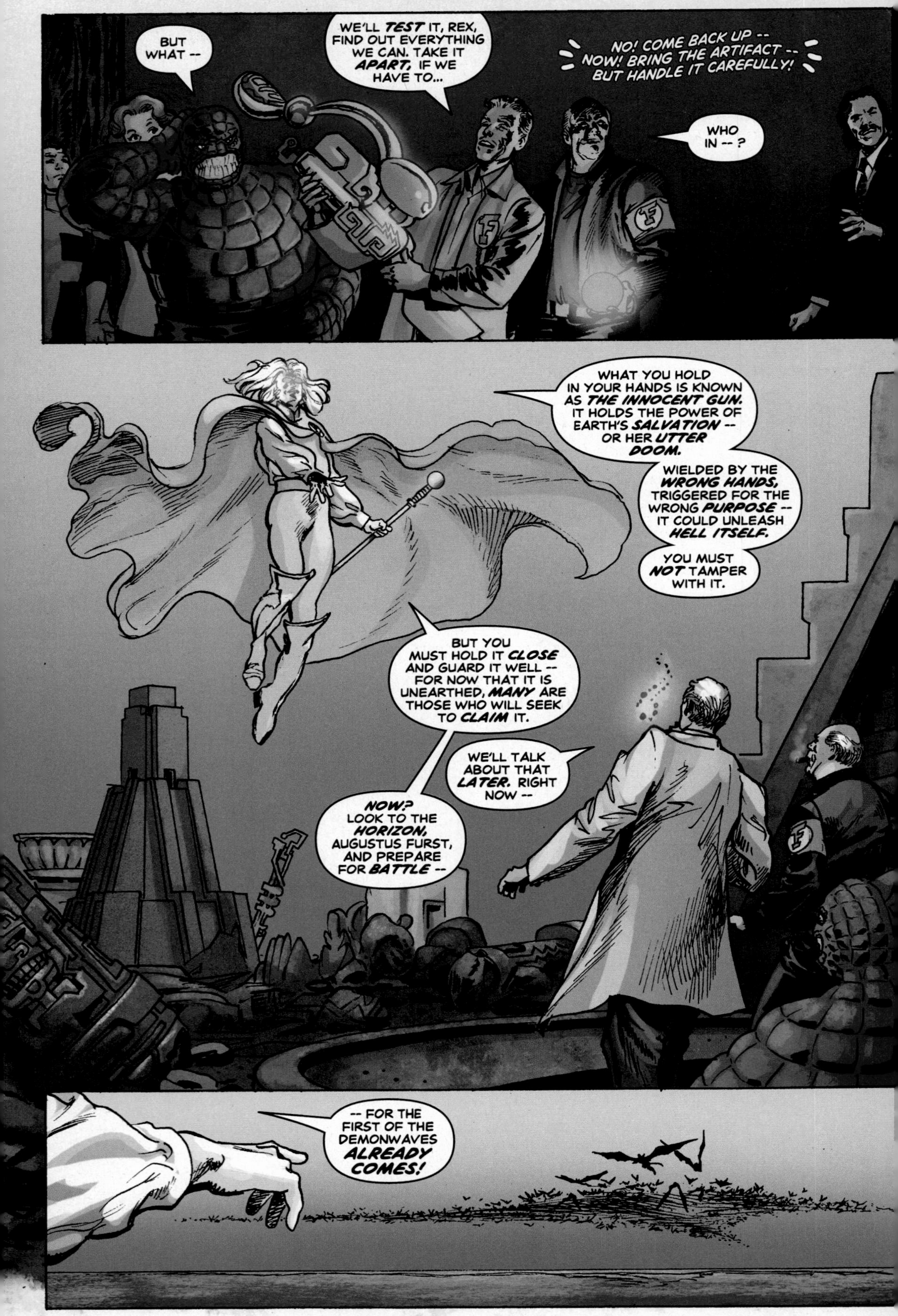
BUT WHAT --
WE'LL TEST IT, REX, FIND OUT EVERYTHING WE CAN. TAKE IT APART, IF WE HAVE TO...
NO! COME BACK UP -- NOW! BRING THE ARTIFACT -- BUT HANDLE IT CAREFULLY!
WHO IN -- ?
WHAT YOU HOLD IN YOUR HANDS IS KNOWN AS THE INNOCENT GUN. IT HOLDS THE POWER OF EARTH'S SALVATION -- OR HER UTTER DOOM.
WIELDED BY THE WRONG HANDS, TRIGGERED FOR THE WRONG PURPOSE -- IT COULD UNLEASH HELL ITSELF.
YOU MUST NOT TAMPER WITH IT.
BUT YOU MUST HOLD IT CLOSE AND GUARD IT WELL -- FOR NOW THAT IT IS UNEARTHED, MANY ARE THOSE WHO WILL SEEK TO CLAIM IT.
WE'LL TALK ABOUT THAT LATER. RIGHT NOW --
NOW? LOOK TO THE HORIZON, AUGUSTUS FURST, AND PREPARE FOR BATTLE --
-- FOR THE FIRST OF THE DEMONWAVES ALREADY COMES!

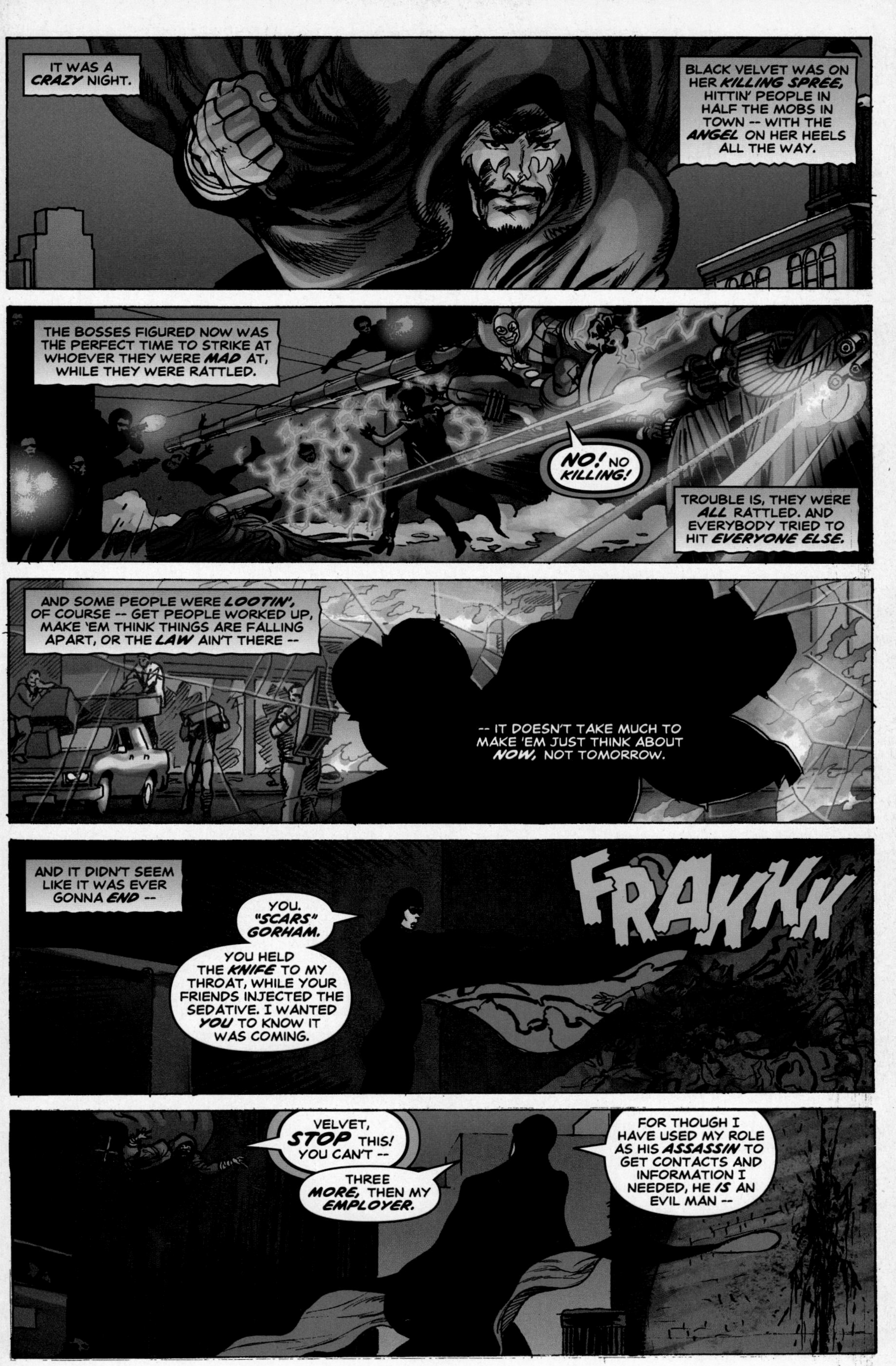

IT WAS A CRAZY NIGHT.
BLACK VELVET WAS ON HER KILLING SPREE, HITTIN' PEOPLE IN HALF THE MOBS IN TOWN -- WITH THE ANGEL ON HER HEELS ALL THE WAY.
THE BOSSES FIGURED NOW WAS THE PERFECT TIME TO STRIKE AT WHOEVER THEY WERE MAD AT, WHILE THEY WERE RATTLED.
NO! NO KILLING!
TROUBLE IS, THEY WERE ALL RATTLED. AND EVERYBODY TRIED TO HIT EVERYONE ELSE.
AND SOME PEOPLE WERE LOOTIN', OF COURSE -- GET PEOPLE WORKED UP, MAKE 'EM THINK THINGS ARE FALLING APART, OR THE LAW AIN'T THERE --
-- IT DOESN'T TAKE MUCH TO MAKE 'EM JUST THINK ABOUT NOW, NOT TOMORROW.
AND IT DIDN'T SEEM LIKE IT WAS EVER GONNA END --
FRAKKK
YOU. "SCARS" GORHAM.
YOU HELD THE KNIFE TO MY THROAT, WHILE YOUR FRIENDS INJECTED THE SEDATIVE. I WANTED YOU TO KNOW IT WAS COMING.
VELVET, STOP THIS! YOU CAN'T --
THREE MORE, THEN MY EMPLOYER.
FOR THOUGH I HAVE USED MY ROLE AS HIS ASSASSIN TO GET CONTACTS AND INFORMATION I NEEDED, HE IS AN EVIL MAN --

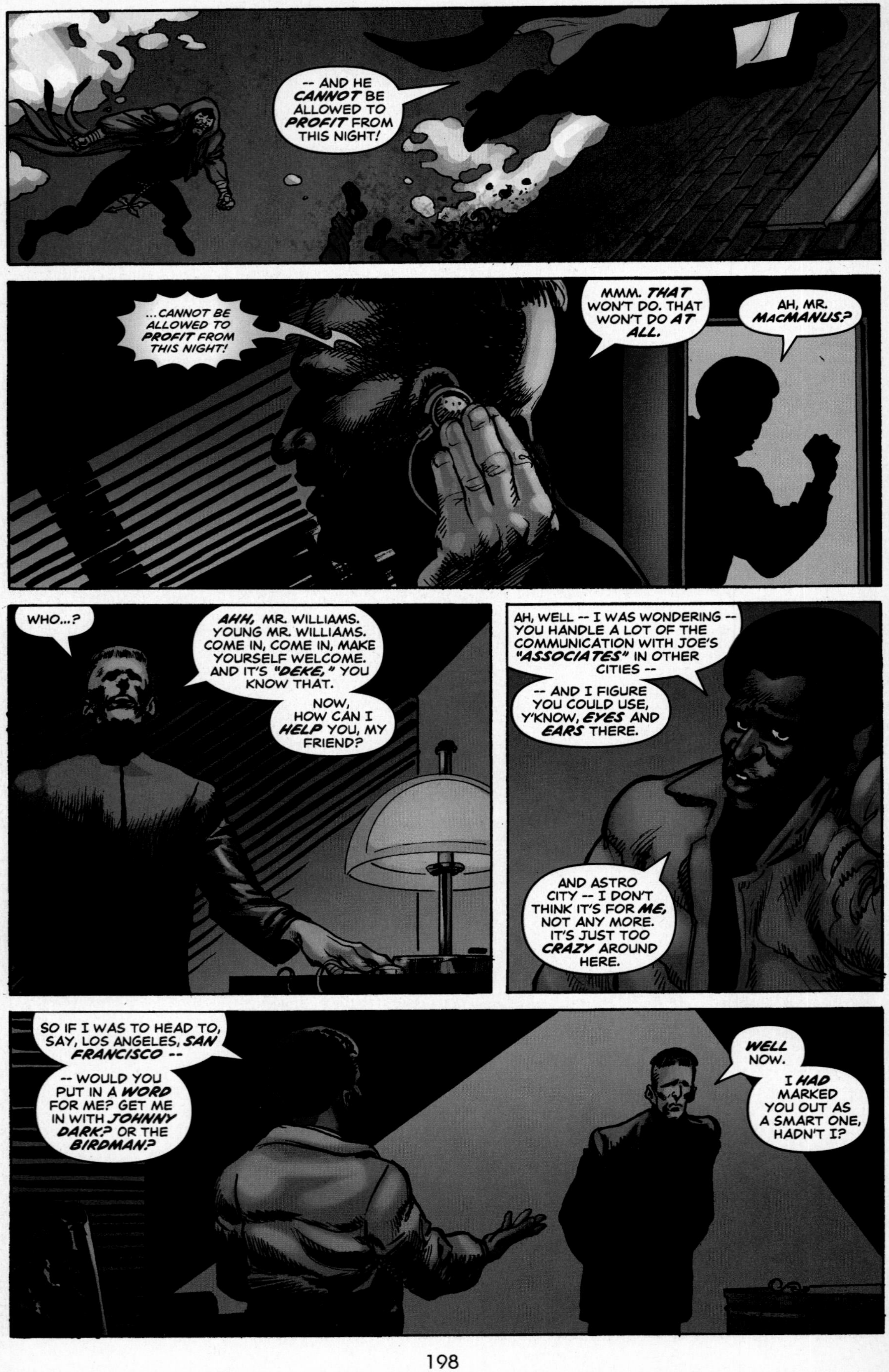
-- AND HE CANNOT BE ALLOWED TO PROFIT FROM THIS NIGHT!
...CANNOT BE ALLOWED TO PROFIT FROM THIS NIGHT!
MMM. THAT WON'T DO. THAT WON'T DO AT ALL.
AH, MR. MACMANUS?
WHO...?
AHH, MR. WILLIAMS. YOUNG MR. WILLIAMS. COME IN, COME IN, MAKE YOURSELF WELCOME. AND IT'S "DEKE," YOU KNOW THAT.
NOW, HOW CAN I HELP YOU, MY FRIEND?
AH, WELL -- I WAS WONDERING -- YOU HANDLE A LOT OF THE COMMUNICATION WITH JOE'S "ASSOCIATES" IN OTHER CITIES --
-- AND I FIGURE YOU COULD USE, Y'KNOW, EYES AND EARS THERE.
AND ASTRO CITY -- I DON'T THINK IT'S FOR ME, NOT ANY MORE. IT'S JUST TOO CRAZY AROUND HERE.
SO IF I WAS TO HEAD TO, SAY, LOS ANGELES, SAN FRANCISCO --
-- WOULD YOU PUT IN A WORD FOR ME? GET ME IN WITH JOHNNY DARK? OR THE BIRDMAN?
WELL NOW.
I HAD MARKED YOU OUT AS A SMART ONE, HADN'T I?

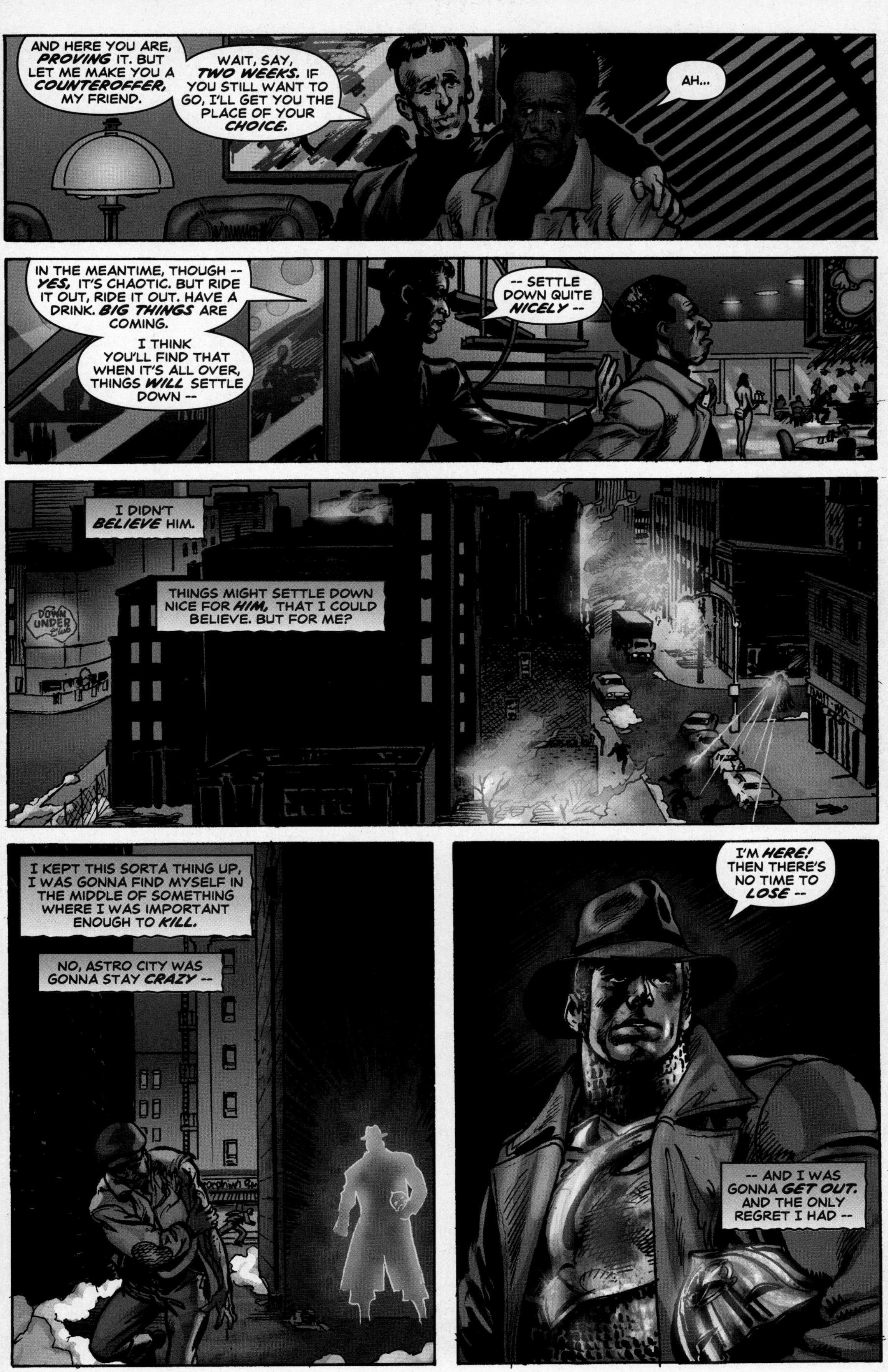
AND HERE YOU ARE, PROVING IT. BUT LET ME MAKE YOU A COUNTEROFFER, MY FRIEND.
WAIT, SAY, TWO WEEKS. IF YOU STILL WANT TO GO, I'LL GET YOU THE PLACE OF YOUR CHOICE.
AH...
IN THE MEANTIME, THOUGH -- YES, IT'S CHAOTIC. BUT RIDE IT OUT, RIDE IT OUT. HAVE A DRINK. BIG THINGS ARE COMING.
I THINK YOU'LL FIND THAT WHEN IT'S ALL OVER, THINGS WILL SETTLE DOWN --
-- SETTLE DOWN QUITE NICELY --
I DIDN'T BELIEVE HIM.
THINGS MIGHT SETTLE DOWN NICE FOR HIM, THAT I COULD BELIEVE. BUT FOR ME?
DOWN UNDER
I KEPT THIS SORTA THING UP, I WAS GONNA FIND MYSELF IN THE MIDDLE OF SOMETHING WHERE I WAS IMPORTANT ENOUGH TO KILL.
NO, ASTRO CITY WAS GONNA STAY CRAZY --
I'M HERE! THEN THERE'S NO TIME TO LOSE --
-- AND I WAS GONNA GET OUT. AND THE ONLY REGRET I HAD --

-- IS THAT I WOULDA LIKED TO TALK TO *CHARLES* BEFORE I WENT --

NOW?

NOW.

BLAM BLAM BLAM

BLAM BLAM

THE WAREHOUSE WAS A KNOWN *TRANSFER POINT* FOR DRUGS AND GUNS. LANNIE SAID IT MIGHT BE GOOD TO *CHECK* IT THAT NIGHT.

I DON'T THINK I BELIEVED HIM, EVEN *THEN.* I JUST -- I DIDN'T CARE. MY JOB, MY FAMILY, MY LIFE -- WHAT WAS WORTH *STAYING* FOR?

FOR WHAT IT'S WORTH, CHARLES, I DON'T THINK YOU *TALKED* TO SAAF. AND I DON'T THINK YOU WERE *GONNA* TALK, EITHER.

BUT WE HAD TO BE *SURE.* SORRY ABOUT THIS.

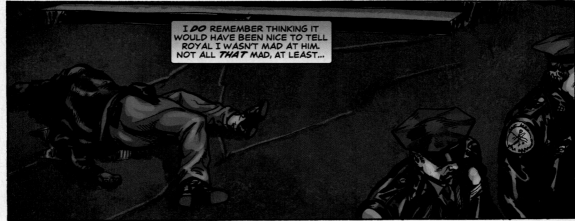

I *DO* REMEMBER THINKING IT WOULD HAVE BEEN NICE TO TELL ROYAL I WASN'T MAD AT HIM. NOT ALL *THAT* MAD, AT LEAST...

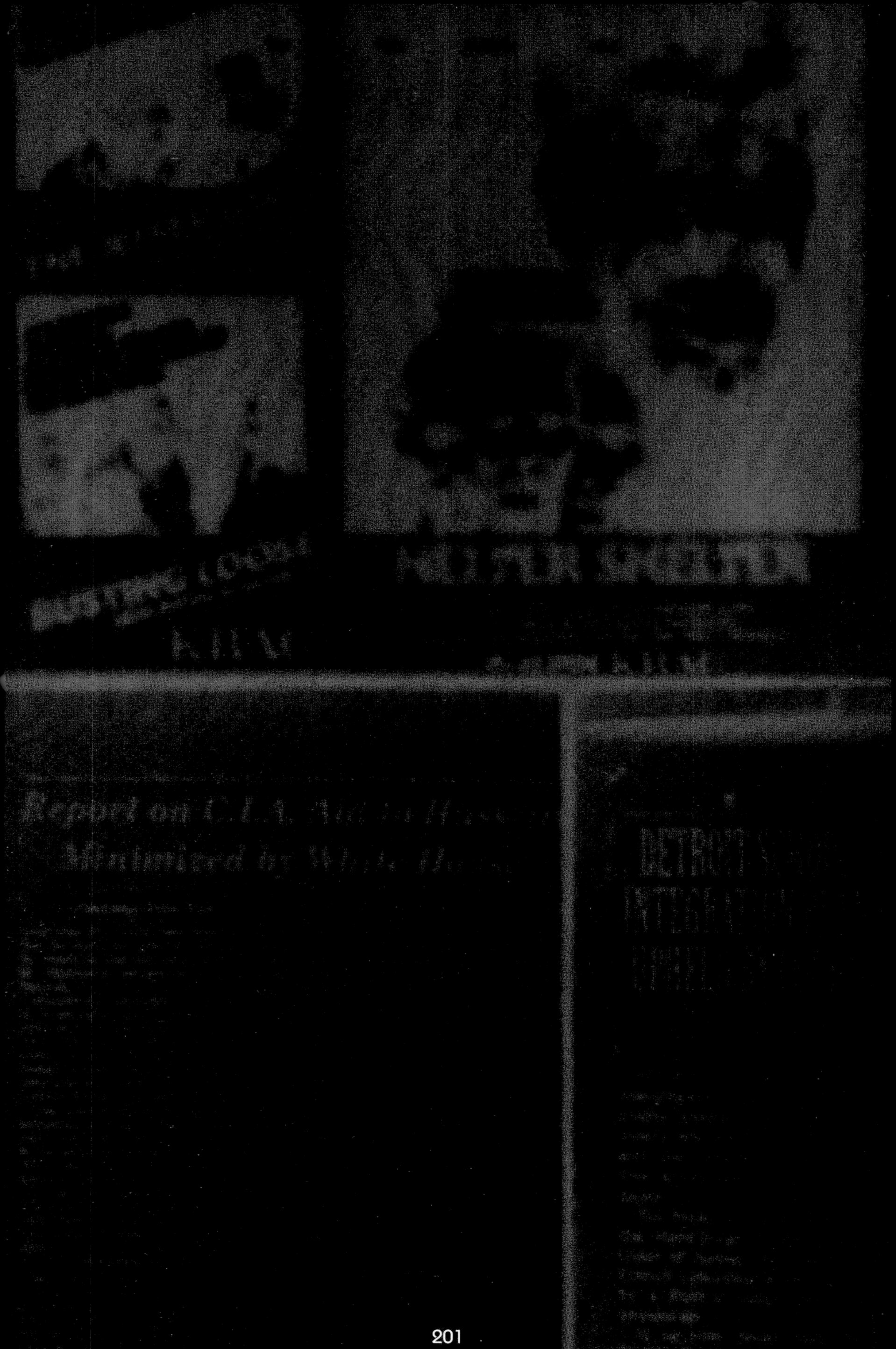

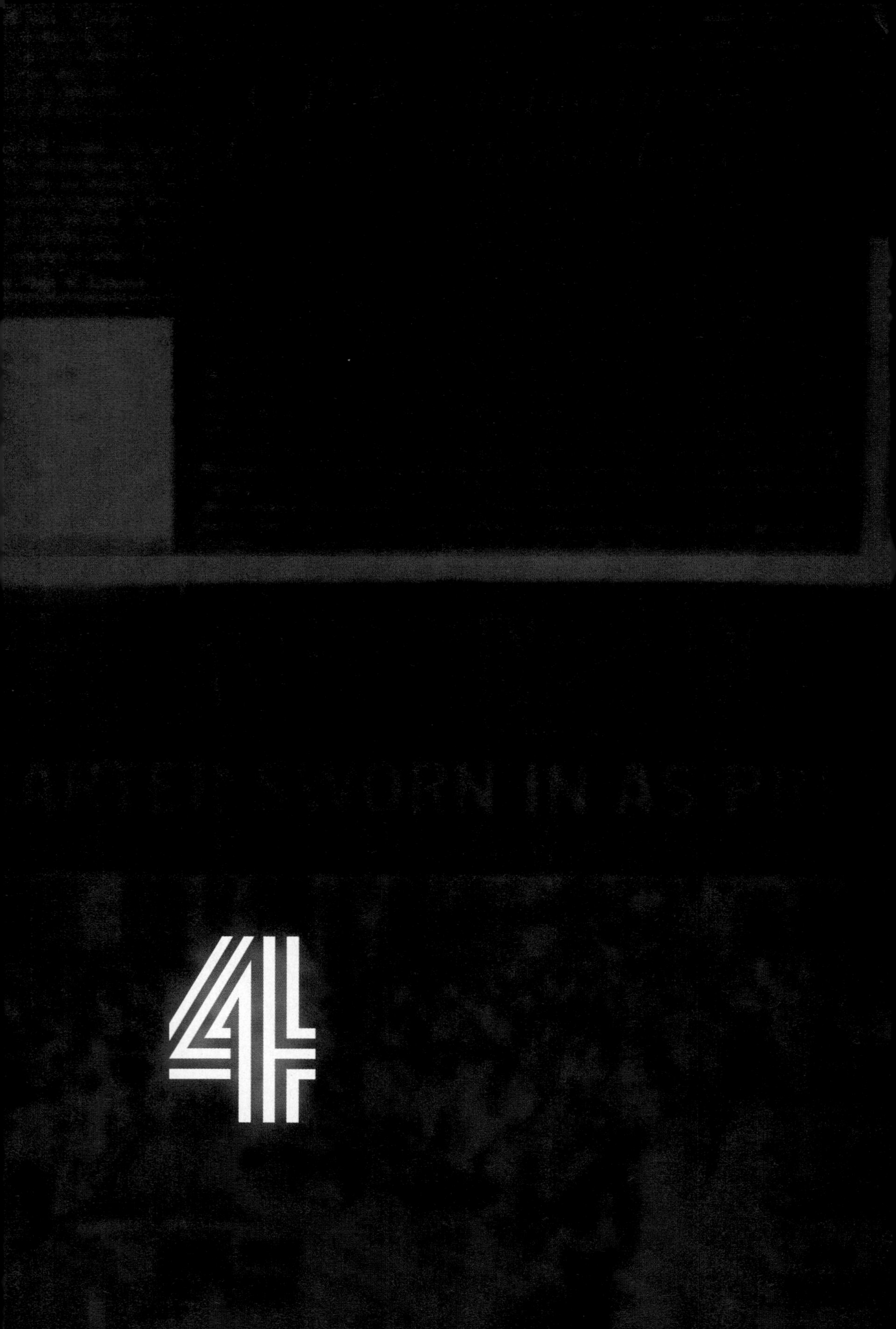

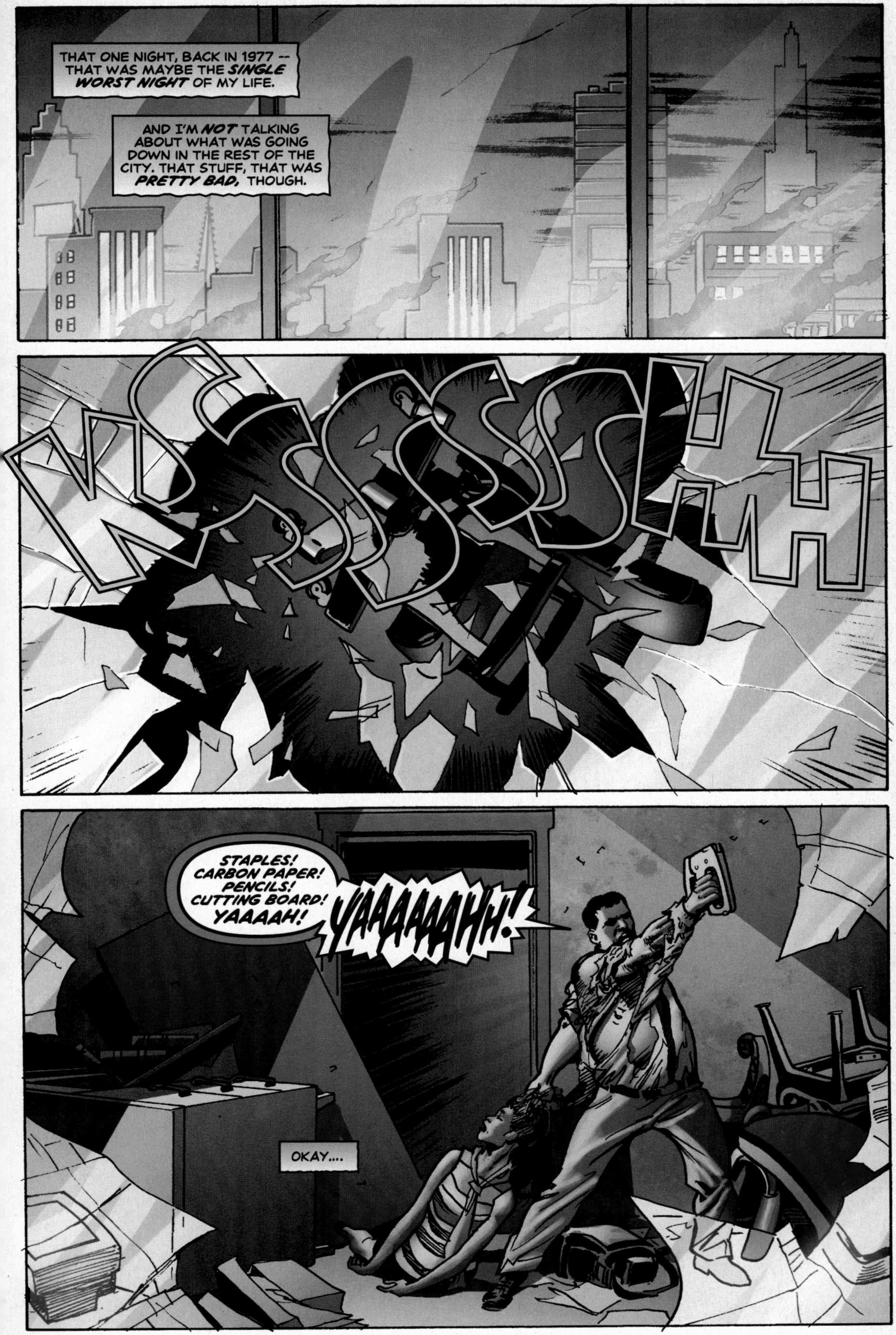

THAT ONE NIGHT, BACK IN 1977 -- THAT WAS MAYBE THE SINGLE WORST NIGHT OF MY LIFE.
AND I'M NOT TALKING ABOUT WHAT WAS GOING DOWN IN THE REST OF THE CITY. THAT STUFF, THAT WAS PRETTY BAD, THOUGH.
KSSSSSHH
STAPLES! CARBON PAPER! PENCILS! CUTTING BOARD! YAAAAH!
YAAAAAAHH!
OKAY....

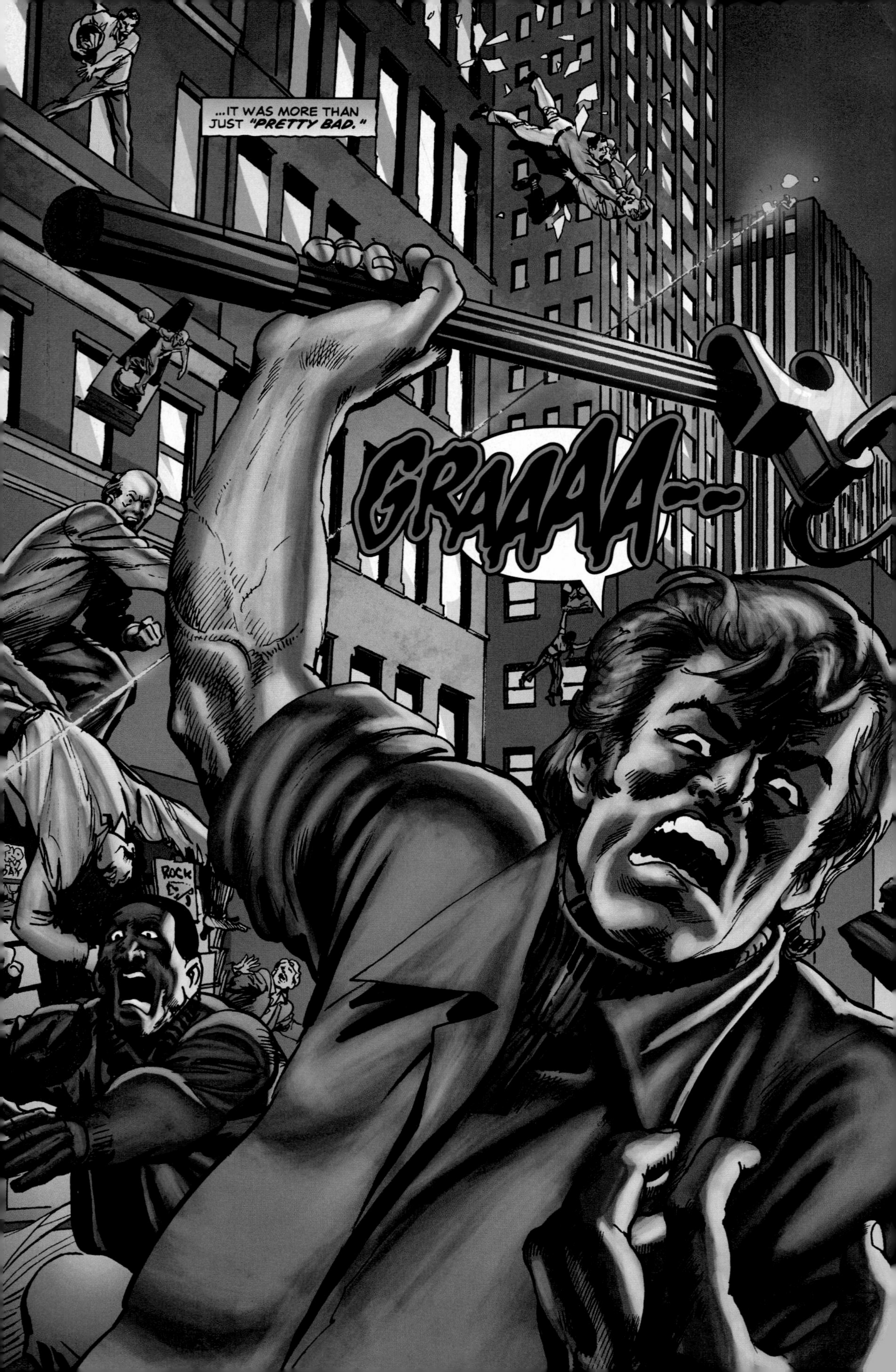
...IT WAS MORE THAN JUST "PRETTY BAD."
GRAAAAA--
ROCK

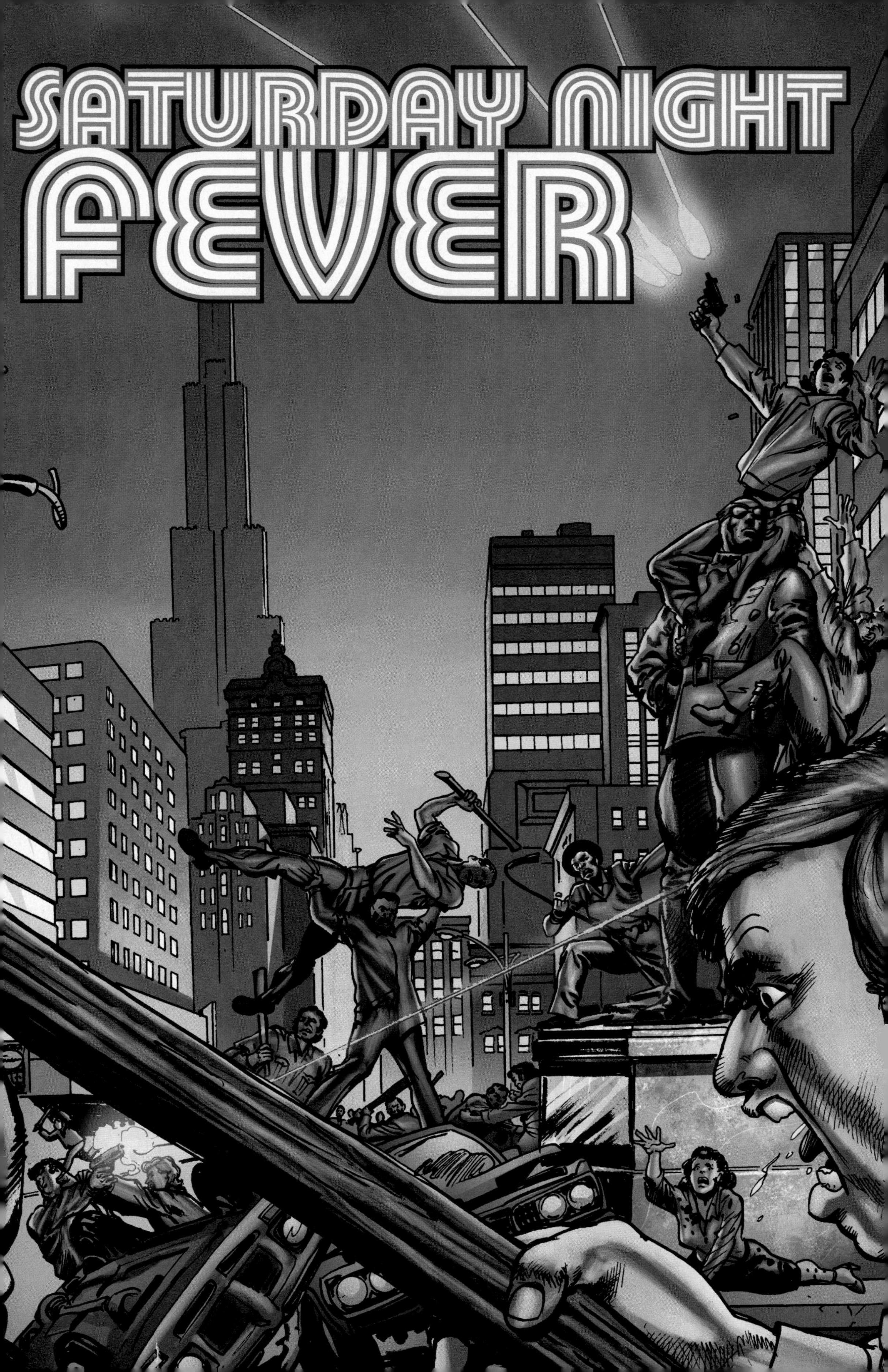
SATURDAY NIGHT
FEVER

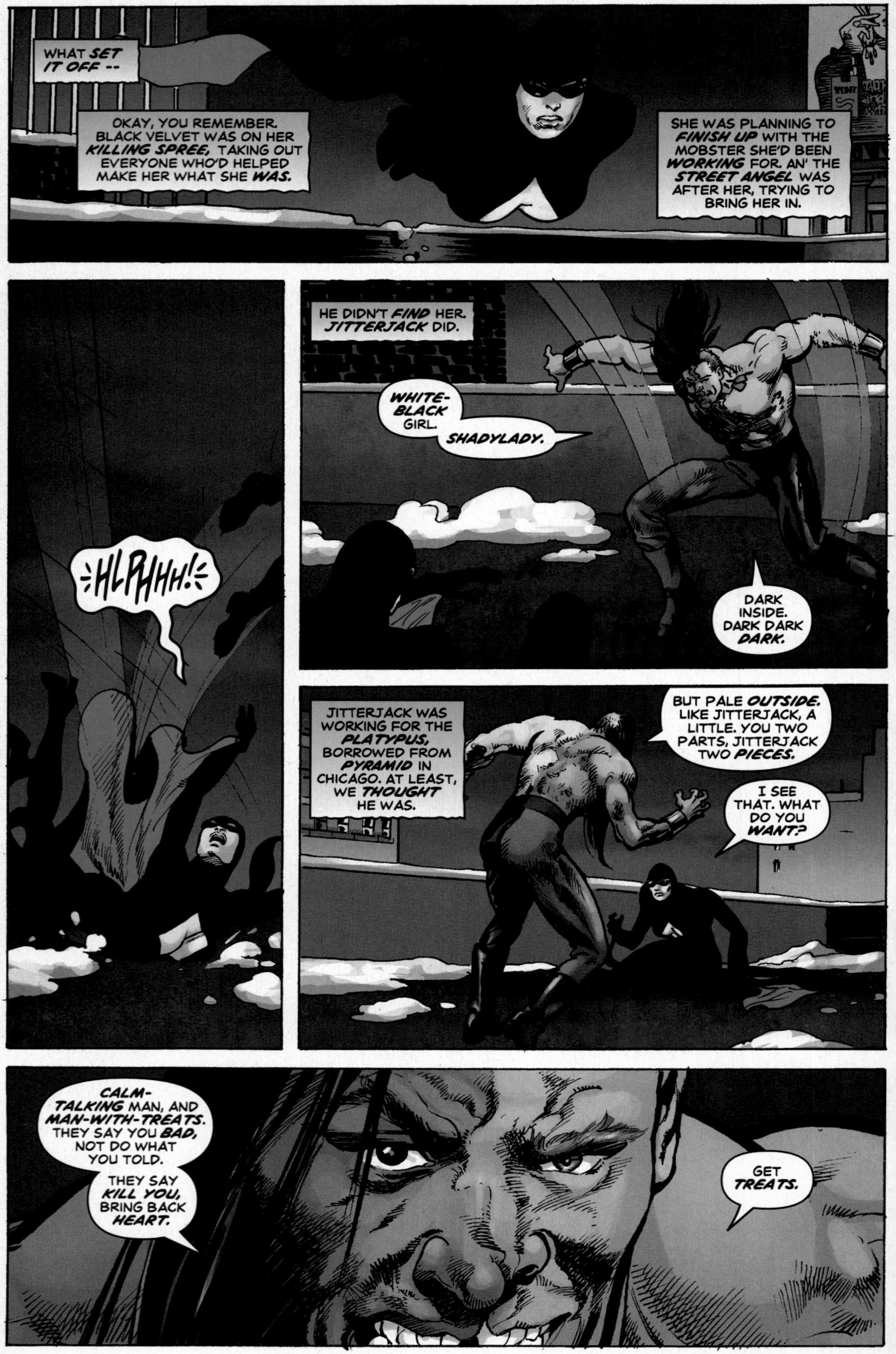
WHAT SET IT OFF --
OKAY, YOU REMEMBER. BLACK VELVET WAS ON HER KILLING SPREE, TAKING OUT EVERYONE WHO'D HELPED MAKE HER WHAT SHE WAS.
SHE WAS PLANNING TO FINISH UP WITH THE MOBSTER SHE'D BEEN WORKING FOR. AN' THE STREET ANGEL WAS AFTER HER, TRYING TO BRING HER IN.
HE DIDN'T FIND HER. JITTERJACK DID.
WHITE-BLACK GIRL.
SHADYLADY.
DARK INSIDE. DARK DARK DARK.
HLPHHH!
JITTERJACK WAS WORKING FOR THE PLATYPUS, BORROWED FROM PYRAMID IN CHICAGO. AT LEAST, WE THOUGHT HE WAS.
BUT PALE OUTSIDE. LIKE JITTERJACK, A LITTLE. YOU TWO PARTS, JITTERJACK TWO PIECES.
I SEE THAT. WHAT DO YOU WANT?
CALM-TALKING MAN, AND MAN-WITH-TREATS. THEY SAY YOU BAD, NOT DO WHAT YOU TOLD.
THEY SAY KILL YOU, BRING BACK HEART.
GET TREATS.

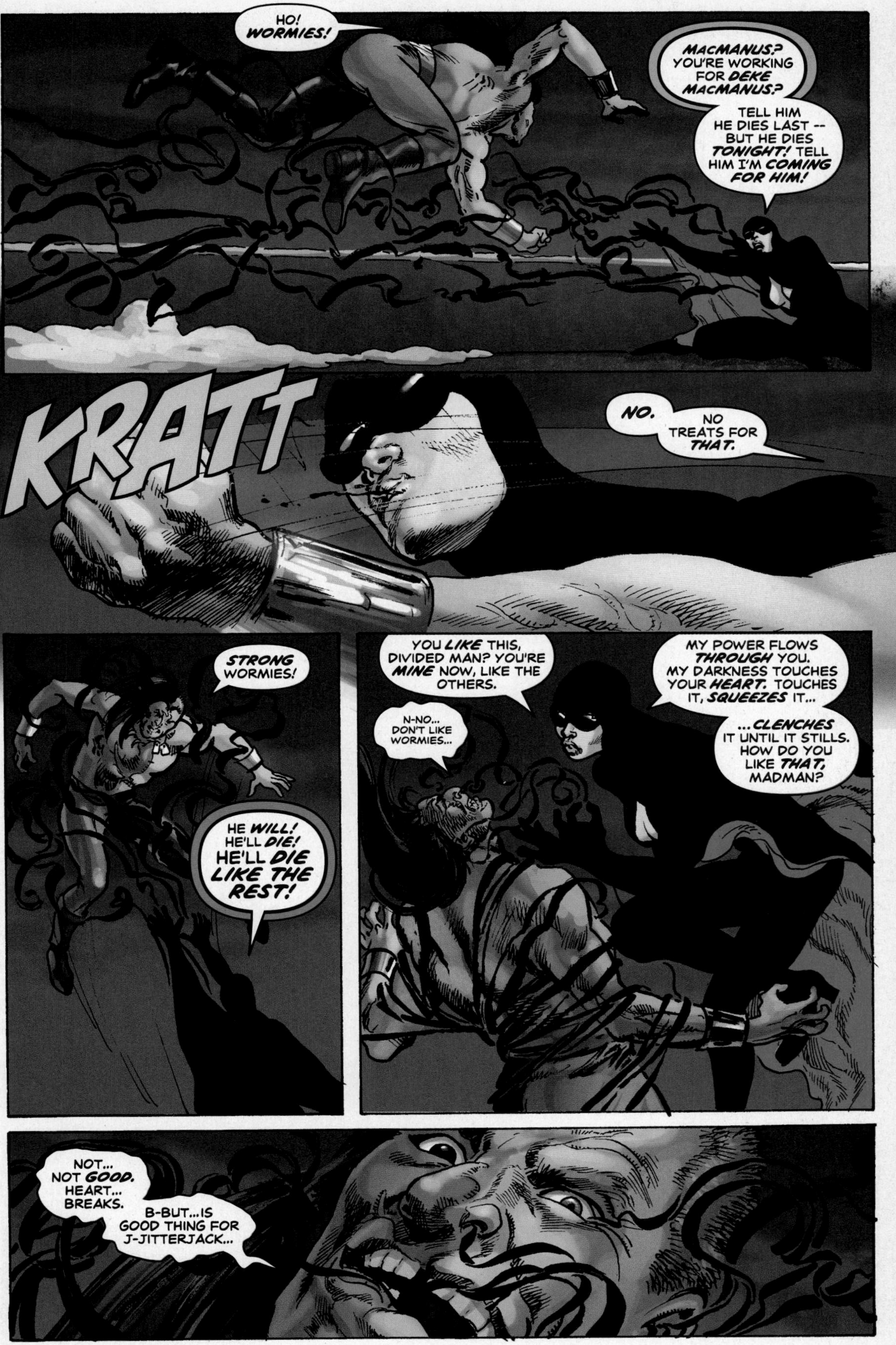
HO! WORMIES!
MACMANUS? YOU'RE WORKING FOR DEKE MACMANUS?
TELL HIM HE DIES LAST -- BUT HE DIES TONIGHT! TELL HIM I'M COMING FOR HIM!
KRATT
NO.
NO TREATS FOR THAT.
STRONG WORMIES!
HE WILL! HE'LL DIE! HE'LL DIE LIKE THE REST!
YOU LIKE THIS, DIVIDED MAN? YOU'RE MINE NOW, LIKE THE OTHERS.
MY POWER FLOWS THROUGH YOU. MY DARKNESS TOUCHES YOUR HEART. TOUCHES IT, SQUEEZES IT...
N-NO... DON'T LIKE WORMIES...
...CLENCHES IT UNTIL IT STILLS. HOW DO YOU LIKE THAT, MADMAN?
NOT... NOT GOOD. HEART... BREAKS.
B-BUT...IS GOOD THING FOR J-JITTERJACK...

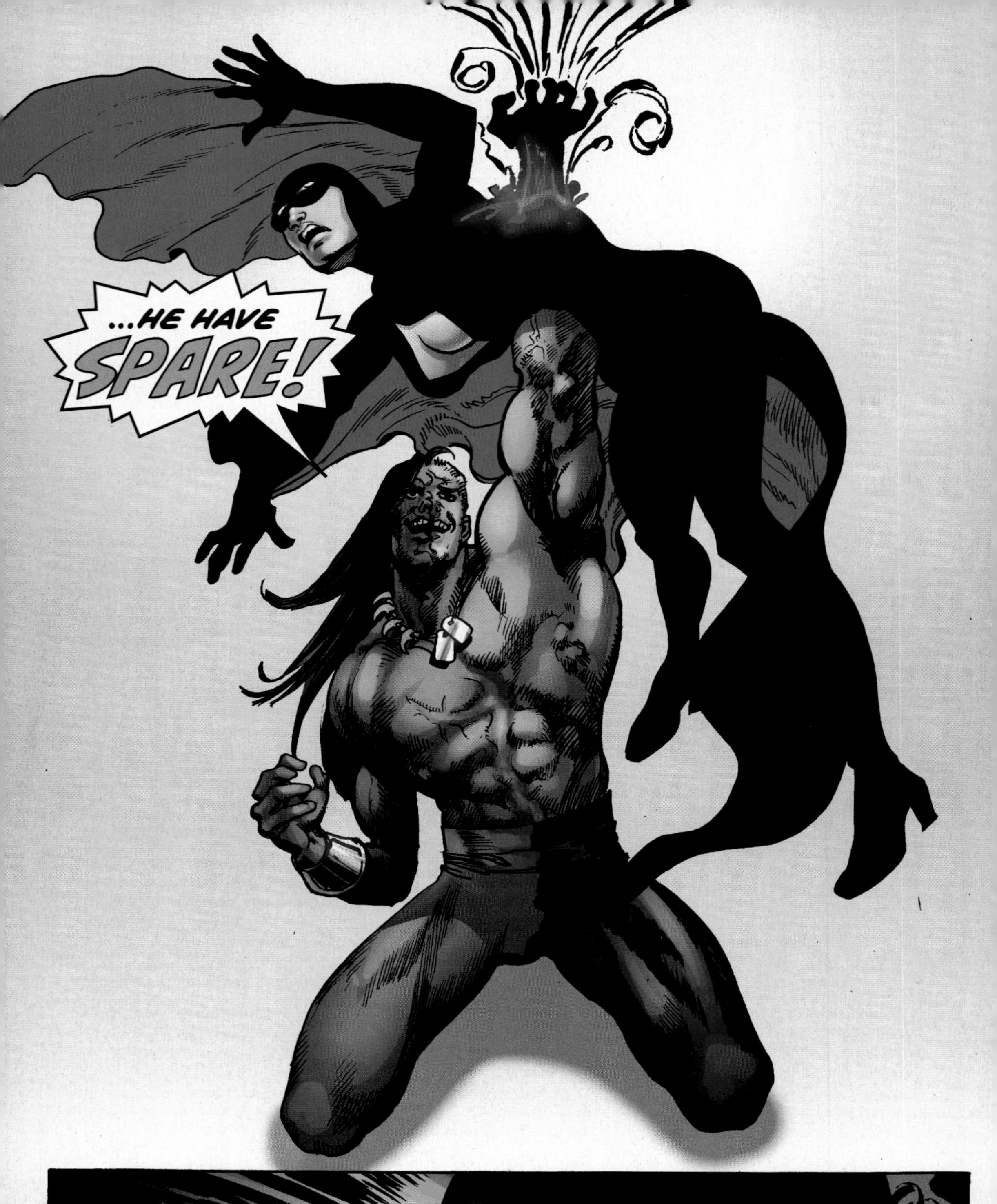
...HE HAVE
SPARE!

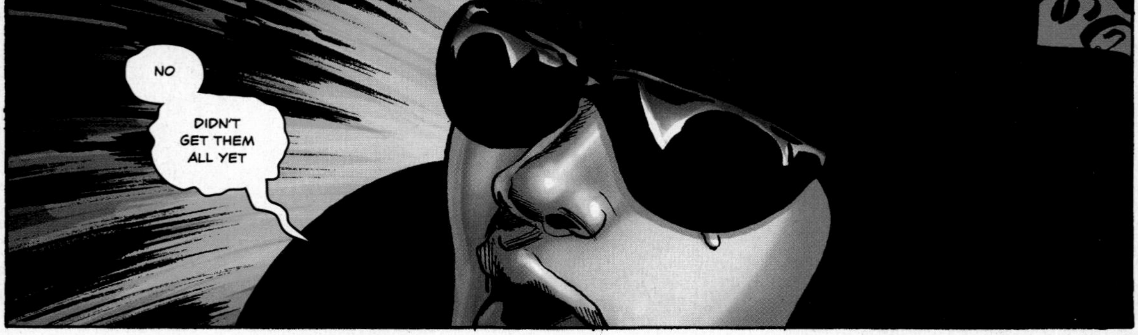
NO
DIDN'T GET THEM ALL YET

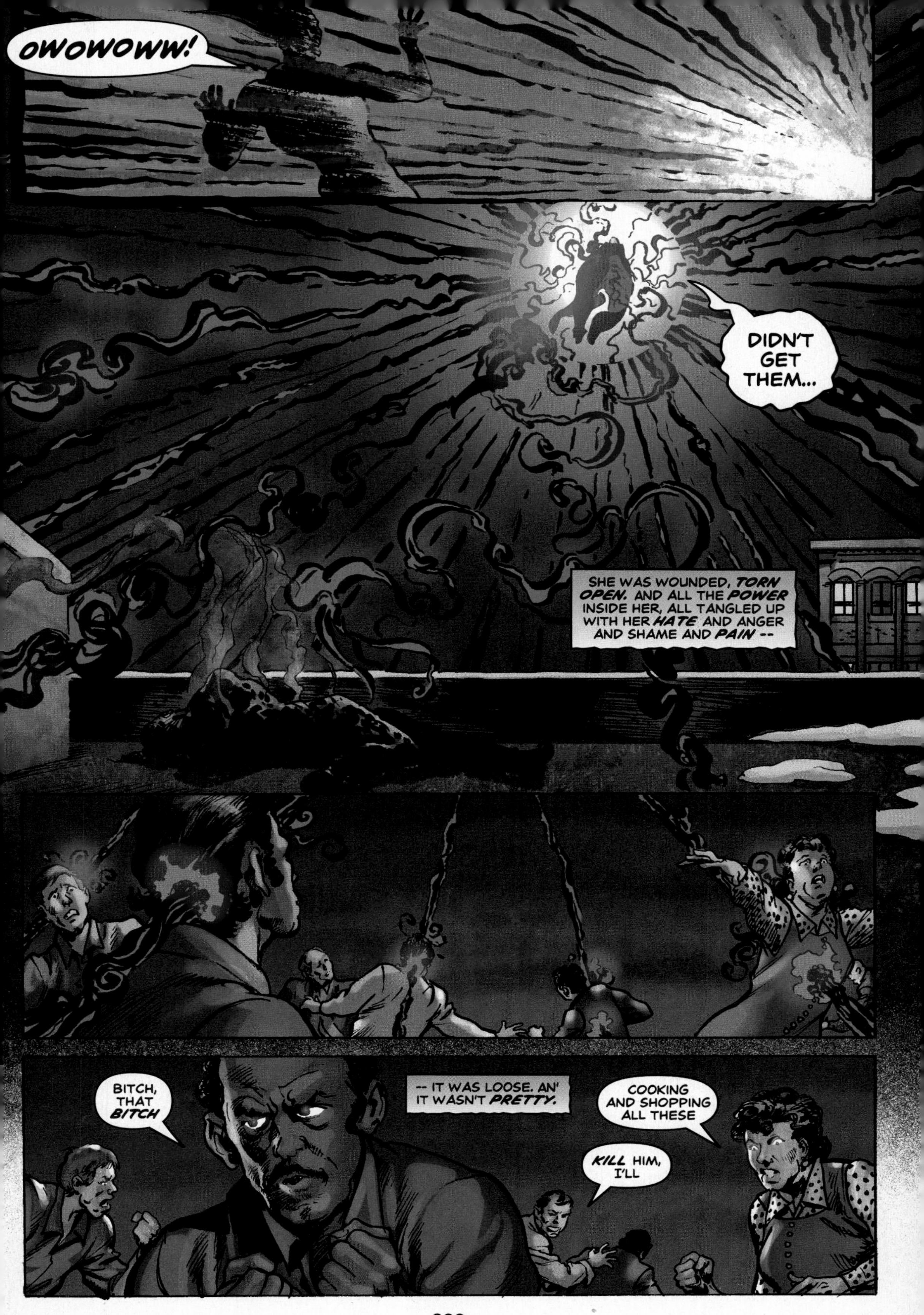
OWOWOWW!
DIDN'T GET THEM...
SHE WAS WOUNDED, TORN OPEN. AND ALL THE POWER INSIDE HER, ALL TANGLED UP WITH HER HATE AND ANGER AND SHAME AND PAIN --
BITCH, THAT BITCH
-- IT WAS LOOSE. AN' IT WASN'T PRETTY.
COOKING AND SHOPPING ALL THESE
KILL HIM, I'LL

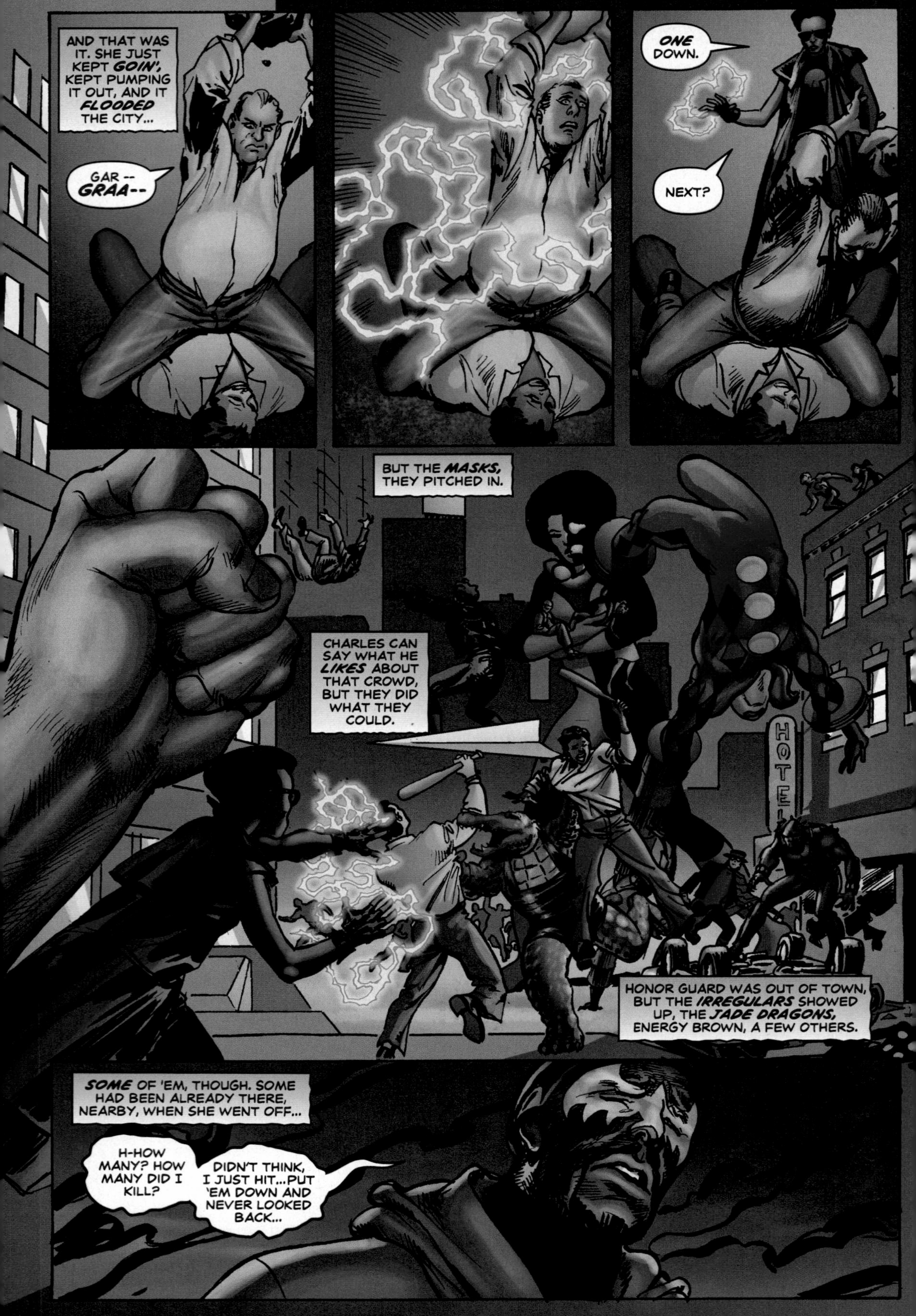
AND THAT WAS IT. SHE JUST KEPT GOIN', KEPT PUMPING IT OUT, AND IT FLOODED THE CITY...
GAR -- GRAA--
ONE DOWN.
NEXT?
BUT THE MASKS, THEY PITCHED IN.
CHARLES CAN SAY WHAT HE LIKES ABOUT THAT CROWD, BUT THEY DID WHAT THEY COULD.
HOTEL
HONOR GUARD WAS OUT OF TOWN, BUT THE IRREGULARS SHOWED UP, THE JADE DRAGONS, ENERGY BROWN, A FEW OTHERS.
SOME OF 'EM, THOUGH. SOME HAD BEEN ALREADY THERE, NEARBY, WHEN SHE WENT OFF...
H-HOW MANY? HOW MANY DID I KILL?
DIDN'T THINK, I JUST HIT...PUT 'EM DOWN AND NEVER LOOKED BACK...

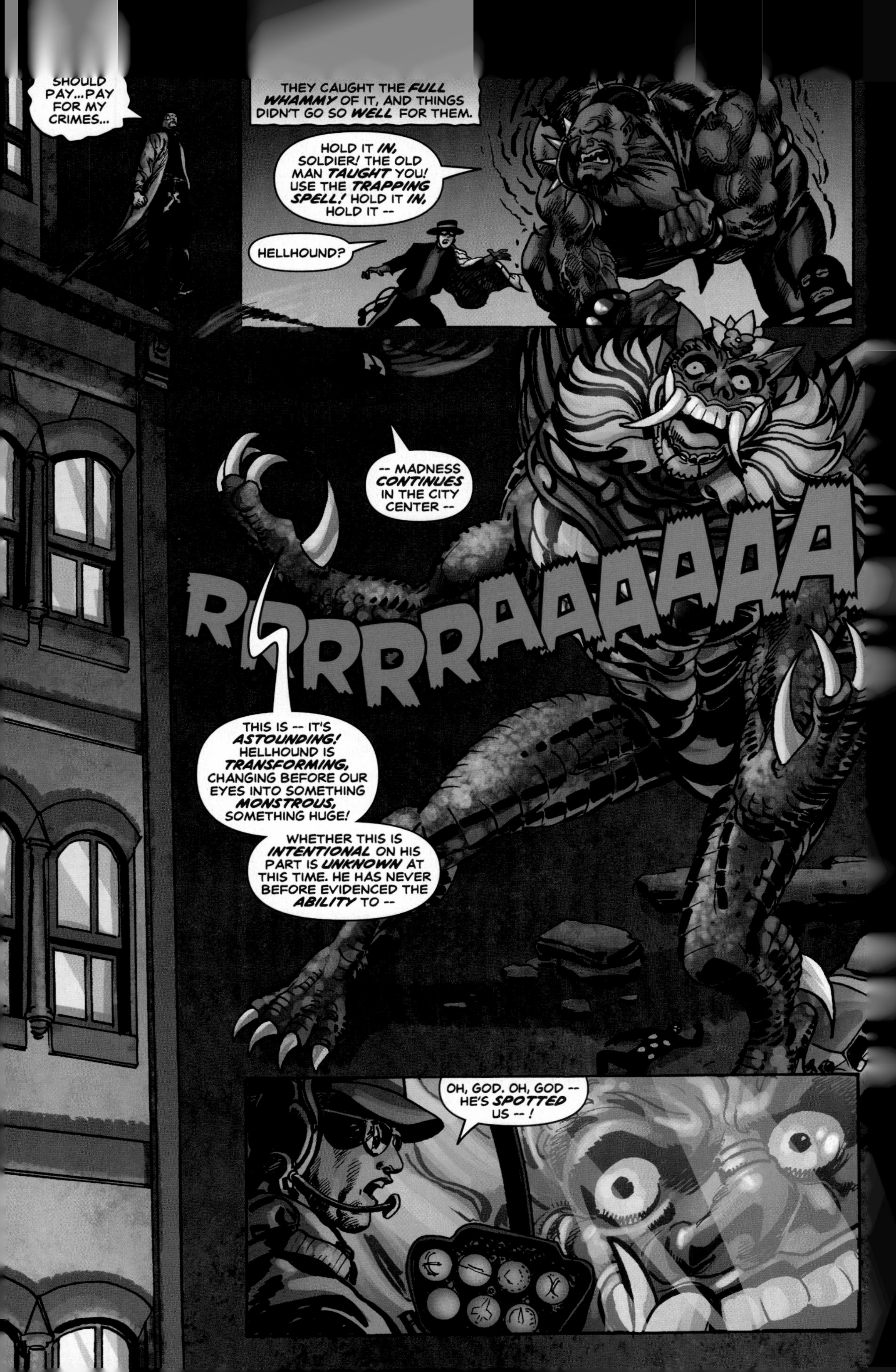
SHOULD PAY...PAY FOR MY CRIMES...
THEY CAUGHT THE FULL WHAMMY OF IT, AND THINGS DIDN'T GO SO WELL FOR THEM.
HOLD IT IN, SOLDIER! THE OLD MAN TAUGHT YOU! USE THE TRAPPING SPELL! HOLD IT IN, HOLD IT --
HELLHOUND?
-- MADNESS CONTINUES IN THE CITY CENTER --
RRRRRAAAAAAA
THIS IS -- IT'S ASTOUNDING! HELLHOUND IS TRANSFORMING, CHANGING BEFORE OUR EYES INTO SOMETHING MONSTROUS, SOMETHING HUGE!
WHETHER THIS IS INTENTIONAL ON HIS PART IS UNKNOWN AT THIS TIME. HE HAS NEVER BEFORE EVIDENCED THE ABILITY TO --
OH, GOD. OH, GOD -- HE'S SPOTTED US -- !

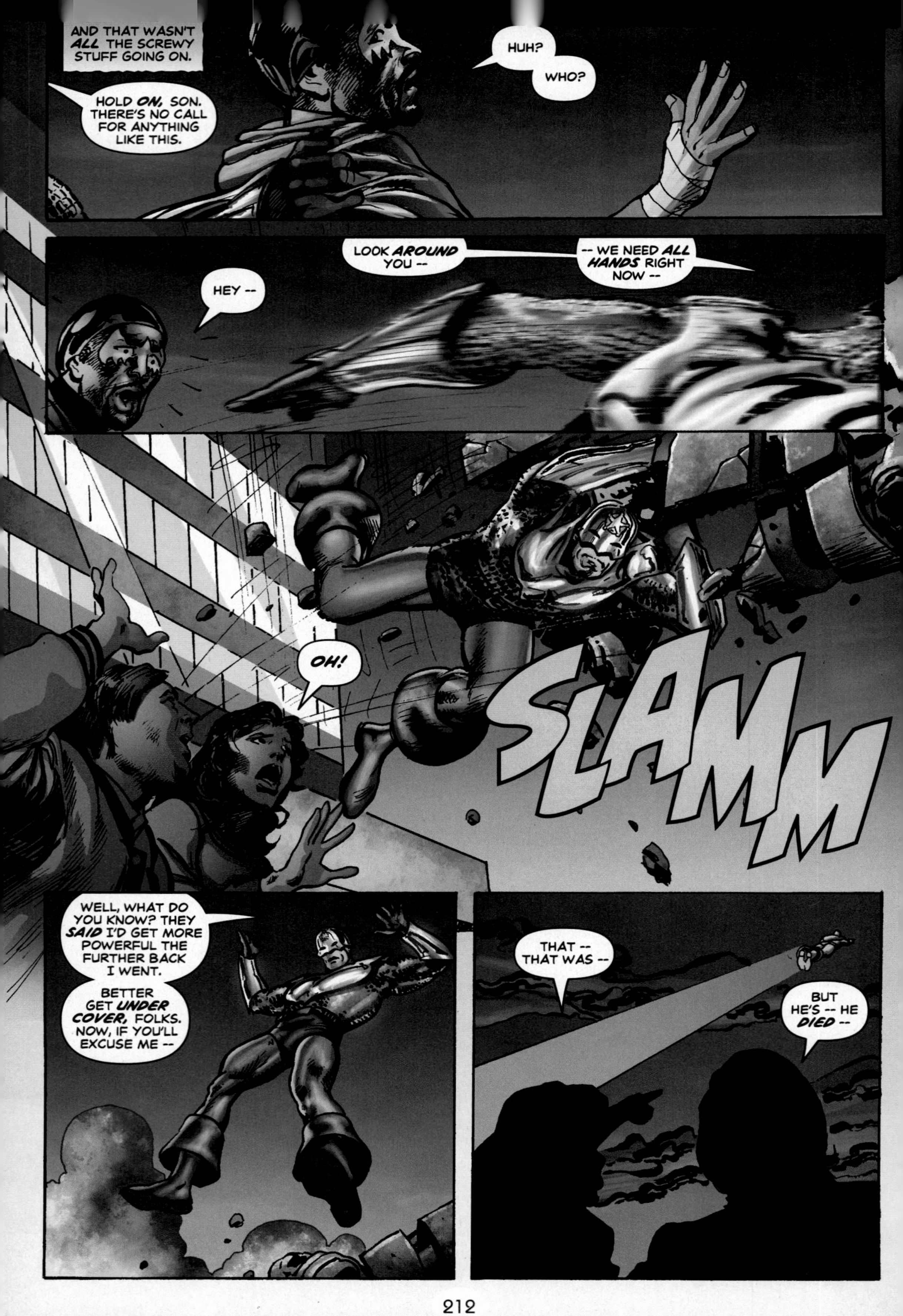
AND THAT WASN'T ALL THE SCREWY STUFF GOING ON.
HUH?
WHO?
HOLD ON, SON. THERE'S NO CALL FOR ANYTHING LIKE THIS.
LOOK AROUND YOU --
-- WE NEED ALL HANDS RIGHT NOW --
HEY --
OH!
SLAMM
WELL, WHAT DO YOU KNOW? THEY SAID I'D GET MORE POWERFUL THE FURTHER BACK I WENT.
BETTER GET UNDER COVER, FOLKS. NOW, IF YOU'LL EXCUSE ME --
THAT -- THAT WAS --
BUT HE'S -- HE DIED --

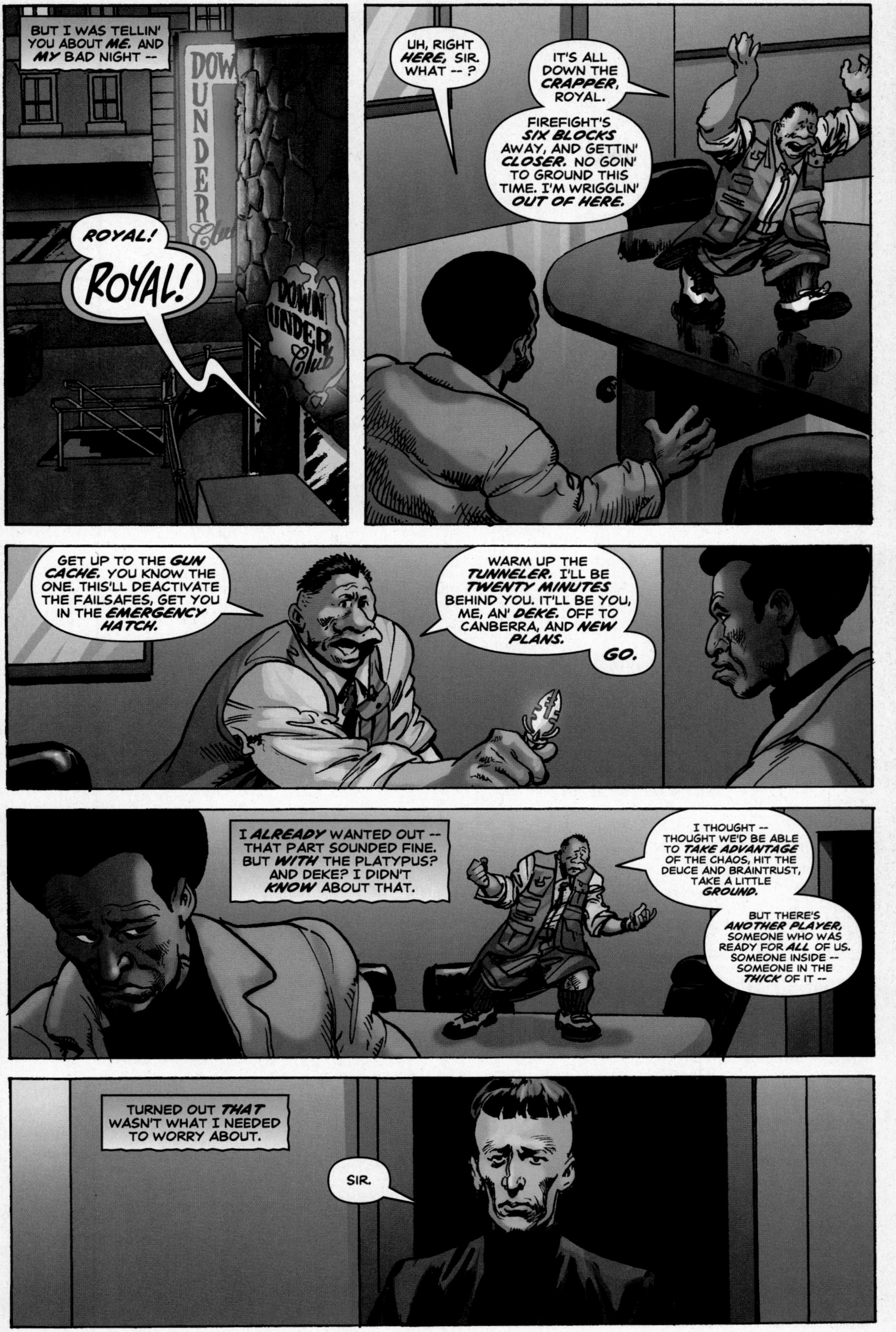
BUT I WAS TELLIN' YOU ABOUT ME. AND MY BAD NIGHT --
DOWN UNDER Club
ROYAL!
ROYAL!
DOWN UNDER Club
UH, RIGHT HERE, SIR. WHAT -- ?
IT'S ALL DOWN THE CRAPPER, ROYAL.
FIREFIGHT'S SIX BLOCKS AWAY, AND GETTIN' CLOSER. NO GOIN' TO GROUND THIS TIME. I'M WRIGGLIN' OUT OF HERE.
GET UP TO THE GUN CACHE. YOU KNOW THE ONE. THIS'LL DEACTIVATE THE FAILSAFES, GET YOU IN THE EMERGENCY HATCH.
WARM UP THE TUNNELER. I'LL BE TWENTY MINUTES BEHIND YOU. IT'LL BE YOU, ME, AN' DEKE. OFF TO CANBERRA, AND NEW PLANS.
GO.
I ALREADY WANTED OUT -- THAT PART SOUNDED FINE. BUT WITH THE PLATYPUS? AND DEKE? I DIDN'T KNOW ABOUT THAT.
I THOUGHT -- THOUGHT WE'D BE ABLE TO TAKE ADVANTAGE OF THE CHAOS, HIT THE DEUCE AND BRAINTRUST, TAKE A LITTLE GROUND.
BUT THERE'S ANOTHER PLAYER, SOMEONE WHO WAS READY FOR ALL OF US. SOMEONE INSIDE -- SOMEONE IN THE THICK OF IT --
TURNED OUT THAT WASN'T WHAT I NEEDED TO WORRY ABOUT.
SIR.

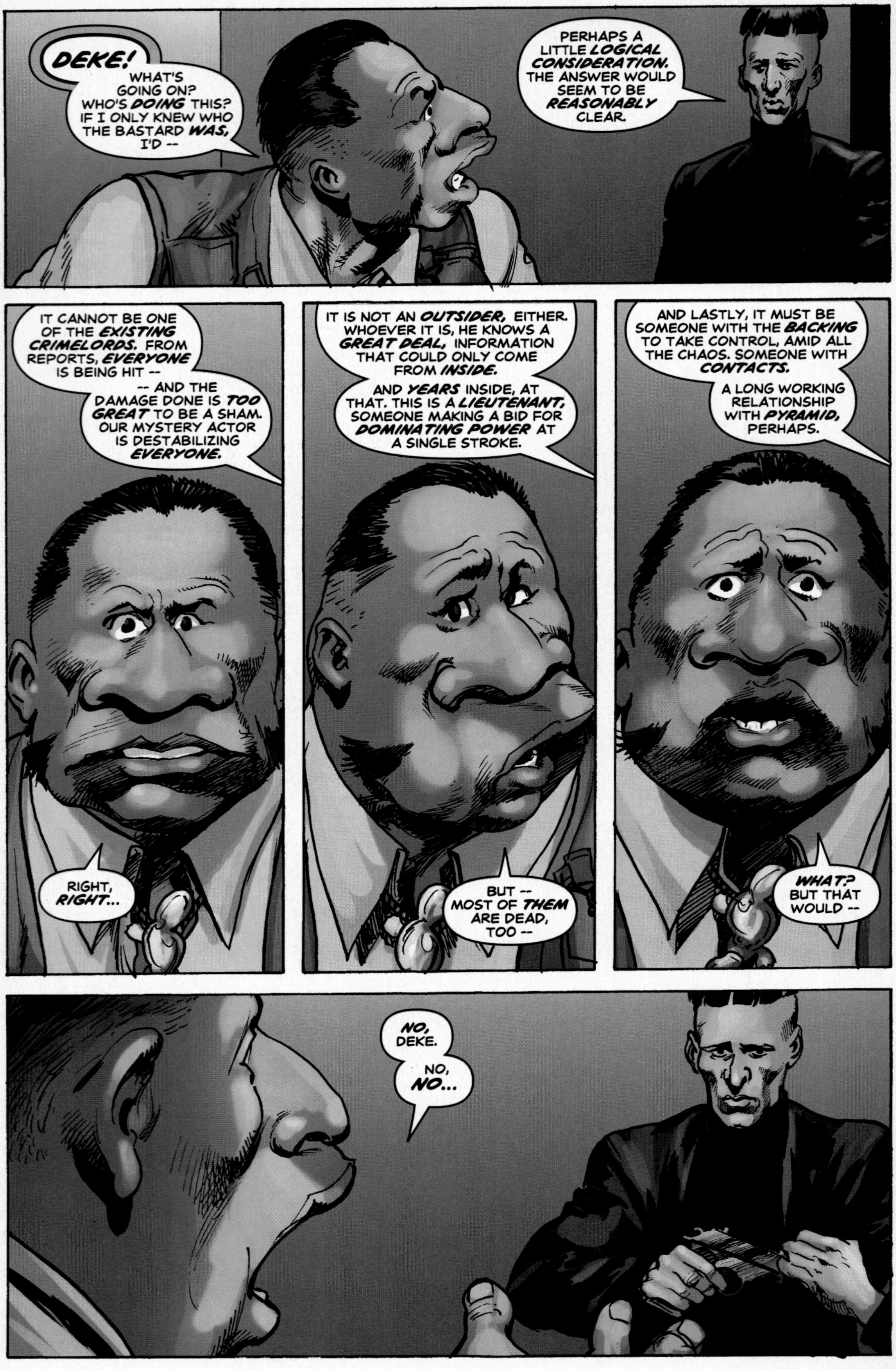
DEKE! WHAT'S GOING ON? WHO'S DOING THIS? IF I ONLY KNEW WHO THE BASTARD WAS, I'D --
PERHAPS A LITTLE LOGICAL CONSIDERATION. THE ANSWER WOULD SEEM TO BE REASONABLY CLEAR.
IT CANNOT BE ONE OF THE EXISTING CRIMELORDS. FROM REPORTS, EVERYONE IS BEING HIT --
-- AND THE DAMAGE DONE IS TOO GREAT TO BE A SHAM. OUR MYSTERY ACTOR IS DESTABILIZING EVERYONE.
RIGHT, RIGHT...
IT IS NOT AN OUTSIDER, EITHER. WHOEVER IT IS, HE KNOWS A GREAT DEAL, INFORMATION THAT COULD ONLY COME FROM INSIDE.
AND YEARS INSIDE, AT THAT. THIS IS A LIEUTENANT, SOMEONE MAKING A BID FOR DOMINATING POWER AT A SINGLE STROKE.
BUT -- MOST OF THEM ARE DEAD, TOO --
AND LASTLY, IT MUST BE SOMEONE WITH THE BACKING TO TAKE CONTROL, AMID ALL THE CHAOS. SOMEONE WITH CONTACTS.
A LONG WORKING RELATIONSHIP WITH PYRAMID, PERHAPS.
WHAT? BUT THAT WOULD --
NO, DEKE.
NO, NO...

BLAM

MM.

AUBREY?

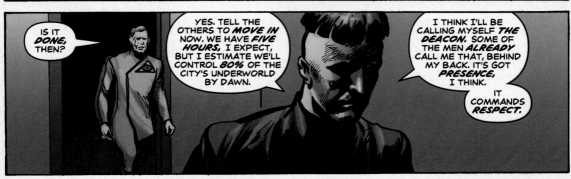

IS IT *DONE*, THEN?

YES. TELL THE OTHERS TO *MOVE IN* NOW. WE HAVE *FIVE HOURS*, I EXPECT, BUT I ESTIMATE WE'LL CONTROL *80%* OF THE CITY'S UNDERWORLD BY DAWN.

I THINK I'LL BE CALLING MYSELF *THE DEACON*. SOME OF THE MEN *ALREADY* CALL ME THAT, BEHIND MY BACK. IT'S GOT *PRESENCE*, I THINK.

IT COMMANDS *RESPECT*.

HUFF

HUFF

HE'D SENT ME TO THE *GUN CACHE*. I'M SURE ALL HE MEANT WAS FOR ME TO GET HIS *ROBO-MOLE-MACHINE*, LIKE HE SAID.

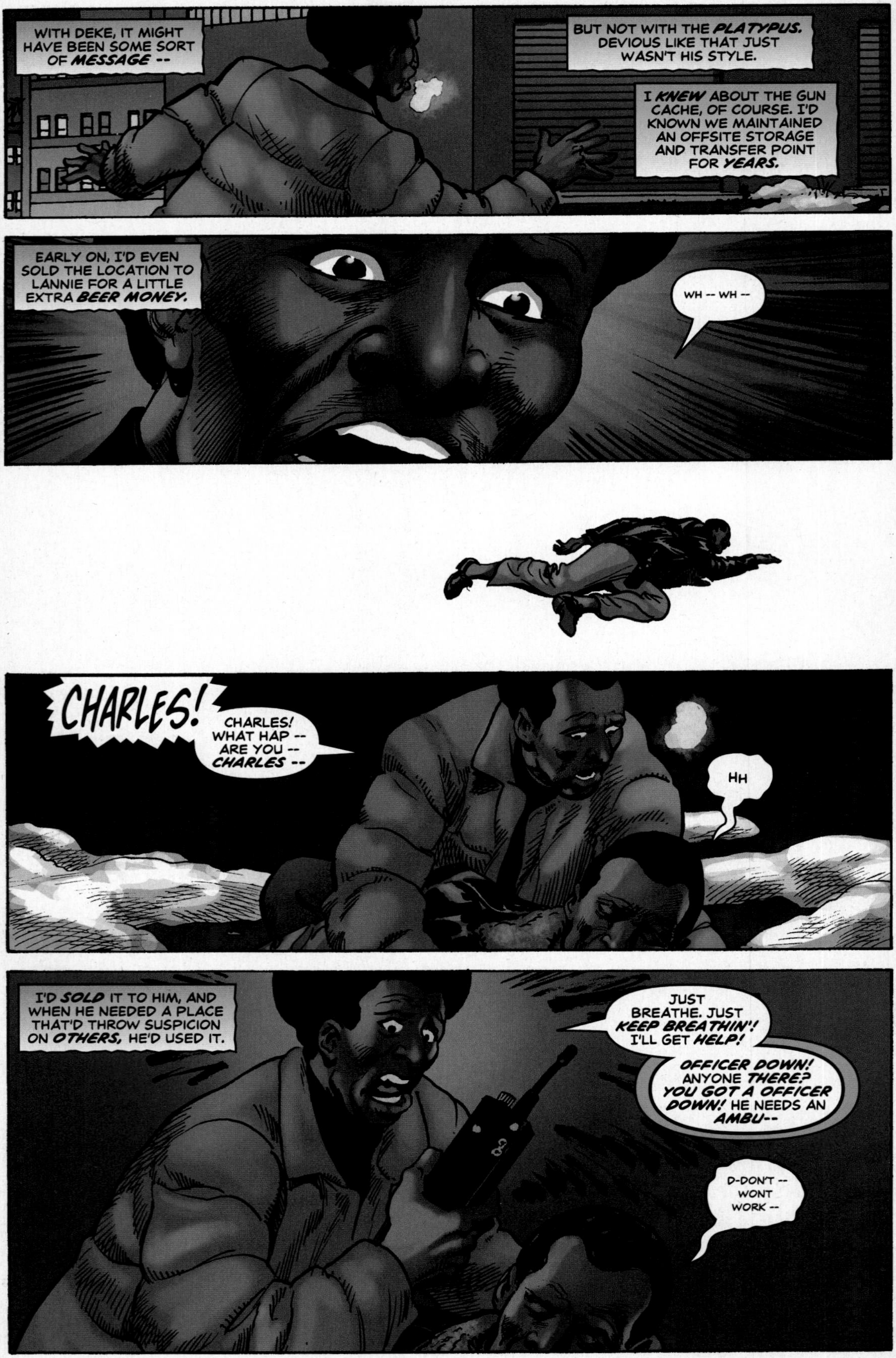

WITH DEKE, IT MIGHT HAVE BEEN SOME SORT OF MESSAGE --
BUT NOT WITH THE PLATYPUS. DEVIOUS LIKE THAT JUST WASN'T HIS STYLE.
I KNEW ABOUT THE GUN CACHE, OF COURSE. I'D KNOWN WE MAINTAINED AN OFFSITE STORAGE AND TRANSFER POINT FOR YEARS.
EARLY ON, I'D EVEN SOLD THE LOCATION TO LANNIE FOR A LITTLE EXTRA BEER MONEY.
WH -- WH --
CHARLES!
CHARLES! WHAT HAP -- ARE YOU -- CHARLES --
HH
I'D SOLD IT TO HIM, AND WHEN HE NEEDED A PLACE THAT'D THROW SUSPICION ON OTHERS, HE'D USED IT.
JUST BREATHE. JUST KEEP BREATHIN'! I'LL GET HELP!
OFFICER DOWN! ANYONE THERE? YOU GOT A OFFICER DOWN! HE NEEDS AN AMBU--
D-DON'T -- WONT WORK --

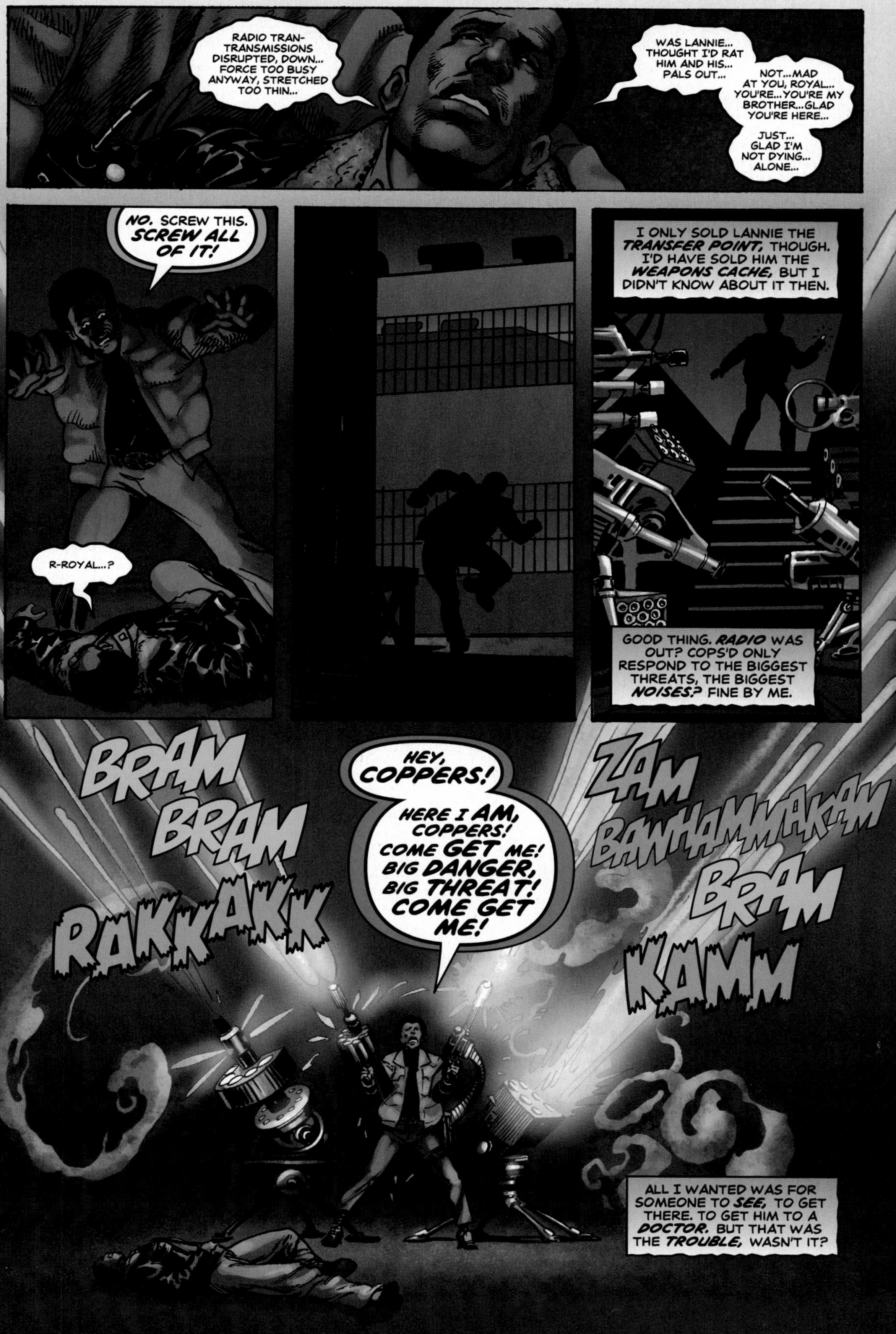
RADIO TRAN-TRANSMISSIONS DISRUPTED, DOWN... FORCE TOO BUSY ANYWAY, STRETCHED TOO THIN...
WAS LANNIE... THOUGHT I'D RAT HIM AND HIS... PALS OUT...
NOT...MAD AT YOU, ROYAL... YOU'RE...YOU'RE MY BROTHER...GLAD YOU'RE HERE...
JUST... GLAD I'M NOT DYING... ALONE...
NO. SCREW THIS. SCREW ALL OF IT!
R-ROYAL...?
I ONLY SOLD LANNIE THE TRANSFER POINT, THOUGH. I'D HAVE SOLD HIM THE WEAPONS CACHE, BUT I DIDN'T KNOW ABOUT IT THEN.
GOOD THING. RADIO WAS OUT? COPS'D ONLY RESPOND TO THE BIGGEST THREATS, THE BIGGEST NOISES? FINE BY ME.
BRAM BRAM
RAKKAKK
HEY, COPPERS!
HERE I AM, COPPERS! COME GET ME! BIG DANGER, BIG THREAT! COME GET ME!
ZAM BAWHAMWAKAM BRAM KAMM
ALL I WANTED WAS FOR SOMEONE TO SEE, TO GET THERE. TO GET HIM TO A DOCTOR. BUT THAT WAS THE TROUBLE, WASN'T IT?

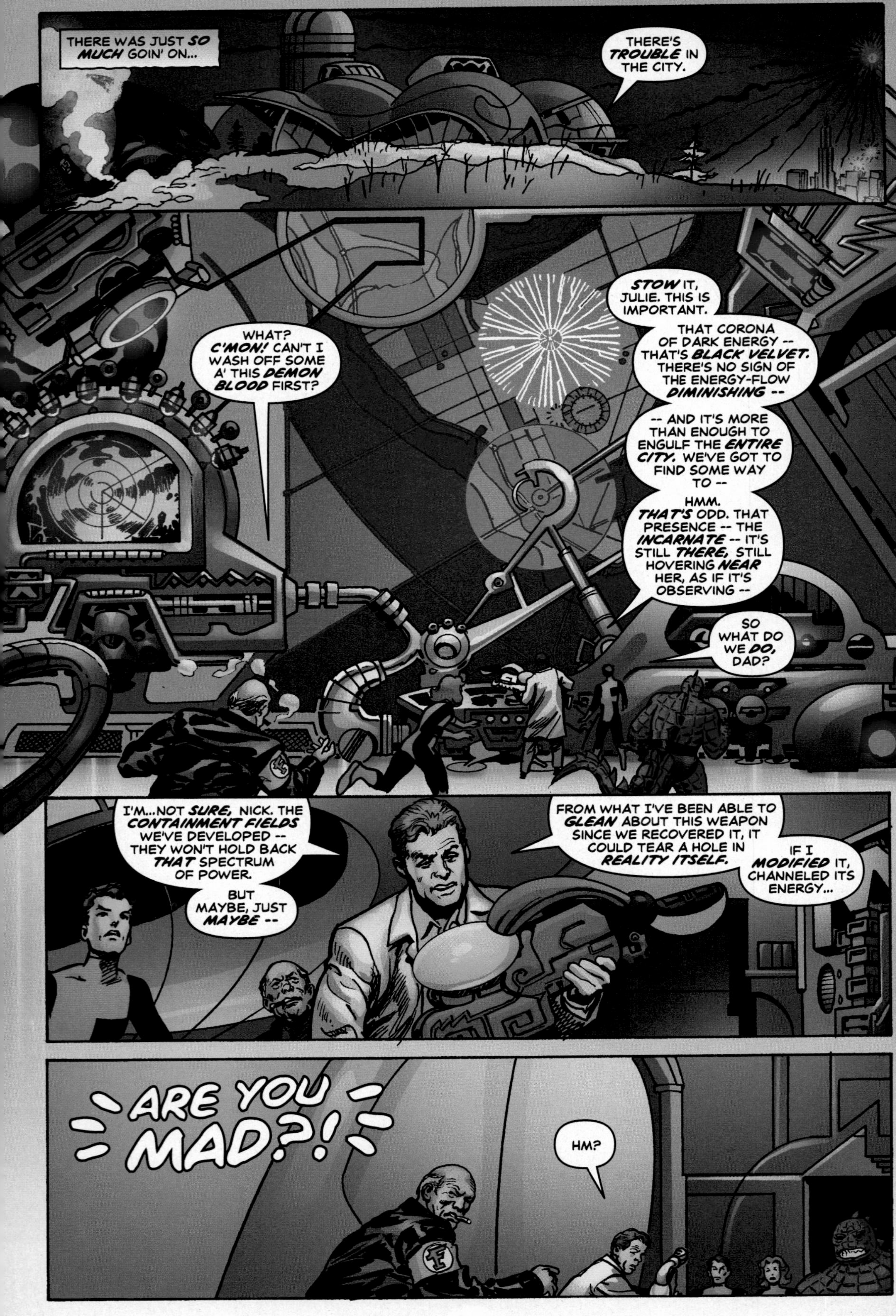
THERE WAS JUST SO MUCH GOIN' ON...
THERE'S TROUBLE IN THE CITY.
WHAT? C'MON! CAN'T I WASH OFF SOME A' THIS DEMON BLOOD FIRST?
STOW IT, JULIE. THIS IS IMPORTANT.
THAT CORONA OF DARK ENERGY -- THAT'S BLACK VELVET. THERE'S NO SIGN OF THE ENERGY-FLOW DIMINISHING --
-- AND IT'S MORE THAN ENOUGH TO ENGULF THE ENTIRE CITY. WE'VE GOT TO FIND SOME WAY TO --
HMM. THAT'S ODD. THAT PRESENCE -- THE INCARNATE -- IT'S STILL THERE, STILL HOVERING NEAR HER, AS IF IT'S OBSERVING --
SO WHAT DO WE DO, DAD?
I'M...NOT SURE, NICK. THE CONTAINMENT FIELDS WE'VE DEVELOPED -- THEY WON'T HOLD BACK THAT SPECTRUM OF POWER.
BUT MAYBE, JUST MAYBE --
FROM WHAT I'VE BEEN ABLE TO GLEAN ABOUT THIS WEAPON SINCE WE RECOVERED IT, IT COULD TEAR A HOLE IN REALITY ITSELF.
IF I MODIFIED IT, CHANNELED ITS ENERGY...
ARE YOU MAD?!
HM?

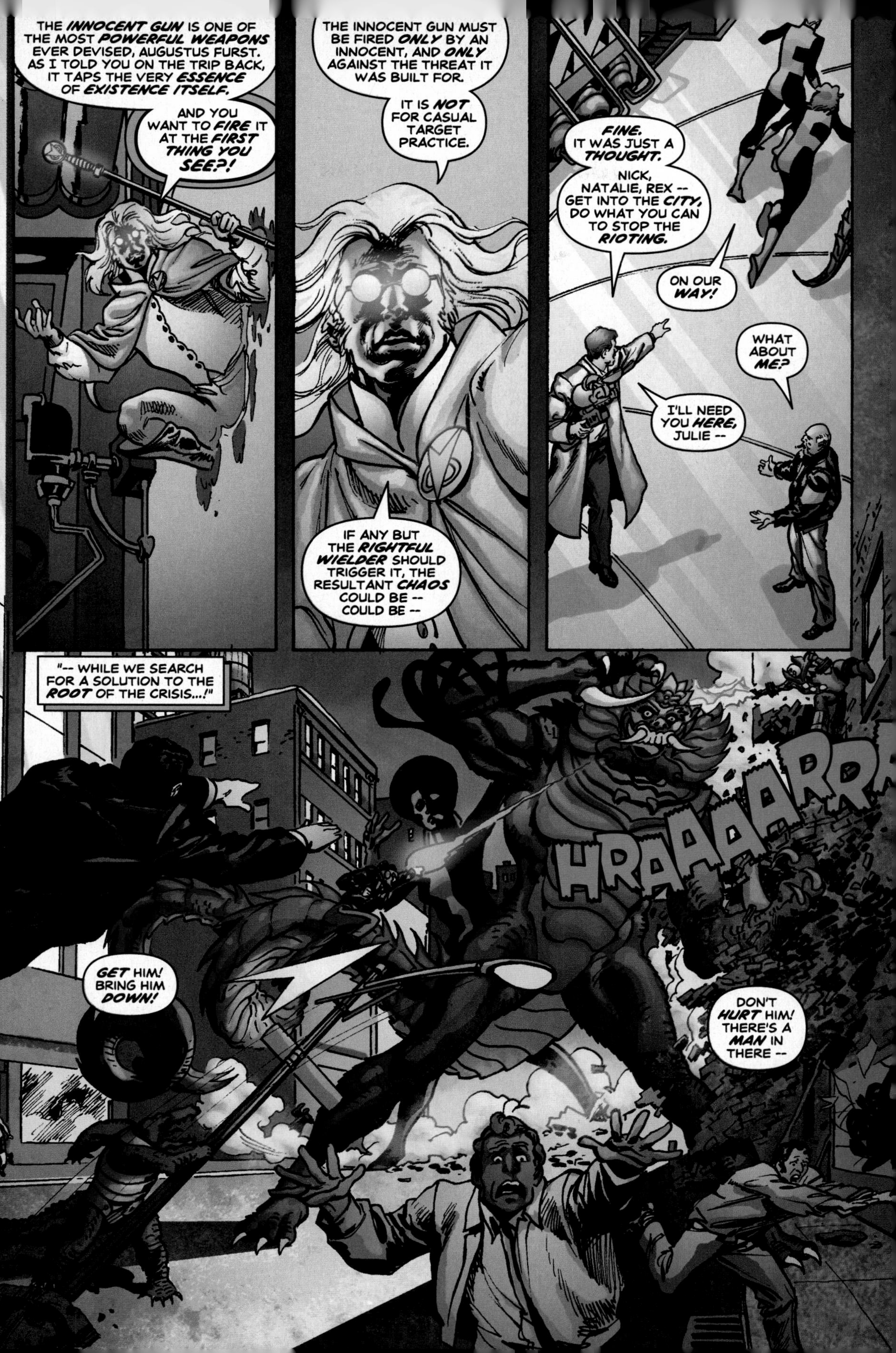
THE INNOCENT GUN IS ONE OF THE MOST POWERFUL WEAPONS EVER DEVISED, AUGUSTUS FURST. AS I TOLD YOU ON THE TRIP BACK, IT TAPS THE VERY ESSENCE OF EXISTENCE ITSELF.
AND YOU WANT TO FIRE IT AT THE FIRST THING YOU SEE?!
THE INNOCENT GUN MUST BE FIRED ONLY BY AN INNOCENT, AND ONLY AGAINST THE THREAT IT WAS BUILT FOR.
IT IS NOT FOR CASUAL TARGET PRACTICE.
IF ANY BUT THE RIGHTFUL WIELDER SHOULD TRIGGER IT, THE RESULTANT CHAOS COULD BE -- COULD BE --
FINE. IT WAS JUST A THOUGHT.
NICK, NATALIE, REX -- GET INTO THE CITY, DO WHAT YOU CAN TO STOP THE RIOTING.
ON OUR WAY!
WHAT ABOUT ME?
I'LL NEED YOU HERE, JULIE --
"-- WHILE WE SEARCH FOR A SOLUTION TO THE ROOT OF THE CRISIS...!"
HRAAAARR
GET HIM! BRING HIM DOWN!
DON'T HURT HIM! THERE'S A MAN IN THERE --

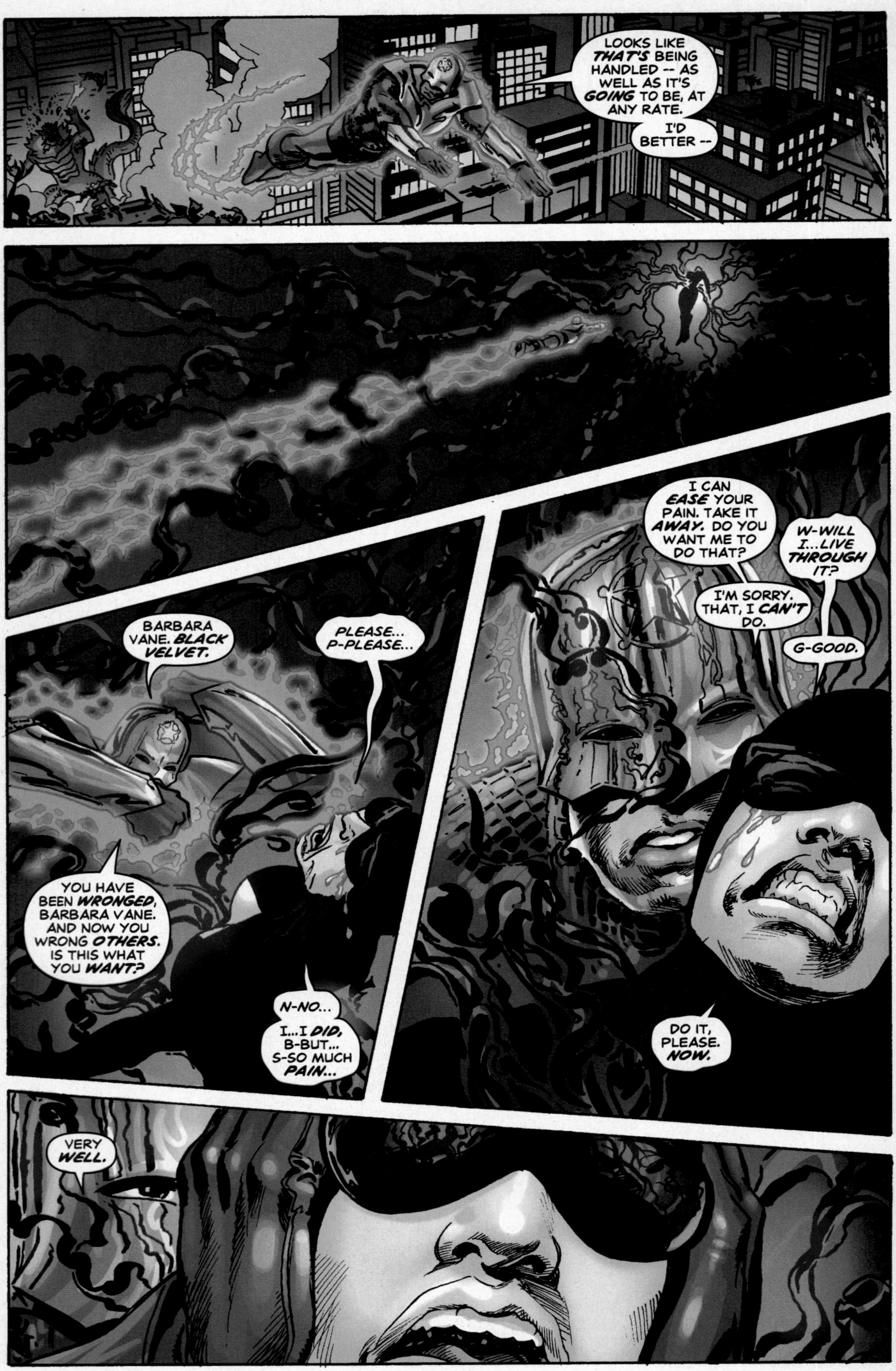
LOOKS LIKE THAT'S BEING HANDLED -- AS WELL AS IT'S GOING TO BE, AT ANY RATE.
I'D BETTER --
BARBARA VANE. BLACK VELVET.
PLEASE... P-PLEASE...
YOU HAVE BEEN WRONGED, BARBARA VANE. AND NOW YOU WRONG OTHERS. IS THIS WHAT YOU WANT?
N-NO...
I...I DID, B-BUT... S-SO MUCH PAIN...
I CAN EASE YOUR PAIN. TAKE IT AWAY. DO YOU WANT ME TO DO THAT?
W-WILL I...LIVE THROUGH IT?
I'M SORRY. THAT, I CAN'T DO.
G-GOOD.
DO IT, PLEASE. NOW.
VERY WELL.

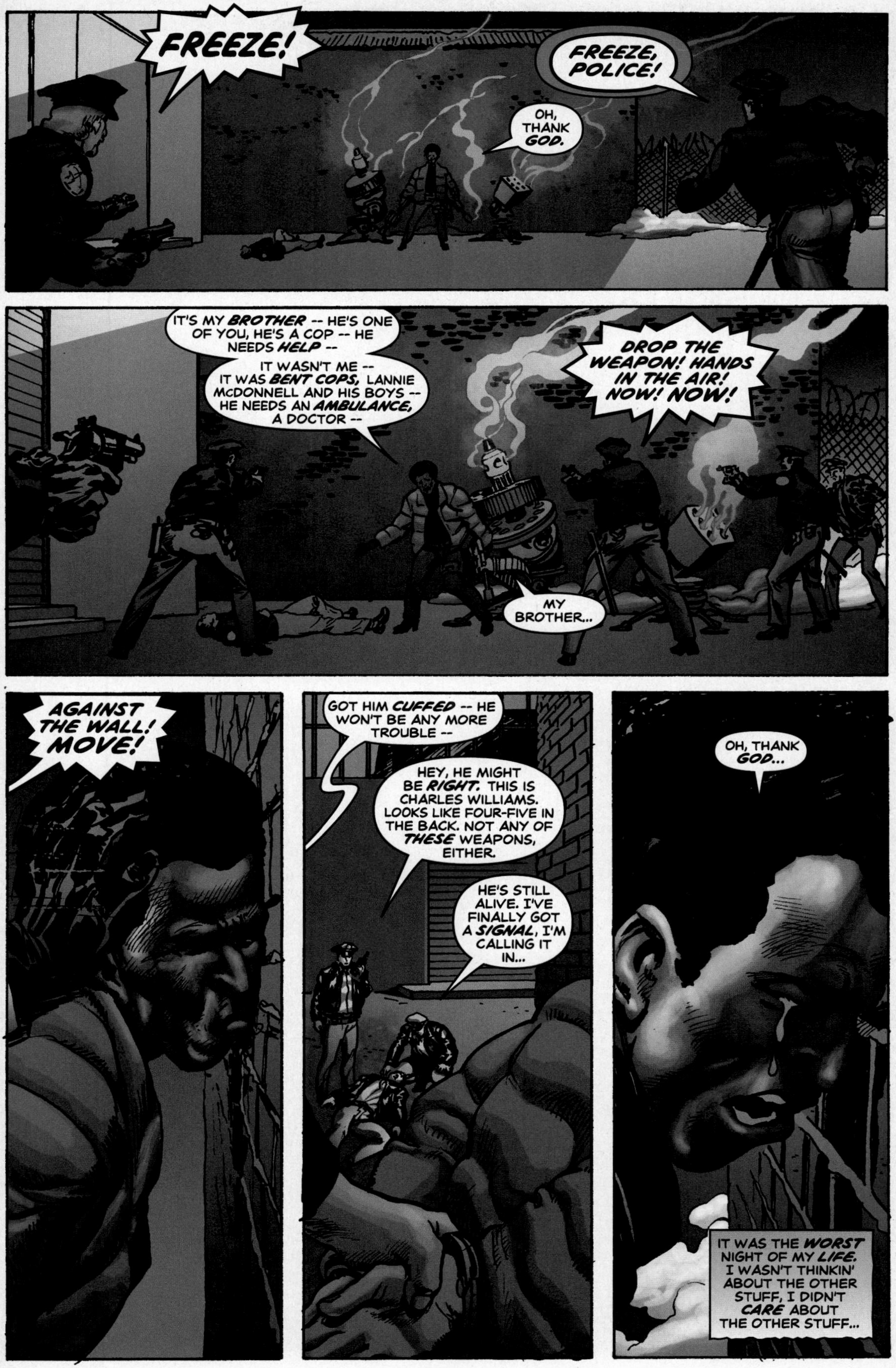
FREEZE!
FREEZE, POLICE!
OH, THANK GOD.
IT'S MY BROTHER -- HE'S ONE OF YOU, HE'S A COP -- HE NEEDS HELP --
IT WASN'T ME -- IT WAS BENT COPS, LANNIE McDONNELL AND HIS BOYS -- HE NEEDS AN AMBULANCE, A DOCTOR --
DROP THE WEAPON! HANDS IN THE AIR! NOW! NOW!
MY BROTHER...
AGAINST THE WALL! MOVE!
GOT HIM CUFFED -- HE WON'T BE ANY MORE TROUBLE --
HEY, HE MIGHT BE RIGHT. THIS IS CHARLES WILLIAMS. LOOKS LIKE FOUR-FIVE IN THE BACK. NOT ANY OF THESE WEAPONS, EITHER.
HE'S STILL ALIVE. I'VE FINALLY GOT A SIGNAL, I'M CALLING IT IN...
OH, THANK GOD...
IT WAS THE WORST NIGHT OF MY LIFE. I WASN'T THINKIN' ABOUT THE OTHER STUFF, I DIDN'T CARE ABOUT THE OTHER STUFF...

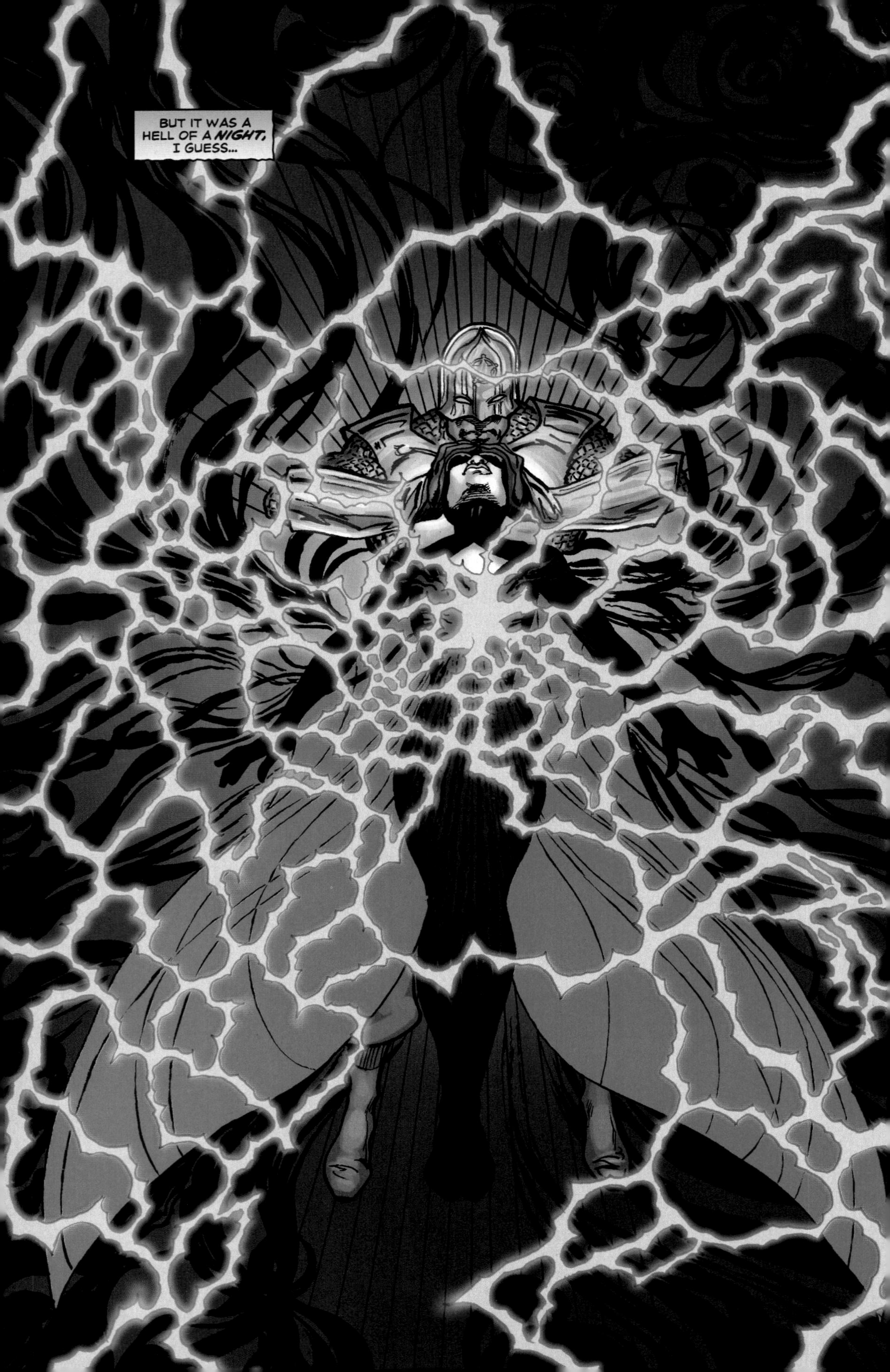
BUT IT WAS A HELL OF A NIGHT, I GUESS...

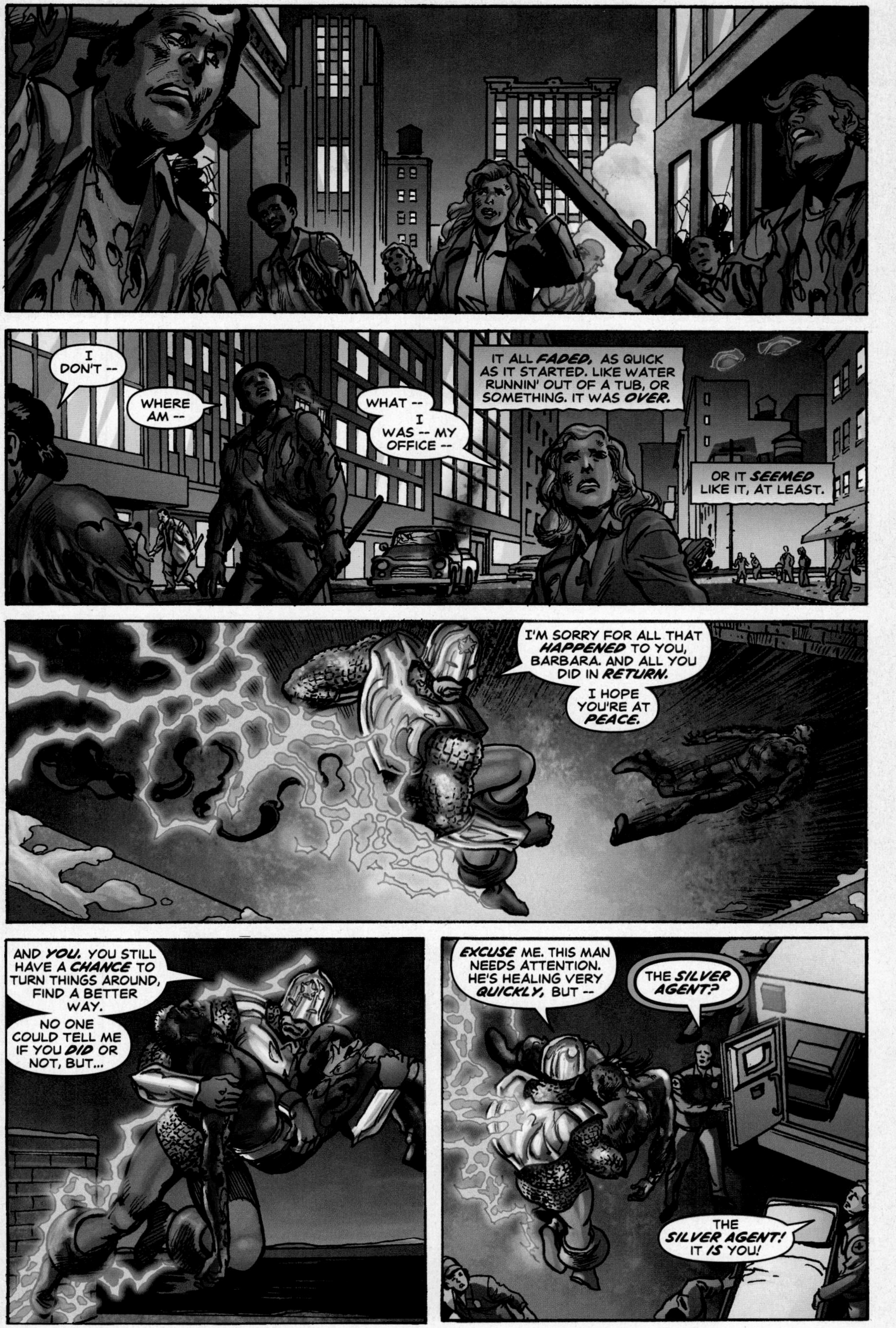
I DON'T --
WHERE AM --
WHAT -- I WAS -- MY OFFICE --
IT ALL FADED, AS QUICK AS IT STARTED. LIKE WATER RUNNIN' OUT OF A TUB, OR SOMETHING. IT WAS OVER.
OR IT SEEMED LIKE IT, AT LEAST.
I'M SORRY FOR ALL THAT HAPPENED TO YOU, BARBARA. AND ALL YOU DID IN RETURN.
I HOPE YOU'RE AT PEACE.
AND YOU. YOU STILL HAVE A CHANCE TO TURN THINGS AROUND, FIND A BETTER WAY.
NO ONE COULD TELL ME IF YOU DID OR NOT, BUT...
EXCUSE ME. THIS MAN NEEDS ATTENTION. HE'S HEALING VERY QUICKLY, BUT --
THE SILVER AGENT?
THE SILVER AGENT! IT IS YOU!

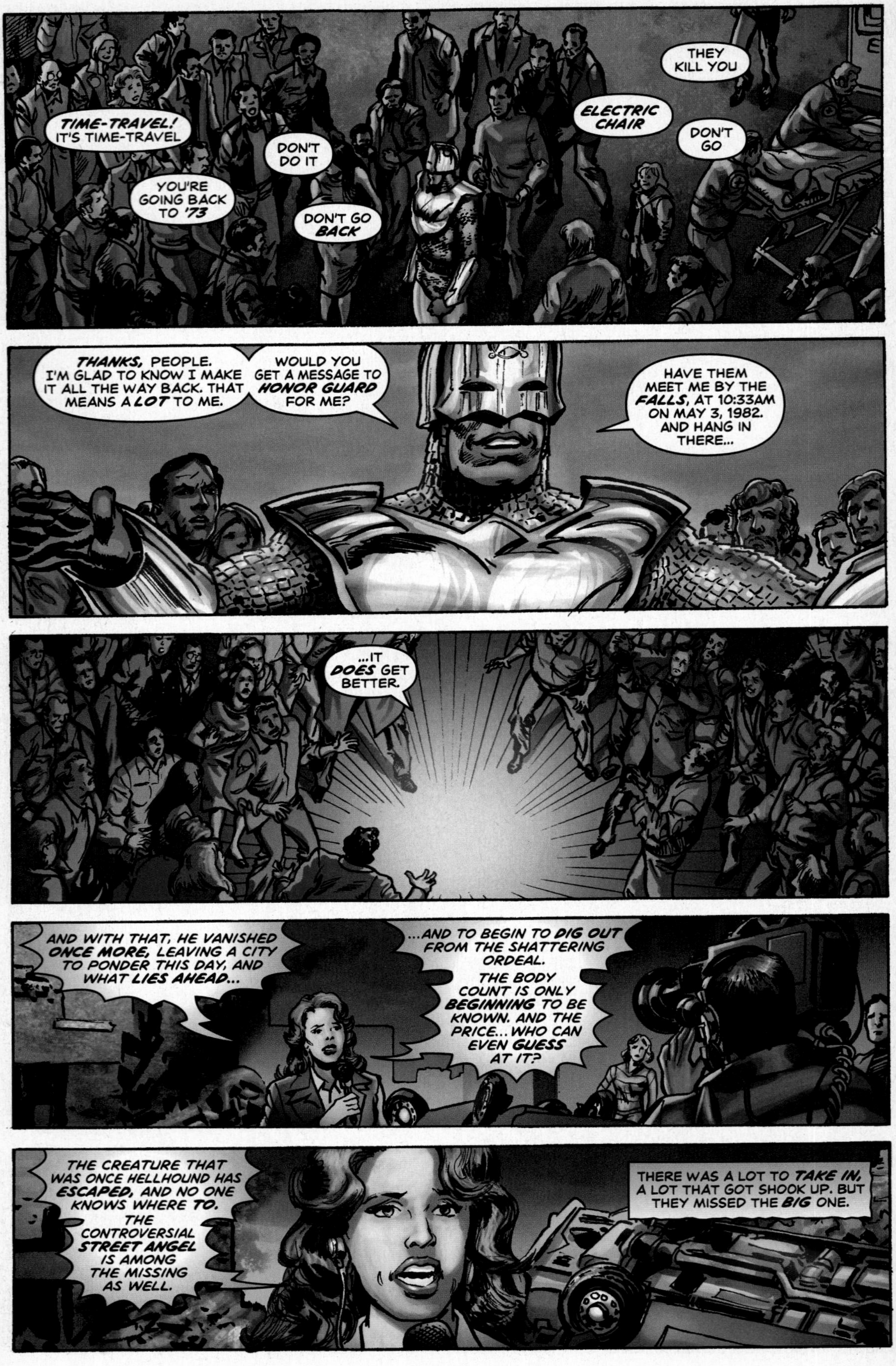
TIME-TRAVEL! IT'S TIME-TRAVEL
YOU'RE GOING BACK TO '73
DON'T DO IT
DON'T GO BACK
ELECTRIC CHAIR
THEY KILL YOU
DON'T GO
THANKS, PEOPLE. I'M GLAD TO KNOW I MAKE IT ALL THE WAY BACK. THAT MEANS A LOT TO ME.
WOULD YOU GET A MESSAGE TO HONOR GUARD FOR ME?
HAVE THEM MEET ME BY THE FALLS, AT 10:33AM ON MAY 3, 1982. AND HANG IN THERE...
...IT DOES GET BETTER.
AND WITH THAT, HE VANISHED ONCE MORE, LEAVING A CITY TO PONDER THIS DAY, AND WHAT LIES AHEAD...
...AND TO BEGIN TO DIG OUT FROM THE SHATTERING ORDEAL.
THE BODY COUNT IS ONLY BEGINNING TO BE KNOWN. AND THE PRICE... WHO CAN EVEN GUESS AT IT?
THE CREATURE THAT WAS ONCE HELLHOUND HAS ESCAPED, AND NO ONE KNOWS WHERE TO.
THE CONTROVERSIAL STREET ANGEL IS AMONG THE MISSING AS WELL.
THERE WAS A LOT TO TAKE IN, A LOT THAT GOT SHOOK UP. BUT THEY MISSED THE BIG ONE.

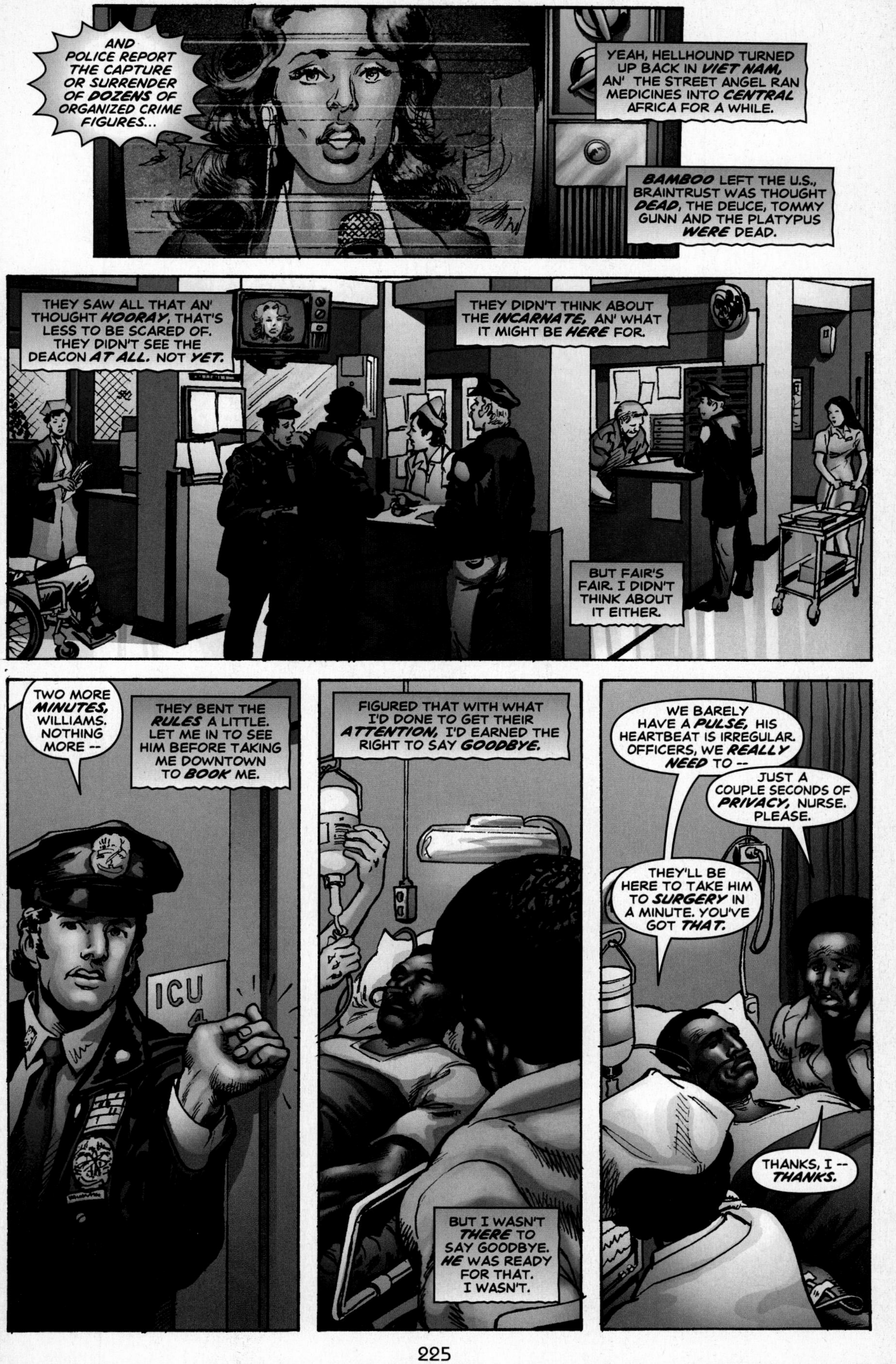

AND POLICE REPORT THE CAPTURE OR SURRENDER OF DOZENS OF ORGANIZED CRIME FIGURES...
YEAH, HELLHOUND TURNED UP BACK IN VIET NAM, AN' THE STREET ANGEL RAN MEDICINES INTO CENTRAL AFRICA FOR A WHILE.
BAMBOO LEFT THE U.S., BRAINTRUST WAS THOUGHT DEAD, THE DEUCE, TOMMY GUNN AND THE PLATYPUS WERE DEAD.
THEY SAW ALL THAT AN' THOUGHT HOORAY, THAT'S LESS TO BE SCARED OF. THEY DIDN'T SEE THE DEACON AT ALL. NOT YET.
THEY DIDN'T THINK ABOUT THE INCARNATE, AN' WHAT IT MIGHT BE HERE FOR.
BUT FAIR'S FAIR. I DIDN'T THINK ABOUT IT EITHER.
TWO MORE MINUTES, WILLIAMS. NOTHING MORE --
THEY BENT THE RULES A LITTLE. LET ME IN TO SEE HIM BEFORE TAKING ME DOWNTOWN TO BOOK ME.
ICU 4
FIGURED THAT WITH WHAT I'D DONE TO GET THEIR ATTENTION, I'D EARNED THE RIGHT TO SAY GOODBYE.
BUT I WASN'T THERE TO SAY GOODBYE. HE WAS READY FOR THAT. I WASN'T.
WE BARELY HAVE A PULSE, HIS HEARTBEAT IS IRREGULAR. OFFICERS, WE REALLY NEED TO --
JUST A COUPLE SECONDS OF PRIVACY, NURSE. PLEASE.
THEY'LL BE HERE TO TAKE HIM TO SURGERY IN A MINUTE. YOU'VE GOT THAT.
THANKS, I -- THANKS.

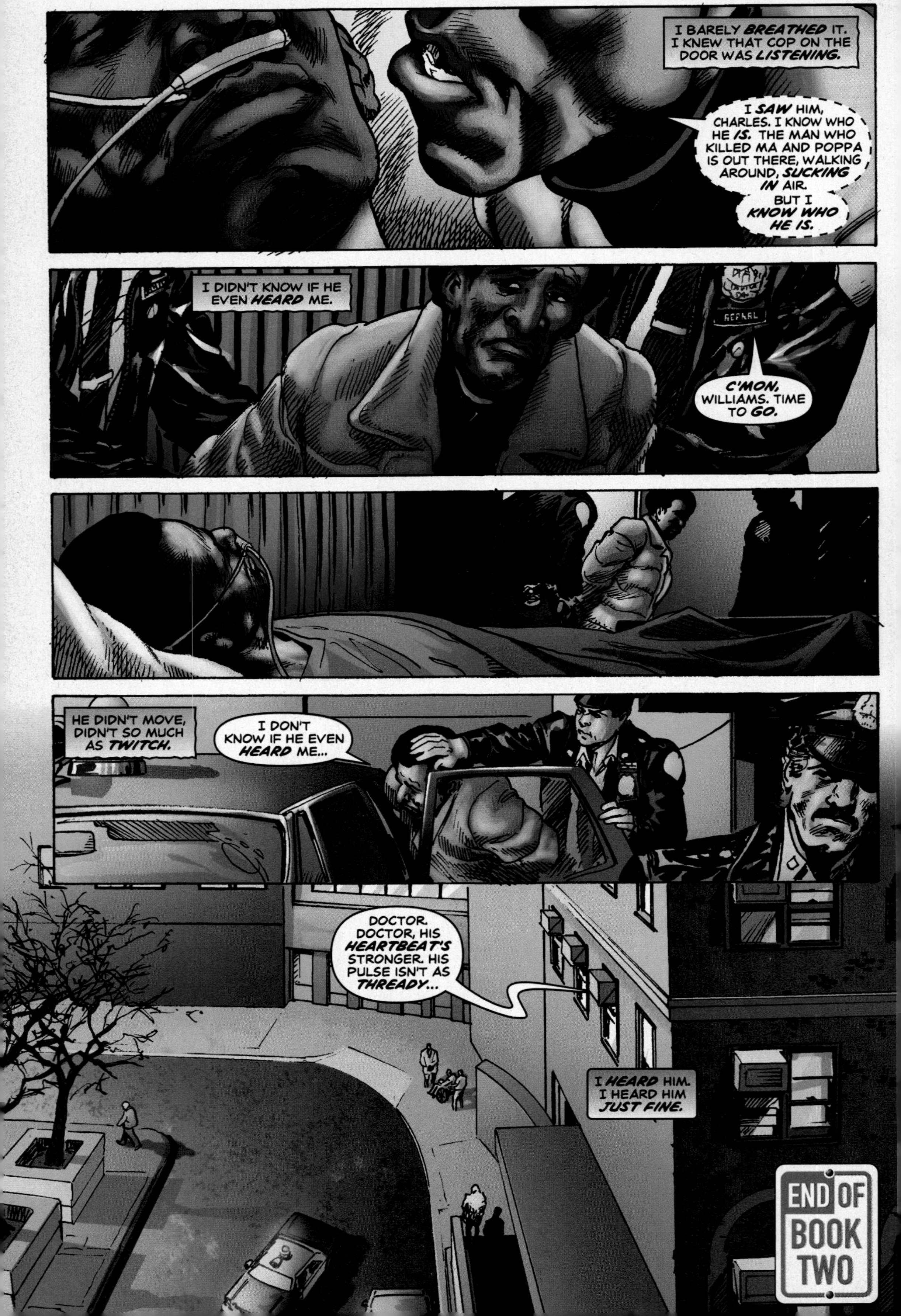
I BARELY BREATHED IT. I KNEW THAT COP ON THE DOOR WAS LISTENING.
I SAW HIM, CHARLES. I KNOW WHO HE IS. THE MAN WHO KILLED MA AND POPPA IS OUT THERE, WALKING AROUND, SUCKING IN AIR.
BUT I KNOW WHO HE IS.
I DIDN'T KNOW IF HE EVEN HEARD ME.
C'MON, WILLIAMS. TIME TO GO.
HE DIDN'T MOVE, DIDN'T SO MUCH AS TWITCH.
I DON'T KNOW IF HE EVEN HEARD ME...
DOCTOR. DOCTOR, HIS HEARTBEAT'S STRONGER. HIS PULSE ISN'T AS THREADY...
I HEARD HIM. I HEARD HIM JUST FINE.
END OF BOOK TWO

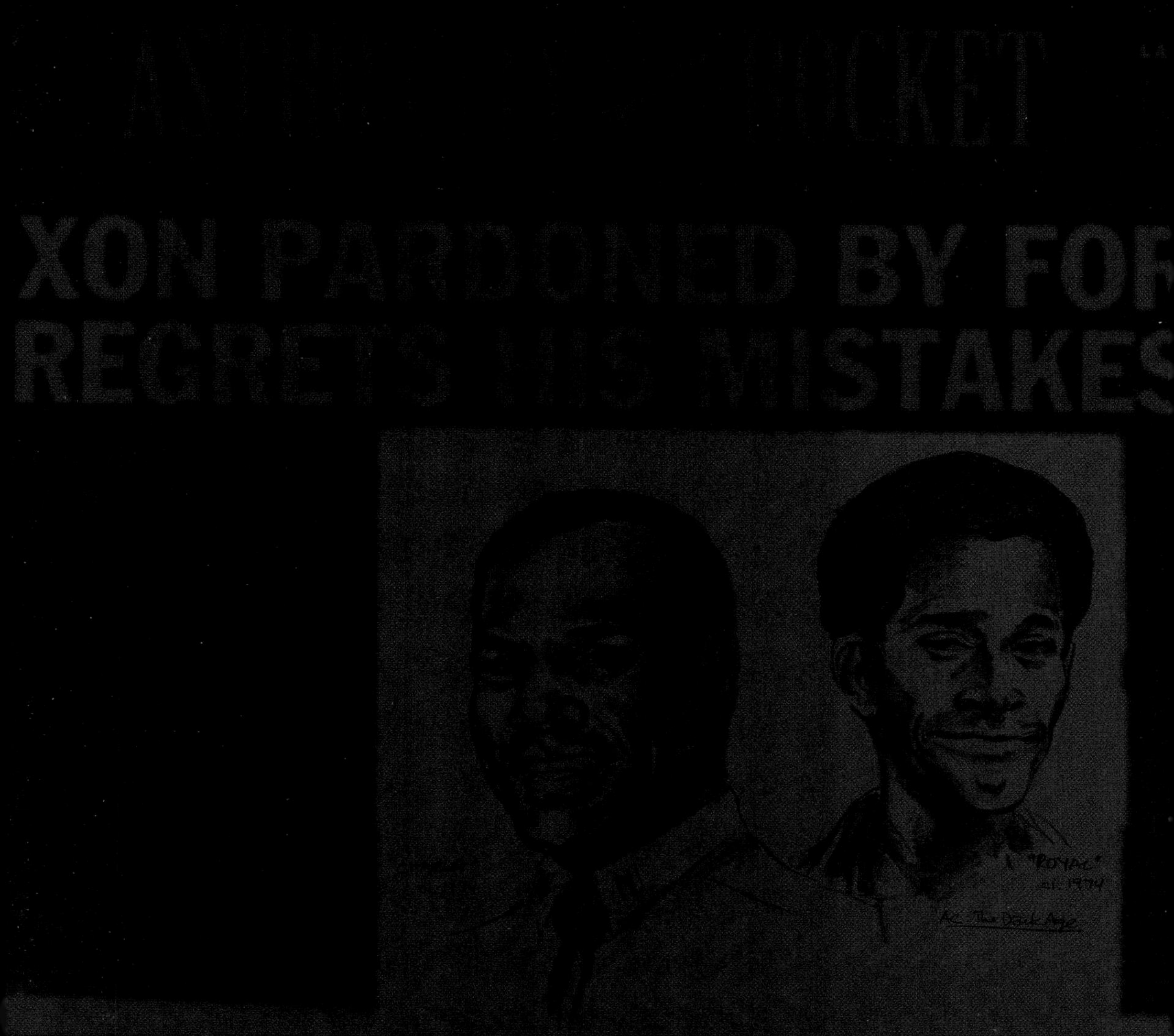
XON PARDONED BY FOR
REGRETS HIS MISTAKES

SKETCHBOOK DARK DESIGNS

A vast, decades-spanning saga with dozen of superheroes in it? Always an enjoyable challenge, particularly when all of the heroes will be period pieces, and need to feel like they belong to their particular era. The Black Badge, for instance. He'd been mentioned before, and seen as an old man -- but to tell a story set in Bakerville in the late 1950s, we needed to see him in his prime, at a time the only outright black superhero in American comic books may have been Lion Man, from All-Negro Comics #1 (and only). He had to have the simplicity of Fifties hero design, feel pre-Silver Age (so he should feel as much like a detective hero as a superhero), look like a character who could have turned up in at least a tryout backup tale or two, and still be cool.

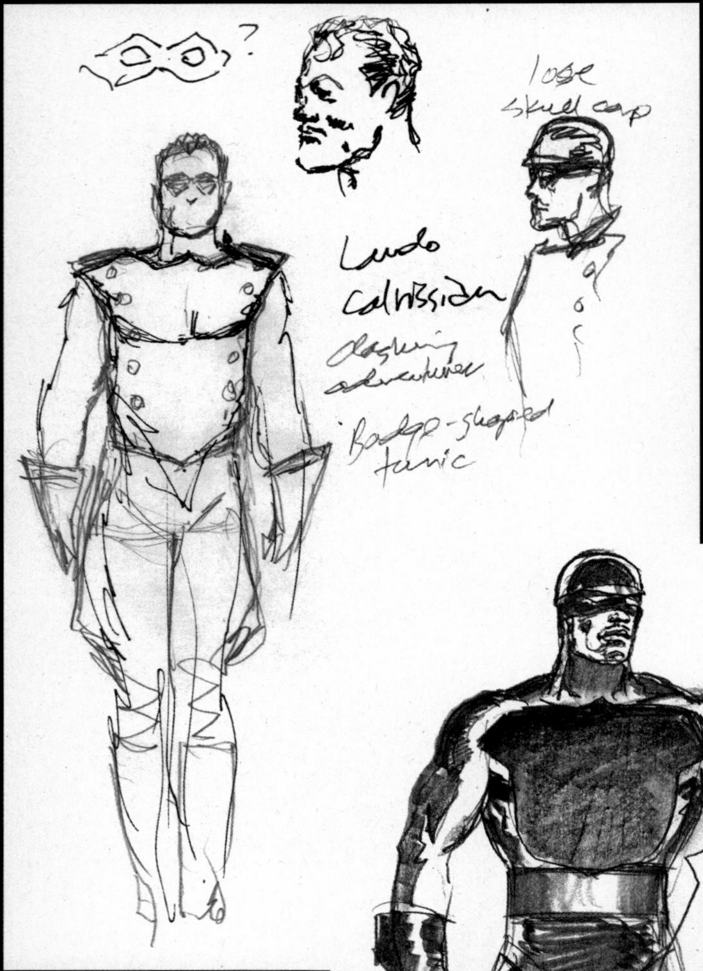

?
lose skull cap
Lando Calrissian
dashing adventurer
Badge-shaped tunic

Previous page: Initial designs for our leads, Charles and Royal Williams.

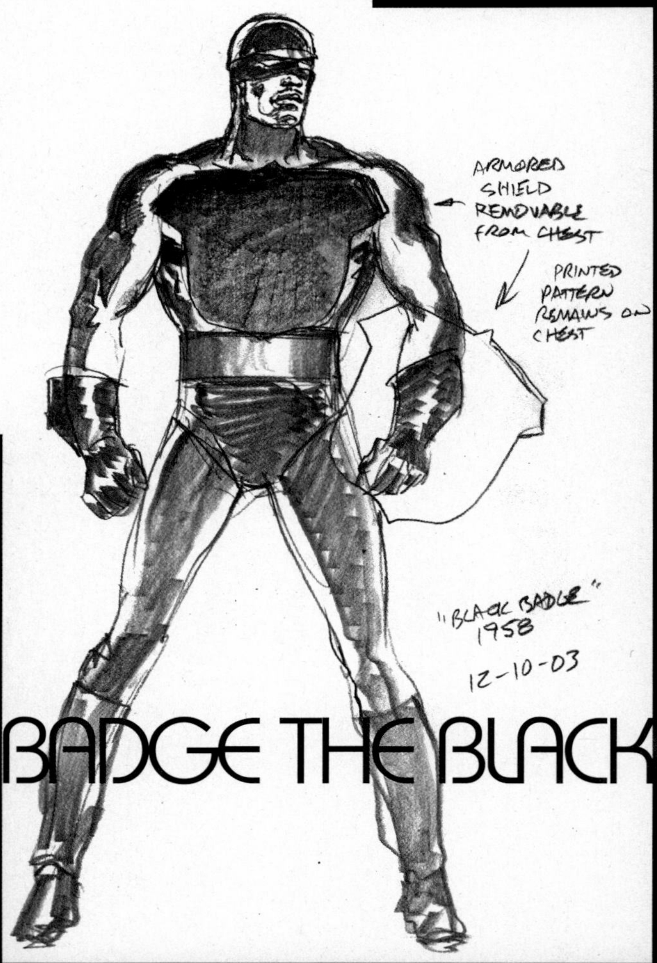

ARMORED SHIELD REMOVABLE FROM CHEST
PRINTED PATTERN REMAINS ON CHEST
"BLACK BADGE" 1958
12-10-03

THE BLACK BADGE THE BLACK BAD

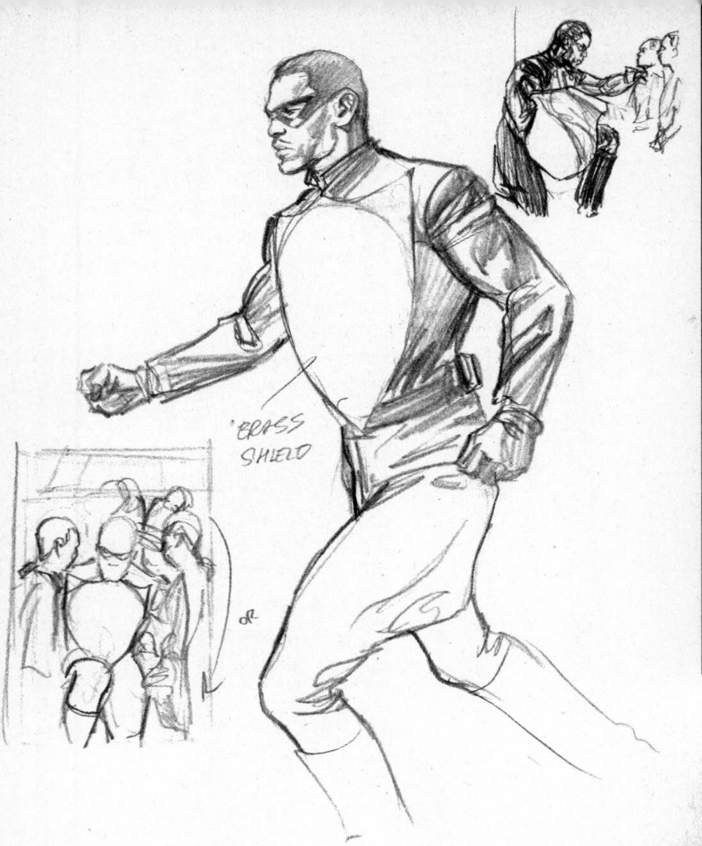

'BRASS SHIELD
OR

It took a few tries, but Brent and Alex nailed it, I think.

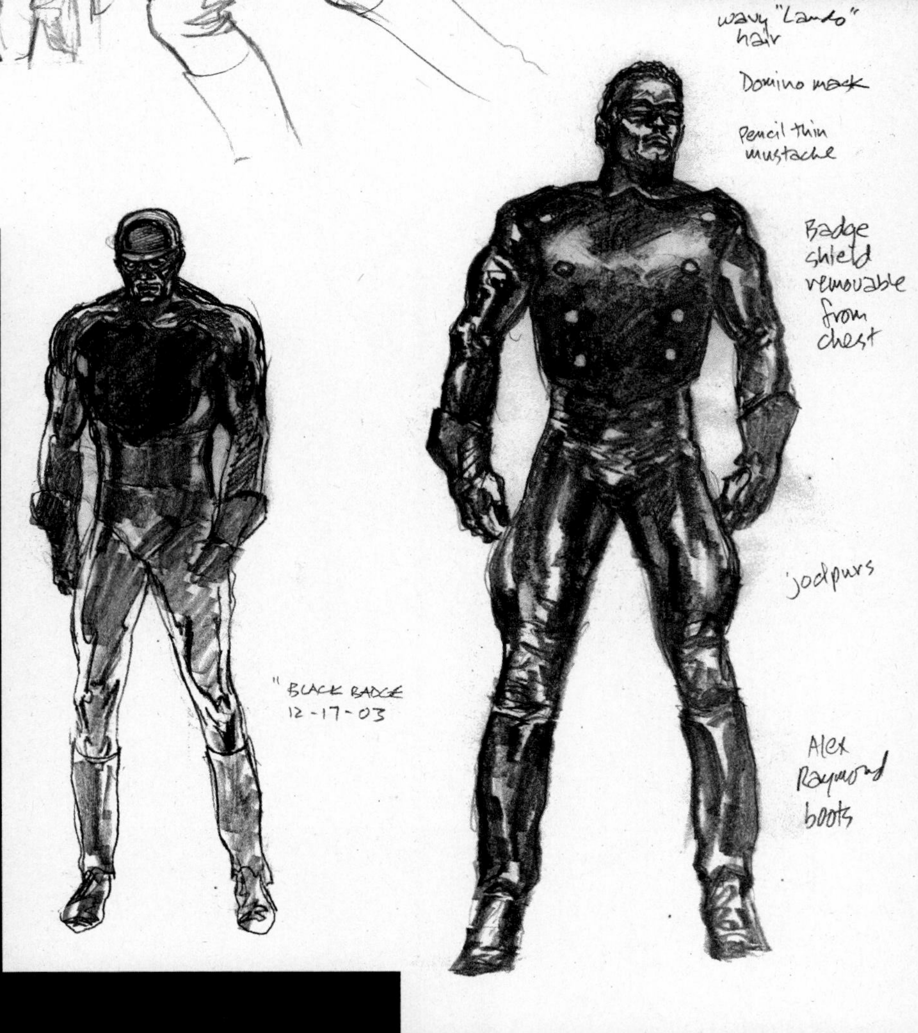

wavy "Lando" hair
Domino mask
Pencil thin mustache
Badge shield removable from chest
'jodpurs
"BLACK BADGE 12-17-03
Alex Raymond boots

THE

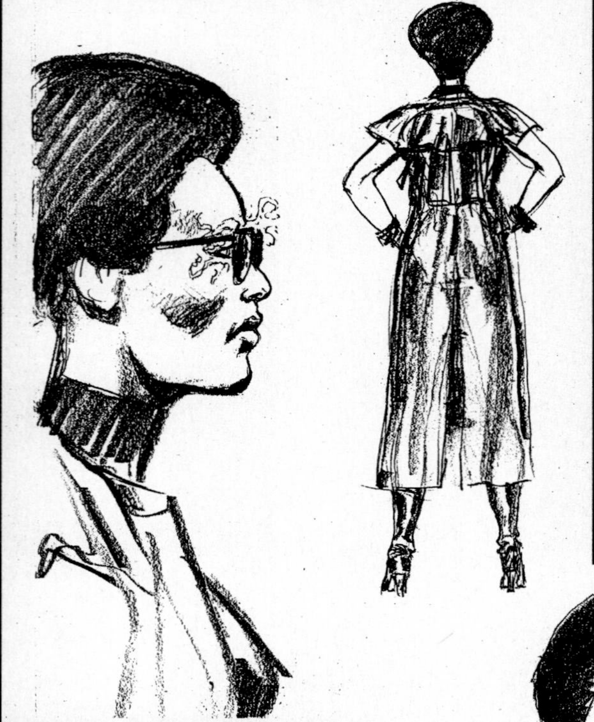

And then it's the 1970s, and we need Seventies heroes, from a troubled biker Vietnam vet-turned-monster (see our cover gallery for sketches of Hellhound), to a no-nonsense street hero (more in the mode of Cleopatra Jones and Coffy than John Shaft, for a change), and kung-fu heroes.

"Energy" Brown became our bad-neighborhood street hero -- or at least one of them.

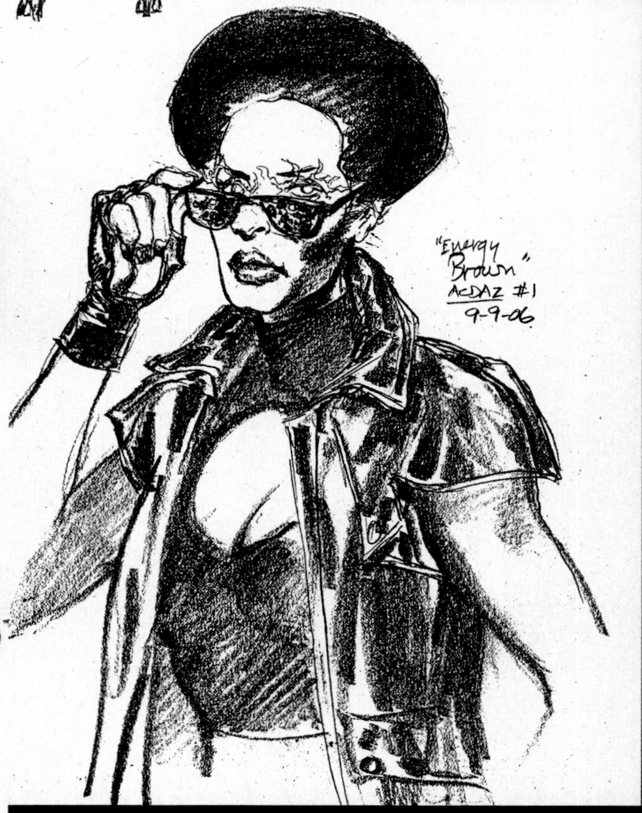
"Energy Brown"
ACDAZ #1
9-9-06

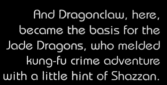

And Dragonclaw, here, became the basis for the Jade Dragons, who melded kung-fu crime adventure with a little hint of Shazzan.

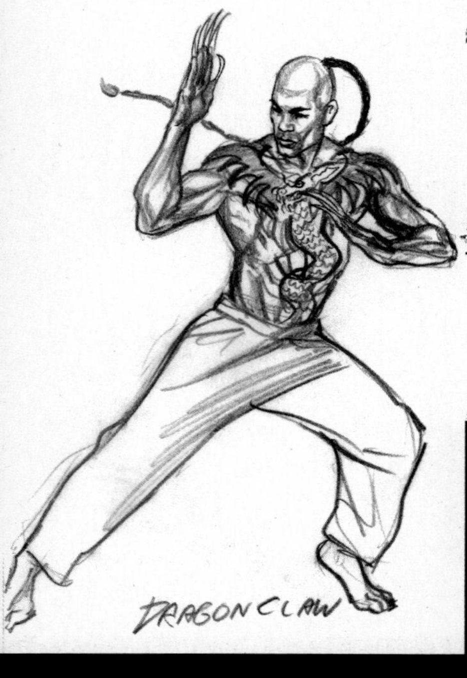
DRAGONCLAW

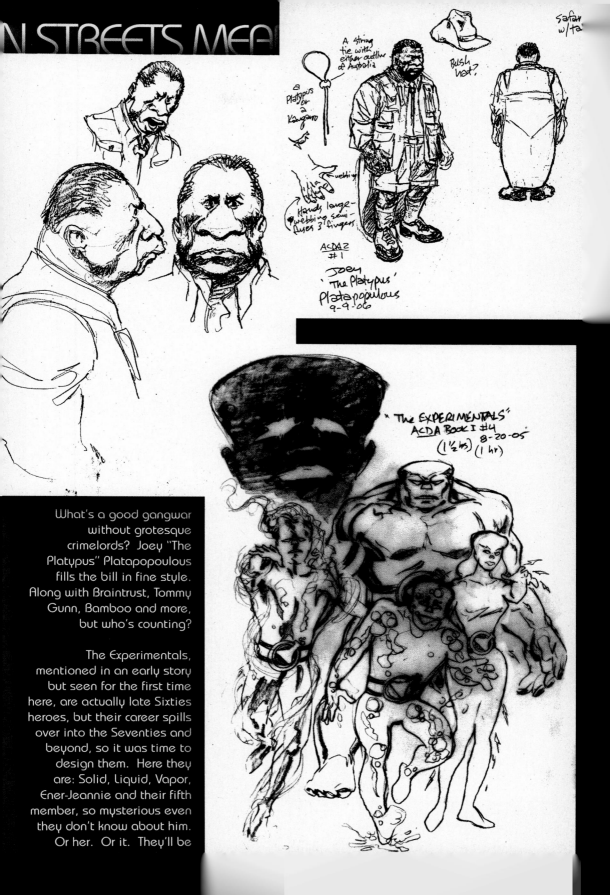

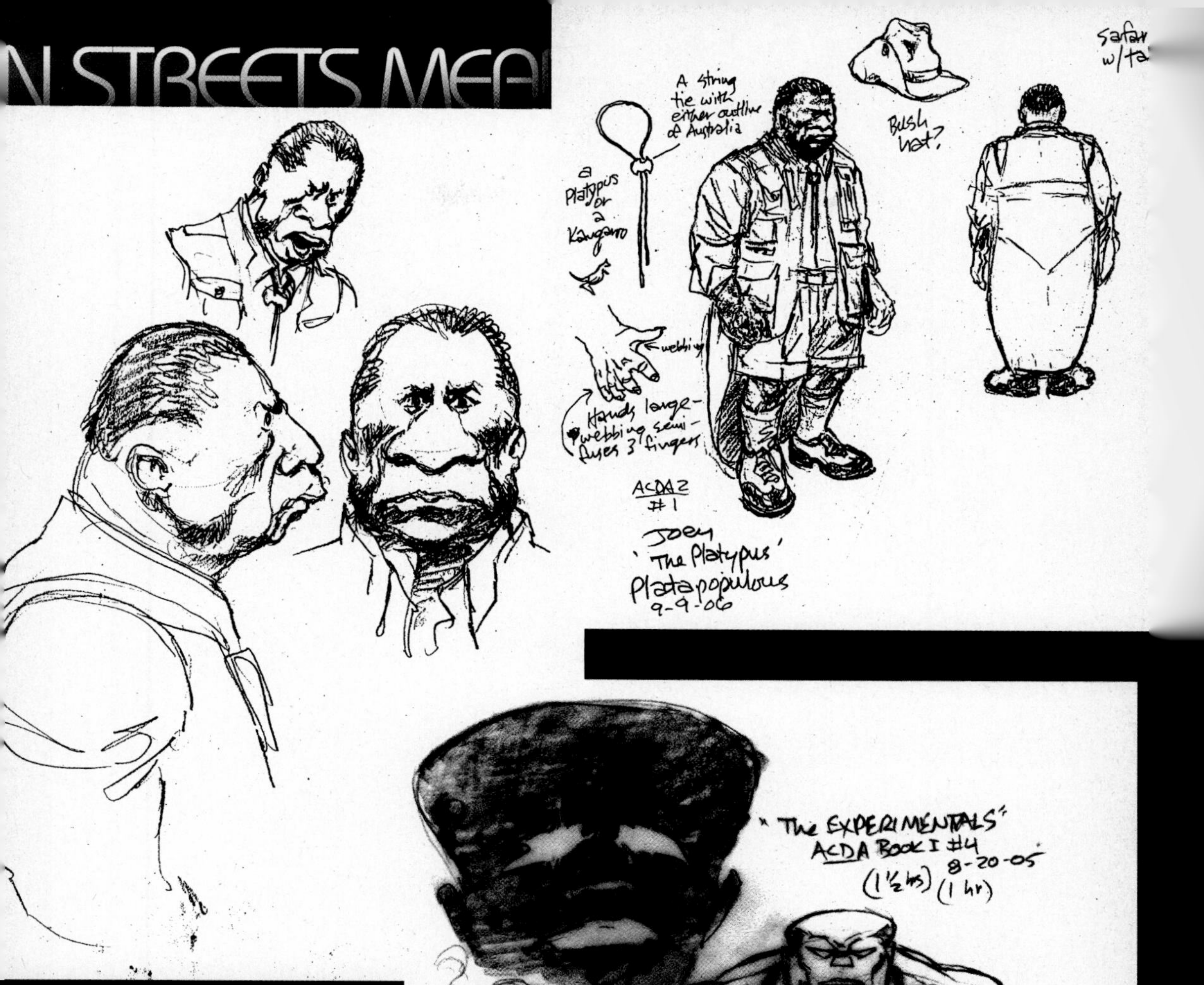
safari w/ta
A string tie with either outline of Australia
a Platypus or a Kangaroo
Bush hat?
webbing
Hands large-webbing semi-fuses 3 fingers
ACDA2 #1
Joey 'The Platypus' Platapopulous 9-9-06

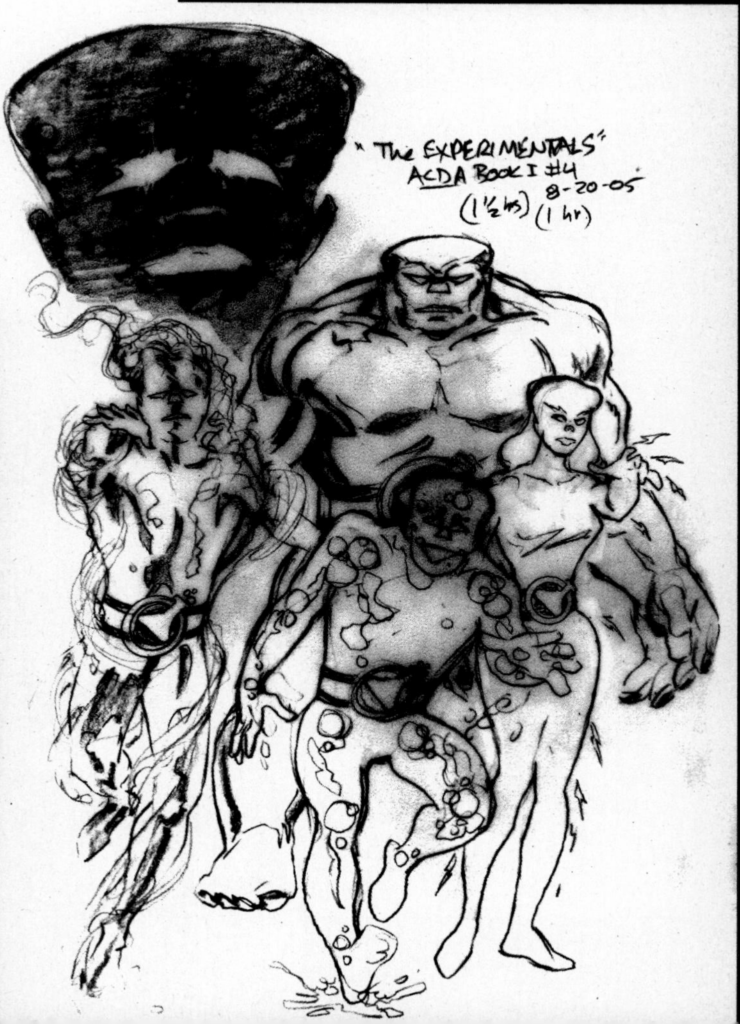
"The EXPERIMENTALS"
ACDA Book I #4
8-20-05
(1½ hrs) (1 hr)

What's a good gangwar without grotesque crimelords? Joey "The Platypus" Platapopoulous fills the bill in fine style. Along with Braintrust, Tommy Gunn, Bamboo and more, but who's counting?

The Experimentals, mentioned in an early story but seen for the first time here, are actually late Sixties heroes, but their career spills over into the Seventies and beyond, so it was time to design them. Here they are: Solid, Liquid, Vapor, Ener-Jeannie and their fifth member, so mysterious even they don't know about him. Or her. Or it. They'll be

SIMON MAGUS

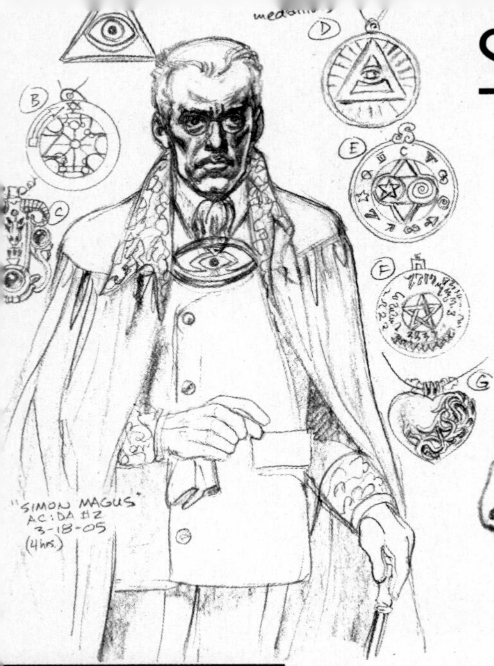

B
C
D
E
F
G
"SIMON MAGUS"
ACDA #2
3-18-05
(4hrs.)

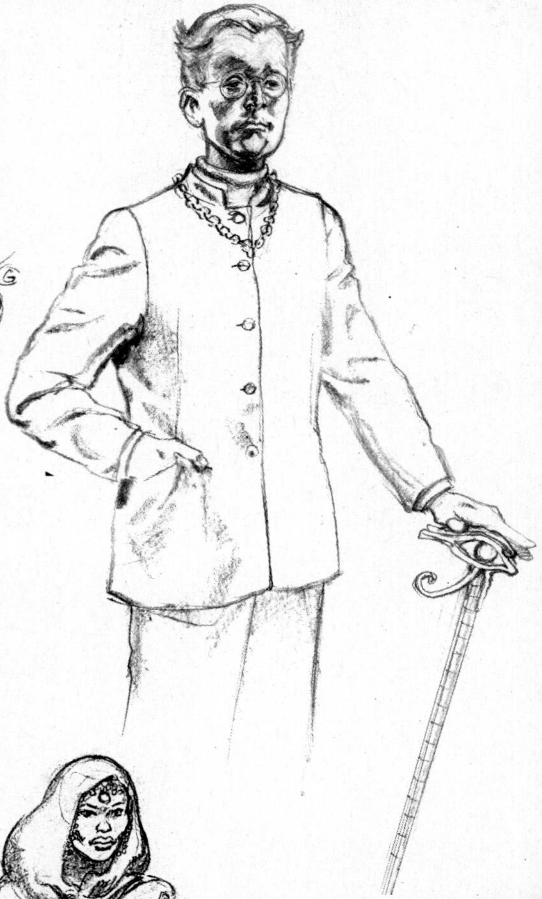

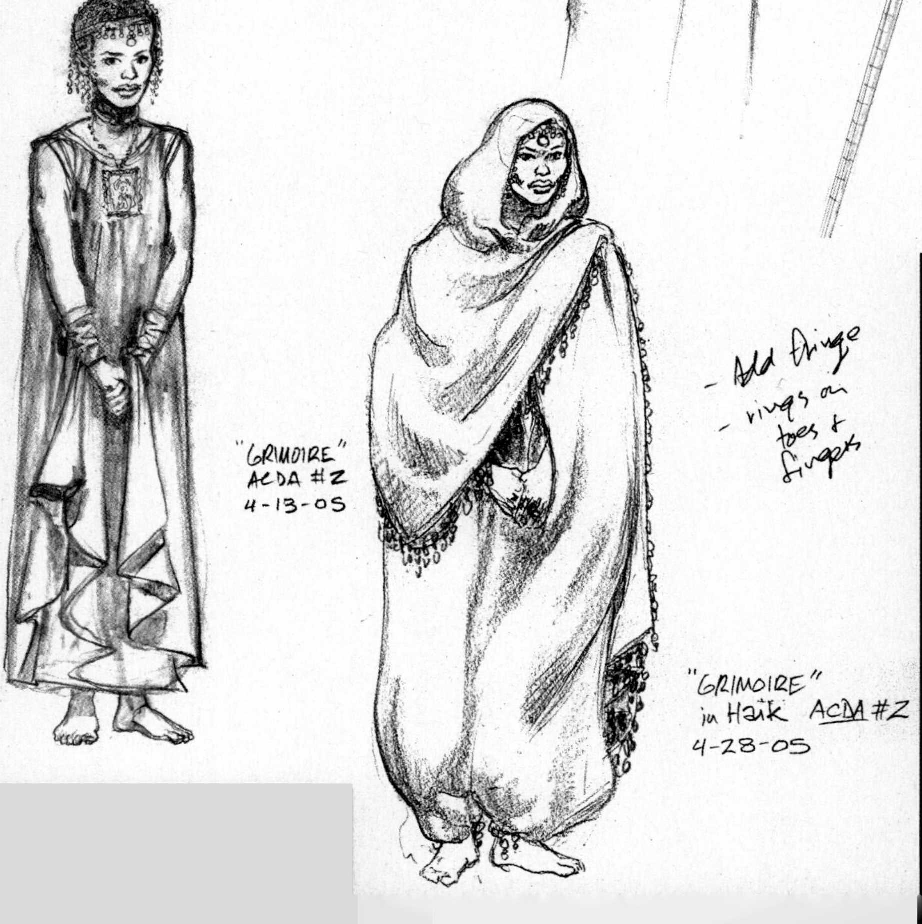

"GRIMOIRE"
ACDA #2
4-13-05
- Add fringe
- rings on toes & fingers
"GRIMOIRE"
in Haik ACDA #2
4-28-05

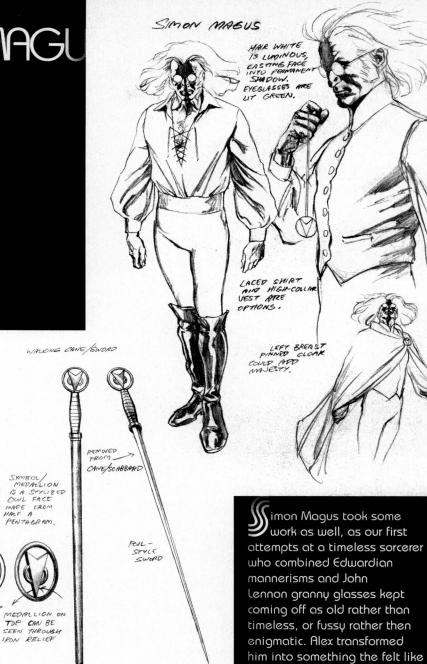

SIMON MAGUS

HAIR WHITE IS LUMINOUS, CASTING FACE INTO PERMANENT SHADOW. EYEGLASSES ARE LIT GREEN.

LACED SHIRT AND HIGH-COLLAR VEST ARE OPTIONS.

LEFT BREAST PINNED CLOAK COULD ADD MAJESTY.

WALKING CANE/SWORD

REMOVED FROM CANE/SCABBARD

FOIL-STYLE SWORD

SYMBOL/MEDALLION IS A STYLIZED OWL FACE MADE FROM HALF A PENTAGRAM.

← 3½" WIDE →

MEDALLION ON TOP CAN BE SEEN THROUGH IRON RELIEF

Simon Magus took some work as well, as our first attempts at a timeless sorcerer who combined Edwardian mannerisms and John Lennon granny glasses kept coming off as old rather than timeless, or fussy rather then enigmatic. Alex transformed him into something the felt like counterculture wisdom drawn from timeless traditions.

And Grimoire, Simon's "assistant" -- Brent realized her beautifully. A female character whose power is given lip service while the men have all the fun. Even the enlightened had some more enlightening to do. But the Eighties are coming like a freight train...

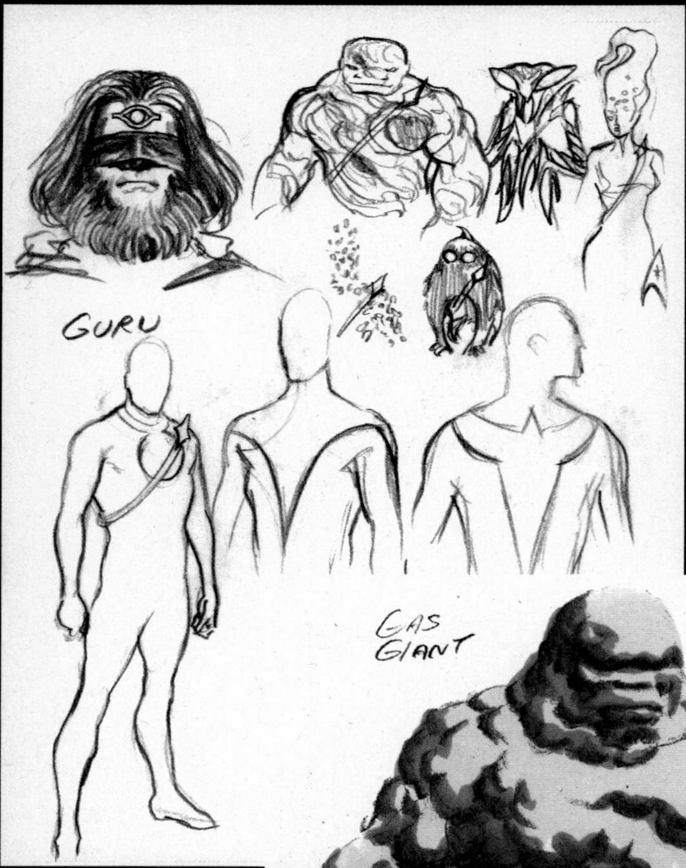
GURU

Alex's name, so he got to bear the brunt of designing eleven superheroes who looked like a 1970s team, looked appropriately alien, and could play the part of the cosmic peace-ambassadors-from-space who seem to spend all their time fighting. A wonderful collection of alien archetypes, assembled around one Earth-hero icon as leader.

OLLO ELEVEN THE APOLLO ELEVEN

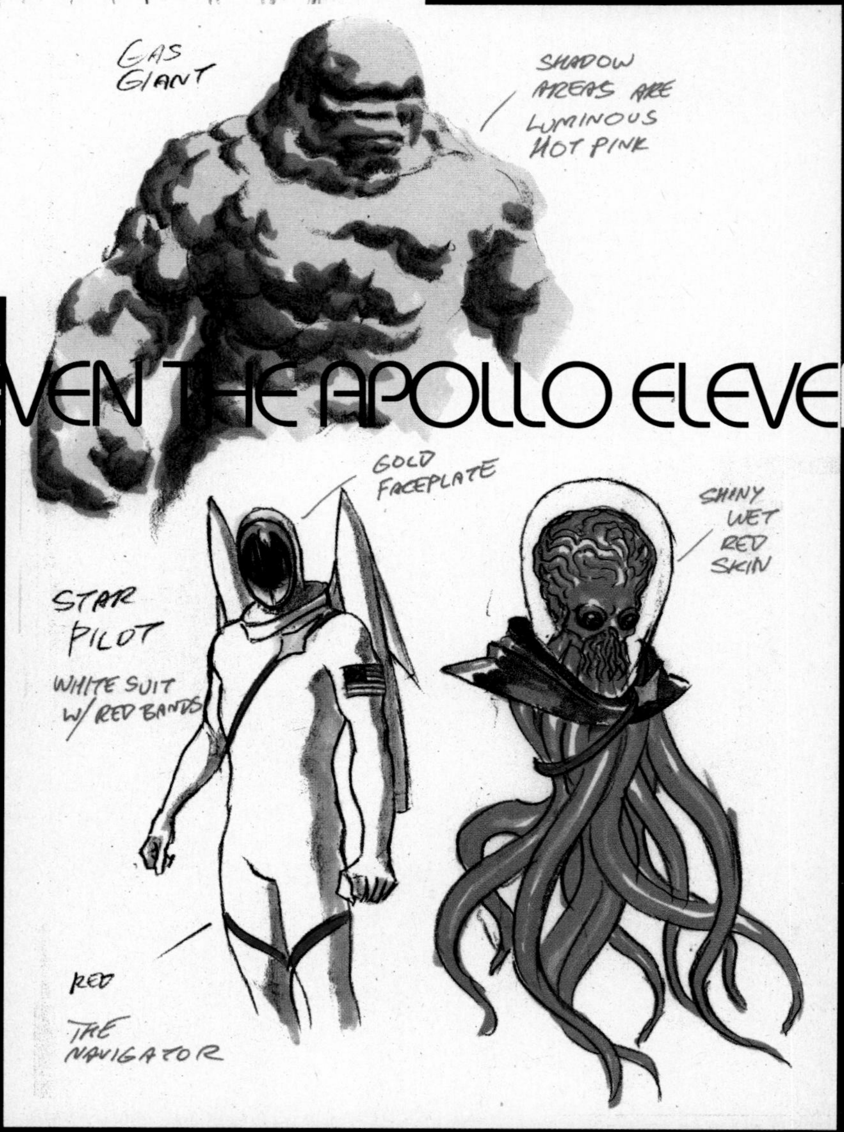
GAS GIANT
SHADOW AREAS ARE LUMINOUS HOT PINK
GOLD FACEPLATE
SHINY WET RED SKIN
STAR PILOT
WHITE SUIT W/ RED BANDS
RED
THE NAVIGATOR

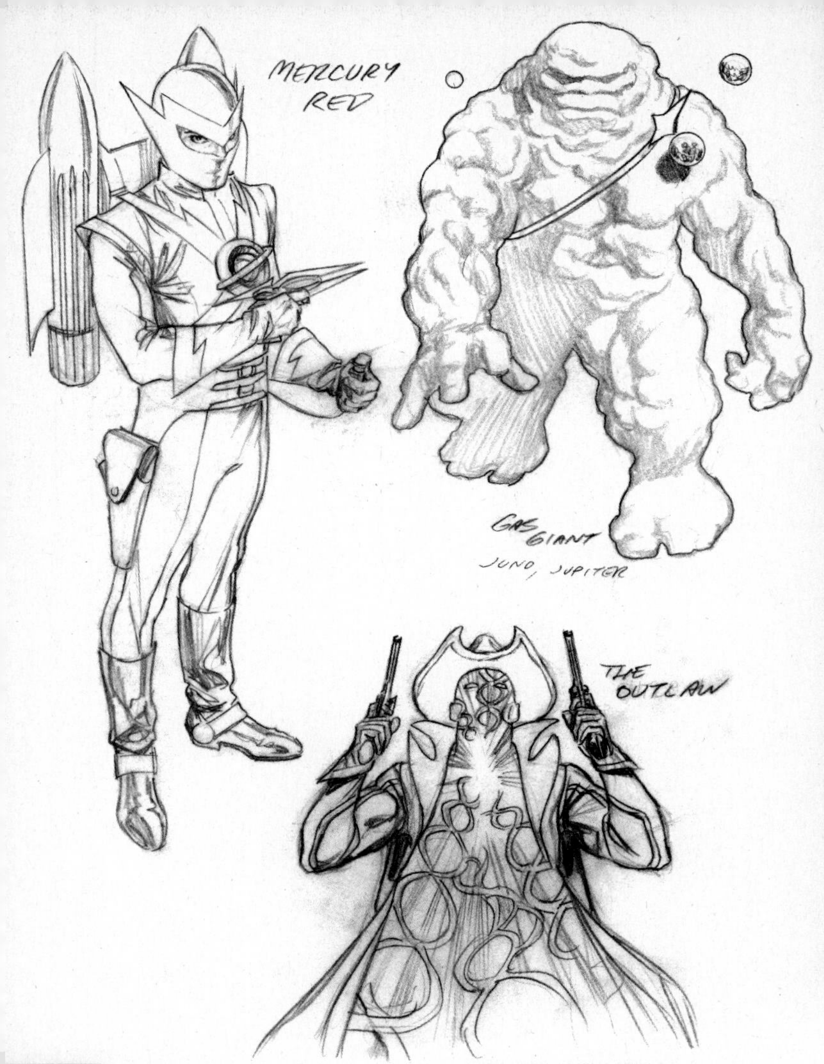
MERCURY
RED
GAS
GIANT
JUNO, JUPITER
THE
OUTLAW

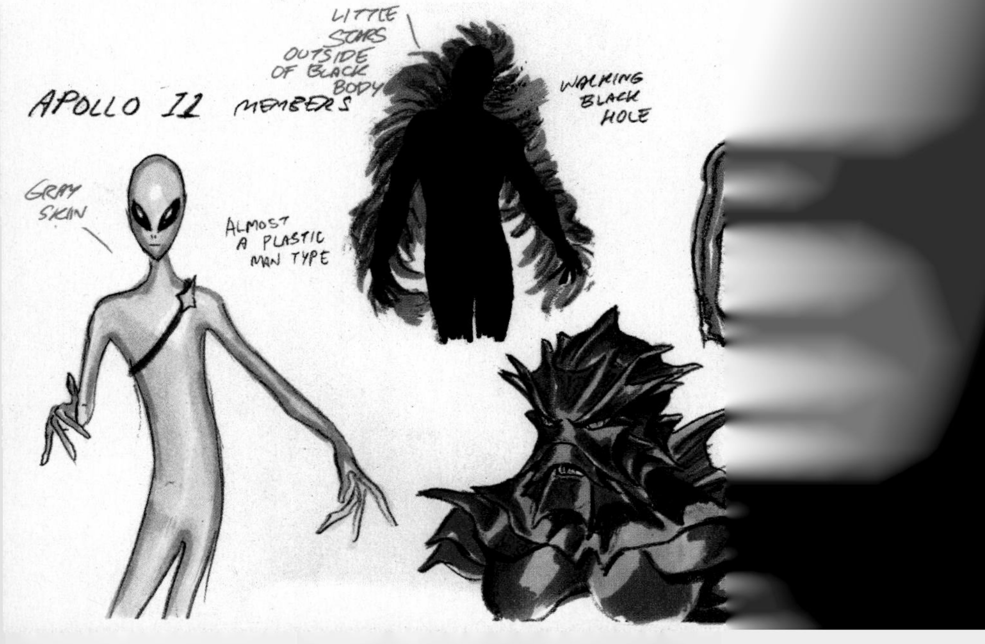
LITTLE
STARS
OUTSIDE
OF BLACK
BODY
APOLLO 11 MEMBERS
WALKING
BLACK
HOLE
GRAY
SKIN
ALMOST
A PLASTIC
MAN TYPE

THE APOLLO 11

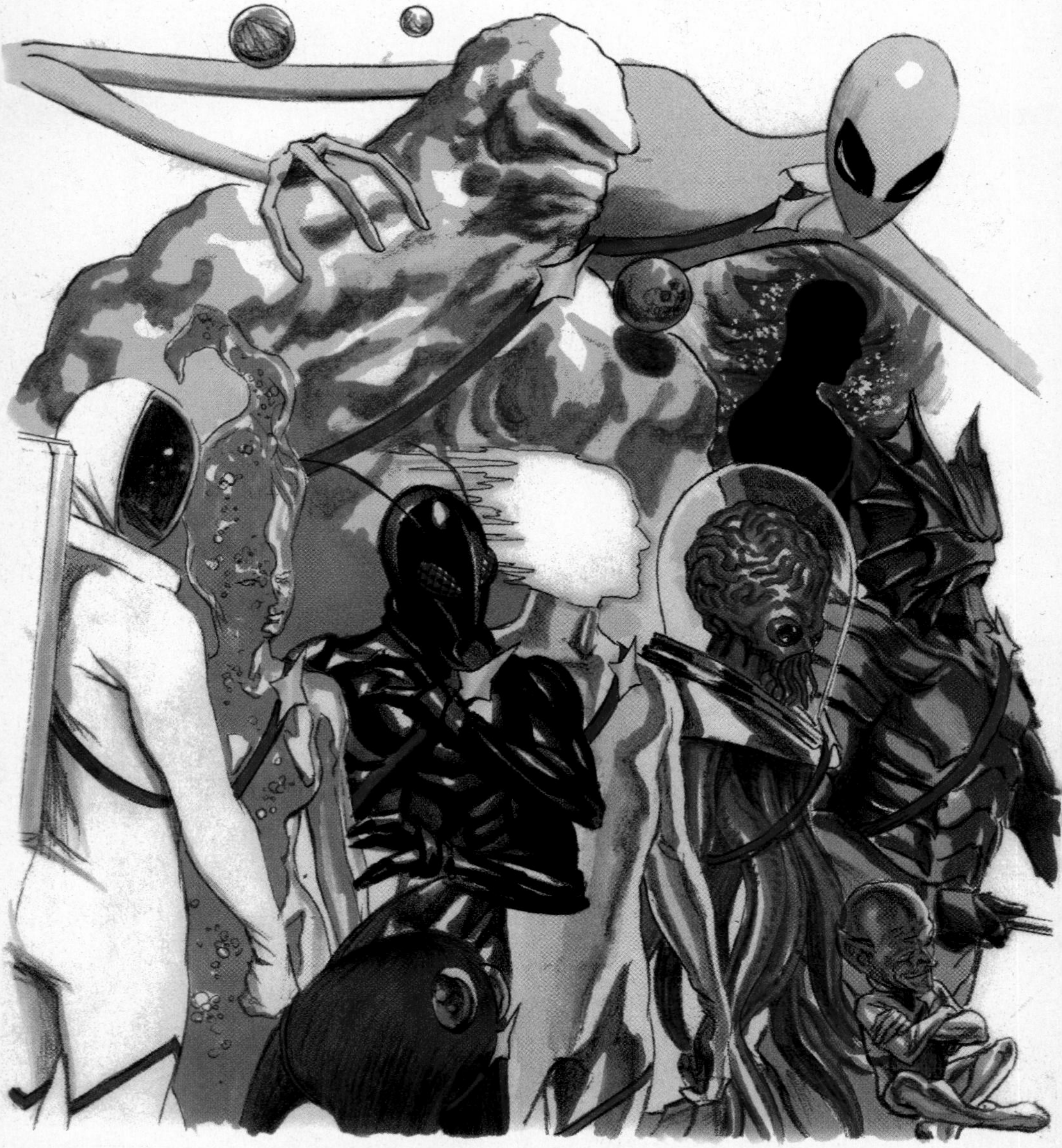

COVER GALLERY

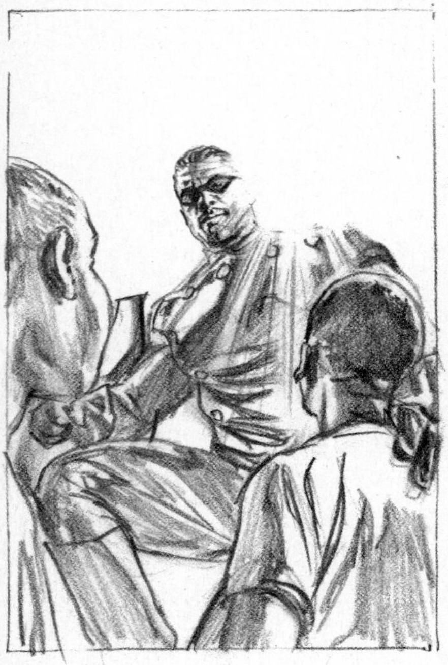

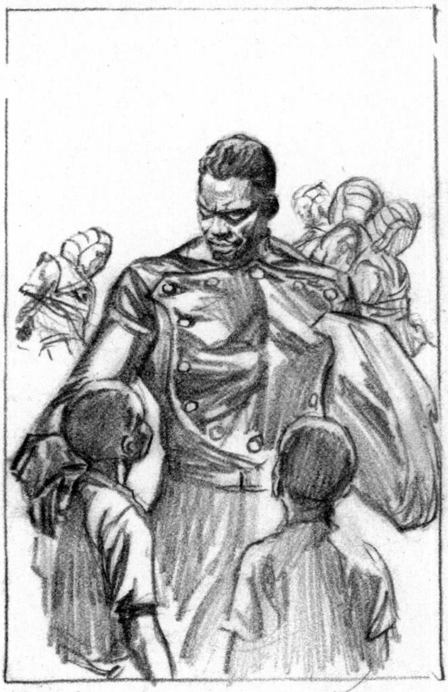

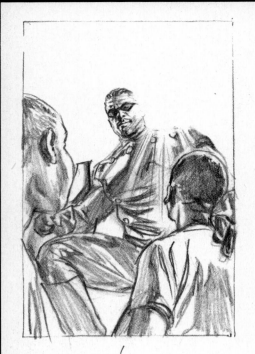

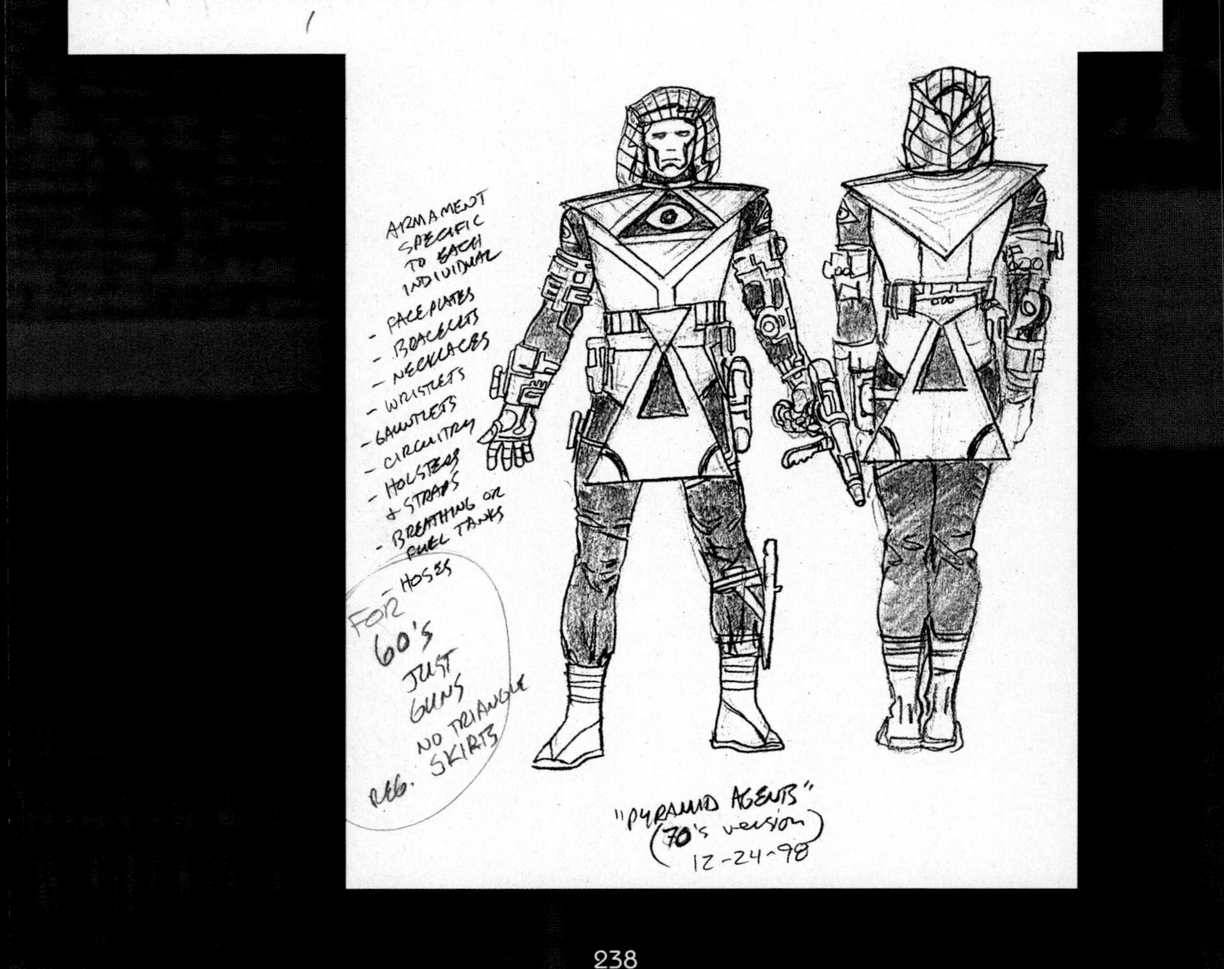
ARMAMENT SPECIFIC TO EACH INDIVIDUAL
- FACE PLATES
- BRACELETS
- NECKLACES
- WRISTLETS
- GAUNTLETS
- CIRCUITRY
- HOLSTERS + STRAPS
- BREATHING OR FUEL TANKS
- HOSES
FOR 60's JUST GUNS NO TRIANGLE REG. SKIRTS
"PYRAMID AGENTS" (70's version)
12-24-98

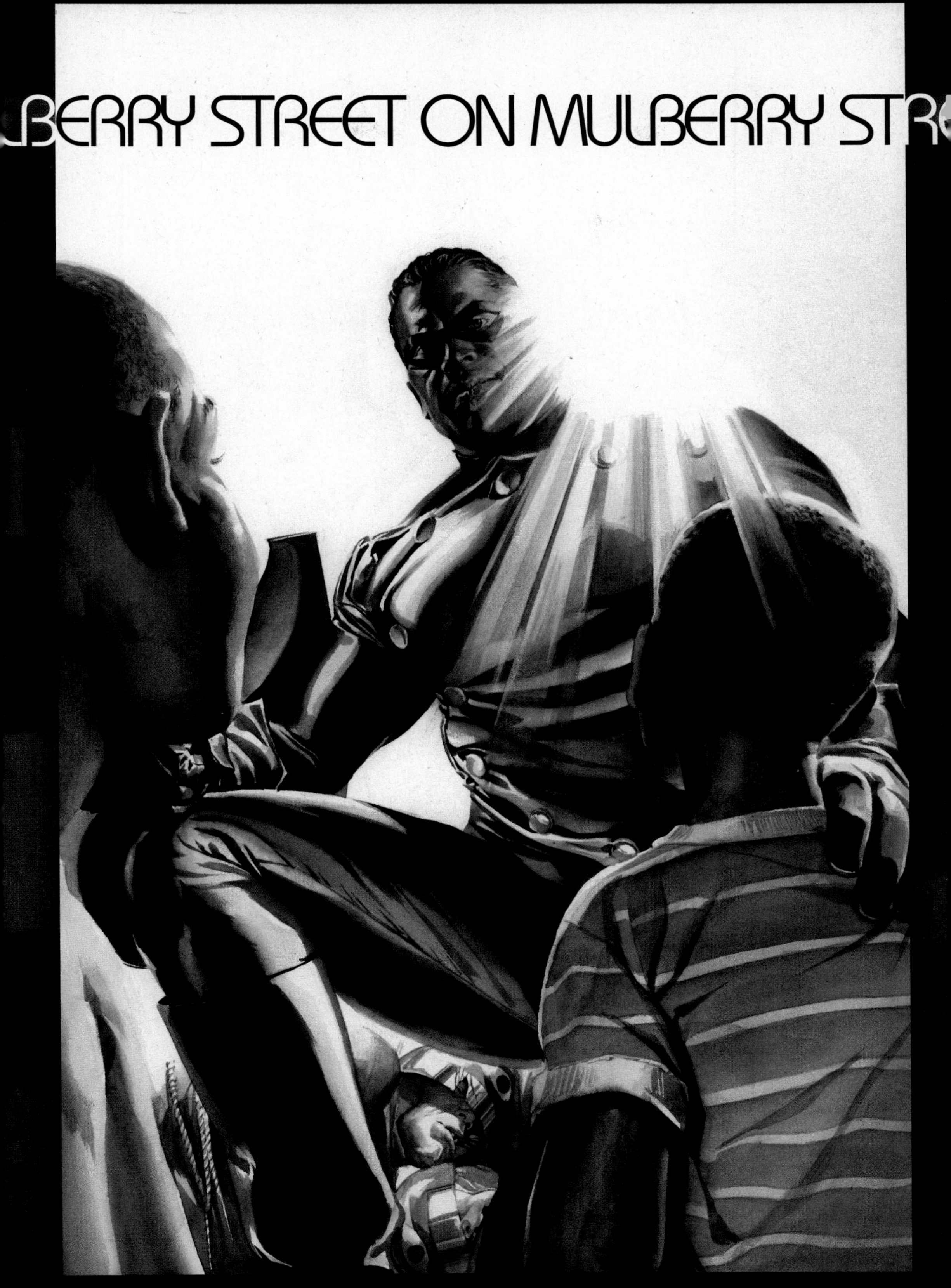
LBERRY STREET ON MULBERRY STR

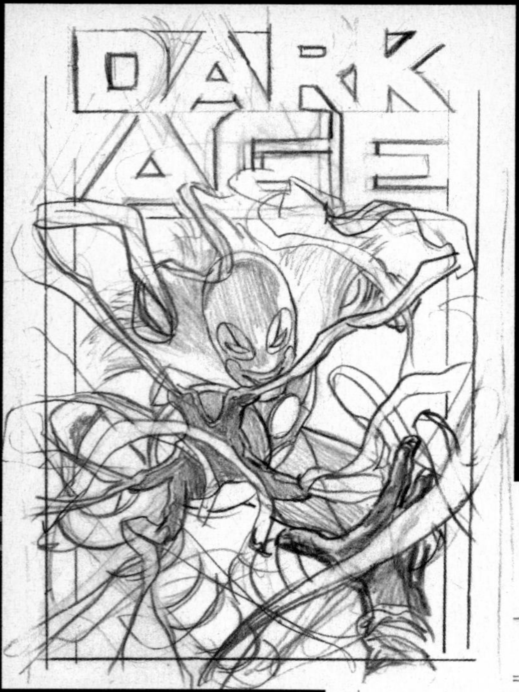
DARK
AGE

DARKNESS FALLS

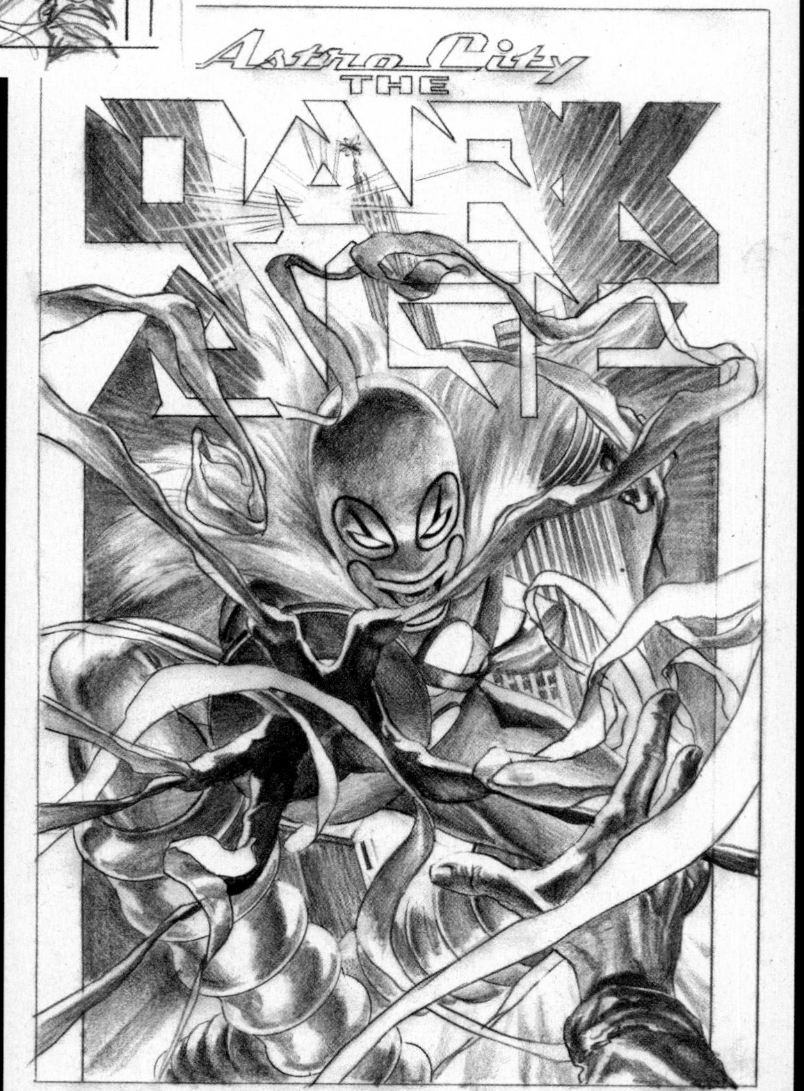
Astro City
THE

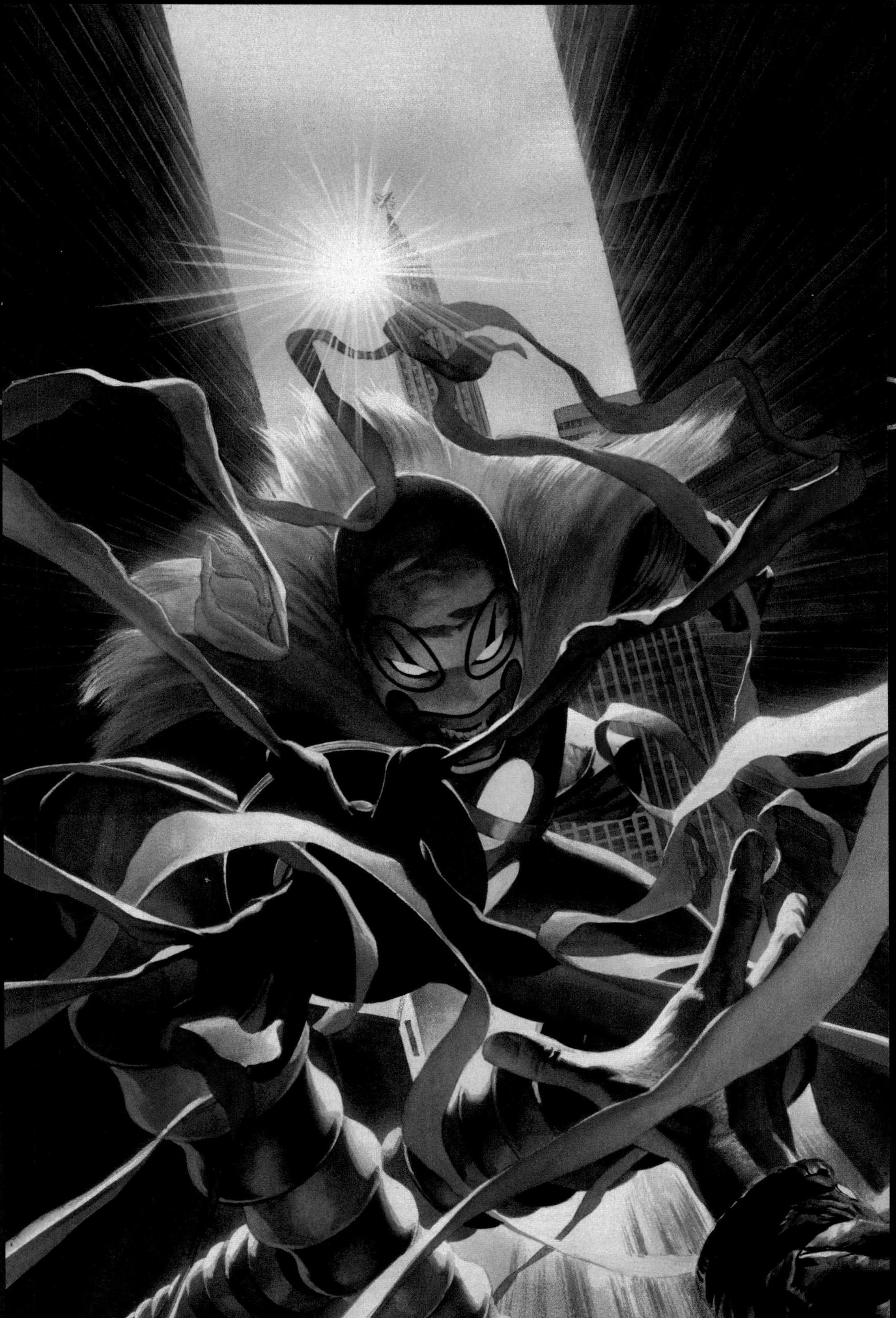

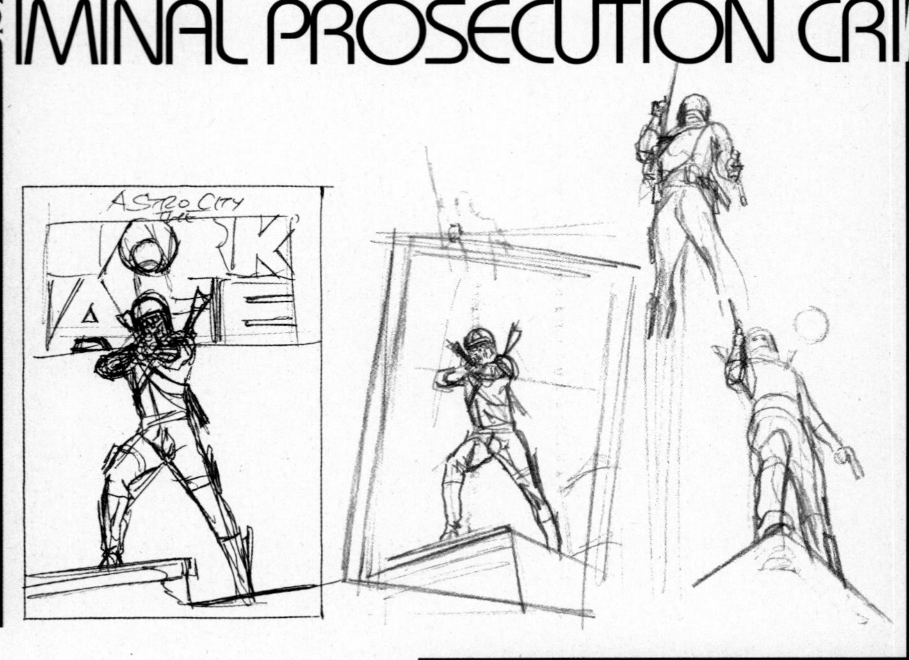
ASTRO CITY
THE

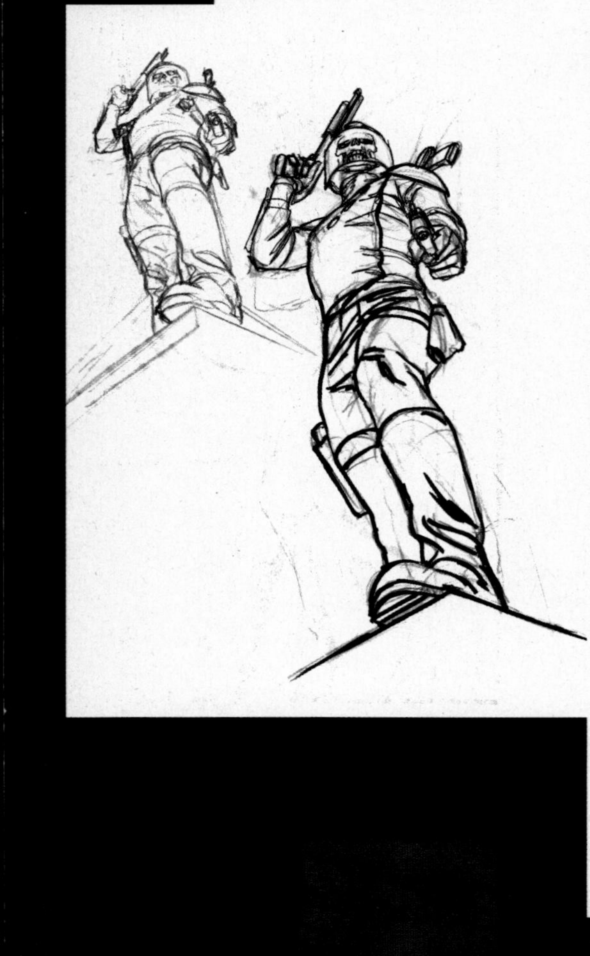

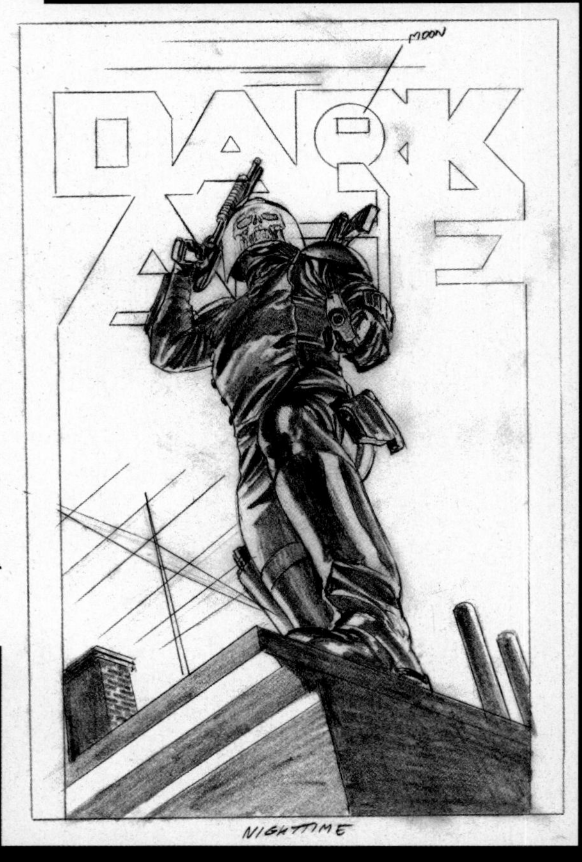
MOON
NIGHTTIME

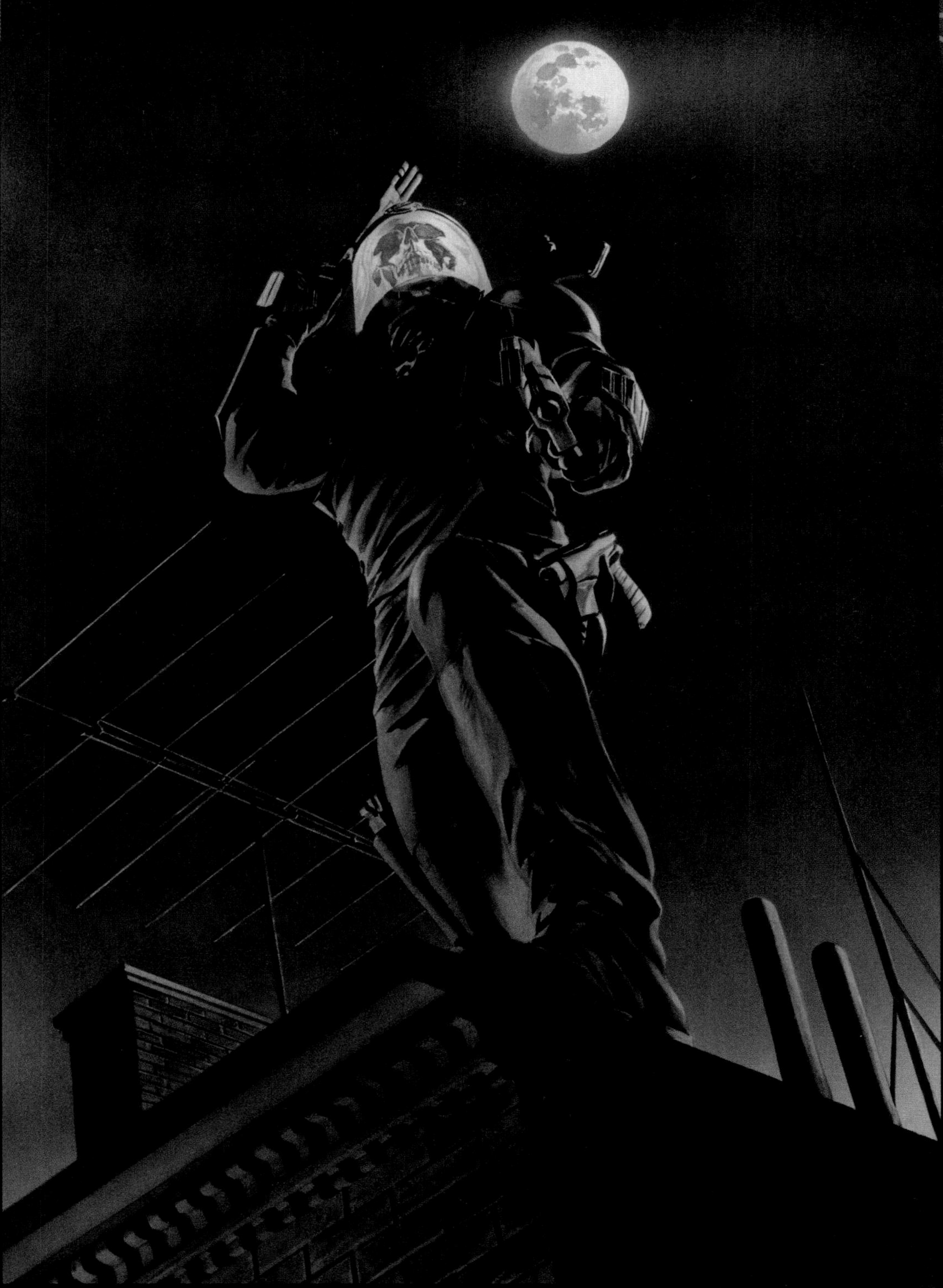

OF WAR CASUALTIES OF WAR CASUF

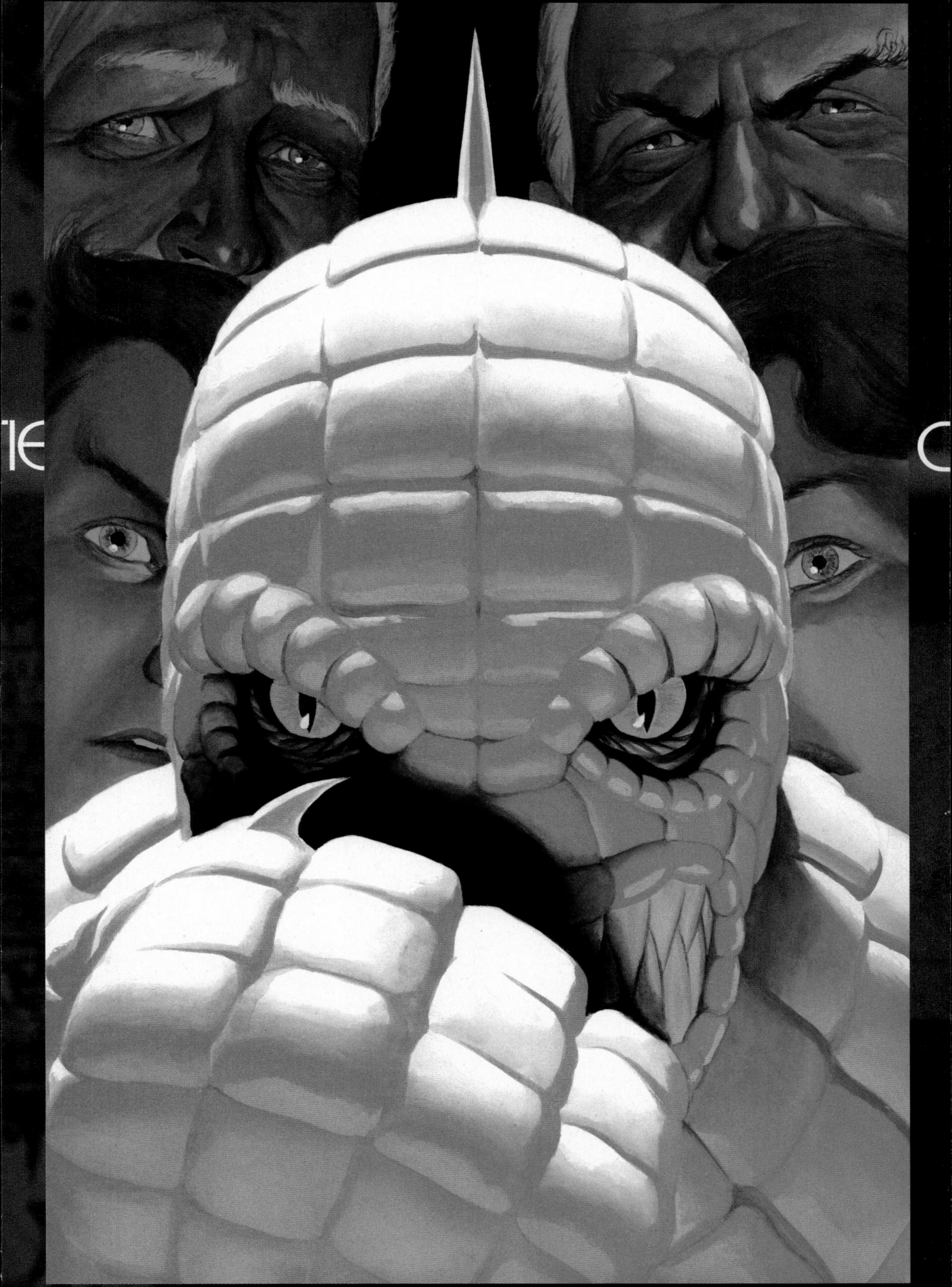

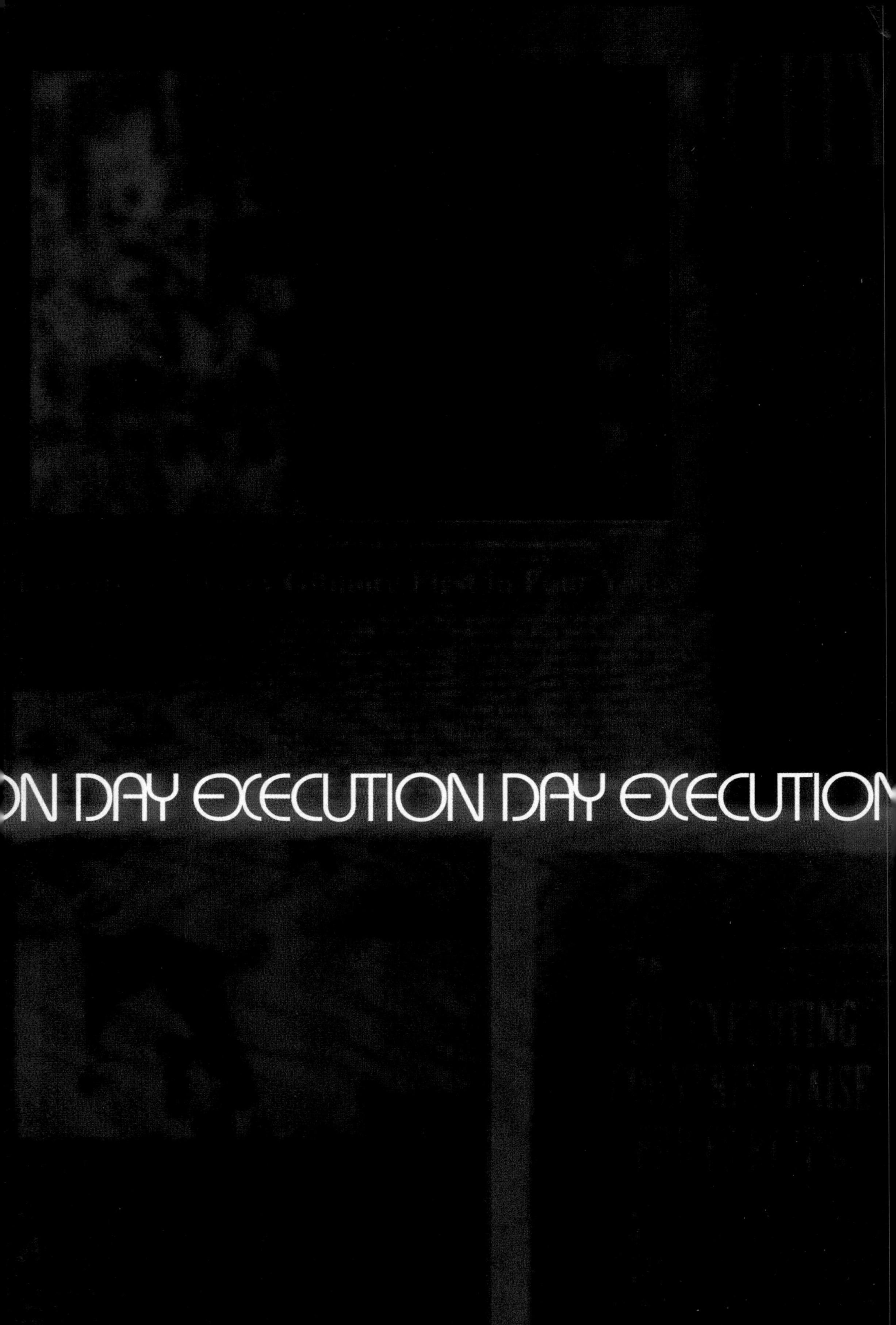
ON DAY EXECUTION DAY EXECUTION

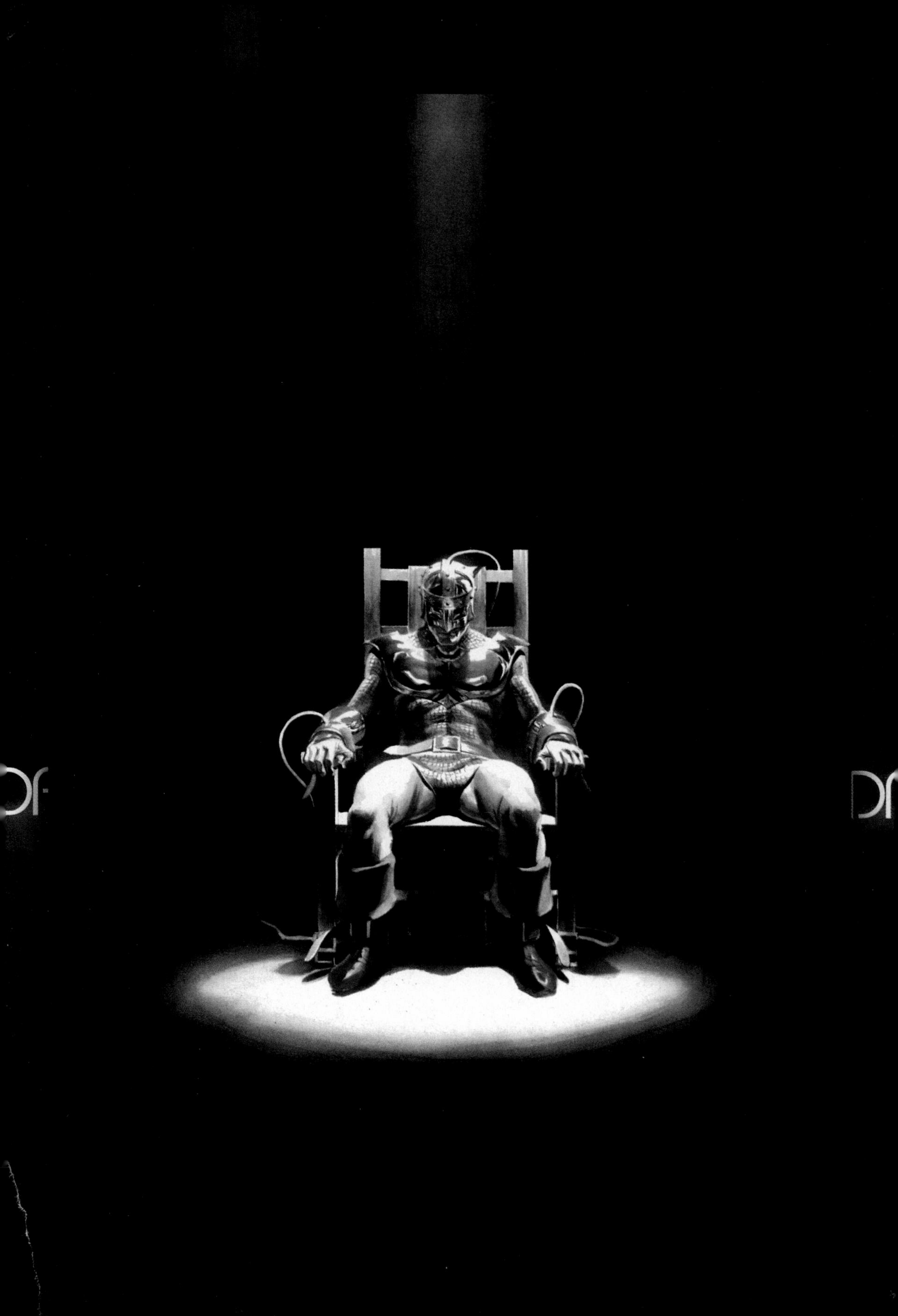

WIND BLOWING A CO LO

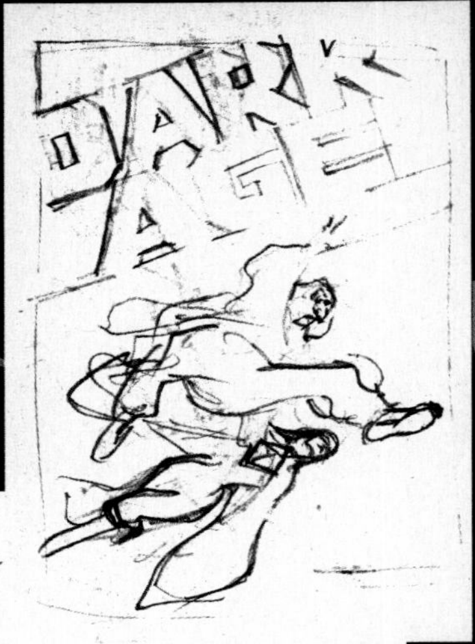

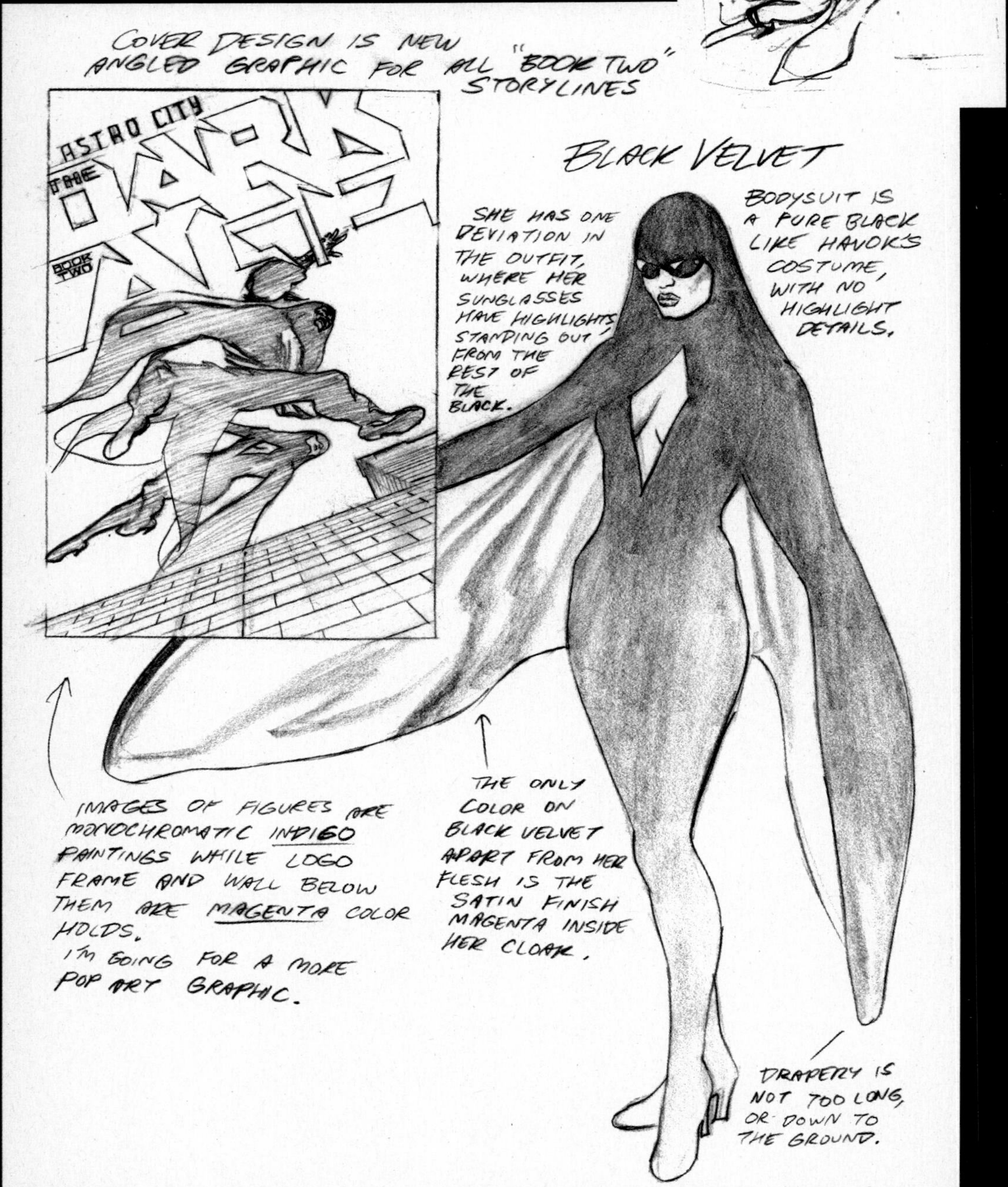
COVER DESIGN IS NEW ANGLED GRAPHIC FOR ALL "BOOK TWO" STORYLINES
ASTRO CITY
THE
BOOK TWO
BLACK VELVET
SHE HAS ONE DEVIATION IN THE OUTFIT, WHERE HER SUNGLASSES HAVE HIGHLIGHTS STANDING OUT FROM THE REST OF THE BLACK.
BODYSUIT IS A PURE BLACK LIKE HAVOK'S COSTUME, WITH NO HIGHLIGHT DETAILS.
IMAGES OF FIGURES ARE MONOCHROMATIC INDIGO PAINTINGS WHILE LOGO FRAME AND WALL BELOW THEM ARE MAGENTA COLOR HOLDS.
I'M GOING FOR A MORE POP ART GRAPHIC.
THE ONLY COLOR ON BLACK VELVET APART FROM HER FLESH IS THE SATIN FINISH MAGENTA INSIDE HER CLOAK.
DRAPERY IS NOT TOO LONG, OR DOWN TO THE GROUND.

NG A COLD WIND BLOWING A

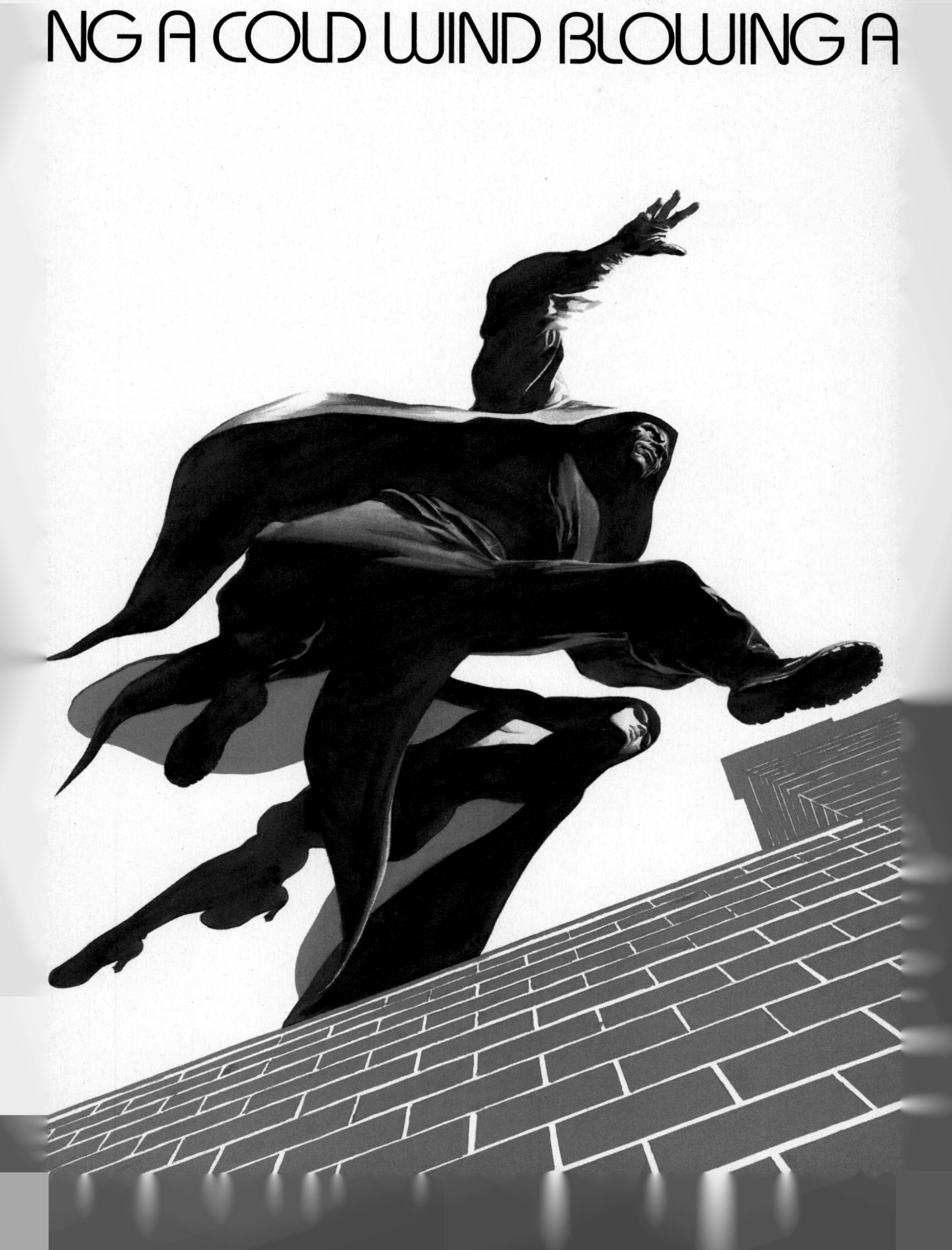

E OUT-OF-TOWN

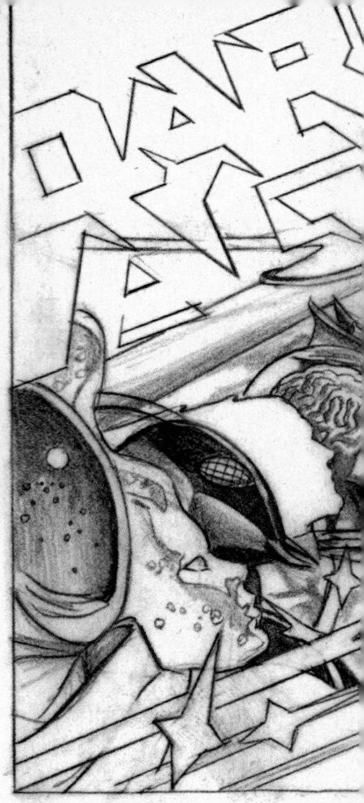

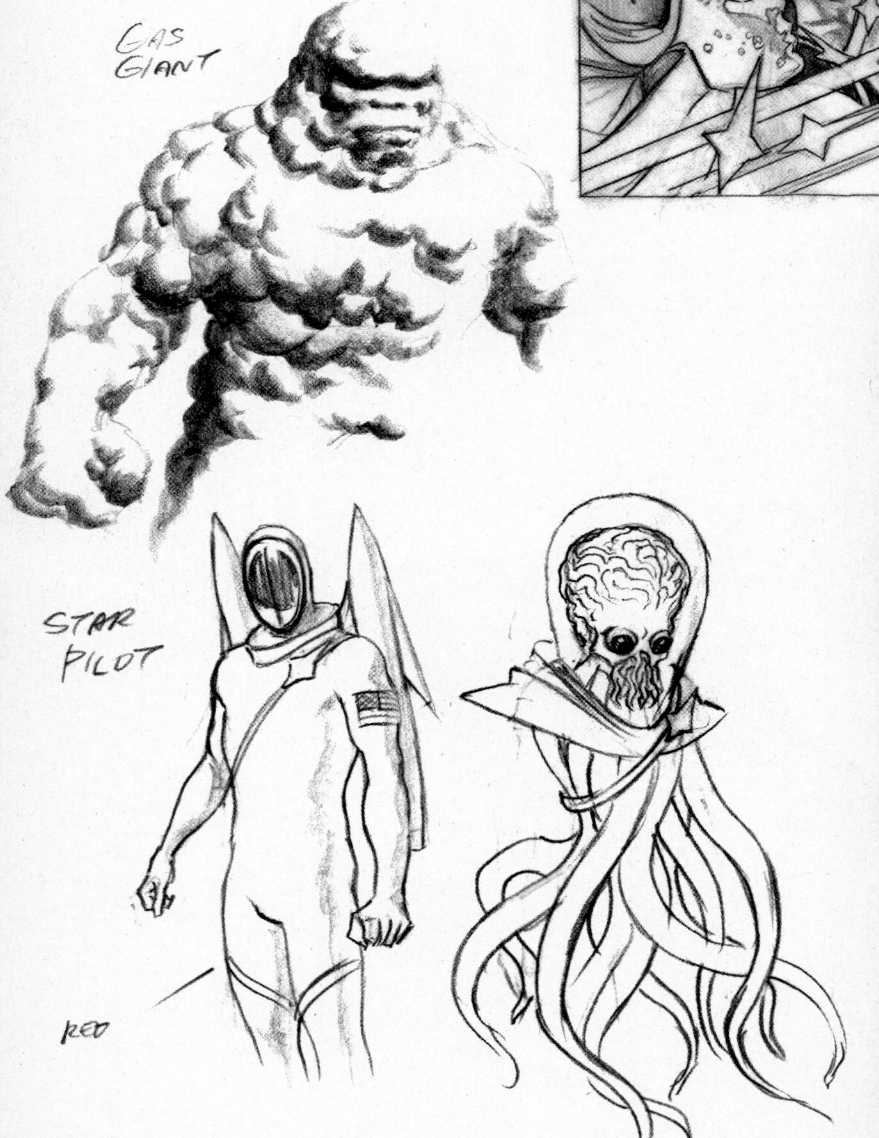
GAS GIANT
STAR PILOT
RED

WNERS THE OUT-OF-TOWNERS

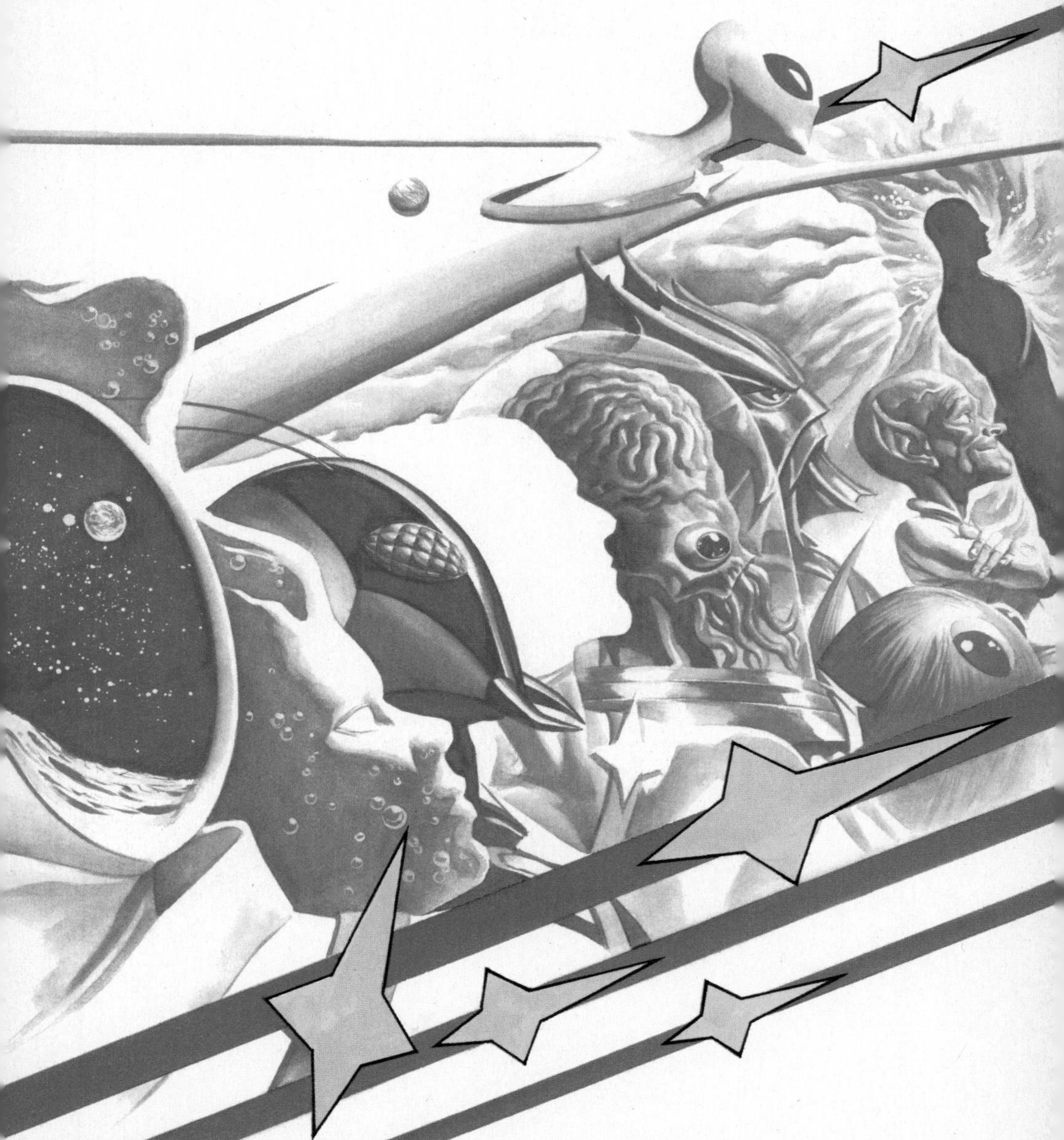

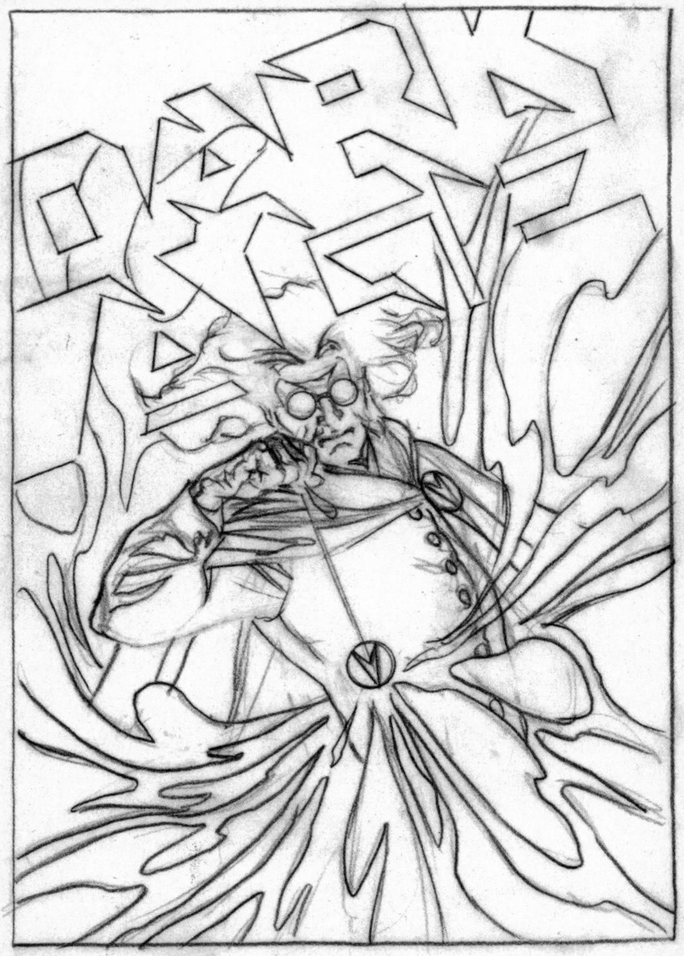

EN STREET FIGHTING MEN STREET

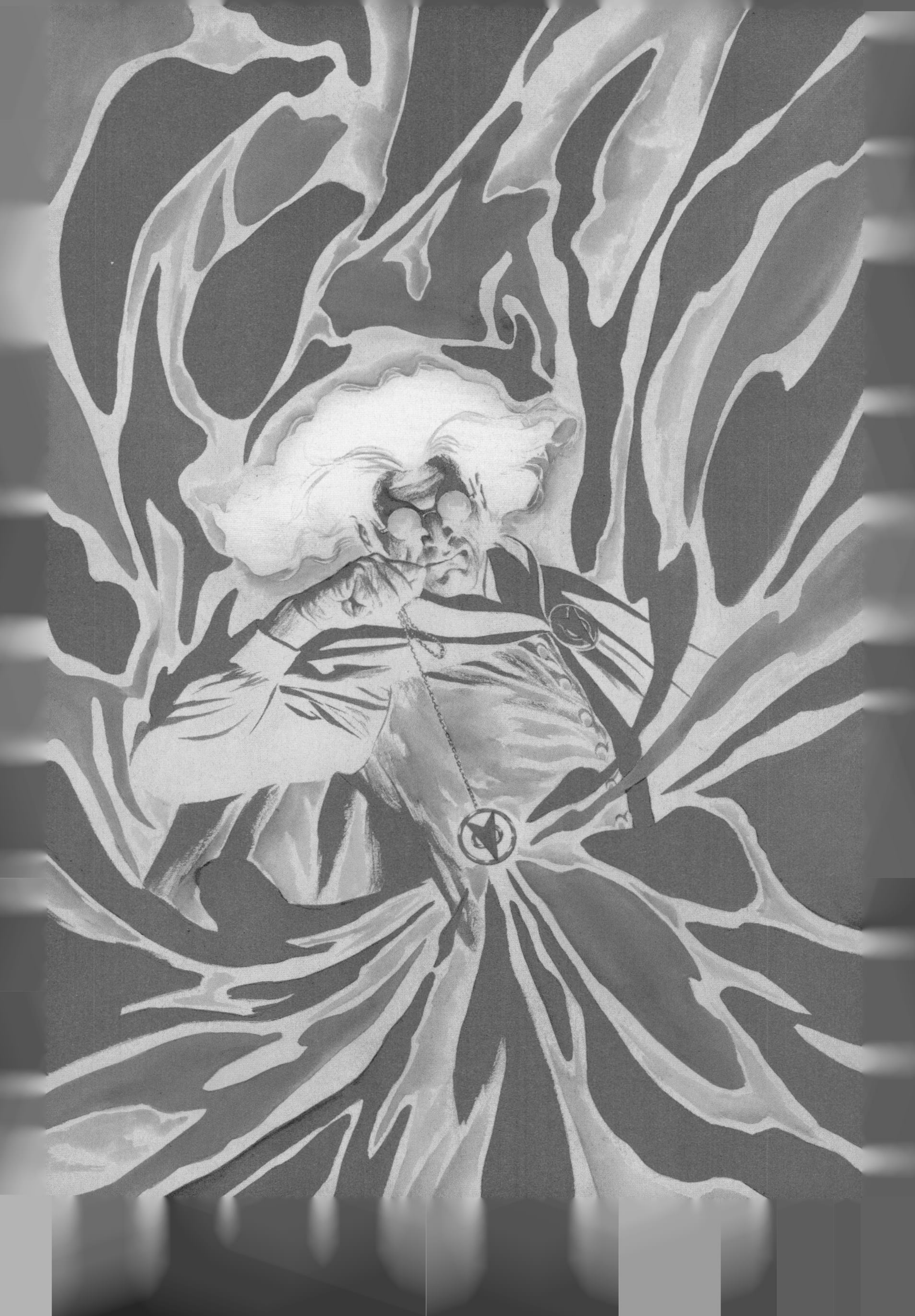

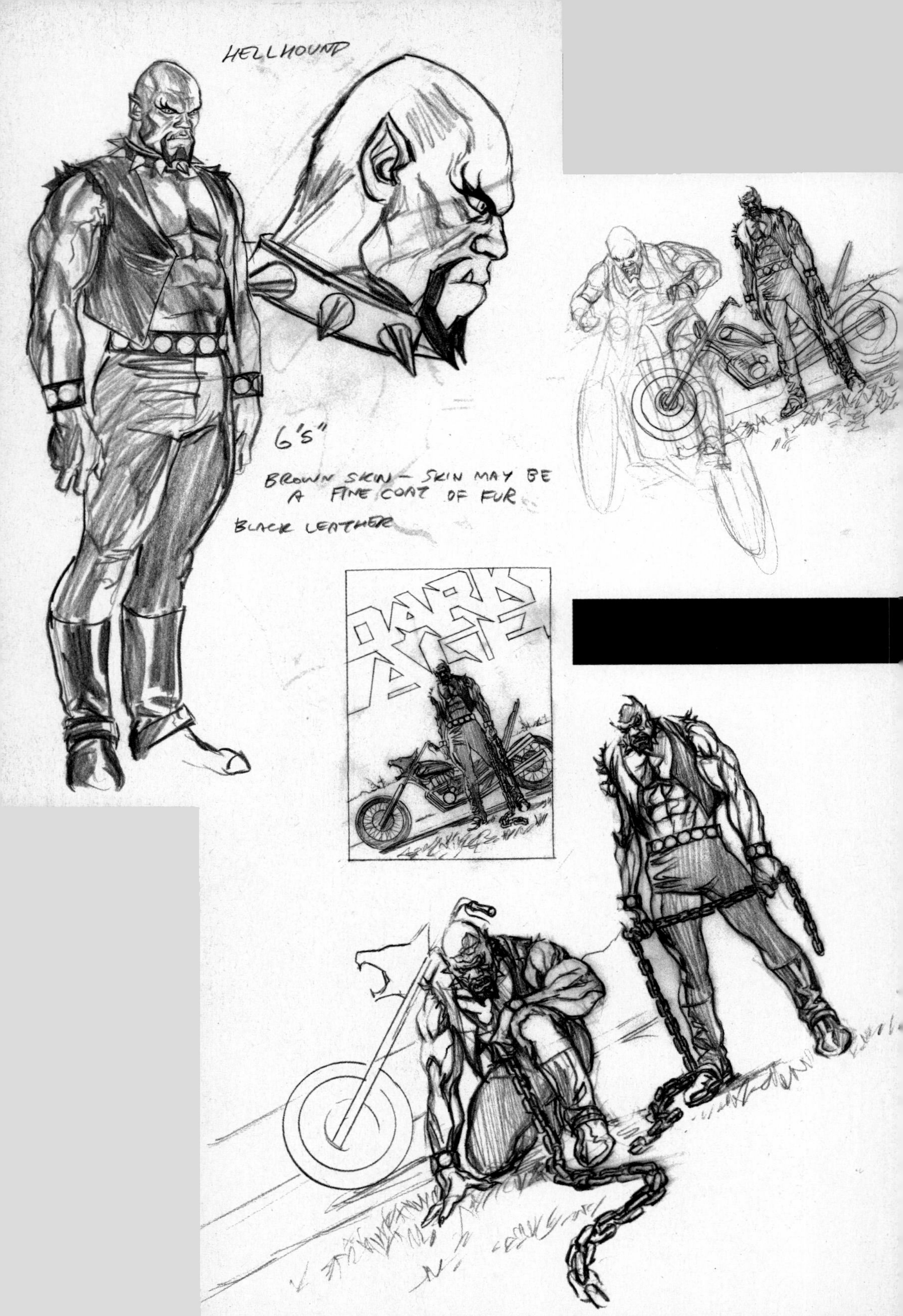

HELLHOUND
6'5"
BROWN SKIN — SKIN MAY BE
A FINE COAT OF FUR
BLACK LEATHER

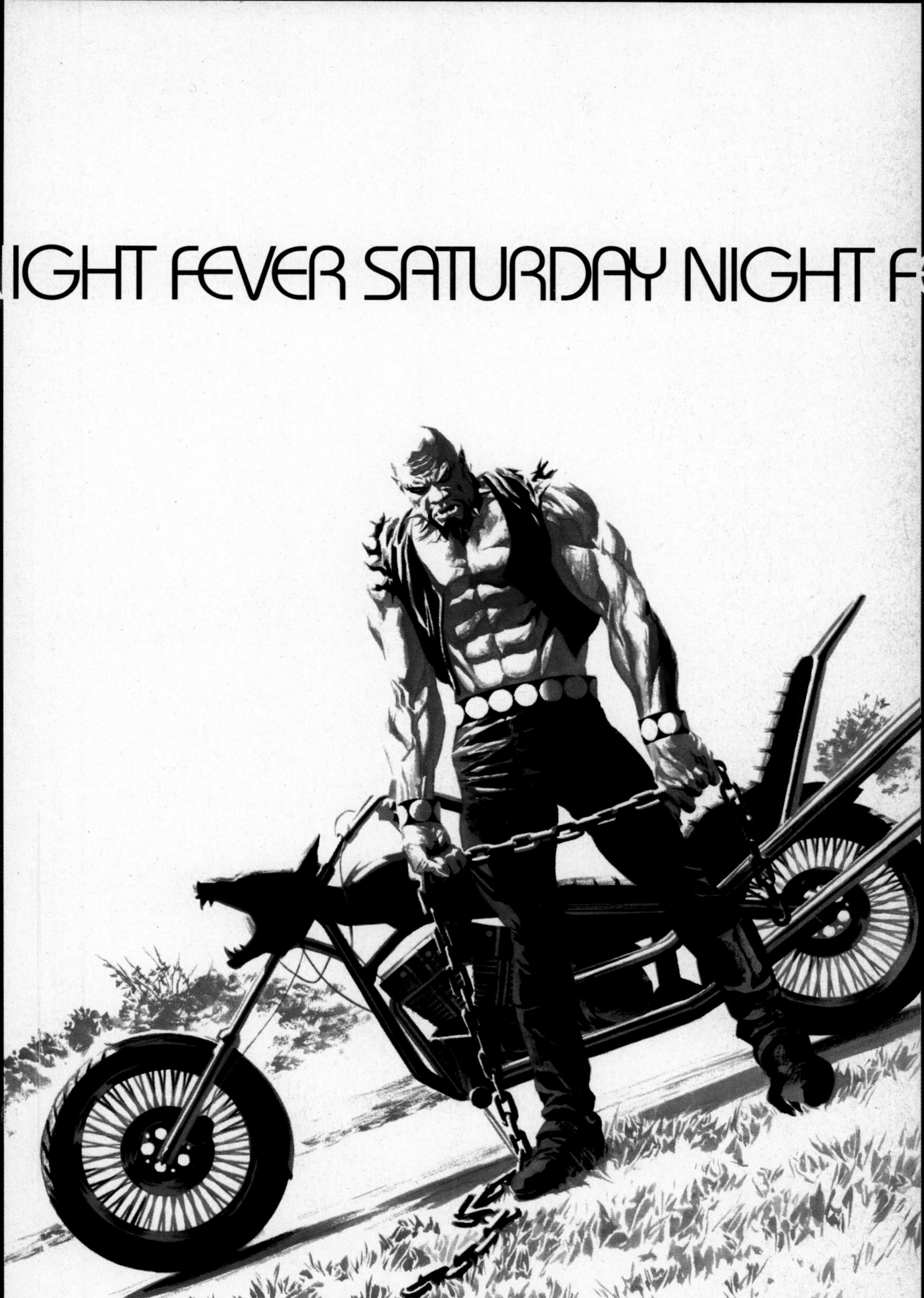
IGHT FEVER SATURDAY NIGHT FE

Thanks to the usual suspects — Lawrence
Watt-Evans, Karl Kesel, Richard Howell,
James Fry and others — for tirelessly
serving as sounding boards. Thanks also
to my mother, for sharing her perspective
on the 1960s and 1970s.
— KURT BUSIEK

I thank the City of New York, which was
in the throes of The Dark Age when
I first arrived there in 1976, for its
immeasurable inspiration in the object
creation of Astro City.
— BRENT ERIC ANDERSON

My thanks to Marcus McLaurin for
allowing Kurt and me a home for our
Marvels project so many years ago and
driving both of us elsewhere to elaborate
upon its inspiration for Astro City. Also
thanks to Bob Schreck, formerly of Dark
Horse Comics, whose embrace of the
Dark Age concept and dismissal of the
previously-agreed upon Astro City series
would cause us to realize the importance
of building up that universe first before
fulfilling this project.
— ALEX ROSS

ACKNOWLEDGMENTS